MARK MAZOWER

Hitler's Empire

Nazi Rule in Occupied Europe

ALLEN LANE
an imprint of
PENGUIN BOOKS

ALLEN LANE

Published by the Penguin Group
Penguin Books Ltd, 80 Strand, London WC2R ORL, England
Penguin Group (USA) Inc., 375 Hudson Street, New York, New York 10014, USA
Penguin Group (Canada), 90 Eglinton Avenue East, Suite 700, Toronto, Ontario, Canada M4P 2Y3
(a division of Pearson Penguin Canada Inc.)
Penguin Ireland, 25 St Stephen's Green, Dublin 2, Ireland
(a division of Penguin Books Ltd)
Penguin Group (Australia), 250 Camberwell Road, Camberwell, Victoria 3124, Australia
(a division of Pearson Australia Group Pty Ltd)
Penguin Books India Pvt Ltd, 11 Community Centre, Panchsheel Park, New Delhi – 110 017, India
Penguin Group (NZ), 67 Apollo Drive, Rosedale, North Shore 0632, New Zealand
(a division of Pearson New Zealand Ltd)
Penguin Books (South Africa) (Pty) Ltd, 24 Sturdee Avenue, Rosebank, Johannesburg 2196, South Africa

Penguin Books Ltd, Registered Offices: 80 Strand, London WC2R ORL, England

www.penguin.com

First published 2008
1

Copyright © Mark Mazower, 2008

The moral right of the author has been asserted

All rights reserved
Without limiting the rights under copyright
reserved above, no part of this publication may be
reproduced, stored in or introduced into a retrieval system,
or transmitted, in any form or by any means (electronic, mechanical,
photocopying, recording or otherwise) without the prior
written permission of both the copyright owner and
the above publisher of this book

Set in PostScript Adobe Sabon
Typeset by Rowland Phototypesetting Ltd, Bury St Edmunds, Suffolk
Printed in Great Britain by Clays Ltd, St Ives plc

A CIP catalogue record for this book is available from the British Library

ISBN 978-0-713-99681-4

www.greenpenguin.co.uk

Penguin Books is committed to a sustainable future
for our business, our readers and our planet.
The book in your hands is made from paper
certified by the Forest Stewardship Council.

Hitler's Empire

To my parents

Contents

PART I:

For Greater Germany

CONTENTS

PART 2:

The New Order

PART 3:

Perspectives

List of Illustrations

Every effort has been made to contact all copyright holders. The publishers will be happy to make good in future editions of this book any errors or omissions brought to their attention.

19. Demolition of the Vieux Port, Marseille, 1943 (Établissement Cinématographique et Photographique des Armées, Ivry, DAM 1414 L6. Photo: Weber (Prop. Eins.))
20. The Kovno Ghetto, 1941 (USHMM, courtesy of George Kadish/Zvi Kadushin)
21. Gypsies in Belzec, 1940 (USHMM, courtesy of Archiwum Dokumentacji Mechanicznej)
22. Marshal Antonescu and his wife, 1942 (akg-images/ullstein bild)
23. Hitler and Mussolini, 1941 (akg-images/ullstein bild)
24. Removing the Royal Yugoslav eagle from helmets, 1941 (akg-images/ullstein bild)
25. Painting on the Ustasa 'U', 1941 (akg-images/ullstein bild)
26. German troops in Serbia, 1941 (USHMM, courtesy of Muzej Revolucije Narodnosti Jugoslavije)
27. Molotov partisan brigade, 1942 (USHMM, courtesy of Museum of the Great Patriotic War (photo: Faye Schulman))
28. The Warsaw ghetto uprising, 1943 (USHMM, courtesy of National Archives and Records Administration, College Park)
29. The Jassy death train, 1941 (USHMM, courtesy of Serviciul Roman De Informatii)
30. Hungarian Jewish deportees, 1941 (USHMM, courtesy of Ivan Sved (photo: Gyula Spitz))
31. Auschwitz personnel, 1944 (USHMM, courtesy of Anonymous Donor)
32. Plaszow concentration camp, 1943–44 Raimund Tisch)
33. The liberation of Dachau, 1945 (USHMM, courtesy of Benjamin Ferencz (photo: Sidney Blau))
34. Soviet troops enter Budapest, 1945 (akg-images/ullstein bild)
35. Danzig, 1945 (akg-images/ullstein bild)
36. Shaving the head of a French woman, 1944 (Roger-Viollet/Topfoto)
37. The Nazi elite, Mondorf-les-Bains, 1945 (*Time* Magazine, 5 November 1945/photo: 'N.C.')

Note: USHMM is an abbreviation for the United States Holocaust Memorial Museum. The views or opinions expressed in this book, and the context in which the images are used, do not necessarily reflect the views or policy of, nor imply approval or endorsement by, the United States Holocaust Memorial Museum

List of Maps

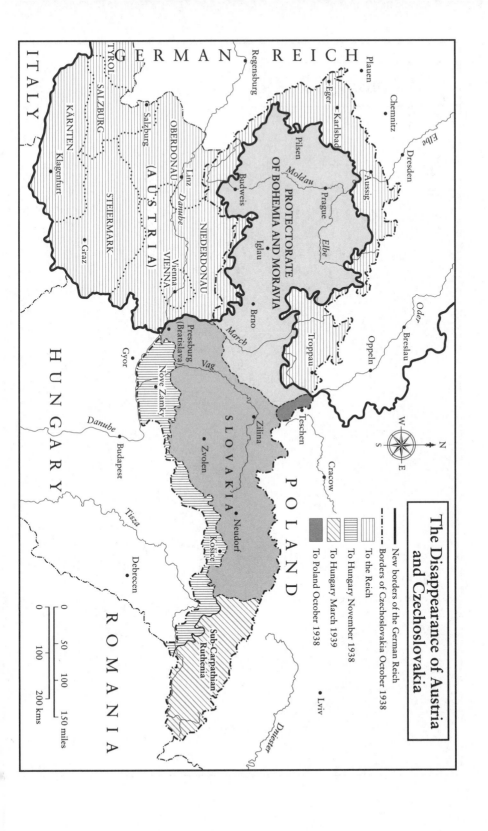

The Disappearance of Austria and Czechoslovakia

New borders of the German Reich
Borders of Czechoslovakia October 1938

To the Reich
To Hungary November 1938
To Hungary March 1939
To Poland October 1938

ITALY

GERMAN REICH

Regensburg
Plauen
Chemnitz
Eger
Karlsbad
Dresden
Elbe
Aussig
Pilsen
Moldau
Prague
Elbe
Budweis
Linz
Danube
Iglau
Brno
Troppau
Oppeln
Breslau
Oder

TYROL
SALZBURG
KÄRNTEN
Klagenfurt
Salzburg
STEIERMARK
Graz
OBERDONAU
(AUSTRIA)
NIEDERDONAU
Vienna
VIENNA

PROTECTORATE OF BOHEMIA AND MORAVIA

March

Gyor
Pressburg
Bratislava
Nove
Zamky
Vag
Zilina
Teschen
Cracow

HUNGARY

Danube
Budapest
SLOVAKIA
Zvolen
Neudorf
Kosice
Tisza
Debrecen

POLAND
Lviv

ROMANIA

Sub-Carpathian
Ruthenia

Dniester

W N E S

0   50   100   150 miles
0   100   200 kms

Poland, 1939–40

Baltic Sea

Memel

Memel

Königsberg

Gumbin

East Prussia

Stolp

Gdynia
Danzig

Elbing

Lötzen

Tczew

Danzig-

Allenstein

Neustettin

Chojnice

Deutsch Eylau

Grajew

Stettin

Pomerania

West

Prussia Grudziadz

Mława

Schneidemühl

Bydgoszcz

Chełmno

Notec

Toruń

Os
M.

Berlin

Warta

Włocławek

Plock

Frankfurt.a.d.O.

Poznań

Kutno

Vistula

Wyszkó

Koscian

Warthegau

Warsaw

20 Sept.

Sk
Minsk
Maz.

Kalisz

Łódź

Skierniewice

Lukó

Glogau

P   **O**   **L**

Oder

Dresden

Görlitz

Wieluń

Piotrków

Radom

Breslau

General

Lu

S i l e s i a

G o v e r

Oppeln

Częstochowa

Kielce

Gielwitz

Vistula

Prague

Katowice

Cracow

Tarnów

Protectorate of

Mor. Ostrava

Bohemia and Moravia

Nowy
Targ

Nowy Sacz

Brno

Zilina

Returned to Slovakia
on 21 Nov. 1939

Kezmarck

S   L   O   V   A   K   I   A

Danube

Kosice

Vienna

Bratislava

H   U   N   G   A   R   Y

LITHUANIA

Daugavpils

Kaunas

Vilnius

Suwałki

Lida

Minsk

Grodno

Njemen

Nowogrodek

Wolkowski

Baranowicze

Białystok

Narew

Słonim

Slutsk

Kamieniec Litewski

Pripec

Bug

Pinsk

Brest-Litovsk

A   N   D

Sarny

Dniepr

28 Sept.

Kovel

Chełm

Korosten

e   n   t

Włodzimierz

Rovno

Kiev

Dniepr

Zamość

Zhitomir

Sieniawa
Radymno

Brody

UKRAINE

Lviv

Przemysl

Tarnopol

20 Sept.

Proskurov

Vinnitsa

Stryj

Dniestr

N

Stanisławow

Kanenets Podolsk

W   E

Kolomea

Mogilev

Munkacs

Cernauti

S

R   O   M   A   N   I   A

	German Reich
	Territories lost to Germany by Poland
	Soviet Union
	Territories lost to the Soviet Union by Poland
	Vilnius territory ceded to Lithuania by the Soviet Union on 28 Oct. 1939
....	Boundary of German-Soviet 'spheres of interest' (23 Aug. 1939)
——	Military demarcation-lines with date of designation
——	Final German-Soviet borders, 28 Sept.

0   50   100 miles

0   50   100   150 kms

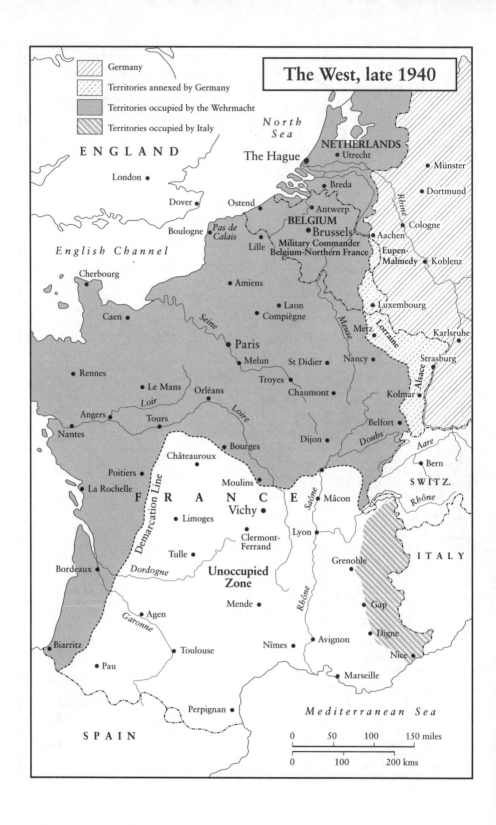

The West, late 1940

Operational Areas and Camps, Autumn 1942

Extermination camps

Major concentration camps

SOVIET UNION

Helsinki

Gulf of Finland

Lake Ladóga

Kronstadt
Leningrad
Nova

Tallinn
Vaivara
ESTONIA
Narva
Luga
Novgorod
Lake Ilmen
Damjansk
Lovat
Volga
Kalinin

Tartu
Lake Peipus
Pskov

Bay of Riga

Ventspils (Windau)
LATVIA
Riga
Salaspils
Cholm

REICH
Liepāja
Šiauliai
Daugavpils (Dunaburg)
Dvina
Nevel'
Vitebsk
Bely

Klaipeda
COMMISSARIAT
LITHUANIA
Postavy
Lepel'
Smolensk
Vjasma

Tilsit
Kaunas
Vilnius
Orsa
Borisov
Roslavl'
Kirov

Königsberg
OSTLAND
Maly Trostenets
Mogilev
Dnepr

Stutthof
Suwalki
Grodno
Minsk

EAST PRUSSIA
OPERATIONAL AREA
Brjansk

Bialystok
Baranowicze
Slutsk
Rogacev

Treblinka
Pinsk
Recica
Gomel
Trubcevsk

Warsaw
Brest-Litovsk
Pripet
Ersk
Ryl'sk

Chełmno
Desna

Sobibor
Kovel
Samy
Cernigov

Lublin
Majdanek
Luck
Rovno
Korosten
Konotop

GENERAL GOVERNMENT
Priluki

Auschwitz
Płaszów
Belzec
Kiev

Cracow
Lviv
REICH COMMISSARIAT
UKRAINE

Jaslo
Proskurov
Cerkassy
Dnepr
Poltave

SLOVAKIA
Stanislawow
Vinnica
Kremencug

Munkács
Kamenets-Podolsk
Uman'
Dnepropetrovsk

Cemauti
BESSARABIA
Kirovgrad

HUNGARY
Pervomajak
Krivoj Rog

Debrecen
South Bug
Prath

Chisinau
TRANSNISTRIA
Nikolajev
Kachovka

Tighina
Tiraspol'
Cherson

Odessa

ROMANIA
Alba (Akkerman)
Black Sea
CRIMEA

0   50   100   150 miles

0   100   200 kms

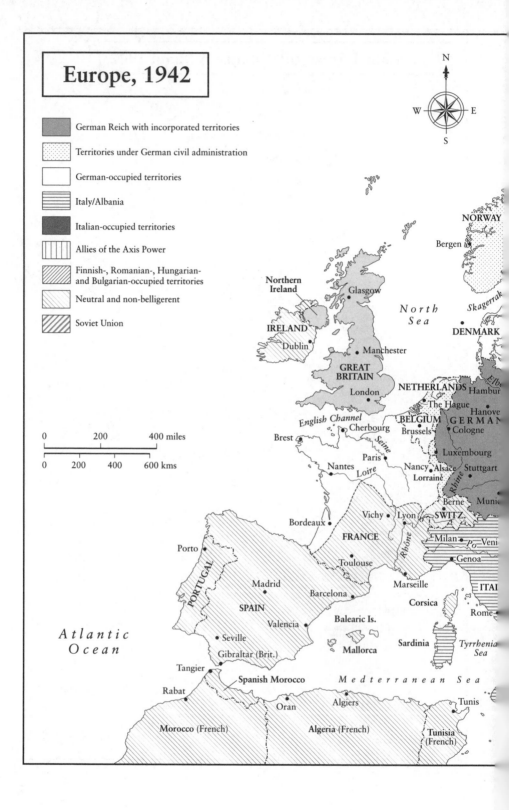

Europe, 1942

Legend:
- German Reich with incorporated territories
- Territories under German civil administration
- German-occupied territories
- Italy/Albania
- Italian-occupied territories
- Allies of the Axis Power
- Finnish-, Romanian-, Hungarian- and Bulgarian-occupied territories
- Neutral and non-belligerent
- Soviet Union

0	200	400 miles

0	200	400	600 kms

N

W — E

S

NORWAY

Bergen

Northern Ireland

Glasgow

North Sea

Skagerrak

IRELAND

DENMARK

Dublin

Manchester

GREAT BRITAIN

NETHERLANDS   Hamburg

London

The Hague

Hanover

English Channel

BELGIUM   GERMANY

Cherbourg

Brussels   Cologne

Brest

Seine

Paris

Luxembourg

Nantes

Loire

Nancy   Alsace   Stuttgart

Lorraine

Berne   Munich

Vichy   Lyon   SWITZ.

Bordeaux

FRANCE

Milan   *Po*   Venice

Porto

Genoa

Toulouse

Rhône

Madrid

Marseille

ITALY

Barcelona

PORTUGAL

Corsica

SPAIN

Rome

Valencia

Balearic Is.

Sardinia

Tyrrhenian Sea

Atlantic Ocean

Seville

Gibraltar (Brit.)

Mallorca

Tangier

Spanish Morocco

Mediterranean Sea

Rabat

Oran

Algiers

Tunis

Morocco (French)

Algeria (French)

Tunisia (French)

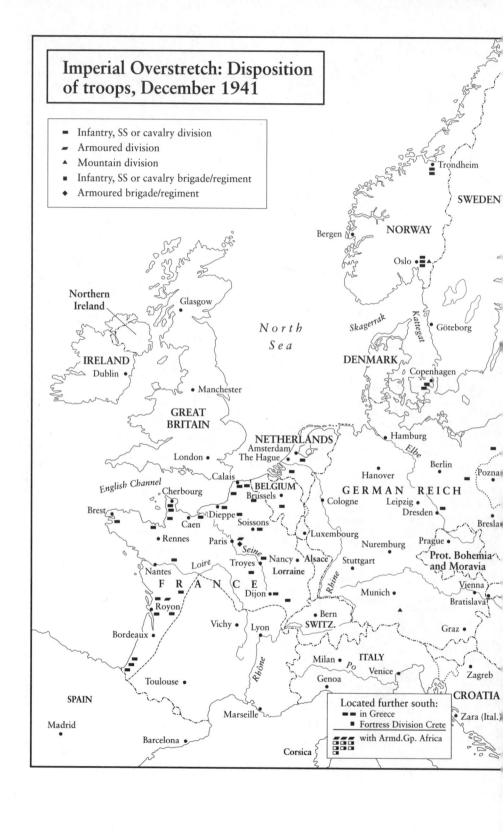

Imperial Overstretch: Disposition of troops, December 1941

- ▬ Infantry, SS or cavalry division
- ◢ Armoured division
- ▲ Mountain division
- ■ Infantry, SS or cavalry brigade/regiment
- ◆ Armoured brigade/regiment

Trondheim

SWEDEN

Bergen

NORWAY

Oslo

Northern Ireland

Glasgow

North Sea

Skagerrak

Kattegat

Göteborg

IRELAND

Dublin

DENMARK

Copenhagen

Manchester

GREAT BRITAIN

NETHERLANDS

Amsterdam
The Hague

Hamburg

Elbe

London

Berlin

Poznań

English Channel

Calais

BELGIUM

Brussels

GERMAN REICH

Hanover

Cherbourg

Cologne

Leipzig

Dresden

Breslau

Brest

Dieppe

Caen

Soissons

Luxembourg

Nuremburg

Prague

Rennes

Paris

Seine

Nancy

Alsace

Stuttgart

Prot. Bohemia and Moravia

Nantes

Loire

Troyes

Lorraine

Vienna

FRANCE

Dijon

Munich

Bratislava

Royon

Vichy

Lyon

Bern

SWITZ.

Graz

Bordeaux

Milan

Po

ITALY

Venice

Zagreb

Genoa

Zara (Ital.)

Toulouse

CROATIA

SPAIN

Marseille

Madrid

Barcelona

Corsica

Rhône

Rhine

Located further south:
- ▬▬ in Greece
- ■ Fortress Division Crete
- ▦ with Armd.Gp. Africa

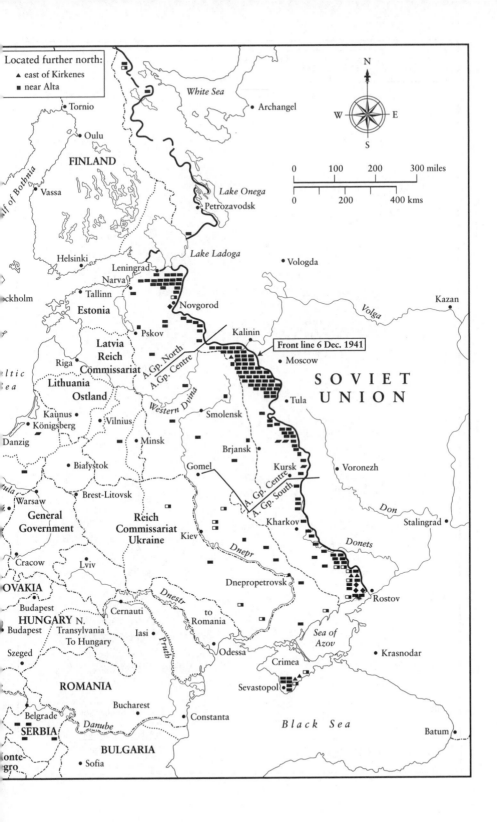

Located further north:
▲ east of Kirkenes
■ near Alta

White Sea

• Archangel

N
W   E
S

0   100   200   300 miles
0   200   400 kms

• Tornio

• Oulu

FINLAND

Lake Onega

• Vassa

• Petrozavodsk

Lake Ladoga

• Vologda

Kazan

Helsinki

Leningrad

Narva

Tallinn

Estonia

Novgorod

Volga

Pskov

Kalinin

Moscow

Latvia
Reich
Commissariat

Riga

A. Gp. North

A. Gp. Centre

Front line 6 Dec. 1941

SOVIET
UNION

Lithuania

Ostland

Western Duna

Smolensk

• Tula

Kaunus

Königsberg

Vilnius

Minsk

Brjansk

Danzig

• Białystok

Gomel

Kursk

• Voronezh

Warsaw

Brest-Litovsk

A. Gp. Centre

A. Gp. South

Don

Stalingrad •

General
Government

Reich
Commissariat
Ukraine

Kiev

Kharkov

Cracow

Lviv

Dnepr

Donets

OVAKIA

Dnepropetrovsk

Rostov

Budapest

HUNGARY N.

Cernauti

to
Romania

Dnestr

Iasi

Sea of
Azov

Krasnodar

Budapest

Transylvania
To Hungary

Szeged

Prut

Odessa

Crimea

ROMANIA

Sevastopol

Bucharest

Belgrade

Constanta

Black Sea

Batum •

SERBIA

Danube

onte-
gro

BULGARIA

Sofia

General Plan East

N

W · E

S

Lake Ladoga

Baltic Sea

Helsinki

Gulf of Finland

0   50   100   150 miles

0   100   200 kms

Leningrad

Tallinn ▲
Rakvere ▲   Narva ▲   Luga △
Paide ▲   Lake
Estonia   Peipus   Lake Ilmen
Tartu ▲

INGERMANLAND

Valga ▲
Pskov △

Riga ▲
Abrene △
Latvia
Rezekne △
Daugavpils
△

Moscow •

Memel •
Lithuania   Šiauliai ▲
MEMEL-   Dvina

NAREW   Vilnius △

Königsberg •   Dnepr   Tula •

Danzig •   **East**
Prussia   Memel

Minsk •

SOVIET
UNION

Vistula

Warsaw •   Siedlce •

P   O   L   Pripet   A   N   D

Czestochowa •   Radom •   Desna
Kielce •   Lublin •
Zamość •

Cracow •   Rovno ★
Tarnów •   Shepetovka ★   Kiev •
Przemyśl •   Lviv •   Belaja Zerkov ★   Kharkov •
Berdichev •
Bobrinskaja ★   Dnepr

Dniester   Bjatichalka ★   Dnepropetrovsk •

Budapest •   Krivoj Rog ★
HUNGARY   R   **GOTENGAU**
O   Nikolajev ★
M   Odessa •   Cherson
A
N
I   Crimea
A

Black
Sea

Pruth

    Area of the three Marches

△   Outer Ostland bases

▲   Inner Ostland bases

•   Bases in the General Government

★   Bases in the Ukraine

–·–·–·–   Pre-1939 boundaries

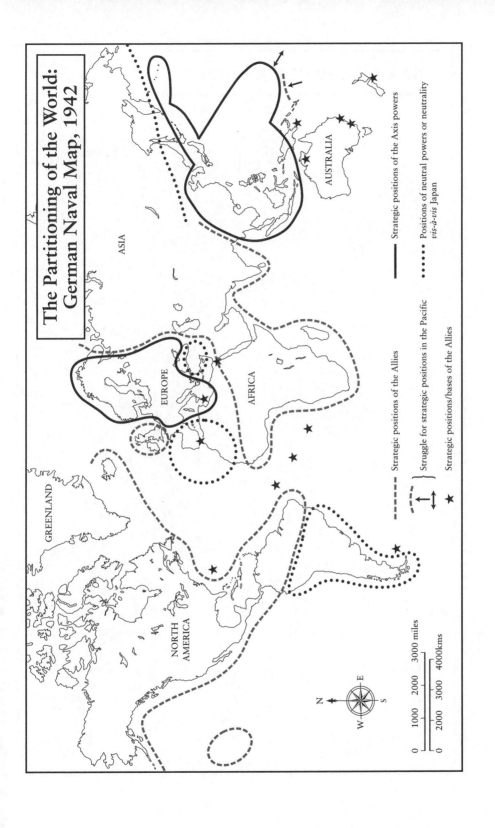

The Partitioning of the World:
German Naval Map, 1942

GREENLAND

NORTH
AMERICA

ASIA

EUROPE

AFRICA

AUSTRALIA

N
W E
S

0	1000	2000	3000 miles
0	2000	3000	4000kms

———— Strategic positions of the Axis powers

· · · · · · Positions of neutral powers or neutrality
          vis-à-vis Japan

– – – Strategic positions of the Allies

} Struggle for strategic positions in the Pacific

★ Strategic positions/bases of the Allies

The Collapse of the Empire

Baltic Sea

Flensburg

Kaliningrad
(Königsberg)
9.4.45

Kolberg
18.2.45

Danzig
30.3.45

NETHERLANDS

Hamburg
3.4.45

18 APRIL,
1945

Stettin
26.4.45

Wałcz
11.2.45

The Hague
liberated
7.5.44

Hannover
10.4.45

Berlin
2.5.45

Poznań
(Posen)
23.11.45

Warsaw
17.1.45

Vistula

BELGIUM

Rhine

Brandenburg
1.4.45

Brussels
liberated
3.9.44

Cologne

Kassel
4.5.45

Leipzig
19.4.45

Torgau

Dresden
8.5.45

Głogów
1.4.45

Łódź
19.1.45

Luxembourg

Frankfurt
am Main

Chemnitz
9.5.45

Cheb
(Eger)
27.4.45

G   E

R   M

Breslau
6.5.45

16 APRIL, 1945

Elbe

BOHEMIA

Prague
9.5.45

Katowice
28.1.45

Nancy
liberated
15.9.44

Nuremburg
20.4.45

Plzen
(Pilsen)
6.5.45

MORAVIA

Cracov
19.1.4

18 APRIL, 1945

Stuttgart

Danube

SLOVAKIA

F
R
A
N
C
E

Bern

SWITZERLAND

Munich
30.4.45

Linz
5.4.45

Vienna

15 APRIL, 1943

Budapest
13.11.45

Berchtesgaden
4.4.45

Graz

FEBRUARY 1945

H U N

Brenner Pass
4.5.45

SOUTH
TYROL

Udine

Lubljana
7.5.45

13 OCTOBER, 19

Szeged
5.10.4

Milan

Po

Venice

Trieste
2.5.45

ISTRIA

Zagreb
9.5.45

Genoa

23 APRIL,
1945

Bologna 21.4.45

Ravenna 6.12.44

Bihac

CROATIA

Jajce

Belgrade
20.10.44

OCT. 1944

Rimini 22.9.44

Zara
2.11.43

Sarajevo
6.4.45

SER

Florence
4.8.44

SAN MARINO

13 JANUARY, 1945

ITALY

5 JUNE,
1944

Adriatic Sea

MONTENEGRO

Corsica
liberated
4.10.43

Rome

1 OCTOBER,
1943

Kotor
23.11.44

Shko
29.11

Cassino
12.2-18.5.44

Tirana
17.11.44

Naples
2.10.43

REICH COMMISSARIAT

COMMISSARIAT OSTLAND

Kaunas
1.8.44

Vilnius
13.6.44

Minsk
3.7.44

OCTOBER, 1944

Białystok

Smolensk
25.9.43

Vitebsk
26.6.44

Drina

Homel
26.11.43

S O V I E T
U N I O N

Brest-Litovsk
28.7.44

Siedlce
3.7.44

Lublin
24.7.44

22 JUNE, 1944

REICH COMMISSARIAT

N   Y

Chernihiv
21.9.43

GENERAL GOVERNMENT

Lutsk
5.2.44

Rovno
5.2.44

Zhitomir
31.12.43

Kiev
6.11.43

1 OCTOBER, 1943

Lviv
27.7.44

Berdichev
5.1.44

UKRAINE

Vinnitsa
20.3.44

Uman
10.3.44

Dnestr

Dnepr

ov
.45

Uzhhorod
(Ungvar)
27.10.44

Cernauti

Prut

Debrecen
20.10.44

R Y

Cluj
(Kolozsvar)
12.10.44

22 JUNE, 1944

Iasi
21.8.44

Chisinau
24.8.44

Odessa
10.4.44

Sea of
Azov

ad
.44

Sibiu
6.9.44

Izmail
(Ismail)
26.8.44

Crimea

Sevastopol

R O M A N I A

Ploiesti
30.8.44

Craiova
26.8.44

Bucharest
31.8.44

Danube

Constanta
28.4.44

Black Sea

Nis
23.10.44

Sofia
16.9.44

BULGARIA

28 OCTOBER, 1944

kopje
.11.44

Varna
9.9.44

Burgas
9.9.44

Istanbul

TURKEY
(Neutral)

eda
nel)
45

Acknowledgements

I owe a great debt to the numerous scholars upon whose works I have relied, and to my many wonderful students at Princeton, Sussex, Birkbeck and Columbia. I should also like to thank the following for giving me the chance to inflict my ideas on them and their colleagues: Florent Bayard, Pieter Lagrou and Henri Rousso; Charles Dellheim; Richard Evans; Ido de Haan and Pieter Romijn; Tony Judt; Erez Manela; Anthony Pagden and Sanjay Subrahmanyam; Robert Pippin; and Gyan Prakash. Marilyn Young, Fred Cooper, Fritz Stern, Sheldon Garon and Phil Nord provided especially useful responses and comments as did participants at the Birkbeck Balzan workshops organized by David Feldman, Jessica Reinisch and Elisabeth White.

I have also benefited enormously from the intellectual support and friendship of my colleagues at Columbia University. My thanks to fellow participants in the Center for International History's research project on Occupation, and in particular to Alan Brinkley, Matthew Connelly, Victoria de Grazia, Isobel Hull, Rashid Khalidi, Martti Koskenniemi, Gregory Mann, Susan Pedersen, Anders Stephanson and John Witt. I received invaluable guidance from Volker Berghahn, Holly Case, Fred Cooper, Tomislav Dulic, Laura Engelstein, Catherine Epstein, Alison Frank, Carol Gluck, Gabriella Gribaudi, Hans-Christian Jasch, Pieter Judson, Simon Kitson, Pieter Lagrou, Mark Lilla, Kiran Patel, Susan Pedersen, Derek Penslar, Rachel Phipps, Pieter Romijn, Lidia Santarelli, Ben Shephard, Leonard Smith, Tim Snyder, Anders Stephanson, Adam Tooze, Mark von Hagen, Yfaat Weiss and Tara Zahra. Many of them took time off from their own busy schedules to read drafts and suggest improvements, and I am very grateful to them all. Jessamyn Abel, Holly Case, Catherine Epstein, Benjamin Martin, Leonard Smith, Tim Snyder and Tara Zahra also shared unpublished work that was of enormous help. Equally, though more indirectly, valuable have been my conversations over the years with the late Francis Carsten, Eric Hobsbawm, Claudio Pavone, Carl Schorske and Fritz Stern – exemplars of the historian's craft who also lived through these years. Most of this book was written while on leave from Columbia, and I would like to thank the Department of History for granting me this time, and David Blackbourn, Patricia Craig, Peter Hall and Charles Maier for making me feel so welcome at Harvard University's Center for European Studies and throwing open to me the quite extraordinary riches of Widener Library. Andrew Wylie, always magnificently supportive, ensured the optimal conditions for the book's production. Simon Winder first suggested I write it and has been a fount of terrific ideas, encouragement and good sense ever since. As always, I could not have done without the invaluable advice, close reading and friendship of Peter Mandler. But as to what I owe Marwa Elshakry, who has lived with the Nazis for these past few years, I am lost for words. All I will say is that without her incredible patience, her sympathy and her deep insight both this book and its author would have been much worse off: *Elfi shukr, ya habibti.* I would also like to thank my parents- and sisters-in-law and Nadeem for the gift of their friendship, and my brothers and their loved ones for their constant support. As for my beloved parents, I have benefited from their support and encouragement for longer than I can remember and in more ways than I can acknowledge. This book is for them.

Abbreviations and Acronyms

AK	Armia Krajowa (Home Army)
BFK	British Free Corps
DAF	Deutsche Arbeitsfront (German Labour Front)
DEST	Deutsche Erd- und Steinwerke GmbH (German Earth and Stone Works Ltd)
DVL	Deutsche Volksliste (German People's List)
EAM/ELAS	Ethniko Apeleftherotiko Metopo/Ellinikos Laikos Apeleftherotikos Stratos (National Liberation Front/ Greek People's Liberation Army)
ECE	Economic Commission for Europe
GPO	Generalplan Ost (General Plan East)
HJ	Hitler-Jugend (Hitler Youth)
HKT	Ha-Ka-Ta (German Eastern Marches Society)
HSSPF	Höhere SS- und Polizeiführer (Higher SS and Police Leader)
JNF	Jewish National Fund
KdF	Kraft durch Freude (Strength through Joy organization)
KONR	Committee for the Liberation of the Peoples of Russia
LVF	Légion des Volontaires Français contre le Bolchévisme (Legion of French Volunteers against Bolshevism)
MSR	Mouvement Social Révolutionnaire (Social Revolutionary Movement)
NKVD	Narodny Komissariat Vnutrennikh Del (People's Commissariat for Internal Affairs)
NS	Nasjonal Samling (National Unity Party)

NSB	Nationaal-Socialistische Beweging (National Socialist Movement)
NSDAP	Nationalsozialistische Deutsche Arbeiterpartei (National Socialist German Workers Party)
OEEC	Organization for European Economic Cooperation
OKH	Oberkommando des Heeres (Army High Command)
OKW	Oberkommando der Wehrmacht (Supreme Command of the Armed Forces)
OMi	(Reich Ministry for the Occupied Eastern Territories)
OSTI	Ostindustrie GmbH (East Industries Limited)
OT	Todt Organization
OUN	Orhanizatsiya Ukrayins'kykh Natsionalistiv (Organization of Ukrainian Nationalists)
RKFDV	Reichskommissariat für die Festigung deutschen Volkstums (Reich Commission for the Strengthening of Germandom)
RNP	Rassemblement National Populaire (National Popular Rally)
RSHA	Reichssicherheitshauptamt (Reich Security Main Office)
RuSHA	Rasse- und Siedlungshauptamt (Main Race and Resettlement Office)
RVL	Reich, Volksordnung, Lebensraum
SA	Sturmabteilung
SD	Sicherheitsdienst (SS Intelligence Service)
SHAEF	Supreme Headquarters Allied Expeditionary Force
SiPo	Sicherheitspolizei (Security Police)
SOE	Special Operations Executive
SOL	Service d'Ordre Légionnaire (Legionary Service for Law and Order)
SS	Schutzstaffel
SSPF	SS- und Polizeiführer (SS and Police Leader)
STO	Service du Travail Obligatoire (Obligatory Labour Service)
UNRRA	United Nations Relief and Rehabilitation Administration
VDA	Verein für das Deutschtum in Ausland (Union for Germandom Abroad)

VNV	Vlaamsch National Verband (Flemish National Union)
VoMi	Volksdeutsche Mittelstelle (Ethnic German Liaison Office)
WVHA	Wirtschafts-Verwaltungshauptamt (Economics and Administrative Main Office)
ZOB	Zydowska Organizacja Bojowa (Jewish Fighting Organization)
ZWZ	Związek Walki Zbrojnej (Union for Armed Struggle)

Preface: The View from Varzin

'Although the gradual decrease and final extinction of the races of man is an obscure problem, we can see that it depends on many causes.'
Charles Darwin, *The Descent of Man* (London, 1871), 230

The storks were already migrating as the first Germans began to flee East Prussia. This was in the late summer of 1944. By the following January, with the temperature twenty degrees below zero, more than three million refugees and their animals were trudging westwards to escape the vengeance of the Red Army. For mile after mile they shuffled through the snows, clogging the roads while the retreating German troops tried to force their way through. The last civilian trains were crowded with 'huddled shapes, rigid with cold, barely able to stand up any more and climb out; thin clothing, mostly in tatters, a few blankets over bowed shoulders, gray, hollow faces'. As the front came closer, the concentration camps were emptied as well, and their surviving inmates were marched deeper into the Reich; their guards shot the stragglers and left their bodies by the roadside.[1]

One young refugee was a German aristocrat fleeing her family's East Prussian estate. After four weeks in the saddle, Countess Marion Dönhoff wearily crossed the Vistula and cajoled her horse along the snow-bound back roads of Pomerania before finding herself passing the gates of Bismarck's former country residence at Varzin. In her memoirs – written many years later – she describes how she turned into the grand oak-lined avenue to protect herself from the violent flurries. Two large horse-drawn wagons packed high with wooden boxes stood in front of the house. The Bismarck family papers were being moved westwards for safety.

Inside she found the eighty-one-year-old Countess von Arnim, who had decided not to leave the home where her children had been born and where her husband, Bismarck's son, had died many years before. That evening over dinner, von Arnim regaled her guest with stories of life at the Kaiser's court. We do not know if she also admitted that she had once hailed the Führer as her father-in-law's successor. But maybe her refusal to leave reflected her disillusionment with the Third Reich and its leader, and her sense that a much older world was passing along with the Nazis. In the garden's frozen earth, a freshly dug grave awaited her. Barely a fortnight after she waved her guest farewell, the Red Army arrived: amid the violent chaos of those weeks, her suicide went unnoticed.[2]

Halfway round the world, another, very different Varzin also faced attack in early 1945. This Varzin was an inaccessible tropical volcano at the south-eastern edge of Japan's wartime Pacific empire. Sweltering beneath its summit, thousands of beleaguered Japanese soldiers, brought in originally to spearhead an invasion of Australia, now found themselves trapped by the Anglo-American advance and subjected to a ferocious aerial bombardment. As wave after wave of Corsairs and Venturas tore in to destroy what had once been the largest naval base in the region, many of the troops took cover beneath the dense canopy of the overgrown coconut plantations. When 85,000 of them surrendered that summer, they left behind miles of tunnels, gun emplacements and bunkers amid the mangrove swamps, some Korean prostitutes, a handful of emaciated POWs and mass graves in the back country.

With its heavy rains and luxuriant humidity, Mount Varzin was a densely forested and still active volcanic peak that loomed above the magnificent natural harbour of Blanche Bay on the island of New Britain. This was the same island which the Germans had once labelled New Pomerania and which had formed a remote outpost of their fledgling colonial empire in what to this day is still called the Bismarck Archipelago. It lay to the east of Kaiser-Wilhelmsland, part of the sprawling prewar Pacific colony of German New Guinea. Bismarck's diplomatic feat in creating this realm was thus commemorated in archipelagos and volcanoes and settlements; one of the main towns on the Gazelle Peninsula was simply named after his eldest son, Herbert. Perhaps the familiarity of these names reassured some of the Lutheran missionaries saving native souls for Christ, the copra traders and shippers who established plantations and turned savages into labourers, the anthropologists and botanists who collected and classified the island's rare trees, orchids and butterflies. But the roughly 16,000 people already inhabiting the Gazelle Peninsula paid less attention to them than did the few hundred newcomers. 'The natives obviously do not know the names given by Europeans,' wrote the island's first ethnographer, 'and the latter know the native designations just as little, and consequently it has come about that natives, adrift in their canoes, who finally arrived at a settlement, could not be sent back to their homeland because the name that they gave to their dwelling place was totally unknown.' To those who actually lived in the villages on its slopes, the name Varzin meant nothing. In fact, the natives often appeared to do without place-names at all. But European colonial settlers could not operate in that way: for them, names meant power.

In the very year that Germany's claim over the islands had won international recognition, Sybille von Arnim had married Wilhelm von Bismarck. In those days her ageing father-in-law still occasionally left Berlin for his country estate at Varzin. The substantial manor house set amid the Pomeranian forests had been his reward for presiding over the defeat of the Habsburg army and turning Prussia into the leader of a unified German Reich. It was there that he had in 1870 brooded on the eve of the war with France, leaving the Kaiser to try to cope without him. Yet Varzin was more than merely a retreat. It was linked to the capital by one of Germany's first telephone lines, and thence Bismarck summoned his colleagues and conducted much of the business of state. Calmed by the proximity of nature, his restless and nervous disposition found an almost mystical confirmation of the power of the land itself that went beyond snobbery; in his mind it represented his real kingdom on earth. It was, says one historian, 'the Reich in miniature'.

In this little state of his own, with its woods, fields and village, he grew tropical fruit in his greenhouses and established a substantial paper factory. Its raw materials came from the 4,000 hectares of forest which surrounded it, and its workforce was housed near by. There were some labour problems on the land, and many local German peasants, chafing at life under something close to feudalism, drifted westwards into the cities. But Bismarck solved this, in the same way that many of his neighbouring landowners did, by employing cheaper Russian and Polish migrant workers instead. Thus the architect of the modern German state pursued a way of life increasingly reliant upon non-German hands.[3]

Names alone did not guarantee control of Germany's new tropical paradise. There were also the natives to contend with – both those who could be trained to collect and process the copra, tobacco and coffee that Europeans introduced, and those who preferred to hunt animals and each other amid the frangipani, palms and candle trees. Understanding these naked 'children of nature' was the first step to knowing what to do with them, and it was important – at least in the eyes of the land's new masters – that Germany show itself capable in this respect too. 'With the now completed partitioning of the earth among the civilized states of Europe and America,' wrote a museum administrator at the turn of the new century, 'the scientific investigation of the earth also has become more and more nationalized.' German readers needed to appreciate the importance of a properly scientific understanding of race for empire-building since

one must first of all get to know a people that one wishes to rule; one cannot expect that a primitive people become familiar with the complicated structures of our civilization, with our fine understanding of completely foreign perceptions of justice or moral concepts; rather we must endeavour to understand their culture, their thoughts and their sentiments.[4]

Mount Varzin's pioneer ethnographer, Richard Parkinson, would surely have agreed. He had started off as a German plantation manager but he had other strings to his bow. He sent six Tolai dancers to Berlin for the 1896 Colonial Exhibition; he amassed the largest collection of the island's native artefacts in private hands; and he helped collect plants, birds and butterflies as well as human remains such as skeletons and skulls (which the local prevalence of cannibalism facilitated), which he sold to museums abroad. Unfortunately, these activities contributed to the eradication of the very traditions he valued. By 1908 a visitor to Mount Varzin noted that many cultures had 'almost or entirely disappeared – in some cases the natives themselves are gone'.

Parkinson himself saw such developments in a longer perspective. According to him, the mountain was the site of an ongoing bloody clash between the two main races that inhabited the Gazelle Peninsula. Over the preceding century or so, immigrants from neighbouring islands had spread inland up its slopes, encroaching on the former dwelling places of the original inhabitants. The result was that 'there now developed a struggle between both tribes which continues to this day'. The coming of the Europeans had only made these tensions worse, and the German press noted 'an irregular and unrestrained *Grenzkrieg* [border war] which is conducted without mercy on both sides'. The logic of a Darwinian competition for life and land seemed to be as fierce as anywhere, an existential fight between two primitive groups with their own rituals, languages and enmities.[5]

It was from the steps of his estate at Varzin, on a September day in 1894, that Bismarck had emerged to sound the battle-cry of German nationalism against the Poles. He was increasingly worried about Germany's growing Polish population and the security threat this posed, especially in its eastern borderlands. Few political issues were more inflammatory. In power, Bismarck had actually encouraged German farmers to buy land in areas where there was a Polish majority. In retirement, he fretted about his successor's lack of concern. The Polish-speaking Bismarck was no racial warrior, and estates like his relied on Slav workers, but he was uneasy, and nationalist lobby-groups pleaded with him to speak out.

Once he agreed, specially chartered trains brought thousands of patriotic 'pilgrims' to Varzin to hear him denounce the subversive activities of the Polish gentry and clergy. He called for a tough response from the Prussian government. The Poles' territorial demands, he told them, were limitless. It was the Germans who had brought civilization to the primitive East, and the mastery was rightfully theirs: 'I am speaking, not with the aim of winning over the Poles, which is hopeless in any case, but with the intention of exterminating the remnants of sympathy for Poland among our countrymen.'[6]

Sounding the tocsin for a new kind of ethnic mass politics, Bismarck depicted the region as a frontier in the racial battle between Germans and Slavs. A highly vocal and effective lobby group in Berlin sprang up to demand that other politicians too 'support Germandom in the Eastern Marches'. Claiming merely to protect German ways and culture, in fact it sought to roll back the wave of Polish immigration and to force Poles – whether migrants or not – to leave Prussia's border regions. As for the local Poles, Bismarck's speech struck them as little short of a declaration of war, and they mobilized too, boycotting German shops, supporting Polish newspapers and cultural groups, and making sure they sold land to each other and not to Germans.

Bismarck himself was not sure he liked where this was leading. After all, he realized that further eastern conquest would not solve the Reich's Polish problem, and indeed could only add further Poles, and therefore, when the country celebrated his eightieth birthday, he counselled moderation. He told a delegation of students that, while they should accept struggle – for 'life is a struggle' – they should bear in mind that Germany itself had no further need for war. 'We had what we needed [after the war with France]. To fight for more, from a lust for conquest and for the annexation of countries which were not necessary for us, has always appeared to me like an atrocity.' At the very end of this birthday speech, the old man raised his glass to the Kaiser: 'I hope that in 1950 all of you who are still living will again respond with contented hearts to the toast, LONG LIVE THE EMPEROR AND THE EMPIRE!'[7]

Dying only three years later, in 1898, he could scarcely have been expected to foresee what lay ahead. At first his estate at Varzin itself became a kind of shrine of the Bismarck cult. An enormous monument was unveiled in the park, a small museum opened in the woods, and there was even a sculpture of his favourite horse. But gradually the clouds darkened, and the wars he had dreaded intervened. The belligerent young Kaiser whose health he had toasted was driven into exile in the Netherlands, Germany's tropical colonies were confiscated, and the monarchy was replaced by a republic. The Nazis then aimed to outdo Bismarck's achievements, but instead Germany itself was ruined, divided and occupied. Prussia disappeared from the map, an independent Poland was restored, and Bismarck's beloved Varzin found itself on the wrong side of the border. Known today as Warcino, it is a school for young Polish forestry students.

During the Third Reich, the German government took little interest in the old German overseas colonies that had been lost in 1918 – the Nazis themselves were much more interested in colonizing parts of Europe itself. But the remaining Germans who had stayed on in what was now Australian-run New Guinea kept a close eye on events at home. In fact, they had been such enthusiasts for the Nazi cause that, when the

Japanese attacked in 1942, the Allies shipped them to an internment camp on the Australian mainland. This turned into a small Antipodean outpost of National Socialism, a last enclave of Germany's Pacific empire. Run by loyalists who decorated their offices with portraits of Hitler, it held festivals commemorating fallen 'martyrs' of the Party, and the swastika flew above the pre-fab barracks. In 1943 there were evening lectures on 'the German East' and German–Italian friendship to keep up the inmates' faith in an ultimate German victory. When the end of the war was announced, their National Socialist memorabilia were burned in 'a gloomy and defiant ceremony' amid speeches and 'songs of German struggles, German courage, German devotion and German faith'. The Australian camp commander made them watch films of Belsen to 're-educate' them, and then tried – with little success – to persuade them to stay in Australia.[8]

Though they did not realize it, the internees were fortunate. Being captured in the Pacific and held in Australia meant that they remained, as Europeans, the members of a privileged ruling caste. Nationalism and war might have fractured the solidarity of the region's European colonial elite, but the assumption of a common superiority remained, and they were the beneficiaries. Between the wars, the Australians had treated the natives brutally; but to the Germans, whatever their political views, they showed respect. In Germany's 'Eastern Marches', their fate would have been different. They would have started out as rulers there too – over a Polish population treated like natives. But at the end they would have found themselves with the defeated side in a Darwinian war of annihilation.

Viewed from the slopes of Mount Varzin, the Nazi New Order looks like the story of Europe's own 'war of the peoples'. But, unlike the fighting between the Baining and the Tolai, this was a war that in its scale, intensity and ambition reflected the modern European will to power – a desire to explore, expand, identify and control territory and peoples that had taken them to Africa, the Americas and the remotest islands of the Pacific. Heirs to this tradition, the Nazis shared that imperial desire but did something with it that was unprecedented and shocking to the European mind of the early twentieth century: they tried to build their empire in Europe itself and, what is more, to do it at breakneck speed in only a few years. If this book is about the first Varzin and the passions that erupted in the German–Polish borderlands, it is written from the perspective of the second. For, in the long run, the significance of Hitler's bid for empire is that it irrevocably altered not only Europe but also that continent's place in the world, and thus the world itself.

Introduction

'Could the war have been won at all, even if no military mistakes had been made? My opinion is: no. From 1941 onwards at the latest it was just as much lost as the Great War because the political aims bore no relation whatsoever to Germany's military and economic possibilities. The only thing Hitler's peculiar method of waging war cost the German people was millions too many people killed. That's the only thing – the war could not have been won. The remarkable thing is this, a thing about which I am always thinking: how is it that a country like Germany, which is situated in the middle of the continent, has not developed politics into an art, in order to maintain peace, a sensible peace ... We were so fatuously stupid as to think that we could challenge the world ... without seeing that that is absolutely impossible in the situation in which we find ourselves in Germany. What are the reasons for it? ... I am no politician, I am no historian. I don't know. I only see the question.

Generalleutnant Ferdinand Heim, in a lecture to fellow POWs,
23 May 1945[1]

In early October 1941, a string of victories brought the Wehrmacht to the outskirts of Moscow and convinced Hitler that the Soviet Union had been beaten. He realized his mistake within days. But by then it was too late. Propaganda Ministry officials in Berlin had already provided journalists with a brutally frank revelation of what Europe could expect under Nazi rule. The war was over, they had told them, and the Reich was going to create a self-sufficient 'Europe behind barbed wire' that could withstand any military threat. Germany would become 'much freer and colder' in the way it treated 'the nations dominated by us' and 'there would be no question of some pathetic little state obstructing

European peace with its special requests or special demands'. As for the German people, they would face new challenges and they would have to deal in particular with the sort of constant skirmishing on their new Eurasian border in the East that the British confronted on India's north-western frontier. In short, they would need 'to be led to the imperial European ideal'.[2]

Hitler as empire-builder: it may not be how we commonly think of the Führer, but it was certainly one of the images he had of himself. The Nazis believed it had fallen to them to establish an empire that would elevate them to the status of a world power. With scarcely any direct experience of overseas colonialism to guide them, and knowing little about the British in India, they were nevertheless greatly impressed with the idea that a tiny group of administrators could run an entire sub-continent. For them, empire was an 'ideal' – or, to put it more bluntly, a violent fantasy of racial mastery, a demonstration of the prowess of a martial elite bred to lord over hundreds of millions of subjects. The Germans would have to be trained in these virtues, Hitler believed, in order to compete with the rulers of 'great spaces' for the globe's resources. They had lagged behind in the Scramble for Africa at the end of the nineteenth century, and they could not afford to ignore the competitive rivalries unleashed after the First World War as well. The British and French had already grabbed the Middle East, the Japanese had marched into Manchuria in 1931, and the Italians had invaded Ethiopia four years later. Germany needed to make up for lost time.[3]

How far Nazi imperial ambitions really extended is an issue that still divides historians. 'Today Germany is ours, and tomorrow the whole world,' sang the Hitler Youth. But what dreams of dominion lay in the mind of the Führer is hard to say. No one seriously believes that he was a mere opportunist, without any foreign policy programme at all. But could he really have envisaged a campaign of world conquest? Believing the Third Reich's appetite to have been virtually limitless, some scholars point to its naval preparations for a transatlantic conflict and argue that Hitler was guided by a foreign policy programme of confrontation with the USA that dated back to the 1920s. Others doubt that things worked so neatly or went so far and stress Hitler's fixation upon Europe and his arguments for eastwards expansion – *Lebensraum*.[4]

The two views are not incompatible, but Europe came first in every sense. The operative difference to bear in mind is surely between domination and conquest. Almost a century before Hitler, Abraham Lincoln's secretary of state, William Seward, talked about making the United States into 'the successor of the few great states which have alternately borne commanding sway in the world'. For Seward, establishing 'control of this continent is to be in a very few years the controlling influence in the world'. He saw power projected through commerce whereas Hitler valued the control of resources, but the two men's hegemonic ambitions were otherwise not far apart. 'Any thought of world policy is laughable,' Hitler commented in October 1941, 'until we are masters of the continent . . . Once we are the masters in Europe, then we will enjoy the dominant position in the world.'[5]

Controlling Europe was what really mattered for the Nazis precisely because they believed it held the pivotal position in the world's geopolitical system. In 1904 the British geographer Halford Mackinder had famously argued that he 'who rules eastern Europe commands the Heartland; who rules the Heartland commands the World Island; and who rules the World Island commands the World'. It was not an implausible idea. By 1942, after all, the Germans were in command of a landmass larger than the USA, and more densely populated and more economically productive than anywhere else in the world. Whatever the challenges that Hitler may have thought would face future generations, there can be little doubt that the conquest and consolidation of this vast area represented the culmination of his own foreign policy.[6]

It was for this reason that the Nazis regarded their own imperial ambitions as compatible with those of other leading powers, and they could never understand why the British in particular failed to see this. 'It seems to us,' commented Alfred Rosenberg, the regime's self-proclaimed philosopher, 'that the British empire too is based on a racially defined claim of dominance.' Did they not share the all-important combination of a sense of racial superiority and hatred of Bolshevism? The Nazis planned to dominate Europe, in other words, much as the British ran Asia or Africa – or so it seemed to them. If the British could be persuaded to give up their hostility to the idea that no single power should be allowed to control the destiny of the continent, there was no reason for the two powers to fight. Africa could be carved up anew along the lines of the discussions that had started in the late 1930s and the more ambitious blueprints that followed the fall of France. But for Hitler, eastwards expansion promised Germany more than overseas colonies ever could, and it was the lands between the Baltic and the Black Seas that he singled out for German settlement.[7]

'Putting it precisely,' commented a German official in the Ukraine in 1942, 'we are here in the midst of negroes.' This was the mysterious, disturbing and hazy realm that the Germans called the 'East' – a supposedly uncultivated wilderness of swamps, impenetrable forests and steppes on Prussia's doorstep – which was only awaiting German energy and discipline to be put into order and made productive. *Ostrausch* – the intoxication of the East – worked its magic on many of those sent in to rule it. But continental empire had one massive disadvantage for a regime that was gripped more than any other by the fear of racial contamination. The Reich's sheer proximity to the detested *Untermenschen* – often physically indistinguishable from Germans, and increasingly important as labourers – alarmed Berlin and brought out its most repressive tendencies.[8]

In the Reich itself, the wartime inflow of Poles, Russians and Ukrainians got the Gestapo snooping round farms and factories and ended up in public hangings and mass arrests. In the newly occupied territories, the war and racial anxiety fused in an infinitely more toxic combination. Europe's eastern borderlands, after all, were where the Nazis staked their claim on the future. This was clear on the battlefield: for whereas British and US military losses totalled below half a million men each, the Russians lost at least eight million. 2.7 million Germans died on the Eastern Front, compared with 340,000 in western Europe and 151,000 in Italy. Behind the front lines the disparities were greater still. Approximately 1,500 French men and women died during the Liberation of Paris, but more than *one hundred* times as many Poles perished during the Warsaw uprising, which was going on at the same time. Of the 8.6 million civilians estimated to have died under Nazi occupation in Europe, the overwhelming majority were in the East, and even more died in the USSR itself. Unlike the war of 1914–18, this was a war against civilians – fought out chiefly in those countries destined for the German *Lebensraum*.[9]

Eastern Europe, therefore, must lie at the heart of any account of the Nazi empire, but there is also the broader question of Europe itself. After all, the Germans, as we saw, were supposedly going to be trained in the 'imperial, *European* ideal', and many of the Nazis' more idealistic supporters in other countries took them at their word. In 1942 the

French right-wing writer Pierre Drieu la Rochelle, for instance, hoped that the Germans would 'lead Europe in the direction of the future'. Goebbels too worked hard to portray Hitler as the commander of a European crusade against communism. Yet despite the barrage of anti-Bolshevik Euro-propaganda from Berlin, Hitler himself remained a Greater German nationalist to the bitter end and in private he repeatedly stressed that the war was being fought for Germany and its people alone.[10] He told army commanders in December 1944 that they were fighting to find a definitive solution to Europe's German question. The war was a continuation not only of the First World War but of the nineteenth-century German wars as well and aimed at the same goal: 'the complete unification of all Germans'.[11]

Such speeches make Hitler sound like a typical nationalist – heir perhaps to the nineteenth-century Pan-Germans. Like other irredentists, their goal had been to win the largest possible state, which left as few countrymen as possible outside its borders. This was the prize Polish and Romanian nationalists won, for instance, in 1919; it was what the Hungarians and Bulgarians hoped the Germans would help them achieve in 1940. But to highlight only this rather traditional dimension to Nazi policy would be badly misleading for it ignores the critical importance of the geopolitical focus on mastery of the Eurasian landmass as the only conceivable way for Germany to rival the United States or Britain and it skates over the rigid biological racism, the unconstrained ruthlessness and the indifference to law that shaped the contours of the Third Reich's nationalism.

By contrast, the idea – which had also surfaced during the First World War – of a specifically *European* mission for the Reich never assumed nearly the same importance except for a brief moment in 1940. As the Wehrmacht conquered much of western Europe, Scandinavia and the Balkans with bewildering and completely unforeseen speed, older plans to regenerate the continent by creating a large German-led trading bloc were momentarily dusted off. It was a prospect – Germany as Europe's 'centre', as coordinator of a large internal market – the roots of which lay in nineteenth-century German thought. But this vision disappeared almost as quickly as it arose. Rationalizing interactions among capitalist economies preoccupied German industrialists and bankers (and those Nazis associated with them such as Hermann Göring) but scarcely interested Hitler. In 1941, the invasion of the USSR redirected his attention eastwards. The rest of Europe henceforth registered in his mind merely as a provider for the German economy, and to the extent that the regime thought in European terms it was because those running the war effort were forced to do so. Ways of fighting partisans that had been worked out in Belorussia were adopted in southern Italy and Finland. Labour tsar Fritz Sauckel travelled from France to the Ukraine to supervise his conscription drives. The wartime postings of a typical Gestapo official took him from southern Austria to north-western Germany, the Caucasus, Poland and Slovakia, and he even at one stage contemplated applying for a job with the new colonial service in Africa. War and occupation became the Nazis' way of integrating the continent, and indeed it eventually contributed roughly one-quarter of the resources consumed by the total German war effort. But this was entirely a consequence of needing to mobilize its resources; no positive vision lay beyond it.[12]

One reason the Germans failed to think deeply about Europe was that for much of the war they did not need to: Europeans fell into line and contributed what they demanded anyway. After 1945, this was conveniently forgotten. Those who had endured the German occupation hailed the heroic *résistants* and passed in silence over the fact that German officials in most of Europe had not been overly troubled by resistance until late in the day. That the Germans had managed to divert the resources of the continent to the benefit of their own war economy was attributed to coercion. Berlin's dealings with cooperative businessmen and civil servants in western and central Europe went unmentioned. So did the fact that thousands of unemployed French, Dutch, Croatian, Spanish and Italian workers had volunteered to work in factories in the Reich before the slave labour programme came in.[13]

Postwar, a collective amnesia seized countries like Italy, Hungary and Romania that had fought alongside Hitler and run parallel occupations of their own. The Croats and Slovaks had acquired their own states, Bulgaria had swallowed up neighbours' lands, and Hungary regained much of the territory it had lost in 1918. Mussolini had dreamed of a new Roman empire and sent his conscripts to the Cyclades if they were lucky and the Sahara, Slovenia or Somaliland if they were not. Romania had administered the Ukraine, festooned Odessa with corpses and hurled hundreds of thousands of soldiers into the struggle with the Red Army. Baltic, Belorussian and Ukrainian nationalists had all fought on the German side too in the hope that they might benefit.

Collaboration itself had been by no means an inexplicable choice, for in 1940 Europe was haunted by the failures of interwar liberalism and democracy and the Germans' economic and military successes compelled respect. Some Europeans hoped against hope that they would unite the continent better than the League of Nations or the British and French had done. Others were merely resigned. What made collaboration seem naive in retrospect was the Germans' almost total incapacity to respond to the political opportunity that opened up for them. As a result, they made themselves almost instantly unpopular. 'It is at all events one of the central problems of Hitler's Europe,' noted the great Dutch historian Pieter Geyl, who spent eighteen months of the war in the Buchenwald camp, 'this conflict between the attraction exercised by certain tendencies of the New Order and the growing disillusionment attendant upon the practice of the conqueror.'[14]

Its fundamental cause was Hitler's nationalism – or more precisely, his conviction that no one mattered or could be trusted politically apart from the Germans themselves. The sovereignty and independence of his allies could be overridden when necessary; the political aspirations of his collaborators could be disregarded at any moment. He completely ignored calls to proclaim a European programme that could compete with the Allies' Atlantic Charter. All that counted in his view was to be feared and obeyed. A Hungarian secret policeman summed up this attitude: 'In the occupied territories, the German government endorses the principle that, thrusting considerations of popularity into the background, only a regime or a government can be tolerated which is permanently at the beck and call of Germany.' For Hitler this was the essence of a colonial policy. Europe existed fundamentally to serve the interests of Greater Germany.[15]

Trying to create an empire on the basis of nationalism was nothing new. The French had their civilizing mission, and so, in a different way, did the Americans. More pertinently, the pre-1914 Russians and Hungarians had tried binding their lands together by spreading their language and culture. What made the Nazis' approach not only unusual but completely counter-productive as a philosophy of rule was their insistence on defining nationalism in such completely narrow terms that it precluded most of the peoples they conquered from ever becoming citizens. 'All states that are liberal of naturalisation towards strangers are fit for

7

empire,' Francis Bacon had written in the early seventeenth century. 'For to think that an handful of people can, with the greatest courage and policy in the world, embrace too large extent of dominion [is wrong for] it may hold for a time but it will fail suddenly.' Never was there a better illustration of the truth of this maxim than the fate of the Nazi New Order.[16]

Of course, the European overseas empires were themselves scarcely shining examples of Bacon's inclusive approach. Full British, French or Portuguese citizenship was hard to obtain if your skin was the wrong colour, and dual systems of legal status were not a Nazi invention. But outside Europe, exclusionary regimes had generally grown up over long periods of time, in what were still largely rural societies. They involved complex accommodations and compromises with local and native rulers, and in any case they were themselves coming under strain in the interwar period from emergent colonial nationalist movements. The Germans imposed their rule very suddenly in the midst of a war and they chose to inflict this on urbanized societies which had powerfully shaped and already formed senses of their own national identity. What was striking was not that Europeans resisted, but that they were mostly so hesitant to do so.

One reason was disorientation: the coming of the New Order shook the legitimacy of Europe's nation-states more deeply than ever before or since. It aimed, after all, not only to bolster German nationalism but to erase other peoples' sense of national identity as well. Countries like Poland, Czechoslovakia and Yugoslavia were wiped off the map. Many of the other conquered nations were also only decades old. Enemy occupation showed how weakly they cohered, and how easily they could fall apart. Deep fault lines ran within them – of class, language, ideology and religion – and total war triggered off lethal internecine clashes over the very image and self-definition of the nation itself. Often civil war was only a hair's breadth away, and in Greece, Yugoslavia, Italy and the Ukraine it cost thousands of lives.

The Germans' murderous retaliatory instincts were also a highly effective deterrent. Their devastating impact can best be seen through the public reaction to little-remembered episodes like the execution of the Czech premier, Alois Eliáš, in 1942, the 1941 reprisals in Serbia that resulted in more than 2,000 civilians being shot in the small town of Kragujevac alone, or the total demolition of the Vieux Quartier in

Marseille with the evacuation of its 40,000 inhabitants after a few roadside bombs had exploded in the city. These terrifying events crushed the spirits of those who learned about them and made the costs of resistance – not only to those who took up arms but to innocent civilians as well – all too evident.

Such memories – alongside those of Lidice, Oradour and the camps – have done much to shape our understanding of Nazism. Instead of being seen as an extreme version of a common modern European phenomenon – nationalism – it is its exceptional, pathological love of violence that is generally highlighted. Theorists of totalitarianism, in particular, portray it as an example of that fortunately rare type of polity in which a small band of men seize and hold power for no reason but sheer lust for domination, stamp out freedom and use terror to perpetuate their rule. They stress the political elite's control over ordinary people, and because they assume that the masses were coerced by terror from the start they do not spend much time worrying about the Nazis' own ideas. Instead the dictator himself emerges as the demonic prime mover in a kind of nihilistic counter-theology.

Now more than half a century old, the totalitarian paradigm has us in its grip still. It does get some things right. Hitler was indeed central both to the running of the Reich and – perhaps even more – to the way the Germans ran Europe: during the war there was no real collective government in any sense, and the continent's administration was run by him in a fashion that prevented that from emerging. His interventions, too, were often decisive – notably in escalating levels of collective punishment. Unsure (with some reason) of how far the German public was behind his long-term goals, he made sure that power stayed in the hands of those he most trusted. 'Working towards' the Führer, these men devised ever more bloody means of overcoming the numerous difficulties that their own ambitions had created. The wartime Nazi state thus operated with relatively little restraint, especially in eastern Europe or in the other occupied territories where checks on arbitrary executive power had fallen away, or had been undermined. One of the Nazis' most articulate opponents, the former French premier Léon Blum, understood what was happening. Of his relatives, who refused to leave Paris, he wrote in 1942 that 'they imagine that the atrocities of last month will be the last, or at least that the universal horror that they have provoked will lead to a long respite. They do not realize, I fear, that the gears move faster and faster and that one can always go further in atrocities; the limit is never reached.'[17]

Yet the totalitarian paradigm also gets many things wrong. Germany certainly needed to coerce the populations it ruled, but the situation was more complex inside Germany itself, especially during the war. Germans, on the whole, did not have to be coerced into fighting, and even in the final days there was no wholesale collapse as there had been in 1918. The country's dogged resistance cannot be attributed to the rapid escalation in terror that unquestionably did take place. Recently, scholars have claimed that the booty of conquest allowed the regime to buy popular backing for the war; the point is debatable, but that the population, despite its evident lack of enthusiasm when war actually broke out, did give its support, is not. Nor can one any longer maintain that there was any significant distinction after 1941 between how the SS and the Wehrmacht treated Jews and Slavs in the occupation. Ordinary German soldiers behaved just as brutally against the Bolsheviks, the Jews and other *Untermenschen* as the '150 per cent' Nazis. The New Order was thus a *German* venture in this sense too – not merely designed *for* the Germans, but reliant upon them and their active participation as well.[18]

Then there is the question of the ideas and debates that shaped the wartime system of German rule. Neither Hitler nor anyone else had anticipated the challenges the war brought. Quite the contrary: although the Nazis dreamed for years of fighting, when it happened they were taken aback by the consequences of their own success. The result was a series of arguments about ends and means that erupted in 1939 and never let up. As one follows these through private memoranda, published articles and the press, it quickly becomes clear that no single Nazi theory of conquest could be deduced either from *Mein Kampf* or from any of Hitler's own pronouncements. Thus we find that SS officials in 1939 wondered how they could seriously claim to be building a racially pure nation when they were pushing the Reich's boundaries beyond the zones of German habitation and ruling over Czechs and Poles. In 1941 others tussled over whether to privatize Soviet state farms or to keep them as they were in German hands. No one ever really decided, either, how far the seizure of power inside Germany before 1933 provided a template for Nazifying occupied countries, or indeed whether Nazism was exportable at all. Nazis believed passionately in their Führer and in National

Socialism, but this ideological commitment generated no simple answers to the problems they faced. For a totalitarian regime, there was a surprisingly vigorous argument about what continental mastery really meant.

Above all, there is a real problem with discussions of National Socialism that fail to take into account the catalytic impact of the war itself. Nothing perhaps illustrates the point better than the evolving terror apparatus. In September 1939, the six main concentration camps in the Reich housed a mere 21,400 prisoners between them; by the start of 1945 the system had metastasized into an enormous and appallingly run network of camps containing more than 700,000. There was, in short, no single system of terror that sprang fully formed from Hitler's brow. It was the policing of conquered territory in the East that allowed the SS to make its dizzying ascent until it became the most feared organization in occupied Europe. It was the war that completely altered the position of the Führer himself, allowing him to trample over what was left of judicial discretion inside Germany and making him simultaneously more remote and less constrained. It took only a few months, in the winter of 1941–2, for the Nazis to allow more than two million Soviet POWs to die in crowded camps, unseen and largely unrecorded. It took only three years – 1941 to 1944 – for them to invent and build extermination camps, kill over five million Jews and press-gang more than six million Europeans to work in the Reich. None of these things had happened – or had even been contemplated – before the war broke out.

The early 1940s are thus a prime example of how the violence of war – especially when short-sighted and ideologically driven political leadership is combined with overwhelming military superiority – may lead to an almost limitless escalation in the use of force and a constant revision of rules and norms. The Nazis embraced the idea of pre-emptive war and did not regard themselves as generally bound by international law; as a result, only their own ethical constraints (which intense racial nationalism weakened where non-Germans were concerned) set limits to what they regarded themselves as justified in doing. Yet if war allowed the regime to conquer territory, it was also a means – as Hitler himself well understood – to change the Germans and their values. For Nazism aimed to break not merely with parliamentary liberalism, but much more fundamentally with what had been until then commonly accepted notions of humanity. 'Man as such does not exist,' Walter Gross, head of the Office of Racial Policy, had written in 1936. 'There are only men belonging to this or that race.'[19] It took the war to bring out the full implications of this. Polish professors and priests were systematically and violently humiliated. When Soviet POWs were reduced to cannibalism, Hitler reacted with disgust. 'The men there are beasts,' he assured a Croatian visitor in February 1942: Germany's war was being waged against 'a bestial degeneration of humanity [*Menschheitsentartung*]'. As for the Jews, they were made to pull carts like horses, and to weed market squares on their hands and knees – as though to proclaim that they were no longer fully human.[20]

Much of today's interest in the New Order focuses on the subject of the Holocaust – the paradigmatic case of Nazi destructiveness. Yet even the 'war against the Jews' essentially grew out of the Führer's 'war for the Germans'. As it was, this entire campaign of conquest and racial annihilation rested on a fantastic illusion. The Wehrmacht's own polls showed that scarcely any German soldiers wanted to stay in Poland, let alone Russia, once the fighting was over: the very men Himmler intended to reward with farms in the East desired nothing so much as to return home. Most of them never got the chance. Millions of Russians, Poles, Jews and Belorussians perished in pursuit of the Nazis' imperial fantasy, but so did the very people who had killed them and were supposed to take their place: it was thanks to Nazism that German soldiers and civilians ended up dying in numbers that were probably not far short of the toll of the Final Solution itself. Far from establishing the Greater German Reich, Hitler left the country dismembered. His empire had premised its salvation on the death of millions, but salvation never came, and as his regime consumed its own, death was all it left behind.[21]

PART I

For Greater Germany

I

Germans and Slavs: 1848–1918

The chain of events that culminated in the creation of Hitler's empire did not begin with the invasion of Poland in 1939, the seizure of power in the Third Reich in 1933 or even the creation of the Nazi Party itself in Munich after the First World War. What unfolded between 1938 and 1945 was the final chapter in the story of a much older idea – the idea of a Greater Germany.

Or so it seemed in 1944, as the V-1 rockets fell on London, and the historian Lewis Namier found his mind back going back nearly a century to the events of 1848 – that extraordinary year when revolutionaries had toppled monarchs, and Paris, Prague, Vienna and Venice had resounded to the cry of liberty. In Frankfurt's Paulskirche, a German national assembly had convened proudly beneath a giant painting of *Germania* – a rather solidly built maiden in classical robes holding a sword triumphantly unsheathed in one hand and the flag of the German nation in the other – while its delegates debated political unity, freedom of the press and the need for a modern constitution. For many people ever since, the Assembly provided a glimpse of the road *not* taken, the expression of a German democratic spirit that was soon to be crushed by Prussian militarism and that might, had it triumphed, have spared Europe a century of wars.[1]

That was not how Namier saw it. In his view, the true spirit of 1848 *had* won out, and the deputies themselves with their dreams of Greater Germany had paved the way for the disaster of Nazism. There was, he argued, no vast gulf separating nineteenth-century German liberals from twentieth-century National Socialists: love of the nation, and hatred of the Slavs, was common to them both. 1848 was the moment when German parliamentary nationalism first revealed its capacity to destroy the peace of the continent. No longer could political differences be adjusted solely among kings and diplomats for now they involved the aspirations of entire peoples – aspirations increasingly defined in terms of land, language and blood.

In those long-forgotten speeches delivered at Frankfurt, Namier discerned the tap-root of German expansionism. Many orators there had hoped to behold a unified fatherland the cultural and economic superiority of which would irresistibly attract Poles, Czechs and other Slavs; they talked about a dominion stretching from the Baltic to south-eastern Europe and, fixated on the idea of a powerful national state, they rejected the very thought that Germans could ever be turned into a minority: 'Are half a million Germans to live under a German government and form part of the great German Federation, or are they to be relegated to the inferior position of naturalized foreigners only?' The mission of an eventual German national state must be to include all Germans within its borders and to save members of the nation from the awful fate of falling under the sway of a Slavic neighbour: 'Our right is that of the stronger, the right of conquest ... Legal rules appear nowhere more miserable than where they presume to determine the fate of nations.' To Namier's audience in London, much of this uncompromising rhetoric – with its demands for a mighty Germany to act as bulwark against Russia, and its talk of 'puny nationalities' likened to destructive 'parasites' trying to 'found their own lives in our midst' – must have had an uncannily familiar ring.[2]

This reading of Germany's past was, no doubt, tendentious and anachronistic. There were plenty of differences between the liberals of the 1840s and the National Socialists of a century later, between those who believed in the power of German culture and those who believed in German blood. But some Nazis did describe their own history in rather similar terms. Only a few years earlier, Professor Reinhard Höhn, one of Himmler's favourite intellectuals, had applauded the '48ers. According to him, they had been right in asserting the principle of civilian rule over the military, something the Third Reich had finally managed to achieve only thanks to the power of the Nazi Party. Hitler singled out the democrats of Frankfurt for praise too. In a speech he made in the city after the *Anschluss* with Austria in 1938, he expressed his happiness at being 'the fulfiller of a yearning which once found its most profound expression here'. He told Josef Goebbels that the '48ers were in no way to be compared to the hated 'November Democrats' who had founded the Weimar Republic for the simple reason that they were 'Greater German idealists', who had believed like him in a powerful German nation with a European mission. According to the Führer, they had tried to build a Germany that could crush the Slavs and dominate Europe. Unfettered by the kings and princes who had defeated them, he would triumph where they had failed.[3]

Nationalism's triumph had been a long time coming, for in the middle of the nineteenth century, the German-speaking peoples were still ruled by a bewildering array of duchies, principalities and kingdoms. What people in central and eastern Europe meant when they described themselves as 'German' varied greatly from place to place, and many of them could scarcely understand one another because regional dialects were so strong. Politically, most 'Germans' professed loyalty to their rulers and did not see themselves as part of a single group, still less one that ought to be unified in a single state. The intellectuals at Frankfurt were thus challenging mainstream opinion not following it. As one journalist complained in 1848: 'The majority of Austrian peasants do not even know that there is a Germany and that it is their fatherland!' Waking Germans up to the truth of nationalism was the self-imposed mission of a minority of troublemakers: it would take them the best part of a century before their message prevailed.[4]

In the loosely organized German Confederation which emerged after Napoleon's defeat, the two most powerful states were Austria and Prussia, and the intimate yet fraught relationship between them was to shape Europe's German question for decades. Less than half the size of its rival, Prussia was far more thoroughly German-speaking in population. It might have only sixteen million inhabitants as against thirty-six million subjects of the Habsburgs, but of those sixteen, fourteen million spoke German, whereas fewer than seven million lived in Emperor Franz Joseph's polyglot domains. In short, from the nationalists' viewpoint, the kind of state they wanted seemed most likely to emerge under Prussian direction.

Following the Franco-Prussian war, the German states were indeed unified in a new German Reich, and Wilhelm I of Prussia was proclaimed emperor. But for many nationalists this was only a halfway house – a so-called 'Little German' solution because it did not include the German-speaking lands of the Habsburg empire. Unfortunately for them, the architects of the new Reich had ruled out the idea of destroying the

Habsburgs. Bismarck was a man who knew where to draw the line – for, as he put it, 'new formations in this area could only be of a permanently revolutionary character'. His conservatism imposed strict limits on Germany's expansion, and the alliance with Austria-Hungary remained the cornerstone of the Reich's foreign policy up to the outbreak of the First World War and beyond: in 1915, a German historian noted that 'the primary and most immediate task of the war [was] the preservation of Austria'.[5]

Inside the empire itself, nationalist movements were also stirring among the Hungarians, Italians, Poles and South Slavs. Not all of them aspired to political independence, for many realized that the most likely alternative to the Habsburg empire was being trapped between 'a Russian universal monarchy' and a powerful new Germany. In 1848 the prominent Bohemian intellectual František Palacký, rejecting an invitation to the Frankfurt Assembly, had famously explained that 'if the Austrian empire did not exist, in the interest of Europe, nay, of humanity, it would be necessary . . . to invent it'. By the end of the century, belief in the empire as a multi-national space spanned the political spectrum from Catholic monarchists to Austrian Marxists who had come round to believing in the need 'to prevent the collapse of Austria and to enable its nations to live together'.[6]

The Emperor Franz Joseph was certainly not interested in wrapping himself in the flag of German nationalism. He knew such a policy would only arouse the antipathy of his – far more numerous – other subjects, and he knew too that religion prevented most Austrian Germans from looking to Protestant Berlin for help. Loyalty to the House of the Habsburgs was more important to him than ethnic background. But as Italians, Czechs and Poles demanded language and cultural rights of their own, some Habsburg Germans formed national clubs and societies to mobilize against them, founding schools, newspapers and gymnastics societies. Duelling fraternities flourished; students would drink and make loud, aggrieved speeches, toasting 'Germania, Mother of Us All!' In their halls, under prominently displayed pictures of Bismarck and the German Kaiser, garlanded with flowers, they would talk about fighting to stop the local Czechs or Slovenes from crushing 'Germandom'. The founding charter of the Alldeutsche Vereinigung opened with the pledge to 'strive for a relationship of the former German Lands of Austria with the German Reich, which will permanently guarantee the preservation of our *Volkstum* [People]'. In Bohemia the German Workers' Party called for 'the maintenance and increase of the *Lebensraum* of its own nationality' in the face of 'pressure from foreign workers of lower culture'. These movements – strongly anti-Slav, often anti-Semitic – marked the milieu from which Hitler emerged. Here – in an uncompromising critique of the empire, in a rejection of its way of accommodating the diverse peoples of central Europe, and in the drive to unify all the Germans in a single state irrespective of existing national boundaries – lay the starting-point of the future Führer's thought.[7]

POLES

Nazism borrowed much from late Habsburg German nationalism, but it borrowed much more from the Prussians, especially as regarded the treatment of Poles. Poland itself had ceased to exist as a result of being partitioned between Austria, Russia and Prussia in the late eighteenth century. But for the Prussians, partition had been a particularly bad idea: it destroyed the buffer state that had cushioned them from the might of Russia, and it had vastly increased the size of the country's Polish-speaking minority. In the province of Posen in particular, Poles remained in a majority despite the Prussian government's efforts to attract German settlers. Drawing on the words of Jean-Jacques Rousseau, a Polish deputy at the Frankfurt Assembly in 1848 warned his German colleagues: 'You may have swallowed us up, but, by God, you shall not digest us.'

Half a century later, Prussia's Polish indigestion was worse than ever. They formed its largest minority – about 10 per cent of the total population – and the fact that they were Catholics only made matters worse. The Kaiser's police tried to keep them under surveillance. But in the East, their numbers grew so rapidly that they started to alarm the Prussian government. Bismarck's anti-Catholic campaign closed down Polish-language schools, confiscated Church estates and led to the arrest of many priests. Yet Polish workers and agricultural labourers still constituted a majority of the population in many border areas. The town of Posen/Poznań was a heavily fortified German island in a Polish sea: in the surrounding province, 800,000 Poles lived alongside half that number of Germans.

In the mid-to-late nineteenth century, an increasingly conflictual and racialized view of the Slavs was in any case spreading among the German intelligentsia. The geographer Friedrich Ratzel, an important figure in turning the public's attention to the importance of agricultural settlement for national vitality, applied Darwinian theories to the rise and fall of the *Volk*, and argued that what he called 'living space [*Lebensraum*]' was needed to ensure its continued growth. Many of his followers gave his arguments a harsh, racialized edge. Explaining his new science of 'geopolitics', the Swedish political scientist Rudolf Kjellén talked about 'the ambition of the state to become organically united with the soil': expansion was 'self-preservation'; large states would flourish while small states would gradually disappear, 'the more the world became organized'. Kjellén praised war and emphasized Germany's ambiguous position as 'Reich of the Middle', both uniquely susceptible to encirclement and urged on by destiny to expansion and leadership.[8]

Bismarck had little time for such ideas. His focus was on internal consolidation; but winning this struggle was much harder than Prussia's battles abroad had been. He expelled Polish workers, but most of them returned fairly quickly. He then established a new Royal Prussian Colonization Commission to strengthen 'the German element ... against attempted Polonization'. The first serious German effort at a state population policy on national lines, this used bank credits and compulsory land purchases to help Germans settle in border areas.[9] Yet its main effect was to merely push up land prices: German sellers profited; German tax-payers footed the bill. Meantime, the Poles organized their own national credit and cooperative groups. They lost 60,000 hectares to the Prussian Commission between 1896 and 1912 but by adding another 100,000 they more than made up for it. Bismarck's policy satisfied nobody and caused huge ill-feeling. The trouble was that it basically wished away the realities of industrialization in favour of a medieval agrarian fantasy that global economic forces were irrevocably destroying.[10]

Behind all this lay a question that was critical to the Nazis' own political goals: how far could a state control where its population chose to live? While some Germans responded to what was drily called 'the Eastern bonus' – state subsidies – this was simply not high enough for the hundreds of thousands more who still went abroad, chiefly to the USA. The 170,000 immigrants enticed on to the land by the Commission were overshadowed by the 830,000 Germans who left eastern Prussia alone after 1895. Depopulation not repopulation was the reality that faced German nationalists. As one journalist from Posen – where the Polish population had grown rapidly since the 1860s – wrote mournfully in 1902:

Officials from the Reich consider it the greatest misfortune to be transferred to our province. According to them, such a transfer is not very much different from being exiled to Siberia. The peasant, so long as he can rub along somewhere, is careful not to be sent to our inhospitable province where the land is not particularly fertile and competition with the Polish peasant strong. He prefers to emigrate to America.[11]

The young Max Weber, who studied the Polish problem closely, felt the outlook was grim. He especially blamed the great landowners for relying on Polish labourers. The large landed estates, wrote Weber, were 'our greatest Polonizer', and the 'violent crisis of agriculture' was leading inexorably to the triumph of 'the least evolved nationality'. A far more extensive colonization programme was needed than anything Bismarck was prepared to consider. It was not enough to put more money in the pockets of wealthy families who did not need it; priority needed to be given to supporting the small German landholder. Forty years later, Weber's arguments found a receptive audience in Nazi circles. In an essay dedicated to SS chief Heinrich Himmler at the very moment that the latter was resettling Germans and expelling Poles with a ruthlessness undreamed of before the First World War, a high-ranking Nazi sociologist drew on Weber's analysis to denounce the lack of seriousness with which the old Kaiserreich had addressed this pressing racial issue. Freed from the reactionary political influence of the Junker class, he argued, the Third Reich was proving itself more effective than any of its predecessors.[12]

As the nineteenth century ended, lobby groups to defend the 'German Eastern Marches' emerged and seized the initiative away from the old Prussian elite. The H-K-T (so-called after the initials of its three founders) organized boycotts of Polish businesses, sponsored lectures (for example, on 'Civilization and the National State', or 'What Unites the Germans, and What Divides Them?'), tours of the borderlands and kitschy 'German Day' festivals. Others reminded people of the glories of the medieval German past – when the crusading Teutonic Knights had Germanized the East by the sword – and published alarming maps showing the demographic threat from the East. One way or another, considerable energy was invested in regenerating what nationalists called 'the consciousness of national kinship'.[13]

Under pressure, German politicians – having briefly abandoned the futile old Bismarckian policy – now went back to it. Yet the Pan-Germans wanted them to do much more – to ban Polish, for instance, on shop-signs and store-fronts, in church records and private associations, or to force Polish newspapers to run a parallel German text for every story. 'The state that surrenders the unity of its state language surrenders its political unity altogether,' wrote a lawyer. This was nothing less than a 'war of the peoples', and time was running out. 'We must support with all our strength the immigration of Germans into the Polish provinces,' wrote one in 1906. 'The Colonization Commission must quicken the tempo of its work because the period of peace is an invaluable time for such achievements and peace will not be endless. The Germanization of the Eastern Marches must be concluded before we go to war with the northern and southern Slavs.'[14] Even assimilation was no longer the answer. On the contrary, according to a writer in 1902: 'For the German who wants to preserve the German type against inferior races such as the strongly Mongolized Slavs, the first commandment is: "No racial mixing with aliens".'[15]

Weber had identified the crucial problem: the Prussian landowners were keen to keep their cheap workers; the racially minded middle-class patriots wanted them gone. Trying to dampen down the passions on both sides, a German-language newspaper in Posen reminded its readers that what was at stake was

not an aggressive 'life and death' struggle waged against the entire Polish population; it is not a question, so to speak, of exterminating the Poles. Rather the government's Polish policy is aimed only at the defeat of those Polish nationalist efforts and designs whose realization would be incompatible with the Prussian state-idea and with the security of the German Reich.[16]

Yet some were indeed thinking of a 'life or death' struggle. Bismarck himself felt strongly that Germany needed peace. He commented in 1887 that 'Russia wishes to conquer no German land, and we desire to conquer no Russian land. It can only be a question of Polish provinces, and of these we already have more than is convenient for us.'[17] He therefore had no time for his own General Staff's plans for an assault on the Tsarist army, complete with support for nationalist insurgencies in Poland, Finland and the Caucasus; the latter idea in particular he regarded as entirely mad. But once he was gone, Germany's politicians became more nervous and belligerent. Liberals and socialists, who had traditionally hated the Tsarist regime, were joined by conservatives who feared that the Reich he had created was more vulnerable to attack from the East than he realized. As a result, they launched themselves into the war that would make their problems worse.

THE FIRST WORLD WAR

In 1914, Bismarck's legacy was completely abandoned. Chancellor Bethmann-Hollweg called for Russia to be pushed back far to the east, and for its hold over non-Russian peoples to be broken.[18] The following summer, the armies of the Central Powers did indeed push the Russians back, and the Germans marched into Warsaw. Suddenly the Polish question became more than merely theoretical, and Russian Poland was divided between the occupation forces of the Central Powers. Austrian military rule was established in the southern part, while the Germans set up a General-Government in Warsaw.

A more striking contrast with the Nazi occupation in the Second World War it is hard to imagine. The University of Warsaw was re-opened, Polish-language teaching was reintroduced after nearly half a century of Russian rule, and large numbers of students were readmitted. Thanks to the Germans, municipal self-government was introduced for the first time – something unknown under the tsars – and elections were held during the war. The German army also had a conscious policy of supporting the Jewish press in Poland and the governor, General Hans von Beseler, set up a Jewish self-government. In short, the Germans tried to present themselves as liberators from Russian tyranny, and Beseler urged the formation of a 'Polish national state' 'in the closest association with Germany' – basically a revival of the post-Napoleonic Congress of Poland but this time under German not Russian rule. In July 1916, General Erich Ludendorff, the chief of staff to the German army in the East (*Oberost*) advocated turning Poland into a principality, with its own army, under Germany's control. The following month, the Central

Powers agreed that they would jointly support an Independent Kingdom of Poland and they set up a Council of State of Polish notables to help run the country.[19]

Yet if these policies offered a stunning contrast with how the Nazis would treat Poland in 1939, others looked uncannily like precursors. Alongside their pro-Polish policy, for instance, the Germans were planning to annex part of Russian Poland in order to carve out a new so-called frontier strip along the Reich's eastern border: the existing population in the area was to be deported to make room for German settlers. The Pan-German lobby was calling for this, and so were the large number of German public figures who signed the so-called Intellectuals' Address in the summer of 1915. Designed to elevate the discussion of war aims above the merely economic, the Address called for increased German colonization in former Russian territory and the building of a human frontier wall.[20]

The whole war was leading armies to uproot populations, especially in sensitive borderlands and front areas. The German army itself cleared a large strip of land of its inhabitants along the Baltic coast, and it also created a dead zone several miles deep in France when it withdrew to the Hindenburg Line in 1917. Scorched earth policies deprived the enemy of all the resources the land had to offer. The extraordinary devastation of the strip in front of the Siegfried Line in France in 1917 was the apotheosis of this approach – the region was turned into 'a desolate, dead desert' in which trees, buildings and hedgerows were systematically levelled by explosives, leaving a completely flattened landscape. Other armies were also clearing their borders. Ottoman forces marched Greeks and Armenians away from the Mediterranean coastline into Anatolia. Serb villages were emptied and burned down by Hungarian soldiers. Above all, xenophobic and fearful Russian officers forced more than three-quarters of a million civilians to follow the retreating Tsarist armies away from the borderlands, creating a huge refugee exodus.[21]

As in the colonies before 1914, and as in Europe after 1939, the German army's policies as a force of occupation combined systematic exploitation with violent pacification. One of the reasons why the Germans failed to conjure up a new Polish army as they hoped to do was the extreme resentment they had aroused, according to a report at the time, by a whole series of military-industrial interventions, such as the seizure of raw materials, factories, machines, the compulsory purchase of houses and the stripping of private forests ... All these measures have given rise to a sense of specific complaints, as have the generally rough handling of the population by German soldier and officials and the imposition of unnecessary restrictions on movement.[22]

In Belgium, the behaviour of the military was, if anything, worse, and the deportation of nearly 60,000 workers to German factories prefigured the policies that were pursued on a much larger scale across Europe after 1941. Half a million French workers, too, were conscripted for war work and a large network of labour camps emerged. Military necessity was an argument that triumphed over all considerations of international law or diplomacy, and the army itself seemed to be indifferent to the uproar that these policies created around the world. It was equally unconcerned about the reaction to news of the atrocities it committed in Belgium in the autumn of 1914, when at least 6,000 people were executed and thousands of buildings were deliberately demolished or burned down. As in the Second World War, the German army seemed little bothered about the plight of the local population, and even with imports of foreign aid malnutrition became pervasive – indeed a considerably more serious problem in Belgium after 1914 than it was in the Second World War.[23]

The Reich's new military masters – Hindenburg and Ludendorff – aimed to use the 'East' to show the 'Westerners' in France and Belgium how to build 'something lasting' through 'German work'. In their vast Baltic fiefdom, *Oberost*, they aimed to colonize the wild forests and marshes and to civilize their inhabitants (exactly as previous generations of Germans had talked about civilizing the Poles). Ignoring the ethnic and logistical complexities of the terrain, they saw military occupation as a way to exploit the under-utilized resources on Germany's doorstep. In Macedonia, the French army had similar ambitions. But Hindenburg and Ludendorff did not only want to conquer nature; unlike the French, they wanted to conquer the region racially as well, keeping Slavs under surveillance and creating new settlements where 'German heroes' could be reborn. As during the period of Nazi occupation, the army tried to mobilize the entire population for forced labour, introduced an extensive system of registration and identity cards and deported tens of thousands of workers to Germany. This was also a culture which demanded the constant acknowledgement of military prestige. Non-Germans had to step off the pavement if they met a German officer and tip their hats; they could not enter railway cars reserved for Germans. Contempt for civilians and the lack of institutional curbs on military behaviour combined with ideologies of completely unrealizable social transformation to allow the German army to treat occupied populations and property as it pleased; when the war started to go badly, the result was pointless destruction on a vast scale.[24]

TO BREST-LITOVSK

In the spring of 1918, however, the war in the East seemed to be going very well indeed, and the vision of a German empire there materialized when the Germans forced a punitive peace on a despondent Bolshevik delegation. Thanks to the Treaty of Brest-Litovsk, signed in a vast, gloomy Russian fortress, a crushing *pax Germanica* emerged across a swathe of Tsarist provinces from the Baltic to the Black Sea – a region which strikingly prefigured that conquered by the Wehrmacht in 1941. On the Western Front, German troops massed for the decisive offensive, intending to finish off the Entente before arriving American troops could tilt the balance. But in the East, a new order was already being established. As the imperial regime collapsed, the Kaiser's army took over. Russia, according to one German officer, was 'nothing but a great pile of maggots; all rotten, all swarming together without order'.[25]

At Brest-Litovsk, the Bolsheviks ceded 90 per cent of Russia's coal mines, 54 per cent of its industry and a third of its rail system and its population. German soldiers marched into the Ukraine and Georgia, and with one million troops occupying the region, Berlin's strategists created a cordon of new puppet states that would buffer Germany from Bolshevism and provide the markets, grain, oil and other resources to guarantee Germany's status as a world power. There would be a 'new order in Europe [which] promised far greater permanency than the outright annexation of foreign territory'. The Germans set up obedient regimes in the Ukraine, Lithuania and Poland, and turned Romania into a satellite as well. The German High Command dreamed of its frontier wall of 'physically and mentally healthy human beings' warding off the racial threat posed by the fast-breeding Slavs. Others imagined marching further east still – turning the Crimea into a German 'Riviera', forcing a way through the Caucasus to Persia, Afghanistan and ultimately India, to bring the British empire to its knees by enlisting the sympathies of Pan-Islamic or Pan-Turkish movements across Eurasia.[26]

There was only one problem: the war had not ended. 1918's western offensive petered out, and with America's entry into the war, the balance of forces shifted rapidly against Berlin. A few months later, with a swiftness the German public found hard to comprehend, Germany's allies sued for peace, and the German High Command followed suit, conveniently blaming civilian treachery rather than their own strategic miscalculations for their capitulation. The Kaiser was forced to abdicate and reluctantly started his long exile in the Netherlands. Over the coming months, Germany's new eastern order crumbled, and Brest-Litovsk became 'the forgotten peace'.

But it was not forgotten by everyone. Enraged nationalists could not believe that this eastern prize had been snatched from their grasp and they fought to reclaim it. Bands of volunteers mobilized in diverse so-called Free Corps to defend the nation's borders: they battled socialists in Munich and the Poles in Posen. In the Baltic, General von der Goltz was backed by the Entente Powers when Trotsky's Red Army took Riga in December. German paramilitaries and ex-soldiers flocked to von der Goltz's headquarters at Mitau in order to preserve what they could of Brest-Litovsk – not only against the Bolsheviks but against Baltic nationalists and if necessary the British as well. Pushing the Bolshevik forces back east, they brought terror and mass executions in their wake. Five hundred civilians were shot without trial in Mitau itself, 3,000 were killed in Riga, the capture of which in May 1919 – the high-point of their venture – they hailed as 'the symbol of the victory of European civilization over Asiatic barbarism'. More or less unknown today, their temporary reconquest of Latvia and Lithuania was among the most violent episodes of the entire war and a precursor of what lay ahead. 'The battles in the Baltic states were more brutal and vicious than anything I had experienced before,' wrote one of the participants, the future Auschwitz commandant Rudolf Höss. 'There was hardly a front-line; the enemy was everywhere. Wherever the opposing forces collided, there was a slaughter until no one was left.'[27]

Claiming to be saving the Baltic states from Bolshevism, the Germans behaved like freebooters. For some the goal was an estate of their own; for others, there was no goal beyond blind obedience to their leaders, 'war and adventure, excitement and destruction'. 'Villages burst into flames, prisoners were trampled underfoot,' recalled one. All of this they remembered in a romantic glow, seeing themselves as crusaders reborn, a new generation of Teutonic Knights. 'The dangerous strangeness of this land which held me in such a peculiar spell enticed me,' wrote one. 'It was a land which imparted to war something of its own turbulent and ever-changing character ... This is perhaps what had given the Teutonic Knights that restless seeking which ever drove them, again and again, from their solid castles to new and dangerous adventures.'[28]

As Nazism consolidated itself in Germany in the 1930s, such men were pushed to the margins; they were too unruly, demanding and unpredictable, and many of them perished in the bloodletting of the Night of the Long Knives in 1934. But war was what they knew best, and after 1939 many of them returned when another German army established a second New Order in those same eastern territories. Hitler's personal secretary, Rudolf Hess, and his successor, Martin Bormann (whom the war turned into one of the most powerful men in the Reich), had been Free Corps men. Höss, helped by his friend Bormann, had committed murder to avenge the death of their Free Corps comrade Leo Schlageter. Erich Koch, Hitler's viceroy in the Ukraine between 1941 and 1944, had been one of Schlageter's honorary pall-bearers. The ties between these 'old fighters' thus went back decades. Occupied Poland was ruled by former Free Corps men too – the governor general, Hans Frank, and Warthegau boss Arthur Greiser. Germany's wartime police chief, Kurt Daluege, had been a section leader in the Rossbach Free Corps, while the undiplomatic minister to Romania, Manfred von Killinger, had planned the murders of several leading Weimar politicians. And there were more – Erich von dem Bach-Zelewski, the SS general in overall charge of anti-partisan operations across Europe, Wilhelm Stuckart in the Interior Ministry (one of the wartime Reich's most important bureaucrats), as well as Reinhard Heydrich and Ernst Kaltenbrunner, the two heads of the Reich Main Security Office. The second occupation of the East was their moment.[29]

One wonders what the Reich's former commander-in-chief, the ex-Kaiser Wilhelm himself, would have felt when German armies invaded the USSR in 1941. He had cheered on the victories in the Low Countries and France the previous year. But less than a month before this second war against Bolshevism began, he died in his Dutch château, aged eighty-two. The Kaiser and the Führer shared the same focus upon eastern Europe as the critical zone for national security, the same obsession with land, colonization and racial settlement. Along with many of their followers, both believed that expanding Germany's borders was necessary to achieve safety in a world of constant struggle against the Slavic danger from the East. The Kaiser, like Hitler, saw Bolshevism as a worldwide Jewish anti-German plot which demanded ruthless opposition: pushing for military-policing operations to wipe out the Bolsheviks, he wanted his men to behave like the 'Turks in Armenia'. His leading generals wanted – precisely as Hitler did later – to deprive Russia of its vital cereals, coal, minerals and oil by occupying the Ukraine and the Caucasus.[30]

But the differences were revealing too. The Nazis went to great pains to show that they were not merely repeating the Kaiser's policies (although they might have fared better if they had). Writing in March 1942, Josef Goebbels, the Nazi propaganda minister, scoffed at those who expected the Nazi New Order, having pushed the Red Army back hundreds of miles, to set up new governments in the 'midget states' of the East: 'One would have to take the imperial regime of Kaiser Wilhelm as a model if one were to inaugurate so short-sighted a policy. National Socialism is much more cold-blooded and much more realistic in all these questions.' And indeed, unlike Hitler, Kaiser Wilhelm II and his government had actually talked the language of national liberation, monarchism and self-determination and countenanced the creation of nominally independent east European states. They spoke sometimes of racial strength, but such a vocabulary carried far less murderous implications for civilians under their authority. Military occupation by the imperial army could be harsh, but, as the experience of Poland showed, it was nothing compared with what the civilians who ran the Nazi occupation machine were ready to do. Those Poles and Jews (and there were many) in 1939 who anticipated that the victorious Third Reich would behave like the Second were horribly disillusioned. Indeed, despite the anti-Semitism commonplace in the Kaiser's entourage, the Jews did not figure centrally in Germany's plans during the First World War. They were less enemies than they were potential allies, encouraged along with the other rebellious nationalities under the tsar.[31]

Most important of all, in the First World War there were still the Habsburgs. Dynastic solidarity constituted *the* decisive brake on the idea of a Greater Germany. But in 1918, the Habsburgs and Hohenzollerns were toppled, and in their stead there arose after 1933 a new, more powerfully centralized state of the German People, with Hitler as its architect, which easily swallowed up the small, rump Austria created at Versailles. Hitler may have been born a subject of Emperor Franz Joseph, but his worldview presupposed a vision of order and nationality in eastern Europe which was not so much post- as *anti*-Habsburg, based on ethnic purity not intermingling, on loyalty to the nation rather than to any supra-national dynasty. The roots of the Nazi New Order, in other words, lay not in anti-Semitism, nor in the blind lust for conquest, but rather in the quest to unify Germans within a single German state. Under the direction of a self-made leader and his mass party, this aimed to succeed where the Kaiser had failed, in establishing a permanent dominion in the East over the Slavs and in this way to become powerful enough to exercise mastery over Europe as a whole.

2

Versailles to Vienna

'The struggle for ethnicity is nothing other than the continuation of war by other means under the cover of peace. Not a fight with gas, grenades, and machine-guns, but a fight about homes, farms, schools, and the souls of children . . .'
                                                    Theodor Oberländer[1]

If 1918 began with the Germans poised to establish a triumphant new order across eastern Europe, it ended with them facing complete collapse. The Habsburg empire disintegrated almost overnight, and the Emperor Charles fled to Switzerland before ending up on Madeira, where he died a few years later. In Germany the monarchy was abolished, and the Kaiser went into exile. Meanwhile, Britain and France came around to the idea that – as one diplomat put it – their 'interests entirely coincide with the principle of nationality'. In 1919, they set up a *cordon sanitaire* of east European buffer states ruled by governments closely allied with London and Paris. Blaming the Germans for starting the war, they burdened them with reparations and punished them with substantial losses of territory. Many Germans who had grown up as Habsburg or Prussian subjects found themselves being ruled by Czechs, Poles, Estonians and Latvians for the first time.[2]

Even before the war had ended at least one British diplomat had asked himself: what if the Germans took the slogan of national self-determination seriously? Would the peace not then lead to an even larger German Reich – especially if the Habsburg monarchy fell apart? In October 1918, it did. As the empire entered its death throes, the prewar representatives of the German territories of Austria-Hungary gathered in Vienna and declared that they constituted a Provisional National Assembly for Germany-Austria: the Austrian Germans wanted unification with Germany and they saw no reason to wait. Shortly after that they passed a draft constitution which stated categorically that 'Germany-Austria is a component part of the German Republic.' It was thus the Central Powers' defeat, not their victory, that brought Greater Germany closer.[3]

Austrian Social Democrats wanted to join republican Germany because they saw it as a sure means of jettisoning the Habsburg monarchy for good. Only a few months earlier, they had still been thinking about turning the empire into 'a state of nationalities' – a kind of alternative to Wilsonian nation-states – as 'an experiment for the future national order of mankind'. But that moment had passed, and defeat had narrowed the options. They were excited by the fact that the Kaiser had been forced off his throne and they believed *Anschluss* would allow them to create that great German republic their grandfathers had glimpsed in 1848. Few people could imagine a tiny independent Austria flourishing; becoming part of Germany would not only guarantee prosperity, but would also show that, as the new chancellor, Karl Renner, put it, 'We are one community sharing a common fate.' For fellow socialist Otto Bauer, the merger of Austria and Germany would help create 'the Germany of tomorrow ... a democratic Germany'.[4] In the telegram he sent Berlin after the proclamation of the new constitution, he noted that the country had 'expressed its will to be reunited with the other Germanic nations from whom it had been separated 52 years ago'. In this way, he suggested, the historical wounds created by Prussia's defeat of the empire in 1866 might finally be closed.

Anschluss – amid the shock of the Habsburg callapse – was not a slogan of the left alone: on the right, too, there had been wartime calls for 'a new order of all political, national and economic-social relationships' with Germany. But the left was really the driving force. In elections for the new Austrian assembly in February 1919, the right mustered only 18 per cent of the votes, compared with 41 per cent for the Social Democrats. Not all Austrians welcomed unification, however, and there was also a large vote – more than one-third – for the Catholic Christian Socials, many of whom feared Prussian domination and the dilution of the Church's influence.[5]

In Paris there was a much bigger stumbling block to German unification than Austrian Catholicism. After all, the Entente Powers had not really fought for four years merely to preside over the expansion of

Germany. While Weimar formally accepted the *Anschluss* resolution, German diplomats fretted about the likely reaction abroad. And with good reason: when the Treaty of Versailles was agreed in June 1919, it insisted upon the establishment of an independent Austria. Less than two months later, the victors also gave South Tyrol to Italy, and parts of Styria and Carinthia to the new Kingdom of the Serbs, Croats and Slovenes, while Bohemia's Germans found themselves in the new state of Czechoslovakia. As if this was not bad enough, further efforts at unification were explicitly blocked: 'The independence of Austria is immutable unless the Council of the League of Nations agrees.' It was in vain that Austria's leaders pointed out the obvious contradiction with the principle of self-determination which formed the basis for the new Wilsonian order in Europe. In Vienna the National Assembly accepted the Treaty under protest, and the name of the state was altered in October 1919 from 'German Austria' to the 'Republic of Austria'. With time, support for independence increased. But *Anschluss* remained a rallying-cry for Austrian politicians throughout the 1920s, and popular anger with Versailles simmered as what had once been the core of a vast empire was forced to cope with the immiserating consequences of imperial collapse: 'Hunger or *Anschluss*!' ran a slogan of the Austrian National Democrats. In private, even smart Catholic politicians like Ignaz Seipel, chancellor of the Republic, were broadly in favour of it. 'Austria in its present form has never had a self-contained existence,' wrote Seipel to a correspondent in 1928. 'Consistent with their entire history and style of life, the Austrians are big-state people.'[6] Yet so long as the Versailles settlement held, *Anschluss* remained a diplomatic and military impossibility.

MINORITIES AT THE LEAGUE

At least in Austria, ethnic Germans were a majority. Elsewhere in eastern Europe the establishment of new states had left them as often sizeable minorities. There were 1.2 million Germans in Poland at the end of the war, 3.5 million in Czechoslovakia, 550,000 in Hungary, 250,000 in Italy, 800,000 in Romania, 700,000 in Yugoslavia and 220,000 in the Baltic states. Versailles had turned Germans into the largest minority population in Europe and by 1930 it was estimated that 8–9 million of the 36 million members of national minorities in eastern Europe were German.[7]

It would be unfair to accuse the war's victors of ignoring their plight. On the contrary, they made Poland and other east European states guarantee them collective rights. The League of Nations itself monitored their compliance and thus identified itself with the proper treatment of Germans, Jews and other minorities in the New Europe, the peace of which it was designed to watch over. This was a hugely ambitious departure in international law for which the nineteenth century provided few precedents. Previously, newly independent states had been told by the Powers to guarantee freedom of conscience and to avoid religious discrimination – provisions which had been applied to Belgium, Greece, Serbia and others before 1914. But the new arrangements spotlit states' behaviour in the realms of education, culture, economy and administration. The problem – and time would show that there was one – lay not in the idea of guaranteeing collective rights, which was in many ways a good one, but in its implementation.

In some countries, Germans – and minorities generally – had few grounds for complaint. Estonia and Latvia in particular treated them well. Considering the annexationist policies of the German army in the region during the war, the chauvinistic attitude of some of the local German barons and the destructiveness of the Free Corps, it is in retrospect little short of astonishing how far these new states were willing to accommodate their diverse populations. The Estonian constitution guaranteed their right to cultural autonomy and in 1925 passed a law by which individuals could choose to identify themselves with a given nationality. This stood as a model of how the new League regime might have worked, with better will, elsewhere. Deputies could address parliament in German, Russian, Yiddish or Swedish, if they chose, and although many German landowners were ruined by the expropriation of their estates, the majority of Estonia's Germans lived more modestly in the towns and were unaffected.[8]

Behind the 1925 law in Estonia were the 'other' Germans – those who believed in ideas of minorities protection and cultural autonomy and wanted to make them work. Ewald Ammende had grown up during the First World War and watched the failure of wartime German efforts to create lobby groups of disaffected anti-Russian nationalities. In the early 1920s, he published numerous articles on the challenges of adjustment

– political, economic and mental – that Germans faced in central and eastern Europe, and he was also behind the Union of German National Groups in Europe. The European Nationalities Congress, which he helped to found three years later, was Europe's main minorities umbrella group. It brought Jews, Ukrainians, Germans and others together to strengthen the League's commitment to minority rights. But its base and its core funding were German, and we need to understand its rise – and fall – in the context of Weimar's approach to the whole troubled issue of the Germans abroad.[9]

In Germany itself, it had become clear that armed resistance to the Versailles settlement was fruitless. The right-wing paramilitaries had been able, in a few cases, to seize small towns; yet without political backing they could not turn this into lasting control. As early as autumn 1919, parliamentary deputies had argued that, whatever the merits of the frontier settlement with Poland, it was necessary for the sake of the existing German minority there to establish good relations with the Polish government. They looked with similar realism upon the situation in Czechoslovakia, where, in the waning days of the war itself, the Kaiser and Ludendorff had fantasized about annexing parts of Habsburg Bohemia. Once the Treaty of Versailles was signed, German diplomats told the Sudeten Germans (now abandoning their older Habsburg identity as 'German Bohemians') that they should cooperate with the Czech authorities. 'Correct relations' remained the watchword, despite anti-German (and anti-Semitic) riots in 1919. Between Czechs and the new Austria, relations were soon on a solid footing, smoothed by extensive mutual trade, with no interference from Berlin.[10]

But the minority rights treaties could not by themselves normalize relations between Germans and their neighbours. Too much previous history was involved – old arguments over language in Habsburg Bohemia, over land in Prussian Poland – and Germans in these new states could not easily accept that they were no longer the ruling class. In Czechoslovakia, where – as the Paris peace conference had presciently warned – the problem of the Germans was 'quite different from the mere protection of other minorities', a new school law forced the closure of some German village classrooms, while Prague's German-language university languished.

The deeply embittered debate which had all but torn the Habsburg monarchy apart was resolved by a law which made Czech the official language of the new country. German officials had two years to learn it or lose their jobs, and after 1926, when the law came fully into force, thousands of former Habsburg civil servants were thrown out of work. In many places only letters with Czech addresses would be delivered; only telegrams in Czech could be sent from Prague; nothing but Czech could be used when conversing with a telephone operator. Streets were renamed after Czech heroes and confrontational local administrators claimed 'absolute mastery' over local Germans. Census officials decided whether people were to be entered as Czechs or Germans, disregarding the feelings of the people involved in order to inflate Czech numbers. And, as in other countries, a land reform targeted German farmers and subsidized the settlement in 'predominantly Germanized regions' of Czech colonists as 'the bearers and promoters of the ideas of the nation and the state'. On the other hand, the Czech story was not just one of repression. There was substantial German representation in the new parliament, and over time Germans and Czechs started to cooperate in business, unions and politics, brought together by a common anti-communism and by the buoyancy of the Czechoslovak economy.[11]

In Poland, the atmosphere and policies were considerably harsher. The newly independent Polish state had acquired 90 per cent of the former Prussian province of Posen, and 66 per cent of West Prussia – with a combined German-speaking population of more than one million; the German port of Danzig became a Free City with a League com-missioner. Amid vicious clashes between German soldiers, who blazoned their trucks with swastikas and death's heads, and their armed Polish counterparts, this transfer of power took place amid a struggle that was fiercer than anything in Bohemia. The Weimar government tried to clamp down on the paramilitaries. But when the Poles disputed German claims to Upper Silesia, Weimar called on them for help. Led by Hitler's future ambassador to wartime Slovakia and Romania, Manfred von Killinger, nationalist volunteers – selected on the basis of race and their hatred of Jews, communists and Slavs – fought off the Poles. After this, Killinger's force was secretly subsidized by the government to train an underground force for eventual use against Poland, and this support was terminated only after some of them went on a killing spree, assassinating the Catholic deputy Matthias Erzberger and Weimar's Jewish foreign minister, Walter von Rathenau.[12]

In Poland itself, the Germans were seen as second-class citizens and traitors. During the Russo-Polish war of 1919–21, there were reports that Germans had greeted the Russians as liberators, and the Poles forced many Germans to choose immediately between Polish and German citizenship. It wasn't much of a choice, as those who opted for the former faced immediate conscription. Following the Red Army's withdrawal, German refugees fled Poland on such a scale that the governor of East Prussia even proposed an exchange of populations.[13]

But the chief Polish weapon against the Germans was land reform. Whereas in the Czech case confiscations chiefly eroded the power of the old Austrian aristocracy, the Poles also targeted farmers with more modest holdings in order to reverse the effects of prewar Prussian Germanization. The land reform itself affected 68 per cent of eligible land owned by Germans but only 11 per cent of that owned by Poles; its role as an instrument of nationalization could not have been clearer. 'Polish land for the Poles' was a common watchword, and Sikorski spoke in 1923 of 'de-Germanizing' the western provinces. Those Germans whom the Prussian Colonization Commission had helped to settle before the war were the first to be targeted.[14]

Not surprisingly, emigration fever swept the German population. Fearful of finding themselves on the wrong side of the border with Poland, thousands fled westwards. Estimates suggest that roughly 575,000 Germans left Poland between 1918 and 1926, including more than half the German population of the ceded portions of Poznania and Western Prussia. This huge proportion dwarfed the less than 10 per cent of Germans who fled the Czech lands, and was even more than the 200,000 Germans the French expelled from Alsace-Lorraine. It is clear that an exodus took place from the western Polish borderlands that in its magnitude had no equal either in Czechoslovakia or anywhere else at this time. Former German towns now shrank and turned into Polish ones.

Yet both the Poles and the Germans realized they needed to prevent matters getting out of hand; each had a substantial minority to worry about in the other's country. And although relations between them were never less than strained during the lifetime of the Weimar Republic, at least they remained manageable. The German Foreign Ministry was no keener than its nationalist critics to accept the Versailles border with Poland as definitive, but it saw the minority as a lever for a future revisionist policy; if no Germans remained, their claim to Polish land would be far weaker. Hence German policy was to persuade members of the minority to stay where they were. Indeed, in the mid-1920s, Weimar Germany went further: it tried to internationalize their plight by joining the League and positioning itself as *the* 'Protector of Minorities' for the continent.

This policy was identified chiefly with the figure who dominated German diplomacy before Hitler, Gustav Stresemann, and it represented a considerable shift in his own thinking. A conservative nationalist who had favoured seizing swathes of Belgium and France as well as eastern Europe during the war, Stresemann had been one of the first German politicians to welcome the union with 'German Austria'. Yet power revealed the pragmatist, and in the mid-1920s he engineered Germany's entry into the League. Participation in it was necessary, in Stresemann's mind, to advance German interests in eastern Europe, and in particular to enforce observation of the minority rights treaties, and he used this argument frequently to counter nationalist criticism of his pro-League policies. While Germany funded the European Nationalities Congress, Stresemann himself mounted a concerted effort to improve the overall system of legal protection, and even proposed that Germany should draw up a new policy towards its own minorities. All this formed part of a broadly revisionist long-term agenda which he privately defined as 'the creation of a state the political borders of which encompass all the German peoples living within the contiguous area of German settlement in central Europe and who wish to be connected with the Reich'. This was not all that different from what the Nazis were calling for. The most obvious difference – and it was no small one – was that Stresemann saw the path lying through the League. And whereas Hitler planned to expel minorities, Stresemann anticipated Germany acquiring more – hence the importance of turning itself into a model state towards those it already possessed. Yet like Hitler, he saw borders and minorities as interconnected issues. That June, he secretly told the leaders of German missions abroad to 'launch propaganda for a revision of the eastern frontiers on a grand scale'.[15]

Stresemann believed the League could be reformed to make it a more effective defender of German interests, and he staked much of his political capital on trying to bring this about. That reform of the minority rights regime was needed was the one thing almost everyone could agree on. Unbound by any of the obligations encumbering the east European states, postwar French governments, for instance, had carried out a blatantly racist assault on the civil rights of German-speakers in Alsace-Lorraine, eventually deporting 200,000 of them with impunity. The Lithuanians – and later the Poles – had not liked being singled out and proposed that the proper treatment of minorities be made binding upon *all* members of the League. The Hungarians wanted minorities to be allowed to present their grievances before the Council of the League. But it was Stresemann's proposal to create a permanent minorities commission along the lines of the existing mandates commission that attracted the most attention. Briand, the French foreign minister, had already warned that expanding the demand for 'rights' might lead Europe to war, when a row erupted at the December 1928 meeting of the League Council between Stresemann and his Polish counterpart, Foreign Minister August Zaleski. After Zaleski criticized the minority Deutscher Volksbund for its incessant complaints, and accused its leader of treason, Stresemann interrupted him in a fury, banged his fists on the table and announced a German campaign to broaden the minority rights regime. Amid an atmosphere of grimly heightened tension, this proposal got nowhere. Meantime, the situation on the ground went from bad to worse. In the months before Stresemann's early death, Polish artists visiting German Silesia were attacked by a group of young Nazis, the Volksbund leader, Dr Ulitz, was put on trial in Poland, and the League Council voted against the German proposals. Fishing in troubled waters, the Soviet *Izvestia* gleefully described Europe under the League as 'a prison for minority peoples'.

Stresemann's very substantial final achievements – the French agreement to evacuate the Rhineland five years early; the revised Young Plan for reparations – overshadowed the paltry fruits of his eastern policy. His early death, the onset of the depression and the astonishing rise of the Nazi Party in the September 1930 elections all marked the end of an era. In the years that followed, Germany seemed to lose any confidence in the League's capability to protect the rights of Germans abroad. But what came next was more than a repudiation of the Versailles borders and the pursuit of territorial revisionism by other means: it was a wholesale rejection of the entire system of minority rights and international legal protection that the League had created. That was the old order that the Nazi New Order would sweep away.[16]

TOWARDS GREATER GERMANY

In Germany itself, nationalist criticism of Stresemann's policies had been unrestrained long before his death brought Weimar's brief period as 'protector of minorities' to an end. Refugee organizations and nationalist groups had conducted a long-running campaign against the League, while paramilitary fraternities such as the Heimatbund Ostpreussen and the Deutscher Wehrverein preserved the networks of veterans who had fought in 1918–19. In Silesia and East Prussia there were excursions by train and bus to the 'bleeding frontier', to mourn the lost territories and the unredeemed brothers who still lived there; by the early 1930s such tours were being organized by the local authorities themselves. Some held military parades and lit fires at the border, and a few went further and prepared for armed confrontation.[17]

Concern about the plight of 'Germans abroad' was not confined to fringe paramilitary groupings or Nazi-style racial theorists. The Poles had been spectacularly successful at 'de-Germanizing' former Prussian possessions. They settled tens of thousands near Gdansk and built up a rival port near by. The departure of many Germans contributed to dramatic shifts in the population balance. In Poznań/Posen Germans made up only 2 per cent of the population in 1930 compared with 42 per cent in 1910; in Bydgoszcz/Bromberg the figure dropped from 77 per cent to 8.5 per cent. There was widespread concern in Weimar for the German refugees, and much support for cultural institutions and welfare organizations strengthening 'Germandom'. The venerable Verein für das Deutschtum im Ausland (VDA) – disbursing state and private funds to German minority schools and other bodies – had more than two million members. The VDA was a mainstream organization, but it too portrayed foreign governments in a hostile light, as waging a continual war of cultural extermination against beleaguered Germans abroad. More extreme views flourished in the new research institutes for the study of the *Volksdeutsch*.[18]

After 1918, there was therefore a renewed interest in the country's mission 'in the East', boasted by the spread of 'geopolitics' as an approach to political geography, and by the popularity of theories of *Lebensraum*. Bismarck's achievement, formerly heroized, now came under the spotlight: in Weimar, he was increasingly criticized for having been content with a Little Germany, excessive friendship towards Russia and having abandoned the *Drang nach Osten*. Bismarck's Hohenzollern empire – said the republican left – had been a vehicle for preserving the power of the Prussian autocracy. A Greater Germany, on the other hand, would reach back to the democratic legacy of the 1848 revolutions and would demonstrate the possibilities of a 'real *Grossdeutschland* that is built on a democratic foundation'. Racial nationalists, for their part, saw the yoking together of Germany and Austria as the synthesis of 'a new German Man', closer to the soil and harmonizing the diverse traditions of North and South. The Catholic Centre Party thought the addition of Austria might counterbalance the North's Protestant supremacy. Right across Weimar's political spectrum politicians and intellectuals preached the need for national expansion, attentiveness to Germans abroad and the need for a new 'community of the people' (*Volksgemeinschaft*). Schoolbooks taught an understanding of the importance of Austria in particular, and ethnic Germans in general. Lobby groups sponsored lectures on 'Gay Vienna' and supported concerts by the Vienna Philharmonic.

In this atmosphere of national humiliation and outrage, anything – even music – could be invoked to prove the Greater German argument. Contrasting Bach and Handel, whose intensity captured 'the melancholy heaths and moorlands, the dusty grey clouds' of the north German landscape, with the gentler 'Vienna Woods' lyricism of Mozart and Haydn, the musicologist Robert Lach concluded:

Both groups are separate, yet both are part of each other through the German spirit that lies in them. Do not Bach, Handel and Schubert, Haydn and Mozart, belong to each other as Germany and Austria? Are they not unified in the common living German spirit as Beethoven united German and Austrian music? And is not Beethoven a symbol of this unification of the German and Austrian soul, a symbol that will eventually stand?[19]

The past was suddenly looking very different. Trying to bridge the divide between Little and Greater German outlooks, the Austrian historian Heinrich Ritter von Srbik advocated a new approach which he termed *Gesamtdeutsch* – the history, that is to say, not of the historical Germany that had existed as the Holy Roman Empire, nor of the political Germany within the borders of 1871, but rather of the entire world inhabited by ethnic Germans, a world which had never existed as a political unit, but which might in the future. 'The task of German history,' he wrote in his epic *German Unity (Deutsche Einheit)*, 'is to help build a new German house.' As late as 1942, von Srbik was still writing lyrically of how 'Germany has [now] carried her thousand-year mission and role of leadership to the very frontiers of the Western World ... Not as imperialism, and not on the basis of a humanitarian ideal, but grounded rather in a new idea, that of *Volkstum*, which recognises the personalities of nations and organically attaches the small nations to the leadership of the great Volk.' It took him until 1944 to realize that Hitler's New Order was not going to recreate an idealized Holy Roman Empire.[20]

Like von Srbik, many nationalist academics came from the fringes of the German world – from Austria, or the Baltic states, or the Prussian borderlands. Even non-Nazis found it easy to see National Socialism, or more precisely Hitler himself, as the vehicle for the national revival they longed for. In the case of the Jewish medieval historian Ernst Kantorowicz, for instance, who, though a conservative nationalist, was certainly no Nazi, this attitude was pronounced.[21] Writing in 1941, an observer of the German intellectual scene noted that:

German historians, save for a republican minority, needed little 'coordination'. The Germany of the future which most historians had envisioned and worked for approximated in many fundamental respects the Nazi state of today. The necessity of power, the primacy of foreign policy over internal affairs, the rejection of 'foreign' ideologies and institutions, the stress on German culture, the subordination of the individual to the state, the devotion of the Reich to its mission in the east, the inclusion of all Germans in the empire, Germany's need for a *Führer* with broad powers, are but the most important features.[22]

Of course, as intellectuals will, most of these scholars became disillusioned when the Nazis failed to implement their ideas – but not before the Nazis had shown the extent of their debt. When, in February 1939, Hitler inaugurated the new battleship *Bismarck*, and spoke in praise of his illustrious predecessor, whose achievements had been limited only by his necessity to share power with the Hohenzollerns, he was not diverging far from the common historical judgement in Nazi Germany. A year later the Führer held forth to Goebbels in the same vein: 'Bismarck could not achieve more. The dynasties stood in his way.' Praising the democrats of 1848, he boasted that Germany would also take up the mantle of European leadership from the Holy Roman Empire: 'because of our organizational brilliance and racial selectivity, world domination will automatically fall to us'. Bismarck, the liberals of 1848, Catholic emperors – all these diverse elements were merely grist to the 'total German' Nazi mill.[23]

About the importance of the concept of Greater Germany to the Nazi movement and to Hitler personally there can be no doubt. Hitler himself described National Socialism as 'the child of the Pan-German League'.[24] Nor could the opening articles of the Party's founding programme have been any more emphatic. Banning Jews and others of non-German blood from citizenship, they called for the creation of a Greater Germany on the basis of the right of national self-determination, the revocation of the peace treaties and colonies to settle Germany's 'surplus population'. Any doubts about Hitler's own commitment to these ideas are laid to rest by a cursory reading of *Mein Kampf*. Hitler and his followers saw the post-Versailles settlement in eastern Europe not merely as national humiliation but as a biological threat to the survival of the German people as a whole. From such a perspective, no other foreign policy was ultimately possible than one of territorial expansion, and the prime justification for the takeover of power and control of domestic policy was to prepare the country for the protracted wars that would win land.

It is surprising, to put it mildly, that the vast scholarly literature that has emerged over the past thirty years analysing the bases of Nazi electoral support in Weimar has had little to say about such issues; concentrating almost exclusively upon domestic factors, historians have tried to ascertain the sociological profile of the 'typical' Nazi voter (only to conclude that such a figure probably did not exist). In fact, the need for expansion, a theme upon which Hitler increasingly elaborated, was very popular. With Stresemann's 'minorities crusade' at the League blocked, and his successor Brüning haunted by his failure to force through an Austro–German customs union, Hitler hammered away in his speeches at the idea of a modern 'eastern colonization' to solve the 'lack of space' in post-Versailles Weimar. The Wall Street crash and growing unemployment, he argued, only confirmed the need for more land as an alternative to Germany's diminished access to world markets.[25]

Hitler had a pragmatic and patient side, and, once in power, apart from withdrawing almost immediately from the League of Nations, his goal in the first few years was to present a moderate image to the world, while the economy recovered and rearmament could get underway. Securing Germany's western borders against the French was critical. At the formal level, relations between Germany and its eastern neighbours remained correct. But the Third Reich centralized control over the numerous groups dealing with German minority affairs, and the Party created a new office – the Volksdeutsche Mittelstelle (Ethnic German Liaison Office) – to coordinate activities connected with ethnic German affairs. Within a few years this had taken over the older VDA and was being run by Heinrich Himmler's SS. No longer interested in acting as 'protector of the minorities of Europe', Nazi Germany's party-state tried to tighten its grip over the leadership of the often doggedly independent ethnic German welfare and lobby groups.[26]

Concern for Germans abroad reinforced the idea of international relations as racial struggle. At the centre for propaganda and irredentist activity against Poland, the Bund Deutscher Osten, Theodor Oberländer, a young lecturer on 'Eastern affairs' from East Prussia (and later a minister in the postwar Adenauer government) adopted a martial tone. 'The struggle for ethnicity,' he wrote in 1936,

is nothing other than the continuation of war by other means under the cover of peace. Not a fight with gas, grenades, and machine-guns, but a fight about homes, farms, schools, and the souls of children, a struggle whose end, unlike in war, is not foreseeable as long as the insane principle of nationalism of the state dominates the Eastern region, a struggle which goes on for generations with one aim: extermination!

A year later, Oberländer was stripped of his positions for being too *soft* on the Polish question.[27]

This idea of foreign policy as 'the continuation of war by other means under the cover of peace' also affected how the Third Reich thought about international law. After 1933 Nazi legal theorists asserted the primacy of each state's self-interest, and, increasingly, of race. They wanted a new kind of law according to which an organic German community would create its own legal norms. The ideal, as one explained, was a national state that was 'racially satiated', for only such a state would enjoy peaceful relations with other states in the international system. But what followed from this was not entirely reassuring: treaties and other agreements were regarded as binding as long as they did not jeopardize the racial health of a people; some racial communities were stronger than others and could 'naturally' exert a hegemonic influence over them; war not law was therefore the ultimate arbiter of international order. Nazi lawyers were deeply suspicious of the whole idea of a universal international law premised upon the formal equality of sovereign states.[28]

Keen to claim the loyalty of Germans abroad, the Nazis racialized the notion of citizenship outside the Reich as well as inside it. 'The concepts "citizen" and "racial comrade" do not coincide,' wrote an adviser to the minister of the interior in 1936. 'The race, or its single member, the racial comrade, must stand in the first place.' In other words, affinity among Germans wherever they might be trumped 'the formal conception of citizenship'. The 'boundless and unalterable loyalty towards one's own race', which another law professor saw as the guiding principle of National Socialist law, supposedly outweighed any loyalty which ethnic Germans might be expected to feel towards Czechoslovakia, Hungary or any other state the passport of which they happened to hold. If, according to such thinking, the Third Reich and indeed the Führer himself were nothing more than the voice of the German *Volk* as a whole, then it was also true that it – and he – had the right to speak for the *Volk* and to expect ethnic Germans everywhere to do its bidding.[29]

Thus German minorities diplomacy was turned on its head. Abandoning Geneva in 1933, Berlin negotiated directly with its counterparts in east European capitals. The British and the French were sidelined, and ethnic German organizations became mouthpieces for the National Socialist line. The Polish government played into German hands by repudiating its League obligations. A few years later, it recognized the minorities question as a bilateral matter, accepting the Reich as an advocate for the German minority. This certainly did not do much to help Germans in Poland; on the contrary, the evictions and confiscations increased, unemployment rates rose, and more and more ethnic Germans declared themselves Poles. What it did illustrate was how the diplomatic order established at Paris in 1919 was being replaced in eastern and central Europe by one minted in Berlin. Inside Poland, as the old elites either emigrated or were driven away, the German community remained politically weak. Their fate would in future be determined by German policy and German strength.[30]

ANSCHLUSS

For Hitler, predictably, the first step in the programme of expansion after the Saar plebiscite and the remilitarization of the Rhineland was into Austria. *Mein Kampf* opens by demanding the restoration of 'German Austria to the great German motherland', and Hitler could not have written more clearly about the significance of his motherland as the springboard for national expansion:

German-Austria must return to the great German motherland, and not because of any economic considerations. No, and again no: even if such a union were unimportant from an economic point of view; yes, even if it were harmful, it must nevertheless take place. One blood demands one Reich. Never will the German nation possess the moral right to engage in colonial politics until, at least, it embraces its own sons within a single state. Only when the Reich borders include the very last German, but can no longer guarantee his daily bread, will the moral right to acquire foreign soil arise from the distress of our own people.

The call for *Anschluss*, as we have seen, was not a monopoly of the right. In 1926, Hitler's home town of Linz had seen the Austrian Social Democrats resolve to pursue '*Anschluss* . . . through peaceful means', and successive Austrian and German governments had sought through quiet diplomacy to prepare the ground. Visa requirements between the two countries were abolished, legal and business practices were standardized. Between 1930 and 1931 the Brüning government pursued the idea of a customs union between the two states even after it provoked a diplomatic showdown with France. Both sides knew this would be a blow to the Versailles order; some senior German diplomats even believed it might force the Czechs and Poles into Germany's arms. But by bad timing the announcement coincided with the Credit-Anstalt bankruptcy which brought the Austrian economy to its knees and made France's enormous gold reserves more important than ever; the resulting humiliation was just one of the reasons for the collapse of the Brüning government, as Weimar's crisis entered its terminal phase.

Even after 1933 there was no straightforward path to Vienna. The year after Hitler came to power, he allowed Austrian Nazis to mount a putsch. Embarrassingly for him, this failed, and the ring-leaders were hanged, and, worse still, it alienated fascist Italy. Afterwards, the Third

Reich pursued a much more gradual 'evolutionary' approach. In July 1936, Austria agreed to follow a foreign policy based on the principle that the country 'acknowledges herself to be a German state'. The following year, speaking to his senior defence staff, Hitler underlined that 'the aim of German policy was to make secure and preserve the racial community and to enlarge it'. He told them, however, that the time for war would come in the early 1940s. As for Austria, he was still worried about Mussolini's reaction. In fact it was not the Führer but Göring who wanted to push ahead. At his estate he showed the Italian leader a map on which Austria was already depicted as part of Germany. When the Duce commented tersely, 'The Reich is fulfilling its programme punctually,' this was taken by Göring as assent.[31]

In early 1938, however, events unexpectedly came to a climax. Hitler had replaced his foreign minister with the more pliable Ribbentrop and dismissed both the minister of war and the commander-in-chief of the army, von Fritsch, who opposed the idea of invasion. He also had himself proclaimed supreme commander of the armed forces, emphasizing the army's subordination to the regime. In Austria, meanwhile, the government's efforts to clamp down on the Austrian National Socialists backfired, and, under enormous German pressure, the Austrian chancellor, Schuschnigg, was forced to lift a ban on the party, to amnesty its convicted murderers and even to appoint Nazi candidates to key cabinet positions. The lawyer Arthur Seyss-Inquart (who later ran the occupied Netherlands) became minister of the interior and Edmund Glaise-Horstenau (stationed in wartime Zagreb) became minister without portfolio. Schuschnigg had already – at Hitler's demand – got rid of the army chief of staff, General Jansa, who had prepared plans for military resistance to a German invasion. This was the 'evolutionary' strategy that Hitler insisted afterwards to Austrian Nazi leaders would make invasion or an uprising redundant; because it would lead to Nazi takeover of the country from within, he did not, he told them, 'desire a solution by violent means'.

Less than a fortnight later, however, he learned to his astonishment that Schuschnigg planned to call a plebiscite. Ironically, an instrument which had been used throughout the 1920s to call for *Anschluss* was now being conjured up to prevent it. While Austrian Nazis rampaged through the streets of Vienna, Hitler abandoned his 'evolutionary' approach and threatened to invade if the chancellor was not replaced by

Seyss-Inquart, the pro-Nazi interior minister. Under immense pressure, Schuschnigg did eventually resign late in the evening of 11 March, and Seyss-Inquart took over the same night, while Austrian Nazi squads ransacked ministerial buildings and arrested members of the former government. To Hitler's enormous relief, Italy indicated it would not object. The Wehrmacht, which had no up-to-date invasion plans, crossed the border the next morning to be met by cheering crowds.

Taken aback by the fervour of their welcome, the Nazi leadership now confronted a constitutional problem to which they had given little thought. Should Austria remain as a centralized state, with its own government, within a larger federal German structure? Or should the country be ruled directly from Berlin? The yawning chasm between ideology and practical implementation, between the unstoppable momentum of German power and the inability to plan ahead – something which was to be a constant feature of Nazi rule in occupied Europe – was evident here at the very start. But so was the energy and the radicalism with which the regime threw itself into resolving such major issues on the spur of the moment. The last time *Anschluss* had been on the agenda, Hans Kelsen, probably the country's most distinguished jurist, had advocated keeping Austria as 'a federal state inside a federal state'; he thought this would enable Austrians to preserve *both* their Austrian and their German identities. But this was probably the least attractive option for Germany's National Socialists, and after Hitler's triumphant reception in Linz, he decided on a 'total *Anschluss*' in which the country, its laws and administration would be integrated within the existing German state. In short, Austria was to disappear.[32]

Austria was therefore completely stripped of its identity (as Czechoslovakia, Yugoslavia and Poland would be after it): it was renamed the Ostmark and treated as a province of the Reich. German law was gradually extended throughout the country, and Austrian government institutions were dissolved or subordinated to their German equivalents. One of the key advisers in this process was Wilhelm Stuckart, a senior civil servant in the Reich Interior Ministry and a man who was to play an important role in the coming years in organizing the administration of other Nazi conquests. A very different but even more important figure was Josef Bürckel, the Nazi *Gauleiter* who had successfully managed the incorporation of the Saarland and who was brought in to do the same thing as commissioner for the reunification of Austria with the

German Reich. Under Bürckel's leadership, the Ostmark itself did not last long. It was broken up into seven smaller provinces, which were each directly subordinated to the Berlin offices of the central government and the Party. 'Red' Vienna's hold over the rest of the country was thus weakened, and the Austrian capital was not even named as one of the five Führer cities of Greater Germany that were singled out for special building projects. (Linz – known officially as the 'Home Town of the Führer' – was preferred.) Soon nothing was formally left of Austria at all.

In the spring 1940, with his work done, Bürckel left for western Germany again; his expertise was needed in the newly occupied French province of Lorraine. Hitler was impressed by Seyss-Inquart too and made him Reich Commissar in the Netherlands. Contemporaries were struck by the smoothness of the whole process. An American political scientist wrote in 1938: 'Another nation has been taken over and incorporated into the German political, economic, and social ... system without confusion, almost as if the details of such a union had been worked out with great care for years in advance.'[33] Meanwhile, the Party enjoyed its triumph. The Nazi putschists who had been hanged by Austrian police in 1934 were celebrated as martyrs of national revolution. Thousands gathered in the Carinthian Nazi stronghold of Klagenfurt to hear Hitler's deputy, Rudolf Hess, and to watch the swearing-in of the seven new Party *Gauleiters*. At the old Austrian Chancellery itself in Vienna, the 1934 plotters' target, a memorial plaque hailed the men who 'stood up for Germany'.[34]

In fact, the process had not been *that* smooth. Even as Austria lost its political identity, its social order dissolved into an orgy of violence and looting. Many Nazi 'old fighters', especially those who had spent years underground, in prison or abroad, saw the toppling of the Schuschnigg government as their moment for revenge. What was startling was the extent to which it was the Jews who bore the brunt. Before the German army had reached Vienna, it was in the grip of a pogrom, as mobs plundered shops and offices, attacked Jews in their homes and carried out their own 'arrests'. 'Hell was unleashed,' wrote the playwright Carl Zuckmayer, describing the evening of 11 March. 'The city turned into a scene from a Hieronymus Bosch nightmare.' It was, he went on, worse than anything he had ever experienced – worse than battles he had fought through in the First World War or the street fighting that followed it, the Beer Hall Putsch in Munich or the first days of Nazi rule in

Germany. 'None of those compared with these days in Vienna.' Photographs of jeering onlookers surrounding Austrian Jews, as they were forced to scrub the pavements on their hands and knees, were soon seen around the world. But these pictures scarcely captured the scale of the looting – a pogrom of enrichment that exceeded even the destruction of Kristallnacht a few months later. This was anti-Semitism as pure robbery, as men wearing swastika armbands or claiming to be from the Gestapo carried out 'searches' of apartments and helped themselves to whatever caught their eye. Viennese Jews themselves were deeply shocked at the onslaught and nearly 500 committed suicide.[35]

The Austrian capital became in effect a laboratory of anti-Jewish violence: figures who would assume enormous importance in the wartime Final Solution four years later played a critical role there in 1938. There was, for instance, the Carinthian Nazi Odilo Globocnik, whom Hitler appointed *Gauleiter* in May. Lasting only a few months until he was sacked for corruption, Globocnik's career was resuscitated when he went on to become Himmler's SS and police commander (SSPF) in Lublin in eastern Poland and the organizer of the extermination camps of Belzec, Sobibor and Treblinka.

Yet the city's degeneration into anarchy under the influence of men like Globocnik worried some powerful figures in the Third Reich. Appalled that individuals had been allowed to carry out their own personal 'Aryanizations' of Jewish property (thereby impoverishing the state), Himmler's deputy, Reinhard Heydrich, threatened to unleash the Gestapo on Austrian Nazis for their lack of discipline. One of the ways Vienna pointed to the future was that it showed the SS how important it was to take anti-Jewish policy away from the Party's street fighters. What became known as the 'Vienna model' was their answer to this – a much more systematic and bureaucratic way of getting rid of the Jews and robbing them of their property. It was developed by one of their 'Jewish experts', Adolf Eichmann, through his new Central Office for Jewish Emigration – something which he later described to an Israeli police interrogator proudly as 'a first for the Reich'. By October 1938, the resourceful, energetic and unscrupulous Eichmann was boasting that 350 applications were being dealt with daily. In less than two years, Austria's Jewish population dropped from 192,000 to 57,000 as Jews were intimidated and despoiled and left the country. Once the Germans conquered Czechoslovakia, Eichmann replicated his system there ('[it]

simply followed the example of Vienna'), and after the defeat of Poland, he established a similar body in Berlin as well. With the outbreak of the war, Eichmann's star rose further: his expertise and experience made him the central figure in the planning and organization of the continent-wide deportation of Jews to the camps.

In Vienna itself he had been helped by a third figure, the senior SD man there, Franz Stahlecker, who also found that the *Anschluss* provided the springboard for a successful SS career in mass murder. He became Himmler's chief SS and police officer (HSSPF) in Prague and Norway before being put in command of Einsatzgruppe A, the death squad which under his leadership killed nearly 250,000 Jews in the Baltic and northern Russia in the last six months of 1941. None of this was even imaginable in the spring of 1938; but arguably none of it would have come to pass without what happened then.[36]

With the Wehrmacht's unimpeded march into Austria, the first breach in the Versailles territorial order was made: the Greater German Reich was emerging, just as Hitler had promised. In the run-up to the plebiscite that was organized on the *Anschluss* question, the Nazis swamped the country with propaganda. Giant banners carrying quotations from Hitler's writings – 'Those of the Same Blood Belong in the Same Reich!' – adorned prominent public buildings. Yet the ringing endorsement for unification that followed was probably not misleading. Even Karl Renner, the Social Democrat who later became the country's first post-war president, admitted shortly before the vote that 'although [it has] not been brought about by the methods which I advocated, the *Anschluss* has nevertheless been completed. It is a historical fact, and this I regard as general satisfaction for the humiliation of 1918 and 1919 . . .'[37]

Many of those who hailed Hitler so enthusiastically during the Wehrmacht's triumphant march into the country soon changed their mind, of course. For a small number, this was connected with the brutality shown towards the Jews. Although there was widespread approval of the regime's anti-Semitism, the sheer violence of those first days and weeks shocked some. Considerably more anger was provoked by the Party's assault on the Catholic Church. The Archbishop of Vienna had met Hitler during his triumphant visit, allowed the swastika to fly over St Stephen's cathedral and signed his letters in the Nazi fashion with a 'Heil Hitler': he could scarcely have been more accommodating. But this was not enough to assuage the Austrian Nazi radicals, foremost among them the young *Gauleiter* Globocnik. They confiscated Church property, dissolved Catholic organizations and deported many priests to Dachau. The opposition of some Catholic Nazis to Globocnik's crusade against the Church was one of the reasons he was dismissed. Outside the movement, the anger spilled into the open. Perhaps the very first act of overt mass resistance to the new regime took place in early October 1938, when a rally of thousands of young worshippers left mass in the centre of Vienna and started chanting 'Christ is our Führer' before being broken up by police.[38]

Embryonic though it may have been, even Austrian nationalism was stronger than the Nazis granted. Demands for *Anschluss* had always masked a complex of motives, and few people actually wanted Austria's identity to disappear as entirely as Hitler wanted. In Vienna, in particular, the incompetence, corruption and ruthlessness of the new bosses did not pass unremarked. The Viennese felt they had been taken over by provincial thugs from Carinthia and – perhaps worse – by Germans like Bürckel, who was accompanied by a retinue of unsavoury followers from the Palatinate. Greater German solidarities could not be forged quite as quickly as Hitler hoped, nor by his methods. 'It was not so much National Socialism they disliked, as things German in themselves,' noted an observer. Soon Germans from the Reich were being 'annoyed and heckled'; there were fights in beer-taverns, soccer riots and even cat-calls directed at Göring's wife when she visited the opera. Bitter fatalistic jokes about the 'Prussian' takeover began to circulate. Two Austrians sit in a café in Vienna, ran one. The first says, 'Hm,' and the second, after a long silence, answers, 'Hm.' The first repeats: 'Hm,' and the second responds, 'Well, we finally got rid of the Turks too.'[39]

3
Expansion and Escalation: 1938–40

In the East lies our tomorrow, lie Germany's years to come,
There waits danger, a people's troubles, and the beat of the victory drum.

There our brothers kept the faith, so the banner never sank,
Five hundred faithful years they kept watch without thanks.

There good earth lies waiting, that carried no seed till now,
There lie no farms or cattle but land crying out for the plough!

There we must win back the foreign soil, which once was German domain,
There there must be new beginnings. Germans, arm and hear this refrain![1]

In February 1933, Hitler privately outlined his future goals as 'perhaps fighting for new export possibilities; perhaps and probably better, the conquest of new *Lebensraum* in the East and its ruthless Germanisation'.[2] New export possibilities did indeed open up shortly afterwards – without the need for fighting – thanks to bilateral barter trade deals between Germany and the Balkan states. But after the *Anschluss*, the focus on *Lebensraum* and Germanization became increasingly clear. In the critical year that followed the occupation of the Sudetenland in October 1938, the Third Reich occupied the rest of the Bohemian lands and Poland and as it did so, it moved from taking over territories with a preponderantly German population to ones inhabited chiefly by Slavs. These developments made the rest of the world question whether the pursuit of *Lebensraum* was really just about guaranteeing Germans' right to national self-determination, as Hitler had so often claimed in the past. The Germans, for their part, were brought face to face with the problem of empire – finding ways, in other words, to govern non-German majorities, a problem rendered more acute by the Third Reich's increasing commitment to racial theory as the basis of law and administration. Many Austrians and Sudeten Germans had welcomed the incoming Wehrmacht troops as liberators. The Czechs certainly did not, though they did not fight. As for the Poles, their fierce resistance took the form of a dogged and courageous if strategically suicidal defence against overwhelming odds. Thus the German military experience in 1938–9 ranged from a peaceful stroll by twenty-four Wehrmacht divisions into the Sudetenland to a full-scale invasion of Poland on several fronts by fifty-seven divisions, over five weeks of heavy fighting which left 16,000 German dead and 28,000 wounded, not to mention 66,000 Polish military fatalities along with thousands of executed civilians.

The Third Reich's voracious expansionism shocked the rest of Europe. But we should not assume the Germans were wholeheartedly behind it either. At least one senior official in the SS privately criticized the march into Prague as 'imperialism'. Public opinion, reported von Hassell on the eve of the Polish campaign, looked on the war itself 'as a sort of Party project'. Once Hitler himself came to realize the extent of popular passivity within the Reich, he felt confirmed in the view he had long held that war was necessary, not merely for the conquest of *Lebensraum* and the security of the Reich, but to test and steel the Germans themselves.[3]

SUDETENLAND: OCTOBER 1938

Even before the *Anschluss*, the Czechs were deeply worried about what might lie ahead. In February 1938 Hitler referred publicly to the 'ten million' Germans living in neighbouring states and warned that the Reich would not 'idly watch their persecution'. And while Göring soothed the Czechs, Hitler was confidentially assuring Konrad Henlein, the leader of the Sudeten German Party, that Germany would come to his aid. Henlein (whose mother's maiden name was the distinctly un-German Dvořáček) was a persuasive advocate for the ethnic German cause abroad, and after the *Anschluss*, large numbers of Germans from other parties flocked to his banner; aware that their old Habsburg identity as 'German Bohemians' lay in the past, they increasingly identified themselves with the cause of Greater German nationalism. In their minds, the old imperial border that had divided the Habsburg empire from Bismarck's Reich had dissolved, and at their rallies there were excited chants of *'Ein Reich, ein Volk, ein Führer!'* The Czech government passed a new Nationality Statute to boost the minority's autonomy and to promote the use of German, but it was not enough, and could not have been: Hitler and Henlein had jointly agreed when they met that, in the latter's words, 'we must always demand so much that we can never be satisfied'. The Czechs themselves had few friends left: even Churchill believed that the Sudeten Germans, in calling for 'Home Rule', were only asking for what they themselves had demanded before 1914.[4]

When Hitler insisted on the immediate cession of the Sudetenland in September 1938 at Munich, the British and French agreed. But Neville Chamberlain's capitulation was not, as he announced, 'peace for our time': it was a disaster for the Czechs and a catastrophe for all those hoping to stem the German drive to war. Deprived of more than one-third of Bohemia and Moravia, and abandoned by its allies, Czechoslovakia – with its vital arms industry and its strategically crucial location in the heart of Europe – was surrounded by hostile forces and rendered virtually helpless. A disillusioned President Beneš made way for Emil Hácha, an eminent lawyer who lasted in his post until 1945, a tragic and broken figure. Hitler had gambled and won. The German army, possessing barely forty divisions, had faced not only thirty-five well-armed Czech divisions dug in along well-fortified lines, but a potentially overwhelming French force of one hundred divisions in the West. Yet both the British and the French felt they needed much more time to rearm and feared their vulnerability to German air power in a long war. They thus handed over the Sudetenland without a fight. The Czech border guards simply stood aside, and the Germans encountered no resistance. When Helmuth Groscurth, an Abwehr officer, toured the region in early October, he found the Sudeten Germans euphoric. In their minds, this was sweet revenge for the humiliations of 1918. To celebrate the collapse of the short-lived Czech state, full military honours were paid at the grave of fifty-six Germans who had been killed during fighting with Czech soldiers at the end of the First World War, and a wreath was also laid at the tomb of the founder of the Sudeten Nazi Party.[5]

Groscurth noticed the disciplined bearing of the incoming German troops, and the officers' generally good and even sympathetic relations with their Czech counterparts. But small, aggressive and poorly trained SS detachments were causing trouble, as were vigilante armed bands of ethnic Germans, keen to take revenge on their Czech neighbours. The SD sent several thousand Jews and anti-Nazis to Dachau. Behind the scenes, relations between the military and civilian administrators, and between the Reich Germans and Henlein's supporters, were confused and tense. A staff officer wrote afterwards that it was in the Sudetenland that 'the State's inability to govern' emerged 'to such a crass extent for the first time'. The smooth cooperation the military had foreseen in their peacetime planning for occupation administration never really materialized, and officers who still imagined they were in the world of the Kaiser's army were shocked to see civilian and Party agencies being granted so much power.[6]

None of this stopped the Sudeten Germans from being digested by the Reich even more rapidly than the Austrians had been. Wilhelm Stuckart, the Interior Ministry expert who had supervised the incorporation of Austria, was brought in, and Henlein was named Reich Commissioner for the Occupied Sudeten Territories. After the army handed over its administrative responsibilities, he was named *Gauleiter* of the new Reichsgau Sudetenland. On 21 November the Sudetenland was formally annexed, and shortly afterwards, new deputies took their seats in the Reichstag in Berlin. Sure enough, political unification brought the inevitable grumbling by those who had thought it would mean the end of all their problems: Sudeten Germans complained at the lack of inward investment, at the conscription of their young men into an army where they faced ridicule for their accents, at their domination by 'arrogant and overbearing Reich Germans', and at the continued presence of Czechs among them. Had they but known it, their problems were only beginning.[7]

TAKING OVER PRAGUE: MARCH 1939

Munich marked the moment when the Third Reich took over from the British, the French and the League of Nations as regional arbiter of central Europe. Smaller states brought in new anti-Semitic laws – a simple way of indicating their willingness to please the Reich – and from late 1938 onwards, many of the boundaries established by the peace-makers in Paris were redrawn in Berlin. The powerful anti-Nazi coalition of states that might well have halted German expansion had catastrophically collapsed because of the British and French loss of nerve. Even Poland feasted on the corpse of the Czech state. A swathe of southern Slovakia and Ruthenia was handed over to Hungary, which thus began the process of recouping the tremendous losses of territory it had suffered after the First World War: within four years, thanks to Berlin's favour, it won back land from Romania and Yugoslavia as well. The Czechs were made to grant autonomy to Slovakia and eastern Carpatho-Ukraine while the remaining Germans inside the Czech lands won the right to Reich citizenship. Prague even had to swallow plans for an extra-territorial German motorway system across the country to guarantee German control (though in fact this was never built). As a new authoritarian government took power and unleashed measures against Jews and anti-Nazis, the tell-tale hyphen inserted into the country's name – it was now officially called Czecho-Slovakia – presaged further fragmentation. In total, Munich stripped it of one-third of its territory and population, its natural frontiers and several costly defensive positions, 40 per cent of its industrial plant, 55 per cent of its coal and, not least, all but 4.5 per cent of its ethnic German population.[8]

For Germany, on the other hand, the year had brought extraordinary gains, and on New Year's Day 1939, the Führer addressed the Germans in a mood of jubilation: 'Who can help being deeply moved, seeing today's Greater German Reich ... as he reflects on the situation we faced a mere six years ago?' In his Order of the Day to the troops, he thanked his men for realizing 'a dream of many centuries' – the birth of Greater Germany: 'I thank you for your dutiful loyalty. It is my firm belief that in the future also you will stand ready to protect the nation's right to life in the face of any type of aggression.' What this meant for Germany's neighbours was gradually solidifying in his mind. There would have to be increased pressure on Poland if Danzig – the German port which had been declared a free city in 1920 and was connected by a customs union with Poland – was ever to return to the Reich. That in itself was an argument for occupying the rest of the Czech state so as to be able to overwhelm the Poles from three sides. But with such a war already in his mind, an invasion of Prague had to be as smooth and swift as possible. His instructions to the army mandated that 'outwardly it must be made quite clear that [occupation] is only a peaceful action and not a warlike undertaking'. Publicly, he sent out mixed signals. At the end of January, he gave the mammoth two-and-a-half-hour speech to the new Greater German Reichstag which today is chiefly remembered for its sinister prophecy that the Jews of Europe would be annihilated in the event of a world war. But in fact mostly he hymned the new Greater Germany. He stressed that the *Volk* still needed more *Lebensraum*; on the other hand, he stated that 'we may consider this process of the formation of the German nation as having reached its conclusion'.

The Czechs had not totally given up. Indeed, they showed signs of taking the Munich guarantees of their borders seriously and they demanded to know whether Germany was committed to these. At the end of February they got the answer they had hoped not to hear: the guarantees had been 'prematurely given' since the area fell 'first and foremost within the sphere of the most important interests of the German Reich'. Berlin's plans for the 'liquidation' of the rump Czech state were now accelerated. The Slovaks were pushed to demand outright independence, and when Czech troops went into the Slovak capital to suppress this in March, the final blow fell. Backed by Hitler, the Slovak priest-politician Father Jozef Tiso declared Slovakia's independence. The same day, the unfortunate Czech president, Emil Hácha, was summoned to Berlin, where Hitler told him the army had orders to invade. Placed under immense psychological pressure, and menaced with threats by Göring to bomb Prague from the air, the elderly Hácha fainted and had to be brought round by Hitler's doctor before he could bring himself to sign a memorandum drawn up by the Germans, placing his country under the Reich's 'protection'. Men from the SS Leibstandarte Adolf-Hitler had already crossed the border, and the following morning, as Czechs woke up, General Blaskowitz led the first German troops into a snow-bound Prague. By 9.30, German field guns covered the city from the heights of the Hradčany castle. Apart from some slashed tyres, and snowballs hurled at German tanks and trucks, there was no resistance.

What German 'protection' really meant no one in Berlin knew, apart from the fact that the Czechs would be obliged to follow Germany's wishes where their foreign policy was concerned. Hitler had decided to expunge the name of Czechoslovakia from the map and to create a new state – the Protectorate of Bohemia and Moravia. Wilhelm Stuckart, the hard-working Interior Ministry expert on the incorporation of occupied territories, was brought in to draft a new 'constitution'. Closeted in Prague's Hradčany castle over the night of 15–16 March, while a triumphant Hitler slept there, Stuckart and his colleagues worked out the details. The decree they drew up establishing the Protectorate justified the occupation historically, on the grounds that 'the Bohemian-Moravian countries belonged for a millennium to the *Lebensraum* of the German people', and politically, because the Czechoslovak state had shown itself incapable of guaranteeing order. The Reich was supposedly endangered by 'a new, stupendous menace to European peace', and it was 'only an act of compliance with the law of self-preservation if the German Reich is resolved to take decisive action for the reestablishment of the foundations of a Central European Order'.[9]

In fact the regime the Germans were setting up bore an obvious similarity to the protectorates established by colonial powers – through the French treaties with Tunis and Morocco, for instance. Like nominally independent Egypt, Iraq or Cuba, the Protectorate of Bohemia-Moravia retained many but not all of the attributes of sovereignty. It kept a president and a government, a militia of 7,000 men and an internal public administration which remained relatively intact. But power had to be exercised 'in conformity with the political, military and economic rights of the Reich', and the interpretation of these lay in the hands of a Reich protector appointed from Berlin with his own district civil administrators, military and police forces, and the authority to confirm or deny office to members of the Czech government. Reminiscent of European colonial practice too was the establishment of a dual system of law by which – much as in French Algeria – Germans of Czech citizenship were allowed to register automatically for citizenship of the German Reich, while the rest remained nationals of the Protectorate. There thus grew up a parallel extra-territorial jurisdiction for the 250,000 Germans in the Protectorate.

But there were some novel features of the Nazi *fait accompli* as well. First and most obvious was the fact that for the first time in the modern period such measures were being applied by one European state to another. This was, in fact, an extraordinary reversal of many of the assumptions upon which the edifice of nineteenth-century international law and the entire world system of states had been constructed, and racism was evident as much in the note of anti-Nazi outrage as in Nazi policy. 'No nation belonging to the white race has ever before had such conditions forced upon it,' wrote Eugene Erdely. 'It constituted the first

German colonial statute in modern history for a white and civilized nation.'[10]

No less significant was a narrower point: Hitler had issued the Protectorate proclamation as a personal decree rather than as a Reich law, providing a striking indication of how the expansion of the Reich was increasing the Führer's personal power. According to one leading German commentator on constitutional law: 'It is clear that the implementation of the Führer's promise ... is entirely up to him ... By Hácha's act, the authority to supply a framework for the political organization of the Czech people was completely transferred to the Führer.' The doctrine of unfettered executive power turned the 16 March decree into a document which Hitler could interpret and reinterpret at will. What it meant by sovereignty remained unclear, as did its definition of the Reich Protector's powers. And the Protectorate's relationship to the Reich was no less ambiguous. It was declared rather confusingly to be 'independent under constitutional law' but an 'integral part of the Greater German Reich'.[11]

These ambiguities reflected a real ideological dilemma. Given that this was the first of Germany's conquests of an 'alien people', no one really knew how to bring the Czechs within the 'area of the Reich' in a fashion that accorded with the principles of Nazi jurisprudence. To the leaders of a state that until that moment had based its nationality policies on the principle of expelling several hundred thousand non-Germans, accommodating several million more of them raised serious issues; they were Slavs, admittedly, not Jews, but the Reich's racial experts worried nonetheless.[12]

Yet in the spring of 1939, Hitler was still acutely aware of the eyes of the world upon him and he wanted his new Czech settlement to advertise as far as possible the benefits of German hegemony. The Führer thus appointed the elderly von Neurath as Protector because, as a former foreign minister, he sent a reassuring signal abroad that Germany had decided 'not to deprive the Czechs of their racial and national life'. 'According to the Führer's will,' Stuckart told civil servants in late March, 'the Czechs should be treated in a conciliatory manner, though with the greatest strictness and relentless consistency ... The autonomy of the Protectorate should be restricted only if obviously necessary.' Later he added privately that the new regime in Bohemia and Moravia 'as the first embodiment of the German concept of the protectorate must avoid everything that would be likely to deter other nations, which might later express the same desire of being added to the German Reich as protectorates'. An acute foreign observer, a young American diplomat in Prague called George Kennan, had already guessed this: the idea of the Protectorate, he wrote in late April, 'was devised at a time when many of the Germans, according to all indications, expected to be able to extend their hegemony peacefully at an early date to Hungary and other central European countries. Thus the terms of the Czech Protectorate would have had importance as a precedent, and particularly as an encouragement to other countries to feel that absorption into the German orbit would not necessarily mean the termination of their national existence.'[13]

The Germans hoped that their Slovak policy too would send the signal that they were supportive of other national movements. After the German army occupied Slovakia temporarily to block any Czech counter-action, the Slovak government signed its own Treaty of Protection with Germany. Onlookers gleefully enjoyed the incongruous sight of an SS detachment providing the guard of honour for a Catholic priest, as Slovakia's veteran autonomist, Father Jozef Tiso, touched down at Berlin's Tempelhof airport for the negotiations that led to his country's independence. Tiso's career could make him look like all things to all men: in his time, he had passed for a loyal defender of Hungary, the monarchy and the Church, a violent anti-Semite, a pragmatic member of the interwar Czech republican system and a defender of authoritarianism. But he had always remained true to his provincial Slovak roots and he had never had any illusions about how far a powerless people like the Slovaks could survive in a world of constant flux without more powerful patrons and allies. Once Hitler came to power, he understood the need to gain Germany's support, if only to ensure that, when Czechoslovakia came under threat, the Slovaks, somehow, preserved their autonomy of action.[14] But the Slovaks must have wondered what German protection was really worth a week later when the Hungarian army suddenly invaded the east of their country and occupied what was left of Slovak Ruthenia – the Hungarians had acted with the Germans' consent. Outwardly, Slovakia enjoyed the trappings of sovereignty and was internationally recognized by twenty-seven governments (including France, Britain and the USSR). In practice there was a heavy German advisory presence and a large mission that controlled trade, the economy and internal policy.

Nevertheless, under Tiso's guidance Slovakia's conservative Catholic politicians adroitly exploited what little room for manoeuvre they had been granted. Taking advantage of Berlin's reluctance to drop its pose as liberator, they created an authoritarian rather than a Nazi-style political system and marginalized their own extreme right. They made the Germans negotiate hard before allowing them to use Slovakia for deployment against the Poles and, while they were happy to pass anti-Semitic legislation in line with the German example, they were otherwise uninterested in racializing their own domestic law. Thus Slovakia became a showpiece for the New Order in more ways than one. The Germans never felt as sure of the Slovaks as they wanted, and while to everyone else it looked like a puppet state, to some in Berlin the country became an example of what could happen when 'small nations' were allowed too much freedom.[15]

The Germans were conscious of international attention for good reason. Far more than Munich, it was the invasion of Prague and the creation of the Protectorate that alarmed the rest of Europe and raised new suspicions about Hitler's plans. In his diary, Italy's foreign minister, Ciano, asked himself 'what weight can be given in the future to those [German] declarations and promises which concern us more directly?' In public, the British prime minister, Neville Chamberlain, wondered what had happened to the principle of national self-determination by which the Germans had laid such store. 'The events which have taken place this week,' he continued, 'in complete disregard of the principles laid down by the German Government itself seem to fall into a different category and they must cause us all to be asking ourselves: "Is this the end of an old adventure, or is it the beginning of a new?"'

Hitler's uncompromising reply came when he launched the battleship *Tirpitz*. 'Providence did not create the German *Volk* so that it might obediently comply with a law, applauded by either the English or the French, but so that it might realize its right to life,' he raged. England was speaking of virtue 'in its old age'. Just as Germany kept out of Palestine, so 'England has no business in the German *Lebensraum*'. By what right did the British shoot Arabs in Palestine 'only because these stand up to defend their homeland', while by contrast, the Germans 'go about regulating our affairs calmly and with order'? This was not support for Arab anti-colonialism but a demand that Germany be allowed some discretion in its own sphere of influence. Highlighting Germany's lack of hatred towards the Czechs, he went on to assert that the Reich 'has no intention of attacking other nations'. And he looked forward to the rise of an ideological community of fascist Italy and Nazi Germany to demonstrate internationally what was already evident in Spain, that the right was superior in strength and will to the forces of 'democratic Great Britain' and 'Bolshevist Russia'. With that, he enjoyed a few days sailing off Heligoland on a new cruiser. It was a voyage which remained among the happiest memories of his life.[16]

WAR OF THE PEOPLES

Even as Hitler enjoyed the fresh air of the North Sea, intense diplomatic activity between London, Warsaw, Paris and Bucharest was transforming the political mood in Europe and it was at this point that the momentum towards the wider war – the war that he had not anticipated fighting for several more years – finally became unstoppable. In January 1939, the Poles had again stonewalled in the face of Hitler's demands. Now a steady drumbeat of German claims heralded conflict. Hitler publicly insisted on the annexation of Danzig and Poznań, and Lithuania was forced by Berlin to hand back the strip of formerly Prussian land known as Memel. Finally, the British and French abandoned the policy of appeasement and gave Poland a guarantee of military support. When the Italians invaded Albania, they issued another guarantee to Greece and Romania.

How much these were really worth was an open question. Neither the British nor the French governments wanted to fight and they hoped fervently that the guarantees themselves would act as a deterrent. But Hitler was not fooled and responded by intensifying Germany's relationship with fascist Italy. 'Firmly bound together through the inner unity of their ideologies and the comprehensive solidarity of their interests,' ran the preamble to their treaty, 'The German and the Italian people are determined also in future to stand side by side and to strive with united effort for the securing of their *Lebensraum* and the maintenance of peace. In this way, prescribed for them by history, Germany and Italy wish, in a world of unrest and disintegration, to carry out the assignment of making safe the foundations of European culture.'

Behind the pose of peace, the German preparations for war were accelerating. The two leaders had agreed (or so the Duce thought) that the optimal time for war would be 1943. But the Italo-German alliance – the most important for Germany during the Second World War – was never a relationship based on trust, and the day after the treaty was signed, Hitler told his generals he planned to attack Poland 'at the first opportunity'. Munich had convinced him of the weakness of the Western powers and Czech weapons, horses, gold and land had strongly reinforced the capabilities of the German army, allowing it to raise the equivalent of another ten divisions. Unwilling to get involved prematurely in a war in which he was convinced Britain and France would intervene, the Duce made Hitler release Italy from its alliance obligations. But by the last week of August, this mattered less to Hitler than it might have done earlier, for, in probably the greatest diplomatic coup of his career, he had reached an extraordinary under-standing over Poland with Stalin. The Ribbentrop–Molotov Pact, which provided for the country's partition, smoothed the way for Germany to invade.

Unlike Mussolini, Hitler believed France and Britain would stay out and that Poland, too, would be quickly crushed. He was, by all accounts, genuinely taken aback when news came in that the British would fight. But one way or another, he believed that – as he put it in mid-August – 'the great war must be fought while he and the Duce are still young'.[17] On 22 August, as Ribbentrop flew to Moscow to sign the non-aggression pact, Hitler was at his mountain fastness in Berchtesgaden, giving a speech to his senior military commanders. Notes taken at the time indicate exactly what kind of war he foresaw:

A life and death struggle . . . The destruction of Poland has priority. The aim is to eliminate active forces, not to reach a definite line . . . I shall give a propagandist reason for starting the war, no matter whether it is plausible or not. The victor will not be asked afterwards whether he told the truth or not. When starting or waging a war, it is not right that matters, but victory. Close your hearts to pity. Act brutally. Eighty million people must obtain what is their right. Their existence must be made secure. The stronger man is right. The greatest harshness.[18]

On 1 September, with nearly two million German troops pouring across the frontier into Poland from the west, north and south, the Führer issued the following proclamation:

To the Wehrmacht!

The Polish state has rejected the peaceful regulation of neighbourly relations I have striven for and has appealed to arms. The Germans in Poland are being persecuted by bloody terror and are being driven from their homesteads. A series of frontier violations, of a nature not tolerable for a great power, proves that the Poles are no longer willing to respect the German Reich's frontiers. To put an end to this lunacy, there remains no other course for me but to meet force with force.

Inside the Reich, Goebbels had been whipping up anti-Polish feeling, running scare stories on the suffering of ethnic Germans. On 11 August, he told newspaper editors that 'as of now, the first page should contain news and comments on Polish offences against the *Volksdeutsche* and all kinds of incidents showing the Poles' hatred of everything that is German'. This propaganda offensive had a huge impact on a population keen to get back the lands that had been lost in 1918. 'Every day the newspapers bring us new reports about the cruel treatment of Germans in Poland, about the threats against Danzig, and the insane, shameless comments made about the Reich by Polish warmongers,' wrote one lieutenant. 'None of us was surprised, therefore, when on 25 August at 6.00 p.m. we received orders to prepare for departure.' 'The *Volk* returns home to the *Volk*,' wrote another. 'Where are those people who at one time wanted to put boundaries around this land? Where are those who hated and scoffed at the voice of the people and thought they could bind the displaced communities of a people in the chains of Versailles?'[19]

There was nothing especially Nazi about welcoming a war to redress the grievances of Versailles; much of Germany was behind this. What was characteristic of the regime – and indeed its military supporters – was the extremism of its plans to turn the conflict into a harsh racial struggle against the Poles. Training manuals gave the soldiers a grim picture of the Pole; now their superiors confirmed it. 'Soldiers of the Twenty First Division! This is for the honour and existence of the fatherland,' proclaimed one general on the eve of the invasion. 'East Prussia is in danger . . . We will be marching into ancient German land that was ripped away by the treason of 1919. In these former areas of the Reich our blood brothers have suffered frightful persecution! This is the living space of the German people.'[20]

The army's high command should not have been surprised by Hitler's rewriting of the rules of war. When the invasion began, General von Brauchitsch, the army commander-in-chief, stressed that civilians were 'not their enemy' and that the German troops would obey the provisions of international law. Although he warned the Poles that saboteurs, partisans and snipers would be dealt with harshly, this was consistent with military policy in the First World War; so was the seizure of hostages to ensure the obedience of the civilian population. Yet Hitler had already given his senior commanders a signal that his plans called for the 'physical annihilation' of the Polish population, and that he planned the targeted killing of thousands of members of the country's intellectual, social and political elite. Uncertain – with good reason it would turn out – of the army's willingness to obey such orders, he turned to Heinrich Himmler's SS to execute them.

As it had done in previous campaigns, the SS mustered special *Einsatz-gruppen* (Special Operation Groups), many of them led by veterans of the 1919 border wars. Officially, their task was to secure the army's rear, to carry out policing duties and combat insurgents. But their instructions were unnervingly vague; following discussions with the army, it was agreed that they should 'combat all elements in foreign territory and behind the fighting troops that are hostile to the Reich and the German people'. In the middle of August, they were told about Polish atrocities against German civilians and warned about Polish plans to mount resistance through secret saboteur organizations. (Pilsudski's underground movement in the First World War provided the model for these.) To pre-empt them, Himmler's deputy, Reinhard Heydrich, was instructed by Hitler himself to arrange 'the liquidation of various circles of the Polish leadership, which ran into the thousands'. Passing these orders on to his men, Heydrich stressed that 'the driving force of the resistance movement could be found in the Polish intelligentsia' and hammered home the point that in the context of this struggle 'everything was allowed'. The laws of war – on any interpretation – were being left far behind.[21]

Having learned from the Czech campaigns, the army high command demanded to be given complete control of all forces in Poland. It wanted to be able to handle the SS in particular, as well as the civilian administrators who would take over regional government as the front moved on. But it failed to get its way. The question of whether the SS and police units accompanying the troops would be entirely under the army's control remained unresolved. And although Heydrich was very careful not to antagonize the generals, he clearly saw the Polish campaign as a chance to prove the SS's value. Hitler's mistrust of the military was also evident; his orders just before the invasion made civilian administrators more independent of them than had been the case in the past. All this fuelled the military's misgivings, and, although the evidence is circumstantial, it seems that anxiety about exactly what Hitler had authorized SS units to do prompted the army to call for further meetings with Heydrich. On 29 August, they finally signed off on *Einsatzgruppen* plans to arrest up to 30,000 Poles.

Invaded from three sides and having mobilized late, Poland was in a hopeless situation; the Germans had twice as many troops and three times as many aircraft and tanks. In addition, there were more than 800,000 Soviet troops on the country's eastern border. Basing their strategy on the expectation that the British and French would quickly come to their aid, the Poles were soon disillusioned: neither of their partners planned to attack Germany during the initial invasion, expecting the fighting to get bogged down as it had done in the last war. Enjoying command of the air, the Luftwaffe bombed Poland's towns and cities and strafed columns of refugees and trains. Nonetheless, the Poles defended doggedly and inflicted heavy losses on the Germans. On 9 September, their government called for general armed resistance, and, even after troops surrendered, civilians continued to fight on, producing precisely the kind of irregular combat that always brought the worst out of German soldiers. For the first time since Hitler came to power, his troops found themselves up against a very determined and elusive enemy.

The shock was palpable from the start. 'A difficult battle with [Polish] bands has erupted ... which can only be broken through the use of draconian measures,' noted Quartermaster General Eduard Wagner as early as 3 September. The policing problem was actually made more acute by the extraordinary speed of the German advance: uniformed policemen suddenly found themselves in a war zone, responsible for 'pacifying' a huge area with little prior preparation or intelligence. The same day, SS chief Himmler issued an order calling for 'insurgents' to be 'shot on the spot'.[22]

In fact, neither soldiers nor SS men had waited for such orders, and from 2 September onwards, Polish civilians of all ages fell victim to frontline troops, at times carrying out reprisals for 'partisan' attacks, at others merely murdering at random. The small town of Złoczew was one of the first to experience what tens of thousands of others across Europe would suffer in the coming six years: it was burned to the ground, and nearly 200 people, including children, were killed. In another case, a military investigator reported that 20 Poles, 'so-called criminals', had been summarily shot. Some of the more egregious outrages were investigated for the army had not become as accustomed to this level of violence as it would be a year or two later. An SS stormtrooper and a police sergeant were arrested by military police for killing fifty Jews. Yet, facing the death penalty, they received lenient sentencing on the grounds that 'because of the numerous atrocities committed by the Poles against the ethnic Germans, they were in a state of irritability'.[23]

These atrocities were not purely imaginary. Indeed, the Poles' treatment of the ethnic Germans played an important part in fuelling 'the war of the peoples'. Worried about Nazi-funded underground organizations and 'self-defence' militias, they had closed down many German cultural and religious institutions after the invasion of Czechoslovakia, and, when the invasion of Poland began, police arrested 10–15,000 members of the minority on the basis of prepared lists and marched them away from the front lines. Attacked by Polish bystanders and soldiers, between 1,778 and 2,200 Germans died, some of exhaustion or maltreatment, others through mass shootings.[24]

When they uncovered evidence of these deaths, the invading Germans were provoked into an even more violent response. In Bydgoszcz – the most notorious case – hundreds of local Germans had been killed because of rumours that snipers were firing on Polish troops. The death toll amounted to 700–1,000 people, and some of the bodies were horrifically mutilated.[25] When German infantry entered the city and found them, they arrested several thousand Poles, including teachers, priests, lawyers, civil servants and other members of the 'intelligentsia', and anyone pointed out by a local German as involved in anti-German activity was immediately shot. Although a court martial was established in the town hall to try those already held, it was quickly overwhelmed.

Hitler himself was outraged by reports that German civilians had been killed on Bydgoszcz's 'Bloody Sunday' and demanded a tougher response. In the days that followed, the army turned over 500 prisoners for execution to the SS, and a sweep of one neighbourhood of the city netted another 900 prisoners, of whom 120 were shot in nearby woods and fields. Fifty students from a local school were executed after one of them fired at a German officer; the army itself shot another fifty 'priests, teachers, civil servants, rail operators, postal officers and small business owners'. New instructions mandated that any civilians found in possession of weapons were to be shot on the spot. In all, it is estimated that 1,000 Polish civilians were killed around the town between 5 and 13 September, and as many as 5,000 in the region.[26]

This one episode, among the most violent of the entire campaign, suggests various motivations for the Germans' brutality during the invasion. Many of those killed were hostages held under draconian but standard military guidelines to be shot in reprisals. They were the victims of the Wehrmacht's mode of combating guerilla war rather than of Nazi racial policy, and German and Habsburg troops in 1914 had behaved similarly when they came under attack from snipers and guerillas. But the troops also saw themselves as avengers in a German–Polish 'people's war'. Standing above everyone, and instrumental in setting the tone, was Hitler himself; it was the Führer who insisted that German crimes should go unpunished and that ever more violence was the answer to any Polish opposition.

Inside the military there were signs of unease. Himmler's shoot-on-sight order of 3 September was not initially known to many army officers and was ultimately rescinded. But the generals were worried about the growing ill-discipline and brutalization of their own men. As one divisional chief of staff noted: 'the first days of the war have already shown that the troops and that part of the officers inexperienced in war were either not taught at all, or insufficiently trained . . . The instinctive nervousness and insecurity and corresponding uninhibited shootings and incendiarism shames the discipline and reputation of the army, needlessly destroys quarters and provisions, and leads to hardships for the populace that doubtless could have been avoided.'[27]

It was now dawning on some commanders just how far-reaching Hitler's intentions for the Poles were and they worried about the army's reputation and the possible impact on foreign armies' treatment of German soldiers in the future if they were involved in 'ethnic extermination [*volkstümliche Ausrottung*]'. Yet they got no support from their superiors. On 7 September, Heydrich issued secret orders to his death squads that the 'liquidation of leading Poles' should be completed by the beginning of November. Five days later, when he tried to get the army to speed up the killing of 'the nobility, the Catholic clergy and the Jews', Admiral Canaris, the commander of the Abwehr, expressed his horror. 'For these methods the world will hold the Wehrmacht responsible, under whose eyes these things would take place,' he warned General Wilhelm Keitel, head of the armed forces high command. But the pliable Keitel merely told him that the policy was Hitler's, and that if the army did not want to be involved, it would be entrusted to the SS and the civilian administrators who succeeded it. After further meetings, including one between General Brauchitsch and the Führer, Brauchitsch told his senior field commanders that 'the *Einsatzgruppen* have been directed to carry out certain ethnic-political tasks in the occupied areas, according to instructions from the Führer' and that these remained 'outside of the responsibilities of the local commanding officer'. The army top brass simply washed their hands of the whole business.

This was no less than the Führer demanded. In early October Hitler issued a general amnesty for all German soldiers convicted of crimes during the invasion itself – a measure widely and no doubt correctly interpreted as a green light for future 'harshness' on the part of the troops. His adjutant noted that he was fed up with the Wehrmacht's 'maudlin sentimentality'; later, he criticized General von Blaskowitz, the military commander in Poland, for his 'infantile attitude' when the latter issued harsh punishments to SS men for war crimes and complained openly about gross violations of international norms.[28]

Amid the violence, the shape of the future that awaited Poland took time to emerge. As the Führer's interpreter subsequently noted: 'The Nazis kept talking about a thousand-year Reich but they couldn't think ahead for five minutes!' The Wehrmacht's rapid advance meant that, as early as 8 September, German units had seized the Corridor, reached the outskirts of Warsaw and cut off large numbers of Polish forces around Poznań. Yet mid-September, with Warsaw still holding out and Mussolini pushing for a negotiated settlement, found Hitler and his advisers wavering between a number of possible scenarios. One was a so-called 'Fourth Partition' between Germany and the USSR; another was to allow the existence of a small rump Polish state after Germany had annexed its western territories; and a third was to divide even this rump Poland (the Czech solution, as it were) in order to set up a small Ukrainian state in south-east Poland. Yet all of these had drawbacks from the German viewpoint, and the latter had no hope of being approved by Stalin. (Having closed the Polish question, the last thing he wanted to do was to reopen the Ukrainian one.)[29]

The Russian factor turned out to be decisive. Alarmed at the ease of the Germans' advance, the Red Army had marched unceremoniously into eastern Poland halfway through the German invasion, giving Hitler in turn a nasty surprise by the speed of its own takeover. Soviet and German troops met along the demarcation line, mostly peacefully, and at Brest-Litovsk, the site of Germany's moment of triumph twenty years earlier, they held a joint victory parade before the Wehrmacht pulled back. But the Red Army was now too close for comfort. Hitler was still holding an olive branch out to the British, and the Italians too wanted him to treat Poland in a way which did not preclude a diplomatic solution with London and Paris. In a surprisingly moderate speech on 19 September, therefore, Hitler stressed that 'our interests are of a very limited nature', and he praised 'the Polish soldier', while bemoaning the murder of 'thousands of slaughtered *Volksgenossen*'.

Stalin, on the other hand, did not want any kind of Polish state at all to survive. Moreover, he offered the Germans additional territory in eastern Poland around Lublin in return for the recognition that Lithuania fell within his sphere of influence, and this too held attractions for the Germans, who started thinking of it as a possible 'reservation' for the Jews. As September drew to a close with no signs of British interest in a compromise, Hitler's private conversations suggested a far-reaching outcome. Poland would disappear from the map, and the territory under German control would be divided into three ethnically homogenized zones, with the Poles in the middle serving as buffer between expanded Reich territories to the west and a small Jewish reservation on the Soviet border:

1. Between the Vistula and the Bug: this would be for the whole of Jewry [from the Reich as well] as well as all other unreliable elements. Build an insuperable wall on the Vistula even stronger than the one in the West. 2. Create a broad cordon of territory along the previous border to be Germanised and colonised. That would be a major task for the whole nation: to create a German granary, a strong peasantry, to resettle good Germans from all over the world. 3. In between a form of Polish state.[30]

Western Poland was thus to become the crucial sector for the expansion of the Reich. Germany would regain former Prussian land, and much besides, and resettle this with colonists. 'Racially valuable' Poles would be Germanized while 'trouble-makers' among 'the Polish intellectuals' would be killed off. 'In thirty years' time,' his adjutant noted, Hitler wanted 'people to drive across the country and nothing to remind them that once upon a time these regions had been the subject of disputes between Germans and Poles.'[31]

Such a murderous task – going well beyond even what it had been asked to connive in during the invasion itself – was clearly not something the army wanted to be associated with. The Wehrmacht retained a large presence in Poland, helping in particular to crush the last sporadic resistance and manning the border with the USSR. But the administration of the occupation was placed in the hands of civilians outside the military chain of command, and Western Poland itself was prepared for annexation. It took more than a month for Hitler and his advisers to decide how far to extend German rule beyond the old Prussian boundaries. Several of the more knowledgeable among them worried about taking over land with largely Polish populations; Germanizing it, they feared, would simply be too difficult. On the other hand several *Gauleiters* in border regions wanted to expand their fiefdoms, while Göring demanded easy access to the industrial city of Łódź. And there were strategic rationales for pushing Germany's border much further east as well. Eventually, after discussions that took up the whole of October, Hitler decreed a new border running deep inside prewar Poland. Łódź's fate was settled following a visit there by Himmler, Goebbels and the interior minister, Wilhelm Frick. Two brand new *Reichsgaue* were established – one around the city of Danzig; the other eventually including both Poznań and Łódź – and the eastern borders of the provinces of Upper Silesia and East Prussia were enlarged. This was Hitler's fantastically expanded version of the First World War's frontier wall idea. He evidently had no qualms about the challenge ahead: in the territory to be brought into the Reich lived 8.9 million Poles, 603,000 Jews and a mere 600,000 Germans.[32]

To Germanize these conquered lands as fast as possible, Hitler bypassed both the army and the civilian ministries and chose Party comrades who answered only to him. Two of them were bitter rivals who had run the prewar Danzig Nazi machine: the Party *Gauleiter* there, Albert Forster, and Arthur Greiser, who headed south to set up a new headquarters at Poznań. Greiser was keen to prove himself in this prestigious new post – not least because he had joined the Nazi Party relatively late and, much worse for Hitler, had once been a freemason – and he embraced the Führer's programme. 'He would liquidate the Polish intellectuals wherever he thought it justified,' Hitler confided approvingly to an aide. 'They had killed us earlier, one should not shrink from the task if it was about getting rid of trouble-makers.'[33]

Hitler still appears to have hoped to persuade the Western powers that German rule would actually bring stability to eastern Europe. On 6 October, the day after his triumphant visit to the bombed-out ruins of newly conquered Warsaw, he made a lengthy victory speech to the Reichstag. Still talking in terms of the continued existence of a Polish rump-state (*Reststaat*) – though this was by now window-dressing – Hitler insisted it would have to conform to the priorities set from Berlin: stable German borders, a new economic order and, most important of all, 'a resettlement of the nationalities' to put an end to 'a cause of persistent international friction'. To listen to him, all he wanted to do was to improve on Versailles and bring peace to eastern Europe. 'The revisions of the Treaty of Versailles that I implemented,' he went on, 'have not caused chaos in Europe. To the contrary, they constituted prerequisites for the creation of clear, stable and above all tolerable conditions here.' Raising the prospect of a peace conference with England, he stressed that Germany and Russia were stabilising 'this zone of unrest'. 'For the German Reich, this mission, which cannot be regarded as an imperialist one, means an occupation for fifty to a hundred years . . . In the end, all this benefits Europe.'[34]

It was a most bizarre conception of what the British were likely to find reassuring. As it was, they no longer trusted anything he said and made it clear they were not interested in any kind of deal. 'Every possibility for an understanding has now disappeared,' noted the Italian foreign minister, Ciano, in a deeply gloomy mood. There were two immediate consequences. First, Hitler prepared for an offensive against France, and second, he made up his mind about Poland. The day after his speech, he put Himmler in charge of a new task – strengthening 'Germandom' by bringing ethnic Germans 'back' into the Reich so that they could be resettled in the newly conquered territories. 'Poland is finished,' noted Propaganda Minister Goebbels (among the most anti-Polish of Hitler's ministers) on 10 October. 'No one talks about a restoration of the old Polish state any more.' Hitler created a rump state known as the General Government, under his former private lawyer, Hans Frank, in that part of the country – between Warsaw and Cracow – that was not slated for annexation. By the end of October, four months earlier than planned, German-occupied Poland was entirely under civilian control. 'The military are too soft and conciliatory,' Goebbels wrote in his diary, adding later after a conversation with Frank: '[They] are pursuing a milksop bourgeois policy rather than a racially aware one. But Frank will get his way.' The army high command was glad to wash its hands of Poland and turned its attention to the forthcoming offensive in the West.[35]

Though the Germans had also set up a General Government in Poland during the First World War, it offered no kind of model for what Hitler had in mind. There was all the difference in the world between a traditional, socially conservative occupation run according to the principles of the laws of war and the far more violent Nazi version bent on radical socio-political and demographic change over 'fifty or a hundred years'. The Kaiser's govenor general had been a military man, General Hans von Beseler, whereas Hans Frank was a Party high-up. Von Beseler had set up an assembly of Polish aristocrats and promised the country a form of independence; Frank presided over the mass murder of the Polish elite and represented the alternative to any kind of autonomy. The Poles were to be turned into a minimally educated slave labour force for the Germans and would have no need for politicians of their own in the future. 'The Führer has no intention of assimilating the Poles,' wrote Goebbels. 'They are to be forced into their truncated state and left entirely to their own devices . . . We know the laws of racial heredity and can handle things accordingly.' Rigid racial demarcation on a properly 'scientific' basis was, according to the Nazis, the only means of achieving a 'perpetual peace' between the two peoples.[36]

This dire fate, however, faced the Poles in particular rather than the Slavs as a whole. Despite the Nazis' rhetoric, in theory, and increasingly in practice, racial scientists and policy advisers distinguished between different groups of Slavs. The Slovaks were allowed to govern them-selves, and even in the Protectorate of Bohemia and Moravia the Germans ruled through a Czech bureaucracy and a figurehead Czech president – something denied to the Poles. 'The principles applied to the Bohemian-Moravian Space could not be applied to the Polish Space owing to the unbridled Polish character, which was sharply revealed during the Polish campaign as an element which requires a different method of domination,' explained a German journalist in Poland later on. It was, in other words, the strength of Polish resistance during the invasion which had been decisive in precluding a Czech political solution there. But it is hard to imagine that the Germans would ever have treated the Poles as they treated the Czechs, given the decades of bad blood between them.[37]

Although after Poland's defeat, some in the SS toyed with the idea of shooting the Czech intelligentsia as well, this idea was never systematic-ally pursued. In November 1939, mass arrests of academics were carried out both in Cracow and in Prague, and several thousands were sent to concentration camps. The universities in both countries were closed indefinitely in accordance with the Nazi decision to eliminate higher education across eastern Europe. Nevertheless, in Prague, von Neurath retained the Führer's ear while hewing a more moderate course. He was an old-fashioned conservative, not a Nazi, and Hitler was happy to allow him to do whatever kept the peace politically and the factories working. The government managed to continue to fund the Czech Academy of Arts and Sciences, and Czech rations remained as high as if not higher than those in the Reich itself. Partial strikes were sup-pressed with relatively little bloodshed. When Hans Frank visited the Protectorate, he noted with surprise that

There were large red posters in Prague announcing that today seven Czechs had been shot. I said to myself: if I wanted to hang a poster for every seven Poles that were shot, then all the forests in Poland would not suffice in order to produce the paper necessary for such posters.[38]

As this comment suggests, the destiny of the General Government was much grimmer. The first new German 'colony', it was to be ruled directly from Berlin – in yet another example of how war and conquest were expanding the reach of the Führer's personal power and shrinking the reach of what one scholar has called 'the juristic conceptual world of German administration'. It was, wrote one Party journalist, 'an entirely new kind of administrative unit within the protective area of the Great German Reich'. The SS lawyer Werner Best, founder of the Reich Security Main Office (RSHA), which was supposed to coordinate security policing across the ever-expanding Nazi empire, saw the General Government as 'the first building block' in a new continental *Grossraum*. Frank himself – ambitious, intelligent, histrionic and deeply corrupt –

established his own mini-government in Cracow with its own cabinet meetings, ministries and state secretaries. He himself was soon known irreverently as 'the King of Poland', his domain as *Frankreich*.[39]

At times Frank talked about the General Government as 'a protectorate-state, a kind of Tunis' and at others as a 'life reservation' for 'the Polish people'. But Poland itself as a term was supposed to disappear, and any reference to the 'occupied Polish territories' – as they had been known in September – was discouraged lest it imply that the country enjoyed a legal half-life. The international theory of military occupation as it had emerged over the preceding century had clearly established the provisional nature of an occupying power's authority and affirmed the continued sovereignty of the defeated enemy; only a peace treaty – from the formal viewpoint – had the power to transfer sovereignty from one state to another. The Foreign Ministry therefore cynically advised dropping any reference to 'occupied territories' in the title of the General Government since this might imply commitments in law 'which we doubtless do not wish to be bound by'.

Army lawyers were the most reluctant to jettison international legal norms. In mid-April 1940, gearing up for war in the West, the Supreme Command of the Armed Forces (OKW) asked whether Poland still existed *de jure* – an issue which bore upon the treatment of any Polish prisoners who might be captured in France. The Foreign Ministry answered that it did not: the war with Poland had ended upon Hitler's decision to wind up the military administration of the country. Treaties with the Soviet Union and Slovakia had referred to 'the hitherto existing Polish state' or the 'former Polish state'. The Swedes, who had accepted to protect Polish interests, were firmly told that Poland no longer existed. Even so, the diplomats cannot have been terribly confident of their case for they asked that their advice should not become publicly known.[40]

After the fall of France, with the prospect of further military occupations looming in the north and west of Europe, the lawyers returned to the subject. In the Academy of German Law, traditionalists argued daringly that the unilateral annexation of Polish territory and the subsequent occupation of the General Government were illegal; others disagreed: they took the Nazi line that the Führer made the law. Middle-of-the-roaders suggested prudently the precise legal status of the General Government remained unclear. Again it was urged to drop any reference to 'the occupied territories' from the title of the General Government itself for fear that damaging comparisons would be drawn with the much more conventional treatment of the French and Belgians under the Wehrmacht. As a result, when he met Frank in Berlin shortly after the fall of France, Hitler mandated the change of title and, from the summer of 1940, rump Poland was known simply as 'the General Government'. Hitler told Frank that this way it would become clear that the territory of the General Government would remain part of the 'German Reich territory [*deutsches Reichsgebiet*]' for ever. Poland had disappeared.[41]

4

The Partition of Poland

'The present war offers the opportunity, perhaps for the last time in world history, for Germany to assume in a decisive way its colonization mission in the East . . . It must not be deterred by words; rather, it must be engaged with resolute action; it calls [for us] in time to get accustomed to the idea of a resettlement of large masses of people.' These sentences could easily have been written in 1939 or 1940. But in fact they come from a much earlier set of plans drawn up in 1915 under the title 'Land without People' (*Land ohne Menschen*), the wartime scheme devised in Berlin to push the German–Slav racial frontier to the east and to create a wall of German farmers on Polish land. As we have seen, this was an idea that attracted numerous German policy-makers, intellectuals and planners, and only defeat prevented its realization.[1]

The Nazis were thus certainly not the first German nationalists to think of radical solutions for the Polish problem through colonization and expulsion. Yet officials in the Third Reich failed to draw much on these earlier discussions to map out what they would do once Poland had been defeated. That former Prussian territories would be reincorporated into the Reich was self-evident. But what of their overwhelmingly Polish inhabitants? And what too of Hitler's sudden decision to annex an enormous amount of land that had never been Prussian at all – a decision that immediately doubled the number of Poles being brought within the new German border? Some academic experts had speculated before the war about 'improving' the Poles by freeing them from 'Jewish domination'. But such a policy was much too pro-Polish for what Hitler had in mind. He wanted to destroy the Poles' leadership class completely, and his discussions in August and September focused on the 'political house-cleaning' necessary to accomplish that. As a result, approximately 50,000 Poles and 7,000 Jews were executed during the invasion. Yet there were no plans – or so it would seem – for what to do with the remaining millions of the Polish population, nor – more astonishingly – for identifying the German colonists who were supposed to come in and constitute a new frontier wall against them. It was as though, compared with the zest with which Hitler and his associates mapped out the destructive dimensions of their task, everything else could simply be left to take care of itself.[2]

Although the Nazis resolutely refused to face the fact, the basic demographic shortfall had remained the same for at least a century. There simply were not enough Germans available or willing to be resettled on Polish land. This problem was especially acute for the Nazis given their extreme biological racism and their dislike of the idea of turning Poles into Germans through cultural assimilation. By Polish estimates, more than 90 per cent of the population of the territories annexed by the Reich was Polish (Nazi estimates were only a little more optimistic). To make matters worse, Germans had been moving westwards in increasing numbers, not only from interwar Poland but even within the Reich itself. In 1937–8, German emigration from eastern Prussia soared; similar migratory trends could be observed in Silesia, Bavaria and, ironically, even in the Sudetenland. From the regime's viewpoint, conquest came just in time to prevent Germans themselves betraying the national interest by their abandonment of the borderlands.

As for the ethnic German communities beyond the Reich's borders, Nazi policy after 1933 had been to keep them where they were and to use them when desired as fifth columns; Berlin's supposed concern for the plight of the large minorities in central Europe allowed it to meddle in Hungarian and Romanian affairs. But by the same token this made it impossible for the minorities themselves to be resettled in western Poland. Only in one diplomatically sensitive case was this policy not followed. After the *Anschluss* brought the Reich to Italy's border, Hitler was keen to reassure Mussolini that he would not use the German minority in Italy against him and in 1938 he started negotiations with Rome to 'transfer' them to the Reich. A basic agreement was signed in June 1939 – a key element in cementing the Axis alliance – and Himmler was put in charge of repatriating the first group of 9–10,000 *Reichsdeutsche* citizens, while negotiations continued over the fate of the rest, who were mostly former Habsburg citizens.[3]

The talks with Italy dragged on, and the numbers involved were not large, but they established a precedent. And only a few months later, the idea of systematically repatriating ethnic Germans suddenly acquired an entirely new urgency thanks to the Molotov–Ribbentrop Pact and the Soviet invasion of eastern Poland. This triggered off nervousness in the Baltic republics, especially once Moscow began demanding to station troops there as well. Terrified Baltic German leaders feared falling into the hands of the Red Army and they reminded Himmler of the massacres the Bolsheviks had carried out in Riga at the end of the First World War. Amid a mood of near panic in Berlin, Hitler decided to arrange for them to be brought 'home to the Reich', if only to ensure there was no conflict with the Russians. A month after his epochal first visit to Moscow, therefore, Ribbentrop was sent back to arrange this. Thanks to the Soviets – or more precisely to the Baltic Germans' fear of them – a new supply of settlers for western Poland had suddenly been found. The regime tried to pretend it had been planning this all along; but in fact it had merely been responding to events.[4]

In early October German liners put to sea suddenly and made for the Baltic ports of Riga, Tallinn and Liepāja. It was while they were still on their way that Hitler delivered his 'offer of peace' speech to the Reichstag. But in the light of these events we can see that his emollient words were not only directed towards London. His statement that the 'splinters of the German nation' would be withdrawn from eastern and south-eastern Europe and brought back to the Reich to prevent further conflict was clearly also aimed at reassuring Stalin and avoiding an unnecessary clash with Russia.

The first ships docked at Baltic ports on 7 October to repatriate those Germans who wished to leave, the same day that Himmler was named head of the Reich Commission for the Strengthening of Germandom (RKFDV). 'The consequences in Europe of the Treaty of Versailles have now been abolished,' the decree appointing him began. 'As a result, the Greater German Reich is now able to bring in and settle within its territory Germans who were hitherto obliged to live abroad and is also able to arrange the settlements of population groups within its sphere of interest in such a way as to divide them more satisfactorily from one another.' Here was the real beginning of the new population policy for occupied Poland. There had been no master-plan; merely a panicked response to a regional crisis which was then repackaged by the regime as a major policy initiative. But Himmler was able to turn this brilliantly into a means of expanding the SS's power in Poland and elsewhere. In many ways it was the real beginning of the wartime transformation of the SS into a state within a state.[5]

The duties of RKFDV were threefold: to supervise the repatriation of ethnic Germans from abroad; to keep Poles and Jews in occupied Poland under surveillance in order to 'eliminate' their 'harmful influence'; and, by evicting them in sufficient numbers, to permit the resettlement of the incoming Germans in the annexed western territories in particular. Starting in the Baltic states, eastern Poland and Russia to prevent clashes with Germany's Soviet ally, the resettlement programme grew under Himmler's leadership into a vast project in population engineering that ended up driving hundreds of thousands of Poles and Jews from their homes in western Poland, fuelling the momentum towards genocide, while simultaneously bringing in hundreds of thousands of ethnic Germans as colonists. The Nazis hardly cared if the new arrivals – especially from Russia – spoke poor German, wore odd clothes and had 'catastrophic' bad teeth, rickets and a high degree of premature senility: they were Germans, they seemed to have safeguarded their racial purity and they could be used to settle the 'newly recovered East'. In a speech made on 6 October, Arthur Greiser, the *Gauleiter* of the new Warthegau province, outlined the goal Hitler had just set him: 'In ten years' time, there will be here no patch of land which will not be German; every homestead will belong to German colonists. They are already on their way from all the provinces of the Reich, from the Baltic states, from Lithuania, Rumania, Russia and the Tyrol to settle down in this region. They came down here one and all to wage a merciless struggle against the Polish peasantry.'[6]

In the Baltic states, German agents painted a rosy picture of what lay ahead for those who embarked for the Reich. Propaganda articles depicted neat but apparently uninhabited farmhouses awaiting new owners. In fact, those awaiting repatriation were not fooled and many of them knew very well that Poles were being expelled to make way for them. Their reason for leaving was not commitment to the Nazi cause but fear of staying if the Soviets took over. Reaching a settlement of economic claims with the Baltic governments took some time; and at least 7,000 Germans refused to go at all. But most were keen to be gone and left within two months. Terror of the approach of Soviet rule led many Latvians and Estonians to apply as well, often claiming that they had German relatives or other connections. The terror was even greater among the Volhynian Germans living in eastern Poland. Many of them had been deported by the Tsarist authorities during the First World War, and they were familiar with the deportations from the Soviet borderlands in the 1930s. When the news was announced that they too would be resettled, they were overjoyed. By the time the first groups of them left at the end of December, three months of Soviet rule had increased their desire to be gone. Indeed many non-Germans – including Poles, Ukrainians and even Jews – risked their lives begging to be included on these convoys: a few Ukrainians and Poles were admitted. Jews were not.[7]

The ships from the Baltic docked at West Prussian ports in mid-October as bands played, and speeches celebrated the new arrivals' 'homecoming'. While teams of Hitler Youth waved flags to greet them, 'wild' expulsions quickly cleared apartments for them and forced out their Polish owners. The victims had little time to pack and were allowed only a single suitcase, a change of underwear, some food and 200 zloty each. Evicted from Gdynia, Mrs J. K. recalled that the German gendarmes who gave her a few hours to leave told her 'that not only must I be ready, but that the flat must be swept, the plates and dishes washed and the keys left in the cupboards so that the Germans who were to live in my house should have no trouble'. She and others in her position were then transported to the General Government in open wagons with only straw to keep them warm.[8]

Poles were the chief victims of this programme of eviction and expulsion. But it also changed the destiny of Poland's Jews. Ever since the invasion, they had routinely been singled out for punishment and humiliation. Jewish shops and homes were targeted by German troops as they passed through, while Gestapo officials made them 'clean up' public squares and streets as though to atone for their polluting presence. The Third Reich had turned young German conscripts into ardent anti-Semites who enjoyed publicly making fun of these 'enemies of the race' by shaving their beards, or cuffing them when they did not salute fast enough. Despite the surge of organized anti-Jewish violence in Poland before the war, many Poles took time to understand the new ethos and to realize who sanctioned it. 'All brutalities have to be tolerated,' one German major told new Polish police recruits in October 1939, since they had been ordered by 'higher quarters'.[9]

Yet for the Reich's 'Jewish experts' the conquest of Poland immeasurably complicated their task. Between 1933 and 1939 their forced emigration policies had led the Jewish population of the Reich to drop by more than half, from 503,000 to 240,000. And although the conquests of 1938 and 1939 brought new areas of Jewish settlement within their area of responsibility – 180,000 Jews in Austria, 85,000 in the former Czechoslovakia – the same policy had worked there too, and around half of these, too, had fled, or been forced out, as a result of Eichmann's operations. By September 1939 the great majority of the 400,000 refugees who had fled Greater Germany since 1933 were Jewish. (Fatefully, almost half remained within Europe, for the opportunities for refugee resettlement outside the continent were shrinking.)[10] Poland changed the equation completely. The Germans now found themselves responsible – having scarcely considered the matter beforehand – for more than two million Polish Jews, the third-largest Jewish population in the world after the USA and the USSR and nearly ten times larger than that in the Old Reich itself.

Having been hit by this unexpected problem Himmler and Heydrich wanted to make it go away as quickly as possible. They proposed to focus on the newly incorporated territories of western Poland and to make them *judenrein* in the space of four months by expelling their entire Jewish population eastwards. When Stalin offered to transfer the Lublin district to the General Government, he opened up the prospect of creating a 'Jewish reservation' on the new border with the USSR.[11] This fired the imagination of Adolf Eichmann, the SD specialist in 'Jewish emigration', and he suggested dumping the remaining Jews from Austria and the Czech lands there too.[12]

Yet only five trainloads of Jews were actually sent to a small transit camp on the San river before Himmler was forced to cancel the entire operation. Anti-Jewish feeling was not the only force driving German occupation policy, as the race warriors now realized. Hans Frank was furious at the idea that his General Government might have to house the Jewish reservation for the Reich and its new territories. And Hitler was worried about installing large numbers of Jews on the sensitive border with the Red Army. Another problem had emerged as well. Once the first transports of Baltic Germans arrived in Danzig, it became clear that deporting Jews – especially from Vienna and the Protectorate – would not free up the housing German immigrants required in western

Poland. With thousands of ethnic Germans on the move, and transportation stretched, Hitler's decision to 'consolidate Germandom' in western Poland took priority over plans for expelling Jews from the Greater German Reich.[13]

Because there were nearly nine million Poles in western Poland and only 603,000 Jews, it made little sense to prioritize the latter's expulsion as Himmler demanded. The Germanization programme aimed to settle the newcomers – whatever their previous professions – on the land; yet western Poland's Jews were predominantly urban. They lived, in short, in the wrong places. And it was not only at this strategic level that the deportations seemed to have been misconceived. The initial round-ups had already deprived farmers of workers and the towns of badly needed skilled craftsmen and Polish civil servants. Within months, grumbling began to be heard among some of Himmler's rivals that his schemes were dogmatic, ill thought through and damaging to the German war effort.

One of the earliest and most troublesome of the dissenters was the young *Gauleiter* of Danzig-West Prussia, Albert Forster, an early Nazi member and a man who had Hitler's ear. Forster had run the Nazi Party machine in Danzig for years, and his appointment as *Gauleiter* gave him what one despairing Interior Ministry official termed 'ducal authority' in the region. Despite the fact that, as an honorary SS officer, Forster was nominally under Himmler's authority, he refused to allow the latter's racial policies to determine his own approach. It was the Polish coastal towns in his province that had been the first to be evacuated. So-called 'wild', and then more organized, expulsions of Poles had turned them into ghost towns and ironically even blighted the port of Danzig itself – the port for which the whole war had supposedly been started. Polish Gdynia opposite had been renamed Gotenhafen. But after the expulsion of its inhabitants on 16 October, it should have been called 'Totenhafen' (Harbour of the Dead) according to a Swedish journalist who described how a mere 17,000 arriving Baltic Germans were supposed to take the place of the town's 130,000 original inhabitants. The port stagnated, machinery was packed up and requisitioned, and only the empty apartments and furniture left behind by the Poles offered any pickings. Forster was perturbed and soon brought the expulsions to an end. Muttering that he did not want old people or 'plutocrats', he allowed only 12,000 of the Baltic Germans to stay; another 50,000 had to move on south. After this, far fewer Poles were ever deported from Forster's *Gau* than from the Warthegau, and far fewer Germans were allowed to settle there. Regarding the settlers as Himmler's stooges, Forster in effect opted out of the entire resettlement policy. With Hitler unwilling to act, there was little Himmler could do but fume.[14]

The attitude of Forster's long-time rival and enemy, Arthur Greiser, could scarcely have been more different. Both men had been appointed by Hitler at the same time, but Greiser hoped to make his giant Warthegau a model for the new racial war. The odds were against him – for of the *Gau*'s prewar population of about 4.9 million people, 4.2 million were Poles, and 435,000 were Jews. Only 325,000 – under 10 per cent of the total – were ethnic Germans. This meant that Germanization would either have to be abandoned or pushed through with extreme force. Greiser left no doubt which option he chose. He embraced Himmler's plans, and it was thus in the Warthegau that the SS carried out its so-called First Short-term Plan in December 1939, the real start of systematic ethnic cleansing. Despite the wintry weather, Heydrich was keen to push ahead – 128,000 ethnic Germans were en route from eastern Poland – and more than 87,000 victims – mostly Poles – were herded on to trains bound for the General Government. Often they were robbed and beaten by the very officials in charge of expelling them; some froze to death en route. But for Himmler this was only the first step in a much more comprehensive programme of deportations.[15]

Unfortunately for the reputation of the SS, the December expulsions did not go at all smoothly. Even the loyal Greiser was critical. The police were supposed to have identified individuals who were regarded as security risks or whose deportation would free up housing and work opportunities for the new immigrants. But the Gestapo had mislaid their card index of Polish intellectuals, and police in Łódź had made up numbers by targeting a Jewish neighbourhood in the city – detaining 7,000 Jews in less than six hours. Their haste had meant they did not have proper facilities to register or question the Jews, forcing 'people with children to stand around for hours in the cold and snow drifts', as SS-Sturmbannführer Richter reported in dismay. Other deportations were held up because local internment camps were already assigned to incoming Baltic Germans. Some deportees had claimed they were really ethnically German, and the lack of proper screening procedures led the SD to fret that perhaps they were.[16]

The economic repercussions of deporting the wrong people were especially alarming. The already understaffed local railways, for instance, employed 12,000 Poles and 4,200 Germans. Railway administrators insisted on deferrals for the Poles, and on being told in advance of any plans to deport their staff, warning that any sudden expulsions would be 'unbearable for the war economy and could bring the various large-scale population movements into question'.[17] Hans Frank and his staff in the General Government were even louder in their protests. They had to cope with a stream of destitute newcomers being pushed across the border and faced the prospect of one million Poles and Jews arriving in a matter of months. It was too much, especially in light of the planned attack on France, which many feared would not be over quickly. To challenge Himmler, Frank got the backing of the far more powerful Hermann Göring, who (even as his own men despoiled the country's economy) worried about the havoc these huge movements of population could cause. The army weighed in too. In an unusually frank statement that led eventually to his being fired, Colonel General von Blaskowitz, Rundstedt's successor as commander in Poland, protested at the short-sightedness of the whole brutal policy:

It is misguided to slaughter tens of thousands of Jews and Poles as is happening at present; because in view of the huge population neither the concept of a Polish state nor the Jews will be eliminated by doing so . . . If high officials of the SS and police demand acts of violence and brutality and praise them publicly, then, in a very short time we shall be faced with the rule of the thug . . . The resettlement programme is causing especial and growing discontent throughout the country. It is obvious that the starving population, which is fighting for its existence, can only observe with the greatest concern how the masses of those being resettled are left to find refuge with them completely penniless and, so to speak, naked and hungry. It is only too understandable that these feelings reach a pitch of uncontrolled hatred at the number of children dying of starvation on every transport and the wagons of people frozen to death. The idea that one can intimidate the Polish population by terrorism and rub their noses in the dirt will certainly prove false.[18]

Hitler was furious but he could scarcely afford to ignore misgivings from such powerful quarters. The showdown came at a conference called by Göring at his Karinhall estate in early 1940. Frank called for an outright halt to the deportations: the expulsion of tens, even hundreds, of thousands of people eastwards was simply impossible while the war was still going on; with rail capacity, police manpower and housing all stretched to the limit, it created too much disruption. Göring backed him: securing the harvest in the incorporated territories would require Polish farm-workers, and it made no sense to get rid of them. He therefore issued a ruling: there were to be no further expulsions unless Frank was warned in advance, and on 11 March Himmler reluctantly announced that the deportation policy had been suspended.

One consequence was that the plight of Jews in western Poland became significantly worse as they were trapped inside ghettoes that had originally been intended only as temporary solutions before deportation. The idea of forcing the Jews into ghettoes had always been present, but the initiative to do so was generally taken by local authorities. Greiser's officials in Łódź, home to the largest Jewish community in the Warthegau, were the first to construct one, once they realized that immediate deportation was not going to be possible; construction started in February 1940 and was finished in April, becoming a model for other towns and a kind of tourist attraction. Others in the Warthegau were also built at around the same time.[19]

That July, the log-jam in deportations started to worry the Warthegau authorities. With more than 160,000 people inside the Łódź ghetto who lacked either running water or a functioning sewage system, a public health crisis was becoming a serious possibility and threatened to spill over into the rest of the city. Greiser warned Frank that 'it would be an impossible situation to keep these Jews, packed together in the ghetto, over the winter'. He had anticipated that they would be gone by October, and his senior police officer reminded Frank that the ghetto had been established on the 'condition that the deportation of the Jews would begin by mid-year at the latest'. Frank did not care. Just as Greiser was keen to make his region 'free of Jews', Frank wanted *his* capital Cracow *judenfrei* by the end of the year, and he did not need Greiser's Jews adding to his task. As it was, Himmler himself had cancelled all Jewish transports east into the General Government shortly after the fall of France, having learned of a new possible solution for eastern Europe's 'Jewish problem' – the construction of a mass reservation of Jews in the French colony of Madagascar.[20] By the summer of 1940, it must have looked as though Hitler's plans for a new racial order in Poland had ended almost as soon as they had begun. Despite the deportations, the vast majority of the non-German inhabitants in the annexed territories remained where they were.[21]

Not everyone thought this was a story of unmitigated failure. For one resettlement boss, it was little short of astonishing that Germany had resettled more colonists in a single year – and during a war, at that – than the Royal Prussian Colonization Commission had managed to do in twenty-eight. Himmler's men had placed the ethnic Germans in over sixty reception camps and provided mattresses and straw, stabling, food and excellent medical care. Schools had been established for their children, and there were language classes for those who had forgotten German. Greiser himself boasted of the Warthegau's productivity, its sterling agricultural performance with a bumper harvest, the way – in short – it had brought to an end 'the unhappy chapter in German history that was characterized by the expression "People without Space" '.[22]

Even so, there were reasons for those policing Germany's new ethnic frontier to worry. There was the impasse in Jewish policy and fears of the financial, health and security costs involved in ghettoization. Another 275,000 ethnic Germans would be shortly heading west following the Soviet march that summer into formerly Romanian Bessarabia and Bukovina; they too would most likely have to be held indefinitely in transit camps. As it was, the Warthegau was already full of ethnic Germans who grumbled they had been waiting around to be resettled since the start of the year, and Himmler himself visited a camp near Łódź to try to calm them. 'You must understand you have to wait,' he told them. 'Before you get your farm, a Polack must first be thrown out. Often they are such holes that we first have to put the buildings in order or to combine farms . . . By summer you will walk on your own land.'[23]

The slow pace of the resettlement programme was thus producing dissatisfaction on all sides. The security police were worried about the threat posed by the Poles themselves and feared rebellion. They noticed that the Poles had started anticipating evacuations and seemed to know when they were coming. (This was not difficult. It took the Germans a while to realize that the appearance of deportation officials chalking marks on houses sent a fairly reliable signal of impending expropriation.) When the authorities arrived to confiscate Polish farmhouses, their owners were nowhere to be found, swelling the ranks of a vagrant population that might, come winter, turn to banditry. By the end of

1940, an estimated 35,000 Poles were on the run. Sealing off the border with the General Government did not seem to help.[24]

As for the newcomers, the grumbling that had greeted Himmler was only the tip of the iceberg. Some of them felt they had been misled into coming and disliked their treatment in the resettlement camps and the bullying and know-it-all manner of the officials in charge. Even when assigned properties, a few people claimed to feel unhappy about taking over what belonged to someone else; others were more upset at their run-down condition and the isolation they felt. Moreover, their political and sexual behaviour remained under strict surveillance, and their property could be reassigned if they aroused the authorities' misgivings. The intense pressure on them to give up older regional loyalties and their religious traditions was another source of tension and one of the factors behind a powerful anti-Church drive by Nazis in the Warthegau. The reported difficulties led social workers to be rushed in, but they too frequently made the situation worse; Reich Germans could not help, it seemed, but talk about the ethnic Germans in demeaning and arrogant terms – as 'settler material' or 'naive, really just like big children'. As relations soured between the settlers and the authorities, there were protests and arrests, and some simply abandoned the farms they had been told to tend and returned to the camps.[25]

In the General Government, it was victory over France that allowed the Germans to reveal their true colours. Up until the spring, the region's fate was still being defined with an eye to international reaction. It was said that it would be a potential Polish homeland in which 'Poles . . . will be under German sovereignty but not as German citizens and will receive a kind of reservation here'. But once victory had been won in the West, and the last prospects of a general peace conference vanished, the reach of Hitler's ambitions became clear. He told Frank that the General Government was to be brought into much closer connection with the Reich itself and to serve as a 'labour reserve' for Germany. There was no longer any talk of a 'Polish homeland'. Under 'the absolute leadership of the German nation', it was declared to be ripe for extensive Germanization of the population's 'completely German racial core'.

In practice, Germanization of the General Government could scarcely get very far when there was still so much to be done in the incorporated territories to the west. For one thing, there were hardly any Germans.

What the new policy really meant was an escalation of the murderous campaign against Polish nationalism. In November 1939, there had been a wave of arrests of intellectuals and notables across the country. Hostages had been seized on the eve of the Polish national holiday and more than 100 members of the University of Cracow had been sent to the Oranienburg concentration camp, where seventeen elderly professors died. After a lull of a few months, a second wave of arrests took place. Frank feared an upsurge of nationalist resistance during the invasion of France. To forestall this, 30,000 members of the Polish elite were rounded up and imprisoned, and more than 3,000 were shot. The so-called AB Action (Special Pacification Operation) was 'intended to finish off at an accelerated pace the mass of the rebellious resistance politicians and other politically suspect individuals in our hands', Hans Frank confessed. 'I must quite openly admit that this will cost the lives of a few thousand Poles ... but all of us as National Socialists have a duty at this time to ensure that no further resistance emerges from the Polish people.'[26]

Frank believed that once the elite had been killed off, the Polish masses would fall into line. His so-called 'splinter policy' aimed to make it clear to the Polish 'working man' that the repression was not aimed at him, provided he remained obedient to German commands. Frank did not much worry about what he termed the Poles' notorious lack of political realism; such small centres of opposition as survived could be ignored so long as they remained uncoordinated. Yet as he gloated at the sophistication of his strategy, how could he not have thought Poles would interpret German rule as anything other than brutish, arbitrary and violently repressive?

In the first place, they faced the daily threat of assault and death. Executions and casual shootings remained commonplace. In Łódź, German soldiers killed a Pole who entered the wrong railway carriage and then fired on bystanders when they protested, killing three. Others were shot for offering deportees food and drink. Collective punishment for any actual or suspected attacks on Germans became the norm. In addition, all Poles were declared liable for compulsory labour service. As Germany's labour shortage worsened, they were rounded up on the streets in random raids and packed off to the Reich or put to work on roads and military installations. Women faced domestic service, farm work or even (at least this was the rumour) service in military brothels.

Prisons and work camps – like the new camp at Auschwitz established around the time of the AB Action – quickly became crowded, and the execution site outside Warsaw at Palmiry became infamous. In the freezing winter of 1940–41, the death toll rose so fast that it took two weeks to get a requiem mass said for a loved one in the churches of Warsaw. From his lavishly decorated headquarters in the Wewel castle in Cracow, Frank occasionally mused that things were spiralling out of control. It was a complete illusion, he insisted, to think that the General Government could be controlled through 'a campaign of extermination [*Ausrottungsfeldzug*] against Polish peasants and workers'. Yet his alternative – a German alliance with Polish workers against the country's 'great capitalists' that would split the masses from the elite – was no less fantastic.[27]

Poland's 'great capitalists' were a figment of Frank's imagination. In practice, the Germans had been systematically plundering the Polish economy from the outset. As economics supremo of the Reich, Göring established a network of agents to grab all moveable assets. His men, together with the Wehrmacht and later the SS, also took over Polish firms. Freed from most legal restraints and encouraged to exploit the country and its resources for their own ends, it was understandably hard for many Germans to know where 'organization' ended and plunder began. As officials helped themselves to whatever caught their fancy, corruption started to erode the authority of German officialdom itself, jeopardizing Frank's efforts to create a model 'colonial administration' that would make the General Government self-sufficient. 'Wild requisitions' had to be brought under control, he insisted in early 1940, if the *Germans'* respect for property was not to disappear altogether. As it was, 'the phrase "to organize" means thieving and robbery'. More concerned with animals than humans, he noted in alarm that the numbers of cows, pigs and chickens had plummeted.[28]

Such considerations would have carried more weight had Frank's own greed not been notorious. As it was, the problem of corruption – which was to become such a pronounced feature of the New Order across Europe – was connected in the case of Poland to two things in particular. One was the confiscation of Jewish property. A common source of enrichment for Party officials in the pre-1939 Reich, it became even more profitable in the East, where the Party and the SS were stronger, and checks on such behaviour scarcely existed. Astonished German state auditors found that SS officials in former Poland had routinely created 'special funds' for their own use. Greiser established a 'deposit account' in a Poznań bank for 'money confiscated from Jews and enemies of the Reich'. In Lublin, Globocnik made 'large-scale transfers of confiscated jewels'. In Stanislau, a search of the SS offices revealed money, gold coins and all kinds of currencies stashed in chests, desks and filing cabinets as well as crates of jewels.[29]

Corruption was also a reflection of the calibre of the Germans staffing the occupation bureaucracy. More than 2,100 civil servants were posted to the newly annexed territories of western Poland by the end of 1940, compared with only 70 in the former Austria, 480 in the Protectorate and 860 in the Sudetenland. Yet their quality was very mixed. Many had been sent by the Party, which saw the annexed territories as a new potential power base; often they had few or no administrative qualifications apart from ideological fervour. Others were attracted by the prospect of enrichment. Quite a few were career civil servants who had been dismissed in Germany for drunkenness or corruption and were amnestied in September 1939 and allowed to redeem themselves through an eastern posting. Such men often tried to prove their credentials by behaving especially harshly towards the Poles.[30]

The Poles themselves, meanwhile, were turned into second-class citizens and hit by a barrage of prohibitions. They were forbidden to use public beaches, swimming pools or public gardens. Their universities were closed and political and cultural organizations dissolved. Their ancient libraries and art collections were systematically looted and the contents sent to Germany. Forbidden from wearing military decorations, or even school uniforms, they were obliged to occupy the rear portions of platforms in stations, trains and buses, and to stand if necessary to allow Germans to sit down. Adults had to salute Germans in uniform and were beaten if they omitted to do so. They had to bare their heads in the presence of German officials and to stand aside when they passed. Shopkeepers were told to serve German customers first, and Poles were allowed to shop only at certain times. They were granted much lower rations than Germans (though they were still higher than those set for Jews); chocolate was prohibited, and milk was often reserved solely for German children on the grounds – in the words of Robert Ley, head of the German Labour Front – that 'a lower race needs less food'. Polish children were not even allowed to watch German fairy-tale films, since 'the conveying of German sentimental values ... appears ... fundamentally questionable'.[31]

Discriminatory decrees were assiduously enforced, and German civil servants who did not take them seriously could be removed. But the Kafkaesque logic of bureaucracy generated rules that were often mutually contradictory. The case of the 'Hitler salute' is a good example. In some areas Poles *had* to use it when a German official passed. In others, Poles were *forbidden* to use it, and officials charted lapses with alarm (since it was 'a privilege of the Germans and of recognized Germanic fellow-racials like the Flemish, the Dutch, the Norwegians etc. . . . but not of those of unequal blood like Poles, Czechs, Ukrainians and so on'). Eventually the security police accepted that its use could not be enforced. But because they feared that an announcement to that effect would damage German prestige, they recommended simply doing nothing. The result was more confusion.[32]

Greiser's Warthegau was the scene of the worst repression as zealous German officials invented ever more imaginative and surreal measures to put the *Untermenschen* in their place. Some punished them for riding bicycles or pushing handcarts or even – in Kutno – for smiling ironically. Regulatory overdrive led to a 'Prohibition on Bystanders Keeping their Hands in their Pockets in the Presence of Military Personnel'. More seriously, the Warthegau also saw a sweeping assault on the Catholic Church in which large numbers of monasteries were confiscated and church organizations were dissolved.

Greiser's deputy, the white-haired August Jäger – an elderly Prussian civil servant – was a veteran of the Reich's anti-Church wars and so vehement in his hostility that he was nicknamed '*Kirchen-Jäger*' (Church-hunter). But the intensity of anti-Polish hostility in the Warthegau also reflected Greiser's success in building up a highly activist Nazi Party apparatus from scratch. The armed volunteer *Selbstschutz* units were disbanded, but local German Nazis and newly arrived ethnic Germans from eastern Poland or Romania, keen to prove their nationalist credentials (especially as they were often ridiculed by other Germans for their accents and customs), acted as pioneers defending the prerogatives of Germandom amid a sea of potentially rebellious Poles.[33]

During the autumn of 1940, as the SS and the Party came to terms with the realization that the region would continue to have a large Polish population for some time to come – the repression acquired a more systematic, bureaucratic and even pedagogic character. 'As we are still compelled to use Polish labour power,' Greiser proclaimed,

it is impossible to avoid the everyday presence and contact of German citizens with Poles belonging to the same sphere of labour. Similarly owing to the shortage of dwellings and domestic staff, it is not yet possible to avoid neighbourhoods with Poles, or even common dwelling in one house. Therefore it becomes indispensable to direct the attention of the German population, with the aid of requisite measures, to the necessity of strict observance of the demarcation in their personal relations with individuals belonging to the Polish national community.

The problem of telling Germans and Poles apart was a constant concern in a society where Germans were billeted in Polish homes and Germans and Poles jointly made up fire crews or workforce teams. Germans were told to wear distinguishing marks to avoid receiving the kind of brutal treatment casually meted out to Poles: those who forgot soon found punches and abuse made them remember. In some towns the Poles were marked out by being made to wear a violet letter P, and pamphlets were distributed warning Germans not to fraternize since: 'There are no decent Poles, just as there are no decent Jews.' The press publicized the prosecution of Germans like agricultural labourer Karl Lossain, who paid for a Polish fellow worker to visit the cinema with him. If friendship was forbidden, sexual relations between Germans and Poles could cost the latter their lives. The guiding principle was 'a ruthless separation of the members of the German nation from those of the Polish nation', announced one senior Warthegau administrator. Germans who flouted this faced protective arrest and even being sent to a concentration camp.[34]

The German assault on Polish nationalism targeted the cities in particular. In the annexed territories, Poles were forced out of urban areas: Poznań (over which Poles and Germans had tussled since the mid-nineteenth century) lost 70,000 of its inhabitants in a few months; Łódź 150,000. The population of Kalisz dropped from 80,000 to 43,000, Włocławek from 67,000 to 18,000. But the most dramatic fate was reserved for Warsaw. Hitler forbade any reconstruction to take place there during the war at all and he approved plans to turn the old Polish capital into a provincial German town once the war was won. Running the city as a communications hub for the empire in the East, 120,000 Germans would eventually enjoy the greenery of an entirely 'new

Warsaw' on the left bank of the Vistula; on the opposite side, a workforce of 'Polish slaves' would be packed into a much smaller area.[35]

Preparations for this policy of separation began during the war. In the autumn of 1940, Warsaw was divided into three districts, with the Germans taking over the centre, with the best hotels, restaurants and boulevards. Life for the Poles became harsher, but the fate of the Jews was worse. The construction of the ghetto took most of 1940, and in November, it was finally isolated from the rest of the city by brick walls, barbed wire and planks. The 80,000 Poles who lived there were ordered to leave, and 150,000 Jews were moved in. Other Jews were brought in from surrounding towns and villages, and in March 1941 its population peaked at 460,000. Although prewar Warsaw had already been over-crowded, inside the ghetto, a mere 15 per cent of the city's housing stock was supposed to shelter one-third of its population. Since most of the inhabitants were destitute, and rations were less than one-tenth those granted Germans in the city, the ghetto was a death-trap. Mortality rates there soared from 23.5 per thousand in 1940 to 90 in 1941 and an astonishing 140 in 1942. A Jewish police force kept order; a Jewish council answered to the German authorities; Jewish soup-kitchens attempted to feed as many as they could. But none of these groups had any real control over the situation.

The ghetto itself – by far the largest in occupied Poland – became an attraction for Germans passing through the city, much as its equivalent in Łódź had done. Spectators gathered, fascinated, along the walls to peer at the 'Eastern Jews' inside. They included 'officers, often civilian German officials in the General Government administration, function-aries in uniform, members of the labour service, railway workers, Red Cross nurses'. A horrified German soldier, Joe Heydecker, described the gawkers.

Most of them stayed there for a long time, silent, impassive, watching people go in and out, the checks and the brutality. Some turned away; others allowed themselves to offer words of encouragement. Most remained silent without giving the least sign that would allow one to know their thoughts or feelings.

Heydecker made his own unauthorized incursions into the ghetto in order to photograph its bleak, snow-bound streets. His camera captured the Polish, Jewish and German police manning the checkpoints behind crude barriers of fencing and barbed wire, the street sellers with their baskets of bread, carts of books and even – one day – balloons. From immaculately dressed professionals in bow-ties and smart overcoats to gaunt, unshaven beggars with their feet wrapped in damp rags, Heydecker caught a spectrum of life on the ghetto streets in the months before most of the inhabitants were deported to the extermination camp at Treblinka.[36]

OCCUPATIONS COMPARED

One way to understand the nature of the German occupation of Poland more fully is to compare it to the earlier occupations of Czechoslovakia and Austria or, indeed, going further back, to the First World War occupations carried out by the Kaiser's army. But perhaps an even more illuminating comparison is with the Soviet occupation of eastern Poland and the Baltic states that took place at the same time. Stalin was certainly not the first Russian leader to want to secure his western borders through an agreement with the Germans. An early proposal to end 'disorders' in western Belorussia and western Ukraine had been made to the Prussians in 1756, and the partitions of Poland had been justified on similar grounds. Tsarist negotiators in the First World War emphasized the strategic importance of this area, and in the 1920s Soviet military planners reaffirmed the need to revise Poland's eastern border. Hence from the Soviet point of view, the Ribbentrop–Molotov Pact represented the fulfilment of long-standing territorial demands.[37]

In the middle of September 1939, the Red Army moved largely unopposed into eastern Poland, and the following year it occupied the Baltic states and Romanian Bessarabia. Coming after the German invasion had already demoralized the Poles, the Red Army lost only 1,000 killed in the fighting, and only round Grodno, where there was serious Polish resistance, did it execute large numbers of Polish POWs. The Germans, by contrast, lost twenty times as many men and executed nearly 60,000 civilians, as we have seen.[38] But Stalin shared Hitler's desire to break the power of Polish nationalism and he had been at least as adamant that no independent Polish state should remain after the country's partition. Both men wanted in effect to revert to the traditional Russo-German approach to the Poles. But there was nothing traditional about the means they adopted: in effect, Poland became a kind of grim laboratory case for the study of comparative totalitarianisms. In the minds of the inhabitants of these imperial borderlands, this may have been the latest chapter in a much longer story of forced population movements, massacres and foreign occupations. But under both occupiers state violence was employed on a scale that had simply been beyond the imagination of the nineteenth-century empires. The murderous culmination came around the time of the Germans' AB Action, when the NKVD itself executed more than 15,000 Polish officers – the bodies of the largest contingent were later exhumed from mass graves in the Katyn Forest by the Germans – as well as 7,305 others, held in NKVD jails. (It is possible, though there is as yet no proof, that the German and Soviet crimes were linked, and that they pooled intelligence on the victims.)

Both sides too organized deportations on a vast scale. The Germans, as we have seen, gave priority to organizing transfers of Germans *into* the newly annexed territories. By the end of March 1941, according to Eichmann's calculations, 408,000 Poles and Jews had been expelled to the General Government while about the same number or more had been sent west into the Old Reich as forced labourers. This was a huge number, but it could have been much higher since only the 1941 military build-up against the USSR prevented Heydrich from deporting another 831,000 people. The Soviet authorities deported hundreds of thousands of civilians too, in a series of four major operations of considerable brutality, though there were no counterbalancing inward migrations.

In February 1940, 140,000 members of the families of Polish ex-servicemen who had been given land in the eastern provinces of interwar Poland were sent to convict camps in the forests of Siberia. In April, in an operation to clear a strip along the Ukrainian border, 66,000 people – mostly women and children – were sent to Kazakhstan; in June, there was a round-up aimed at targeting 'counter-revolutionaries' and 'spies' who had entered the Soviet zone fleeing from the Germans. (Not surprisingly, perhaps, many of these 76,400 individuals were Jewish.) And finally, on the very eve of the German invasion in June 1941, another 88,000 were deported from Poland and the Baltic states. The total given by internal Soviet data suggests approximately 380–390,000 Poles were sent east as 'special deportees'. Other estimates run as high as 1.25 million.[39]

But even if the two partitioning powers pursued what were in some respects similar policies, they did so for different ends. The Third Reich had annexed land with a population of 10.7 million, of whom more than 90 per cent were Poles and barely 6 per cent Germans; yet the absurdly ambitious purpose of the annexation – indeed of the war itself – was to reverse this demographic imbalance by getting rid of as many non-Germans, which meant in this case chiefly Poles, as possible. The land occupied and then annexed by the USSR, in contrast, was one where even according to the official interwar Polish statistics Poles were not in a majority – perhaps 5.3 million out of a total of 13 million: large numbers of Ukrainians, Belorussians, Jews and others also lived there. More importantly, Soviet policy, while aiming to crush Polish national-ism, and to prevent any security threats it might pose, especially near the borders, did not aim to get rid of any particular national or ethnic group *in toto*. Its purpose was social revolution, not national purifi-cation. That is one reason why the German deportations aimed to expel non-Germans from the Reich entirely, while the Soviet round-ups drove those they caught deep into the country's interior.

The categories of enemy targeted by the two sets of secret police, though overlapping where their concern with the Polish elite was con-cerned, differed in other respects, most obviously regarding the Jews. This surely explains the steady trickle of Jews trying to cross the demar-cation line *into* the Soviet-occupied zone while Poles moved in the opposite direction. There was no equivalent on the Soviet side to the sporadic, unsystematized and almost invariably unpunished shootings of Jews which German soldiers and SS units carried out. German policy, by contrast, made it clear that Jews had lost all their rights and were no longer protected by law. This was evident well before any decision to murder them had been taken, and was underlined in a report sent from occupied Poland as early as February 1940 to the Polish government in exile.[40]

More broadly, the whole basis of Nazi law was racial and national difference. Although Poles might be led by the Germans to feel they were in a superior position to the Jews, they were always treated under the law as second-class subjects. In the Soviet case matters were different. Officially at any rate ethnic and religious distinctions did not matter. This was, of course, why many left-wing Polish Jews, especially the younger ones, greeted the Red Army with enthusiasm. Having felt the chill wind of an increasingly anti-Semitic Polish nationalism, they welcomed the promise of civic equality. That Soviet rule spelled doom for the traditional institutions of *shtetl* life (not to mention other political parties) bothered their elders but not them.[41]

But it was not only young Jewish leftists who welcomed the Soviets' arrival. The Red Army proclaimed that it had come to liberate its 'kindred nations' – Ukrainians and Belorussians – from the disintegration of the Polish state, and this rhetoric did not fall entirely on deaf ears. Peasants in eastern Poland were courted by the newcomers, invited to join in the destruction of 'Polish fascism' and enticed with the parcelling-out of large landed estates. The Soviets dropped leaflets urging them to 'drive the landowners out with scythes and axes', and some massacred well-off Polish families and took over their property. In country areas, Belorussians and Ukrainians were encouraged to enter the Party and the local administration; in the towns, where they were few, Jews were asked to play a similar role.[42]

Put another way, the two occupations promised their victims very different political and economic futures. In the German case, the annexed territories were to be ruled for the benefit of less than 10 per cent of the population. On the other hand, there would be no social revolution, capitalism would continue to operate, and the main impact was felt in arbitrary violence and ad hoc confiscations of labour, land and other property. Citizenship was to be confined to Germans, and the key issue lay in deciding who was a German. In Soviet-occupied eastern Poland, citizenship was almost immediately imposed upon the population and the machinery of mass participatory politics – assemblies, elections, plebiscites, constitutions – was introduced with the aim of demonstrating the popular desire for incorporation into the Soviet Union. If German law was kept from non-Germans, Soviet law was an instrument for extending Moscow's power. In the East there was thus an explosion of politics; in the West, its elimination. Both were being governed by one-party systems, but in one case the party was closed to the majority of the population. Neither offered the virtues of liberal democracy, and both were brutally repressive, but that does not mean they were alike in their effects.

Force was employed, of course, on a massive scale in the Soviet zone too, and that was because Soviet plans in their way were just as ambitious and single-minded as the Nazis. Where the nationality card could not be played, as for example, in the Baltic states (where the Red Army took over in June 1940), Soviet rule was often much harsher than in eastern Poland. Moreover, the idea of social revolution, of replacing capitalist private property with communal ownership, was fuelled by the envy of incoming Soviet officials: if western Poland was Germany's primitive East, eastern Poland, ironically, was the Soviet Union's first taste of capitalism and prompted nationalizations of banks, commercial enterprises and such industry as there was. Private estates, and land parcelled out by the interwar Polish state, or belonging to monasteries and churches, was expropriated, while ambitious land reform policies were directed at winning over local peasant opinion. In Belorussia, in particular, a sweeping land reform tilted ownership of the land decisively towards the peasant smallholder. In the General Government, the Germans continued to use the prewar zloty; in the Soviet zone, it was abolished, causing huge disruption and losses to those with savings – a move which assisted the assault on capitalism and the extension of the Soviet economic system.[43]

After the Germans launched their invasion of the USSR in June 1941, it quickly became apparent that the Soviet occupation had left behind it a bitter legacy. One of the first things the Germans did in the former Soviet-occupied areas was to film the gruesome handiwork of the Soviet secret police in one NKVD prison after another: Wehrmacht war crimes investigators found thousands of corpses in the jails of Lviv alone. Latvians, Lithuanians, Ukrainians, Romanians and Poles were fired with hatred for the Bolsheviks, and many of them pinned the blame for their sufferings on their Jewish neighbours. German propaganda encouraged them, and they thereby primed themselves and the local population for further massacres.[44]

Eventually, the German army's advance drove it deep into the Katyn forest and brought it face to face with the most gruesome handiwork of their erstwhile partners in the Polish partition. Villagers told them about the Soviet killing grounds in the woods, and in April 1943, once the soil had thawed, the Germans uncovered the well-preserved bodies of more than 4,000 of the Polish army officers shot on Stalin's orders three years earlier. The discovery was an international sensation. The Germans brought in Swiss, Hungarian and Croatian forensic experts and British and American POWs and publicized the remains of the site as evidence of 'Bolshevist crimes against humanity'. They were right, of course, although the world understandably refused to take their word for it. To win the battle for international opinion, and hoping to split the Anglo-Soviet alliance against them, the German Foreign Ministry actually prepared a diplomatic presentation on the Katyn discoveries. Published by the Nazi Party in 1943– even as Himmler was systematically eradicating the evidence of German atrocities on a far greater scale – it described the mass burial site at Katyn as a kind of 'monument for Europe'. The struggle for Greater Germany had unleashed a grisly spiral of state brutality. And even worse lay ahead.[45]

5

Summer 1940

Hitler had regarded a general European war as inevitable. But far from imagining that this would start in 1939, he and his planners reckoned they still had another three or four years to rearm. He invaded Poland, believing that Britain and France would remain aloof, as they had during the Prague crisis. Yet characteristically, as soon as he realized they would not back down, he immediately began planning to take the war to them. Only bad weather and the horrified objections of senior generals stopped him launching an offensive in the West before 1939 was out. It was obvious, therefore, that the decisive struggle would begin the following spring. As Hitler told Mussolini that March, there was 'no other possibility of ending the present conflict'.[1]

No one anticipated what followed. Memories of the Great War and the protracted stalemate on the Western Front were still vivid, and Germany's opponents substantially outnumbered the Wehrmacht in numbers and equipment. Moreover, its mobilization of resources was chaotic and armaments production was below target. Yet thanks to poorly marshalled opposition, some inspired strategic decisions, high morale and luck, German troops swept all before them: the Netherlands surrendered in only four days, Belgium in eighteen, and the French lasted scarcely more than a month. Having anticipated a long war, the Germans were now credited with the secrets of the *Blitzkrieg*. British soldiers retreated from the continent, leaving behind huge quantities of equipment, and at the end of June, the Wehrmacht even seized the Channel Islands. Along the way, it also managed to improvise a Scandinavian campaign in which German troops occupied Denmark without a fight. Although they met much fiercer resistance in Norway, they had crushed this too by early June. It was, by any standards, a remarkable military achievement.[2]

Europe was transfixed by this truly astonishing turn of events, and everyone waited to see what the Germans would do next. The political challenge which faced the Reich now went far beyond consolidating *Lebensraum* in eastern Europe. In the words of Wilhelm Stuckart, the Interior Ministry's constitutional expert, Germany had to move from constructing a *Volksgemeinschaft* (Community of the *Volk*) within its borders to building up a *Völkergemeinschaft* (Community of Peoples) across the continent. With almost no prior preparation, the Third Reich would have to forge a political strategy for defending its gains in the West and for shaping a future New Order for Europe as a whole. In these tasks, Nazi racial goals – the *raison d'être* of the war in the East – mattered less than military, diplomatic and economic considerations. But in the mood of extraordinary euphoria that took hold of the Berlin leadership, it seemed as though sheer will and force could overcome any opposition. Planners no longer believed that any combination of states threatened the Reich politically: 'the economic resources of the north, west and the south-east are all equally available to her'. England continued to fight, but most assumed it would see reason soon. In this intoxicating summer of 1940, when the war seemed won, German thoughts turned to the future and the shape of an eventual Nazi Europe was discussed more fully than any time before or after.[3]

TOWARDS A NEW ORDER

On 9 April, Denmark became the first country to capitulate. The invasion was over in a few hours, before the Danes had even had time to declare war: resistance was patently futile. As a result, compared with Poland, they were handled with such a degree of moderation by the Germans that it is difficult to imagine the same state was responsible for dealing with both. In the case of Poland the Nazis trampled on international law and erased the country from the map, whereas the Danes negotiated the mildest form of German oversight anywhere in Europe. The country remained formally independent, and King Christian stayed on his throne: Copenhagen continued to be the political centre of Danish life throughout the war, and those politicians who fled abroad found themselves marginalized. The parliament continued to function, and there were even surprisingly free elections in 1943 – we know this by virtue of the fact that the Danish Nazi Party won barely 2 per cent of the vote and was trounced by the old prewar parties. German wishes were transmitted through the former ambassador, Cecil von Renthe-Fink, who became Reich plenipotentiary, supervising Danish affairs with a tiny staff and a light touch. The country's territorial integrity was guaranteed, and the small German minority was firmly told not to make trouble.

Renthe-Fink emphasized the importance of keeping the 'outward appearance' of independence in order to weaken opposition to the Germans elsewhere. Keen to move on to Norway, the Führer agreed: in Denmark there was to be no civilian administration, and even the army played only a modest role. It was 'political window-dressing' perhaps – as one Nazi official termed it later on – but first impressions were important at a time when the Germans did not know how the invasions of Norway and the Low Countries would turn out. Such an arrangement also promised to guarantee what Germany really needed from the Danes – dairy produce and foreign policy compliance – at very low cost. German hegemony, it turns out, was exercised in more complicated and indirect ways than is often imagined. The Danes ended the war as members of the United Nations; but for at least three years, they found a comfortable niche in Germany's New Order.[4]

Although the Germans planned to treat Norway similarly, it turned out to be a much tougher proposition militarily and politically. After a surprise assault, which allowed Oslo to fall into German hands, the Norwegians fought back staunchly. To complicate matters, Vidkun Quisling – a right-wing extremist with little support in the country – seized the opportunity to declare the formation of a provisional government headed by himself. Hitler sympathized with his views, but he pushed him aside and appointed an old Party comrade instead as Reich commissioner. The man he chose, Josef Terboven, was already provincial governor of the Rhineland, where he enjoyed a well-deserved reputation for ruthlessness. He had won the Iron Cross in the First World War, before dropping out of college, taking part in the 1923 Beer Hall Putsch and marrying Goebbels' former secretary. Establishing himself in the residence of the crown prince (where, five years later, he would commit suicide by blowing himself up), the unpolished Terboven was not endowed with the gifts of persuasion that would have been necessary to get Norway's shaken deputies to form a new, pro-German government. The head of parliament did call upon King Haakon to abdicate, but he angrily refused and fled to London, where he formed a government in exile. Meanwhile, the political interregnum in Oslo dragged on. At the end of September, Terboven lost patience: he unilaterally abolished the monarchy, dissolved all parties except Quisling's Nasjonal Samling (NS) and announced the formation of a state commission, made up mostly of NS members, to run the country. It was a terrific rebuff to the country's ruling class and it condemned the new government to illegitimacy from the start. Although there was much popular criticism of the king for having fled, Quisling was detested far more, and virtually the whole of Norway was against him.

There was a similar mood of disorientation in the Netherlands, whose monarch and ministers also fled to London. The Dutch army had tried to resist, but on easy terrain they did not last nearly as long as the Norwegians. On 14 May, a massive Luftwaffe bombing raid took barely ten minutes to turn the centre of Rotterdam into smouldering rubble and charred timber, killing nearly 1,000 people and leaving more than 78,000 homeless. Coming after the devastation German bombers had inflicted on Warsaw the previous September, it was a terrifying reminder of the power of the bomber, and the Dutch quickly capitulated. A German military commander was appointed by Field Marshal von Brauchitsch because Hitler had promised the Wehrmacht that in western Europe – unlike in Poland – they would be allowed to run a more traditional military occupation.[5] After only a few days, however, he changed his mind and, as in Norway, he brought in a civilian administration. Because civil commissariats had already been the prelude to incorporation into the Reich in the Sudetenland and western Poland, the Dutch were worried, especially as the man Hitler chose to head this was Arthur Seyss-Inquart, the slippery lawyer who had played a prominent role in the Austrian *Anschluss*. Army staff themselves felt disgusted at 'the utter dishonesty of our top leaders': coming on the heels of similar arrangements in Norway, Seyss-Inquart's appointment did not bode well for their plans to keep the SS and the Party out of western Europe.

In fact, Seyss-Inquart's rather vague instructions from Hitler were far from radical: he was told to reassure the Dutch and encourage collaboration. Unlike Germany's previous conquests, the Netherlands was a colonial power, and Hitler was particularly anxious to prevent its colonies from breaking away and escaping German control. Without a big enough fleet of his own to secure them, he had to treat the Dutch relatively gently. Seyss-Inquart therefore tried to assuage the Dutch by immediately proclaiming that Germany had no 'imperialistic' designs on the country. A short while later, he emphasized that the occupation was exclusively military and implied no claims on Dutch territories. He allowed most of the political parties to continue in existence and he held conversations with conservative politicians. Meanwhile, senior Dutch civil servants carried on the real business of administering the occupation under German supervision, and Dutch law remained in force unless explicitly revoked or amended. As a result, the occupation proceeded at first with only a relatively small German staff to oversee it.[6]

Against the advice of his ministers, and unlike his Dutch and Norwegian counterparts, the young Belgian King Leopold did not leave. He may have been impressed by Germany's treatment of Denmark, but if he hoped for something similar, he was mistaken: Belgium was much more important than Denmark strategically and territorially. He was not allowed to form a new government as he had hoped, and the districts of Eupen and Malmedy, which Belgium had gained at Versailles, were reincorporated within the Reich. Even before the invasion Hitler had refused to commit himself to preserving Belgian independence and he was clearly contemplating expanding Germany's borders further. 'Ideas are . . . in the air concerning Belgium,' Göring confided to his closest subordinates. Leopold was worried, but when he finally met the Führer in November 1940, Hitler simply said that Belgium's 'internal political independence would be the greater, the more clearly and unequivocally she aligned herself with Germany in foreign policy and military matters'. Germany would 'never again' allow Belgium to become 'a springboard for an attack on the Reich or on the European continent'. Would Belgium's political independence be restored? Leopold persisted doggedly. All Hitler would say was that Belgium would 'occupy a position of some sort within the framework of economic and political cooperation with the German Reich'. 'Such a statement,' he continued, 'could not be issued before the public at large, since it would certainly be interpreted as a sign of weakness.' It was not a reassuring outlook.[7]

Yet despite the political uncertainty which shrouded their future, in some ways the Belgians were better off than they realized. Because of the country's strategic significance for the continuing campaign against Britain, the Wehrmacht managed to stay in charge of the occupation for almost the entire war. Two northern French departments – Pas de Calais and Nord – were also attached for administrative purposes, and the whole territory of some twelve million people was run by a military commander for Belgium and Northern France, the hard-drinking General Baron Alexander von Falkenhausen. Despite being nephew of the man who had run Belgium during the First World War, von Falkenhausen was an unusual choice. Formerly military attaché in the Ottoman empire, Japan and Chiang Kai-shek's China (where he had acquired a devotion to the Confucian classics), Falkenhausen was a conservative of the old school. He had been pulled out of retirement and he was one of the more worldly members of what was generally a rather parochial and blinkered military caste. His chief of administration, Eggert Reeder, was no Nazi either, but a former Prussian civil servant whose Army Study Commission had planned the occupation. Despite his (honorific) SS membership, the resourceful Reeder – the real power behind Falkenhausen's throne – hesitated to oppose neither the SS nor the Nazi Party, whose members he regarded as disruptive and dangerous fantasists. He and Falkenhausen managed initially to get the better of Himmler, who wanted to accelerate Belgium's Nazification, and they kept the Party at arm's length too. They allowed the Belgians to run the country as far as possible and were helped by its businessmen and its senior civil servants, whom the out-going government had told to stay on. Belgian courts continued to serve as sounding-boards for the constitutionality of bureaucratic decrees, providing – for a time – something close to legitimacy to the new arrangements. Some civil servants were purged, and many mayors fled in panic during the invasion and were dismissed, but basically, as in the Netherlands, the prewar machinery of state remained intact.[8]

The big prize, of course, was France: compared with this, none of Germany's other gains came close in significance. Despite a fairly even contest initially along some parts of the line, the Germans advanced astonishingly fast. Within a week they had reached the Channel; Dunkirk fell less than two weeks later, and on 14 June they entered Paris. Marshal Henri-Philippe Pétain, the aged but lucid hero of Verdun in the First World War, took over as French premier and announced he would seek an armistice. With between six and eight million civilians fleeing south, clogging the roads and spreading panic, France's demoralization was complete. So sweeping, so swift was the German victory that few could believe it had really happened.[9]

News of the catastrophe reverberated around Europe. 'When Paris fell, people wept in the streets,' remembered a young Jewish girl in Warsaw. For democrats it meant that the war against Hitler was now likely to stretch on indefinitely; Polish and Czech émigré politicians were overwhelmed with gloom since resistance to German rule was clearly not going to be a short-term affair. Fascists, on the other hand, everywhere from Portugal to Romania hailed the Reich's triumph as the sign of the international shift to the right: the fading legacy of the French Revolution had finally succumbed to the authority, youthful energy and discipline of National Socialism. From the Netherlands, the ageing Kaiser Wilhelm II sent his former corporal a message of congratulations. After the humiliation of Versailles, the symbolism of the victory was inescapable, and negotiations for the Franco-German armistice even took place in the same railway carriage that had been used by the triumphant French generals in 1918. Yet while Hitler enjoyed his moment of victory and toured some of the Great War battlegrounds, he was careful not to overplay his hand: it was, at all costs, vital to avoid the kind of situation that had arisen in Norway. Pétain must be encouraged to remain in France to head the country and to prevent the war spreading to the French colonies. Keeping a French government to run the occupation on the Germans' behalf was the priority. Thus for all his draconian initial demands – extortionate 'occupation costs', the deportation of 1.5 million French POWs to Germany – Hitler judged carefully what the French would accept and restrained his initial impulse to carve the country up through annexations.[10]

This certainly did not mean they were off the long-term agenda. After all, the Nazis did not merely want France's defeat, or the collapse of its alliance with England: France was to be permanently broken so that it could never again pose a threat to Germany. On 12 July, Goebbels laid this out for his Propaganda Ministry colleagues in terms which bore the unmistakable imprint of Hitler's thought:

The new order for Europe is to be quite consciously placed under Germany's sole auspices . . . In future France would only play a role as a small Atlantic state . . . Apart from Italy's territorial demands on France, our demands too will be very large . . . As far as France is concerned, the maxim will be: the destruction of the

Peace of Westphalia. Some people are even talking of a revocation of the partition agreed in the Treaty of Verdun of 1843. For this reason, everything which serves to encourage a political or economic revival of France will be destroyed . . . The peace treaty will eliminate France not only as a great power but as a state with any political influence in Europe.[11]

Dramatic future border changes – lopping off much of northern France as far as the mouth of the Somme – were secretly drawn up by the ever-reliable Stuckart. In addition to bringing territory into the Reich, German officials dreamed of a deliberate decentralization of the French state – cooping up the government in Vichy fitted this idea well – in order to weaken French nationalism, a milder version of the Polish policy. Their racial analysis showed France to be a 'mixture' (*Vermischung*), in which the cities and industrial centres had allowed the 'worst elements' to corrupt the best in the name of an 'abstract state': under German guidance, the regions would be given greater freedom from central government. Stuckart's plans were justified in the same way: releasing the strength of 'healthy racial elements' would weaken the power of 'Parisian France'. Calling for a '*völkisch* New Order' for Europe, which would allow the Germans to create grateful allies among the regions' minorities, others recommended giving self-determination to the Bretons and the Basques. They even looked forward to putting similar ideas into effect across the Channel once the British had surrendered: they would detach Scotland from the United Kingdom, create a unified Ireland and give autonomy to the West of England. It was, in short, a vision of securing German hegemony in the West through a nationalities policy, a kind of mirror image of what the French and British had tried to do in eastern Europe after 1918.[12]

All this lay in the future and remained both speculative and confidential. The actual armistice terms were not nearly as draconian. Pétain would have almost certainly baulked at a full occupation of the country, or being forced to hand over the French fleet, but he was never put to the test. France was divided into an occupied and an unoccupied zone, with the French government nominally sovereign in both. This permitted key strategic areas – the Atlantic coast, the Channel and a land route into Spain – to remain under the operational control of the Wehrmacht while allowing the French government to run the country. Unlike in Poland, the Hague and Geneva Conventions *were* regarded as remaining in force, and although the Wehrmacht interpreted the law of occupation to mean that its decrees were the ultimate source of law, in practice Vichy issued so many ordinances that hard-pressed German officials ended up simply setting guidelines for policy and intervening when they felt these were threatened. French civil servants ran the country, supervised rather loosely by a small Wehrmacht staff stationed with the military commander in Paris. German power was further diffused by the fact that – as so often – the occupiers did not speak with one voice. The only real initial indication of the Reich's long-term intentions towards France was that Pétain himself was refused permission to establish his administration in the French capital; to the delight of the hoteliers of Vichy, he chose the sleepy spa town as the new seat of the national government.

In France, therefore, as in Denmark, the Germans managed to follow their military triumph with a significant political achievement: tempering ideology with pragmatism, they managed to create a loyal and more or less nationally accepted government to work alongside them and run the country. France was much more important than Denmark, to be sure, and the Wehrmacht occupied much of it. Nevertheless, its troops were spread thinly, and only a small number of German officials were needed to coordinate policy with Vichy. For the first two years of occupation the Germans were generally satisfied with the results. But in one respect their victory had a truly dramatic impact. For whereas the Danish political system barely changed as a result of the war and defeat, in France, Pétain's rise spelled the end of the old Third Republic and the emergence of a new constitutional order. Pétain himself was granted unprecedented executive powers as head of state, parliament was adjourned until further notice and former ministers from the prewar Republic were blamed for the nation's lack of preparedness in 1940 and brought to trial. A new constitution was talked about (though it never materialized), and the regime proclaimed a national revolution – with strong anti-republican and anti-Semitic overtones – in the name of family, work and fatherland. German victory had allowed authoritarianism to triumph in France: but that political transformation had been a product of the decisions of the French themselves.[13]

The extension of German power into western Europe had basically been prompted by Berlin's strategic needs. No grand ideological programme was at stake, and the sheer variety of occupation regimes established in 1940 indicated Hitler's uncertainty about where they fitted in his larger scheme, with its predominantly eastern orientation. Denmark, after all, had only been attacked as a launch-pad for the invasion of Norway; and Norway itself was only brought into German plans in order to forestall Anglo-French plans for occupying the northern Swedish orefields.

It was equally unclear in the summer of 1940 where Germany's western campaign should end. There was the problem of Switzerland, for one thing. The Swiss had shot down several German planes during the invasion of France when they strayed into Swiss air space and Swiss politicians feared that after the French they would be next. They had in fact drawn up plans for a joint defence against Germany with the French, plans which undermined their claim to 'armed neutrality': the Germans had learned about these and were furious. Moving Swiss politics to the right, as some conservatives had wanted to do for a long time, was one means of appeasing them. But in fact the Germans were again rather restrained in their demands. They did not insist on the Swiss passing new racial laws, or measures that might have challenged Switzerland's policy of neutrality. They protested at criticism of the Reich in the Swiss press, but they did not go further, largely because they knew that France was watching how they treated the Swiss and they wanted above all to bring Vichy fully on to the Axis side. Military invasion plans were shelved too – not because the Germans feared the Swiss army but because they did not want a row with the Italians over how to divide up the country. As a result, the Swiss remained outside the war, peacefully and prosperously (if sometimes a little nervously) offering trading, banking and invaluable transit facilities to the Axis and, much later on, discreet meeting points for Axis and Allied intermediaries.[14]

A much more important piece of unfinished business was the problem of Britain, on which issue Hitler dithered uncharacteristically. His basically pro-British stance did not change after Dunkirk and he made several more attempts to reach a settlement. In the midst of the invasion of France he confessed that he expected an agreement with London 'on the basis of the division of the world' and he made a public offer of peace in the middle of July in a speech to the Reichstag that was quickly and publicly rejected. Increasingly, however, he was realizing the difficulty of separating Britain from the US and contemplating more dramatic steps. A few days before his peace offer he ordered preparations for a naval assault across the Channel, and detailed operational plans were drawn up by the army in August. There were to be landings in Sussex, Kent, Dorset and the Isle of Wight, before German forces pushed up to a line running from Colchester to the Severn, and then into the Midlands, encircling London. But the German naval chiefs were extremely worried by the risks of an invasion, and Hitler himself was oddly diffident and hoped that a 'show of force' by the Luftwaffe would suffice to change British policy. German military intelligence overestimated the forces available for defence, and Hitler seems anyway to have been reluctant to embark on a step which could have brought down the British empire.[15]

While the planning for a cross-Channel invasion was going ahead, Major Walter Schellenberg of the SD, a young personal aide of Himmler's and foreign intelligence chief at the RSHA, was compiling a handbook on Britain for Gestapo use. Apparently assisted by information from two MI6 officers who had been kidnapped near the Dutch frontier the previous November, Schellenberg's classified *Informationsheft GB* offers a glimpse of Britain that is both oddly perceptive and utterly bizarre. 'Democratic freedom in Britain' was described as a sham. The trade unions were said to be 'not concerned with politics', while the Archbishop of Canterbury and the Church of England Council on Foreign Relations were held responsible for anti-German propaganda; so was Oxford University, whose 'Oxford Pamphlets' on current world problems were singled out for mention. Libraries, universities, individual scholars and émigré anti-Nazi politicians were all described if they were of interest to German intelligence. England itself was supposedly run by freemasons, Jews and a small public-school-trained elite. The English gentleman was described as someone 'who has never thought about philosophical issues, who has hardly any knowledge of foreign culture, who thinks of Germany as the embodiment of evil but accepts British power as inviolable'. At the end, the 'Special Search List GB' (*Sonderfahndungsliste GB*) listed 2,820 individuals for special Gestapo attention, of whom thirty were to be arrested on sight. Had they ever taken over in England – in the fashion imagined by Len Deighton in his novel *SS-GB* – the Gestapo would have come after not only politicians, union activists and military officers but also such sinister figures as Noel Coward, Nancy Cunard and Sigmund Freud (who had died the previous September, but still made it on to the list).[16]

A few of these so feared invasion that they fled across the Atlantic:

the writer Stefan Zweig went to the USA and thence to Brazil, where he committed suicide in 1942 after completing his moving lament for the Europe that he considered irrevocably lost, *The World of Yesterday*. But the 'Special Search List GB' soon became nothing more than a historical curiosity. Late that autumn, after abortive attacks on British airfields and heavy bombing raids which left more than 23,000 civilians dead, the Luftwaffe abandoned the Battle of Britain, and Hitler shelved the idea of invading. He had already decided to attack the USSR the following year as an indirect means of putting pressure on the British. Meanwhile, German diplomats tried to keep abreast of morale from across the Channel, but reports were fragmentary, and even the German ambassador in Dublin found it hard to work out what was going on. 'Organised life in London' during the Battle of Britain was said to 'have completely broken down; even plundering and sabotage have been noted.' On the other hand, recovery was said to have been 'surprisingly fast'. Some travellers from the UK said the British would never capitulate; others predicted that they were nearing the end of their resistance. Hitler himself seems to have been completely uninterested.[17]

INTO AFRICA

Before moving against the Soviet Union, Hitler did turn his attention to the British position in the Mediterranean. Although the German navy was keen on this new 'peripheral' strategy, seeing in it a last chance to shine before the land war with the Soviet Union, it was not in fact powerful enough to carry the war to the English unaided. Hitler had launched a general European war while the programme which was supposed to give the Reich the largest navy in the world was still in its early stages. The navy that he did have had not even been capable of carrying his invasion force across the Channel. In the case of the Mediterranean, therefore, and of north Africa in particular, Europe's new master found that he had to act as diplomatist and statesman rather than as a commander-in-chief; he had to arbitrate and cajole where he could not compel, in order to make the best use of Germany's partners. But this turned out to be a far more difficult task than conquering half of Europe had been. Both his ally, Italy, and Spain, which he desperately hoped would enter the war, wanted to take advantage of France's defeat and coveted its north African possessions. His conundrum was how to satisfy both of them without at the same time alienating the French, who were potentially more important than either. Bismarck's ability to play one enemy off against another was not one Hitler shared, and his own greed for territory got in the way as well.

In the war against Britain, Spain's support was obviously vital. On 19 June – in the days between Pétain's appointment and the signing of the armistice – Madrid had actually offered to go to war with Britain in return for Gibraltar, French Morocco and several other African territories. Spanish troops had occupied French Tangier a few days earlier, and Franco wanted to enlarge his north African empire further. The British were worried enough to train a stay-behind team, who would have been sealed in a hidden observation bunker for a year or more to keep watch over Axis shipping movements from the Rock. Fortunately for the men involved, they were never put to the test. For while Hitler was delighted to have the Spaniards in the war, he was simply not prepared to make the concessions they were demanding.

One reason was that, if he had done, it would have become impossible to entice Pétain into the war as well. Pétain was playing a weak hand cleverly, and Hitler feared that if he handed some of the French possessions to the Spaniards, the rest would defect to the British and the Free French. But another reason was that Germany had its own Moroccan wish-list, and German agents were secretly in Casablanca scouting French airfields. As for the German navy, it even wanted bases in the Canary Islands. When Hitler met Franco at the crucial meeting at Hendaye on 23 October, the two men talked past each other. The Spaniards read the German terms for their entry into the war and they were astonished to find that they were being offered nothing definite in Africa. As ever, Hitler was reluctant to pin himself down. Franco talked at enormous length about Spain's historical right to Morocco and refused to contemplate entering the war without a German commitment to honour this. This annoyed Hitler; he later told Mussolini that he would rather have teeth removed than another such conversation.[18]

In Spain itself there was enormous excitement among fascists at the thought of participating in the war, and they could not understand Franco's hesitation. For them, victory in the Civil War had meant the chance to rebuild Spanish grandeur at home, while the defeat of France was an opportunity to extend it abroad and take part in the construction of an anti-communist Europe. The 'New Europe', according to Rafael Garcia Serrano, a member of the fascist Falange movement, was based on three conceptions of Europe: (1) as the West (against the Asiatic Bolshevik barbarians); (2) as Civilization (based on Roman and Christian principles); and (3) as Empire. There were, wrote another right-winger, two kinds of nations: those born to rule, and those born to obey. How could Spain not 'mobilize aggressively' and become one of the 'four, five or six great units which . . . are called to govern the world in this century, in which all fiction of freedom for the tiny national states is going to disappear'? Yet although large numbers of Spaniards were allowed to volunteer to fight, especially after Germany invaded the USSR, Franco was more realistic and prudent and he refused to commit the country on the Axis side. Playing for time with Berlin, he had come to realize that the Germans were very likely to use any Spanish entry into the war as a reason to send their own troops to Morocco. Hence his police stepped up surveillance on Germans in north Africa and made life difficult for German engineers helping to rebuild Spain's defences in the Canaries as well. It was thus thanks basically to Germany's greed that Gibraltar was never attacked. The Germans drew up plans for taking it, but shelved these in the run-up to the invasion of the Soviet Union. They even had contingency plans to invade Spain itself in the event of a possible British landing and only abandoned them in 1943.[19]

What Franco had come to realize was that being allied with Germany could be more dangerous than remaining neutral. It was a lesson that the Italians learned too late. They too coveted France's possessions in north Africa; indeed their demands were even greater because they saw the war as their chance to dominate the entire Mediterranean. But Mussolini was less astute than Franco and he did not realize that being Hitler's closest ally counted for little in the new scramble for Africa: in fact, Italy's claims could be discounted by the Germans precisely because it had already entered the war, and all it won that summer by declaring war on France late in the day was an occupation zone between Grenoble and Nice. Ribbentrop assured the Italian trade minister that Africa was to be divided into two spheres of interest between the two Axis partners, whose friendship – he predicted – would last 'for centuries'. But they were pledged only Oran and neither the rest of Algeria nor French Morocco, as they had hoped. Too late the Italians realized, as Franco had done, that the Germans would always put their own claims on Africa first.

Historically, Germany had been ambivalent about its colonial destiny. Before the First World War, under Kaiser Wilhelm II, devotees of Samoa and German South-west Africa had clashed with the lobbyists for eastwards expansion into the Slav lands. But by the 1930s, the 'ideological reconciliation' between *Lebensraum* and German colonialism had been worked out in the former's favour. *Kolonialpolitik* and *Ostpolitik* were now seen not as alternatives but as a 'complementary necessity' – the former guaranteeing access to scarce raw materials that were necessary to ensure the survival of the German *Volk*, the latter providing the land for settlement. But the colonial enthusiasts now thought their time had come. The Party's colonial expert, Ritter von Epp, had participated in the bloody international repression of the turn-of-the-century Boxer rebellion in China and the annihilation of the Herero in German South-west Africa. In the autumn of 1939, he hailed the outbreak of war as 'the resurrection of the German colonial empire'.[20] Men like him had never got over the loss of Germany's colonies after the First World War and looked forward to creating a new German *Mittelafrika*. They studied British and French colonial policy and explored ways of increasing the productivity of the African worker by intensifying the *corvée*. Although they admired the British, they thought that their policy of indirect rule was much too soft. In Nigeria, they wrote, the British had unfortunately allowed native populations a degree of self-administration which even a tough-minded 'German colonial government' would find hard to reverse. In short, they planned a regime for Africa that would have made the existing empires look tolerant, progressive and fair-minded.[21]

In the summer of 1940, Hitler ordered preparations for a future German colonial administration to be accelerated. The late 1930s had seen an international discussion about the value of colonies as resource bases for their European masters, and Berlin's diplomats talked readily about developing a policy in Africa for Europe's economic well-being. What was needed, they claimed, was 'to rationalize colonial development in Africa for the benefit of the whole of Europe'.[22] But the Foreign Ministry scarcely spoke for the Third Reich. What others in Berlin really envisaged for Africa had little to do with the rest of Europe at all. They wanted a solid bloc of German-controlled territory across the heart of the continent that would link the Reich's new central African empire with navy bases in the Indian Ocean and the Atlantic. The Wehrmacht incorporated projected missions in the African colonies into its ongoing rearmament plans, and the Reich's Africanist experts prepared themselves for service in the tropics. The University of Hamburg began running courses to train colonial administrators, new uniforms were designed, and hundreds of applications were received. A law setting up a Ministry of Colonies was drafted but never published, and decrees were drawn up, extending Nazi racial laws to Africa. Civil servants worked on warnings about tropical diseases and the dangers of sex with native women. German industrial firms provided specialists in African commodities. Such plans developed a life of their own, and long after the new German empire to the south had been overshadowed by the ongoing struggle in the East, the colonial bureaucracy continued to plan for a future which would never come. Even local decrees forbidding blacks wandering around by themselves in wartime Germany – there was a small community of German-Africans in the Reich, and a travelling entertainment troupe called the German-African Show which performed in 'native' costume – were repealed in case they led to unfavourable publicity in Africa. Only near the end of 1942 did Martin Bormann bring the whole colonial propaganda effort to an end.[23]

German dreams of a 'Euro-Afrika' were basically a product of the summer of 1940. That was the Africanists' high point and the moment when Africa also revealed the limits of German might and the costs of Hitler's impetuosity. Much of continental Europe had been crushed by the Wehrmacht. Yet although Germany claimed to be a world power, in fact it found it hard to project Hitler's will outside Europe. The north Africa campaign was the single, temporary exception. But the giant new fleet of the future was not planned to be ready before the mid-1940s, and in this sense Hitler's victories had come too early. Germany's weakness worked to France's advantage, allowing Vichy to pose as all that stood in the colonies between the Nazis and Gaullism, an argument which was strengthened when Vichy loyalists repelled Anglo-Gaullist raiders in Dakar in September 1940. The Spaniards could, at one point, have perhaps been brought into the war if German diplomacy had been more astute and Hitler had been less grasping. But that moment passed, and the result was that he managed to get neither France nor Spain into the war alongside him. As Germany's attention turned east once more, France remained a considerable (if much weakened) force internationally, and the Atlantic and Mediterranean seas remained contested by the British and their allies. Only the Italians were fighting alongside him, and that looked increasingly like a very mixed blessing.[24]

In that summer of 1940, one of the ways in which it looked as though Africa could serve Europe was by providing a homeland for the Jews. Tucked away at the bottom of a Foreign Ministry memorandum written that November was a small item that read: 'Madagascar should be acquired by the German Reich, not for reasons of colonial policy but for the purpose of settling the Jews.' Six months earlier, an ambitious desk officer in the Foreign Ministry had reacted to Germany's victory over France by proposing just such a way out of the impasse of 'the Jewish question'. On 3 June, and with SS plans to expel Germany's Jews eastwards into Poland blocked, the Ministry's new man for Jewish affairs, Franz Rademacher, made a proposal: instead of Palestine or the Lublin region, why not use the French colony of Madagascar as a Jewish reservation? In occupied Poland, this seemed like the solution they had been looking for, a way of restarting the prewar forced emigration policy. Hans Frank told his staff that instructions would shortly be issued that 'all Jews, including those in the General Government, should be sent to African colonies that the French state would hand over for this purpose to the German Reich'.[25]

Rademacher was certainly not the first to talk about Madagascar in this connection. The island had featured in nineteenth-century anti-Semitic fantasies, and similar ideas had been discussed in the 1930s by the Poles and the French. The latter were receptive to the idea of settling Europeans in their colony, but the Poles could not decide if they wanted to be rid of their Jews or to help Polish farmers. Only after the *Anschluss*, as the Polish government veered in a sharply anti-Semitic direction, did it seriously explore the possibility of a mass transfer of Jews to Madagascar with French officials and Jewish groups. But the failure of the League powers to deal properly with the refugee crisis of the late 1930s left the Madagascar option adrift. Rademacher now saw it as a way to demonstrate the Foreign Ministry's ideological usefulness, and to put the Ministry back in the centre of German postwar planning. Here was another area in which Germany could succeed where the League of Nations had failed.[26]

His 3 July memorandum 'The Jewish Question in the Peace Treaty' argued that, with victory 'imminent', the Foreign Ministry should be mandated to make the necessary diplomatic preparations. The peace treaty with France should ensure that territory was made available for German use overseas, and diplomats should fix 'the position of the new Jewish overseas settlement area under international law'. Talking about the Reich as though it was a successor to the League of Nations, Rademacher proposed transferring Madagascar to Germany 'as a mandate', resettling the 25,000-strong French population, turning Diego Suarez Bay into a naval base and leaving the rest to the Jews under an SS governor. 'In this territory the Jews will otherwise have self-administration, their own mayors, police, postal and railroad administrations.' They would exist in a legal limbo – as citizens 'of the mandate of Madagascar', under German control and unable to create a fully sovereign state of their own. And Rademacher concluded by parroting the paternalistic language of the League's own mandatory powers:

We can utilise for propaganda purposes the generosity which Germany shows the Jews by granting them self government in the fields of culture, economics, administration and justice, and can stress that our German sense of responsibility to the world does not permit us to give a race that has not had national independence for thousands of years an independent state immediately: for this they must still prove themselves to history.[27]

Very soon the idea was circulating widely. Foreign Minister Ribbentrop mentioned it to the Italians. Hitler himself spoke in early August of a complete 'evacuation' of European Jewry after the war. The question also came up in discussions with the new Romanian prime minister, the white-haired, monocled Ion Girgurtu. When Girgurtu, a wealthy man with close ties to Germany, said that Hitler should carry through 'a total solution for all of Europe', Ribbentrop replied that they were thinking along these lines. Feasibility studies from a geologist and a statistician gave a favourable verdict. Himmler's deputy, Heydrich, agreed that, given the huge numbers of Jews now in German hands, a 'territorial solution' was called for, and the SS began working on similar plans. An island location would 'prevent lasting contact between the Jews and other nations': Jewish farmers, labourers and builders could be sent first as 'pioneers'.[28]

For as long as an Axis carve-up of Africa was on the cards, Nazi officials thus saw a chance to send the entire Jewish population of Germany – possibly of the rest of Europe – overseas. They were certainly not, at this point, thinking in terms of mass extermination, still less constructing death camps. In fact, much to French annoyance, some 29,000 Jews were expelled from Baden, the Saar and Alsace-Lorraine in October 1940 into France itself, pushing Vichy into developing its own 'massive emigration policy for foreigners', one which would have dumped Jews and other undesirables in the French Caribbean. (The plan was eventually scotched by French colonial officials, who did not want to overcrowd Guadeloupe and the Antilles.)[29]

But as the British retained control of the seas, the Madagascar Plan came to look less and less plausible. Rademacher planned a conference to discuss it, but this was never held. In February 1941, Hitler was still mulling it over. The war, he noted uncertainly, had brought new difficulties, forcing him to deal with the Jews not merely in Germany – as he had originally intended – but 'in the entire Axis commonwealth'. 'If only he knew where the couple of million Jews could be sent,' his adjutant records him saying. 'With so many it was difficult to know. He would approach France and ask them to make space available for a settlement on Madagascar.' By this point, the whole discussion had an air of unreality. When Martin Bormann asked Hitler how they were to be shipped there, Hitler answered ironically: 'A KdF [*Kraft durch Freude* = Strength through Joy] fleet?' He then went on to add that 'he had pondered on many other ideas which were not quite so nice.' Even before the invasion of the USSR, in other words, the Madagascar plan had fallen into abeyance. By October 1941 Rademacher's Foreign Ministry boss knew that its underlying premise – the desirability of forcing Jews to leave Europe – was outdated: SS death squads had been shooting tens of thousands of Soviet Jews since the end of June. A few months later, Rademacher himself wrote to a colonial affairs specialist that 'the Führer had decided that the Jews shall be deported not to Madagascar but to the east. Madagascar thus no longer needs to be provided for the Final Solution.' 'Deportation to the east' was a euphemism. The possibilities of 1940 had disappeared in the mud and snows of Russia and, with it, the chance of 'territorial solutions'.[30]

ORGANIZING THE GERMAN-EUROPEAN ECONOMIC AREA

'If anyone asks how you conceive the new Europe, we have to reply that we don't know,' Goebbels told German newspapermen bluntly on 5 April. 'Of course we have some ideas about it. But if we were to put them into words it would immediately create more enemies for us ... Today we talk about *Lebensraum*. Anybody can interpret it as they wish. When the time comes we will know very well what we want.' Hitler – like his British rivals, Chamberlain and Churchill – wanted to avoid the whole pointless First World War debate over war aims for as long as possible.[31] Partly that was because he had not fully formulated his ideas; partly it was because – as Goebbels suggested – the annexations and border changes he did intend to make were best kept under wraps. But Hitler's silence seemed only to inspire his followers, since some kind of planning for the eventual peace settlement was obviously necessary. As early as 23 May, the elderly state secretary for foreign affairs, Ernst von Weizsäcker, was musing on how Berlin could hold together 'the Pan-German continent as an economic entity but also politically and morally' [*die Methode den pangermanischen Kontinent zusammenzuhalten*]. 'One must reckon,' wrote another diplomat, the anti-Nazi Ulrich von Hassell, 'with a new structure for Europe, in Hitler's image, achieved through a peace supporting his wide aims'.[32]

With the regime's long-range political goals shrouded in deliberate ambiguity, and with peace treaties adjourned *sine die*, discussions of the New Order mostly focused on economics, taking up ideas about how to reorganize the European economy that dated back to the First World War and even earlier. Germany's military triumph and the aftermath of the depression across Europe had made German plans for continental rationalization and reform more plausible than ever. While the Reich faced a labour shortage, unemployment rates were still high in much of western Europe, and the New Order seemed to offer a way to bring them down for everyone's benefit. For German technocrats and businessmen, the Reich's mission was to guide Europe out of the slump of the 1930s and to demonstrate the superiority of the fascist model of an organized trading system over the failed and fragmented liberal gold standard. German economists had long seen the basic assumptions of free market economics as nothing more than an outmoded theoretical rationalization for English supremacy and suggested that fascist systems of controlled trade were more likely to produce prosperity across Europe. As they saw it, Germany's victory over the French promised a more prosperous future and a stronger and more self-sufficient role for Europe in the world. Werner Daitz's Society of European Economic Planning and *Grossraumwirtschaft* wanted a European mark bloc to compete with the Japanese, the Americans and 'the surviving remnants of the Pound bloc'. Andreas Predöhl, the director of the internationally renowned Institut für Weltwirtschaft in Kiel said that now that England was out of Europe, its version of economic theory should be jettisoned too so that the continent could profit from Germany's leadership and move towards a 'new world economy'. Keynes and the Swedes were not the only ones heralding the end of laissez-faire; Nazi economists were on the same track.[33]

As one victory followed another, position papers, policy briefs and unsolicited memoranda proliferated. On 30 May – while the German army pressed at Dunkirk – the deputy director of the Foreign Ministry's economic policy department synthesized the emerging consensus. His basic assumption, he declared, was 'that the final victory has been won, and that therefore England accepts all German conditions'. Whether or not countries such as Holland, Belgium and Norway were to be politically incorporated within the Reich he regarded as a secondary issue. Economic integration was what mattered, through clearing trade and controlled cartels, and perhaps even through economic and monetary union. England and Russia would be compelled by their own self-interest to continue dealing with the Reich. As for the Balkans, the Reich's interests were already well served without the need for military conquest by existing bilateral trade relations.[34]

Yet politics kept rearing its troublesome head. Could countries be trusted to satisfy German desires while remaining nominally independent? After all, Greece and Romania had been caught up in the Reich's commercial web before the war and yet they had both accepted Anglo-French military guarantees in 1939. One of the Reich's model satellites – Slovakia – was showing signs of independence; that July, unsubtle political pressure had to be applied to Father Tiso to accept German 'advisers', and key ministers in his government were replaced. 'The time has now come to make it perfectly plain once again,' wrote the minister to Slovakia, 'particularly with reference to the countries of south-eastern Europe, that Slovakia is in our *Lebensraum*, that is, our wishes alone count.' The other 'model protectorate', Denmark, too, was initiating trade negotiations with other countries without consulting the Germans and blowing hot and cold over the idea of a customs and currency union.[35]

As if to indicate that notions of formal sovereignty or independence belonged to diplomacy's past, Hitler took the task of planning Europe's future away from the Foreign Ministry and handed it over to Göring and Economics Minister Walter Funk. Göring himself was the most important of that group of figures in the Third Reich whose vision for Europe was based on older, pre-Nazi ideas of continental German economic hegemony rather than on Himmler's fantasies of racial purity. It was in keeping with such ideas that he told Funk – who had previously proved his reliability supervising the Aryanization of the German economy, and helping to organize the rearmament effort – to prepare proposals for a 'central European economic bloc'. Criticizing Versailles for having split European markets up into a mass of unviable smaller units, separated by customs barriers and economic nationalism, Göring looked forward to the 'large-scale unification of Europe' under Germany's leadership into a bloc that could compete with the United States.

Funk was a seedy, indolent former business journalist but in July he made a grandiloquent speech that attracted international attention. Announcing that 'gold will have no future role' as basis of the European monetary system, Funk talked about European reconstruction, German pragmatism, planning for the continent as a whole and creating a 'stronger sense of economic community among European nations'. Just as Germany had shown the world how to emerge from the Depression, so it would now lead 'a united Europe' to prosperity and higher living standards. In private, of course, his emphasis was slightly different: winning the war and serving German interests came first. Behind closed doors, Funk had rejected the thought of making the unification of Europe a priority. He was more concerned about getting the economy moving again after the war and ensuring that Berlin became the centre of the continent's financial and trading system. A working group inside the Economics Ministry consulted widely with German, Dutch, Belgian and Swedish business leaders and recommended a unified transportation system, free capital flows and the establishment of a 'European economic union' based chiefly on arrangements between business and trade groups rather than between governments. An undercurrent of mistrust towards the Nazi leadership ran through these ideas. Afterwards, many of them seemed uncannily prescient: the stress on establishing common tariffs on imports from outside Europe, on finding areas of complementarity among different European economies, and on the need to be guided by business interests – these and other themes would be picked up again after the war, when many of these men played important roles in helping to build the Common Market.[36]

Yet the fact remained that, in the Third Reich, the political leadership could not be taken for granted, and what Funk really meant by a 'unified European *Grossraumwirtschaft* under German leadership' remained ambiguous. When asked for his reaction, the British economist John Maynard Keynes said that there was little wrong with the idea of planning for European recovery, the only question was whether a National Socialist regime could be trusted to do it. (It was a reasonable observation: as time went on a more and more coercive tone crept into the discussions inside the Economics Ministry.) For their part, German economists were well aware of Keynes' ideas, and saw them as confirming their view that even in the 'so-called liberal countries' economists were coming to accept that the fluctuations of the market should be controlled by state policy. But the Führer himself reprimanded Funk for encouraging public discussion of these issues: in economic as in political affairs, Hitler preferred to tie his hands as little as possible.[37]

Bored by discussions of European patent law or tariff reform, Hitler was much more interested in 1940 in promoting his real passion for gigantic building and infrastructural plans. Thanks to Speer, his favourite architect – who later became the Reich's armaments tsar – we have been able to glimpse his fascination with cities from both sides. On the one hand, he watched newsreels of the devastation of Rotterdam, Warsaw and Coventry with indifference and even pleasure. Near the end of the war, furious and humiliated by the Anglo-American bombing of Hamburg and Dresden, he fantasized deliriously about destroying New York 'in a hurricane of fire'. He described the skyscrapers being turned into 'giant burning torches, collapsing upon one another, the glow of the exploding city illuminating the dark sky'. Yet the other side of this callousness was his enraptured attentiveness to the future of Germany's cities. 'London will be a rubble heap,' he told Speer flatly, even as he contemplated turning Berlin into 'Germania' – the centre of the empire. It would be bifurcated with colossal boulevards, leading in the centre to a great triumphal arch. When Speer's father saw the room where Speer and Hitler pored over their scale models into the early hours of the morning, he merely shrugged and told his son: 'You've all gone completely crazy.'[38]

With victory in the West, the craziness increased: Hitler did not only want Berlin's new railway station to be bigger than New York's Grand Central, he now planned a plaza – 3,000 feet long, 1,000 wide – to greet newly arrived travellers; modelled on the Avenue of the Rams at Karnak, it would be lined with captured artillery pieces and other trophies of war. In 1941, as the Wehrmacht invaded the USSR, he told the army he needed 200 Soviet heavy guns and some specially large tanks to put on display.[39] The new bridge across the Elbe was to be modelled on San Francisco's Golden Gate – but bigger – so that Germans entering Hamburg by sea would say: 'What is so extraordinary about America and its bridges? We can do just the same.' The regional Nazi Party headquarters was to be housed in a skyscraper that would be visible for miles, with a huge neon swastika to guide shipping. A similar gigantism characterized the naval facilities planned for Trondheim and St Nazaire. The regime had already all but completed work on the world's largest holiday camp at Rügen, with its monstrously vast concrete residential apartment building: it took more than an hour to walk along, its 11,000 rooms and mile-long corridors. In the all-conquering Third Reich, even the beach resorts were to be the largest in the world, and America would be put in its place by German know-how. Dozens of other cities were to get wide avenues suitable for military parades. New administrative buildings, housing estates and gargantuan indoor assembly halls would allow tens of thousands of people to attend Party rallies. As the planning frenzy swept Germany, dozens of local authorities demanded that their towns be rebuilt and submitted their own plans for urban improvement.[40]

The demand for building materials was growing intense. In the summer of 1940, so many German purchasing agents were bidding for Scandinavian granite that a buyer from Hamburg wondered whether every city in the Reich had 'come grabbing stone in Norway'. (Hitler himself ordered some for his own buildings.) Huge contracts were also placed with Finnish, Italian, Belgian, Swedish and Dutch stone companies; an entire fleet of shipping with its own shipyards was planned to transport the heavy blocks to the Reich. Himmler's SS now woke up to the economic potential of its camp system. Old camps were expanded with the addition of works sheds and factories, and entirely new ones like Mauthausen, Natzweiler and Gross-Rosen were situated near quarries and brick-works. The SS even created a special company, the German Earth and Stone Works (DEST), to supply stone for Hitler's own construction needs; it was not a great success, and a disappointed Hitler supposedly suggested the SS stick to making slippers and paper bags, as prison labourers had done for decades.[41]

A Europe-wide communications system was another of his pet schemes. The Todt Organization (OT), a state-run engineering group, had emerged out of the Third Reich's earlier motorway construction projects; by 1940 it was building fortifications and bridges as well. Fritz Todt himself had risen from being inspector of roads to minister of armaments and munitions, and although he became increasingly convinced that the war could not be won, especially after the invasion of the USSR, he also oversaw a number of projects designed to last into the peace. One was a continental motorway that would link Austria and Germany with Scandinavia – Sweden would in this way be peacefully incorporated within the Reich's orbit; another would stretch from Calais to Warsaw and even as far eventually as Moscow; a third went via Lublin to Rostov on the Don. At the same time, with an enthusiasm that left the Reich's hard-pressed railways minister exhausted, Hitler spoke about turning Germany into the hub of a standardized European rail network. He ordered railway planners in Munich to design a vast new station and envisaged trains that would terminate, like the motorway, in Rostov: carrying hundreds of passengers in double-decker carriages, they would be capable of speeds up to 200 kilometres per hour and would need only a few hours to complete the journey. As for the new station, this was naturally to be the biggest steel-frame building in the world.[42]

ARBITER OF EUROPE

But a single superpower is always mistrusted, and Germany's rise to power was so fast and absolute that it elicited concern, even among potential allies. The German ambassador in Turkey, von Papen, reported that the Turkish president harboured 'fears regarding a future German world hegemony'. The Portuguese dictator, Salazar, openly questioned whether Hitler might not be intoxicated by victory and Germanize Europe in ways unacceptable to the Catholic South.[43] And while Laval and other French politicians wanted to place their eggs in the German basket, some of Pétain's men were worried too.

Such anxieties led more and more neutrals across Europe to hope that Mussolini would be a moderating influence upon his more powerful ally. In Lisbon that August the French ambassador to Portugal had a frank conversation with his Italian counterpart. The two men's acquaintance stretched back over many years, and the Frenchman felt able to insist quite openly that in his opinion Italy had to be preserved as a counterweight to the Germans. It seemed hard to imagine, he went on, that 'in the political organization of the new Europe, Italy, which has always had a decisive weight in the European balance, would not make sure to restabilize the balance which the war has already shaken and which may be shaken still more'. If the Axis won the war quickly, Germany's power would be 'hallucinatory'. Italy might have a great African empire, but 'the Moloch of Europe will be Germany'. The result would be that 'we the conquered and you the conquerors will find ourselves by a mathematical relationship of forces in a subordinate position'. Seeking no doubt to drive a wedge between the Italians and the Germans, the canny French diplomat was in fact only voicing concerns that many Italians themselves shared.[44]

No power was more desperate to define its position vis-à-vis the Reich than its main ally and ideological partner. In retrospect, Italy could have best exploited the European struggle by remaining as the arbiter between the western powers and the Reich: Munich was the high-point of this approach. Yet it was not a very glorious position for the founder of fascism to adopt, and once the war began, Mussolini made it clear that he would stand alongside his ideological pupil. The reality was, of course, that his country was virtually bankrupt: greed, pride and fear of being shut out of the postwar settlement were the only reasons why Mussolini decided to join in.[45] The Italians swiftly learned the cost. In June, after Ciano 'almost fell over himself' to lay out Italy's claims against France, Hitler 'paid no attention to them at all but simply uttered a long victory monologue'. Funk's discussions of the coming new economic order also terrified the Italians: they feared that the Germans had thought the whole thing through without consulting them and sent officials to Berlin for reassurance. As Mussolini's ambassador in Berlin, Alfieri, noted, *Lebensraum* was one thing, *Wirtschaftsraum* quite another – diffuser, larger, and vaguer. Germany *said* it wanted to divide Europe, Africa and the Near East between the two Axis partners. But when asked where Italy's *Wirtschaftsraum* would lie, Funk referred vaguely to the Mediterranean. And where exactly the borders dividing the two zones of influence would run – in north Africa, the Levant and south-eastern Europe – was unclear. It seemed doubtful whether a lira-bloc could ever be a viable partner to a Reichsmark-bloc, or that there would be sufficient alignment of economic interests for a partnership between the two to work long into the peace.[46]

Precisely because the idea of a parallel empire seemed so fraught, and a recipe for permanent subservience to German demands, some Italians wanted a very different relationship with the Third Reich. For passionate fascists, after all, Europe's very future was at stake. The fall of France seemed to validate the values for which they had been fighting since 1922 but it also raised the question of whether the New Europe would be truly fascist or merely Nazi. If Italy did not exert a permanent influence on Germany, they felt, the danger was that it would be the latter and that fascism and Nazism might even end up fighting one another. This was why Italy's education minister, Giuseppe Bottai, advised Mussolini in August 1940 not to pursue a 'bi-imperial arrangement'. Such a scheme was motivated, Bottai wrote, by 'initial diffidence toward Germany and ... terror of her predominance'. He criticized those who hoped for 'a victory of the Axis in the sense of the constitution of two separate spheres of influence, of two relatively autarkic economic units, of two autonomies, that is, that would allow Italy to pursue a future political manoeuvre that could eventually be anti-German'. In his view this would be a mistake because it would 'strengthen [Germany's] racism in its most materialistic sense and its imperialism in the sense of the greatest arrogance'. As such outspokenly critical comments indicate,

Italian fascists were capable of penning some of the most scathing exposés of Nazi ideas to be found anywhere in Europe at this time. Bottai himself was conscious of the expansionary nature of German imperialism and the destructive impact of its 'racist pride'. Italy's distinctive contribution to Europe, he suggested, should be to temper this by drawing Germany into a system of collaboration with other states. It was on the basis of such reasoning that Bottai and other Italian commentators devoted themselves during the war to bringing together like-minded Europeans from the spheres of culture and intellectual life. They wanted the Duce's Italy to act as Greece to Berlin's Rome.[47] But then Bottai's ideas rested on a delusion of grandeur: he imagined that a European mission still remained possible for Italian fascism and, even less plausibly, that the Germans would take notice. In fact, the 'bi-imperial' model of Axis rule originated in Berlin, and the Germans certainly had no intention of allowing the Italians any real influence over how they ran Europe.

Germany's unchallenged primacy also caused a much more consequential strain with the Soviet Union. In August 1939, Stalin had believed he could watch the European powers fight themselves to exhaustion. Less than a year later, this prognosis had turned out to be horribly wrong, and Germany had unexpectedly emerged as master of the continent and arbiter of its fate. Fearing that the Baltic sector of its border with the West exposed the USSR to a future German attack, Stalin also embarked on a disastrous war with Finland at the end of 1939 that pushed that border westwards at an enormous cost in lives and prestige. In June 1940, shocked by the scale of the Wehrmacht's success in the West, he took advantage of the drama being played out in France to occupy the Baltic states, and then Romanian Bessarabia and northern Bukovina. Much of this had been foreseen under the terms of the agreement with Germany, but the Germans had not expected him to move so fast. Although the Germans proclaimed their 'political disinterest' in both regions, and the last thing Stalin wanted at this stage was conflict with his new partner, there was no real trust between the two powers. In fact, at the end of July, Hitler secretly ordered planning for a campaign in the East the following year in order to bring home to the British the hopelessness of their situation: 'Russia is the factor by which England sets the greatest store . . . If Russia is beaten, England's last hope is gone. Germany is then master of Europe and the Balkans ... Decision: As a result of this argument, Russia must be dealt with. Spring 1941.' Incredibly, the indications are that Hitler did not believe such a campaign would require more than a few months at the most.[48]

The Soviet move into Bessarabia and northern Bukovina in particular prompted further unwanted trouble in the Balkans and more difficulties for the Germans. One of the more unexpected effects of France's total defeat was that Romania was left without a continental patron, and the vultures gathered. Following the Red Army's takeover in the north of the country, Hungary and Bulgaria advanced territorial claims of their own for border revisions, and a regional war loomed. Having just agreed an oil-for-arms deal with Bucharest, Hitler wished the whole dispute would go away – the last thing he wanted was fighting over Transylvania – but it fell to him and the Italians to sort things out. At the end of August, following a conference at Vienna, the Axis powers handed over 16,000 square miles and nearly two and a half million former Romanian subjects in northern Transylvania to Hungary; a few days later, a chunk of the country was ceded to Bulgaria. Both areas were ethnically mixed, and in both large numbers of people fled into Romania across the new borders. Yet interestingly, the Germans made no attempt to urge a wholesale population exchange on the Hungarians and Romanians, even though this would have been consistent with Hitler's rhetorical support for the idea of ethnically pure states. On the contrary, a German–Italian commission was established which ended up behaving much like the old despised League of Nations had done, monitoring the plight of refugees, reporting on conditions in camps and trying to persuade both governments in Transylvania to treat their minorities properly.[49] In Romania itself this dramatic loss of territory set off a political upheaval. King Carol was forced to abdicate in favour of his son, Michael, but real power was wielded by the country's new dictator, General Ion Antonescu. He had once been an ardent Francophile but was now equally pro-German; indeed he would shortly become Hitler's most trusted and admired ally. After the Vienna Award, the Germans guaranteed what was left of Romania – chiefly to prevent the Hungarians invading and creating a crisis that could bring the Russians further into Romania and jeopardize Germany's access to the oil fields there. But these events left the country badly destabilized by the rapid rise of the Iron Guard, one of Europe's nastiest fascist movements.

Oil was in many ways the key, and Hitler sent a military mission to secure the oil fields themselves – a full division rather than the training units originally requested by the Romanians. This deeply annoyed Stalin. In July, the British had tried to make mischief between him and the Germans by telling him they thought it was the task of the Soviet Union to maintain the unification and leadership of the Balkan countries. Stalin had sharply rebuffed them, denying that there was any danger of a German bid to rule over eastern Europe. But that was before German troops arrived on the Black Sea. The Soviets protested that they should have been consulted and they questioned the need for a German guarantee to Romania. Who, they asked, was the guarantee supposed to be against?[50] The sudden announcement of the Tripartite Pact – an agreement between Germany, Italy and Japan – only made matters worse: the Russians could have been forgiven for wondering where and if they fitted into what looked rather like a revival of the old Anti-Comintern Pact.[51]

Yet at this point, Germany was still dependent on Soviet grain and other raw materials, and even as German military exercises took place for the planned spring invasion, an invitation was sent to Soviet Foreign Minister Molotov to come to Berlin and patch things up. His meeting with Foreign Minister Ribbentrop and Hitler, which took place in November 1940, turned out to be one of the decisive diplomatic encounters of the war. The Germans sought to keep the discussions on a lofty plane, pontificating about a new division of the world's territories and offering the Soviet Union its share of the spoils. Ribbentrop and Hitler tried to demonstrate to the taciturn Soviet diplomat that there was really no difficulty including Russian ambitions in the coming world order. The Russians could extend their influence southwards towards the Indian Ocean – here Ribbentrop waved vaguely at the map – while the Axis would confine themselves to Africa and the Japanese to east Asia. Molotov was unimpressed and retorted in his own precise, dogged, schoolmasterly style. What, he asked, did the expression 'New Order' really mean? The Germans had not conquered India, so how could they dispose of it? Unable to extract a coherent reply, he went on to identify the territorial concerns which had lain at the heart of Russian foreign policy since Tsarist times – control over Finland, the Black Sea, the Balkans and the Straits. Would the Germans object, he asked, if Russia provided a military guarantee to Bulgaria along the lines of the one they themselves had given Romania? Molotov's pointed questions were not easy to answer, and, although the Germans came away from the meeting convinced that there would be no immediate rupture, the grounds of division were all too clear.

Also alienated by Germany's Romanian deal were the Italians. It infuriated Mussolini because it provoked his always lively fear of being locked out of the division of the spoils in the New Europe. After all, he had very little to show so far for his decision to enter the war, and south-eastern Europe was supposed to be in *his* sphere of influence; he had even toyed with the idea of an Italian-led 'Balkan bloc' there. 'Hitler always faces me with a *fait accompli*,' fumed the Duce when he heard that the Germans had sent 'advisers' to Romania. 'This time I am going to pay him back in his own coin. He will find out from the papers that I have occupied Greece. In this way, equilibrium will be re-established.'[52]

A fit of pique thus started off the disastrous Italian invasion of Greece in October 1940, the first Axis setback of the entire war. Foolishly and impatiently – not even waiting for his own deadline to expire in Athens – Mussolini launched 140,000 ill-equipped Italian troops over some of the most rugged mountains in Europe at the onset of the winter snows. The timing was spectacularly bad, the outcome devastating. The Greeks fought back, surprising everyone with the tenacity of their resistance, and soon it became clear that they had held the Italian advance and were even, in some quarters, repulsing it. Hitler appreciated the psychological delicacy of the situation – made worse by the success of British operations against the Italians in Libya, Eritrea and Ethiopia – and he realized that, despite having wanted to keep out of south-eastern Europe, he would have to come to Mussolini's assistance. In November, he sent the Duce a thinly veiled reproof for having embarked on an ill-advised venture that had produced 'very grave psychological and military repercussions', casting doubt on the strength of the Axis in the minds of neutrals, and bringing the English into the Balkans. Another diversion of German troops would now be needed even as he planned for war against the Soviet Union. That winter, he sent a military mission to Bulgaria to pave the way for the troops that would be required against Greece.[53]

What followed was the last victorious German campaign on the European continent. Greece was the primary target since the British military build-up there threatened the Romanian oil fields. But Yugoslavia was added to the list at the last minute too. In March the country's adhesion to the Axis triggered off a popular coup in Belgrade, and, although the new government also professed its loyalty to Berlin, Hitler decided to topple it. Beginning on 6 April, the German military advance was unstoppable, and the fighting was soon over. The former Habsburg officers now commanding the German forces were determined to preclude any repetition of the Serbs' resistance in 1914. Belgrade was heavily bombed by the Luftwaffe, and the country was occupied after eleven days' fighting at a loss of only 151 German dead. Shortly afterwards, Greece fell too. It had all happened so fast that, despite the claims of some historians, there is in fact little evidence that these Balkan operations had any significant effect on the build-up to the attack on the Soviet Union.[54]

As a result, Italy finally got its own mini-empire in south-eastern Europe (though Hungary and Bulgaria also had to be accommodated). The Germans wanted to leave as few troops of their own there as possible and rushed divisions north to the Eastern Front. But the costs were heavy in term of administrative efficiency. Yugoslavia was carved into more occupation zones than any other country in Europe; like Czechoslovakia and Poland, it was a creation of the hated Versailles system and erased from the map. Italy and Germany took over strips of territory; Hungary and Bulgaria helped themselves as well. While Serbia was put under German military occupation, Croatia became a satellite state stretching into Bosnia and Hercegovina. Italy had 'predominance' in much of the country, annexed the Dalmatian coast and incorporated Kosovo into Italian-run Albania; Germany had 'predominance' in the east. Greece too was carved up – into Italian, Bulgarian and German zones – though unlike Yugoslavia it remained under the nominal control of a weak quisling government in Athens. It was not an arrangement to encourage rational government or to ensure stability.

TOWARDS BARBAROSSA

On 18 December 1940, Hitler issued his secret directive to 'crush Soviet Russia in a rapid campaign'. The overall objective was 'to erect a barrier against Asiatic Russia on the general line Volga–Archangel' which would definitively eliminate the USSR as an industrial and European power. Initially Hitler had wanted to defeat England and France first so that the Reich could build up towards the inevitable reckoning with the Bolsheviks. Now, it was his failure to defeat England that prompted the opening of this front much earlier than planned. The unexpectedly speedy victory over France offered the model of a new kind of offensive – the *Blitzkrieg* – and Hitler seems to have been confident that, following the army's triumphs in the West (and basing his judgement too on the Red Army's lamentable performance fighting against Finland earlier in the year), the war would quickly come to a victorious conclusion. 'The entire Bolshevism will collapse like a pack of cards,' Goebbels predicted in May 1941.[55]

Even before the invasion against the USSR had actually been launched, Hitler was looking ahead beyond his enemy's demise. He now stood on the verge of realizing the continental vision he had first outlined in the late 1920s: by the late autumn of 1941, he expected the Axis to be the uncontested military masters of Europe. Germany would hold sway from the Atlantic to the Caucasus. Ongoing border wars beyond the Urals with what was left of Russia he regarded as Germany's equivalent to the Raj's North-western Frontier – a testing ground for German manhood. The 'newly conquered territories in the East' would be held by a 'security force' of some sixty divisions, and the Ukraine would become 'a common food-supply base' for the Axis. Fortress Europe itself would no longer face any serious threat from the land and could be defended with much smaller forces than had been necessary until then. Secure in the East, the Greater German Reich could direct its full attention to defeating the British, driving them to the negotiating table through operations conducted across a vast arc from the Maghreb to Afghanistan. There would be an October assault on Gibraltar, France would help defeat the British in north Africa, and the Spanish would have to come off the fence. In the Middle East, light mobile motorized units would undermine enemy positions in Palestine and Egypt. The British empire would be brought to its knees.

Not many of Hitler's most senior advisers shared his confidence. Having avoided a two-front war in 1939 'by a miracle', they regarded it as mad to start one needlessly in 1941. Foreign Minister Ribbentrop viewed the 1939 agreement with Molotov as his greatest achievement. Moreover, the Russians were still honouring their all-important supply contracts, providing the Reich with badly needed grain and other goods. Traffic with Japan too would be made much harder if the land route through the USSR was cut off. More influential than the lightweight Ribbentrop, the second most powerful man in the Reich, Reichsmarschall Göring, also felt Germany needed time to consolidate its gains. The New Order was still on the drawing-board, and Göring knew that extending the war would quickly bring the Reich up against some hard economic constraints. As it was, manpower was stretched thin, food reserves were low, and lines of command were confused and chaotic. German troops were on patrol from the Arctic Circle to the Aegean, often in regions that offered no obvious benefits of any kind to the Reich.

Yet in the speed of victory during that summer of 1940, and in the West's lack of resistance, Hitler saw a historic opportunity. Russia could be eliminated once and for all without exposing Germany's position. He hated having to rely on Stalin's goodwill for food and other materials and preferred to secure them through conquest. The high grain quotas that Stalin agreed to supply him in January 1941 – and their punctuality in fulfilling their promises over the coming months – convinced him only of the need to grab the riches of the Ukraine for himself. At this point, England posed no threat. It was better to invade the Soviet Union at once and bring the war to an end before American support for the UK became too great. Already bombing raids on German cities, and the continuation of British resistance, were subduing the German public and encouraging opponents across the continent. And alongside such strategic considerations were ideological concerns that loomed much larger than at any time previously. Even the attack on Poland, which prefigured the racial violence of the anti-Bolshevik *Vernichtungskrieg*, paled in comparison with the scale and sheer intensity of the coming engagement. This was the best prepared of all the German campaigns, and the preparation extended to specifying how the enemy population was to be treated. Merciless new codes of conduct were drawn up; new SS killing squads were formed: this was to be an existential struggle to the death against Germany's ultimate racial-ideological foe. On the morning of 22 June 1941, without any prior warning, the invasion began. Following a massive artillery bombardment, an army of more than three million soldiers, one million horses and 600,000 vehicles moved forward along a front over 2,000 kilometres long, running from Finland to the Black Sea. An even larger force confronted them, caught totally off-guard. With this epic, murderous and unremitting conflict as the catalyst, the very character of Nazi rule across Europe was to be irrevocably altered. Already, Hitler had shown that his programme was incapable of winning over Europe politically; as the veteran diplomat Weizsäcker had noted, 'the ideological unity of Europe is reduced to Germany, Italy and Spain' – and even the last of those was doubtful. Now all that was left was force.[56]

6

War of Annihilation: Into the Soviet Union

The principle of ruthless brutality, the treatment of the country according to points of view and methods used in past centuries against coloured slave peoples; and the fact, defying any sensible policy, that the contempt for that people was not only expressed in actions against individuals but also in words at every possible and impossible occasion ... all this bears ample testimony to the complete lack of instinct with regard to the treatment of alien peoples, which in view of its consequences can only be called pathetic and disastrous.

Gauleiter and Generalkommissar Alfred Frauenfeld, 10 February 1944[1]

When Hitler decided to tear up the Molotov–Ribbentrop Pact it was initially for strategic reasons. He reckoned that knocking out the USSR would remove London's one potential ally of any significance on the European continent and force the British to come to terms. But the idea of a surprise military strike soon metamorphosed into his long-held dream of permanently extending Germany's *Lebensraum* deep into the East. Invading Russia had probably been the army's idea to begin with in 1940, and its planners emphasized the likely economic benefits: the occupation of European Russia, they claimed, would deprive the Bolshevik regime of its most valuable resources and bring them under Germany's control. Such a message was music to Hitler's ears. He simply ignored the dissenters. Finance Minister von Krosigk, doubted (correctly as it turned out) whether war would actually improve the Reich's food supply. Most of Göring's economic advisers had serious concerns as well. As for the German embassy in Moscow, perhaps best placed of all to judge, it objected that not only was Stalin no threat, since he had no plans to fight Germany, but occupying even the fertile Ukraine would prove to be highly costly since the mechanized Soviet collective farms would grind to a halt for lack of fuel. It was an assessment Hitler probably never even saw.[2]

Even if he had done, he would have probably disregarded it. Far from anticipating the long, agonizing and ultimately fatal struggle that ensued, he was completely confident of achieving a lightning victory like the one he had just won in France. 'If we get to grips with this colossus the right way the first time,' he predicted in August 1940, 'then it will collapse far quicker than the world expects.' But history had yet another surprise in store: just as the French surrendered sooner than anticipated, so the Red Army turned out to be a far more formidable foe than Hitler ever imagined. The *Blitzkrieg* dragged on to Christmas, then into another year, and another.[3]

The USSR's refusal to give in turned the European war into a global one. In August 1941, less than two months after the German invasion had begun, Churchill and Roosevelt had little confidence in the durability of the Bolshevik regime as they signed the Atlantic Charter that laid the foundation for the subsequent postwar international order. By December, they had changed their minds. Their diplomatic contacts with Moscow intensified rapidly, and the partnership between the Big Three, which would henceforth shape the strategy of the war and the peace, came into being. Before 1941 was out, British Foreign Secretary Anthony Eden had been sent to Moscow. The campaign that had been designed to force the British to capitulate had in fact cemented the new alliance that would ultimately defeat Germany.

Touring the front lines just outside the Soviet capital, shortly after a successful counter-offensive had pushed the Wehrmacht back, Eden and his hosts came face to face with the devastation the Germans had inflicted: 'It was a frightening spectacle,' wrote Ivan Maisky, the Soviet ambassador to London, who was travelling with him.

Not a single house, not a shed or a fence! A plain covered with snow, and strung out along it, as though on a death parade, long rows of village stoves and chimneys which had escaped the fire. One could not help wondering what had happened to those who had quite lately been living in those houses which had ceased to exist.

Bodies of German and Russian soldiers littered the roads, ditches and snow-covered fields, frozen stiff in strange poses, with their arms outstretched or on all fours.

In the town of Klin, Eden's party visited the modest wooden house that had once been Tchaikovsky's summer retreat. 'The house itself had survived,' wrote Maisky,

'but inside everything had been turned upside down, broken and befouled. One of the rooms on the first floor had been turned into a toilet. In other rooms, there were scattered on the floor heaps of half-burned books, pieces of wood, sheets of torn up music-paper. The German fascists had evidently paid tribute in their own way to one of the greatest geniuses in the musical history of mankind. Eden and I slowly walked from room to room. Finally Eden could not restrain himself and said, with an expression of disgust on his face: 'This is what we could have expected if the Germans had landed in our islands.'[4]

It was actually far worse. For Hitler, there was all the difference in the world between the British and the Soviets: *this* was the decisive clash he had predicted for twenty years and he planned to wage it accordingly. To his senior commanders at the end of March 1941, he talked about a 'war of annihilation' – a war 'between two ideologies' – in which the normal rules ceased to apply. At stake was both the defeat of Nazism's most dangerous enemy – Bolshevism – and territorial control of 'the East', the lands between the Baltic and the Black Seas which Greater Germany supposedly needed for its very survival. To the military, he emphasized the great difference with the campaigning in western Europe: 'in the East, toughness is softness for the future'. In short, this was to be the 'moment of destiny', not only for the Führer but also for his army, which had grown since he seized power in 1933 from 115,000 to 3.8 million men.[5]

Most of this army was sent to the Eastern Front, and most of it would perish there too in a struggle in which the casualties dwarfed anything seen till then. Against the Soviet troops, the Germans died in unprecedented numbers, and by March 1942, one-third of frontline units had been killed, lost or wounded; more men had already frozen to death than died during the entire war on the British or American sides. By then, too, more than three million Soviet soldiers had been captured, of whom astonishingly more than two million had *already* starved to death in German hands. Another 100,000 or more Soviet POWs had been executed in cold blood by the German security police. Indeed even more than the epic struggle at the front, it was the conduct of forces behind the lines – towards prisoners of war, partisans and non-combatants –

that testified to the ideological impact of National Socialism on the German military and society.[6]

The subject of much recent controversy, the brutality that many ordinary German soldiers demonstrated towards Soviet civilians reflected much more than the customary strains of war. Stretched supply-lines and lack of resources did not help, nor the fact that there were far too few troops to properly secure the rear areas, which were mostly manned by thinly dispersed, poorly trained, over-age conscripts. Had the Wehrmacht won all the territory it anticipated – it never gained more than half – securing it would have been harder still. Yet the lethal effects of this logistical shortfall were worsened both by the military's long-standing commitment to retaliation through counter-terror and by the regime's intense racism. The violence that was now unleashed could not be compared with anything that had happened until this point – not even in Poland. Hundreds of thousands of civilians were shot or hanged and thousands of villages burned as the Germans and their local auxiliaries chased the elusive partisans. The region's Jewish inhabitants, who were reckoned to be supportive of Bolshevism and the partisans, were killed in growing numbers, first in sporadic reprisals, then more systematically. By the end of 1941, it had already become clear that this was a war of annihilation in no merely figurative sense.[7]

PLANNING THE WRONG WAR

In many ways, the mindless and counter-productive cruelty of the German occupation was prefigured from the start. Neither the military nor Hitler himself had anticipated a lengthy struggle, and, based on surprisingly bad intelligence, the mainstream view in Berlin was that the purges had weakened the Red Army and that its poor performance against Finland in the Winter War of 1939–40 had demonstrated this. In late July 1940, when Hitler first confidentially pronounced there would be an eastern campaign the following year, the navy felt both that 'Russia is still a mystery to us', *and* able to assert confidently that 'the Russian forces can be regarded as far inferior to our battle-hardened troops'. In a handbook on the Soviet military published a few months later, planners depicted their foe as 'unsuited for modern warfare and incapable of decisive resistance against a well-commanded, well-equipped force.'

Russian officers had all the faults of their national character – 'slow-wittedness, schematism, fear of responsibility and of taking decisions'.[8]

Few in Berlin therefore – whatever their views on the political wisdom of the war – doubted that the Wehrmacht would manage to push the Red Army back far into the east. Of course, the generals wanted more men to do the job – as they usually do – and fretted about the lack of reserves. Fears of a two-front war had not completely vanished. The commander-in-chief of Army Group Central, von Bock, presciently warned Hitler that, while they might be able to achieve battlefield victory, he doubted whether 'we can force the Soviets into making peace'. But Hitler himself was not worried; as we have seen, he imagined several dozen German divisions keeping a weakened Russia permanently at bay behind a new border from Archangel to Astrakhan in a kind of colonial 'quasi-peace'. More to the point, the prestige he had won as a result of the lightning victories in western Europe in 1940 had made his position unchallengeable.[9]

All subsequent operational planning was based on the initial highly questionable assumptions. In the run-up to the attack, supply lines were stretched to their limits, and the strain on the Reich's already over-taxed transportation system was ignored. In autumn 1939, the Reichsbahn actually had fewer trains than in 1914, but Hitler's preference for motorized tactics blinded him to what the potential consequences might be, especially amid the autumn mud and winter snows. Nor was the blame solely Hitler's; it also reflected the shortcomings of a military caste which downplayed the importance of logistics (and intelligence) in favour of operational expertise. Staff planners assumed that German troops would be able to make use of the Soviet rail system and infrastructure and they did not foresee the scorched earth tactics employed by Stalin once he had got over the initial shock of the invasion.

The German military also gave almost no thought to the subsequent occupation itself. Presented with the army's proposals to run Russia along the lines of the French and Belgian model, Hitler had exploded: it understood nothing of politics, and military administrations served no useful purpose. Himmler, speaking 'with a respectable and regretful demeanour', had weighed in, deploring the army's wishy-washy handling of the occupations in Poland, Holland and Norway and calling for the replacement of insufficiently motivated officers by SS men. Once the Führer made it quite clear that he wanted a swift hand-over to civilian

rule, the military abandoned the whole subject. 'The planned administration and exploitation of the territory are concerns that may be left to
a later date,' ran the army high command's key instructions of 3 April.
'*This is not the business* of the army.' But that was another miscalculation: more than half of the territory which fell into German hands –
no less than two million square kilometres – remained under military
control to the bitter end.[10]

Keen to curry favour with the Führer, the top brass simultaneously
sanctioned a far more sweeping repudiation of the laws of war than
anything they had agreed to in Poland. One step in this direction was
the so-called Barbarossa Order, which mandated the 'utmost severity'
towards any 'enemy civilians' who tried to 'interfere' with military
operations. Officers had the right to order reprisals against any village
from which hostile fire had come; soldiers would not be punished even
for acts against enemy civilians that constituted military crimes. Anxious
to protect military courts from Hitler, who they feared might simply do
away with them if, as in Poland, they acquitted civilians, the high
command suspended them indefinitely for civilian offences in Russia:
officers were now free to decide the fate of Russian civilians on their
own.

The second order, the so-called 'Commissar Decree', went much
further. The Nazi leadership had already decided that, following the invasion, Party officials must be killed, and on 6 June, the troops, together
with the SS, were therefore instructed to execute captured Soviet commissars. As 'originators of the barbaric, Asiatic fighting methods' of the
Red Army, the latter were denied combatant status and ordered to be
shot on the spot or handed over to the SS. Some appalled German
officers saw the draft decree as 'the systematic transformation of military
law concerning the conquered population into uncontrolled despotism
– indeed a caricature of all law'. To their credit, a few protested privately.
But their superiors obediently followed Hitler's wishes and ignored
their misgivings.[11]

Finally, on 12 June, less than a fortnight before the invasion, came
the 'Guidelines for the Conduct of Troops in Russia', which cast the
war as a life-or-death struggle against an ideology, not a state. Bolshevism was described as 'the mortal enemy of the National Socialist German
people', and the fight against it 'demands ruthless and energetic measures
against Bolshevik agitators, irregulars, saboteurs and Jews, and the total

eradication of any active or passive resistance'. Many field commanders immediately echoed this in their own pre-invasion directives. General Hoepner, who would later be executed for his part in the July 1944 bomb plot against Hitler, advised his troops that:

The war against Russia is an important chapter in the struggle for existence of the German nation. It is the old battle of the Germanic against the Slavic peoples, of the defence of European culture against Moscovite-Asiatic inundation, and the repelling of Jewish Bolshevism. The objective of this battle must be the destruction of present-day Russia and it must therefore be conducted with unprecedented severity. Every military action must be guided in planning and execution by an iron will to exterminate the enemy mercilessly and totally. In particular, no adherents of the present Russian-Bolshevik system are to be spared.[12]

But despite such bloodthirsty talk, Hitler had little faith in the Wehrmacht's ideological reliability and regarded the task of entirely eliminating the 'Judeo-Bolshevik intelligentsia' as one that 'could not be demanded from the regular army'. In March he had therefore entrusted Himmler with 'special tasks resulting from the struggle which has to be carried out between two opposing political systems'. That spring, four mobile SS Special Operation Groups (*Einsatzgruppen*) were created to liquidate opposition in newly occupied areas. Similar groups had been set up in earlier campaigns but never for such a murderous purpose. Nominally placed for their policing duties under the command of territorial army commanders, the *Einsatzgruppen* answered only to the RSHA in Berlin where their so-called 'political tasks' were concerned.[13]

In April 1941, the *Einsatzgruppen* were given instructions to clear the newly conquered territories of 'suspect elements', to shoot all party functionaries, as well as 'other radical elements' and 'all Jews in state and party positions'. Their commanders – highly educated senior SS officers – were made aware of the terms of the agreement with the army and told to 'ensure the most loyal cooperation with the Wehrmacht'. The army itself probably did not know that Reinhard Heydrich had secretly instructed his men to incite pogroms against the Jews. 'It had to be shown that the local population themselves had taken the first measures on their own as a natural reaction against decades of suppression by the Jews,' the head of Einsatzgruppe A wrote several months later.[14]

This caution probably reflected Heydrich's uncertainty as to how much he could count on the army's understanding. But he need not have worried. The army, overstretched as it was, could only commit very few troops of its own to its so-called rear areas, and was grateful for help in policing them. Although its commanders possessed authority over Heydrich's men not only in combat areas but also in the rear areas behind the front, they generally worked smoothly with the SS. Manpower was scarce: by October 1943, of the 2.6 million-strong German army in the East, only 100,000 were patrolling the vast rear areas furthest behind the front. In fact the *Einsatzgruppen* themselves only numbered a few thousand men each, since the SS itself at this point did not have access to larger forces, except from among those thugs, policemen and fanatical anti-Bolsheviks that it was able to recruit once inside Soviet territory. But what the Germans lacked in numbers, they made up for with terror. 'In view of the vast size of the conquered territories in the east,' insisted Hitler a month after the invasion, 'the forces available for establishing security in these areas will be sufficient only if, instead of punishing resistance by sentences in a court of law, the occupying forces spread such terror as to crush every will to resist among the population.'[15]

POST-SOVIET FUTURES

How the newly conquered territories were to be administered was regarded by Hitler as a much less urgent question than how they were to be policed. One thing was clear to him: the area was of such vital strategic, economic and racial significance – its conquest was, after all, the very *raison d'être* of the war – that the task of administering it had to be placed in the hands of reliable Party men. The Foreign Ministry was kept away, and its long-treasured plans to liaise with Ukrainian, Georgian and Baltic nationalists were put back in the drawer. Reich commissars would be appointed to run the former Soviet territories along the lines already established in Norway and the Netherlands. The only real question was whether they should report directly to Hitler – as there – or whether some new body should also be created as an intermediary to coordinate policy across the whole post-Soviet area.[16]

It was a sign of how little importance Hitler attached to the whole issue that the man he chose to think this through was Alfred Rosenberg, a metaphysically inclined Baltic German hack who had studied in Moscow and had some familiarity with the USSR and its nationality problems. Rosenberg regarded himself as 'the philosopher of the [Nazi] movement' and was the author of a verbose best-selling racial tract, *The Myth of the Twentieth Century*. Hitler disliked his writings – calling them 'stuff nobody can understand' – but valued him as someone who had joined the Nazi Party at the very start. More significantly, he regarded him as a weakling and had entrusted the leadership of the Nazi Party to him for this very reason during his period in prison after the Beer Hall Putsch. Goebbels, who thoroughly despised him, called him 'Almost Rosenberg' because he 'almost managed to become a scholar, a journalist, a politician, but only almost'. Despite his many jobs – running the Party's foreign policy office, pronouncing on racial theory and Nazi ideology – Rosenberg was certainly not one of Hitler's inner circle. But he had been about to deliver an inaugural speech on one of his hobby-horses, 'the Jewish Question as World Problem', at the opening of his new Institute for Research into the Jewish Question (stocked with rare items plundered from the continent's leading collections of Judaica) when he was summoned to see the Führer. In early April they met for two hours, and following this meeting Rosenberg was entrusted with the 'central direction of all east European space'.[17]

Drawing up his administrative and political blueprints for the post-Soviet peace, Rosenberg surrounded himself with a circle of men who, like himself, thought the Germans should arrive as liberators from Bolshevism. The memorandum he gave Hitler at their first meeting proposed that they should build an anti-communist alliance, work with anti-Soviet émigrés in Berlin and establish a coalition of satellite states in the former USSR. There would be 'complete annihilation of the Bolshevik-Jewish state administration', and Russia itself would take over from the General Government as the place to expel the racially unwanted masses. Hitler himself had been thinking in not dissimilar terms. In July 1940, he had talked about setting up a 'Ukrainian state, federation of Baltic states, Belorussia, Finland'. Operational studies produced on his orders envisaged breaking the USSR up and creating independent, non-Bolshevik states under German control. Two weeks before he met Rosenberg, Hitler was still talking of 'Stalin-free republics' outside Russia, while relying on the 'most brutal force' in the 'greater Russian realm'. Such plans took the settlement of the Treaty of Brest-Litovsk as the basic model and did not look so very different from what the Kaiser's men had been aiming to achieve in 1918.[18]

Organizationally, Rosenberg started off proposing the creation of four new Reich Commissariats with himself as a kind of coordinator and liaison man with the ministries in Berlin. Within a few weeks, his plans had become more ambitious: now he advocated a separate and fully fledged East Ministry for the region, with himself running it. But there were several reasons why this was a very bad idea. One was that Rosenberg himself was a terrible administrator – Goebbels commented that he 'could only theorize not organize'. Another was that, as the state secretary in the Interior Ministry, Wilhelm Stuckart, pointed out, it was bound to lead to all kinds of jurisdictional disputes with the ministries that already existed. But Hitler was not impressed by their objections – the last thing he wanted was the old civil service ministries trying to run the USSR like Germany – and went ahead with his appointment.

Yet it was as though he was setting Rosenberg up to fail. After all, by this time sweeping responsibilities in the East had already been assigned to much more powerful men than him – men who had absolutely no intention of fighting on behalf of Ukrainians or Belorussians, and who wanted land for Germans alone. One of these was Heinrich Himmler, who regarded the East as his special preserve and spent more time there than Rosenberg himself: in 1942 he even transferred his headquarters to the Ukraine. Hitler had already entrusted his SS with 'political matters' in the occupied Soviet territories, and 90 per cent of all matters in that region, Himmler remarked, were political. He wanted nothing to be promised to non-Germans which could in any way compromise his grand scheme of Germanizing the East. Reconciling this with Rosenberg's idea of a coalition of anti-communist Slav nationalists was obviously impossible.

An even more powerful enemy was Reichsmarschall Göring, who had already been told – before Rosenberg's appointment – that he would run economic affairs in the occupied Eastern territories. Göring's goal was to exploit the conquered lands for Germany's immediate benefit, and one week after the invasion, Hitler formally made him responsible for this, further eroding Rosenberg's authority. As if the new minister's position was not already weak enough, Göring dealt Rosenberg another blow by going behind his back and engineering the appointment of the *Gauleiter* of East Prussia, Erich Koch, as Reich commissioner for the

Ukraine – perhaps the key post in the new civilian administration. Whereas Rosenberg believed strongly that the Ukrainians should eventually gain some kind of independent state, Koch, who had once been an ardent lover of Dostoevsky, had changed his views completely and had become deeply and ostentatiously contemptuous of the Slavs. But in Berlin Rosenberg was criticized as a man who cared more about Ukrainians than he did about Germans, whereas Koch's reputation was that of someone who got things done. Rosenberg might have his Ph.D and his books. Stocky, working-class, loud-mouthed Koch, however, had a brilliant record raising pigs in East Prussia and was promising to replicate this in the East.[19]

For, as Koch knew, the food situation inside Germany was much on Göring's mind. In early 1941, planners were predicting problems as a result of the poor harvest and threatening cuts in rations. The German population was complaining about shortages and high prices, and this increased the determination of the Reich authorities to make the invasion of the USSR pay off fast. Herbert Backe, the state secretary in the Ministry for Food and Agriculture, actually told Hitler that 'the occupation of the Ukraine would liberate us from every economic worry'. He did also remind him that, apart from the Ukraine, the rest of European Russia was not a food surplus area. But the regime was perfectly ready to see famine spread among the civilian population in the occupied territories so long as Germans were nourished. On 2 May, it was agreed that the successful continuation of the war would require the Wehrmacht to 'be fed at the expense of Russia', even if the consequence was that 'thereby tens of millions of men will undoubtedly starve to death'. 'Support of the war economy' was 'the highest law', while the newly occupied territories were to be regarded 'from a colonial viewpoint and exploited economically with colonial methods'. Göring predicted 'the biggest mass death in Europe since the Thirty Years' War'.[20] Backe even drafted a set of 'Twelve Commandments' for future administrators in the East. 'We wish not to convert the Russians to National Socialism but to make them our tools,' he wrote. 'The Russian has stood poverty, hunger and austerity for centuries. His stomach is flexible; hence no false pity!'[21]

Rosenberg – his powers over security and the economy by now whittled away to nothing – was still keen to commit the Reich to a political vision for the future of the territories once ruled by the USSR.

He felt it was important that the differences between the Russians and the rest should be emphasized from the start: while German propaganda should mention 'the Ukrainian people and its freedom', or 'the salvation of the Estonian, Latvian and Lithuanian nations', it should never 'speak of Russia or of a Russian territory'.[22] On the eve of the invasion, he summarized his basic political conception as:

To resume, in an intelligent manner . . . the aspirations to liberation of all these peoples and to give them shape in certain forms of states, i.e. to cut state formations out of the giant territory of the Soviet Union and to build them up against Moscow, so as to free the German Reich of the Eastern nightmare for centuries to come.[23]

Even if it was necessary to keep these territories provisionally under the rule of German civilian administrators, 'the conquered territory as a whole must not be treated as an object of exploitation'. As he warned, 'the worst that could happen from the political point of view would occur if the people, in the face of our measures of economic exploitation, would come to the conclusion that the present regime causes them greater want than did the Bolsheviks'.[24]

That this was precisely what happened was because Hitler himself never took Rosenberg's approach seriously. He wanted the Russians kept down, but had little time for raising up the Ukrainians. Shortly after the invasion, his contempt for the political aspirations of the inhabitants of the occupied territories became abundantly clear. By the first week in July, he had come round to the view that Moscow and Leningrad should be made uninhabitable in order 'to deprive not only Bolshevism but also Muscovite nationalism of their centres'. Like Rosenberg, Hitler saw this as a double struggle against both an ideology and a country. Unlike Rosenberg, he believed Germany did not need the help of any anti-Russian forces to keep Russia down. The war would be over in a trice, and he was already thinking of the minerals and crops that Germany would gain and looking forward to opening up the 'beauties of the Crimea' to German tourists, who would speed there on new autobahns, taming the primitive Slavs with Aryan energy and foresight.[25]

In February 1944, as the German occupation in Russia neared its end, one of Rosenberg's closest collaborators gave a damning indictment of their overall approach, referring to that masterpiece of wrong treatment and the most remarkable and astonishing achievement – to have, within a year, chased into the woods and swamps, as partisans, a people which was absolutely pro-German and had jubilantly greeted us as their liberator and to have thus influenced the course of events in the East in a decisively negative way . . .

But it was Hitler himself who had laid down the lines of this policy at the crucial meeting he had held with Göring, Rosenberg, Bormann and Keitel two and a half years earlier at his Rastenburg headquarters in the Masurian forests. The date was 16 July 1941, and he was confident that the war would not last long, for the Wehrmacht had already won a number of crushing victories, while the Red Army was falling back so rapidly that hundreds of thousands of Soviet troops were being encircled and captured.

Hitler could scarcely have been blunter. He started the meeting by emphasizing that this was a campaign whose fruits would benefit Germany alone. In the short run, it might be tactically useful to play the role of liberators. But the important thing was to avoid superfluous declarations and, above all, for the Germans to know what they wanted as they divided up 'this vast cake'. They needed to prevent any other military power emerging in the region, and beyond that, 'first to rule, secondly to administer and thirdly to exploit' the people and resources they found there. This was a programme for a colonial war of extraction. Germans should be the only ones to bear arms; looking to other nationalities for support was a false illusion. Pacification would be achieved by 'shooting everyone who looked in any way suspicious'.[26]

As if all of this was not enough, a far cry from Rosenberg's dreams of seeing Germany lead a coalition of Slavic states, his plans suffered a further blow when Hitler decided to truncate the Ukraine by attaching formerly Habsburg Galicia to the General Government and giving some of the southern Ukraine, including Odessa, to Romania. So much for winning over the Ukrainians. The lands between would exist solely to serve Germany, while the Germans themselves would 'Europeanize' the steppe, draining marshes, building motorways, establishing plantations and founding new 'German towns'. 'Two or three million men' would come to live in them, Hitler predicted, 'from Germany, Scandinavia, the Western countries and America'. In the past he had often argued that Europe had been harmed by the mass transatlantic migrations of the

previous century; his policy would reverse the direction of the transcontinental flow and send millions eastwards. The ultimate result would be
'to Germanise this country by the immigration of Germans and to look
upon the natives as Redskins'.[27]

It was surely small consolation for Rosenberg that the same conference
also approved his basic blueprint for the civilian administration. Once
the army handed over control, the entire area was to be ruled by four
civilian Reich commissars – one for the Ukraine, another for the Baltic
states together with Belorussia (forming a previously non-existent territorial entity to be known as the *Ostland*), a third for the Caucasus and a
fourth for Russia itself. (In fact, only the first two were ever established.)
Rosenberg, now named minister for the Occupied Eastern Territories,
was placed in overall charge.

As we have seen, his real position was very weak. His appointment
was not even announced publicly as Hitler wanted to wait for a great
victory – one sufficiently emphatic never came – before making the
announcement. Meanwhile Hitler retained for himself the power to
appoint the Reich commissars and the general commissars below them,
and these were the men who would wield power on the spot; indeed
Rosenberg was expected to delegate his power to legislate by decree to
them. He had even less chance, of course, of ordering around Himmler,
Göring or the army. As one of his more knowledgeable subordinates
commented apprehensively, 'It will be hard for the civil administration
to rule a land without having full control over the police and the economy.' As for Rosenberg's political goals, Göring dismissed them breezily
in his instructions to the army economics staff: 'Whatever is to be put
to use, must be put to use immediately. Purely economic considerations,
not political. The Führer has not finalized a political outcome. No
consideration should therefore be taken regarding a future political
order.' And in fact, Hitler always attached much greater importance to
plundering the region of its resources and crushing any resistance than
he did to thinking about how it should be governed.[28]

Rosenberg continued nonetheless to talk about building a New Europe
liberated from Bolshevism. It was the sort of language that some of
his subordinates later adapted quite easily to American needs in the
propaganda battles of the Cold War. But it did not get far in the Third
Reich. Lacking Hitler's ear, Rosenberg saw him again scarcely half a
dozen times – the Führer's gate-keeper, Martin Bormann, held views on

the Slavs that made Hitler look moderate – while his subordinates mostly ignored him and went their own ways. When he complained to Hitler about Koch in the autumn of 1941, the Führer put him firmly in his place, telling him 'not to meddle in the internal administration of the Reich Commissariats, but to confine yourself to broad, general directives which are first to be agreed on with me'.[29]

In fact, the new East Ministry itself became something of a joke. Housed initially in the offices of the former Soviet trade mission, then relocated because of Allied bombing raids, the Ost-Ministerium ('OMi') was soon nicknamed the 'Chaos (Cha-Ost) Ministry' instead. Himmler's mole, the SS officer Gottlob Berger, started out as SS liaison officer but ended up more or less running the political department. It was Berger who memorably described Rosenberg's deputy, the Nazi *Gauleiter* for Westphalia-North, as 'too weak to do any good and too cowardly to sin'. More impressive was the first head of Rosenberg's political department, Georg Liebbrandt, whom Berger described as 'a mixture of businessman, intellectual and horse trader'. But Liebbrandt was eventually forced out because of his pro-Ukrainian reputation.

In general, the Ministry attracted cast-offs and rejects from other departments and was flooded with applications from ill-qualified, over-age recruits keen to head east. An observer acidly pointed out that, whereas Stalin had selected his best political officers for duty in the western provinces of the USSR, the Nazis chose the worst. Recruited through the Party, many of the so-called *Ostnieten* (Eastern failures) were ageing street-brawlers, drawn from the ranks of the SA; they were, according to one SS man, 'blockheads and ass-lickers whose career for the most part had depended on that of their *Gauleiter*'. Rosenberg liked them only because, as SA men, they hated Himmler and his SS. There were also former anti-Nazis seeking a 'second chance' to redeem themselves, farmers looking for more land, 'colonial' carpet-baggers and ethnic Germans looking for the opportunity to become *echte Deutsche*. Few spoke Russian, or had the faintest idea of what awaited them. Attracted by a gaudy uniform which won them the nickname of Golden Pheasants, they seemed more concerned with hierarchy, decorations and the perks of office than with the responsibilities of government. 'The little German, often from the racial point of view himself rather an Eastern type', was how a jaundiced press officer described a typical East Ministry administrator in a private memo in 1944.

Now in the expanses of the East, with pretentious uniforms, titles, salaries, daily allowances and rations . . . a type who decks himself out with revolver and whip or whatever he feels will lend him a natural mastery, superior bearing and genuine manliness. The idle and worthless type of . . . bureaucrat . . . the eternally hungry 'Organiser' with a swarm of like-minded Eastern hyenas, his whole multitudinous clique, recognizable by the two big 'Ws' – women and wine . . . people who enjoy Eastern luxury in food, lodgings and transport all the more the more modest their original circumstances.

These were scarcely the 'real masters' and the 'viceroys' Hitler had foreseen running the East.[30]

Rosenberg's most frustrating run-ins were with his own subordinate, Reichskommissar Koch. Koch detested the Ukraine and he ruled the vast province with a tiny staff from the small town of Rovne, mainly because there were good connections from there to East Prussia, where he remained *Gauleiter* and spent most of his time. He thought about moving to Kiev, but Hitler was so determined not to give the slightest encouragement to Ukrainian nationalists that he told him not to. Koch was nothing if not loyal, and he clamped down harshly on Ukrainian nationalist groups previously tolerated or encouraged by the army. His view, expressed with brutal clarity in his first address in December 1941, was that the Germans were the master race (*Herrenvolk*) and everyone else had the duty to serve them. 'I will pump every last thing out of this country,' he said. 'I did not come here to spread bliss but to help the Führer'. Ukrainian émigrés, visiting the Reichskommissariat from Berlin, were taken aback at his casual references to the Ukrainians as 'niggers'. When Rosenberg's men compiled studies of agrarian systems in the former USSR, Koch scoffed. 'I have to work out how to obtain the harvest from the Ukrainians so as to feed homeland and army. Meantime, Rosenberg sits in Berlin and commissions books!' His view was that Rosenberg's work in the Ukraine would only begin once the war was won; until then he was in charge, and would organize 'the greatest plundering possible'.[31]

Koch's conception of government did not go much beyond repression, organized looting and surveillance: mandatory identity cards helped monitor the population's movements, a new currency was introduced with its own central bank, and the economy was tightly regulated with controls on prices, wages and working hours. Koch himself was appointed trustee of all former Soviet property which was administered in the name of Germany. He rejected outright the chance to privatize large sectors of the economy, which would have been the simplest way to exploit anti-Bolshevik feelings, and clashed repeatedly with Rosenberg over this critical issue. But Rosenberg was not the only official the loud-mouthed Koch feuded with; his relations with the army and the SS also soon deteriorated too, and Berger, who dealt with him on Himmler's behalf, described him as 'a drunkard, incapable of decent behaviour'. In a hard-hitting indictment which landed on Himmler's desk three years later, one of Koch's subordinates, Alfred Frauenfeld, slammed his 'tactics of brutality born of stupidity and inclination ... supplemented by a complete misunderstanding of political and ideological concepts'. It was all very well, he went on, to have kept saying that the Germans were simply behaving like the British in their colonies; but the outcome could not have been more disastrous for German interests had the British planned it themselves.[32]

After all, despite his outspoken and contemptuous attitudes, Koch depended on Ukrainians for help. His own staff, less than 1,000 strong, was completely reliant on village headmen, mayors and intelligence agents. So were Himmler's policemen. The SiPo/SD branch in Kiev, which ran the province from the old NKVD building in Korolenko Street, had a strength of about 120 officers and seventy interpreters and drivers. Clearly, monitoring Kiev's population of several hundred thousand, let alone the four million inhabitants in the surrounding region, would have been impossible without the expertise of Ukrainian policemen, security detachments and informers. It was their agents who tracked down Jews in hiding and helped uncover stay-behind NKVD cells and underground communist resistance groups.[33]

Rosenberg's influence was greater with the army officers running Heeresgebiet Süd, which controlled much of eastern Ukraine even after the western part passed to Koch in September 1941. Like Rosenberg, the Wehrmacht was inclined to draw a sharp distinction between Ukrainians and Russians. Many of its senior officers remembered supporting the Ukrainian nationalist cause in the First World War, and before Koch's arrival, General Karl Von Roques had stressed to his troops that 'the Ukrainian region is to be viewed as the Lebensraum of a friendly people'. Rosenberg's Wehrmacht liaison officer, Hans Koch (no relation to Erich), was a strong influence. He had been born in Lviv under the

Habsburgs and fought alongside the Ukrainians during and after the First World War. For men like him, the German occupation offered a chance to rebuild the kind of imperial relationships with the Slavs that broke down after the collapse of Franz Joseph's empire.[34]

Unlike Reichskommissar Koch, therefore, the military did often see themselves as bringing 'freedom' to the Ukrainians. They also understood the propaganda value of satisfying the latter's desire to be emancipated from Bolshevism. At the end of November, when the Ukrainian question was discussed at army high command, their agreement with Rosenberg remained undiminished: 'No "Nigger attitude" [*Negerstandpunkt*] – towards Ukrainians, rather rational handling in accordance with the guidelines of Minister Rosenberg,' noted a senior officer there. He was particularly anxious about the impact of requisitioning by Göring's men scouring the Ukraine for foodstuffs: 'If the economic teams ruthlessly deprive the population of their daily bread, reasonable treatment by us is useless. The population will just be driven into the arms of Russian propaganda.' It was thus not only the politically motivated racial contempt of Erich Koch that undermined German–Ukrainian relations; even in areas under military control, the plundering of the region's food supplies in accordance with the ruthless guidelines laid down in Berlin got in the way of a genuine collaboration.[35]

Erich Koch's less aggressive counterpart in the Ostland was Hinrich Lohse, another of Hitler's favoured early Party members. Lohse was 'the very essence of a Nazi small-town big shot', according to one eyewitness, 'a gross, vain, silly man, walrus-like in appearance'. Like Koch, he combined his new posting in Riga with work as a provincial governor back in the Reich (in his case running Schleswig-Holstein); like him, he surrounded himself with cronies from his existing post. He too was a heavy drinker and a gourmand and soon built up a vast and mostly redundant bureaucracy in the Baltic states, where most of the real work of government remained in the hands of local officials. Both men combined a kind of genius for the infighting skills necessary to succeed with Hitler with a hopeless inability to establish an enduring basis for German rule.[36]

But the Baltic states, where the German army was greeted with genuine jubilation, occupied a different place from the Ukraine in the Nazi racial imagination. Hitler and Rosenberg both emphasized that their destiny was to become German. 'Seven hundred years of German activity had already made the Baltic region part of the *Lebensraum* of Greater Germany,' Rosenberg instructed Lohse. 'The goal of a *Reichskommissar* for Estonia, Latvia, Lithuania and White Ruthenia must be to achieve the form of a German protectorate, and then to transform this region into part of the Greater German Reich . . . The Baltic Sea must become a Germanic inland sea under the guardianship of Greater Germany.' In the towns, there was the usual process of Germanization, and the occupiers' popularity quickly sank. In Riga, Hitler, Rosenberg, Göring, Bismarck, Wagner, Moltke, von der Goltz and even the Freikorps lent their names to major thoroughfares, and a German Museum was set up to explain how culture had been brought to the Baltic states by the Germans.[37]

Yet Balts ranked much higher in the Nazi racial hierarchy than Slavs: Germans were not forbidden from marrying them, as they were Poles, for instance, and Latvians, Lithuanians and Estonians were allowed to volunteer for service on the Eastern Front. In the three former Baltic states, the Germans left day-to-day government in the hands of small groups of indigenous senior civil servants and acted in more of a supervisory capacity, especially once they came to appreciate the high calibre of many of those working beneath them. Latvians and Lithuanians continued to run their own police forces, carried out the Germans' anti-Bolshevik and anti-Jewish campaign for them and used their own language on official business except when dealing with Germans. Only Riga itself – home to 10,000 or more German officials – remained under the direct rule of a German mayor.[38]

German rule in the Baltic region thus contrasted with Koch's unrealistically brutal regime in the Ukraine and his determined crushing of all national aspirations. But so, more surprisingly, did another part of the *Ostland*. White Ruthenia – the German term for the huge region mostly carved out of pre-1939 eastern Poland and Soviet Belorussia – formed the southern part of Lohse's huge Reichskommissariat. Based in Minsk, the *Generalkommissar* there was another old Nazi, Wilhelm Kube, a man who had been convicted of embezzlement back in the Reich and stripped of his Party functions. Yet despite numerous shortcomings, he managed to combine genocide with a certain minimal political realism. By the time he was blown up by a bomb placed under his bed by his Belorussian maidservant (who was working for the resistance) in September 1943, the immensely vain and corrupt Kube had come to identify himself with the region and to depend upon a Belorussian political adviser.

Kube liked to imagine himself as a patron of the local culture and to play the potentate. But, unlike Erich Koch, Kube also understood the realities imposed by the shortage of German manpower and he saw the local Slavs were worth cultivating as an anti-Russian force, especially in the face of a growing partisan nuisance. While his policemen massacred the region's Jews, he set up a private guard of young Belorussians and allowed the establishment of political and welfare organizations, relying for advice chiefly on anti-Bolshevik émigrés who had returned to Minsk from Berlin and Warsaw. 'The cultivation of White Ruthenian (in other words, Belorussian) culture, civilization and education is an urgent task of the schools in the province of White Ruthenia,' he proclaimed. He told the locals they owed this cultural revival to Hitler, the creator of the New Europe, and made classes in Belorussian compulsory; Russian and Polish were explicitly forbidden. Rosenberg's policy of an anti-Russian nationalities policy could here be seen emerging in embryo.[39]

But only – one should emphasize – in embryo. Few parts of Europe suffered more under German rule than Belorussia; the official estimate is that more than one in four members of the population died, and 9,000 villages were burned down. The occupation itself always remained precarious and fragile in a marshy and thickly forested terrain that was poorly served with roads or other transportation links. Under Kube, the same battery of repressive decrees came into force as elsewhere, and hundreds of thousands of Belorussians were forcibly rounded up for slave labour in the Reich. And then there was the indiscriminate collective punishment of entire communities, the sadistic treatment of local peasants and the massacres which spread across the countryside in 1942 and 1943. The scale of the destruction was so great – a product of the anti-partisan war, in particular – that even postwar relief workers coming in from devastated Germany and Poland were shocked: Belorussia was far worse than anything they had seen.

In the memoirs which he wrote in prison after the war, Alfred Rosenberg scarcely mentioned any of this. Perhaps this was not surprising since he had spent much of his time as minister commissioning endless plans for how Germany would rule in the East once the war was over, poring over the arcane minutiae of the region's ethnic and economic complexities. As he nostalgically reviewed his wartime experiences, he was especially lyrical about the official tour he had made through the Ukraine in the summer after Stalingrad. Accompanying him were two *Gauleiters*, old friends of his, who

were wide-eyed as, from my special train, they saw the vast spaces of the East. Everything there simply burst out of the accustomed dimensions: the wheat fields, the Tauric steppe, the cherry orchards. They heard the reports of the district commissioners on the great improvements made in handicrafts and support for farmers, and the worries and wishes of the local population. They listened to the blustering of Reichskommissar Koch, who more than once displayed his peacock-like vanity. Then we visited Askania Nova, the tree and bird sanctuary in the steppe, the work of the German colonist Falz-Fein. Shortly thereafter we were in the Crimea, in its magnificent Botanical Gardens, and in the peaceful mood of the evening drank some of the sweet wine of the country. We visited Livadia, and slept where it had once been Schinkel's artistic dream to build a castle above the Black Sea. We passed through Simeis where, twenty-six years ago, I had spent a summer, and looked down on the Black Sea . . .

Apart from the shadow cast by his *bête noire*, Erich Koch, this was a picture of Nazi rule as colonial improvement, the war as the fulfilment of dreams of civilizing the 'great space' in the East. Rosenberg portrayed himself as the heir to the great German creators of the past. There was the wildlife preserve with its protected bison, wild horses, ostriches and antelopes, and the orchards, vineyards and fields of wheat made fruitful by expert cultivation. There was the tourist trip to Tsar Nicholas's famous castle, where, only one and a half years later, Stalin would host Churchill and Roosevelt at the Yalta conference. It was the occupation Rosenberg wished he had shaped, almost a parody of Hitler's own fantasies of the East, an occupation without the burned and empty villages, the piles of bodies, the man-hunts, the ghettoes and the starving cities.[40]

PRISONERS OF WAR

And indeed it might have all been different. As it stormed across the border, the Wehrmacht was welcomed joyfully by much of the population in the western USSR, especially in those areas of Poland and the Baltic states that had been occupied by the Red Army in 1939 and 1940. There was good reason for these emotions for in the final days of

Soviet rule terrible things had happened and worse had been planned. Thousands of people had been murdered by the NKVD before it pulled out: more than 1,500 supposed 'anti-Soviet elements' were slaughtered in Lutsk; over 500 in Dubno. Others were on lists for another round of deportations. In many places the Soviet evacuation itself triggered off unrest and looting. Some officers refused to obey the Kremlin's scorched earth directives, worried about their impact on the civil population left behind, and there were occasional shoot-outs with Party officials. More than once, after the Germans arrived, resentful locals fingered Party members, and they were taken away and shot. Soviet society was breaking down under the impact of invasion, much as French society had done the previous year.[41]

It was scarcely surprising, then, that in numerous areas the Germans were greeted with relief or that deputations of smiling peasant girls met the troops with the traditional flowers, bread and salt. They hoped to get their land back, and put bitter memories of collectivization, famine and deportation behind them. In western Ukraine and the Baltic states, many local nationalists even fired on retreating Soviet soldiers to help the Germans. 'Everybody was glad the Germans had come,' recalled one Ukrainian. 'We greet the German army as liberators from Bolshevism,' others proclaimed. 'Heil Hitler!' An *Einsatzgruppe* report noted in early July that, especially in the areas occupied by the Red Army in 1939, 'the German troops were ... most frequently treated as liberators, and at least with friendly neutrality'. Even the anti-Slav General Hoepner was impressed by the warm welcome his troops received. The local population helped wounded German soldiers and served as guides and carriers under fire.[42]

Within the ranks of the Red Army, many felt similarly, of course. The idea that there was an instantaneous and unanimous Soviet resistance to the Germans is a myth. In fact, while numerous units did fight hard against the invaders, others mutinied and killed their commissars. Soviet reservists tried to evade mobilization, and in general many units manifested little desire to fight. The Soviet high command was sufficiently troubled to set up special units blocking troops from retreating and treated those who straggled back roughly. In mid-July Stalin himself noted that 'on all fronts' many men were 'given to panic and even oriented towards the enemy' who 'at the first pressure throw away their weapons ... and drag others along with them'.[43]

The speed of the Wehrmacht advance was extraordinary. Within two days of launching the invasion, the Germans had captured Grodno, Vilnius and Kaunas; by the end of June, Lviv had fallen too. Army Group North sped through the Baltic states, where conscripts deserted the Red Army to join 'partisan' units fighting with the Germans; Army Group Central pushed eastwards, taking Smolensk in the middle of July, while Army Group South drove into the southern Ukraine. Along the way they captured unexpectedly large numbers of prisoners: 320,000 around Bialystok and Minsk alone in early July; another 300,000 during the battle for Smolensk. By the first week in August, the total number of Soviet POWs was estimated at 900,000; it was one and a half million by the end of the month. Another 660,000 were captured during the struggle for Kiev in September and about the same number in October around the Brjansk-Vjasma pocket. As the rains came and the temperature suddenly plummeted, the Wehrmacht found itself responsible for more than three million Soviet soldiers.[44]

German soldiers had already received mixed messages about how to treat their surrendering Russian counterparts. The Wehrmacht propaganda branch urged soldiers to 'drive a wedge between the Soviet regime and the Soviet people' and even referred to 'the potentially friendly Russian population'. Hitler, in his address to the Germans on the morrow of the invasion, had declared that 'the German people have never harboured any hostile feelings against the nationalities of Russia'.[45] Yet at the same time, he reminded his soldiers that communists were 'no comrades' of theirs, and the army issued warnings about 'the treacherous Soviet way in war'. 'In contrast with the chivalrous way the war was fought in Norway,' one stated, 'every German officer and soldier must bear in mind during the war against Russia the treacherous, deceitful and unsoldierly tactics of the Soviet method of waging war,' Soldiers were especially alerted to look out for intellectuals, commissars and Jews and to expect 'unworthy, sadistic and brutal treatment of the wounded and prisoners of war'.[46]

The soldier's image of the Red Army was hopelessly, and confusingly, racialized. Sometimes it was the Jews whose pernicious influence was held responsible, but often, especially in the early phases of the war, it was also 'Mongols', 'Tatars' or other representatives of the 'Asiatic' hordes from whom the Nazis believed they were saving Europe. The Wehrmacht supreme command's instructions for the conduct of the troops in Russia noted that 'the Asiatic soldiers' of the Red Army in particular are 'impenetrable, unpredictable, insidious and cold-blooded'. Hitler himself talked about a *Mongolensturm*, while German propagandists referred to the 'spineless Slavic-Mongol pap' that comprised the human matter of the USSR. Sometimes it sounded as though Barbarossa was a duel between Goths and Nordic peoples on the one hand and Tatar *Untermenschen* on the other. These racial stereotypes played an important role in the tragedy that unfolded.[47]

The Wehrmacht had considerable experience handling large numbers of prisoners of war. In the Polish campaign, it captured more than half a million soldiers; in the summer of 1940, it held another two million after the collapse of the Dutch, Belgian and French armies. Unable to look after them all, the Germans had quickly released all the Dutch prisoners on parole, as well as Flemish Belgians, and almost one-third of the Frenchmen. Arguing that because Poland had ceased to exist as a state, Polish soldiers could no longer legitimately be regarded as POWs under the Geneva Convention, the Germans used them instead as civilian workers. This bending of the international rules regarding prisoners of war put the Poles (like the Yugoslavs and (in 1943–4) the Italians) in a disadvantageous position, but it was nothing compared with what lay in store for prisoners from the Red Army.[48]

During the summer and autumn of 1941, German military lawyers fought a long and ultimately unsuccessful battle with their own superiors over the treatment of Soviet POWs. They insisted that whether or not the USSR had fully adhered to the Hague Convention and the 1929 Geneva Red Cross Convention on POWs was irrelevant: the Germans should treat captured Soviet soldiers properly. But General Field Marshal Keitel, head of the OKW, lived up to his nickname as Hitler's 'Little Lackey' (*Lakeitel*) and rebuffed their advice. 'These doubts correspond to military ideas about wars of chivalry,' he wrote. 'Our job is to suppress a way of life.' The lawyers had a small success in getting the idea dropped of threatening to deport 500 Jews to the East for every German soldier killed in Soviet custody. But Helmuth von Moltke, the Abwehr's international law expert, had sleepless nights. 'My memory of the last two days is none too good,' he wrote in November. 'Russian prisoners, evacuated Jews, Russian prisoners, shot hostages, the gradual extension into Germany of measures "tested" in the occupied territories, evacuated

Jews again, Russian prisoners, a nerve clinic where SS men are cared for who have broken down while executing women and children. That is what the world has been for these two days.'[49]

OKW had reckoned on approximately 1.35 million Soviet POWs in camps in the General Government and Germany itself, as well as others in the occupied territories. Yet several factors conspired to throw these calculations badly out. In the first place, the war did not end in a matter of weeks or months, as Hitler had intended, and this put a strain on food, transportation and supply. Second, Hitler himself prohibited the transportation of Soviet POWs to the Reich on racial grounds, increasing bottlenecks and intense overcrowding in transit camps far from the developed infrastructure found further west. And thirdly, the numbers turned out to be much greater than OKW had ever envisaged. At Nuremberg, Keitel and Jodl tried to defend themselves by stressing the logistical difficulties. More recently, some historians have echoed them. In the words of one, this was 'mass starvation' but not 'mass murder'. But it is not so easy to disentangle what happened from the ideological attitudes described earlier.[50]

Racialism and policy reinforced one another, for instance, in the case of early prisoner releases. Even before Operation Barbarossa, the army had released only Flemish Belgians, treated French colonial troops far worse than white ones and had planned to hold Jewish POWs captured in the Polish army separately from non-Jews. In the Russian campaign, too, racial and political concerns dictated who would be allowed to return home. Soviet POWs of Baltic nationality got preferential treatment as did Ukrainians, especially farmers – whom Göring and the army wanted for the harvest. On the other hand, the army high command ordered that 'Asiatics (depending on their race), Jews and German-speaking Russians' were to be deployed as frontline labour battalions. Overall, the numbers of those released remained less than 10 per cent of the total number. Of the more than 3 million Soviet POWs who died in German custody during the entire war, two-thirds never left the occupied territories and remained under the supervision of the Wehrmacht in one form or another.[51]

From the earliest days of the invasion, as long lines of prisoners were herded away from the front lines, guards shot stragglers and even – as in Poland previously – local peasants who left food by the roadside. A young Polish boy, Waldemar Lotnik, watched a column of 15,000 men trudge slowly past him for over an hour; guards killed them if they collapsed and opened fire when they fell greedily on the vegetables he and his grandfather were carrying on their cart. Some senior German officers were shocked. 'It is horrible, the impression made by the ten thousand Russian prisoners of war who, scarcely guarded, find themselves marching from Smolensk,' wrote Field Marshal von Bock in October. 'Deathly pale and half starved, these unfortunates stagger hence. Many of them have collapsed dead and exhausted along the road.' After the war, Bock's adjutant was more graphic: 'Columns of men marching, kilometres long, were guarded by 10–20 *Landesschützen*, who kept up the rear and shot with a machine pistol anyone unable to keep up . . . This was not the result of the heat of the battle but rather the orders issued by the highest leadership from a kind of irreligious arrogance.'[52]

Perhaps nothing changed the civilians' perceptions of the Germans' intentions so much as these death marches with the emaciated corpses they left behind them. 'We have lost all sympathy of the population,' wrote an observer in the Ukraine. 'The people cannot understand the shooting of exhausted prisoners of war in villages and larger localities and leaving their bodies there.'[53] Marching starving Soviet soldiers through the heart of Kiev and other cities seemed deliberately designed to intimidate the local inhabitants. The guards received conflicting instructions, sometimes told to save their fire only for those seeking to escape, at others reminded to show 'extreme alertness, the greatest caution and deepest mistrust'; they were to respond to the slightest signs of resistance with 'ruthlessness' and to make 'unsparing use' of their weapons. Some enjoyed their power and tormented the prisoners with pieces of bread.[54]

Eventually, the Soviet POWs were crowded into holding pens, surrounded by barbed wire, filled many times beyond their intended capacity. There were, by the second half of 1941, no fewer than eighty-one POW camps in the German operational zone, of which forty-seven were transit camps. With hundreds of thousands of men stranded in them, medical supplies quickly ran out, and typhus and other diseases spread. As the steppe sun beat down, extreme dehydration and the summer heat drove some prisoners mad. They were guarded by tiny numbers of Germans, and poorly trained Ukrainians and other non-Russians, keen to prove their reliability to their new masters. A mere ninety-two guards watched over 18,000 prisoners in Dulag (Transit Camp) 131, thirty men over 8,550 in Dulag 220.

From August, things got worse still. The Wehrmacht was now entering areas devastated by the Red Army's scorched earth tactics, and food was in short supply. As the weather worsened and turned the roads to mud, the huge numbers captured in the massive encirclement operations in September and October intensified the logistical strain. 'The numbers of POWs in Brjansk are increasing critically . . . and their transportation is not possible,' recorded one unit in the field. A week later, things were more desperate still: 'The POW problem grows ever more serious . . . There are also provisioning problems since the personnel in the transit camp cannot cope . . . To make matters worse, the rainy season is upon us, hindering the use of lorries except on good roads, and the fact is that in the immediate vicinity of Brjansk there are no more supplies of food to be obtained.'[55]

By this point, rather than waiting for Berlin to organize long-range transportation, some commanders set up POW work units to search for provisions, enlisted the help of local villagers and reminded their own men of the need to treat the prisoners properly. But it was much too little, too late. The death toll rose inexorably. As early as July, there had been mass starvation among the prisoners in Minsk, site of the first major encirclement, and death rates rose sharply after outbreaks of dysentery and typhus. 54,000 had died in camps in the General Government alone by 20 October; another 45,690 died in the next ten days. Further east, by November, the mortality *daily* in the Brjansk-Vjasma pocket was between 0.6 and 2.2 per cent. In Bobruisk, starving prisoners attempted to break out at night and were shot; the following morning 1,700 – one in ten – lay dead. Long before the world discovered the grisly sight of the overcrowded SS camps in the Reich in 1945, the Wehrmacht's own POW camps – unseen by any journalists – had contained horrors that were, if anything, greater still in their magnitude. By February 1942, only 1.1 million Soviet POWs remained alive (of the 3.9 million originally captured), and of these only 400,000 were able to work. The overall mortality rate for Soviet POWs in German hands during the Second World War was 57.5 per cent; as many British and American soldiers died in German captivity during the whole war as died in these camps in one day. It was hardly surprising that German generals themselves believed that 'the Führer wishes for the decimation of the Slavic masses'.[56]

Food shortages were one of the key problems. In September 1941, State Secretary Backe in the German Food Ministry ordered the Wehrmacht to feed itself from the occupied territories. Given the disruption to the harvest already caused by the war, this would not have been easy in the best of circumstances. By October, it was widely appreciated in Berlin that it meant many POWs would die. In the General Government a staff officer noted that 'mass deaths among the [Soviet] prisoners of war cannot be prevented because the prisoners are at the end of their strength'. When Backe blocked proposals to move large numbers of POWs westwards, fearing the impact on food consumption in the Reich itself, the army's quartermaster-general introduced a distinction significant primarily for the assumption that lay behind it: the army could try to feed POWs in labour details, but 'non-working prisoners . . . are supposed to starve'.[57]

In fact, the entire Soviet population was affected, not just the POWs – especially in the towns. Many urban areas had been devastated by the fighting, by sabotage or by the explosives that the NKVD planted to detonate after they withdrew. But Hitler in any case planned to raze the major Russian cities, and to use hunger to depopulate them. He ordered Kiev to be reduced to rubble, and was furious when he was disobeyed. As it was, German roadblocks were set up to prevent food entering the city, and illegal markets were broken up. The regional army commander protested, and others too criticized what they called the 'extermination' policy, but it was upheld by Göring. Kiev's population fell from 850,000 in June 1941 to 400,000 in October and 295,000 by mid-1943. By November 1941, the chief Wehrmacht armaments inspector in the Ukraine was in despair. 'In the last analysis,' he warned, 'only the Ukrainians can produce objects of economic value through their work. If we shoot the Jews, let the prisoners of war die, allow much of the big city population to starve to death, we cannot answer the question: *Who will then produce economic assets here?*' What even he did not apparently realize was that the policy was deliberate. Other cities were also to be allowed to starve, whether through occupation or siege. The Kiev experience led Göring to state that it was more trouble than it was worth to occupy big cities, especially as Germany would then be 'responsible for the food supply'. 'The greater the chaos in Russia,' ordained Hitler in early October, 'the easier for us to administer and exploit the occupied Eastern territories.'[58]

As the spring of 1942 approached, Rosenberg – who had no real influence in this area of policy – warned that the death of millions of Soviet POWs would be likely to have catastrophic consequences. It would strengthen the resistance of the Red Army and prolong the war. It would also hinder the proper administration and exploitation of the occupied territories. Although in some cases, he alleged, camp commanders had welcomed help in feeding the prisoners, mostly they had rejected this, preferring to let the inmates starve or freeze. Like several of the army's field commanders, Rosenberg even criticized the excessive number of executions on 'political' grounds. Hitler had refused to withdraw the Commissar Order, even though it stiffened resistance and deterred many communists from changing sides.

Rosenberg charged Himmler in particular with racial and political naivety. The SS had picked out and killed groups among the POWs (such as Soviet Muslims) who were potentially an important source of pro-German support. Although his ministry had constantly drawn Himmler's attention to this, an execution squad turned up in November at a POW camp near Nikolajev to 'liquidate "Asiatics" '. Criticizing the attitude that, because the Poles had been harshly treated, those further east must be more toughly treated still, Rosenberg complained that the result had been to alienate a population more anti-Bolshevik and therefore potentially pro-German than the inhabitants of western Europe, whose own treatment had been much milder. He concluded optimistically, 'Every camp commander should henceforth be responsible for turning his POWs into propagandists for Germany when they later return home.'[59]

By February 1942, though, the propaganda war was the last thing on POW camp commanders' minds. Johannes Gutschmidt, for instance, was a sixty-five-year-old former officer in the Wilhelmine army and a confirmed royalist. Although he had fewer than 200 men under his command he found himself guarding as many as 30,000 POWs at a time. Doing his best to find food and medical supplies for his detainees, he worried about their lack of shelter from the rain as well as the camp's vulnerability to partisans reportedly gathering in the woods near by. At the end of October, Gutschmidt recorded the first act of cannibalism in his camp; several prisoners had eaten part of a dead comrade. By mid-November, many of them were dying despite some food being available: they were worn out and suffering from the lack of proper accommodation. As the thermometer plummeted below freezing, the mortality rate approached 1 per cent daily. A typhus epidemic was raging across the camps of the area. Elsewhere, things were even worse: at another camp in Vjasma, there had been 4,000 deaths, and the commander had been threatened with investigation by his shocked superior. On 21 January 1942 Gutschmidt had two Russian soldiers who had been surprised eating corpses shot; the next day, he marked the anniversary of the Kaiser's birthday. The final entry in his diary, in early March, is a gloomy one:

8 March 1942 [Smolensk]
Now all the POWs capable of work are to be sent to Germany to free up armaments workers there for the front. Of the millions of prisoners only a few thousands are capable of working. So unbelievably many have starved to death, many are ill with typhus and the rest are so weak and pitiful that they can't work in this state. The German administration failed to provide them with enough provisions, and there's likely to be a nasty bust-up when so few come to Germany to work.[60]

From the German point of view, this was indeed the most counter-productive aspect of the whole business. Not its impact on the horrified local population, which now rightly read into the emaciated corpses a wider programme of deprivation which ultimately targeted them too. Not the impact on the Red Army, the soldiers of which resisted with much greater determination. Rather it was the fact that Soviet POWs had been allowed to die in enormous numbers while the Reich suffered from a huge and growing shortfall of manpower. Had the war been over as quickly as Hitler hoped, this would not have mattered, and the winding-down of the war economy would have seen the shortfall shrink. Labour was simply not a priority as long as victory seemed imminent. Even when things changed, in the autumn, when Berlin's planners – faced with 2.6 million vacancies – realized they needed to think ahead, the fear that Soviet POWs would spread disease or Bolshevism blocked their transportation to Germany. Reports that they were dying en masse were not taken very seriously, and Göring awoke too late to their potential value for the Reich war economy. The result, as Rosenberg noted bitterly, was that, of what he estimated as 3.6 million captives, only a 'few hundred thousand' were capable of work.[61]

THE PARTISAN WAR

As the Germans battled east, their instructions left them in no doubt how to deal with resistance. While the combat troops thrust ahead, security divisions and SS *Einsatzgruppen* would crush any opposition through mass executions and reprisals. How ironic it was, then, that there were no prewar Soviet plans for resistance at all, since Stalin believed that in any future war with Germany, the struggle would be waged on the enemy's soil. He regarded talk of partisan warfare as tantamount to defeatism, stopped planning for it in the late 1930s and ignored Zhukov's warning early in 1941 that Germany might occupy Soviet territory in the event of war.

After the invasion, however, attitudes in the Kremlin changed fast. Within a week it had called for Party and Soviet officials to 'establish partisan detachments and diversion groups'; bridges, roads, phone and cable lines and supply depots were to be destroyed to disrupt the advance. By mid-July, there were plans to foment resistance by sending help behind the German lines, and instructions to Party leaders in districts threatened with imminent occupation to prepare by organizing underground cells. They were ordered 'to personally lead the struggle in the enemy rear ... by example'. 'Destruction battalions', which had been initially formed to deal with German parachutists dropped behind the Soviet lines, were to be converted into partisan formations once the Germans had occupied their area.

Yet in the chaos of the first phase of the invasion, it took time for these instructions to take effect. The first partisan detachments were often formed by local Party members or soldiers on their own initiative and lacked expertise, equipment and coordination. These were problems that could not easily be overcome, even in regions where the terrain favoured irregular warfare. Whilst it would be an exaggeration, as some historians have claimed, to suggest that the Germans were facing an imaginary enemy in the remaining months of 1941 – they were not – they were certainly not facing the coordinated and effective partisan force that began to emerge only a year later. South of Leningrad, for instance, there were about 4,000 partisans in the winter of 1941, mostly sabotaging rail lines and bridges rather than killing Germans. By mid-December, finding food and shelter and coping with the hostility of local peasants had become at least as urgent for them as attacking the occupiers.[62]

Hitler himself was delighted that Stalin had called for resistance. It opened the door, he decided, to the possibility of 'exterminating all that stands against us'; pacifying the vast areas so far won required shooting 'anyone who even looks askance at us'. The military high command followed the Führer's lead. Resistance should be broken by such terror that the population lost 'all inclination to resist', Field Marshal Brauchitsch warned of Bolshevik 'bestiality', and mandated 'harshness' through summary executions and the burning of entire villages.

Yet standing orders did not in themselves determine the troops' behaviour and in fact many frontline units behaved more reasonably towards civilians than their orders suggested they should. 'During the first days after the occupation of these *raioni*,' ran a Leningrad regional report, 'the Germans conducted a policy of sweetening the population. Initially ... the Germans didn't take anything from the population. Even more, they gave children sweets, peasants sugar.' Army officers encouraged the opening of churches and promoted the idea, readily believed in some areas, that 'Soviet power will not return'. 'Soviet power is clearly finished,' peasants warned would-be partisans, 'since almost all of Russia has been captured by the Germans': escaped POWs were turned away by villagers who feared the German reaction if discovered. In other cases villagers requested German protection to stop partisans stealing their crops and kidnapping local people. The early summer of 1941 saw many army commanders soft-pedalling the harsh orders they had been given, realizing a conciliatory policy made better sense. In July, OKH issued advice to avoid reprisals against local communities for attacks which were not carried out by them.[63]

Yet as the front swept onwards, it left ever-larger areas of forest, marsh and steppe to be policed by rear-area security detachments, which faced immense difficulties in restoring order. This was the first time the Wehrmacht had faced resistance lasting more than a few weeks, and the unpleasantness of the experience was multiplied by the heavy losses it was suffering on the front. Deserters, escapees and POWs released from German captivity roamed the roads and were seen as a potential security threat. Reliable intelligence was scarce, and the troops themselves were hopelessly stretched. 707 Infantry Division, with only 4,500 men, was initially responsible for the entire Generalkommissariat Weissruthenien

– a territory of 60,000 square kilometres and two million inhabitants. To make matters worse, heavy losses at the front drained manpower: 281st Security Division, in north-west Russia, dropped as a result of transfers from 11,449 to 3,137 men between June and August 1941. Since the best troops went first, the division ended up with middle-aged reservists roaming the back roads on bicycles. Concentrated in 'strongpoints' along the main roads and railway lines, they felt themselves surrounded by spies and saboteurs, estranged from the local population by their ignorance of languages, their racism and fear.[64]

As the summer progressed, these depleted German security units faced new problems. The Red Army's scorched earth tactics had left ruins behind, and civilians behind the pre-1939 borders were much less friendly than those in the western territories. Worse, the psychological advantage had shifted, and the end of the war no longer appeared imminent. With huge numbers of ex-Red Army personnel trapped behind the German lines, the conditions for resistance coalesced, and by the end of August, the first real signs of partisan activity appeared. It was now that the troops in the Army Group Centre rear area started behaving far more ruthlessly than they had before, shooting civilians in larger numbers and killing any Red Army soldiers that they encountered. General von Schenckendorff demanded that after 16 September every 'escaped Red Army soldier still roaming around' between the Beresina and Dnepr rivers be shot on sight. But even before this, officers in 221st Security Division had called for harsher measures and stepped up the killing of 'suspected partisans'.[65]

Through October and November, the civilian death toll in Belorussia and the Ukraine rose fast. Troops of 403rd Security Division, which had a reputation for ferocity, were at one point burning several villages a week as well as shooting dozens of 'partisans' – often they were really Red Army soldiers cut off from their unit hiding in the woods trying to avoid capture. There was a clear linkage between the German treatment of POWs and the partisan threat: many soldiers were only trying to return home when the Germans arrested or shot them, hoping to avoid the starvation that awaited them in German POW camps. Escape into the woods often seemed the safer option, turning the Germans' suspicion into a self-fulfilling prophecy. According to 286th Security Division,

In part, these people are prisoners who have escaped from or been left behind by the prisoner-of-war columns marching through the locality. In part, they have been sent to the rear by front-line troops accompanied not by German personnel but only by the general instruction to 'go west'. Most were wandering around weaponless. However, that doesn't rule out the possibility that vagrant individuals, particularly officers, might join partisan groups that they stumble across.

Some units ordered refugees 'as a matter of principle' to be arrested or 'liquidated'.[66]

One other factor helped reduce the troops' inhibitions against widespread killing of non-combatants and that was their ready identification of their enemy with the Jews. Their May guidelines had specified ruthlessness against 'Bolshevik inciters, guerillas, saboteurs, Jews and the complete elimination of all active and passive resistance'. Even General Lemelsen, who – unusually – protested the 'irresponsible, senseless and criminal' shootings of prisoners of war and civilians, saw Bolshevism as the product of 'a Jewish and criminal group'. Such views made it seem logical to single out Jews for collective punishment, either for what the Bolsheviks had done already or for attacks on German troops. This was the rationale behind the army's abortive proposal to deport Jews in retaliation for any reported killings of German POWs. And from the start of the invasion, there were mass shootings by Wehrmacht units as well as by the *Einsatzgruppen* and their local helpers. Starting in the Baltic in late June, such massacres spread through eastern Poland into the Ukraine.

The SS was pushing hard to make the connection between Bolshevism, the partisans and Jewish civilians and demanding the killing of women and children. In late July, Himmler ordered a 'mopping-up operation' around Pinsk and suggested driving the Jewish women and children there into the nearby swamps to drown. When the troops reported that the water was too shallow, they were shot in mass executions. Himmler's orders shocked even some of the SS men themselves, and, although they talked of being involved in anti-partisan operations, it was clear to them, as to everyone else, that this was something very different. A few days later there was particularly grisly confirmation of this. In a small Ukrainian town, a group of ninety abandoned small children was discovered who had accidentally been overlooked following the visit of one of the *SS-Sonderkommandos* there. When General von Reichenau decided that 'the operation . . . had to be completed in a suitable way', they were shot by Ukrainian auxiliaries. The Wehrmacht officer who had found them likened the idea of shooting them to an NKVD atrocity; his comrades, however, explained that 'the elimination of the Jewish women and children was a matter of urgent necessity whatever form it took'. [67]

But the Wehrmacht still generally understood these killings as part of a war against partisans and saboteurs. At the end of September, more than 33,000 Jews from Kiev were shot in the Babi Yar ravine outside the city. The Babi Yar massacre itself is notorious. What is less well-known is that it came at the start of the German occupation of the city, after delayed Soviet mines blew up many members of the newly installed military administration there and created chaos and panic among the German troops. In fact, much of the city's population was relieved to see the back of the NKVD and helped the Germans track down and defuse other mines. Both the Germans and many Ukrainians readily blamed the Jews for the explosions and linked them to the 'partisans'. The Wehrmacht had already made plans to round up the remaining Jewish men for forced labour when the explosions took place. Together with the SS, they decided instead to carry out a mass 'punishment action' on a hitherto unprecedented scale. The shooting in the ravine itself was carried out by German SS police and Ukrainian guards, who then covered up the site by setting off explosives in the ravine walls, before getting down to the business of sorting through the clothes and money that had belonged to their victims. By this point in the invasion, mass killing of Jews was sufficiently commonplace for the executioners to have known how to organize things to maximize the spoils. [68]

In short, by the autumn of 1941, Jews were being massacred in great numbers under the guise of the anti-partisan war. As one of Himmler's closest associates, Artur Nebe, commander of Einsatzgruppe B, told the troops, 'Where there are partisans there are Jews and where there are Jews there are partisans.' In the Ukraine, the pro-Nazi Field Marshal von Reichenau – one of Hitler's favourite senior generals – issued an order commanding his men to show 'full understanding of the necessity for tough but just atonement of Jewish *Untermenschentum*'. 'The war against the enemy behind the front,' he went on, 'has not been pursued toughly enough.' Coming days after the Babi Yar massacre, this was a green light for mass murder and a strong indication to the troops to give the SS their unquestioning support. Other senior generals followed suit.

'This struggle against the Soviet Armed Forces is not to be pursued only according to the European rules of war,' declared the 11th Army commander, von Manstein, the following month.

> It will also be fought behind the front: partisans, snipers in civilian clothes, attack isolated soldiers and small units ... Jewry [*Das Judentum*] forms the intermediary between the enemy in the rear and the still-battling remainder of the Red Army and the Red Leadership ... The Judeo-Bolshevik system must be exterminated once and for all and never again allowed to assail our European *Lebensraum*.[69]

From October onwards – as the new tougher guidelines coincided with intensified partisan activity – the civilian death toll rose sharply. The hostage policy also developed an anti-Jewish dimension of its own. In the Balkans, the entire Jewish population of Belgrade was rounded up by the military commander there to serve as hostages. In the Ukraine, the commanding general of Army Rear Area South, Karl von Roques, instructed troops to select Jews and Russians for reprisal executions in preference to Ukrainians. This certainly did not mean an end to the killing of Ukrainians (or indeed Serbs); on the contrary, peasants continued to be killed in vast numbers in reprisal raids – women and children included. But the latter, unlike the Jews, were generally being targeted in the context of an actual anti-partisan war.[70]

By October and November, German soldiers and police units had instructions to make the Jews 'disappear' from the countryside, and counter-insurgency had become a cover for genocide. Early in the morning of 6 October, for instance, a squad of fifteen members of an infantry regiment stationed in a small Belorussian town was told to shoot the approximately 1,000 Jews who lived there. This they did, in batches of ten, before they moved on to villages near by. Volunteers among them participated eagerly in these 'Jew games'; on their return, their commanding officer announced that 'partisans had been shot in action'. Yet as one of the perpetrators confirmed after the war, 'In reality, it was generally known in the company that this meant Jews who were in no way partisans.' By early December, such units, together with police detachments, had shot approximately 20,000 Belorussian Jews. Six months later, Generalkommissar Wilhelm Kube wrote from Minsk that with 'Jewry . . . the main bearer of the partisan movement' in the region, 55,000 Belorussian Jews had been 'liquidated' in ten weeks and anticipated that the few who remained alive would eventually also be shot, ruling out – as he put it – the risk that the partisans 'can still rely to any real extent on Jewry'.[71]

By this point, the identification of Jews as partisans had become a self-fulfilling prophecy: with no other refuge available, the handful of survivors of the region's prewar Jewish population of nearly one million gravitated towards the partisans. Yet despite the existence of Jewish partisan brigades and encampments, Jews made up barely 5 per cent of the overall partisan strength. Killing Jews was effective because it was so easy. But it had little impact in practice against an enemy made up mostly of Belorussians, Ukrainians and Russians.[72]

TOWARDS THE FINAL SOLUTION

Even where there was no partisan threat, Jews were being singled out from the earliest days of the invasion and executed. Following a fierce struggle to capture the key Baltic port of Liepaja (Libau) from the Soviets at the end of June, the Wehrmacht encouraged the defenders to surrender by letting them know that: 'We won't do anything to you. We're only killing Jews and communists.' Ordinary soldiers as well as members of SS-Einsatzkommando 1a murdered Jewish civilians in the town and nearby villages over the next few days. Army commanders introduced the first discriminatory decrees against Jews, forcing them to present themselves for work and to wear a yellow star and banning them from public places. And it was the garrison commandant in Liepaja who instructed a local SS execution squad to start mass executions which ran into mid-July and which eventually numbered no fewer than 2,500 victims. These events were exceptional only in their timing; six months later, they had become commonplace right across the occupied territories.[73]

The Liepaja massacres pointed to the close cooperation between the army and the SS, fired by an ideological fervour that identified Jews with criminality and Bolshevism. 'The struggle against Bolshevism,' ordered OKW on 12 September 1941, 'requires a ruthless and energetic assault above all against the Jews, the main carriers of Bolshevism.'[74] One should also note the spectacular character of much of the killing itself, which frequently took place in full view of soldiers and civilians alike. In the eastern Latvian town of Daugavpils, 13,000 Jews were killed partly in public gardens in its centre, and partly at a nearby weekend recreation spot. This was not the secret killing of the Polish death camps in the following year; on the contrary it formed the sequel to a kind of murderous martyrology. For as the Germans marched into one town after another in the region occupied by the Red Army after September 1939, the corpses left behind by the NKVD would typically be brought and laid out in public view, and other victims of Bolshevism would also be commemorated. The Jews would be singled out as responsible and forced to exhume the bodies and rebury them before themselves falling victims to the Germans and their helpers. Bringing the killing openly into the market-places of villages and towns, the Germans were implicitly warning local non-Jews of what could happen to them, and at the same time making them complicit.[75]

Despite the involvement of the Wehrmacht in the killing itself, anti-Jewish policy was the preserve of the SS. Heydrich's instructions to the *Einsatzgruppen* initially defined their 'self-cleaning campaign' chiefly in terms of the struggle against Bolshevism. On 2 July they were told to liquidate communist officials and 'Jews in party and state positions' as well as 'other radical elements (saboteurs, propagandists, snipers, attempted political murderers, agitators, etc.)'. But they were also to encourage local populations to begin 'attempts at self-cleansing on the part of anti-communist or anti-Semitic elements in the areas to be occupied' – a green light for the massacres that erupted in several parts of western Ukraine and the Baltic in the first weeks of occupation. This second set of orders suggested a much wider targeting of Jews than the first and meant getting local anti-Semites to do the SS's dirty work without leaving a potentially incriminating paper trail behind.[76] Thus the *Einsatzgruppen* quickly encouraged pogroms and massacres among what they initially described as 'Lithuanian partisan groups' (meaning pro-German militias) and 'independent groups'. Even so, the pace of the killing was too slow for the SS. On 13 July, the head of Einsatzgruppe B reported that 'only 96 Jews have been executed in the first few days' in Grodno and Lida; as a result, 'I have ordered that greater efforts must be made.' In Latvia, the Germans were initially disappointed at local passivity, though the murderous energy shown by the police and fascist groups soon changed their mind.[77]

Latvia and Lithuania, with their relatively small Jewish populations and widespread popular bitterness at the short-lived but severe Soviet occupation, became the initial laboratory for genocide. Rosenberg's civilian administrators eyed Jewish property and hoped to concentrate the Jews themselves in ghettoes as a captive labour force. But the SS, which was deeply frustrated by the impasse of Jewish policy in Poland and wanted to avoid similar delays in the Soviet case, had something far more dramatic in mind. According to Himmler's representative, the former Gestapo official Franz Stahlecker, who arrived in Riga after serving in Vienna, Prague and Norway, the Baltic region offered the chance of a truly 'radical handling of the Jewish question' for the first time: Baltic Jews *could* be eradicated because they were not nearly so important in the economy as they were in the General Government; moreover, they *had* to be eradicated because, unlike there, they functioned as 'carriers of Bolshevism'. Stahlecker told Rosenberg's men they would 'cleanse the countryside' and concentrate Jews in a few towns, where they would be 'selected' according to their ability to work. It was a recipe for systematic mass murder that merely nodded to the needs of the local war economy.[78]

Stahlecker was as good as his word, and his Einsatzgruppe A unleashed a murderous wave of killings across the region. Pushing for total annihilation, urged on by Himmler himself and helped by the appointment of the murderous Friedrich Jeckeln as higher SS and police leader in Riga in October 1941, the SS overrode all the objections of Rosenberg and Lohse. By early 1942, according to Stahlecker's own reckoning, it had killed 229,052 Jews, and only 3,700 remained as labourers in camps and ghettoes in Latvia, and 34,500 in Lithuania: the Baltic region had the grim distinction of becoming the first part of Europe to be declared *judenfrei*. It was – from the SS's point of view – an achievement and an opportunity: the fast-emptying ghettoes of the *Ostland* now beckoned as the place to which they could deport and ultimately kill the surviving Jews of Germany itself, bypassing the General Government. Transports from Germany, Austria and the Protectorate went through the winter of 1941–2 to Riga and Minsk, where many were shot immediately. Half of those sent to Riga were dead within a few months. Of the thousands of German Jews who reached Minsk, only ten were still alive at Liberation.

Native auxiliary units did much of the actual killing, led by men like Latvian policeman Viktors Arajs. In the Baltic, policemen and their families had been previously singled out by the NKVD. But some conception of revenge was not the only motive for sadistic 'Jew-haters' like Arajs: national fervour, the intoxication of power and greed drove them too. Often drunk, he and his men tortured, raped and killed their way across the Latvian countryside. Regular police units also helped by arresting and guarding Jews until the killing squads could arrive. Dutiful village constables received their orders, drove out to farms where Jews were reported to be hiding and shot them in the fields or woods near by, ordering farmhands to bury the bodies.[79]

The other SS killing squads did their best to keep up with Stahlecker. In the middle of October, when Einsatzgruppe A was already reporting 118,430 Jews shot in the *Ostland* (alongside 3,387 'communists'), Einsatzgruppe C further south boasted a tally of approximately 75,000 Jews. A month later, Einsatzgruppe B estimated its victims to the end of October at 45,467, and on 12 December the southernmost Einsatzgruppe D reported 54,696, of whom the vast majority were Jews. If we bear in mind that other SS detachments and – as we have seen – Wehrmacht units too, were also targeting Jews in mass shootings and 'mopping-up operations', it seems likely that by the end of the year at least half a million Jews had been killed by German forces behind the front lines, a figure that had probably risen by another 50 per cent when spring came.[80]

Historically, Eastern Europe was not a place where the killing of civilians was unknown. Nevertheless, these huge numbers dwarfed the death toll in either the ongoing anti-partisan war or previous anti-Jewish campaigns in territories under German control. Nothing like this – whether in terms of numbers or systematic organization – had been experienced in Tsarist pogroms or during the bloody interregnum of 1918–19, when thousands died at the hands of Polish and Ukrainian bands. Local anti-Semitism was often on display; it allowed the Germans to recruit helpers and it made it hard often for the victims to escape or hide. But it was not the prime cause. That was a series of German policy decisions. What these events show is that some time in the early autumn, the Nazi leadership resolved to try to rid the occupied Soviet territories of their Jewish population.

Yet although half a million Jews may have already perished by the end of 1941, there were perhaps another two million in former Soviet territories who still remained alive. *Einsatzgruppen* leaders themselves believed that, while they were 'wiping out the Jews to the greatest possible extent', outside the Baltic 'a complete liquidation of the Jews is not feasible, at least not at the moment'. It was not just the sheer size of the USSR's Jewish population, compared with the rather small number of SS units – scarcely 3,000 men in total – assigned to the task. Nor was it only the winter which slowed things down, nor the population's increasing unwillingness to support German killers the further east they went. It was also the crucial role played by Jews as craftsmen and workers in the local economy of many towns. Even some Germans felt that the Jews were not the sole source of 'political danger' and argued that 'we should not neglect the main task of destroying the communist system in favour of the easier job of destroying the Jews'. According to others, the fact that large numbers of Jews had fled across the Urals 'represents a major contribution to the solution of the Jewish question in Europe'. In other words, to many involved in the killing machinery of the occupation itself, there were compelling political and economic reasons not to aim for a total annihilation of the region's Jewish population.[81]

But this was not how the policy-makers in Berlin saw matters. For them, economic considerations took second place to extermination, and over the winter of 1941/2, the killing apparatus was reinforced. Gas vans from Berlin toured the Belorussian and Ukrainian countryside, providing mobile gassing facilities; at the same time, as the killing accelerated, the strain on the small *Einsatzgruppen* units was gradually eased by a huge build-up of gendarmerie forces and their auxiliaries in the areas of civil administration: by mid-1942 they numbered 165,000 and by early 1943 rose to a maximum of some 300,000. It was these German policemen and their Ukrainian helpers who carried out many of the executions from 1942 onwards.[82]

In Belorussia, where most Jews had survived through into the winter of 1941, administrators launched a new round of massacres in early 1942, held up only by the frozen earth, which 'prevented the digging of pits as required by mass graves for the Jews'. Once the thaw came, the shooting intensified. Generalkommissar Kube, who needed time to get used to the idea of executing Jews transported from Germany – among them decorated war veterans, who came 'from the same cultural circles as ourselves' – did not show the same concern for members of 'the bestial hordes' of the region. The crowded Minsk ghetto was soon home to tens of thousands of shivering, destitute and terrified people, sheltering amid the ruins that had survived the German takeover. Most of these were murdered in a series of executions that took place during 1942. By early 1943 Kube was proudly showing horrified Italians inside the church in Minsk, where vast mountains of suitcases and packages testified to the success of the genocide.

In the Ukraine, Koch too was keen to see the Jews killed off to reduce the local demand on food and he encouraged his men to cooperate with the SS. Himmler himself urged his SS and police leaders to implement in full his orders to kill all the Jews in order to 'clean the Ukraine for the future settlement of Germans'. At the end of July 1942, he impatiently resolved a long-running argument over definitions of Jewishness with the injunction not to get lost in definitions: the main thing was that 'the occupied Eastern territories must become free of Jews'. Rosenberg's civilian administrators cooperated readily registering Jews, and forcing those living in isolated country areas into makeshift ghettoes. In fact, Rosenberg's men gradually regained control of their own police forces from Himmler's SS. But this did not mean any lessening in the pace of the murders. On the contrary, the second wave of killings, which lasted through 1942 into the following year, was even more lethal than that of 1941–2. One recent estimate suggests that twice as many Jews died after April 1942 as before it.[83]

By the time the Germans withdrew, well over two million Jews inside the borders of 1941 had been killed. Of these perhaps 1.6 million had lived within the territories taken over by the USSR after 1939. Thus geography turns out to have been of crucial importance. Jews bore the brunt of German violence everywhere, but it was where the Red Army had taken over relatively recently that they died in the largest numbers. That was where the German execution squads struck earliest and with least warning, and where they successfully exploited the Polish, Baltic and Ukrainian populations' hatred of the Soviet occupiers. The *shtetl* culture of the old Tsarist Pale of Settlement, heartland of Russian Jewry before 1939, never recovered.[84]

7

Make This Land German for Me Again!

'The most radical and theoretically most perfect solution of the problem would be the complete expulsion of all Czechs from the country and its settlement by Germans. This solution, however, is impossible because there are not enough Germans for the immediate occupation of the territories which belong in the foreseeable future to the Greater German area. [Expelling all the Czechs] would leave the fields fallow and the cities deserted.' Reich Protector von Neurath, Prague, 1940[1]

Arriving in 1941 as the new mayor of the small town of Poniatowec in the Warthegau, a Prussian civil servant called Franz Bock found himself in the wilds of the Reich's frontier lands. It was a backward, rough-and-ready kind of place. The county prefect, his superior, was a former butcher; the last mayor had used the local bar as an office. Life seemed odd and unfamiliar. Why, he wondered on the first day, did the town's inhabitants greet him so obsequiously and step aside to let him pass? Why was it that the only people in the town who spoke proper German were Jews, while the German who ran the local cement factory responded to his questions in an incomprehensible half-Polish dialect? And who were these Balkan arrivals in strange outfits, claiming to be ethnic German refugees from somewhere beyond Romania?[2]

Bock had been keen to do his bit to restore 'Germandom'. Much 'national work' was obviously needed to set the place to rights. But the arrogance and thoughtlessness of his Nazi colleagues kept getting in the way. Two SS men drove in to screen Goebbels' most recent propaganda film, *Homecoming*, which depicted Poland's prewar German minority as brutalized and helpless victims, saved by the Führer, and Bock wondered what the point was of whipping up resentment against the Poles, especially as locals had slipped into the cinema illegally and were watching. 'What I have built up in months, this film will destroy in hours,' he fretted. Things did not improve the next night when the two film men drunkenly woke up the town's 'Jewish Eldest' and ordered him at gunpoint to send a couple of girls round to their rooms. Some Jewish girls were indeed sent, there was a fight, and as news of the story spread around the town, the two Germans were arrested and locked up for infringing the race laws. A little later, after that fuss had died down, a Gestapo team drove in and ordered Bock to select some of 'his' Jews for a public execution. It was too all much, and he quit, convinced things had been better managed in the Kaiser's time. Working to make former Polish land German again was an infinitely harder, more unpleasant and more disorderly business than he had ever imagined.[3]

Like other Germans of his generation and class, Bock did not need films such as *Homecoming* to remind him of the sufferings of ethnic Germans in eastern Europe after the First World War. Everyone knew how, after 1918, their land had been confiscated or surrounded with subsidized clusters of new settlements. Hostile officials had discouraged them from speaking German or declaring themselves as Germans in censuses and even the landscape itself had been de-Germanized through changes to the names of families, streets and entire towns. In many areas Germans had been deliberately expelled; in others they had sold up and left, or bowed to the pressure to change their nationality. The Nazi regime saw reversing the effect of these decades as its priority. 'Make this land German for me again!' Hitler had ordered an official after the conquest of northern Yugoslavia in 1941. His message to those he appointed to the Reich's other borderlands was basically the same.[4]

But Hitler's goal was not just to reverse the losses suffered by Prussia and the Habsburg empire in 1918, it was to create a German state on a scale never seen before and to make all Germans, whatever their political views or loyalties, play their part in this. With the resources of Europe's most powerful state and police apparatus behind them, the Nazis took forced population transfer and colonial resettlement to new extremes. They brought nearly 800,000 ethnic Germans 'home' to the Reich and planned new towns for millions more to live in. At the same time, they planned to rid eastern Europe of much of its existing non-German population to free up farms and pastures for German settlers.

Two eminently modern ideas drove the entire vision. One was an intense nostalgia for the past, in particular for that long-vanished medieval past that provided the template for the society the Nazis dreamed about and that offered their main historical justification for what they were doing. Heirs to nineteenth-century romantic historians – Himmler had grown up on their stories – the Nazis saw themselves *re*conquering land that the German knights had won and settled many centuries before. This infatuation with history distinguished Nazi colonialism from its European overseas rivals – the British and French rarely if ever claimed to be taking back land that had once been theirs. Why else invade the USSR in the name of a crusading twelfth-century emperor (Barbarossa)? Why else would Himmler have taken the Teutonic Knights as the model for the SS or spent so much time over devising rituals and composing speeches in memory of the man he came to believe incarnated the 'most German of all German rulers', Heinrich the Fowler, travelling dutifully every year to honour him in the cathedral of Quedlinburg? Greater Germany was, in short, a conscious attempt to turn back the clock, a hatred of modern life that could only emerge from modernity itself. The Third Reich – and the SS in particular – highlighted the purity of the example set by Germany's ancestors and dreamed of restoring their way of life – agrarian, self-sufficient, hierarchical, sword in hand. Hitler could see the value of motorways and the need for compromises with industrial society, not least in the shape of modern armaments. Himmler was far more obsessional than his Führer: he staffed his well-funded German Ancestral Heritage Society with high-powered historians and archaeologists and he was trying to turn his followers into yeomen farming their plots in fake medieval village communities even before the war broke out.[5]

The other modern element in Nazi policy was their commitment to the 'science' of race. Leaving what they saw as the half-hearted misconceptions of the Kaiser's prewar nationalities policy behind them, they wanted to turn race and biology into the guiding principle for administration. 'Our mission is not to Germanise the East in the old sense – bringing the German language and laws to those living there,' stated Himmler, 'but rather to ensure that in the East dwell only men with truly German, Germanic blood.'[6]

This commitment to a strict policy of racial difference broke new ground. Many European countries before the Nazis dreamed of rescuing 'their' minorities by conquering their neighbours' land. In the nineteenth century, Serbia, Greece, Bulgaria and Romania all aspired to fulfil their national mission through expansion, and exactly the same logic had led Polish politicians after 1918 to fight the Ukrainians and Lithuanians for as much land as possible. The historian A. J. P. Taylor once mischievously remarked that 'in international affairs there was nothing wrong with Hitler except that he was a German'. From this point of view, he was right. Taylor laughed at those who described the German dictator as a man of unique wickedness. But what was important about Hitler was not his wickedness; it was his commitment to biological racism.[7]

Prewar Germany funded racial science well – as it did the sciences in general – and the Third Reich was a particularly generous sponsor. After 1939, the Third Reich's racial experts were no longer consulted merely on the health of Germany's own population but helped to make decisions affecting the continent as a whole. Men in white coats ran classification panels and training programmes to decide which of the Slavs or ethnic Germans they stripped and measured were 're-Germanizable'. Their decisions dictated whether people would be sent to work-camps or settler colonies, whether their pregnancies would be permitted or aborted, and whether they could keep their children or see them sent away for adoption. Yet allowing them to pronounce on policy had unexpected results. The discipline of racial science itself was in turmoil, and many German scholars had already become aware of the difficulties. Old-fashioned racial determinism seemed hard to square with new findings in genetics, and it was not particularly helpful either when explaining the characteristics of a given people or *Volk*. These debates had not really reached the German public, which had been carefully sheltered from them by the regime. But knowing how to distinguish a German from a non-German – the key concern for those running the new empire – was not something upon which it was possible to get expert consensus.[8]

'Every German had his own ideas of race,' comments a recent historian. The subject was certainly in flux. The 'Breslau school' believed in tracking blue eyes and blond hair, but Otto Reche and Fritz Lenz – two luminaries of academic racism – thought physical characteristics were crude markers since most individuals were themselves mixed racially. For Hans Günther, a popularizer of Nazi science, even Germany contained strains of all the major European races – the Nordic, East Baltic, Alpine and Dinaric – as well as fortunately small quantities of

Mediterranean and Inner Asian blood. A few heretics solved the problem of matching up the categories of race and *Volk* by talking about a 'German race', but this simple solution was criticized by most of the academics as unscientific. There were similar doubts about the usefulness of talking about 'Slavs', whom experts thought were made up of a variety of much smaller sub-groups of differing racial 'value'. The value question itself was divisive – some believing in racial hierarchies, others insisting that difference carried no connotation of worth.

All of this spelled enormous confusion, regarding not only the Germans but also the Jews. Experts like the geneticist Otmar von Verschuer, wartime director of the Kaiser Wilhelm Institute of Anthropology, Human Heredity and Eugenics and Josef Mengele's boss, strongly doubted that Jews were originally a race at all. He listed what the racial anthropologists had determined were their identifying characteristics – their rolling gait, love of garlic, their neuroses, intellectualizing, jabbering talk and tendency to white-collar crime. But Jews were according to him a mongrel breed, basically indistinguishable in terms of blood from the Germans. Verschuer did wonder if they were perhaps in the process of becoming a separate race through inbreeding and isolation. What was clear to him was that their negative traits outweighed their positive ones and threatened the health of those they lived among.[9]

By committing itself to a policy based on biological racism, the regime was thus in fact condemning itself to extreme uncertainty, and this gave discretion to the policy-makers and permitted wide variation in nationalities policy from place to place. The case of the Jews was, from this point of view, exceptional: a set of rigid guidelines was applied, allowing almost no exceptions. In other cases, the Germans followed criteria for national and racial identification which were not always very different from those used elsewhere. Sometimes they screened people in a highly selective way – as in the Warthegau, the authorities of which tended to follow Himmler's elitist line. But next door in West Prussia, they simply dragooned as many local people as possible into declaring themselves Germans. Assimilation – the policy which was supposed to have been abandoned – was thus brought back, as supposedly watertight racial criteria were in fact merged with more old-fashioned cultural and political determinants of national belonging.

But the arbitrariness of Germanization was accompanied by the appearance of technological sophistication and comprehensiveness. The rotten foundations of racial science were obscured beneath a vast and increasingly mechanized wartime bureaucracy dedicated to perfecting the systematic methods of population identification and control that the regime's police and statisticians had been working on through the 1930s. Ten days after the war began, Germans were required to carry ID cards. The long-delayed census of the Greater German Reich was carried out, allowing for easy identification of Jews and other minorities, and new offices of population statistics were established to carry out similar censuses in Prague, Cracow and Riga. German statisticians also co-operated enthusiastically with their counterparts in technologically advanced countries such as the Netherlands. When he was shot in Prague, Reinhard Heydrich – the Acting Protector of Bohemia and Moravia – had been working on a scheme for the total racial screening of the entire population. In fact, no other country ever attempted so ambitious a policy of classification, separation and colonial resettlement in so short a time across such a vast area. None devoted such resources to implementing it, or adopted such murderous and sophisticated methods in its pursuit. In short, wartime Germanization constituted the single most forceful and ambitious attempt at nationalizing people and territory in Europe's history. It explains why the Nazi conception of occupation involved something far more permanent, wrenching and destructive than the temporary abeyance of sovereignty mandated by liberal international law, and it contributed more than any other single factor to the increasingly violent transformation of life in the Reich itself and to the rise of the SS – the motor of Germanization – as its major political and military institution.[10]

ORIGINS

Little of this was foreseeable in 1938, and an observer of events in Austria and the Sudetenland could hardly have guessed the scale of the regime's wartime nationalizing ambitions. Both regions, after all, had preponderantly German populations already. People from the Old Reich might laugh at their accents and odd ways – insults against 'Sudeten donkeys' in the ranks of the expanded Wehrmacht were frequent enough for the army to worry. Yet even so they would likely have voted for incorporation into Germany had they had the chance to do so back in 1918. There was relatively little, therefore, for the nationalizers to do.

The Sudetenland, with its large Czech population, posed its own dilemmas. Henlein, the Sudeten Germans' leader, wanted to Germanize the region by reversing the interwar land reform, expelling the Czechs eastwards and reducing the use of the Czech language. Ethnic German activists initially drove out many Czechs and made it clear that they would not be welcome to return. But their frustration that things were not moving faster boiled over during Kristallnacht with shouts of 'First the Jews, then the Czechs!' and 'Out with the Czechs!' The fact was that Berlin had its own reasons for wanting local Czechs to stay put. Despite a 'transfer of population' clause in the Munich agreement (recalling the 1922–3 Greco-Turkish population exchange), Hitler's key concern, looking east, was to keep the tiny German minority in rump Czechoslovakia. Because he did not want to give the Czechs any reason to expel them, the Sudeten Germans were told to behave. Henlein restrained his cohorts and assuaged them with 'Borderland Welfare' subsidies for Sudeten swimming-pools and libraries.[11]

Bringing millions of non-Germans under German rule for the first time, it was the conquest of Prague in the spring of 1939 that raised a new and urgent question for the Nazis: on what terms should an 'alien people' be incorporated within the 'area of the Reich' in a way that accorded with the principles of racial jurisprudence? Hitler himself, a little more than a year earlier, had raised the possibility of forcing many of them out. At the start of the invasion itself, a senior army commander went even further by musing about organizing the 'physical annihilation' of the Czechs; it would not be possible under normal conditions, he admitted, but how else to solve the problem? This was too extreme, but the expulsion option did not vanish. By October 1941, Heydrich was talking about eventually deporting half the country's population to Siberia. But this was for the future: meantime the increasing wartime value of the Czech economy necessitated a less drastic approach.[12]

In Bohemia and Moravia, there were few Germans in lands that seemed fitted to be on the front line of Germanization. For obvious reasons, the Nazis could not contemplate counting those self-professed Germans – rather a large proportion of the total – who unfortunately happened to be Jewish. (Many German-speaking Jews declared themselves German in the interwar Czech census; after 1945, Jewish survivors were expelled by the Czechs for this reason.) Thus the Nazis faced a serious numbers gap for the first time, for Germans made up barely 3 per cent of the population. Once the Protectorate had been created, the SS managed to expropriate a huge amount of Czech land, but finding Germans to farm it was the hard part. Instead of the 150,000 families that they had anticipated, they settled just 6,000 in five years. Czech hands still tilled the soil and harvested the crops that Germans ate.[13]

The Reich also relied on Czech workers to keep the production lines rolling. Reich Protector von Neurath and his deputy Karl Frank stressed that Germany would remain dependent upon Czech labour into the foreseeable future. 'Humans are the empire's capital, and in the new Reich we cannot do without the labour of seven million Czechs,' wrote Frank in 1940. He emphasized that the Czechs could not as a whole be 'reduced to a servant nation on racial grounds', and proposed that 'sugar and the whip' – in other words, material inducements and threats – should be used to encourage candidates for Germanization. Large numbers of Germans could be created, where they did not already exist, by screening the Czech population for traces of German ancestry. Expelling Czechs, as some racial purists in the Nazi Party and the SS wanted, would simply have been economically self-defeating for the Reich as long as it had a war to win.[14]

Citizenship laws offered another useful way of making the numbers look better. After the First World War, after all, many European states had introduced systems of forcible classification. In Czechoslovakia in 1921 the authorities had fined thousands of people for declaring themselves Germans and had unilaterally reclassified them as Czechs. Similar policies were followed in French Alsace, Slovenia and Poland. What was striking about the new citizenship law that the Nazis now introduced was that it was actually *less* coercive than these predecessors, following the pre-1914 Bohemian German preference for voluntary assignation instead. It distinguished between (German) Reich citizens and second-class (Czech) 'members of the state', but left it to individuals to choose which to opt for. Evidently, the authorities were affected by considerations of racial purity and could not bring themselves to use the law as a means of turning large numbers of Czechs into Germans. But their approach had the disadvantage of allowing Germans not to declare themselves either. In fact many Germans did *not* rush to become Reich citizens, fearing obligatory work duty, conscription and Nazification. 'It had been assumed that all ethnic Germans would demand to become

Reich Germans,' wrote a perturbed German civil servant in Prague in August 1939. 'This reckoning . . . was a mistake . . . One must say that in this respect the ethnic Germans have disappointed us.' Ironically, therefore, the Nazis found that not even conquest sufficed to stem the slow decline of the numbers of self-declared Germans in Bohemia.[15]

Desperate to boost their numbers, the Germans targeted the so-called 'amphibians' – a term originally used in the Habsburg empire and employed by Nazi social scientists to designate people (often bilingual) whose ethnic identity was ambiguous. They represented a phenomenon that had been regarded as perfectly normal in the nineteenth century but that nationalism's triumph had turned into an oddity. 'Amphibians' (sometimes also called 'hermaphrodites') were thick on the ground throughout the German borderlands, and the Protectorate was home to hundreds of thousands of them. According to a German administrator, there were many Czechs who 'in their racial and ethnic worth do not appear to be that bad, often because – due to the fact that their parents belonged to both nationalities – they do not know to which side they should belong'.[16]

The Nazis' official definitions of Germanness in the Protectorate reflected a surprisingly open-ended and non-biological understanding of nationality. 'A German national is one who himself professes allegiance to the German nation, as long as this conviction is confirmed by certain facts, such as language, education, culture, etc.,' noted Karl Frank in March 1939. 'Any more precise elaboration of the term "German national" is not possible given current relationships.' Leaving things open in this way allowed him to try to win over the 'amphibians' by enticing them into German-language schools or attracting them to German welfare services. In fact, 80,000 – roughly 1 per cent of the population – did declare themselves for the German side between March 1940 and December 1941 alone, and more than 300,000 did so by the war's end.[17]

Offered new incentives and penalties to opt for one side or the other, ordinary 'amphibians' exploited wartime opportunities or bowed to new realities much as they had done in the Czech republic previously. A widow, whose Czech husband had died in the 1920s, received welfare support because – in her own words – 'she raised her children to be upstanding Germans in purely Czech surroundings, in spite of the most bitter poverty, without ever succumbing to the influences of Czechdom'.

Much later, a Czech novelist recalled being dragged to a German school by his father: 'For the first time in my childhood, I rebelled against my father's authority and shrieked to the open windows of the Czech town hall in Schlesisch Ostrau: "I don't want to go to a German school! Let me go to my Czech school!"' He was backed by his former Czech teacher, who 'leaned out from the window on the first floor of the town hall, and yelled to my father in Czech: "Let go of the boy, you Ersatz Teuton!"' Such decisions pitted children against parents, wives against husbands, and pro-Protectorate Czechs against anti-Nazis. 'The Germans are opening new German schools where there used to be none,' warned an underground Czech journal in 1939. 'This is your business, women. It is in your hands whether our children grow up to be Czechs or Germanized, patriots or traitors.'[18]

Overall, this first experiment in Germanization turned out to be a chastening experience for the Nazis. Not only did they find that many ethnic Germans were unenthusiastic about declaring themselves, but they suspected many so-called 'amphibians' of enlisting solely out of opportunism. After the fall of France, Nazi officials became especially worried that 'undesirable elements' were registering as Germans. This was 'an opportunistic element', 'the worst of Czechdom' (they feared) who were prompted by crass materialism; often their children did not even speak German. Briefly, under the reign of Reinhard Heydrich, the authorities steered a far more coercive course, screening and seizing Czech children by force. After Heydrich's assassination in 1942, children from the village of Lidice, which had been razed to the ground in reprisal, were sent to an SS adoption home near Poznań, where they were given German names. Yet what is striking is how few such cases there were, compared with the tens of thousands of child-kidnappings in Poland. Even though some 50 per cent of the Czechs were thought to be German-izable compared with barely 3 per cent of Poles, it was the Poles who bore the brunt of forced Germanization. The Czechs were simply too important economically, and too obedient politically, to make it worth alienating them.

By late 1942, the Germans had more or less come to terms with their failure, and were reduced to promoting their own bizarre brand of Czech nationalism. They founded a new youth organization and tried to foster what they called 'Reich-loyal Czech Nationalism'. Schoolchildren marched along under the swastika singing Czech songs and spent their vacations on 'Heydrich's Summer Relaxation Camps'. By the summer of 1944, they were helping organize a Week of Czech Youth in Prague. Neither the SD nor the Czech resistance were quite sure what to make of this deeply ambiguous movement, which looked like collaboration one minute and national revival the next. But one thing was clear. The early confidence of the racial theorists had been misplaced: Germans were in short supply, and it was not easy to make more, especially as the war began to turn against the Reich.[19]

WINNING BACK POLAND

In the entire Germanization drive, nowhere possessed such importance as Poland – in particular those territories that were annexed. Bringing them into the Third Reich raised the stakes for racial policy because it meant they had to be Germanized as fast as possible; in fact, in October 1939, this became *the* wartime priority for Hitler and for those he entrusted with the task, one they would force through with every means at their disposal.

Yet the demographic challenge was nearly as large as in the Protectorate to the south. Officials in the Nazi Party's Racial-Political Office pointed out nervously that conquest was bringing ever larger Slavic populations inside the Reich's borders. Economic and security considerations had pushed the new German boundary far beyond the old 1914 lines, giving the Reich most of the Polish iron, steel and textiles industries but simultaneously including many more Poles and Jews. Emphasizing that Germans comprised only 7 per cent of the population in the new territories, compared with 86 per cent Poles (and 5 per cent Jews), they called for 'a ruthless decimation of the Polish population'. Only the pitiless 'transfer' of most Poles could help avoid the nightmare scenario of creeping Polonization within the Reich itself. They advised closing Polish schools and banning religious services in Polish: Polish restaurants, cafés, cinemas, theatres, newspapers and books, associations and unions were also targeted. In short, Berlin should aim for the 'ruthless elimination of all elements not suitable for Germanization'.[20]

In May 1940, Himmler borrowed from these ideas when he offered Hitler his own thoughts on how to treat 'the alien population in the East'. Seeking to restore his authority over population policy, following the chaos he himself had caused by trying to drive hundreds of thousands of people into the General Government, his basic advice was to split the non-Germans up into as many 'ethnic splinter groups' as possible, to deprive them of all sense of national identity and to trawl them for 'the racially valuable people' whose German blood made it worth bringing them back to the Reich for re-education. The Jews would be sent abroad through 'a large-scale emigration' to Africa 'or some other colony'. Eventually Ukrainians and Poles too would disappear as collective units through fragmentation and cultural deprivation, surviving only in the General Government as an 'leaderless labouring class', providing the Reich with migrant and seasonal labour to build roads, quarries and construction and thereby 'participating in [the Germans'] eternal cultural deeds'. All that could be said for Himmler's approach was that it eschewed physical extermination as 'Bolshevik', 'un-German' and 'impossible'. At this point, in the spring of 1940, he was still more than a year away from the world of the Holocaust.[21]

Such plans obviously rested on the ability to define Germanness and to isolate it from its surroundings. But on this the Nazi Party's own racial experts were in two minds. On the one hand, things seemed fixed and obvious: a German national was one 'who in folkdom, custom and family community, lives as a German, if he is of German or related blood'. (Such people had the right to German citizenship, though they would have to change their names if these betrayed signs of Slavonic origins. Everyone else would 'have no political rights'.) Yet the experts did accept the need for some kind of policy 'to extract the Nordic groups from the remaining population and to Germanize them'. Anticipating that only small numbers would fall into this category, they recommended sending them – 'and especially their children' – to Germany proper. As for Polish children who appeared to be 'racially valuable' officials should sever their ties with their parents and transfer them into German care with new names. Clearly, Germanization meant one thing in the Protectorate, where the Czechs still enjoyed a substantial measure of self-government, and something much more coercive in those parts of Poland that were to be turned into new provinces of the Reich itself and where the ethnic struggle between Germans and Slavs had for decades possessed a harshness absent elsewhere.

This was why Hitler swiftly marginalized the role of the regular civil service and the army in these areas. Fearing that they were too hidebound and inhibited to take the kinds of measures he had in mind, he placed his trust instead in his Party officials, and above all in Himmler's fast-growing SS. Through the newly created Reich Commissariat for the Strengthening of Germandom (RKFDV) and associated agencies, Himmler's officials expelled Poles and Jews, repatriated ethnic Germans from abroad and arranged their temporary housing and eventual resettlement. Refugee welfare specialists, agronomists and doctors cooperated with policemen, racial anthropologists and urban planners for the sake of what Himmler called 'the real Germanization of the land' – their occupation 'from the racial point of view'. In January 1940 Konrad Meyer, the urban planner who would later write the blueprint for the Germanization of European Russia, anticipated the expulsion of at least three million Poles and more than half a million Jews from western Poland in order to make room for similar numbers of German colonists. Nazi Party experts made Meyer look moderate; they wanted to get rid of even more.[22]

Between the wars the Polish government had itself settled farmers on German land. Hitler did not, however, want to banish only them; Himmler's men hoped to remove all the existing Polish and Jewish landowners and to replace them with German settlers. Working fast and enthusiastically 'to make this land German again', they took over four-fifths of all the land in the incorporated regions, roughly 626,000 farms on some six million hectares. Some 536,951 ethnic Germans came to the Warthegau – 85 per cent of all those brought to the annexed territories. Yet once the first wave of expulsions in 1939–41 had tailed off, many Poles continued working under German direction on the lands that had once been theirs.[23]

Because the Führer demanded that new colonists be of 'only the best, the soundest German blood', the bureaucrats in the Central Immigration Office were painstaking in screening incoming ethnic Germans and selective about who they allowed to stay permanently in the area. Officials scanned an increasingly complicated set of instructions which intensive courses in biology, anthropology and eugenics were supposed to have clarified. There was body type (on a scale from 'ideal figure' (9) to 'malformed' (1)), racial type (from 'purely Nordic', through 'a balanced cross of Nordic, phalian or dinarian' to 'non-European blood strain'), character, intellect, political record and hereditary background. Assessors started off with physical features but ended up by trying to evaluate a bewildering mixture of personal, social and psychological characteristics. Entire families were photographed, medically examined and interrogated about their ancestry and their political beliefs. At the end of this process, the elite were deemed suitable for resettlement, while the rest were sent on into Germany proper for further monitoring and education.[24]

In fact, the ethnic Germans from Italy and the USSR who were allowed to stay were joined in many areas by Germans from the Reich. Initially hesitant to settle in the East, they were attracted by tax breaks the regime introduced in late 1940. Their numbers never came close to the two million farmers envisaged by Agriculture Minister Darré in early 1940, but they did amount to several hundred thousand people. Although Himmler talked about holding the land in trust till after the war for veterans, these 'land hunters' moved in, hoping to enjoy quick pickings and besieging the civil servants at the land registry. They were drawn by the prospects of participating in a free-for-all on a vast scale, thinly disguised by a veneer of legalism after Göring issued a decree making all Polish farms liable for confiscation. Often they came with influential letters of recommendation – sometimes so influential that they could not be ignored. In fact, the regime was itself using Polish estates to buy the loyalty of its leading figures. On the border with East Prussia the *Gauleiter*, Erich Koch, simply took over some properties and added them to his already large private domains. General Guderian took time off from his military duties to tour the Warthegau looking for an estate of his own. When asked by von Manstein how he came by the one he eventually chose, Guderian told him that 'he had been given a list of fine Polish properties which he had viewed over a few days before deciding on the most suitable property'. The Polish owners had initially still been living there; but when he had taken over their estate, they had already gone and – so he told Manstein – he had no idea what had become of them.[25]

Germanization was transforming the Polish towns as well. When ethnic Germans arrived at Łódź after their long journey from eastern Poland, Jews with yellow stars carried their baggage for them and looked after their horses. In Łódź itself – now called Litzmannstadt – resettlement specialists requisitioned Polish and Jewish homes as well as schools and other buildings to accommodate the newcomers and organized Jewish labour details to clean up the properties. Even as the planners prepared blueprints for the postwar rationalization of former Polish 'space', separate German zones were being established. And from the ubiquitous 'Adolf-Hitler-Platz' – as the central market square was generally now called – outwards there was a wholesale renaming of streets and buildings. Eventually, the deportation of huge numbers of Polish and Jewish residents was going to allow the realignment of Łódź's town centre on an entirely different axis; new industrial zones and suburbs for German workers would spring up with modern theatres, cinemas, parks and concert halls. Christmas cards from German managers in Auschwitz depicted the kind of new model settlement that was planned for the rapidly expanding industrial belt in Silesia as well.[26]

Once Hitler mandated the eventual political integration of the General Government into the Reich, such schemes became official policy there too. Hans Frank dreamed of getting the Jews out of the cities, cleaning up the ghetto in Cracow, his capital, and replacing it with 'clean, German residential quarters in which one can breathe German air'. Yet the scarcity of ethnic Germans was even more of an obstacle than further West. Frank hoped to seek out the scattered 'racial kernels' of 'Germandom' and recover them for the nation. 'I speak openly of Germanization,' he told his staff. 'How often have we not seen with astonishment some blond, blue-eyed child speaking Polish? To which I say: "If this child learned German, it would be a pretty German girl." ' But the other pillar of Germanization was the Nazi Party itself, whose network spread across the country. Opening a Party House in Cracow, Frank talked of Germanizing the region in a few decades, 'perhaps less', so that one day the Führer would say of it what he had recently said of Essen, that it was 'the most Aryan *Gau* in the German Reich'. The General Government, he went on, must become as German as the Rhineland: 'And if someone tells me: "That is impossible," I can only ask: "Is the fact that we are sitting here in Cracow, that we have Party Houses in Warsaw and Lublin, any less implausible than that this land, if we rule it properly, should become German?" '[27]

The likelihood of these fantasies materializing obviously depended on the regime's conception of who was, or might become, German. The re-settlement schemes of 1939–40 chiefly concerned those ethnic Germans who had come under Soviet control and left most German minority groups in central Europe untouched. But as it was, the overall number of Germans available for resettlement was not large. In *Mein Kampf* Hitler had rejected the idea of assimilating 'racially foreign elements' and criticized Prussian Germanization policy for making this mistake. Yet translating such attitudes into policy meant ending up with a form of racial screening which excluded large numbers of people who might otherwise have swollen the German *Volksgemeinschaft*.

This did not bother Himmler. An aesthete, like many racists, he attached great importance to physical appearance. 'The racial enquiry should prevent the development of Mongol types in the newly settled East,' he ordained. 'I want to build a blond province here.' In order to 'liquidate' the Polish minority in regions that were now to become part of the Reich itself, Himmler ordered, children 'whose racial appearance indicates Nordic blood' were to be kidnapped and 'subjected to a racial and psychological process of selection'.[28] As these comments suggest, his primary concern was purity of 'blood'. 'We have to see to it that now, in these days when we are strong,' he declared after Poland's fall, 'people who are of our blood will be brought back to us, as much as is in our power, and that we see to it that none of our blood is ever lost to the outside world.'[29]

Yet in Poland itself such an exclusive quasi-biological understanding of nationality complicated the forging of a coherent policy towards the so-called 'Germanizables'. After all, many Polish citizens had family connections with Germans; populations were as mixed in many areas as they were in the Protectorate. Himmler – lost in his own historical theories – might talk about a 'racial selection' (*Auslese*) and 'sieving' (*Siebung*) in order to make sure that 'Mongols, mixed Mongols and Huns' were carted off into the General Government. But there were many bases upon which such a screening could be made. Facing the prospect that the whole resettlement programme would end up depopulating the Reich's new eastern borderlands by getting rid of Poles before enough Germans had been found to come in, the local authorities in the Warthegau moved back towards an assimilation policy and sought to introduce new citizenship guidelines in order to work out whom to give German ID papers to. Less dogmatic than Himmler, Hitler himself understood the problem and once he clarified that he *would* tolerate some degree of assimilation the guidelines were finalized. Even in Poland, as it turned out, the Nazi regime was being forced to retreat from its hardline insistence on biology as a criterion for nationality.

The so-called German People's List (DVL) that was introduced by decree in March 1941 was designed, in the words of Gauleiter Forster in Danzig-West Prussia, to help all those who 'had been overwhelmed and lost because of the Polish pressure in the course of the centuries . . . The real content and aim of the decree is to ensure that not one drop of German blood is lost to the German nation.' Stripped of the rhetoric, this really involved the introduction of a surprisingly flexible approach to German nationality, one that allowed large numbers of people to claim citizenship, even if they did not speak German. The List established no fewer than four categories: the elite – Class 1 – covered former German-speaking Polish citizens who had been members of German societies or unions between the wars; class 2 were people of 'German racial descent' who had maintained their German characteristics, for example, by speaking German under Polish rule; class 3 included both Germans in mixed marriages and their children, while the 'renegades' in class 4 had 'actively worked in a manner hostile to Germany' despite their own German origins.

If people were accepted in one of the first two groups they received blue ID papers and German citizenship – those in class 1 could also join the Party; class 3 received green papers and 'state membership' – they were essentially on probation, while class 4 did not even obtain this, though they remained susceptible to future examination for 're-Germanization'. The chief incentive for entering classes 1 to 3 was that their property was exempted from confiscation and that they were most likely to benefit from the plundering of Polish property; on the other hand, they automatically became liable for conscription into the armed forces. Someone from category 3 or 4 could not marry someone from category 1 or 2. And category 4s were often marked for police surveillance.[30]

Even this complex system did not exhaust the possible permutations, and a special court system, headed by Himmler, adjudicated on especially thorny DVL cases. Someone who applied for *Volksdeutsch* status on the basis of her pro-German activities in Poland before the war had a Jewish father. The court decided she could not be admitted, but she was given a certificate which stated that she was not a Pole but a 'privileged, protected inhabitant of the Reich' (yet another category, this time one which fell outside existing citizenship boundaries). Here racial considerations were trumped by pragmatic political ones as the court did not want to drive a person of initiative and 'leadership' potential into the anti-German camp. In another case, a man from 'pure' German background in Poland had married a woman whose father was Indian. Although racial inspection showed that the woman and children betrayed evidence of 'foreign and in fact Negro blood', the man had been a member of pro-German political groups between the wars, and the family had been forced to flee to Germany in 1939 as a result. The man was placed in category 1 and his wife and children in category 2, thanks to their 'sacrifices' for Germany. This seemed pragmatic, but there was a harsher reality: the court instructed that the man be told 'in a friendly way' not to have any more children with his current wife.[31]

By the beginning of 1944, approximately 2.75 million people out of a total population of 9.5 million had successfully passed through DVL checks in the incorporated territories. For the racial purists, the results were disheartening:

Population in the Former Polish Territories (January 1944) (thousands)

	Warthegau	Danzig-West Prussia	Upper Silesia	East Prussia
Reich Germans	194	c.50	c.100	6
German settlers	245	52	38	8
Germans [DVL]:	493	938	1,420	46
Class 1	218	113	97	9
Class 2	192	97	211	22
Class 3	64	726	976	13
Class 4	9	2	54	1
Poles and others	3,450	689	1,040	920
Total Population	4,382	1,729	2,598	980
Germans/Total Population	21.2%	60.0%	60.0%	6.2%
DVL 3–4/German Population	7.8%	78.1%	66.1%	24.8%

Note: Numbers as in original (not all totals add up correctly).
Source: NO-3568 in International Military Tribunal, *Trial of the Major War Criminals*, vol. 4. (Washington, 1949), 937–9.

What the figures in the table show is that with an acute shortage of Germans of any kind in the new provinces – whether from the Reich, locals or new settlers – the DVL lists played a crucial role in swelling the numbers. They had the least impact in Greiser's Warthegau, which had welcomed more settlers than any other *Gau* and had been correspondingly strict in granting citizenship to former Polish citizens. Yet what were the fruits of this racial orthodoxy? A still huge numbers gap which all the efforts of the RKFDV and the SS had been unable to bridge, and a large and alienated Polish majority, now mostly dispossessed and living in temporary camps or specially assigned villages.[32]

Understanding where this would lead, Greiser's bitter rival, Albert Forster, in the neighbouring province of Danzig-West Prussia, had gone in an entirely different direction and taken full advantage of the possibilities offered by the DVL system. Ignoring the SS racial experts, he kept settlers away and swelled the List with huge numbers of mixed class 3s. Forster had his own theory, which was that many locals were not Poles at all but 'Kashubians', ripe for Germanization. He thought Himmler's emphasis on rigorous racial selection a lot of nonsense, and saw a virtue in avoiding the protracted upheaval of deportation and resettlement. From 1941, he was inclined to admit any former Polish citizen on to the List who spoke German reasonably well – soon even that condition was relaxed – and had done nothing politically to cross the authorities.

In fact, Forster was not simply allowing Poles to become Germans, he was actually forcing them to. 'During the process of Germanizing Poles on the basis of the Ethnic Register,' recalled an official after the war, 'there were many cases where whole villages or towns were compulsorily entered in the register according to fixed quotas laid down by Forster. For example, a local branch leader or mayor was instructed to enter eighty per cent of his village although it was at least eighty per cent Polish.' Nearly two-thirds of the former Polish population of Forster's *Gau* was brought, by one means or another, on to the DVL. Storm-troops of barely Germanized Poles could be seen marching through the streets of his towns singing Polish national songs.[33]

'If I looked like Himmler, I would not talk so much about race,' Forster was reported to have said. But it was not just the insult that made Himmler furious; it was also the policy, especially as his rival Greiser fed him a steady stream of complaints about the thuggish and inefficient way the new *Gau* was being run. Himmler was unamused that two of Forster's closest and most boorish Party colleagues should have insulted an ethnic German 'of unimpeachable ancestry' as a 'Polack' even as they turned Poles into Germans by administrative fiat. Forster was fastidiously reminded that there was no competition for who could Germanize his *Gau* first; the important thing was to ensure that Germanization produced a 'racially impeccable' population since 'one drop of false blood which comes into an individual's veins can never be removed'. But Hitler was apparently less bothered, and racial specialists in fact backed Forster's claim that a large proportion of the native population in West Prussia was descended originally from German settlers. Between Himmler's idea of a small, carefully selected racial elite lording it over a Polish underclass and Forster's equally National Socialist vision of Germanization through forced conscription in mass organizations there was in fact an unbridgeable chasm.[34]

Less contentiously than Forster, the provincial administration in Upper Silesia also held Himmler's resettlement teams at arm's length, arguing with great success that keeping the regional economy running smoothly should be the wartime priority. After a few initial expulsions of Poles, it decided that Upper Silesia was far too important as an industrial base to risk destabilizing it through Himmler's grand demographic ventures. 'The settlement opportunities in Upper Silesia are extremely limited – or rather, almost entirely exhausted,' its *Gauleiter* regretfully told the head of the RKFDV in January 1943. There too, the huge number of class 3s provided the tell-tale sign as to what he really thought of the SS racial guidelines. He preferred to hang on to his Polish workers by any means and did not even introduce the racial classification system until more than a year after the Warthegau. Under fire at the start, this policy of retention rather than liquidation of a substantial section of the Polish population seemed more and more compelling the longer the war went on.[35]

Hitler himself thought Himmler's race mysticism was impractical and, while hostile to Serbs and Russians in general, he felt differently about other groups of Slavs. He praised the Czechs as 'industrious and intelligent workers' and speculated that blue-eyed Ukrainians might be 'peasant descendants of German tribes who never migrated'. In fact, he came round to the view – common among German anthropologists – that there was, racially speaking, no such category as 'Slavs'; it was a linguistic term, nothing more. That did not stop it continuing to be used. But it helps explain why the Führer allowed Himmler and Forster each to define Germanness in his own way.[36]

THE GREATER GERMANIC REICH

There was, of course, precious German blood to be found in Western Europe as well. As early as mid-October 1939, Hitler had told his party chiefs to anticipate the eventual incorporation of Belgium and Switzerland into Germany. Six months later, Rosenberg hailed the victory over Denmark with the words: 'Just as Bismarck's Reich was born in 1866 so will the Greater German Reich be born from what is going on today.' Almost immediately, the shadow of annexation fell westwards over regions which Hitler intended eventually to claim on historical or racial grounds.[37]

In France, as they regained the territories that had belonged to the prewar Kaiserreich, the Germans were in no mood for forgiveness. In the wake of the First World War, the French had purged the provinces of Alsace and Lorraine, classified their population according to 'blood origins' and driven out more than 90,000 people in barely a year: the German population of the Moselle department dropped from 164,502 in 1910 to under 45,000 in 1921. France's defeat in 1940 offered the chance for the Germans to take their revenge. Outside Strasbourg cathedral that June, Hitler stood next to the man who had been the last German mayor of the city in 1914. 'What do you think?' the Führer demanded of his euphoric troops. 'Must we give France back this jewel?' 'Never,' came back the response. Putting trusted *Gauleiters* in charge of the French borderlands, and ignoring French protests, Hitler told them to Germanize the area within a few years.[38]

In Alsace, where Robert Wagner – the *Gauleiter* of neighbouring Baden – was appointed civilian governor, French POWs from the region were released provided they signed a declaration stating that they were of German blood. Civilians who had fled the fighting returned to find banners across the streets with slogans in German welcoming them home to the Greater Germany. Annexation did not seem far off. At the same time, the process of expelling undesirables began: roughly 10,000 Jews were expelled westwards into France, along with tens of thousands of non-Jews. Nazi organizations were established and German law came into effect. In Wagner's mind, most of the province's population was already German, whether they realized it or not. Although the German language was made compulsory, he recognized that many inhabitants still felt loyalty to France; yet in his mind, this merely demonstrated their German ancestry since 'fidelity is the distinctive quality of the Germans'. Culture rather than race thus became his focus. He ordered street- and business-names to be changed to German equivalents, pulled French books from public libraries and used them for a Christmas bonfire. Those who spoke French in public were sent to concentration camps while tens of thousands of young men were conscripted into the Wehrmacht and the Waffen-SS.

The former trainee-teacher micro-managed the transformation, illuminating the more farcical side of the nationalist mind-set by laying down the law on personal names. 'Non-German' names were henceforth banned, as the secret police scanned the telephone directories. Sensing the possibility of backsliding, Wagner prohibited 'René' being turned into 'Renatus', or 'Marcel' into 'Marcellus', published lists of acceptable German names and unacceptable French ones, and laid down transcription rules (to avoid a situation in which different members of the Dumoulin family ended up with Vondermühlen, Zurmühlen, Müller and Dümuler). Nationality politics turned into onomastics.

In little more than six months more than 2,000 inhabitants of Strasbourg alone 'volunteered' to have their names changed. But not even his own staff could agree on what a real German name was: some found 'Johann' too Jewish; when another insisted changing 'Robert' into 'Rupprecht', a critic observed that the *Gauleiter* himself was called Robert. And wasn't the Reich minister of agriculture the very French-sounding Darré, and the health leader a certain Leonardo Conti? When Monsieur 'Boulois' was forced to alter his name to 'Bulwa', another official complained that it contained 'nothing Germanic': 'names like Bulwa are not even European, but would fit the chief of an African tribe better'. A chauffeur called Houillon was 'Germanized' to Hüller and then Hujung, while a Boulanger was torn between Bäcker and the experts' preference for Bulanger. (Wagner himself had the last word, deciding on Hujung and Becker.)

By the autumn of 1943, everyone – Wagner apart – was thoroughly fed up with the whole charade. One Nazi official – a long-time Alsatian autonomist – asked sarcastically whether 'in a phase of total war, it is absolutely necessary that officials and specialists scratch their heads to decide if a Charpentier should be called Scharpenter or simply Zimmermann, and whether the fact that a certain Caquelin became Kagel is decisive for the outcome of the war'. Laughable though such measures might seem in retrospect, by the time that the Germans got round to passing the ordinance which made the whole renaming demand legal – in early 1943 – more than 50,000 applications had been received. Whether they did what Wagner (whose family name was originally Backfisch) hoped, which was to 'liberate the Alsatian from the odium of being only a half-German', is more doubtful.[39]

The deadly earnestness of the war for nationality thus had its ridiculous side. Just as some racial theorists actually worried that Germans in the Reich might get an inferiority complex if ever confronted by the magnificent racial specimens who would be selected to settle in the eastern territories, so others believed that Wagner's overblown purism risked rousing ill feeling inside the Reich. Wagner himself fretted that many of the Germans coming into Alsace from the Reich themselves bore French-sounding names: fearing complaints from Alsatians who had been forced to change their own names, he tried to insist that only Germans with properly German names worked in the province. This made Interior Minister Frick furious. Even after the war, he told Wagner, there were no plans to make Reich Germans change their names, except perhaps in the case of Slavic ones, and the Führer himself saw no need to Germanize the names of families descended from Huguenot refugees, either in Germany or in Alsace itself. Such was the power of the *Gauleiters* that Wagner simply took no notice. So far as he was concerned, all names had to be Germanized, and the statistics proclaimed the policy a success.

Next door, Gauleiter Josef Bürckel in Lorraine was much less bothered with names. He was busy expelling Frenchmen and Jews as well as keeping out ethnic Germans (who were, in his view, often less racially desirable than those already on the land). He preferred to find settlers, if they were needed, from among the peasantry of western Germany. Bürckel was another of those *Gauleiters* who attached great importance to keeping the SS and its racial fantasies at bay. When Bürckel deported more than 60,000 French speakers – almost 15 per cent of the region's population – without examining them racially first, the SS were furious. When he proposed deporting 40,000 more undesirables to the Ukraine as settlers, they objected that the resettlement programme was not a dumping ground or a punishment: eventually a 'controlled deportation' of around 10,000 took place under SS supervision. But it was only a temporary victory for Himmler in his more or less constant struggle against the Party bosses whose own rough and ready views of Germanization so often crossed his own.[40]

The clash between Himmler and the Party over Germanization was also going on in the Low Countries and Scandinavia. The populations of these countries were not Germans (*Deutsche*) but they were 'Germanics' (*Germanen*) in the eyes of the regime and therefore ripe for eventual political incorporation. How this was to be achieved was where the Party and the SS diverged. The Party wanted to help sympathetic Dutch and Norwegian Nazis to build up mass movements: they wanted a replay of the National Socialist revolution as it had taken place in Germany and they saw figures like Norway's Quisling or Holland's Anton Mussert as natural Führers of their people.

The trouble was not only that such men were deeply hated and politically marginal; they were also nationalists, with their own conception of a future relationship with Germany. As early as 1 May, Quisling was urging on Hitler a political programme for 'a constitutional union of all Germanic countries': this, as he explained, would not mean Norway's absorption into a Greater Germany but 'a free Germanic federation under the leadership of Germany'. Similarly, Mussert advocated a Greater Holland (swollen by the addition of Belgian Flanders) not joining the Reich. In August, he proposed a 'League of Germanic Peoples' to be led by Hitler. The Dutch would rule a territory racially purified of Jews (to be sent to Guyana) and Walloons. Mussert's Dutch Nazi Party would guarantee Dutch sovereignty, and this was definitely *not* what the Germans had in mind.[41]

Well aware of such men's limitations, Himmler's strategy was very different. In keeping with his whole conception of the elitist nature of politics, he rejected the very idea of establishing pro-German mass parties. After all, the Dutch Nederlandse Unie had been set up in 1940 to help the Nazification of Holland but had quickly turned into an obstacle to it. Instead he encouraged the formation of small loyal elites, armed groups of volunteers, who would learn German, fight for the Reich against the separatist schemes of their rivals and take power as 'champions of the Greater German idea'. There was to be no federation of allied National Socialist states but, rather, one single Greater Germany united by racial solidarity. In September 1940, he set up a small Dutch unit; the following year he poached Quisling's deputy (and rival), Police

Chief Jonas Lie, to command the new SS force there, making him *SS-Standartenführer*. Mussert's head of security also defected to the SS. Mussert himself was worried about what this all meant: 'The higher SS leadership considers the Dutch people German,' he lamented. 'It is terrible. What will come of it?' In fact, the Party and the SS basically fought each other to a stalemate in the Low Countries. The main consequence was that the small and dwindling number of people there who wished to be identified with the Nazi cause was split down the middle by the infighting, weakening the Germans' ability to control events and helping those who either opposed them, or simply wished to follow a more pragmatic line.[42]

Yet the Germanization of northern Yugoslavia after April 1941 showed that Party and SS were not always at loggerheads. Perhaps it was because the stakes were so much lower here that they found it easier to get along. In this part of Europe, the argument for national self-determination was an embarrassing irrelevance since even in Habsburg times less than 8 per cent of the population spoke German, and things had only got worse: the 1931 Yugoslav census had shown that 29,000 Germans – a fourfold drop over twenty years – were living amid more than a million Slavs.[43]

But as usual in the areas he wanted Germanized, Hitler took no notice of the demographic realities and handed northern Slovenia over to two Austrian Nazi Party officials – Siegfried Uiberreither and Franz Kutschera, a former ship-boy and gardener. Both men also accepted appointments from Himmler and made sure that the Germanization of the South Slavs would take place in conjunction with the SS. The annexation of these territories to the adjacent Austrian *Gaus* was planned for early 1942 but it was postponed several times, following partisan attacks on German patrols, and never formally implemented. Still, that did not impede the Germanization drive. Hundreds of German teachers were rushed into Slovene kindergartens, and the Slovene language was banned for official use. Courses in German were made compulsory, and eventually nearly 400,000 people registered for them. The Germans set up a single new mass nationalist organization in each province and made entry as easy as possible.

Within a few weeks of the occupation, drastic deportation plans – originating in all likelihood with Himmler himself – were also drawn up. To secure the Reich's new southern border, he wanted to expel one

Slovene in three, southwards into the newly established state of Croatia. It was a disastrous idea. Eventually 80,000 Slovenes were deported – fewer than the 260–280,000 originally envisaged by Himmler, yet as many, in terms of the proportion of the total population, as anywhere else. But unlike in France or Poland, these deportations provoked almost immediate resistance. The Germans carried out mass arrests and reprisal shootings and burned entire villages. In fact Slovenia became one of the earliest sites of a bitter partisan war. Nothing worked, and Himmler had to scale the deportations back. In Croatia itself there was a knock-on effect as the Ustaša government began expelling Serbs to make way for the Slovenes. When Serbia refused to take any more, they started killing them instead. In this way, Himmler's Germanization schemes triggered off genocide and provoked an uprising.[44]

By the summer of 1942 Himmler's expulsion plans had completely ground to a halt, and even the few ethnic Germans he had resettled in Slovene homes along the new border strip with Croatia were complaining: their new dwellings were not as good as those they had left behind, the fields were poorer, and to make matters worse, some said, it was hard to sleep at night in a house whose owners had been evicted. Once the partisans started targeting them, they had much more to worry about: by the time the SS got round to addressing their complaints, several had been killed and others thrown out by the guerillas. After the settlers asked to be moved away from the frontier, the SS offered them rewards to stay. Himmler can scarcely have noticed, for his mind was set on much bigger things. But it would have been good had he done so, for the failure of the resettlement programme in Slovenia was a warning of what was to come.[45]

GENERAL PLAN EAST

In the summer of 1942 – the last time the Germans would feel truly confident of victory – Himmler was at full stretch. One minute he was dealing with plans to resettle the ethnic Germans of the South Tyrol hundreds of miles away on the Black Sea, the next he was addressing the problem of how to confront the growing partisan movement in the Ukraine and Belorussia. There was the question of who would replace the assassinated Heydrich in Bohemia-Moravia, an upcoming trip to

Finland to arrange, intelligence to process from the Middle East and the USSR. There were staff birthdays – Himmler was always a generous present-giver to those who worked for him – and decorations to hand out. The rapidly expanding Waffen-SS also needed his attention – one of its elite units was earmarked to take part in the assault on the Caucasus. Not least there was the 'Jewish Question' – transports, ghettoes (more than 160 in Belorussia alone), labour policy, sterilization and a top secret new murder programme. It was on 17 July that he visited the newly expanded camp at Auschwitz and inspected the land improvement projects, the fish-ponds and crop stations as well as the camp complex itself. At nearby Birkenau, he and his entourage witnessed a 'selection' of newly arrived Dutch Jews, and the subsequent murder by gassing of dozens of them. It was after this experience, according to the Auschwitz commander, that he gave the order to stop digging mass graves and to burn the bodies instead.[46]

Around the time of his Auschwitz visit, Felix Kersten, Himmler's Finnish physiotherapist, found his patient in a state of such excitement that it was impossible to get him to relax. A conversation with Hitler had left Himmler so euphoric that he felt as though it was 'the happiest day of my life'. Hitler had finally given his blessing for the comprehensive plans Himmler had laid before him for the Germanization of 'the East'. 'It's the greatest piece of colonization which the world will have ever seen,' boasted Himmler. And indeed the limited visions of 1940 had been left far behind, and the question was no longer merely what to do with Poland. For Kersten, Himmler conjured up a vision of settlements of armed farmers planted across the former Soviet Union as far east as the Urals. Linked with Germany by transcontinental motorways – sections of these were already being built by Jewish workers – they would constitute a border wall protecting Europe from 'an irruption from Asia'. Plans and maps in his bulging briefcase marked farmsteads and forested plantations, model villages and towns, and all the necessary amenities to secure the livelihood of a new class of 'financially powerful and independent' farmer-soldiers. 'When he has accomplished that, the name of Adolf Hitler will be the greatest in Germanic history,' Himmler exulted, 'and he has commissioned me to carry out the task.'[47]

Hitler was just as captivated. One quiet evening a few weeks later, he sat down with Albert Speer on the bench under the trees outside his wooden bungalow in his Ukrainian headquarters. The tranquillity was disturbed only by the Führer's low, hoarse voice as he predicted that the Wehrmacht advance would continue through the Caucasus into Iran and Afghanistan. 'If in the course of the next year we manage to cover only the same distance . . . by the end of 1943 we will pitch our tents in Teheran, in Baghdad and on the Persian Gulf. Then the oil wells will at last be dry as far as the English are concerned.' Behind the front, in European Russia, the Germanic peoples of Europe would settle and breed. Telling Speer to write it all down, he started to do the sums – eighty million Germans, ten million Dutchmen ('who are really Germans'), 300,000 from Luxembourg and so on. Impressed by the blond-haired, blue-eyed Ukrainian children he had met – obviously the stories that the Goths had settled in the region 1,600 years earlier were correct – he added a round ten million supposed Slavs who could be 're-Germanized'. Coming up with a grand total of 127 million real or potential Germans, the Führer then started projecting birth rates far into the future. Speer heard all this unemotionally; but Hitler himself was intoxicated by the numbers. This was, for him, the real birth of the empire.[48]

General Plan East had been gestating for several months with a small cluster of bright young SS-affiliated academic researchers – experts in agricultural settlement, racial science and economic geography. Professor Konrad Meyer, who ran the Planning and Soil unit in the RKFDV and who later enjoyed a successful postwar career in West German town planning, was in charge. His colleagues included the young economic geographer Walter Christaller, whose influential and much-acclaimed theories about the spatial optimization of settlements and 'central places' were taken up internationally after 1945 in development projects everywhere from the Punjab and the West Bank to the Midwest. Meyer and Christaller's specialism was the rational mapping of space and populations: how and where to plan new settlements and the linkages between them. For them the East offered a tremendous opportunity to put their theories into practice. As Christaller wrote in 1940 (in the journal *Raumforschung und Raumordnung*): 'a careful planning and a loving development of the "Main Villages" in the new East is especially urgent in order to root the future settlers from the West and South of the Reich, and to allow them to find a new home in the open spaces of the East'.[49]

Meyer and his team had been working in the annexed Polish territories. But shortly after the invasion of the USSR, Himmler told Meyer-

Hetling (his surname had lengthened as his ambitions grew) to put aside his team's work there and to draw up a long-term 'General Plan East'. In October 1941, they presented an exhibition in Posen on 'Planning and Reconstruction in the East', and Meyer showed Himmler and Heydrich the displays of model villages and farm-complexes complete with modern interiors and rationalized agrarian systems. They evidently liked what they saw for, a few months later, Himmler told Meyer-Hetling that his new plan should expand to cover the entire region from Leningrad to the Crimea.[50]

Demographers and security experts were also making their contribution. In early October 1941, Heydrich made a important programmatic speech about Europe to his colleagues in Prague which marked one of the early signs of the SS's new ambitions for the East: first, he said, there were those countries – Norway, the Netherlands, Flanders, Denmark and Sweden – inhabited by 'Germanic men' 'of our blood and our character', that would be incorporated or associated in some way with Germany. Secondly, there were the Slav countries of eastern Europe; and third, there were the 'spaces' as far as the Urals which would be exploited for their labour and raw materials. Heydrich described a 'German wall' of 'German blood' standing against 'the Asian storm-flood' (just as Himmler would the following summer to Kersten). The whole orientation of German racial policy, he went on, would shift eastwards, from the Protectorate, the Warthegau and West Prussia into Russia itself. And this meant that Poland, the Protectorate and the Baltic states, too, would have to be Germanized with 'the old colonial spirit' which had seen Germans settle the same regions in medieval times.[51]

Such an ambitious reworking of German settlement plans raised many problems in the minds of more practically minded men, men less obsessed with the Teutonic Knights or stories of the Wild West. Rolf-Heinz Hoeppner, head of the Central Resettlement Office in Posen, was well aware of the difficulty of translating grand visions into practical terms in the midst of a war. On 3 September, he sent Eichmann, the RSHA's expert on the Jewish question, a long memorandum which makes it clear that, even before Heydrich's Prague speech, deportations from eastern Europe were being planned on a vast scale for the coming peace, targeting all those who were not 're-Germanizable'. According to Hoeppner:

After the end of the war, a large-scale deportation of population groups that are undesirable for the Greater German Reich will be necessary in the various territories taken over by Germany. This concerns not only the final solution of the Jewish question, which will pertain to, in addition to the Greater German Reich, all states under German control; in addition, it includes above all the deportations of racially non re-Germanizable members of primarily eastern and south-eastern peoples within the German settlement sphere.

There was clearly a huge question-mark hanging over the fate of *all* 'non re-Germanizable' peoples in eastern Europe, not just the Jews. Hoeppner himself suggested – in self-confessed ignorance of the leadership's proposals – that vast areas of the USSR ought to be made available for these populations under the administrative control of the SS. There was the practical issue of whether it would be possible to initiate such transportations, especially for Jews, while the war was going on. But a more basic question needed to be settled first. As he put it:

It would be sheer fantasy to discuss further organization in these intake areas, since fundamental decisions must first be made . . . it is essential that we be totally clear from the outset as to what is to be done in the end with these displaced populations that are undesirable for the Greater German settlement areas. Is the goal to permanently secure them some sort of subsistence, or should they be totally eradicated?[52]

Subsistence or extermination? On this crucial long-term question, Hoeppner was still in the dark. And not only him. Given the numbers involved, this is scarcely surprising. According to the Wannsee conference statistics, the Jews of Europe numbered eleven million people; but the overall non-German population of eastern Europe was many times larger than that.

Hitler was not the only one feverishly counting bodies. The demographic complexities also weighed on the mind of Dr Erhard Wetzel, a Nazi Party race expert seconded to Alfred Rosenberg's Eastern Ministry. Commenting on the calculations produced in Heydrich's RSHA, Wetzel noted that, although he agreed with the overall goal of Germanizing the East, the RSHA had underestimated the demographic odds against it working. It was basing its calculations on some highly wishful birth-rate projections when it hoped to resettle as many as ten million Germans across the East by the 1970s.

He also thought it was too sanguine about the numbers of non-Germans that would have to be deported. The RSHA estimated that forty-five million people already inhabited the target regions, more than thirty million of whom were designated as racially undesirable and slated for expulsion: this included more than 80 per cent of the population of Poland, 64 per cent of Belorussia and 75 per cent of the Ukraine. (The fate of the remaining fourteen million was unclear – they would presumably either be Germanized, killed or used as 'helots'.) But according to Wetzel's calculations, there would in fact be some 60–65 million people to deal with, and at least 46–51 million to deport. He singled out the Poles in particular as 'numerically the strongest and therefore the most dangerous of all the alien ethnic groups which the Plan envisages for resettlement'. Reckoning their population at 20–24 million, Wetzel feared that resettling them in western Siberia would create 'a source of continual unrest against German rule'. Yet mass murder did not seem possible either. In his revealing words, 'it should be obvious that one cannot solve the Polish problem by liquidating the Poles in the same way as the Jews' since the Germans would be burdened with guilt 'for years to come' and would alienate their neighbours as well.

On the other hand, Germanization, even if one avoided excessively strict criteria, would by no definition cover more than a small fraction of the population. Looking further ahead, Wetzel worried that a radical resettlement of the notoriously fast-breeding Russians would merely sow the seeds of another race war in twenty-five or thirty years' time. And on the horizon, Wetzel discerned a bigger enemy still – 'a Great Asia and an independent India' which, with hundreds of millions of inhabitants, posed a greater long-term threat to Europe's racial purity than even the Slavs. Was there any way of averting this gloomy prospect? Not to judge from Wetzel's own rather hopeless solution, which was to force Slavs to emigrate, perhaps to Brazil, which 'urgently needs people', exchanging them with Germans who had settled in Brazil and could be used instead as settlers in the Crimea.[53]

The RSHA, as Wetzel's comments indicate, seems to have been primarily concerned with establishing the numbers of Germans available for settlement, and of those non-Germans slated for deportation and death. Coming out of the heart of the security police apparatus, its plans were unsurprisingly light on the legal, geographical and economic dimensions of the resettlement itself. What form of landholding should be introduced, and what kinds of trade and industry should be factored in? What were the optimal population densities and what balance between urban and rural zones? How many settlements should there be, of what size, and how far apart? What roads would be needed to connect them? How many workers would be needed – at what cost – and what would the budget look like? This was where Meyer-Hetling and his youthful economists and geographers made their contribution. By May 1942 they had reworked the RSHA materials and drawn up a blueprint ('Legal, Economic and Spatial Foundations for the Reconstruction of the East') for the resettlement of three major areas of German colonization – 'Ingermanland' south of Leningrad, the southern Baltic zone, and 'Gotengau' in the Crimea and southern Ukraine. A line of 'strong-points' was to be strung across Galicia and the Ukraine, linking the three zones. Rings of German villages would encircle entirely new modern towns of 15–20,000 people each at key railway and road junctions. There would be a state monopoly of land, farmed out by the SS on long leases, and major Slavic cities such as Warsaw and Leningrad would be permanently reduced in size.[54]

Hard though it might have been to fault this plan for lack of ambition, Himmler did just that and sent its architects back to the drawing-board. He did not like the idea of three discrete zones of settlement and said that Latvia, Estonia and the General Government should all be earmarked for German settlement as well. (It was at this very point that Himmler ordered the immediate and total destruction of the General Government's Jewish population.) In fact, they should be thinking, he told them, of a 'General Settlement Plan' which linked up the proposed eastern settlements with Alsace-Lorraine, Slovenia, Poland and the Czech lands. He needed detailed costings for labour and materials for the entire project of the kind Meyer had already prepared for the annexed Polish territories. And finally, he needed the time-frame to be shortened from thirty to twenty years. This was Himmler's much-prized 'optimism' in action, an optimism indistinguishable from a refusal to face the facts when they flew in the face of his political obsessions.

The debate over the feasibility of these demands, and the attempt to satisfy them, continued for many months. As the war went from bad to worse, the racial experts lost themselves in ever more grotesque flights of fancy. They ignored the practical difficulties that the wartime Germanization of border lands had already demonstrated – the economic costs, the violence, enmity and unrest, the growing unhappiness of the settlers languishing in transit camps for months and years – and speculated instead on how many of some seventy million Slavs should be killed, expelled, 'de-nationalized', or accepted in partnership. Meyer's office calculated the numbers of Germans 'available' for settlement, making demographic projections thirty years into the future, arriving simultaneously at truly astronomical projections of the eventual costs involved. Himmler's mania for planning covered every detail. He even called in his favourite landscape architect so that future settlers would 'not be deprived of that harmonious picture of manor-house and garden, settlement, fields and landscape' which characterized 'the German essence'. As order was imposed on the Russian steppe, dirt, dust, impoverishment and disorganization would give way to wide, clean roadways lined with hedgerows, cottage gardens brightened with vines and 'traditional blooms', and small graveyards, shaded by oaks, lindens, birch, ash, yew and juniper, which would stand guard over the rows of simple tombstones facing East.[55]

MAKING A START: RESETTLEMENT AND MASS MURDER

From one point of view, this is the story of a blueprint that was never realized, an exercise in utopianism of the kind for which both Himmler and Hitler were notorious, noteworthy only for its toxic combination of romantic nationalism and social scientific expertise. Meyer's defence during his trial after the war was precisely that his schemes had never been put into effect. Yet because there was such confidence in the imminence of victory – at least until Hitler banned all further postwar planning at the start of 1943 – such ideas in fact did not remain only on the drawing-board: Himmler tried to make a start where he could, and to block any wartime policies that threatened to obstruct its eventual implementation.

One of his victims was Alfred Rosenberg's Eastern Ministry. The 'Chaos-Ministry' had never been enthusiastic about wholesale Germanization. Rosenberg's political strategy of conscripting non-Germans into an anti-Bolshevik crusade ran directly counter to Himmler's racial policy to keep them as an underclass. When he visited the Baltic region in September 1941 Himmler immediately ordered the relocation of Russians in Estonia 'to the East' to make room for future German settlement and insisted that the children of those unfortunate enough to have been deported by the Soviets in 1940–41 should be brought to the Reich to be screened for 'Germanizability'. In Lithuania, the SS confiscated more than 6,000 farms to resettle some of the ethnic Germans from that country who had been waiting patiently in transit camps since leaving Lithuania two years earlier. By the autumn of 1943, around 30,000 Baltic Germans had been brought back from the Reich, while it was clear to the Lithuanians themselves that what lay in store should the Germans win was likely 'deportation to the East'.[56]

In Ukraine, supporters of the existing ethnic German communities faced an uphill battle. 'We are not wholly enraptured with your *Volks-deutschen*,' one of their SS advocates was told. They seemed to be racially inferior and inter-married with Ukrainians. Where were the neat, clean villages of blond-haired, blue-eyed Germans that the men from Berlin had expected to find? Officials complained that 'they are poor and raggedly dressed and look disorderly, and one does not take them for Germans. Also the homes and villages look wrecked, wild and derelict, no longer like clean, well-kept German villages.' As Nazi welfare services reached them, they seemed to become lazy and dependent on hand-outs. At *Volksdeutsche* Christmas celebrations, supposedly German children 'stood around the tree and sang Ukrainian songs'. Propaganda encouraging ethnic Germans to enlist in police forces had to be translated into Ukrainian to reach its targets. Undeterred, Himmler pushed ahead with plans to resettle Germans around his field headquarters in Hegewald – eventually some twenty-eight villages in an area of 200 square miles were set up – and he also made a start on the planned settlement in Crimea, though many of the unfortunate ethnic Germans who were sent there had to be sent back to the Warthegau camps again after only a few months, because of the Red Army's advance.[57]

General Plan East shaped policy even outside the former USSR. In Bohemia-Moravia, which was also slated to become an integral part of the Reich, Heydrich pressed for the early deportation of Jews, concentrating them in Theresienstadt as an interim measure (the fortress-town was to be turned later into a German settlement), and ordered that the confiscation of land and the racial classification of Czech children be accelerated. There might have been only 23,000 Germans in Prague's one million population, but Heydrich was not deterred. In Meyer's outline, the Germanization of Bohemia-Moravia was to be achieved by Germanizing half the Czech population and deporting the rest (roughly 3.6 million people) to the East. Nor did such schemes vanish on Heydrich's death. On the contrary, it was at his funeral that Hitler himself scared Czech President Hacha by threatening to deport the entire Czech population if there were any more serious attacks on German interests. As he boasted one evening afterwards to his companions: 'I added that as we had accomplished the migration of several million Germans, such an action would present no difficulty to us.'[58]

General Plan East left its mark in Poland too. In fact, while the pace of resettlement in the Warthegau slowed down dramatically, it intensified in the General Government. Himmler was anxious to push ahead with pilot schemes, and the main testing-ground he chose was the Lublin region in the East, where Himmler's SSPF, Odilo Globocnik, aimed to 'imprison' the Poles and 'crush them economically and biologically' by intensive German settlement. The elegant Renaissance provincial town of Zamość – now a UNESCO World Heritage site – was to serve as the regional capital for 60,000 new German colonists. In August 1942, Himmler walked around it with the local German administrator and told him to tear down the old town immediately and replace it with a new German settlement which would be called Pflugstadt (City of the Plough). Playing for time, his companion, who treasured Zamość's architectural unity, asked the Reichsführer what a 'German town' should look like: there was, after all, Nuremberg's medievalism or the neo-classicism that Speer favoured. To sort it out, Himmler sent in a team of architects and town planners, who were still working on their blueprints when the Red Army marched in. It was a small triumph for the delaying tactics of one of the saner of the civilian administrators running Poland.[59]

The stakes were high. Frank had wanted to wait for the end of the war before beginning to bring in German colonists, arguing that the disruption was bound to jeopardize the Polish contribution to the war economy. But Himmler, always pushing ahead, saw no reason to wait. He had the powerful support of Martin Bormann, the Nazi Party leader, who was even more anti-Slav than he was, and both men may have been hoping that a successful settlement of the Lublin area would allow them to go even further, to break up the General Government itself into three new Reich *Gaus*, and perhaps even to persuade Hitler to disband Rosenberg's Ministry for the Eastern Territories and thus expand the control of the SS and the Party there as well.[60]

But this turned out to be a huge miscalculation and the beginning of the end for Himmler's entire colonization plan. In Lublin the thuggish Globocnik himself was a recipe for disaster, and his callous and incredibly violent methods provoked exactly the backlash that Hans Frank had feared. Between late November 1942 and the summer of 1943, in order to clear room for incoming colonists, his troops uprooted no fewer than 100,000 villagers from at least 300 villages: thousands of them were sent to the camps at Majdanek or Auschwitz. Families were racially screened, and parents separated from their children; some even ended up in the gas chambers. As in Slovenia, this fanned the flames of resistance and brought new challenges to the overstretched German authorities.

Within weeks of the first drive, the region around Zamość was in turmoil: farmers were fleeing to join partisan bands in the woods, and there were attacks on the new settlers, leaving several dead. Partisan warfare now threatened to spread across the General Government, which had previously remained rather quiet. Himmler ordered vicious reprisals including, 'if necessary', the 'annihilation' of complete villages, but this failed to stamp out the unrest. Nor was Himmler any more adept at the colonization itself: although thousands of Polish and Ukrainian farms were identified for expropriation, he brought in only 10,000 instead of the anticipated 50,000 settlers. They turned out to be a rag-bag – from Serbia, Bukovina, Belgium and elsewhere, including 'anti-German' families from Luxembourg, and city folk with no farming experience. Back in Berlin, Goebbels talked about 'the massive political idiocy' of the whole resettlement idea.

Hans Frank and his civil administrators were furious: thanks to Globocnik's inept savagery, Poles and Ukrainians had lost their former hostility towards the Bolsheviks and were now nervous that under the Germans they would be 'treated like the Jews'. What this meant was well known in the Lublin region, where only 20,000 of the 250,000 Jews who had lived there in April 1941 were still alive at the end of 1942. Nor was it a completely baseless fear: Frank himself, speaking confidentially to Nazi Party leaders at that time, had speculated that some people, wondering what was to be done with the Poles who had lost their homes, might say that those who could not work could be 'exterminated'. His own hardly reassuring view was that 'an extermination of millions of human beings depends on conditions that we cannot at present meet'.[61]

In May 1943, Frank complained that the 'newly settled areas [were] ... in a state of open rebellion'. Villagers were being expelled with only minutes' warning and sent to camps where they were divided up on the basis of their fitness for work: 'These measures caused an indescribable panic among the population', leading half of those earmarked for expulsion to flee; rumours rippled like shock waves through the countryside, and things only got worse when local police forces retaliated with mass shootings, killing children and elderly people. According to reports in the émigré *Polish Fortnightly Review* that summer, entire districts were depopulated leaving

only cattle ... roaming the fields. Large numbers of people are being killed on the spot. Some children have been kicked to death, the rest are segregated – children up to thirteen, women and old people over fifty being carried off to be destroyed. It has been confirmed that two trainloads, each of thirty trucks, of children, women and old people were murdered in gas chambers in Majdanek alone, on July 2nd and 5th ... People are roaming about the countryside and hiding in woods, being fired at with guns and from aeroplanes.

Ignoring the political turmoil and economic dislocation, Himmler's reply was that Germanization must go on: Lublin itself was only 10 per cent German, and he wanted this to rise to 25 per cent by 1944.[62]

How unlikely this was to happen was revealed in the unhappy testimonies elicited by the SS's own racial examiners. Maria L. was '100 per cent of German blood', married to a 'pure Pole'; nevertheless she refused to be categorized as a German, saying defiantly she had married a Pole, was awaiting his return and 'did not want him to find her a German'. Johanna W. was 'racially worthy' but 'refuses to learn the German language or to become a German'. Brunhilde M. 'showed when screened an attitude which may be called thoroughly anti-German ... Her husband had been killed in action as a Polish officer. She rejected any tie to Germandom and did not want to have anything to do with it.' That ordinary people could take such a brave stance despite the likely consequences – Brunhilde M. faced the camps, and her children were ordered to be taken away, sterilized and farmed out for adoption – suggests that, by 1943, 're-Germanizable Poles' were a vanishing breed. Given the shortage of ethnic Germans, and the reluctance of most candidates to venture as pioneers into what was turning into a war zone, Himmler and Globocnik's scheme seemed set to fail.[63]

In the Warthegau, meanwhile, the repression of the Poles was even harsher than in the General Government. The secret police sought to 'break the biological forces of the Polish people' by raising the marriage age – to prevent Poles having children – and supporting illegitimacy. It was as though nothing was barred in the war of populations, no institution – marriage, the family – safe when the security of the German nation was at stake. At the end of 1942 came a new policy of targeting Polish children for Germanization from orphanages; they would be sent to SS-run nursing homes for eventual adoption by German families, a policy which was extended on a smaller scale to several other countries as well. But Polish children were at risk more widely. Himmler was concerned about the 'racially good types' to be found among the Slavs and declared it was the Germans' 'duty to take their children with us, to remove them from their environment, if necessary by robbing or stealing them'; all that mattered ultimately was to accumulate the human material to push the borders of Germany far to the East and to become 'the decisive power in Europe'.[64]

A few years later, at his postwar trial, Werner Lorenz, the easy-going head of the VoMi resettlement agency, defended his activities by putting them into historical perspective. The problem of moving populations, he explained, was nothing new. Germans had been wandering across Europe since medieval times. What the creation of new nation-states at Versailles had done was to turn them into disadvantaged minorities. Instead of following the helpful precedent of the 1923 Greek–Turkish population exchange, the League of Nations had mistakenly encouraged minorities to stay where they were behind unfairly drawn boundaries. Yet it had not protected them – hundreds of thousands of Germans had fled Poland in the 1920s without compensation – and international instability had been the result. All Germany had been trying to do – in many ways the whole point of the war, he explained – was to 'exchange such minorities' in order 'to secure a peaceful development in Europe'. And Lorenz could not resist pointing to the ongoing expulsion of

1. Enthusiasm in Salzburg as German troops march in: a family with a photo of Hitler and a swastika flag, 13 March 1938.

2. Angry Czechs watch German troops entering Prague, 15 March 1939.

3. Birth of the Protectorate: Hitler, with (*left to right*) Bormann, Frick, Lammers and Stuckart in the Hradcany castle, Prague, 16 March 1939.

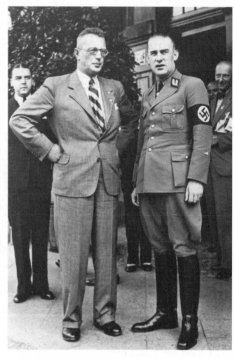

4. Arthur Seyss-Inquart (*left*) with Odilo Globocnik, 1938.

5. SS personnel lead a group of blindfolded Polish prisoners to an execution site in the Palmiry forest near Warsaw, late 1939.

6. Reluctant host: Hans Frank (*right*) with Heinrich Himmler in Cracow, 1940.

7. Ideal home: Himmler and Rudolf Hess visit the 'Planning and Reconstruction of the East' exhibition, Berlin, 20 March 1941.

8/9. Theorists of occupation: Werner Best (*left*) and Reinhard Heydrich (*right*).

10. Talking with the Soviets, 12 November 1940: (*left to right*) Molotov, Frick, interpreter, Ribbentrop, Himmler.

11. The Anti-Comintern Pact, Berlin, 26 November 1941: (*left to right*) Ribbentrop, Witting (Finland), Goebbels, Tuka (Slovakia), Raeder, Lorkovic (Croatia), Frick, Scavenius (Denmark).

12. Jean Cocteau (*left*) and Arno Breker at the Orangerie, Paris, May 1942.

13. The black market in the rue Lombard in Brussels, 1942.

14. A picture of Pétain adorns the headquarters of the collaborationist Ligue Française d'Epuration, d'Entraide Sociale et de Collaboration Européenne, March 1941.

15. Longchamp fashion, October 1941.

16. Heatwave: cooling off at the Pré Catelan pool, Paris, June 1941.

17. 'The Jew and France' exhibition at the Palais Berlitz, Paris, 1941.

18. 'Pioneers': a transit camp holds the wagons of Bessarabian Germans prior to their journey by ship up the Danube to the Reich, October 1940.

19. A crowd on the quay watches the demolition of the Vieux Port, Marseille, 1 February 1943.

Germans from eastern Europe, approved at Potsdam in 1945, to argue that such measures were not in themselves illegal. What really mattered, he suggested, was the manner in which they were carried out.[65]

Humanitarian considerations had never bothered Lorenz or his colleagues while the war was going on. On the contrary, they had seen humanitarianism as a sign of weakness. The whole point of Nazi resettlement schemes was that they were going to produce definitive solutions by the application of state power and tight control over individuals' lives. Their architects were well aware of the fate of previous German attempts, and that was why they tried to learn instead from permanent population movements like the Greek–Turkish exchange. As the head of the wartime Settlement Research Unit in Posen put it, such 'radical measures are only to be understood out of the spirit of a new age'. Ancient and far-flung ethnic German communities would have to be uprooted in order to create a brand-new 'united and combative Germandom'. This was the dream of a 'human wall' that had emerged at the end of the nineteenth century and now seemed within reach. The Japanese colonization of Manchukuo was closely studied as an example of 'creating settlements in the midst of alien population', and the German settlement specialists tried to apply the lessons of Asia in eastern Europe.[66]

Nobody paid much attention to the complaints of the ethnic Germans themselves, who were supposed to sacrifice their traditions, homes and communities for the greater good of the Reich. Even within National Socialist circles, however, Himmler's Germanization plans were attacked for their lack of feasibility, their undesirable wartime consequences and their lamentably poor management. His racial experts, excessively in thrall to the SS's own elite conception of politics, were accused of setting the bar for Germanness too high, and alienating from the very start individuals and groups that could have been and perhaps needed to be Germanized, given the shortage of actual Germans. The Germanization of western Poland was at least a goal upon which the regime agreed and which Hitler had made an unambiguous priority. But when it came to the still larger idea of founding colonies in the Baltic states, Galicia and the Ukraine – and beyond them of General Plan East itself – the doubts were much greater even before the bloody debacle of Zamość and the retreat from the Crimea and the Ukraine.

Perhaps the most searching internal critique was that which came from inside the SS itself, in March 1942, when SS-Hauptsturmführer

Helmut Schubert, an economist posted to the RKFDV, was asked for his thoughts on General Plan East. His reaction was the opposite to Himmler's: far from being too modest, the Plan was too ambitious, dangerously divorced from the bigger economic picture and riddled with internal contradictions. The key failing was manpower, or more precisely the lack of it. Schubert predicted that 'after the war the gulf between the far greater political and economic possibilities for Germany on the one hand, and the size of the German labour force on the other, will be the central problem'. It was not just that the Plan's demographic prognosis was implausible, that few of the 'Germanic' peoples Himmler set his hopes on – the new Dutch East Company helped recruit barely 1,000 Dutch farmers; the Plan banked on three million – were likely to want to head east. How could the authors talk about a 'total settlement' of Lithuania when 'even today' in the incorporated territories, 40–60 per cent of the Poles remained as workers? What did they think 'total Germanization' would achieve in Estonia, Latvia and the General Government when wartime experience showed how painfully slow Germanization was and how meagre the results? And did they not realize that an effective settlement would require more urban workers than peasants if the latter were to be properly catered for?

The draft, Schubert alleged, thus betrayed a complete lack of concern for manpower levels and the overall direction of the German economy. The many millions needed for the 'total Germanization' of the East – Schubert agreed that a piecemeal approach would simply result in 'racial mixing' – could only be found 'on condition that certain very drastic presuppositions are fulfilled'. Schubert's main point was that Germany's secular drift from the land into industry was set to continue after the war; indeed it would accelerate if Germany became, as many business-men hoped, the manufacturing hub of Europe, and relied on eastern Europe for its raw materials and food. Postwar Germany would become 'a large industrial zone', increasingly urbanized (Schubert worried about the racial and social threat implied) and, most worryingly of all, depen-dent upon 'a permanent and growing presence of foreign workers', especially on the land. The German peasantry inside Germany would be replaced by larger farms with hired workforces of non-Germans, the 'total Germanization' of the East through resettlement would become impossible, and there would be a 'progressive infiltration of lesser blood'.

To put it simply, Germany had to choose between a higher standard of living (and economic control over Europe) or deindustrialization, colonial settlement in the East and racial purity. No political theorist of late twentieth-century capitalism could have posed more starkly nationalism's fundamental dilemma: prosperity and globalization, or ethnic homogeneity and stagnation. Schubert himself concluded that the latter option was not impossible, but it would imply a much greater degree of state control over industry and manpower than had been seen so far. Without a quasi-permanent peacetime management of the economy by the Party and the SS, market forces and selfish industrialists would make General Plan East unworkable and destroy 'the German-Germanic blood value' into the bargain.[67]

Schubert's lengthy memorandum was imbued with the racism of the regime but it was also sharply perceptive. Its author was one of a small chorus of settlement critics clustered around the increasingly marginalized agriculture minister, Walter Darré, who felt there were not enough Germans to satisfy everyone and saw Himmler's agrarian expansionism as likely to lead to the extinction of the peasantry inside Germany itself. They supported the ideal of an ethnically pure peasant nation but argued that imperial overstretch would make that harder to achieve, not easier. But the inefficient Darré was sidelined in May 1942, and anyway Himmler hated 'pessimists'.

Of course the regime could not afford to ignore the question of manpower that Schubert had raised. Indeed at that very moment, Hitler was paying new attention to the Reich's overall labour needs and appointed a plenipotentiary for labour to address them. But *his* function was not postwar planning but the wartime conscription of even more foreign forced labourers into the Reich economy. In other words, the wartime economic crisis looked set to increase not diminish the danger of 'racial mixing' that so alarmed Schubert and other Nazis. Hitler himself was willing to tolerate this for the sake of victory, and one of Himmler's closest aides, Gottlob Berger, responded to the young analyst in the time-honoured fashion of political appointees who know what their master wants to hear: things were really not so bad, Berger told the sceptical SS economist, the birth rate was actually rising, and there were German peasants who could be shifted from the Reich eastwards. The real danger, Berger concluded, was – lawyers! Shortly afterwards, Schubert was reassigned to the Eastern Front.[68]

Himmler went on regardless, as we have seen. That September he told his closest associates that their chief task in the first twenty years after the peace would be to bring together 'the Germanic peoples' so that their numbers would grow from eighty-three to 120 millions – the very figure Hitler had arrived at with Speer. They had to resettle the entire General Government, the Baltic, 'Ingermanland' and the Crimea; to build roads, motorways, railway links, and a 'string of pearls' of small towns reaching the Don and the Volga. Eventually this 'Germanic East' would stretch to the Urals, so that when Europe – half a millennium hence – came eventually to settle scores with other continents, a solid phalanx of 500 to 600 million 'Germanic' peoples would bar the way to its enemies.[69]

The idea of a 'frontier wall', which had first emerged during the First World War, had grown in Himmler's fertile imagination to something which bore less and less contact with reality. The war showed that there were few limits to the Third Reich's ability to expel or even exterminate entire populations; but not even the Nazis could conjure up Germans where they did not exist, at least not while prioritizing race and blood over cultural assimilation. The 'Germanic' peoples of the Netherlands and Scandinavia showed no desire to settle in the Ukraine or the Baltic – only a few hundred ever did – and increasingly hated their German masters. Racial solidarity was a myth, undermined by the brutality of the very people who talked about it most. Finding volunteers within Germany was no easier: the furthest east most were willing to go was to the Warthegau or the Sudetenland: they preferred to head west into Lorraine. As a result, the Reich's nationalization schemes became more and more open to non-Germans; only in the case of the Jews did they remain as murderous as ever.

In practice, Himmler's resettlement schemes in western Poland ground to a halt at the end of 1942. His efforts to embark on the first stages of General Plan East during the war were a dismal failure. His pilot project at Zamość brought turmoil to the General Government and made Hans Frank look far-sighted and moderate in comparison; the smaller Hegewald project in the Ukraine suffered a similar fate, and the ethnic Germans who had been settled there were driven away by Ukrainian militias and partisans. More and more *Volksdeutsche* were looking for ways out. In Soviet Volhynia in the winter of 1939–40, numerous Ukrainians, Belorussians, Poles and even Jews had begged to be counted as Germans and brought to the Reich; five years later, Sudeten Germans could be seen ostentatiously speaking Czech, and in Silesia and the Warthegau many DVL category 3s were actually applying to have their designations reversed. When Greek guerillas took deserters from the Wehrmacht, many of these supposed Germans suddenly professed to be Poles or Russians.[70]

By the summer of 1944, the pioneer colonies from the Baltic to the Crimea had been abandoned, and the Warthegau's transit camps were filling up once more with colonists fleeing the Bolsheviks for the second time in four years. The front crept closer and closer to the pre-1939 borders of the Reich itself and then crossed them, gradually shrinking the once Greater Germany until it entirely disappeared under an enemy occupation in its turn. In the following three years, east European countries wreaked their revenge and, by expelling the remaining ethnic Germans among them, they shifted the settlement border between Germans and Slavs decisively hundreds of miles to the west. The German minorities of eastern Europe were uprooted, and most of their communities vanished. Himmler's achievement in resettling 800,000 ethnic Germans between 1939 and 1944 was dwarfed by a refugee crisis involving ten times as many people.

Even in defeat, however, memories of Nazi population policies and the mentalities that had produced them did not vanish. In West German universities and think-tanks, one found echoes of the frontier farmer idea into the 1950s. Academic specialists who sailed through the transition from Hitler to Adenauer now talked about resettling the refugees from eastern Europe to form a new 'border wall' of peasant smallholders inside the country: they would act as a bulwark against communism on the Cold War's front line with East Germany and the Czechs. The race language dropped away, but the anti-communism remained – invoked in the service of democracy and the Free World. Agricultural subsidies, one of the core policies of the Common Market, would wed German peasants to parliamentarianism again, and preserve a healthy nation.[71]

The durability of such language indicates that what we think of as Nazi nationality policies in fact formed part of a broader European tradition. Across the Rhine, for instance, fears of population decline still gripped the French well into the 1950s (and for longer still, once their fear of fast-breeding Germans was replaced by a fear of fast-breeding north Africans). Their leading demographers warned that the Nazis had been all too successful: decimating the Poles and others of France's traditional eastern allies, the Germans had preserved their own high birth rate through the war, the readier to launch their revenge. There was widespread apprehension too that the postwar expulsion of the German minorities from eastern Europe and their concentration inside German borders had simply increased the threat of instability.

And it was not only the French who feared this. 'The demographic foundation of the German danger is being reconstructed,' stated Eugene Kulischer, author of the most serious analysis of European population history, in 1948. 'It would have been an imitation of Nazi cruelty to exterminate the *Volksdeutsche*. But it was disastrous to crowd them into rump Germany.' Many commentators anticipated a Nazi revival and had vivid memories of the revisionist movement in Germany that had followed defeat in the First World War. Kulischer himself advocated 'a drastic demographic policy' of curtailing the German birth rate and encouraging large-scale emigration from Europe. Former German Economics Minister Hjalmar Schacht wrote helpful memoranda after the war proposing to settle Germans in colonies in west Africa as a kind of population safety-valve. Himmler's plans may have been unique in their ambition and brutality but they were certainly neither the first nor the last to regard demography and colonization of the land as the key to national security. It would take several decades before Europeans learned to see things differently.[72]

8

Organizing Disorder: 1941–2

At the end of 1942, Germany occupied approximately one-third of the European land-mass and ruled nearly half its inhabitants. The swastika flew over the Channel Islands in the west and over Mount Elbrus in the Caucasus, from northern Norway to the Sahara. Yet this vast dominion was not formally administered as a whole, and the Germans never created anything comparable to the Greater East Asia ministry through which the Japanese ran their wartime empire. Hitler personally appointed officials to run the conquered territories, and they were in most cases answerable only to him. Not since Napoleon had a single figure held such absolute sway.[1]

To help him, Hitler looked first to the Party comrades who had shared in the struggle for power. 'I know only too well how difficult it is to find the right man for the more important posts,' he told Martin Bormann, head of the Party chancellery. 'One is compelled again and again to appeal to the same individuals. When selecting our commissars for the occupied Eastern territories, I kept coming back to the names of my old *Gauleiters*.' To the thirty-eight regional Party chiefs who held office in the Old Reich itself, another ten were added after 1938 in formerly Austrian, Czech and Polish territories. But these numbers actually underestimate the extent of the Party's wartime involvement because long-time Nazis were also picked as chiefs of civilian administrations in Luxembourg, Bialystok and the Slovene borderlands, and others became Reich commissars for Norway, the Netherlands, Ukraine, the Baltic states and Belorussia, and even Reich plenipotentiary for south-eastern Europe. Mostly already holding provincial positions of authority in the Reich, these men acquired new powers abroad that they had previously only dreamed about.[2]

Others lost out or were passed over. The commander-in-chief of the air force and head of the Four Year Plan, Hermann Göring, was perhaps still the second most powerful man in the Reich when the Polish campaign began. But although he remained in charge of the economic exploitation of the conquered territories, his appointment as Reich field marshal after the fall of France marked the apogee of his influence, and he spent more and more time hunting in the woods of his luxuriously appointed estate. (A knowledgeable contemporary biographer listed his first visitors of the day as his tailor, barber, art dealer and jeweller.) The Foreign Ministry, beset by infighting under the petty, peacock-like Ribbentrop, was sidelined, as the room for traditional diplomacy narrowed: squeezed out of west and eastern Europe, its emissaries remained influential only in Denmark, France and the Balkans. As for the army generals, Hitler never fully trusted most of them. He had even less time for the Ministry of the Interior, which had hoped to use the war as the chance to carry out the centralization of government it planned for Germany as a whole. Ironically, it turned out that centralizing state power was easier for civil servants to do in countries like France or Belgium than it was for their German counterparts, locked in a losing battle with the multi-headed Hydra that was the Nazi Party.[3]

The Party was in the ascendant because Hitler regarded its leading men as the key to prosecuting an effective racial war and to constructing the new Greater Germany. For these tasks, he wanted officials who were 'constantly on the alert', 'a new type of man, a race of rulers, a breed of viceroys' – 'political leadership' not 'administration'. The civil service struck him as hidebound and attached to outmoded ideas of law. The results of running this kind of dual state were predictable. Even before the war, by setting up his *Gauleiters* in numerous fiefdoms answerable only to him, Hitler had caused bureaucratic chaos. 'It was easy to see,' wrote one well-placed observer, 'that our allegedly highly centralized Führer state had already begun to break up into dozens of satrapies and scores of tiny duchies.' As the Reich expanded and became an imperial power, Germany's civil servants watched the confusion grow worse.[4]

There was only one possible refuge for those who saw disaster looming and sought a less personalized and more efficient means of running things, only one man who had sufficient prestige and dynamism to challenge the Party – Heinrich Himmler, the head of the German police and the SS. A long time before, the SS had started out as a small security service for the Party leadership. Mixing state and Party duties, however, and inculcating in its members a sharp sense of internal discipline and *esprit de corps*, it emerged by 1941 as perhaps the most powerful single body in the Reich, and an alternative and a competitor to the Nazi Party itself. Himmler was an unlikely figure to have accumulated such extraordinary power; colourless and uncharismatic, he was an obsessional pedant far happier talking about Tibetan Buddhism, race breeding and the Indo-Germanic roots of civilization than he was about economics, law or war. Yet he had proved his organizational capabilities over many years, he surrounded himself with capable if unscrupulous assistants and he knew how to take advantage of the opportunities the war provided better than anyone else: by the time it ended, 'loyal Heinrich' had also been appointed Reich commissar for the strengthening of Germandom (RKFDV), minister of the interior, head of the political and military intelligence services, commander of the Home Army, and supervisor of the POW administration. He was even in charge of customs and borders.

If the Party was a mass organization, held together only by loyalty to its Führer, and never able to impose discipline on its powerful *Gauleiters*, Himmler's SS – an exemplar of centralized governance by a carefully selected elite – espoused a very different vision of National Socialism. The SS certainly ended the war with more than its fair share of sadistic psychopaths, trigger-happy camp guards and drunks, but its higher echelons – especially inside its intelligence wing, the SD – included highly educated analysts and policy-makers who hoped that their ruthless professionalism could rescue Germany's European mission from the Party's amateurish mismanagement. (After the war, the lesser-known of these men washed the blood off their hands and became industrialists, lawyers, professors and management consultants.)

Some of them were intellectually confident enough of their view of National Socialism to pen trenchant critiques of the way the war was being managed. They were deeply committed to the goal of a new racial order in Europe under German leadership; what they wondered was whether the wartime *Führerstaat* was sufficiently well run to bring it about. Unfortunately for them, Himmler was not a man who welcomed criticism. Moreover, the SD elite was submerged in the pell-mell wartime expansion of the SS itself. Between 1939 and 1941, the reformers – inside the SS itself as well as in the civil service – still hoped it could become the engine of a properly organized racial state; by 1942, they were losing hope. To make matters worse from their viewpoint, the expansion of the SS produced its own counter-reaction, and many Party *Gauleiters* lost no time in warning of the dangers of allowing Himmler too much power. The Party promised decentralized chaos, the SS threatened a lethal excess of centralized order. It was between these poles that the National Socialist debate about how to rule the New Order took place.

THE REVIVAL OF THE PARTY

Nineteenth-century Germany and Italy were both states that had won national independence through integration. But integration was a process not an event and was far from complete when fascism and Nazism emerged half a century later. The two movements promised strong executive government after periods of parliamentary fractiousness and appealed to civil servants looking for efficiency and national strength. But Hitler and Mussolini rode to power on the back of mass parties. These were movements based in the provinces, the cadres in which mistrusted the state and its servants and sought to retain power in regional towns far from the corrupting influence of the national capitals. Implicitly, therefore, the Party constituted a challenge not only to the state's monopoly of violence but also to the very idea of strong centralized executive power outside its ranks. Party or state? This was fascism's fundamental dilemma.

In dealing with it, the regimes in fascist Italy and Nazi Germany moved in entirely different directions. In Italy, where Mussolini never held a firm grip over his unruly party, membership soon became little more than a meal ticket for advancement, the price of entry to office, as Mussolini consolidated all power in the state apparatus. In Germany, on the other hand, Hitler's political and ideological leadership of the Nazi Party was unquestioned, and the Party remained as indispensable to him as the civil service was suspect. In his eyes, the Nazi revolution would not be complete until the establishment of Greater Germany, and while he needed the army to defeat Germany's enemies on the battlefield, Germanization – not to mention keeping morale high on the home front – would require the Party. The war, in this sense, was 'the second stage of the National Socialist revolution'.[5]

Once Austria and the Sudetenland had been annexed, the civil servants tried to impose their control over the new regions (*Reichsgaue*). In fact, it looked initially as though the Interior Ministry could use Austria to test the new centralized system of rule over the provinces which it had been trying for years to introduce inside the Reich itself. But the newly appointed *Gauleiters* in Austria appealed directly to Hitler for protection from the 'bureaucrats', and, after the conquest of Poland, this tilt towards the Party intensified. Mandating the newly appointed *Gauleiters* – Forster and Greiser – to Germanize their territories as fast as possible and as brutally as necessary, Hitler did not want them held up by ministerial red tape. To help them, the two men were granted powers not enjoyed even by their equivalents inside the prewar Reich: to the civil servants' fury, they ran all branches of the administration personally, including 'special administrations' for justice, finance, railways and the postal service (which elsewhere remained under Berlin's control). Thus they were able to treat the former Polish provinces as zones where 'National Socialist theory could be put into practice 100 per cent' (as one German newspaper put it).[6]

In 1940, Hitler made his broader annexationist intentions plain by entrusting Luxembourg to the *Gauleiter* of Coblenz and Alsace to the *Gauleiter* of Baden. Lorraine was governed by the most forceful of the three, Josef Bürckel, *Gauleiter* of Saarpfalz, who had just overseen the annexation of Austria.[7] Norway and the Netherlands were handed over to Party men too: as we have seen, they formed part of the 'Germanic' zone that extended far beyond the confines of the 'German' Reich. The following year, Austrian Party appointees took over the Slovene borderlands. The establishment of the Ministry of the Occupied Eastern Territories under Party theorist Alfred Rosenberg, and especially the appointment of *Gauleiters* like Koch, Lohse and Frauenfeld as commissars, represented merely the culmination of this trend.

The Party's rise could not be divorced from the growing wartime concentration of power in the hands of the Führer himself. Of the 650 major legislative orders issued during the war, only seventy-two were formal laws; the rest were decrees or orders issued in the name of the Führer, mostly in secret. In other words, the Third Reich was not run like other states, nor even like other dictatorships. The cabinet did not met after February 1938 and was superseded in September the following year by a ministerial Reich Defence Council. But this too was undermined by Göring's laziness and Hitler's lack of support: after December 1939 it scarcely ever met, and efforts to revive it later failed. Increasingly the war itself was directed from Hitler's remote east Prussian headquarters, and those appointed to run the newly conquered territories answered to him personally. Hardly ever brought together en masse, they were not encouraged to compare notes on their experiences and they did not submit regular reports to Berlin; in fact they were not obliged, Hitler insisted, to answer to any state official at all. The person of the Führer became the court of appeal for all their problems.[8]

The *Gauleiters* themselves were mostly First World War veterans, radical and impatient men with few airs and graces and a fairly basic education. If some were unobtrusive nonentities, more were 'tyrants', like Bürckel in the Saar/Lorraine, 'King Mu' Mutschmann in Saxony, or Erich Koch in East Prussia/Ukraine – quick to anger, competitive and protective of their personal authority. Many had a weakness for alcohol and money. Not without energy and dynamism, they were definitely not organization men. Rather, they placed their trust in individuals – the Führer above all, but secondarily their own cliques of subordinates, whom they generally took with them from one assignment to another. Hitler was extremely loyal to them and kept them in office for long stretches of time – some had run their *Gau* since the late 1920s – thereby increasing their sense of immunity. When forced to get rid of the corrupt and inefficient Odilo Globocnik in Vienna after only a few months, Hitler muttered that he preferred to 'dispose of a *Gauleiter* only under the direst circumstances'.[9]

THE FAILURE OF CENTRALIZATION

Looking on in horror were the civil servants. Interior Minister Frick and his energetic state secretary, Wilhelm Stuckart (described by a colleague as 'the real minister of the interior'), had been trying to streamline Germany's administration before the war. The expansion of German-controlled territory and the growing influence of the Party made the task both much more urgent and difficult. By giving his *Gauleiters* free rein, Hitler undermined Stuckart's hope that the Interior Ministry could function as the clearing-house for all ministerial contacts with the newly occupied territories. Equally disturbingly, Himmler's appointment as

overall Germanization tsar also bypassed existing ministerial departments and established a new office of racial settlement entirely run by
the SS. So far as the bureaucrats were concerned, in other words, they
had to contend with not one but two non-state organizations – the Party
bosses and the SS. Hans Kehrl, one of Göring's trouble-shooters, told
Stuckart that in his view the Reich, despite being 'in a life and death
struggle', lacked a 'functioning government'; Hitler was never in Berlin;
there were no cabinet meetings, and different ministers were wasting
time trying to work out who was responsible for what. To his dismay,
Stuckart agreed.[10]

The Interior Ministry tried to fight back. In 1939, it sought to rein in
Himmler's fledgling RKFDV and to clarify its remit. In 1940, it offered
to help supervise the territories newly taken from France. Yet Hitler –
as we have seen – preferred his old Party comrades to run Alsace,
Lorraine and Luxembourg and backed them over the Interior Ministry
when the inevitable arguments broke out over who was really in charge.
Governors and *Gauleiters* weighed in against the civil servants from
Berlin. One described himself as 'the government's postman'; another
referred angrily to 'the exaggerated centralism and bureaucratization of
the administration since the takeover of power'. Martin Bormann himself acerbically criticized the 'desolate centralism' of the ministries.[11]
Hitler agreed: he rejected the idea of a central office run by civil servants
to coordinate occupation policy, or to supervise the introduction of
Reich law. The last thing he wanted was a standardization of rules and
procedures that would tie the hands of his men.[12] Everything depended
on the individual, not on some impersonal structure. His model rulers,
the British, were wheeled out time and again to support this conclusion:
'Today there are small nations which have more people than the British
world empire!' A few evenings later, he grumpily revisited the subject:
'Among us, the conception of the monolithic state implies that everything
should be directed from a centre . . . The English in India do exactly the
opposite. A hundred and forty-five thousand men govern three hundred
and fifty millions. In their place we'd need millions of officials!'[13]

Drawing the opposite conclusion, therefore, to the Interior Ministry's
reformers, he argued that conquest required 'massive decentralization':

even the mere extensiveness of Reich territory forces us to do this. One mustn't
suppose that a regulation applicable to the old Reich, or part of it, is automatically

applicable to Kirkenes [in northern Norway], say, or the Crimea. There is no possibility of ruling this huge empire from Berlin, and by the methods that have been used hitherto.

There was, in other words, to be no centralized imperial bureaucracy at all. When Göring did eventually stir himself – in January 1942 – to back the cause of the Interior Ministry, Hitler blocked him at once.[14]

The civil servants were unconvinced. The establishment of an entirely new and unnecessary ministry to run the former USSR – under the incompetent wind-bag Rosenberg, no less – was, in their eyes, a giant step towards catastrophic mismanagement; it would have been better, Stuckart argued, to rule each region of the conquered USSR under a Reich commissar answerable only to the Führer, just like the Netherlands and Norway. The indefinite extension of the war beyond the winter of 1941 reinforced their qualms. Looking at the problems created by Rosenberg's corrupt Party second-raters – the 'Golden Pheasants' – civil servants emphasized the costs of squandering manpower through the duplication of tasks and the arbitrary creation of new offices: 'Everyone does this work just to be sure that some other office doesn't grab it.'[15] Stuckart himself was scathing about the impact on German authority in Europe if nothing was done to end waste and rein in the Party:

It is not conceivable that if the current prodigal use of manpower continues we will be capable of an effective reconstruction of Europe or leadership of the continent. As a result of the existing double and treble organization of business in Germany, not only are people being detained in the *Altreich* when they are urgently needed for the development of new territories, but we face the danger that the error of overlapping organization will be exported to the new territories and will lead to the same failings there.[16]

The pressure on skilled manpower was certainly acute. As early as November 1939, roughly 70–80,000 officials had been posted to occupied Poland alone. By 1943, there were more than 263,000 German civil servants in the occupied territories as a whole, the majority in the East. Yet Hitler's mistrust of the civil service was so deeply ingrained that it stopped him from taking its warnings seriously. 'In the case of any difference of opinion,' Stuckart recalled after the war, 'we had to take account in advance that Hitler would decide against the opinion of the Ministry.' Time and again, the Führer stubbornly refused to do anything that automatically bound the hands of his personal emissaries. In the East, above all, he refused to make 'the mistake of eternal regimentation' from Berlin.[17]

It is not surprising, therefore, that during 1942 an Interior Ministry team reached some gloomy conclusions about the impact of Hitler's personalized mode of rule:

It is one of the most characteristic organizational principles of the National Socialist state that tasks of great political priority, which can be solved in a timely fashion only by deploying maximum resources of power, are assigned not to agencies with clearly defined competencies, but to a *trusted individual furnished with sweeping powers.* In organizational terms this is unobjectionable if the existing administrative agencies are put at the disposal of this kind of commissar and if – functioning simply as a central authority – he makes use of them and does not create a new apparatus of his own. But it leads ineluctably to the gravest difficulties if commissars of this kind turn up at *Gau* or *Kreis* level, and if sooner or later they acquire the form of a new authority equipped with its own comprehensive powers.[18]

Despite the verbiage the basic problem emerged loud and clear: too much personalized rule, too much making things up along the way, too many new bodies and new acronyms. What the civil servants called 'special administration' (*Sonderverwaltung*) – was turning into a huge headache thanks to such brand-new creations as Rosenberg's new ministry, Göring's separate economics agency for the East (*Haupttreuhandstelle Ost*) and Himmler's RKFDV. And that was only in the East.

The civil servants' solution remained the old one: administrative efficiency through centralization. All agencies other than those which time had demonstrated required specialist management – the railways, finance, the postal service and justice – should be brought under the central management of the Interior Ministry. If this did not happen, they concluded – and it did not seem likely to any time soon – the Ministry's only hope lay in attaching itself to one of those institutions that had demonstrated their ability to prosper amid the infighting. This meant either the Party or the SS, and there could be little doubt which one looked most suitable to them.

THE CRITICS: TOWARDS THE SS?

It is in this context that we should understand the significance of a fortieth-birthday volume that Heinrich Himmler received in June 1941, exactly five years to the day after he had taken over the German police. Though little read these days, the *Festgabe zum 40. Geburtstag des Reichsführers SS Heinrich Himmler* is a handsome collection of essays, authored mostly by a close circle of senior SS men, that takes stock of what had been achieved so far, hails Himmler as the architect of the New Order and recommends – elliptically but unmistakably – a new direction for German rule.

The first contribution – on the forbidding topic of 'Central Authority, Decentralization and Unity of Administration' – was by none other than the Interior Ministry's Wilhelm Stuckart. Although a hard-working civil servant, Stuckart was also one of the Third Reich's main theorists of Nazi administration and law and he held a position in the SS. In fact, he had been known as Himmler's man in the Interior Ministry for some time. The expert draftsman of Austria and Czechoslovakia's new relationship with the Reich, he was also responsible for the commentaries on the Nuremberg Laws and later played an important role in the Wannsee Conference.

Stuckart's overriding concern, however, was not racial policy but administrative coherence. Described by a colleague as the 'guardian of the Holy Grail of Unity of Administration', he aimed in this essay to demonstrate to Himmler that the civil service was not the hidebound, legally inhibited corps of the past. It *could* take the initiative and show creativity and dynamism; civil servants could be 'pioneers of culture, colonizers and economic innovators in the best sense of these words'. 'It is now high time,' he wrote in 1940, 'for the senior administrative civil servant to be liberated from the odium of the jurist.' To Himmler, he argued that a dynamic civil service, remade in the image of National Socialism, would provide the strong single central leadership which Germany so badly needed.[19]

It was at first sight strange that Stuckart should have addressed himself to Himmler. The need to abolish all the new agencies which had sprung up like mushrooms during the war was one of Stuckart's overriding recommendations, while Himmler himself was one of the most successful exponents of the black art of 'special administration'. Yet other aspects of the SS made it attractive to the rationalizers. In the first place, it was closely connected with the Interior Ministry through Himmler's appointment as head of the German police: by the late 1930s the SS had taken the amalgamation of state and Party agencies further than anyone else in the Reich. From the very start, Himmler's takeover of the police itself had involved extreme centralization, stripping the provinces of their traditional control of policing to create a genuinely national force: to that extent, Himmler was also a brilliant exponent of the unitary administration which Stuckart was arguing for. Indeed, many of the complaints which regional Party officials made against Berlin bureaucrats targeted Himmler in particular. Typical was Martin Mutschmann, the long-term *Gauleiter* in Saxony, who highlighted the tyrannical oversight of Himmler's police bureaucrats in Berlin and complained about the mounds of paperwork required for 'every new tooth for a policeman or for every police dog's death'.[20]

Himmler's belief in the value of an ideologically reliable, youthful and efficiently organized elite and his suspicion of the Party (and the street-fighters associated with it) also made the SS a magnet for many politically engaged professional civil servants who did not necessarily like what the Party itself stood for. It is noteworthy that two of the key figures in the Gestapo – Heinrich Müller, its head, and Franz Joseph Huber, Gestapo head in Vienna from 1939 onwards – reached high rank in the SS without ever joining the Party at all. In fact, there was powerful anti-Party sentiment inside the SS that actually broke to the surface at unguarded moments. Himmler's deputy, Heydrich, had declared starkly after March 1933: 'We do not need the Party any longer. It has played its role and opened up the way to power. Now the SS should infiltrate the police and create within it a new organization.' The bloody reckoning of the Night of the Long Knives the following year was the first brilliantly successful test of this strategy.[21]

The war rekindled this old animosity as the *Gauleiters* and Himmler tussled for control of racial policy, and the SS quickly came to share the civil service view that the Party was a disorderly force incapable of managing the territories it had won properly. 'In my long Party experience,' wrote Higher SS and Police Führer Richard Hildebrandt, of his impressions of Forster's rule in Danzig-West Prussia, 'I have never met with a *Gau* in which things are done so arbitrarily and with so little reason and sense.' One could offer dozens of similar verdicts, and not only for that particular region. By January 1941, the well-connected von Hassell was noting in his diary: 'The Party and the SS are sharply antagonistic.'[22]

Disdain for the Party was especially pronounced in the SS's intelligence arm, the Sicherheitsdienst (SD), the young, highly educated cadres of which had turned it not only into a watchdog over National Socialist ideology, but also into a kind of informal think-tank as well. Its monopoly on domestic surveillance made the *Gauleiters* uncomfortable, not least as they were sometimes among the victims. The men running the SD were also very different – in age, background and outlook – from the *Gauleiters* and had little in common with them: on average a decade or more younger, most had not long been associated with the Party (though they were rightist nationalists to a man) and they were indifferent to its ancient sectarian fissures. While the *Gauleiters* liked the limelight, the thirty-somethings in the SD saw themselves as self-disciplined members of a highly centralized elite and they were convinced that their expertise would help defend National Socialism better than the ageing street-fighters' famous instincts. Heydrich – the organization's founder – followed the model of the British secret service (as he understood it) and recruited heavily in the universities, ensuring a supply of young lawyers, sociologists and philologists, many with freshly minted doctorates.[23]

The 'spiritual father' of the so-called 'Intellectual SD' was a fellow contributor to the birthday volume for Himmler. Professor Reinhard Höhn, who was sometimes referred to as Himmler's 'scientific adviser', was a politically ambitious young sociologist and law professor. After the war, he founded the Harzburg Academy for Economic Leadership, where he put SS ideas of management to good use by drilling businessmen in his theories of 'non-authoritarian leadership' (*Führung*), becoming in the process *the* management studies guru of 1950s West Germany. Unmentioned at the time was his rapid ascent, thanks to his SS connections, through the academic ranks barely twenty years before – an ascent which had marked him out as a sinuous tactician and a fearsome watchdog of Nazism's ideological purity. Höhn had set up the SD's 'spheres of life' project, an ambitious, sociologically inspired surveillance programme which analysed the public mood 'for the benefit of the leadership'. And though forced out of this post when some of his youthful criticisms of Hitler were disclosed, he remained very close to Himmler.[24]

When the war broke out, Standartenführer Höhn was running an SS-funded think-tank exploring problems of territorial expansion and occupation. By the summer of 1940 his research project on the history of Germany's pre-1914 struggle against the Poles was well underway, and his contribution to Himmler's *Festgabe* the following year drew upon this. In 'The Struggle for the Winning Back of the German East: Experiences of Prussian Eastern Settlement, 1886 to 1914', he pointed out the 'numerous fatal mistakes' committed by the Wilhelmine state. Following Max Weber, Höhn argued that Prussia had been unable to protect German land against the Poles because it was hampered by the lack of unified government, the hegemony of the Junkers and a liberal reluctance to intervene in the market. Parliamentarianism was chiefly to blame, and the multiplicity of political parties. But so was the dominance of the landed class, whose need for a cheap Polish workforce constantly undermined the greater needs of the nation.

Himmler was interested and commented that this was where the Third Reich could prove itself superior to prewar Prussia: Weber simply could not have envisaged the degree to which Hitler's Reich could use the power of the state against the Poles. Not everything needed to be left to the market, and, if necessary, Germanization would be guaranteed by the imposition of compulsory land service in the East for all young men. This time, in other words, with the aid of the RKFDV, the Poles would be cleared off German land for good, and the SS, spearhead of an empowered central state, would prove its vital importance for the definitive securing of *Lebensraum*. The German–Polish wars that dated back to the mid-nineteenth century would thus be brought to an end.[25]

A third contributor offered Himmler the most wide-ranging analysis of all – nothing less than a National Socialist theory of continental occupation. Like his friends Höhn and Stuckart, SS Brigadeführer Werner Best was dedicated to the national-racial cause. The archetypal administrator of the Nazi terror apparatus, Best was the hard-working son and grandson of civil servants, a man who prided himself on his 'impersonal objectivity'. But he had been radicalized as a young man by the French occupation of the Ruhr. He was trained as a lawyer, and Himmler and Heydrich relied on him heavily in the 1930s, using his conception of National Socialist law as a justification for a doctrine of virtually unrestricted police power. In 1938 he had interrogated the commander-in-chief, General Fritsch, over accusations of homosexuality, and in 1939 he had been instrumental in setting up the Reich Main Security Office (RSHA).[26]

Had he stayed to run it, the RSHA might have amounted to more than an ambitious idea; it might have turned into the core of a highly centralized SS, something which it never really succeeded in becoming. But Best's career in the SS had hit the rocks. Typically for him, the dispute was triggered off by an article he wrote in a Nazi law journal. His defence there of the role of lawyers in a National Socialist society infuriated his boss, Reinhard Heydrich, a man who saw law as little more than a nuisance, and who probably feared Best as a rival too. The two men had once been close colleagues, but things between them got so bad that Best left, and he found a post as chief administrative officer with the military occupation authorities in Paris. Although his Wehrmacht colleagues were uneasy initially at having such a notorious SS figure in their midst, they soon appreciated his virtues. The adaptable and capable Best became a highly effective overseer of the Vichy bureaucracy, and this experience, reinforced by a study trip to other capitals in occupied Europe, provided the inspiration for his remarkable analysis.[27]

In his contribution to the volume (his relations with Himmler were apparently unaffected by his quarrel with Heydrich), Best analysed the administrative challenges facing the Reich abroad and proposed a typology of occupation regimes. When the Germans had marched into Prague in March 1939, the well-known lawyer Carl Schmitt had talked about the Reich's right to its own 'great space' (*Grossraum*) but had not said anything about how it ought to be ruled. Best proposed to fill this gap. He argued that there were four ways to administer a 'great space' in accordance with National Socialist principles: one was what he called associative – Denmark in 1940 being the best case of an 'informal' German mastery run with a light touch through the Foreign Ministry. Another was supervisory – the examples here being his own bailiwick France as well as the Netherlands and Belgium, where German officials worked through the national civil service, preserving it largely untouched. The third was a 'ruling' occupation – as in the Protectorate of Bohemia-Moravia, where the German reshaping of the local bureaucracy was much greater and had to remain more watchful for threats to the German interest. Best's final category was 'colonial' – the General Government, for instance – where the inferior civilizational level of the inhabitants required the occupiers to take up the burden of government themselves, while reducing its functions to the minimum for the sake of 'order and health'.

Best was basically making a plea for a self-limiting and restrained approach to occupation. Never inhibited from saying what he thought, he was critical of Party ideas regarding eastern Europe and distinguished the idea of a colonial government from servitude. He warned against turning 'inferior' peoples into slaves, predicting that this would lead only to their destruction or to mass resistance, neither of which would serve Germany's interests. He warned too – this time with western Europe in mind – that one could not rush the conversion of a foreign country's political institutions. Nazification must proceed slowly and in some cases not be attempted at all. In this respect, his analysis was based on his racial relativism – each race should be allowed to develop its own institutions.[28]

One should not get the wrong idea about Best. He was no liberal, he was far from opposed to extermination per se and in fact he tackled head-on the thorny issue of what to do about those – 'one or more' – races that might be entirely unwanted within the *Grossraum*. Though speaking abstractly, and without referring specifically to the Jews or the gypsies, Best was unambiguous: it might well be necessary for the *Führungsvolk* (master race) to 'totally destroy (or totally expel from its sphere) such undesired groups'. A year later he repeated his words in a prestigious political science journal: 'Annihilation and expulsion,' he stated, do not, 'according to historical experience, contradict the laws of life, if done totally.' As Best's biographer has noted, there was no parallel in the Reich at this time for this open call for systematic racial extermination, an appeal that was all the more chilling for its scholarly and abstract language.[29]

It is scarcely surprising that one of Best's colleagues in Paris described him as a 'theorist of destruction'. Yet destruction was not his answer for all racial problems. On the contrary, having – as he saw it – summarized all the options for the 'rational' governance of other peoples on racial lines, Best pleaded for extending the principles of 'supervisory administration' as widely as possible. In the former Poland, ruled at the point of a gun, German rule required tens of thousands of Reich officials.

By contrast, there were only about 200 German officials in Paris, and under 1,000 in the occupied zone as a whole. The ratio of German to local administrators varied from 1:43,000 in Denmark and 1:15,000 in France, to 1:3,700 in Norway and 1:790 in the Protectorate. Occupation French-style thus looked both cheap and effective.

Best's blueprint for indirect rule under German leadership linked up neatly with Stuckart's drive for administrative efficiency. In his ideal world, only small teams of German policy-makers would be needed to keep an eye on French, Belgian or Norwegian civil servants; the grateful Scots, Bretons and Welsh – like the Slovaks or Croats – would need even fewer: most European states would police themselves – under German supervision. Indeed this ideal was not, from the Germans' viewpoint, far from the reality in 1940–41. There were disputes with those they ruled, to be sure, but not on the essentials. The Danes were proving reliable suppliers of meat, butter and fish; Slovak farmers and Czech workers delivered what the Germans wanted. French, Belgian and Dutch civil servants identified communists and Jews and cooperated with their German partners, keeping the call on German manpower to a minimum. With Best in charge, the Reich was able to cut its occupation forces in France by two-thirds in the final months of 1941, allowing it to shift troops to the Eastern Front and the Balkans. This looked in fact rather like what Hitler was calling for – a German equivalent of British rule in India.

SUPERVISORY OCCUPATION
UNDER STRAIN

From Himmler's point of view, however, Best's conception of a supervisory administration had one serious drawback. By arguing that non-Germans should be allowed to police themselves, it gave the SS – the key agency concerned with policing and security – no entry-point into much of occupied Europe. Indeed, in 1940 and early 1941, his men had usually been rebuffed whenever they tried to muscle in to tell the *Gauleiters* or generals running the Reich's new conquests what their policing policy should be. But only a few days after Himmler's birthday volume appeared came the invasion of the USSR, and with it an escalating problem of resistance and sabotage across the continent. How serious the situation really was in Europe in the summer of 1941 was a matter of dispute. In France, for instance, Best's Wehrmacht colleagues believed they had the situation under control. But Himmler and Heydrich saw an opening and insisted they were too soft. They wanted to appoint their own higher SS and police commanders (HSSPF) to take over policing and they also wanted to bring in their broad conception of security as 'political administration' across the continent. Until then Hitler had shown little interest in Himmler's obsessive plans for Germanic unity and he was more anxious to keep things quiet in the West so that he could focus on winning the war. But when Himmler claimed that the Wehrmacht or the Foreign Ministry were failing to crack down on the Reich's opponents and underestimating the continental linkages in the war on Bolshevism, that attracted his attention. Best had hoped to persuade Himmler of the need for a relatively light touch, but Himmler was in no mood to listen.[30]

It was events in the former Yugoslavia, where rebellion flared up quicker than anywhere else that summer, that gave Himmler his first real chance of taking over Europe. Caught by surprise, especially after the ease with which they had conquered the country some months earlier, the overstretched Germans tried to quell the uprising that broke out in Serbia, Croatia and Montenegro. But the needs of the Eastern Front made it hard to bring in enough troops, and at one point the military commander in Belgrade seriously questioned whether they could hold the country. Hitler himself was convinced that only draconian punishment would prevent opposition to German rule spreading across Europe. On 16 September he called for 'the most drastic means' to be employed against any provocation and demanded that fifty to a hundred hostages be shot for every German soldier killed. Existing 'political relationships', according to the order, were to be ignored.

Softness was in fact the last charge one could level at the German military in Serbia and they were more than happy to comply with Hitler's decree. On 4 October, after partisans ambushed and killed a group of German soldiers, Franz Böhme, the Wehrmacht commander in Serbia, demanded that hostages be killed on the maximum end of the scale at 100 to 1 and, with communists and Jews already interned, he decided to execute the latter as hostages. A few days later, the chief administrative

officer with the military commander in Serbia, Harald Turner, described
the results in a letter to an SS friend in Danzig:

That the devil is loose here you probably know . . . Five weeks ago I put the first
600 against the wall, since then in one mopping-up operation we did in another
2,000, in a further operation again some 1,000 and in between I had 2,000 Jews
and 200 gypsies shot in accordance with the quota 1:100 for bestially murdered
German soldiers, and a further 2,200, likewise almost all Jews, will be shot in
the next eight days. This is not a pretty business. At any rate, it has to be, if only
to make clear what it means even to attack a German soldier, and for the rest,
the Jewish question solves itself most quickly this way. Actually, it is false, if one
has to be precise about it, that for murdered Germans – on whose account the
1:100 ratio should really be borne by Serbs – 100 Jews are shot instead; but we
had the Jews in the camps – after all, they too are Serb nationals, and besides
they have to disappear.[31]

By the end of 1941, thanks to reprisals more brutal than anywhere else
in occupied Europe, the rebellion in Serbia had been largely crushed.[32]

Now the way seemed clear to set up a 'supervisory administration' in
Belgrade, along the lines hammered out in France. German diplomats
and intelligence officers had already picked General Milan Nedic, the
former Yugoslav chief of staff, to head a new Serbian government.
Harald Turner himself – who had been posted to Belgrade from Paris –
hoped the Nedic government would run the country under his supervision, much as Pétain was doing for Best. Asked by Stuckart in 1942
how more and more territory could be governed by fewer personnel,
Turner replied that: 'The German administration [in Serbia] is carrying
out its tasks in the form of a so-called supervisory administration
[Aufsichtsverwaltung] . . . These methods are proving themselves day
by day.' The only trouble was the usual one – although Serbian civil
servants were proving to be reliable much as the French were, German
agencies were feuding among themselves and getting in each other's
way. The moral was music to Stuckart's ears: 'The simpler and clearer
the German chain of command, the greater the manpower savings.'[33]

Like Best in France, Turner recognized the possibility – indeed the
necessity – for the Reich to enlist nationalist Serbs in a common campaign. The logical consequence of trying to introduce a political aspect
to the reprisals policy was to make Jews and communists the victims.
To Himmler, Turner boasted in April 1942 that 'already some months

ago, I shot dead all the Jews I could get my hands on this area, concentrated all the Jewish women and children in a camp and with the help of the SD got my hands on a "delousing van" that in about 14 days to 4 weeks will have brought about the definitive clearing out of the camp'. Thanks to these gassings, by the summer of 1942, Turner was proudly claiming that Serbia was 'the only country in which the Jewish question and gypsy question' had been 'solved'. For Turner, Best's prescription – mass murder of the Jews combined with hegemonic control of other nationalities (in other words, 'supervisory administration') – fitted the Serbian case perfectly.[34]

For Himmler, however, this was all much too clever. As he reminded Turner: one ought not to forget that 'the Serb remains a Serb', and that the Serbian *Volk* had been 'practised and experienced in revolt for centuries'. Incredibly, Himmler tried to argue that the Wehrmacht and Turner were not being tough enough and in January 1942 he appointed an HSSPF to Belgrade – a violently anti-Slav Austrian called August Meyszner whose watchword was: 'I like a dead Serb better than a live one.' Meyszner thought Turner was being naive in trying to enlist pro-German Serbs in a common campaign. Yet Turner's approach had its own grim political logic, and although Himmler managed to have him withdrawn it was a pyrrhic victory, because Turner's policy was effectively continued by the man who took over from him, a well-connected Austrian Nazi called Hermann Neubacher. Neubacher was contemptuous of what he termed Meyszner's 'totally primitive extermination thesis' and also sought to build up a solid Serbian anti-communist front against the partisans. The Germans were stretched to the limit as the war went from bad to worse in Russia and the Ukraine, and Neubacher – like Turner and Best – understood that the Reich simply could not afford to police entire countries by themselves. The SS thus lost its battle in Serbia, and the principles of the 'supervisory administration' and the Nedic government remained in place until the Germans left. Himmler's first effort to take over a European country had failed.[35]

Much more important was the situation in France. The military commander there was watching the situation in Serbia closely, for in France too – though on a very much smaller scale – the invasion of the USSR had led to an upsurge of armed attacks on German military personnel. Before the summer of 1941, things had been rather quiet, and only twenty-five death sentences had been carried out by the Germans since they had arrived. Yet as they drew down their troop numbers and transferred units eastwards, so there came a series of high-profile assassinations and assaults that culminated in the field commander of Nancy being shot in the street in October by a young member of the communist resistance. The Wehrmacht did not believe there was cause for concern, but Hitler was furious at its softness and intervened directly to insist on the implementation of his order on reprisal quotas.

Unlike in Serbia, the Wehrmacht fought back against these orders. The French did not arouse the same antipathy that the Serbs did, and Pétain was a more considerable force than Nedic. There was a functioning government, and it seemed foolish to undermine it. Hence the German military commander in Paris, Otto von Stülpnagel, argued strongly that reprisals should be calibrated so as not to jeopardize good relations with the mass of the population that was working on behalf of the German war effort. Existing 'political relationships' should not be ignored, despite the Führer's wishes. Hence he proposed something similar to what the Wehrmacht would also come up with in Serbia. After shooting ninety-five hostages on Hitler's instructions, and arresting hundreds more, he proposed fining the Jews of Paris instead and deporting 1,000 of them, together with 500 communists, to 'the East'. Yet this was not enough to assuage the Führer, who was keeping an eye on the situation there and demanding further punishment: Best's 'supervisory administration' was clearly under fire for softness. Von Stülpnagel himself was forced to resign in February, and Best eventually quit too.

For Himmler the outcome *seemed* far more satisfactory than in Serbia. Best and the Wehrmacht lost the crucial right to supervise the French police, and this passed to the SS. In the spring of 1942, an HSSPF was appointed for France – Carl-Albrecht Oberg, who had been running the Radom district in occupied Poland. The SS seemed to be ready to take over western Europe as well as the East, and to introduce its own conception of occupation policing there too. Best himself left France and moved on to run Denmark, a much smaller and less important country whose loose relationship with the Reich suited his own views of occupation perfectly. The result was a triumph for Himmler, or, more precisely, for his deputy – and Best's *bête noire* – Reinhard Heydrich.

BEST OR HEYDRICH?

Best's former boss and nemesis, Reinhard Heydrich, was the second-in-command in the SS and an energetic, ruthless and ambitious infighter. So far as occupation policy in Europe was concerned, he was the rising star. In May 1942, when he travelled to Paris in triumph to install the new HSSPF there personally, there was no longer any love lost between him and Best. 'I once promised your wife,' Best wrote to Heydrich in April 1942, shortly before the latter's visit to Paris, 'that I would be a true friend to you. But you do not want a friend. You want a subordinate.' Heydrich himself put it differently. It had all been about whether 'the lawyers' – men like Best – should have the power to decide on all matters, or merely advise. It was nothing personal; after all, Best, too, was 'an Old Nazi'. He had broken with Best, he told Kurt Daluege, the commander of the regular German police, because he was determined to separate his conception of 'police administration' from Best and the 'regiment of jurists'. Heydrich was a strategist of occupation government in his own right, and a politically much more effective and more powerful one than Best.[36]

After organizing the death squads for the invasion of the USSR, the violin-playing architect of the SS's expansion into the East had been at a loose end. Himmler was alarmed to hear that in the early weeks of the attack his restless deputy was flying over the front lines; on one occasion he was actually shot down, but managed to make his way back safely. In September 1941, however, at the age of only thirty-seven, Heydrich suddenly won a new prestigious appointment as acting protector of Bohemia-Moravia. This was his chance to step out of the shadows and demonstrate his abilities in government.

He had engineered it by taking advantage of the scattered signs of resistance, sabotage and unrest that had multiplied among the Czechs since the invasion of the USSR. The protector in Prague, von Neurath, believed he had the country well in hand. But Heydrich encouraged Neurath's deputy, Karl Hermann Frank, to feed the Führer a very different picture. Alarmed by what was happening in the former Yugoslavia, Hitler was receptive to calls for tougher leadership, and Frank believed he might get the nod over von Neurath. Frank was half-right: only a few days after issuing his draconian hostages decree, von Neurath was withdrawn, supposedly for reasons of health. But it was Heydrich not Frank who replaced him.

Having installed his young family in a luxurious estate outside Prague (where his wife immediately consigned camp labourers to dig a swimming pool in the grounds), Heydrich threw himself into his new task. His basic goal was to crush all opposition to German rule while keeping the Czech workforce obedient and productive. Like Best, Heydrich wanted 'a governing machine with the smallest possible number of capable (German) workers and the devolution of administrative business, the focus of practical administrative work, ever more to the Czech ministries'. But his approach was more draconian. Unleashing the Gestapo in a brief but unprecedented reign of terror on his arrival, Heydrich shocked the Czechs into quiescence. Alois Eliáš, the Czech premier, was arrested and sentenced to death for espionage (like most Czech politicians, he had indeed remained in contact with London); 400 people were executed in two months. This was repression on a scale far exceeding anything the Wehrmacht was carrying out in France. Hitler completely approved, however, commenting that Eliáš's fate would send a signal to politicians in other countries that they would have to watch their step. At the same time, Heydrich tried winning over the Czech workers, laying on free entrance to football matches on May Day and increasing food rations. Martial law was lifted in January, and some students were released from the camps. It seemed to work. 'The Protectorate is now in the best of spirits,' Goebbels noted approvingly in February 1942. There might be trouble elsewhere – the German ambassador in Ankara was attacked, Soviet partisans killed the commander of Einsatzgruppe A, and the Gestapo feared a terrorism campaign across the continent – but the Protectorate looked like a model of tranquillity.[37]

Himmler admired the way this adroit combination of police terror, protected living standards and discreet but firm administrative control had returned the Czechs to obedience. Hitler too was very satisfied. Heydrich now hoped his record in Prague would be the springboard to further advancement. In May 1942, he told his deputy that Hitler might well put him in charge in France – which would have meant a definitive SS takeover in western Europe. His trip to Paris that month thus signalled his desire to extend the Prague model of occupation to the most important country under German control. In fact Heydrich's ambitions went even further. For some weeks before his death he was working on a plan to reform the German administration of the continent as a whole and was actually on his way to see Hitler to discuss this with him when he was assassinated by Czech commandos flown in from London.[38]

NATIONAL SOCIALISM AND EUROPEAN NATIONALISM

Through late 1941 and early 1942, Himmler and Heydrich – with Hitler behind them – thus pushed for tougher policing and collective punishment at the same time as Best, the erstwhile theoretician of unlimited police power within the Reich, was preaching the opposite. At stake was the whole basis for German occupation across the continent. It is easy to see the lack of realism in Himmler and Heydrich's iron fist approach. On the other hand, Best too was scarcely the realist he imagined himself to be either. For there was a basic question he never really answered: why should Europeans accept the leadership of National Socialist Germany at all except under coercion?

Only some ninety million – at the very most – of the 244 million people under the sway of the Third Reich in 1942 were actually Germans. What of the rest? Should there be no acknowledgement of their own national aspirations? Indeed was this exploitation of an entire continent for the benefit of an imperial *Herrenvolk* really what National Socialism was about? Hitler, Heydrich and Himmler had no difficulty with such an idea; they were essentially German nationalists who regarded all other national movements as a potential threat. Not so the Stuckart–Höhn–Best group. Opponents of what they called 'imperialism', they feared that somewhere along the way National Socialism had lost sight of its original purpose, which was the creation of a nationally homogeneous Germany. What distinguished them from their opponents – whether the *Gauleiters* inside the Nazi Party, conservatives like Schmitt or members of the opposition like von Hassell – was their belief that the German conquest of territories that were not, and were never intended to form, part of the Reich's *Lebensraum* posed a real ideological and organizational challenge for National Socialism.[39]

Characteristically, they tried to think through this problem in print. They founded a journal in 1941 (called *Reich, Volksordnung, Lebensraum*) to argue for a 'stronger linkage between practice and theory' in the way Germany ran her *Lebensraum* and the *Grossraumordnung* around it. Their articles tried to show how a New Order established on national-racial lines could be run efficiently and in accordance with the principles of modern administrative science. Stuckart himself even helped set up an international academy of administration to establish common standards of what a later generation would call 'good governance' across Europe. As the war went on, they became critical of the regime's excessive and indiscriminate use of force.

In particular, they distinguished between a crude policy of 'mastery' (*Herrschaft*) and the desired goal of 'leadership' (*Führung*), which, in the words of the legal scholar Carl Bilfinger, 'neither orders nor compels'.[40] The difference between the two had been widely discussed since 1933 among Nazi political theorists. For them Hitler was not the 'dictator' he was falsely labelled by liberals abroad but a figure in close communion with the needs and aspirations of his *Volk*. However, applying this dubious theory to foreign policy involved quite a stretch, for the basis of the *Führerstaat*'s claim on its subjects' loyalty – that the Führer expressed the will of his People – obviously ended on the Reich's borders, or at least on the borders of 'Germandom'. What the benefits for non-Germans might be of German continental leadership needed spelling out separately. This was the task the *RVL* group saw ahead of it, though their woolly pseudo-biological jargon – the intellectual devastation inflicted by Nazism on German thought had taken its toll – hardly helped them to come up with a convincing answer.

In their view, National Socialism's potential contribution to regional and continental peace depended in the first place upon its ability to force through ethnic separation. Different peoples simply could not live harmoniously together: that was their basic premise. The League's approach – with its reliance on international legal protection for minorities and its ultimate gamble on assimilation – had destabilized Europe. In accordance with the 'laws of life' – their writings are suffused with such natural concepts and metaphors – these National Socialists ruled out assimilation because it led to 'blood mixing', which was fatal for a 'ruling race'. Keeping population groups apart was therefore essential (and an argument often used against Germany's growing reliance on imported slave labour, or in favour of draconian new race laws to keep foreigners in their place). Hitler himself, in his 6 October 1939 speech to the Reichstag, had referred to 'a new order of ethnographic constellations, meaning a resettlement of nationalities so that ... better lines of division arise than exist today'. Nearly three years on, although the policies had become even more violent, the underlying rationale had stayed much the same: the systematic mass murder of the Jewish population of the General Government was described by Himmler as part of the 'necessary ethnic separation of races and peoples in the European New Order as well as in the interest of the security and purity of the German Reich'.[41]

All of them agreed that toughness would be needed with the most primitive, inferior or racially poisonous peoples; even extermination might be necessary, as we have seen. But they insisted that in general German hegemony should not mean denationalization or repression: in this sense Turner's support of the Nedic government in Serbia was entirely in keeping with their principles. Stuckart claimed that National Socialism – by virtue of its own explicit nationalism – respected national differences and would offer freedom from domination. The SS, charged with overseeing the policing of the continent, should ultimately both keep different peoples apart and hold the whole together. But force should not be automatically the first resort even against 'race-hostile peoples' (rassefremde Völker), and there were no general rules for its application. Germany's organization of Europe would differ from France's in that no single set of norms would be imposed; each 'worthy' racial group would be allowed to develop independently and enjoy its own Lebensraum. The solution to the problem of European nationalism was thus a continent of nations, each in its own space, working together under the rule of the region's 'natural' leader, Germany. Such sentiments underpinned proclamations issued by the German administration in the Netherlands in November 1941 and in Norway (on the formation of a Quisling government there) three months later. Both talked about cooperation, construction and mutual aid, contrasting this with the 'egoism' and 'boundless profiteering' of international relations under capitalist Anglo-American leadership.

Yet Hitler himself was totally uninterested in leading any attempt fostering cooperation among nations. Nothing could have been further from his mind. The fact that other Europeans were nationalists he dismissed as unimportant if not problematic. Men like Erich Koch in the Ukraine were clearly pursuing a denationalizing policy at Hitler's behest, while more accommodating approaches were ignored. When Hans Frank in the General Government or Kube in Belorussia inched towards an acknowledgement of local nationalist groups they laid themselves open, as Turner had done in Serbia, to the charge of 'softness' or, still worse, 'misplaced humanitarianism'. Discussing German plans for Poland, Best had warned Heydrich against turning partner peoples into slaves; yet, two years on, this was exactly what some SS resettlement theorists were recommending on an even grander scale. In future the Germans would have to play the part of Spartans, one put it in discussions on the Baltic region, the Russians that of helots.[42]

By 1942, the *RVL* group was having the kind of second thoughts common to disgruntled intellectuals who see the world belying their theories. Germany's hegemony – *Führung* – had been undermined, they feared, by a *Herrenvolk* attitude that had called into question the durability of German rule. An anonymously published article, 'Ruling Class or Leading People' ('Herrenschicht oder Führungsvolk') expressed their disillusionment. Written by Best, this searing critique ostensibly explored the reasons for the collapse of ancient Rome. Between the lines, however, it foresaw the failure of National Socialism's continental mission because of its abandonment of the racial 'laws of life'. The Germans had been lording it over other peoples, relying excessively on slave labour and increasing the danger from 'race mixing'. They had learned nothing, after all, from the Bismarckian struggle against the Poles; it was the Poles who had won, because they had remained closer to the land. In addition, the Germans had become indiscriminately and excessively violent: one could not expect to 'expel or annihilate' *all* the other peoples in the *Grossraum* since that defeated the purpose of establishing hegemony in the first place. A true 'ruling People' did not lose sight of the importance of establishing 'a tight cooperation with its *Bundes-genossen*'. In short, the Germans had thus lost sight of the crucial difference between 'leadership' and 'domination'. Best concluded with an unmistakable attack on Hitler himself. In a radio address in October 1941, a triumphant Führer had likened the defeated Bolsheviks to the hordes of Genghis Khan. Now Best gave the same reference a very different spin: Genghis Khan was the ruler whose destructive powers had outstripped his constructive ones, and whose extensive conquests failed to cohere and fell apart after his death.[43]

HANS FRANK AND THE
RULE OF LAW

Heydrich's assassination in the spring of 1942 was a major turning-point in the SS bid to take over the continent. In Belgium, the Wehrmacht blocked the appointment of an HSSPF. And as in Serbia, so in France the SS's apparent takeover had in fact only a limited impact upon reprisal policy: 471 hostages were shot between September 1941 and May 1942, a huge increase compared with the previous period; but in the year and a half after that, the number dropped to 254, and the Wehrmacht was once again sanguine about the state of public order. HSSPF Oberg himself worked closely with the new military commander – they were comrades in arms from the time of the First World War. Deportation of the Jews, which Heydrich had hoped to use as a wedge to expand SS control of occupation in western Europe in general, remained a special case, since everyone else was happy to wash their hands of this unpleasant task. By late 1942, Himmler himself was getting alarmed at Oberg's failure to impose himself on the country.[44]

In the East, however, the SS was always in a far stronger position. As we have seen, Himmler quickly neutralized the hapless Rosenberg and won enormous power in the former Soviet Union. In western Poland, he had the full cooperation of Greiser in the Warthegau; his simmering row with Forster in Danzig-West Prussia continued, but relatively little was at stake, not least since there were hardly any Jews there. There was only one place where he faced a really serious struggle for power and that was in the General Government.

With only the vaguest of instructions from Hitler to guide him, its ruler, Hans Frank, wanted to turn what was left of Poland – once he had killed off its old elites – into a model of colonial government in Best's sense. In 1940 he noted that an 'imperial consciousness' was growing in the Reich, and that the General Government was where it had to prove itself. Despite the theatrical belligerence of his rhetoric, and wave after murderous wave of campaigns against Polish national institutions, the governor general was coming to realize that he still needed Polish workers, peasants and local administrators if the quotas of grain and labour and other materials were to be met. Although thousands of Germans were posted there, Frank constantly complained of being under-staffed and he relied upon Polish civil servants to keep local government going. As an advocate of the German civilizing mission in its new *Grossraum*, Frank went so far as to tell his subordinates that they had the responsibility of showing non-German peoples that their way of life could be preserved under National Socialism, thus encouraging other peoples to come under the Reich's 'protection'.[45]

However, Frank's colonial pretensions – insofar as we should take them as anything more than theatrical expressions of his own notorious vanity – were complicated by the awkward fact that Poland was also vital to the SS and to Himmler personally in his new capacity as resettlement tsar. In 1940 the two men had fought over whether the General Government could take all the Poles and Jews whom Himmler's men wanted to evict from the annexed western territories. In 1941 they struggled over plans to establish German settlements in the eastern part of the General Government itself. In each case, Himmler's aims contradicted Frank's, since they destabilized the region, caused economic havoc, and targeted the Poles en masse, thus undermining Frank's goal of ruling with some degree of Polish support. A clash between the two was inevitable. What was not was that it should eventually raise the issue of what foreign conquest was doing to the rule of law in the Third Reich itself.

Proud of his ministerial status, Frank, like the other Party satraps, interpreted the slogan of 'unity of administration' to mean keeping all powers in his hands. No authority was higher than his in the General Government, he liked to remind his men, and he frequently told the police and the SS that he expected them to obey him, not Himmler.[46] If in this respect, Frank was behaving like any other *Gauleiter*, in another key respect he was unique. Formerly Hitler's private lawyer, he was a relatively senior figure in the Reich and one who identified himself strongly with the Nazification of German law. He was president of the Academy of German Law, which he had founded (and into which he brought Best, Höhn and Stuckart), headed the constitutional law section of the Nazi Party and once described himself with characteristic pomposity as a 'helmsman in the sea of legal feeling'. Seeing the General Government as a 'model province' for his theories of governmental rationality, he had established a legislative office to supervise the 'unified development of law' and staffed his administration with place-men from the Academy. Introducing German courts and jurisdiction, he abolished the Polish supreme court and made the verdicts of the lower Polish courts subject to 're-examination' by German judges. In short, he hoped to develop Germany's 'imperial mission' through the elaboration of a colonial justice system. The General Government would be colonized by Nazi judges.[47]

Yet it was precisely here that the 'King of Poland', as Frank came ironically to be known, lost Hitler's sympathy. For the Führer, the main reason for not annexing the General Government to the Reich was precisely so that the German authorities there should *not* feel bound by law. Like Himmler and Heydrich, he loathed lawyers, and the longer the war lasted the more bitter this loathing became. 'Not the least important of the reasons why I have succeeded in filling the key posts with men capable of performing their duties,' he stated, 'is the fact that they were recruited not on the grounds of having had juridical training but because they had successfully passed through the school of life.' 'I never miss an opportunity of being rude to jurists,' he told Himmler in November 1941. They knew about nothing except 'paragraphs', certainly not about the necessities of racial policy: 'The *Volk* lives despite jurists not because of them.'[48]

In the autumn of 1941, the struggle between Frank and the SS escalated rapidly after Himmler started constructing his pioneering German settlement colony around Zamość without informing Frank. Frank accused Himmler's representative, Higher SS and Police Leader Wilhelm Krüger, with whom he had long had a troubled relationship, of going behind his back and building a 'state within a state'. A few weeks later, lecturing on 'The Technique of the State', Frank made the charge public. In a classic statement of the Party's critique of the overly centralized SS, he contrasted outmoded French traditions of state centralization with the superior German way of unity under the leader principle. 'Here we now have a great school in the East, the great, gigantic East of our Greater German Reich,' he boasted. 'I can calmly say that the purely technical-logical construction of a new kind of administration that we have been building in the Eastern *Gaus*, in the General Government and in the new Reich Commissariats, may become to a great extent the model for a future administrative structure for the Reich.' And, taking an overt dig at the SS, he reiterated his accusation: 'No official area can have its own rules for action, which would exempt it from controls [and make it] like a state within a state . . . The particularism of offices must be eliminated!'[49]

Himmler had his own weapons, however, and he was also prepared to hit below the belt. Party corruption was a favourite concern of the SS, and nowhere was there more to be found than in 'Frankreich' (as wags termed the General Government). That winter, the SS compiled a damning dossier on the governor general himself. Frank had filled warehouses with chocolate, coffee and other luxuries. His wife had ordered a large number of furs – moleskin and ermine jackets, coats of beaver, musquash, ermine, broadtail and silver and blue fox capes – at well below their real value from the evidently un-Aryan firm of Apfel-baum in Warsaw. His own agents traded in the ghetto for jewellery, coffee machines, rings, gold bracelets, tinned food and many other items. 'In German government circles,' the Gestapo's report ran, 'it was a daily conversation topic that the governor general's family went shopping in the ghetto.' There were even regular convoys from Frank's Polish estate to his German home in Bavaria, carrying massive quantities of eggs, dried fruits, furniture, poultry, cooking oil and dairy produce. It even transpired that Dr Lasch, the governor of Galicia, with whom Frank supposedly shared a Polish mistress, had been commissioned to trawl occupied western Europe for art treasures for Frank's residence: paint-ings, furniture, building materials. In March 1942, Frank was sum-moned for a meeting with Himmler, Bormann, head of the Party Chancellery, and Lammers, head of the Reich Chancellery, at Hitler's headquarters.[50]

Frank defended himself staunchly but eventually allowed that Lasch, who was an old associate of his, should be investigated. What emerged was damning. Under interrogation by the SS, Lasch revealed that Frank regarded Himmler and Heydrich as responsible for 'a whole world of injustice, police authority, oppression of the people, concentration camps, cruelty'. As if that were not bad enough, Frank had been worried by the Prague trial of Czech premier Eliáš, the trial that Heydrich had engineered. According to Lasch, Frank saw himself as a defender of the law, standing up for 'justice' against Himmler's 'injustice', and preparing the ground for a postwar campaign to rein in the SS, with the help of the army and the SA: this was the basis for the struggle already underway in the General Government itself. A poseur, superstitious, and always drawing attention to his supposed likeness to Mussolini, Frank criticized even the Führer for failing to rule through his cabinet, as Frank prided himself on doing in Cracow.[51]

In May, Lasch died in custody – a rather unusual occurrence for a regime which killed few of its own after 1934 and something which can only have intensified Frank's hatred for Himmler. But Frank's credibility in Berlin was badly damaged. What was surprising was that as SS officials started issuing orders to Frank's district administrators, he counter-attacked, and with some panache. Speaking to university students and professors in Berlin, Munich, Heidelberg and Vienna, he insisted that 'a nation does not allow itself to be governed by force . . . The German nation lives freely by virtue of its law and can never be compelled to become a *Volksgemeinschaft* by force.' Not confining his remarks to Poland, he worried openly about the meteoric rise of the SS, and its impact on Germany itself. It was as though he was warning his audiences of what the war had done to National Socialism; glorious victories in the East had brought with them an unforeseen and dangerous shift in the balance between police power and law. This had become visible first in the General Government; but there were warning signs ahead for the Reich as a whole. Brutality, he told astonished students in Munich, 'is never synonymous with strength'.[52]

Frank also turned his attention to what was at stake for Europe. Sounding much like Best, he reminded his listeners that Germany was not merely embarking upon a new chapter in the history of empire. It had no interest – he maintained – in enslaving peoples or preventing the development of their cultural life. There could be no New Order without law. Law would have to preserve the life of Europe's smaller nations. And, speaking with unusual clarity, he warned that it would be a disaster if the ideals of National Socialism should become those of a 'police state'. Lawyers might make mistakes, he declared to ringing applause, but they were 'still better than any kind of police state'. The speaker's credentials were threadbare: Frank had after all presided over the destruction of German law, profited from the rise of Nazism and was proving to be a pitiless and murderous ruler of Poland. But the words themselves clearly struck a chord.[53]

Inside the SD, Frank's arguments were analysed at length over the coming months. They were dismissed for their outmoded 'liberalism': the question was not whether the rule of law should prevail, but what kind of law. Judges did need to ensure greater conformity to the needs and wishes of the People. But Frank's reminder that the Reich needed to do a better job of presenting itself as law-maker for the continent as a whole was largely accepted. It was obviously undesirable that people should see the Germans as vandals, and fascist Italy as the new Romans: 'We can only build a durable New Order for a continent in the path of Law. We can of course destroy an old rotten order by force, but a New Order must grow and Law must serve it.' According to the SD, which as so often did not hide unpleasant truths from those allowed to read its increasingly pessimistic reports, Frank's opinions were not his alone; they were shared, not only by 'our enemies' but even by 'numerous of our *Volksgenossen*'. And opinion in occupied Europe was not encouraging either: 'Certainly we must free ourselves of the odious charge that we want only to plant an army boot on the neck of the other Peoples of Europe, who ought to be led by us towards a New Order.' As it was, in the Nordic lands, 'our methods of shooting enemies of the Reich are compared to Bolshevik methods, and indeed people often even compare National Socialism and Bolshevism'.[54]

The author of the above remarks certainly knew what he was talking about. The ghoulish Otto Ohlendorf was a gloomy, driven, self-righteous Prussian who had just come back from the southern Ukraine, bitterly critical of German policy there. His had been no ordinary tour of duty: as commander of Einsatzgruppe D, he had overseen the murder of as many as 90,000 Jews. He had not particularly enjoyed his work but he had stayed there conscientiously, longer than any of his comrades. In fact, as with Frank himself, it was not the fate of the Jews that prompted Ohlendorf's view that Germany was on the wrong path politically: neither man is on record as protesting the mass killing in which both were deeply implicated. For them, the Jews always remained a case apart, and there were bigger issues to worry about. What really made them angry was the idiocy of suppressing the national aspirations of the peoples of the former USSR and their concern at giving too much power to a man like Himmler so lacking in political realism.[55]

The row between the SS and Frank could scarcely have come at a more critical time. Inside the Reich, the fate of the German legal profession was hanging in the balance. The German judiciary had been in limbo since 1941, when Justice Minister Gürtner, one of the few surviving moderates among the Reich's ministers, had died. Nearly two-thirds of

Germany's judges had been appointed before 1933, and Party radicals were now calling for a thorough purge.[56] In April, there was an extraordinary session of the Reichstag. In what would be his last speech before it, a grim-faced Hitler demanded – and the deputies obligingly affirmed – recognition of his role as supreme arbiter of German justice, granting him the right to dismiss any judge 'who failed to understand the needs of the moment'. This speech did not go down well with the German public, which could not understand why Hitler felt he needed more powers, and heralded new pressure on the legal establishment. Frank's warnings against 'police state ideals' and his call for Hitler to protect the judiciary thus left his Führer unmoved, especially as the industrialized mass murder of Polish Jewry was simultaneously entering a new and more intense phase. 'Let me issue a word of warning to our legal gentlemen,' Hitler stated on 22 July 1942, the day after Frank's speech at Heidelberg. 'They should refrain from attempting to impose their mania for regulations on the administration of our eastern territories'. At the end of August, Frank was stripped of his Party honours. He offered to resign as governor general, sending Hitler a letter in which he denounced the growing power of the secret police and the erosion of law in the Reich. But Hitler simply ignored the letter and kept Frank on.[57]

Justice inside Germany became far harsher in the final phase of the war, just as Frank had foreseen. Death sentences in the courts soared from 250 in 1939 to 4,457 in 1942 and 5,336 the following year. The Reich was importing not only racially undesirable slave labour, but also the intensified racial violence and terror which the SS was unleashing across the border. At the same time, the SS accelerated the extermination of Polish Jewry, so that by the end of 1942 barely 300,000 of the two million Jews in the General Government were still alive. (Far from worrying about *this*, Frank joked about it publicly.) The police and terror apparatus became more powerful – and more murderous – both in Germany and in eastern Europe. Himmler himself recognized the connection. 'The political development of the Reich is accelerating as a result of wartime experiences,' he noted in June 1942, apparently linking together the controversy over the judiciary with the accelerating Final Solution. 'We have to push through some decisions especially in the newly occupied territories which are also of decisive importance for the future political direction of the Reich itself.'[58]

Yet as Frank's criticisms suggested, the SS did not have it all its own way, and the old Party–state dilemma remained. In fact, the Party *Gauleiters* were still as entrenched as ever. With their Führer behind them, men like Koch and Forster defied Himmler with impunity. Even Frank, after all he had said, remained in office. Heydrich's assassination – and the resettlement fiasco – hit the SS badly, and Himmler struggled to control what was rapidly becoming less an organization than a collection of disparate mini-empires. When he finally became minister of the interior in 1943, this did little to resolve the struggle between state and Party more broadly. The new minister promised to square the circle, just as his predecessor had done, pledging 'a strong central force' on the one hand, 'uninterrupted by special offices', and 'decentralization and strong local government on the other'. But the old stalemate remained. In Ohlendorf's disillusioned words, Himmler was 'really organizing disorder'.[59]

PART 2

The New Order

9

Making Occupation Pay

At the Reich Chancellery in November 1937, a very select group – Germany's war and foreign ministers and the three heads of the armed services – listened as Hitler expounded at enormous length his vision of the next five to eight years. But the basic message was straightforward. There was little time to lose, for across the world, he told them, 'the primitive urge to colonization' was visible once more. Economic need was the real driving force. It had recently pushed both Japan and Italy to expand, and Germany needed to follow suit. The Reich with its 'tightly packed racial core' could never be self-sufficient in basic raw materials or foodstuffs, and overcrowding was a real threat to the country's future. Raising its standard of living meant gaining access to other people's resources.

But participating in the world economy would make the country vulnerable to British pressure – neither he nor any of his listeners had forgotten the blockade in the Great War – and so the only safe outlet for Germany lay within Europe: 'If we accept the security of our food situation as the principal point at issue,' he said, 'the space needed to secure it can be sought only in Europe, not – as in the liberal-capitalist view – in the exploitation of colonies. It is not a matter of acquiring population but of gathering space for agricultural use. Moreover, areas producing raw materials can be more usefully sought in Europe, in immediate proximity to the Reich, than overseas.' He had Austria and Czechoslovakia in mind in the first instance, predicting that taking them over would improve the Reich's food supply – especially if, as he anticipated, Germany was able to force three million Czechs to emigrate. If they got the timing right, Britain and France would stand aside, and Germany would then emerge bolstered economically and in a strong position to expand further.[1]

Hitler tended to think about economics in terms of how much coal, iron and steel, edible fats and grain he could extract from a given territory. He saw international economics as a zero-sum game, not one in which the fortunes of all were bound together through mutual interdependence. This was certainly how he viewed eastern Europe in particular. But after the fall of France, a much larger prospect suddenly opened up – that of continental hegemony. Economic policy experts, who were acutely aware of the strains upon the German economy since the early 1930s, were hugely relieved. 'Today we administer a territory from the Arctic Ocean to the Black Sea, from the Gulf of Finland to the Atlantic,' boasted the German minister of economics shortly after the invasion of the USSR. 'Never before in the history of the world has there been such an economy to administer [*Wirtschaftsverwaltung*].' This territory – soon to be supplemented with the new lands conquered from the USSR in 1941–2 – offered a resource base superior in almost every respect to that available to Stalin: only in oil did the Soviet Union remain ahead.[2]

Yet resources were not the whole story. Europe's GDP was collectively larger than that of either the British empire or the USA (even before taking into account the potential contribution of French, Belgian and Dutch colonies) but its wealth was generated not so much through extraction as through the performance of sophisticated open and interconnected financial markets. The interwar economic crisis had hit trade among countries within the continent and reduced their dealings with the rest of the world. Nevertheless, these networks and trade interactions remained crucial to European prosperity. The real challenge for the Germans, in other words, was less how to extract resources than how to manage them.[3]

Anxious to build Fortress Europe, however, Hitler underestimated the costs of breaking its international linkages. Once the war broke out and it was cut off from its overseas trading partners by the British blockade, the continent's acute dependence on foreign supplies of grain, animal feeds, oil and coal was starkly revealed. There was often no short-term substitute for imported goods, and coping with their disappearance would, at the best of times, have required skilful management, foresight and a willingness to compromise – not the most prized virtues in Hitler's Germany. Far from helping the German war effort, conquest left some of the Reich's victims in need of German assistance to prevent them starving: net importers like Norway and Greece were, from a strictly economic viewpoint, hardly worth invading. But the rush to war and the fact that the Reich was fighting on the very slimmest of margins only intensified the Nazis' tendency to prioritize plunder policies. As a result, German occupation unsurprisingly triggered off fiscal and monetary crises in one country after another, crises that eroded the authority of the state, stoked inflationary pressures and destroyed fragile internal markets. Nowhere in Europe outside the Reich itself did national income rise during the war. In short, the continent's economic performance was disastrous, and it was worst of all in the very areas that Hitler had believed it was most vital to conquer. A fine recent economic history of the German war economy emphasizes the harsh reality: while US output sky-rocketed, Fortress Europe was a 'basket-case'.[4]

Yet in the short term, Hitler got much of what he wanted for, although the continental pie was shrinking, the Reich was able to consume a growing chunk of it. Despite being only a medium-sized world power, brute force allowed Germany to reorient a very substantial proportion of European trade and production towards itself. Between 1940 and 1944, the contribution of the conquered territories to overall German steel consumption rose from 3 to 27 per cent, and the proportion of foreign workers in the Reich's labour force rose from 3 to 19 per cent, allowing the country to throw millions of its own men into the Eastern Front. At the same time, German consumption increased by one-eighth, as a result of contributions from the occupied lands – *not* including the crucial role of foreign labour. Poles, Czechs and Frenchmen were especially important. An astonishing 7.4 per cent of the *total* population of the General Government worked in the Reich. By 1943 more than half the French workforce was employed for the German war effort, and more than one-third of its national income was being siphoned off for German benefit. In the Protectorate of Bohemia-Moravia, increasingly incorporated within the German economy, national income even rose above prewar levels despite massive net outflows of resources to the old Reich; thanks to significant industrial growth, not to mention 600,000 workers in Germany (and more than 200,000 in the camps), unemployment vanished, and wages kept pace with inflation.[5]

If New Order economics worked at all, it was only in the short term and only because capitalist cooperation between Germans and other countries in the West proved far more productive than the colonialist modes of extraction Hitler demanded in the East. Even occupied countries like Belgium and the Netherlands that needed German assistance to keep their economies afloat proved substantial net contributors to the German war effort. Goebbels was impressed, for instance, by the way Dutch factories obediently churned out the Reich's wartime orders. A scholar of German–Belgian relations refers to the Germans' 'extraordinary success' in putting north-western Europe in general to work.[6] The value of the plundered materials alone from there amounted probably to nearly four times that obtained in the East and western Europe also contributed the lion's share of the financial tribute paid in the form of occupation costs and other taxes. Even for the all-important food supply, the dismal failure of German agricultural policy in the Soviet Union was offset by high deliveries received from France and the General Government. All of this again demonstrated the limitations of Hitler's colonialist vision and showed that densely administered industrial societies could be more profitably exploited than poorly connected agrarian ones.

It was non-Germans who bore the brunt, of course, in the form of sharply cut rations and impoverished diets. Long queues were to be found everywhere, as were the spivs and black marketeers. Housing was in short supply, thanks to requisitioning and bombing, and many goods became a distant memory, obtainable only in fashionable restaurants confined to the Germans and those who served them. Nevertheless, food production in Europe overall did not drop as much as in the First World War, and if the French and Italians were worse off than in 1914–18, the Belgians, Germans and central Europeans were probably not – at least until the war's final year. Severe rises in infant mortality and epidemics were localized, and birth rates rose substantially in many areas: rationing and the black market between them kept most people alive. Famine was rare, striking only in Greece in the first occupation winter and in the Netherlands in the last. In eastern Europe it was a completely different story. Partly because German policy targeted entire groups for death by malnutrition, people starved in great numbers – in camps and ghettoes in the General Government, and throughout the Soviet territories.

The way Germany ran the European economy – like its approach to race and nationalities policy – was shaped fundamentally not only by ideology but also by the course of the war itself. In 1938–9, the Reich built up its commercial and industrial domination in central-eastern Europe and after the fall of France, confident it had won in the West as well, it began to mull over the long-term shape of the continent's peacetime New Order. But from the winter of 1941/2, with the realization that the Soviet Union was still undefeated, the short-term needs of the war economy became very much more pressing. This was the real turning-point in the German management of the occupation overall because it signalled a far more violent exploitation of the continent and its resources. Taking advantage of the collapse of the German judicial system, the SS presided over an astonishing growth of the camp population – from 21,400 in 1939 to over 100,000 in mid-1942 and more than 700,000 by early 1945 – turning itself into a major provider of slave labour. Göring squeezed food consumption in the occupied territories in order to make sure German living standards did not suffer, while Fritz Sauckel, the new plenipotentiary for labour, conducted a series of brutally effective drives from France to the Ukraine, which forced more than five million people into the Reich even as it sparked off resistance across the continent. The victims were dragooned into factories where working conditions had become as grim as in the camps themselves. Hitler's newly anointed minister for armaments, Albert Speer, worked thousands to death in underground missile factories, coal mines and machine-tool plants. 'Do you want total war?' Goebbels had screamed at his hand-picked audience in Berlin in the spring of 1943. Whether they wanted it or not, by that point they had it.

CONQUEST

In the late 1930s, Germany's rearmament effort was bumping up against the resource constraints of the Reich. The countries of central-eastern Europe that had been exporting their raw materials to Germany and seen huge credit balances piling up in their accounts were starting to turn away in favour of customers who could pay in hard currency. Conquest offered another way of grabbing money and goods.

Austria's gold and foreign exchange reserves thus went to the Reichsbank; so did the Czech reserves – worth an estimated $100 million – which were helpfully sent back from London by the British after the capture of Prague. Large stocks of raw materials were seized from

Austria, Czechoslovakia, Poland and western Europe, relieving the scarcity of metals back in the Reich and allowing 40 per cent of German industrial output to remain directed to consumers right up to the invasion of the Soviet Union. One of Hitler's first orders at the time of the invasion of Czechoslovakia was for the army to take control of the huge Ostrava iron and steel works. Horses were especially vital for the Wehrmacht, and it requisitioned more than one million. Finished products, especially weapons and ammunition, went the same way: in two weeks, Czechoslovakia was stripped of enough weaponry to fit out ten Wehrmacht divisions, and more than 1,000 aircraft were also among the spoils. It was the same story elsewhere. One-third of all the goods seized from France were for military use – over 314,000 rifles, 3 million shells and 2,000 tanks. In the case of the General Government, Göring ordered that 'all raw materials, scrap, machinery and so forth which can be used in the German war economy must be removed'. His booty specialists worked fast. In Greece, four million Reichsmarks' worth of commodities were sent back within five months, while another special booty unit sent into the Ukraine in 1941 removed thousands of machine tools for the German aircraft industry.[7]

The German army's impact on conquered economies was felt in other ways too. Mobile credit agencies issued temporary, and overvalued, occupation marks to the troops, giving them huge purchasing power that allowed the 'locusts' to transfer substantial quantities of goods back home. After the fall of France, these 'Colorado beetles' (as Parisian shop-girls also called them) swarmed into Hermès and other *haute couture* outlets, photos of their wives and girlfriends in hand to make sure the size was right, and stripped the shelves bare. In Belgium, 'long processions of soldiers bending under the weight of their innumerable purchases' were a 'daily sight'.[8] Göring and Hitler always stressed the importance of allowing the German rank-and-file to bring back loot from their service abroad, well aware that Party high-ups were looting the continent on a much larger scale. An economist might have said that all this was not *entirely* counter-productive: since invasion generally triggered off a temporary deflationary crisis and even sometimes caused the prices of goods to fall, the German paper money helped inject liquidity and restart economic life. But very quickly the threat of deflation disappeared and was replaced by inflationary pressures that never let up.[9]

After invasion, the Wehrmacht generally encouraged a resumption of 'normal' economic activity. Its task was in some respects easier than in the Great War since in 1940 many civil servants in conquered states took the view that the war was over and that it was their duty to work with the Germans. Thus they ordered businesses and shops to reopen, freezing wages and prices to prevent any sudden price rises. Many businessmen, too, saw little point in not cooperating: the 'Politics of Production', which Belgian industrial magnates launched in June 1940, was emulated across western Europe. Meanwhile, direct military requisitioning was replaced by centralized purchasing and provisioning. In the Netherlands, the Arms Inspectorate was up and running even before the arrival of the Reich commissioner, Seyss-Inquart, scouting out Dutch businesses to which it could 'sub-contract' German military needs. A strict reading of the Hague Conventions would have precluded making the population work for the occupier in this way. But in general, such objections – though raised by Dutch, French and Belgian officials – were ignored. For business owners, there were profits to be made and competitors to worry about. Moreover, the fear that the Germans would simply deport workers to the Reich if they did not return to work by themselves led policy-makers, workers and employers all to see resuming production as the lesser evil.

At least in western Europe they had some kind of choice. In much of eastern Europe, the Germans plundered everything in sight. Göring's vast Reichswerke HG took the lead. It had established a dominant position by the end of 1939 in Austria and Bohemia-Moravia, seizing key coal, iron and steel works and turning itself into probably the largest industrial conglomerate in the world. After 1941, his holding companies also took over Soviet mining, metallurgical and manufacturing concerns. By mid-1944, the Reichswerke HG had over 400,000 employees, most of them outside the Reich. All of this formed part of a deliberate strategy to evict French and British capital from central-eastern Europe and to build up a new state-supervised German zone of armaments production, chemicals and mineral extraction between Linz and Upper Silesia. Firms like chemicals giant I. G. Farben joined in. They had not been especially in favour of the war. But once it broke out, they too took full advantage of it. Following close behind the troops, they fired Jewish employees and accepted Nazis on company boards in return for being allowed to take over non-German businesses.[10]

The long-term goal was to release the Reich – and the Party in particular – from the energy monopoly of the old independent coal and steel barons of the Ruhr and bring key sectors of the Greater German economy more firmly under the control of the state. From the *Anschluss* onwards, Göring stressed that the Reich was not at war just to help a few businessmen make larger profits. The Austrian economy, he stated for example, must be kept 'firmly in the hands of the state'. For Göring, the area under German occupation in central-eastern Europe formed 'a homogeneous economic area' which required Berlin's supervision.[11] His plunder policy in the General Government was soon countermanded, and his own holding company began running firms instead of dismantling them. From Cracow, Hans Frank claimed the credit for effecting the change:

> On 15 September 1939 I received the commission to take on the administration of the conquered eastern territories with particular orders ruthlessly to exploit this area as a war zone and a land ripe for plunder, to turn its economic, social, cultural and political structure into a heap of ruins, so to speak. The work of enlightenment undertaken during the past months has produced a complete change of attitude. Nowadays the area of the General Government is regarded as a valuable part of the German living space. The principle of total destruction has changed into one of developing this area to the extent that it can produce benefits for the Reich.[12]

Yet Frank was far too self-congratulatory, and the Polish national income dropped by a catastrophic 40 per cent following the German invasion. The country's economic life could scarcely be kick-started by a change of heart when prewar markets had been so violently carved up by partition, and a substantial proportion of the surviving business sector lay under obviously temporary management. More fundamentally, the Poles had lost all autonomy and found themselves at the mercy of German plans for their country that offered them no incentive to cooperate.

German policy in Denmark, on the other hand, showed what could have been done in eastern Europe had the Nazis followed what one disillusioned business executive called 'contenting oneself with the attainable'. The contrast with Poland was scarcely believable. Hitler had said that the Danes should be treated 'in the friendliest manner' in view of their lack of resistance, and as a result business contracts were drawn up 'following normal practices'. What this meant was that the Danes largely ran the economy themselves, through a German–Danish Government Committee, which enabled the Germans to make extensive but by no means overwhelming use of the country's shipyards, machine-tools plants and other key industries. The Germans trusted the Danes to play along. There was no 'reorganization' of the economy along Nazi lines, no mass buy-up of assets, or plundering of stockpiles and exchange reserves, nor even the forced conscription of labour. Aware of the sceptical, not to say hostile, attitude of the Danish public, and anxious to secure continued access to the country's dairy produce, fish and meat, the Germans intervened as little as possible in business transactions. They got what they needed, but, as a result, their share of Danish industrial output probably never exceeded 10 per cent of the total, compared with as much as 30–40 per cent in France.[13]

Nowhere else got off this lightly. So far as Hitler was concerned, the military resistance displayed by other European powers sufficed to place them in a different category. Nevertheless, the consequences for western Europe were less serious for the first year or two than might have been supposed. German occupation authorities placed a premium on political stability and limited the asset-grab that threatened to follow conquest. Because Berlin saw Europe's industrial capacity as a safety-valve for the Reich's overheated economy, it tried to avoid damaging its existing infrastructure by excessive intervention, plunder and restructuring. German heavy industry's wish-list of demands was actually rather modest compared with the ambitious war aims they had formulated in 1914. It was thus western Europe that the Economics Ministry chiefly had in mind when in the summer of 1940 it forecast the emergence of a Pan-Europa based not on the merger of states but rather on a 'union of national economies', with private-sector deals being carved out under the supervision of government officials. Building on the close contacts that had sprung up among prominent businessmen across western Europe before the war, the Ministry sponsored cosy meetings and promoted the idea of a coordinated Americanization of regional industries; some industrialists even fantasized briefly about a European industrial parliament under German auspices.

The advantages of such cooperation and mutual understanding were soon evident. Following the fall of France, Göring wanted the Reichswerke to take over west European industries, much as it had done in central Europe. But this time he was far less successful. Having tried to block German industrialists from travelling to scout the pickings in June 1940, he was out-manoeuvred in his bid for a Luxembourg steel combine, Arbed, by a partnership of the Deutsche Bank and the giant Belgian holding company Société Générale, under its adroit governor, Alexandre Galopin, a man the Germans called the 'Uncrowned King of Belgium'. Taking the long view, German businessmen and their West European partners wanted neither Göring nor the *Gauleiters* disturbing their long-established relationships – relationships that predated the Nazi regime and, so far as they knew, might well outlast it too, and they saw the war was an opportunity to build on these. Gustav Schlotterer, the man Funk had delegated to build the new economic order in the region, met with French, Dutch and Belgian industrialists in the late summer of 1940 and discussed the possibilities for long-term co-operation. The ambitious Belgian banker Baron de Launoit, described by a German admirer as 'a veritable Euro-visionary', was keen: 'The Ruhr, South Holland, Belgium, Luxemburg, Lorraine and North France ... constitute a natural economic unit with regard to coal and steel ... We businessmen should burst state borders and learn to cooperate.'[14]

What allowed them to get away with this was Hitler's lack of interest in the region. His eyes fixed firmly eastwards, what mattered to him was that coal and steel continued to be produced, and, so long as they were, the Ruhr interests and their partners abroad got their way. This was fine with the technocrats at the Ministry of Economics. Nominally subordinated to Göring, in fact the Ministry was encouraging German bankers to propose foreign firms ripe for takeover. But it wanted this done strategically and discreetly, avoiding an unseemly scramble. It deplored the unplanned confiscations that had taken place in some countries and recommended 'tactful stock purchases' made on 'a purely commercial basis'. As a result, canny Dutch, French and Belgian corporate executives were able to play German firms off against one another. Wheeler-dealers like the Dutch magnate Fentener van Vlissingen or the Belgian de Launoit cooperated with German partners in banking, trade, heavy industry, chemicals and construction. Sometimes even the German armed forces protected non-German interests from German corporate attack, as when the Luftwaffe prevented I. G. Farben from moving in on the Belgian film manufacturer Gevaert. The result was that none of the really large concerns (such as Unilever and Philips) in Belgium and the Netherlands suffered a significant German takeover, and in general German economic penetration was held up by a tangle of legal difficulties and a shortage of capital.[15]

It is therefore not surprising that employer organizations in the occupied countries responded positively to the German call for 'economic entente' and seemed happy to 'work in common' so long as this kept the Party at bay. 'Better the worst industrialist than the best *Gauleiter*' was their motto. The German Foreign Ministry, together with the Wehrmacht, were willing to help them. When the French Assembly made capital exports illegal, the Germans only confined themselves to a mild protest. 'Collaboration' soon shaped fields as diverse as insurance, chemicals, automobiles and artificial textiles: between the French and their German business partners there was a tacit understanding. As a French civil servant noted, the latter were not always motivated by a

desire for hegemony or domination, but on the contrary a desire to insure themselves against all eventualities. The fact is that some of them are uncertain of a German victory and of a continued Nazi regime, or are acting as bourgeois seeking association with foreign bourgeois so as to influence the social state of their own country.[16]

This kind of cooperation left Göring frustrated. Despite the immense productivity of the Reichswerke's stake in French steel, France provided only 8 per cent of the labour force and 2 per cent of the conglomerate's net worth, compared with some 68 per cent (of both labour force and net worth) represented by the lands the Germans conquered in 1938–9.[17]

As they looked on, National Socialists fumed that the west European businessmen were not being treated like the defeated side. But neither Hitler nor the military saw any reason to alter their pragmatic course: the Belgians were following their 'politics of production', with the country's giant holding companies accommodating the Germans' wishes. The Dutch policy of 'cooperation', under the reliable eye of senior career civil servants (including one, Max Hirschfeld, who was Jewish – surely a unique case in the entire history of the Nazi occupation), allowed heavy guns and machine guns, transmitters and seaplanes to roll off production lines with exemplary reliability. The German Central Contract Office in the country kept its eye on 20,000 firms and stressed that in general they had 'offered no resistance to the acceptance of German contracts'. In short, the system worked.[18]

After the war, a German official who had served in the Netherlands talked up the benefits of their 'cooperation':

In the war there was the chance to modernize one's own [i.e. Dutch] industry, extend lines, gain modern technical procedures at no cost, develop one's ideas further, keep people in work, and not least, to make reasonable profits, which enabled the national budget to fulfill its duties through taxation.[19]

It was difficult to square this Panglossian verdict with the exploitative policies that drove German economic strategy, and even more difficult to take it seriously after the wholesale dismantling and destruction that accompanied the German retreat everywhere from southern Ukraine to central France. Nevertheless, it was not completely wrong; occupation *did* sometimes promote modernization and it certainly allowed a few businessmen to make lavish profits. In France, it boosted the production of artificial textiles, for instance. Reorganized under German super-vision, and taking advantage of German technical expertise and even capital, factories producing viscose and rayon laid the foundations for an industry that would expand fast after the war. In Upper Silesia, new investment in mining, chemicals and arms industries led to a rapid increase in output and employment that formed the base for Poland's chemicals-based industries in the 1950s. More broadly, Göring's policy of state-led industrialization in central-eastern Europe benefited its post-war heirs, the new communist regimes of the region, who found they did not need to squeeze the private sector very hard; the Nazis had already done it for them.[20]

German plans to dominate the continent were not confined to the sphere of business and industry. Seeking to make the Reichsmark the 'most important European currency', Berlin forced countries to channel their trade and money flows through the German capital, while simul-taneously it tried to centralize and standardize the continent's financial services. Only during the war could this have happened alongside a deliberate and systematic overvaluation of the Reichsmark itself. France and Belgium had to suffer the most egregious misuse of the exchange rate, but it was nearly as bad in the Netherlands. In the Protectorate, overvaluation helped Germans to buy up Czech property on the cheap, but it also helped the export of Czech goods. In the General Government, it depleted stocks and left the country stripped of its assets.[21]

Above all, it added significantly to the fiscal burden the Germans imposed upon the conquered countries. According to the laws of war, armies had the right to raise money in the occupied territories to cover their expenses. Since the 1870–71 Franco–Prussian war, it had also become customary for victorious states to levy reparations upon their defeated enemy, supposedly to pay for war-related costs more generally. The Germans now combined these principles and made their so-called occupation costs one of the chief means of financing their war effort. What started off as one-time payments turned quickly into regular demands, dwarfing the forced loans that were sometimes also required. By March 1944, according to OKW calculations, France – easily the single largest contributor – had paid 35.1 milliard Reichsmarks, amounting to between a quarter and a third of its national income over that period. The Netherlands was next, with 12 milliards, then Belgium, with 9.3. The Norwegians carried a huge burden – as much as one-third of national income – considering the poverty of the country and its limited resources. In eastern Europe, where occupation costs in the strict sense were not applied, equally pressing financial demands were made. The General Government paid over an estimated 5.5 milliard RM, and the occupied eastern territories 4.5 milliards, mostly in the form of booty. In the Protectorate of Bohemia-Moravia, more than half the government budget went on contributions to the Reich.[22]

As if this was not enough, German purchasing power was also boosted by expanding the system of clearing agreements which it had developed before the war in eastern Europe. In July 1941, Economics Minister Funk hailed barter trade as Europe's future, something that would liberate it from the constraints of the gold standard era. In the meantime, it was certainly an effective means to exploit countries bound to the Reich. Before the war, the Netherlands had run a small trade deficit with Germany; within a few years this had turned into a large surplus, and the Reich was taking 79 per cent of Dutch exports, compared with a mere 15 per cent in 1938. Belgium, with 72 per cent, was not far behind, and its credit balances amounted to nearly as much as its occupation costs. Prewar France had sent Germany 3–4 per cent of its exports; by 1943 the figure was 17 per cent, and its huge trade surplus far outstripped any other country's.[23]

This was basically organized despoliation, and what the Nazis regarded as essential for Germany's own wartime effort spelled enormous disruption for everyone else. Throughout occupied Europe, existing markets were broken up as civilians fled their homes and overseas trade stopped, while requisitioning depleted farmyards and stockpiles and labour conscription emptied the fields and factories of workers. Acute uncertainty about the future led to hoarding and shopping sprees, which exhausted stocks. While the new occupation authorities sought to encourage a resumption of normal economic activity as quickly as possible, this was hindered in practice by the proliferation of military checkpoints and wartime controls and by the creation of new temporary or permanent borders which destroyed old national distribution channels. The manifold partitions of France, Poland, Yugoslavia and Greece raised new barriers to trade and business and cut suppliers off from their customers. Forced deliveries, an efficient clearing system and fixed exchange rates allowed huge sums to be transferred into German hands but only at the cost of exposing the countries concerned to intense inflationary pressures. Taken together, these factors encouraged fears of imminent chaos or collapse and posed a huge challenge to wartime administrators. As protests mounted in France at German demands, the military commander there, Otto von Stülpnagel warned of expecting too much and wrecking the French economy as a result: 'If you want a cow to give milk, you have to feed it.'[24]

In Germany itself, wage and price controls ensured stability, especially as they were combined with a rather effective rationing system; at the same time, increased taxes soaked up excess liquidity. In France, too, former Finance Minister Pierre Cathala prided himself (after the war) on the stability of the franc, and the continued creditworthiness of the French treasury, which had prevented a panic. 'The currency, the credit, and the financial system of France had ... resisted,' he stated without irony, 'in the fullest sense of these words.'[25] But in the worst cases, inflation led to the collapse of state authority and the abandonment of a monetary economy altogether. Relatively mild in the Protectorate and Slovakia, inflation was a far more serious problem in Belgium, and worse still in Serbia, Croatia and Greece. Hyper-inflation was caused by the government's inability to raise more than a small fraction of its needs from taxation and the huge increase in the money supply caused by the central bank's printing of banknotes. By the end of the war, tax revenues in Greece covered less than 6 per cent of government spending, a far smaller proportion than anywhere else, and a sure indication of the disintegration of the state. Gold sovereign prices rose fifteen-fold in the first two years of the occupation and soared again as it neared its end.

Greece stood as a warning of what could happen when occupation economics went badly wrong and when German demands could only be met by printing money. In July 1942 Finance Minister von Krosigk warned Göring that 'in Greece . . . a legal market no longer exists, nor a price mechanism which could act as a basis for stabilization and reorganization . . . If the war drags on, it will be necessary to prevent the countries whose potential we are exploiting, from premature economic ruin.' A few months later, when the German commissar at the Belgian central bank wrote of dangerous inflationary pressures because of the difficulty of controlling the black market, he highlighted the risk of making 'a monetary "Greece" out of Belgium'. German administrators did not care too much one way or the other about Greece itself, which they had not really wanted to invade, and whose value to the war effort was minimal, but they knew that the costs for the German war effort of allowing Belgium or France go the same way would be much higher.[26]

The longer the war went on, the more considerations of stability and production took precedence over planning for the postwar peace. (Indeed, by 1943, the latter had been officially stopped.) Most of the administrators of occupied western Europe were too concerned to keep output flowing to want to embark on sweeping changes. In 1940, the Ministry of Economics had been full of schemes for a sweeping transformation of European production and distribution systems. Two years later, these had few backers. As a result, those German believers and their foreign supporters who had looked forward to occupation as the chance to Nazify the European economy were increasingly frustrated. As one disillusioned Dutch Nazi reflected in 1941, 'The German agencies help us as well as they can, but they cannot disorganize economic life in the middle of the war for a vague possibility, in order to give the economy to the 3% of NSB members.'[27]

In fact, a reluctance to experiment was visible everywhere. Prewar farmers' organizations were often disbanded and replaced by new unitary pro-German equivalents; but when farmers shunned them and turned instead to the black market, there was little either the Germans or their partners in Belgian, Dutch and French bureaucracies could do. In the occupied eastern territories, the Soviet collective farms were kept together in order to facilitate control of the harvest. After 1940, a

European economy existed only on paper. There was no generalized planning to speak of, at least before the emergence of Speer's powerful Armaments Ministry (and that only for highly specific wartime purposes). Austria, the former Czech lands and the territories of western Poland and eastern France were absorbed fairly smoothly into the Reich economy; but there was no overall strategy for Europe as a whole: the Ministry of Economics was too weak, Göring was too erratic and overstretched, and the Wehrmacht focused understandably upon the short-term and increasingly hopeless task of winning the war. The old idea of a continent-wide customs union was put on hold, and instead what was implemented was partial and piecemeal: the Protectorate was made part of the Reich trading zone, but not Denmark, whose policymakers refused the idea of a union; exchange restrictions with the Netherlands were abolished, but not with Belgium. Bilateral clearing agreements made Germany the centre of European trade, but its perennial shortage of capital prevented it from advancing long-term investment plans. Meanwhile, the level of exploitation generated economic pressures that weakened state bureaucracies everywhere and threw into question their ability either to levy taxes or to keep their own citizens alive and safe.

FOOD

Few issues demonstrated this more starkly than the question of the supply of food. In the First World War, the British blockade, together with the protracted mobilization of millions of men in combatant armies, had caused a serious food crisis across central Europe. This was why the Third Reich from the very start regulated domestic agriculture much more tightly than industry. Indeed it was because they were convinced that the shortages of the First World War had caused the German collapse that the Nazis pursued autarky both as a war strategy and as a goal for the peace to follow. They strove to win the 'battle for production' domestically, but since Hitler believed that the country could not attain self-sufficiency within its existing borders, he never doubted the necessity for a war of conquest. The fruits of such a war would be German 'food security' and the liberation of the European continent from the failures of an interwar international agricultural policy which had made it dangerously dependent upon overseas imports and endangered the livelihood of its own farmers. By thus solving the fundamental problem of the only continent in the world to be so dangerously lacking in its own food supply, fascism would demonstrate its superiority to liberalism, and show how the tyranny of the market could be subdued by political will and state management.[28]

Yet this rosy picture rested on deeply problematic assumptions. In the 1930s, the collapse of international trade spurred protectionism in Europe and freed its farmers from the threat of cheap imported overseas grain. Wheat production soared. On the eve of the war, however, it was still not enough to allow the continent to feed itself. Of an estimated population of 355 million (in 1942), about 100 million lived in food surplus countries – chiefly in eastern Europe; 44 million lived in countries unable to meet three-quarters of their needs, mostly in north-western Europe. Germany itself was slightly worse off than average; despite a substantial increase in self-sufficiency since 1929 it still needed to import about one-fifth of its grain. The position looked worse if Europe's much greater deficit in fats, animal feeds and oils was also taken into account. There were only two possible outcomes. Either the Germans would succeed in raising the productivity of European agriculture in wartime – something which in fact they tried but failed hopelessly to do – or else guaranteeing Germans food from the rest of Europe would mean other Europeans eating less. The Reich's war nutrition plan of April 1939 in fact envisaged precisely this: anticipating a precipitous drop in the supply of food two years into an eventual war, it mandated the extreme exploitation of defeated powers to keep German food intake at a satisfactory level.[29]

Through trade and then conquest, eastern Europe's output of food was indeed redirected towards the Reich. Following the defeat and partition of Poland, the abundant 1940 harvest in the annexed western territories demonstrated the potential contribution the new conquests might be able to make. Had it not been for Nazi racial resettlement schemes which threatened Polish farmers with either eviction or Germanization, this contribution could have been greater still. As it was, a contradiction existed between Germany's ambitious racial and ethnographic resettlement plans, with their inevitably disruptive consequences, and the need to guarantee a reliable and constant supply of food to German consumers in the Reich itself. It was no coincidence that Germany's most successful farming partner in eastern Europe was newly independent Slovakia, where output flourished thanks to the intense German demand and the lack of any real threat from Nazi ideologists to Slovak farmers themselves.[30]

In the Protectorate of Bohemia-Moravia, the SS and their resettlement schemes had only a minor disruptive effect and were generally held at bay by the more pragmatically inclined Protector, the Foreign Ministry and the Ministry of Agriculture. As a result, falls in output were kept within bounds, and deliveries to the Reich maintained. In the General Government, too, many Polish peasants initially took a more sanguine view of the invasion than one might have thought likely. Whatever the mood in the towns, where the catastrophic economic consequences of the occupation were felt right from the start, Polish farmers were prepared to see how things developed. 'Until the end of 1939 or the beginning of 1940 the Germans had not harassed us yet so some of the farmstead masters began saying among themselves that "a good master has arrived here" and "this is the Western culture",' recalled one villager. 'Most of the inhabitants of the village did not hide their contentment about how matters turned out,' recollected another. 'They rejoiced over the "magnificent masters" that the Germans were considered to be.' Inspired by the desire to civilize the Poles, the General Government Food and Agriculture Department – staffed by no fewer than 2,000 German agronomists – aimed to modernize and mechanize Polish farming, improve yields, consolidate land-holdings and free up surplus labour for German industry. It won local approval at first by handing over some of the proceeds of expropriated properties, cracking down on crime, offering administrative jobs, and setting relatively low quotas for initial grain deliveries.[31]

Yet Polish agriculture remained in the hands of Polish farmers, and with Poland's political future a bleak one, they needed incentives to join in the 'battle for production'. Since Frank's long-term plans included the eventual creation of giant farms, to be handed over to German tenant-farmers in reward for wartime service, with the Poles a landless labouring class, it is not surprising that it took time for grain output to rise. What is surprising is that it rose as much as it did. The failure of compulsory requisitions in 1940 forced Frank to adopt a new policy of bonuses, and, although peasant resistance against his draconian laws continued, these incentives – combined with an SS presence in the countryside at harvest-time and harsh new collection laws which led village headmen to be shot if they failed to bring in their quotas – pushed up the delivery of grain from 383,000 tons in 1940/41 to more than one million tons two years later. Polish peasants quickly came to hate the Germans; but the latter could live with that hatred as long as they obtained the harvest. As grain supplies from established suppliers such as Hungary and Romania declined, Polish and Czech farmers became crucial to political stability inside Germany.[32]

Western Europe was in a very different situation, for even more than Germany it needed to import food to stay alive. The springtime invasion itself, with its call-up and its panicked aftermath, affected the 1940 crop badly. And with livestock requisitioned, hundreds of thousands of men in POW camps, and fertilizer and other inputs running short, the longer-term outlook was not good. Belgium – the 'arsenal of fascism' – needed help if starvation was to be avoided, and Norway, too. In the autumn of 1940, as a worrying summer (for Berlin's agriculture experts) drew to a close, Göring summarized the situation pithily: Germany should not have to worry about the food situation there, and the French in particular should do more to boost output. France, which had never figured in German calculations as a food supplier for the Reich, was primarily expected to feed itself and the one million soldiers stationed there. Norway, the Netherlands and Denmark might, however, need attention. In the event, catastrophe was averted, and neither Norway nor Belgium endured real famine. But neither did they do anything to ease the Reich's food needs. The Netherlands did, by switching from grain to potatoes, and as for Danish farmers, the luckiest of all, their incomes soared as a result of exporting to Germany. Occupation, writes one historian, 'was what was needed to pull Danish agriculture out of the prolonged depression of the 1930s'.[33]

Because farmers were more numerous and harder to control than businessmen, agriculture tested the managerial capabilities of the New Order even more than industry did. As national markets disintegrated, checkpoints proliferated, and transportation costs rose astronomically, food supplies became harder to deliver to those who needed them, and rich areas were cut off from poor ones. States that had been weakened by the impact of defeat and subservience could not easily exert their power over farmers, who could ignore their demands, or even meet them with sabotage or – as happened with increasing frequency – guns in hand. If the main mechanism for collecting crops was officially fixed quotas at set prices, then getting the prices wrong, or allowing them to lag far behind the black market rate, would give farmers incentives to divert their crops into illegal channels. Set the collection prices too high, and workers in the cities might not be able to afford food and would protest. Moreover, delivery prices presupposed that confidence in the currency remained intact; in fact, the opposite was true. Because inflation was everywhere, even state purchasing authorities were forced to move by the middle of the war to a barter system, in which they exchanged crops with the farmers for scarce consumer goods.

With delivery prices kept high in order to maximize peasant deliveries, it was usually towns that came off worst. Wartime diaries and memoirs frequently testify to the astonishment of city dwellers at the way people lived in the countryside: what struck the leader of the Polish underground when he travelled from Warsaw into the Warthegau was exactly what impressed a Belgian lawyer when he spent a weekend outside Brussels near the end of the war, tucking into solid local fare. In this conflict of interests between relatively well-off food producers and malnourished urban consumers, high prices created a political strain in the towns which only efficient rationing could check. Introducing rationing in September 1940, Marshal Pétain insisted that 'everyone must assume their share of common hardship'. But the new system of checks and controls merely intensified people's awareness of social inequity.[34] When this broke down, the resulting anger often scared the authorities. In Norway workers struck over their wage freeze, protesting at inadequate rations, and the same thing happened in France during the winter of 1941/2. Rationing had to function in a 'socially just way', the Reich commissar for Norway, Terboven, told the Norwegian authorities, but the latter simply lacked the foodstuffs or the manpower to ensure this. Halting initiatives to introduce rationing in the towns of the occupied eastern territories suffered similarly. Civil servants were among those urban middle classes whose incomes were crippled by inflation, and this increased the incentives for corruption and further damaged public confidence in their ability to distribute food fairly. 'If you want butter, housewives,' a French underground newspaper told its Lyon readers in 1942, 'go to the regional prefect. He's just had sixty pounds delivered from the black market. Help yourselves to half a pound.' In countries where the population broadly supported the war effort – Germany or the UK – rationing worked and was sometimes even popular. But under occupation, rationing was far less effective, since state authorities lacked the popular legitimacy or the police forces at their disposal to secure the necessary supplies. Indeed, they often found themselves relying on national charities and welfare organizations – the Germans even licensed these in Poland and further East – whose soup kitchens and distribution systems offered the only alternative to complete social collapse.[35]

The black market was the other essential source of foodstuffs, especially as in most countries official rations were not set at levels high enough to guarantee health. The starvation noted among the thousands of inmates of Belgian and French prisons and mental asylums unable to gain access to alternative sources of supply demonstrated just how crucial this was. The ghettoes of eastern Europe were the extreme case: in Warsaw, the Jewish population understood, as a German official put it in August 1941, that 'if they remained in the ghetto they must die of hunger'.[36]

Indeed even in the ghettoes there was illegal trade with the world outside, at extraordinary risk. Elsewhere the war saw a constant traffic between town and country as townspeople swapped furniture, valuables, and heirlooms for food. The Germans themselves sold surplus goods to black marketeers, and Wehrmacht provisioning officers bought up food from them too. 'It should be stressed that in principle all offices willing to buy regulated articles should not turn to the black market,' Hans Frank reminded his subordinates. In fact, corruption was rampant among them – the hope of enrichment was, after all, one of the main reasons many of them served in Poland – with Hans Frank himself leading by example. 'Corruption among the Germans is indescribable,' according to an underground Polish source. 'For money one can get a foreign passport, be excused from work and even from wearing the armband prescribed for Jews; for money one can get news about the fate of people who have been arrested. Gestapo agents, who have been given the task of fighting the black marketeers, do business with them and so on.'[37]

Wiser heads recognized it was better to work with the black market than to try to suppress it. In northern Russia, rigorous policing of black marketeers 'had a completely negative result,' according to a German military expert at the time. 'Goods disappeared from the markets . . .

and the urban population lacked the most basic foodstuffs. With the readmission of these markets, these dangerous symptoms vanished.' In Belgium, too, the military administration largely ignored the anti-black market drives of Belgian civil servants, thereby probably helping save the country from the starvation their very presence might otherwise have provoked. The German administration also intervened decisively in Greece in October 1942 in order to transform 'the black market . . . into a completely free market'. The strategy was worked out by the former Nazi mayor of Vienna, Hermann Neubacher, a successful businessman, who managed to bring prices down sharply for several months.[38]

The stakes were high in Greece, a country which, like Belgium and Norway, relied on imports for survival. In the first winter of occupation, it had already suffered the first serious famine anywhere in Europe: the combination of requisitions and hoarding, soaring inflation and high distribution costs had led to a catastrophic breakdown in national food supply. By the early autumn, the first emaciated corpses on the streets of Athens revealed the tragedy to come. In the next six months, tens of thousands died of hunger, or related causes. Most of them lived in Athens, or on one of those spectacular but parched Cycladic islands that now host summer tourists. No one had wanted, or planned, the famine – but neither could the Germans be bothered to do very much about it. They continued confiscating foodstuffs throughout and provided little assistance: according to officials in Berlin, if Germany had any food to spare, Norway, Belgium and the Netherlands were higher priorities. 'We cannot worry unduly about the Greeks,' commented Göring. 'It is a misfortune which will strike many other people beside them.' In the spring of 1942, as food threatened to run short in Germany itself, the tone harshened. 'Are the people in the Greek cities, who at present seem only to consist of dealers, black marketeers, receivers of stolen goods, thieves and work dodgers, really worth being kept alive with the food supplies of the Axis powers?' asked a German-language newspaper. 'How long the Axis powers in their hard struggle can continue to feed a population of millions of idlers remains to be seen!'[39]

Occasionally, famine and starvation struck in western Europe too. The only actual famine took place in Holland in the closing weeks of the war, when the cities on the Dutch coast were temporarily cut off by a German embargo. Amid freezing weather, rations slumped to some

450 calories daily, far below subsistence levels; those who could fled
into the fields searching for food, and an estimated 10,000 – mostly
elderly or infants, and poor – died.[40] In France, urban centres like Paris
and Lyon, and areas of monoculture like the Herault, saw the first signs
of acute distress in rising mortality rates among the most vulnerable
sections of the population – the elderly, the ill, beggars and all of those
who lacked access to the black market for one reason or another. In
October 1942, Vichy introduced special food supplements in the towns
to ward off hunger, and economists warned of serious health risks ahead.

Although there was no outright starvation in occupied Poland – outside the ghettoes, where thousands certainly did die of hunger – the scale
of dislocation and discrimination placed a huge strain on food supplies.
A list of foodstuffs forbidden to Poles but available to Germans included
wheat bread, veal and pork, rice, honey, fish of all kinds, berries, fruit
juices and even onions. Children were especially badly affected, and
their rations dropped below 500 calories daily. A Polish woman
explained that they had avoided starving only by exchanging clothes for
butter, flour or barley meal. Sugar and salt were rarely available. Turning
scraps of ground into vegetable plots, people grew potatoes and rye.[41]

But it was in the USSR that famine had the most devastating consequences. As in the ghettoes, soaring mortality rates indicated deliberate
policy, only the numbers in the occupied Soviet territories who died
were even higher. Part of the problem was a breakdown in planning.
German estimates of exactly what the Russian grain surplus amounted
to were as cavalier and mistaken as their war preparations in general.
They badly overestimated its size, just as they entirely failed to predict
the Soviet scorched earth policy which the Red Army implemented on
its retreat. This left the economic infrastructure in such disarray and
destroyed so many tractors and other farm machinery that even a far
more sophisticated administration would have struggled to restore production to prewar levels. With the Wehrmacht living off the land – in
the expectation of instant victory – Russian and Ukrainian farm holdings
were further decimated by massive requisitioning and slaughter of
animals.

But the starvation basically reflected the fact not that German planning
had failed but that it had succeeded. The rising power in the Agriculture
and Food Ministry, Herbert Backe, was a long-time advocate of deindus-
trializing Russia. His goal was to weaken the urban working class which

Stalin had built up and turn the country back into the wheat supplier for western Europe that it had been before the Bolsheviks seized power – after all, before 1914 it had exported more than ten times as much grain as in the 1930s. In Backe's view, Stalin had taken the country in the wrong direction, crippled Russian agriculture and condemned the rest of Europe to reliance on transatlantic grain. By taking control of the Soviet grain supply, Germany could create a genuine continental *Grossraumwirtschaft* and engineer a more efficient division of labour between industrial West and peasant East. Fixated upon the Russian and Ukrainian granary, Backe attached little or no importance to the 70 per cent of Soviet cast iron capacity, 58 per cent of steel and 64 per cent of coal that were also to fall into German hands.[42]

Nor did he care about Russian food consumers. For the inhabitants of Soviet cities in particular, the implications were grim beyond belief. Whereas the German military in the First World War had set the needs of the local civilian population in eastern Europe above those of Germany itself, the Nazis placed them last. When a planning meeting chaired by Backe before the invasion anticipated a surplus of 8.7 million tons of grain, subject to 'the level of domestic consumption', it also spelled out what this meant: millions of people in the food-deficit regions in the north, including Moscow and Leningrad, should be cut off from the grain producers of the Ukraine and left to starve. A 'most serious distress from famine' was predicted. This, then, was how the Russian clock was going to be turned back to its deindustrialized and deurbanized past; there was no room for 'false humanitarianism' for this would 'reduce Germany's staying power' in the war. And since west Europe's manufactures were more important for Germany than Russia's, the planners concluded, Russian grain surpluses should be used to keep west European not Russian industrial workers alive. A year and a half later, the policy remained unaltered. 'The food supply situation in Europe as a whole,' stated Göring, 'makes it necessary to procure the largest possible agricultural surplus from the occupied eastern territories to feed the troops and the population of the Reich for the foreseeable future. In order to achieve this, the local food consumption of the indigenous population must be kept as low as possible.'[43]

Backe's 'hunger strategy' sheds a different light upon the Germans' treatment of Russian and Ukrainian cities: the stranglehold round Leningrad and the cordons thrown up around Minsk and Kiev were all designed to starve the population, destroy urban culture and force the inhabitants back to the land. Money gave way to barter, and the towns emptied as their inhabitants took to the roads for food. As if to remind them of what lay ahead, they passed the emaciated corpses of POWs and famished civilians laid out on the verges. Just as in western Europe, but on a far larger scale, and in freezing temperatures, this exodus clogged the highways. 'He who flies over or rides through the occupied Soviet territories today,' wrote an Eastern Ministry official in the winter of 1942, 'will notice crowds of people moving along the roads: there are hundreds of thousands of them, and according to the experts, their numbers may often reach a million. These crowds are on the move, either to look for food, or to bring food to the cities in order to sell it.'[44]

The terrible consequences were that the population of a city like Kharkov, one million strong before the war, plummeted to some 250,000 within two years. The Soviet withdrawal had had its effect. From the very start, the Red Army had left little behind and had blown up many of the city's factories on leaving. But the Germans in their turn doomed the city to a slow death. As one survivor remembered a few years later:

The town is void of eatables like a desert, like a long-besieged citadel cut off from the outside world. All the bridges and railroads are blown up, every kind of communication and transportation facilities is totally destroyed. The entering and leaving of the town is strictly prohibited . . . There are no stores, no markets, no shops of any kind. All the stores were either destroyed or plundered and robbed in the last days before the retreat of the Soviet army . . . Who was able and stronger, tried to flee from the town as from a place haunted by pestilence, leaving behind his properties, houses and his relatives . . . There were also other people who, exhausted and extremely weak from the loss of their strength caused by long starvation, risked their lives to save their dear ones. In frosts of 30–40 degrees below zero, carrying heavy loads, scarcely moving, their feet wrapped in old rags, they went 200–300 kilometres in drifts facing the snow-storm to far off villages to exchange their last warm clothes for corn or flour . . . Many of them died, were frozen, lost their way.[45]

Yet because the economies of town and country could not be severed as neatly as Backe imagined, the cumulative result was that wartime farming production never lived up to German expectations. Most of what was collected went to feed the Wehrmacht. A grain surplus *was* delivered from the Ukraine after the 1942 harvest and again the following year. But Erich Koch's repressive hard line alienated the entire population and undercut the army's faltering efforts to enlist the Ukrainians for the German cause. The Agriculture Ministry sent in thousands of agricultural experts to no avail. Deciding *not* to break up the collective farms, on the grounds that their existence made it easier to collect the harvest, the Germans issued a New Agricultural Decree in early 1942 which put off any decision on their fate. The Decree promised to liberate the peasants from the 'tyranny' of the 'Jewish Soviet government in Moscow' but its lack of clarity aroused their suspicions, and within a year it was obvious to many German observers that they had thrown away their main chance to win the peasants over.

A barrage of criticism came from army economists and from Rosenberg's Eastern Ministry. 'Large sections of the Ukrainian peasantry are under the influence of enemy propaganda,' noted one of Rosenberg's aides that October, 'and have lost faith in the seriousness of our intent.' The Agrarian Decree had been botched, and the similar German hesitation over restoring private property in the Baltic had been 'contrary to all political sense'. He warned starkly that by exterminating Jews, and killing off peasants in reprisal for partisan raids, Germany risked losing Ukraine 'as the source of our food supply'.[46] But by the time policy-makers began to contemplate alternatives, the harm had been done. Grain deliveries from the USSR simply never lived up to Backe's (or Hitler's) expectations, and the result of the invasion confirmed all the doubts and hesitations of those who had opposed it. As it was, Nazi rule over Germany's 'California' in the East consigned millions of Soviet citizens to death and made the Reich's task in western Europe harder by shifting the burden of providing Germany with food there instead.

In Germany itself the spring of 1942 brought the realization that food rations inside the Reich would have to be cut. Given Hitler's conviction that the regime's very security was bound up with maintaining German living standards, this was certainly one of the most serious political crises the regime experienced during the entire war. It was at once understood abroad as a sign of weakness, and news of the cuts was immediately exploited and exaggerated by Soviet 'hunger propaganda'. Confidentially, the SD reported that public morale had 'reached a low ebb never previously observed'.[47] Determined that the cuts be reversed as quickly as possible, Hitler was worried enough to replace his increasingly ineffectual agriculture and food minister, Walther Darré, with the dynamic Backe. Darré was a man who was fundamentally driven by romantic racial dreams of reviving peasant life in Germany itself, while Backe was a hard-nosed expansionist and a pragmatist who, like his close colleague Heydrich, believed in getting things done. Food was what mattered at this point, not peasants. Clamping down on the black market in the Reich, he turned his attention to improving grain deliveries from the East.[48]

The murderous results were almost immediately visible. In the General Government, which could not have fed itself in the best of circumstances, Frank's administration was at a loss how to increase deliveries, especially since it regarded Polish rations as already too low. Bonuses for farmers might help. But as in the Russian case, Backe had another answer – cut back sharply on local consumption. One group above all was already starting to starve and could be dispensed with. 'In the General Government,' he told Frank's officials on 23 June, some weeks before the harvest was due, 'there are currently still 3.5 million Jews. Poland is to be sanitized within the coming year.' Just a few weeks earlier, Himmler had announced to his most senior SS men that the 'wandering of the Jews' would be over within the year. He now instructed SSPF Globocnik in Lublin to murder all Jews in Poland not required for work: thanks to the new death camps at Treblinka, Sobibor and Belzec this was achieved. In this way, the food crisis helped to accelerate the Final Solution. In order to help Backe, Himmler's men also took charge of the collection of the Polish harvest. According to his instructions, Warsaw was to be isolated, and peasants who did not meet their delivery quotas were to be shot.[49]

Göring played his part, too, and called a crucial meeting in Berlin in early August. This was one of the very few occasions when the heads of the different occupation administrations were actually brought together, and it allowed the Reich field marshal to lay out the new hard line. Berating the assembled Reich commissars and military commanders for putting the interests of non-Germans above Germans, he signalled a much tougher stance ahead. Germany had conquered 'enormous territories', and yet food consumption in the Reich was descending to the 'miserable rations of the First World War':

In all the occupied territories I see the people living there stuffed full of food while our own people are starving. For God's sake, you haven't been sent there to work for the well-being of the people entrusted to you, but to get hold of as much as you can so that the German people can live. I expect you to devote all your energies to that. This continual concern for the aliens must come to an end once and for all. I have the reports of what you are planning to deliver in front of me. When I contemplate your countries, it seems like nothing at all. I could not care less if you tell me your people are collapsing from hunger. They can do that by all means so long as no German collapses from hunger.[50]

He could not have been more forthright: 'In former times, the matter appeared to me to be comparatively simpler. Then one called it plundering.' He then turned to each country in turn: the Dutch were 'a nation of traitors to our cause', and weakening them would not matter, provided it did not harm farmers and workers in armaments factories. France should deliver 1.2 million tons of grain, not 550,000 as in the previous year. Belgium was not as poor as it claimed. Numbers were hurled around. For Norway: 'They've got fish: 400,000.' When Terboven interjected that this was below the previous year's delivery, Göring responded: '500,000!' The inevitable protests from politicians and civil servants in the occupied territories did not interest him. He was not, he emphasized, in favour of 'collaboration': 'collaboration is a thing which only Mr Abetz [the German ambassador to France] does'. Only the Danes escaped: their special economic relationship was yielding the desired results.[51]

While this crude bargaining was going on, Hitler's mind was ranging over the future, fired by the vistas of General Plan East. Throughout the month of August he continued to elaborate upon this to his dinner guests. Germany was driving forward into 'empty spaces' and would have to learn how to rule them. The local Slavs would deliver the harvest in return for trashy German manufactured goods; any talk of civilizing them was to be punished with a spell in a concentration camp. 'No power on earth will eject us!' he boasted, and the partisans would go the same way as the 'Red Indians' in America. The East would produce a surplus of ten to twelve million tons of grain a year – as indeed it had done before the Great War – and Germany would become 'the most self-supporting state' in the world with millions of German peasants responding to the call of the earth.[52]

Luckily for the Germans, the 1942 harvest results were more than satisfactory. Helped by fine weather over the summer, and increased policing of the harvest, total European grain deliveries rose from two million tons to more than five million in 1942–3: by this point Germany was obtaining no less than one-fifth of its grain from the occupied territories. The General Government and France were the key: supplies from both were sharply up. As a result, in mid-September the regime was able to announce that rations in Germany would rise again. The food crisis was over, and Göring was upbeat: in a 'Harvest Thanksgiving' speech in early October, he predicted further increases ahead since 'eggs, butter, flour exist in the Eastern Territories in quantities you can't even imagine!' Hitler had claimed that, if they managed to raise the rations by October, the British would have to 'abandon any hope they had of starving us out'. Thus the regime presented its achievement as a British failure and confirmation of an eventual German victory.[53]

Goebbels, the propaganda specialist, knew Göring's boasts did nothing to help Germany politically and he instructed German journalists to change the subject. As it was, Europeans – along with those German administrators responsible for public order abroad – reacted angrily to the increased demands. In France, for instance, Ambassador Otto Abetz, the Foreign Ministry man in Paris, warned of 'riots, the gravest disturbance of public order and the immediate resignation or overthrow of the present Government'. One had to work with the French, he stressed, since Germany lacked the manpower to physically collect the harvest without them. The policy of collaboration could not simply be jettisoned, as Göring had implied. From the occupied USSR came similar warnings: the 1942 harvest had proved invaluable, but as food became scarcer, the population was being pushed into the arms of the partisans and was starting to see Bolshevism as the lesser of two evils. The future would show that Goebbels was right and that Göring had been foolish to tempt fate: 1942–3 was in fact the high-point for food deliveries to Germany. They fell slightly the following year and much more sharply the next, and not even continued increases in output in Germany itself were able to compensate.[54]

'The health of Europe today is . . . "not too bad",' wrote a commentator in *International Affairs* in the summer of 1944, warning that only the possibility of epidemics being spread at liberation gave cause for real concern. And indeed, if we attempt to gauge developments in health and living standards across occupied Europe as a whole, some unexpected features of the continent's experience emerge.

Insofar as the goal of German policy was the preservation of a reliable supply of food into the Reich, this was largely attained through a combination of tight controls inside Germany and sharp increases in deliveries from outside. The crisis of 1942 represented, in retrospect, a temporary wobble which was then corrected by increasing the pressure on foreign consumers. Not until very late in the war did Germans start to endure a precipitous drop in calorific intake; and it was after the war that the real collapse took place. Food imports became more and more important: one-fifth of German grain consumption (compared with 10 per cent before the war), one-third of meat (compared with 7 per cent), and a quarter of fats were imported – mostly from France, the USSR, Denmark and the Netherlands. Because racializing food policy meant not only killing off unwanted consumers but sustaining the health of those 'worthy of life', the Reich also paid close attention to nutrition. Its campaign for wholemeal bread ('Wholemeal bread is better and healthier!'), complete with advertisements of chubby-cheeked children with healthy teeth, was matched by incentives to farmers not only inside Germany but also in the Protectorate, the Netherlands, Belgium and France to produce brown bread. Despite consumer resistance, the wholemeal campaign was extended to cereals and biscuits. Muesli was promoted as a healthier form of breakfast. All of this contributed to a vastly improved German demographic record compared with 1914–18: then the birth rate had halved whereas at its lowest point in the Second World War – 1942 – it dropped by less than one-fifth. If Hitler's goal was to avoid the demographic damage of 1914–18, he succeeded.[55]

Elsewhere, while ration levels and overall food intake varied sharply, and despite German requisitioning, health across much of the continent also remained surprisingly good. In general, the basic problem was one of distribution not production. This was most successfully overcome where the state was strong, and communications were relatively easy, which is to say, in western and central Europe. Here rationing was introduced and kept intake at levels lower than they had been before the war but high enough to avoid mass hunger. Some of the societies worst affected were actually allied to Germany: in Karelia, in Finland, some rural populations hovered only just above subsistence levels; in

Italy, official rations were among the lowest in Europe, and the regime's pathetic failure to guarantee the country's food supply after many years of shouting about 'the battle for grain' contributed enormously to popular disaffection and anger with fascism. Only in the former Soviet Union, and in parts of Yugoslavia and Greece, did malnutrition spread widely and threaten mass death from hunger – and these were lands where the state was weakest and German racial ideology had had the most devastating impact. Overall, however, the drop in food intake could not compare with the First World War, at least until the dramatic final months of the war. For most Europeans, improvements in farming and good weather helped keep hunger at bay.

People remained remarkably healthy too. There were few epidemics, and the demographic data suggested an unexpectedly low impact upon infant mortality or birth rates. Denmark – protected by its benign situation in the New Order – was best off and saw a continued ascent in birth rates to well above the levels of the 1930s. But even in France, where most people felt the shortage of food all the more acutely for not having experienced anything comparable in the Great War, the catastrophic drop which took place in 1914–18 was not replicated: on the contrary, there was a rapid, historically unprecedented and substantial increase in births after 1941 – something which postwar demographers attributed to 'the resistance of wartime natality' but which continued after the war, as it did almost everywhere. Similar trends were visible in more food-deprived countries like the Netherlands, thanks to relatively low mortality rates and high birth rates.[56] Overall population – which grew slightly in the UK and more quickly in the USA – dropped only slightly in western Europe. In Yugoslavia, Greece and Poland, the drops were much more marked. Worst off was certainly the USSR: recent studies indicate that the wartime catastrophe in the Ukraine, for instance, outstripped even the famine of 1933; in Belorussia, the figures are less certain, but the outcome may have been even worse. Thus German policy succeeded both in insulating its own people from demographic disaster and in inflicting it on those it most feared and despised. The rest of Europe escaped major epidemic damage: yet the strain food shortages put on the legitimacy of state institutions, and the very real fear of starvation across the continent, make it easily understandable why this could not really help the Germans politically.[57]

At best, the relatively limited impact of German food policy upon health in much of west and central Europe helps to explain why the impact on public order was not as great as one might have expected, at least before the winter of 1942/3. The evolution of popular attitudes may be traced through the reports of the German secret military police in Belgium. In October 1940, they reported public anxiety at provisioning arrangements for the coming winter, and doubts about the competence of the Belgian authorities. At the same time, some 80 per cent of the population was reckoned to 'accept the fact of the German occupation' and to look to the Germans to enforce a fair distribution of foodstuffs. By March 1941, anti-German sentiment was on the rise, mostly because of food shortages. A year later, the black market had become a fact of life, and people were generally convinced the Germans would lose the war in the East. Yet they were still 'passive', and there was thought to be little likelihood of serious trouble. Such strikes as did break out were reckoned to be over rations and poor wages rather than against the Germans directly. By mid-1942, it was becoming harder to separate the deteriorating supply situation from German rule. Yet even in September, the GFP was reporting that 'the general calm, order and security are not threatened'. In France, the Wehrmacht assessments of threats to public order were very similar. Until the end of 1942, in other words, western Europe's immunity from complete economic breakdown seems to have successfully kept it quiet. Mass overt opposition there would not emerge for some time, once the tide of war had clearly turned against the Nazis.[58]

RESOURCES

Energy not food was the real Achilles heel of the German war effort. In 1943, the US produced 67 per cent of the world's oil, while the USSR produced about 10 per cent – approximately equivalent to the output of California. The British controlled nominally independent Iraq and Persia, but so long as the Royal Navy was beating the U-boats in the Battle of the Atlantic, it was American oil that allowed Britain to keep fighting. The Germans, on the other hand, controlled only the oil fields of Romania, the declining wartime output of which was less than 2 per cent of the world total, and a few ageing pumps in Hungary and Galicia. Europe generally – the focus of Hitler's imperial ambitions – was completely reliant on oil imports, and this placed the Third Reich at a tremendous disadvantage, and made fighting a long war virtually impossible. Contrary to the mythology, it was reduced to fighting a twentieth-century war on nineteenth-century technology – horses and coal.[59]

For a moment in 1940 it looked in Berlin as though the petrol-rich Arab world might be in play. Realizing that victory in the First World War had left the British in control of the Middle East's oil reserves, some Germans hoped that France's fall would give them an entrée there. A new state oil holding company was established – Kontinentale Öl AG – (it was intended to take over Polish and Russian oil fields as well), and in May 1941 a German team was sent out to Syria. Foreign Minister Ribbentrop was a key supporter of the expedition – desperately hoping to avert the invasion of the USSR and to keep the pressure on Britain by supporting pro-German forces among Arab nationalists. Hitler, on the other hand, scarcely took the idea seriously, since he was convinced that the defeat of Bolshevism would speedily offer much greater riches and make concessions to the Arabs unnecessary. The contrast with Churchill's decisive intervention could not have been greater. Moving rapidly, over the next few months, the British crushed a pro-German coup in Iraq, occupied Syria and Lebanon (together with the Free French) and forced the abdication of the Shah of Iran. The Axis failure to conquer Egypt, and the tightened British grip over the country, effectively ended Hitler's prospects in that direction. This made the conquest of the Soviet oil fields in the Caucasus – the same ones which had been supplying Germany peacefully in 1939 – all the more urgent, especially since from May 1942 onwards, Hitler was being warned by his senior military staff that without them no offensive operations would be possible the following year. Hamstrung by the Führer's meddling, the Wehrmacht got to Maikop in August, and to Grozny in October, but the failure to take Stalingrad forced the troops to pull back a few months later. There would be no military solution to Germany's energy problem.[60]

It was in vain that Hitler looked to the scientists. Hydrogenation, in particular, was supposed to fill the fuel gap by producing synthetic fuels. Investment in plants like the chemicals complex that was built around Auschwitz – responsible by the end of 1944 for 15 per cent of Germany's methanol production – did allow the Luftwaffe to keep going. But hydrogenation is a massively expensive process with heavy fuel needs of its own, and the quantities required would have consumed a very large proportion of Germany's coal; as it was, the production of synthetic fuels peaked in 1943. Allied bombing damage in 1944, together with the loss the same year of the Romanian oil fields, made Germany's energy predicament insoluble. Increasing the number of fighter planes was little use without the fuel to run them.[61]

For coal, the outlook was better, though not by much. Conquest of Belgium, Holland, France and Czechoslovakia had brought significant mining capacity into German hands. Yet continentally, the position was still not good: Germany was Europe's major coal exporter, but France was the largest coal importer in the world, and Denmark, Italy and Norway too depended totally upon imports. Thanks to the cooperation between German administrators and Belgian and French mine-owners, output recovered quickly in 1940 and continued until it peaked in 1942–3. But thereafter it fell remorselessly, with knock-on effects on steel production and jeopardizing Speer's strategy for industrial co-operation. Hitler himself was very well aware of the implications. In August 1942, he had sharply warned the head of the Reichwerke, Hermann Göring, and head of the German coal producers, Paul Pleiger, that the war was lost if coking coal shortages held back increased steel production. The sustained Anglo-American bombing raids on the Ruhr the following spring targeted the crucial node of the German energy economy and disrupted the entire Speer rearmament strategy.[62]

As defeat loomed, the coal and steel compact of 1940 between Germans, Belgians and Frenchmen started breaking down. Miners had protested low rations from the first occupation winter – Belgian miners' wives waved empty sacks of potatoes in protest outside city halls – but the Germans would not increase rations sufficiently to win them round. From 1943, absenteeism increased, and the productivity gap between German and foreign miners widened. Average daily output in French coal mines dropped by 39 per cent between 1938 and 1944. Whereas the share of foreign food and labour in overall German output continued to rise, foreign coal production declined from 28 to 20 per cent of Germany's total. It was here that the suffering of Europe's urban populations in particular came back to haunt their masters, By the autumn of 1943 strikes had become commonplace, and the decline in output accelerated. Coal reserves reached dangerously low levels, making it ever harder for the Reich to keep the rest of Europe supplied with the fuel necessary for production to continue. In fact, this became more or

less impossible after the Allied bombing raids on German communications infrastructure at the end of 1944 wrecked the country's coal
distribution system and shut down its factories.[63]

So can we say that occupation paid? A recent assessment concludes that
in general it is more likely to do so when the areas concerned are modern
industrial economies, since their resources are more easily tapped, and
communications and control are relatively inexpensive. The argument
looks plausible in the Nazi case: for all their dreams of empire in the
East, it was western Europe that contributed most to the German war
effort. But there are two caveats. One is that not even the most efficiently
run occupation will suffice if certain vital commodities are missing. Had
they won the war in 1941, the Germans could no doubt have bought
the oil and other commodities they needed abroad. Hitler's vision of
extreme self-sufficiency would have been moderated, and Germany's
international economic policy would have been closer to that proposed
by its chemical and shipping industry executives, who never abandoned
the idea of trade with the rest of the world and indeed continued dealing
quietly with American and other firms. But declaring war on the USSR
made that hard, and bringing in the USA made it impossible. Once the
war dragged on and became a slogging match of industrial giants,
Germany's critical energy deficiency began to count. The other thing is
that a purely economic analysis misses the all-important ideological
dimension to the Third Reich's management of the war economy. If
it managed western Europe's economy somewhat better than eastern
Europe's this was not only because it was easier to do so. It was above
all because the ideological stakes were lower. Himmler's SS was weaker,
more traditionally minded men had greater sway, and Hitler himself
had less far-reaching ideas for the future of the region.[64]

10

Workers

Nowhere did the gulf between ideology and reality generate more dilemmas for the Third Reich, and more violent attempts to solve those dilemmas, than in the question of labour. Because the Nazis' primary political goal was the creation of a racially pure state, they abhorred the idea of having to bring foreign workers into Germany, especially from eastern Europe. Yet once the struggle with the Red Army raised the prospect of a prolonged war of attrition, it became clear that the conflict could not be won without them. From 1942 onwards in particular their numbers grew rapidly and by 1944 had risen to more than seven million. The sudden arrival of a vast and largely Slavic population inside the Reich itself represented an unexpected and deeply unsettling social revolution in a country where people were constantly being bombarded with the message that those who lived in the East were primitive, pest-ridden and dangerous. The regime's way of reassuring them was to make workers wear badges, to keep them behind barbed wire, police their every movement and punish them harshly for stepping out of line. In short, the need for foreign workers led directly to a radicalization of the Reich's own racial laws.

FOREIGN WORKERS, 1939–42

In the late 1930s, tightening labour markets inside Germany were already leading farmers to report they were short of hands. By November 1938, there were fears that this was endangering the German food supply. Foreigners formed a quarter of the agricultural workforce in 1936–7, a figure which rose to no less than 43 per cent in 1938–9. Göring supported the influx, and did not think that 'considerations of racial policy' should be paramount. In his view, foreign workers were a necessary evil. But as more German men were called up, their importance grew even further: by 1940 no less than 60 per cent of the agricultural labour force in Germany was non-German. Hundreds of thousands of Polish POWs in particular were stripped of their ex-combatant status, recategorized as civilian workers and assigned to German farms. Given Hitler's obsession with Germany's food security, it was little short of extraordinary that the Reich was depending ever more heavily upon Poles to feed itself, especially as it was simultaneously expelling them from their own farms in the Warthegau and West Prussia. Ironically, many of those same Poles were being made to go into the Reich to work there. Hitler was convinced the Germans needed more land to survive. But even on the land they had they needed Poles to bring in the harvest.[1]

Whatever the craziness of Nazi economic logic, no racially conscious German took the security implications of these developments lightly. To prevent them from contaminating the German population, Polish workers were singled out: not only made to wear badges (a precursor of the later yellow stars for Jews), they were also barred from restaurants, forbidden to ride bicycles and provided with separate brothels to prevent the defilement of German women. Their wages were fixed below German rates until farmers responded by getting rid of their German workers, at which point the regime imposed a 'social compensation tax' to remove this incentive. But the regime was still not overly bothered by Germany's dependence on the newcomers: the manpower shortage had been tackled, and the ideological objections could be countered as long as strict policing kept them in line, and they remained in country areas.

Anyway, after the next round of conquests in the West, it looked as if this reliance on Poles would prove to be only a temporary necessity. The defeat of France and the Low Countries led to the capture of many more prisoners of war as well as to access to European labour markets depressed by years of slump and unemployment. There were more than one million unemployed in France and Italy alone at this time. Others arrived looking for work on a voluntary basis from as far afield as Hungary, Bulgaria and Spain. By the summer of 1940 it seemed therefore as if Germany's needs could be completely satisfied for the foreseeable future. As a result, the Reich released its Belgian, Dutch and Norwegian POWs and some Frenchmen too. The 1.2 million who remained in captivity were deployed in agriculture or screened for the mines and industry.

Attitudes to the increasingly multi-national army of newcomers inside Germany were mixed. The Reich Security Main Headquarters (RSHA) tried to distinguish between 'workers of Germanic stock' and 'racial aliens' and established different sets of punishments for them. But this led to some odd results: Dutch workers were members of a defeated enemy nation, for instance, yet in theory they were racially superior to the Croats, Italians and Slovaks who were coming to work in the Reich as volunteers. The German public did not make subtle distinctions: people generally disliked any foreign workers who refused to conform or made themselves conspicuous. Italian youths were supposedly 'boisterous and rowdy': they complained about the food and clogged-up toilets. French women were 'immoral', the Dutch 'arrogant'. The foreign workers were said to make travel by train unpleasant by their 'insufferable stench', their filthy clothes, their clutter, litter and tendency to burst into song. But in contrast to the Nazi Party's wishful idea that they were only a temporary evil, a senior Labour Ministry official warned that they were not about to leave and he predicted (correctly) that large movements of labour were likely to characterize Europe's economic development well into the postwar era:

Even after the end of the war, it will not be possible to do without foreign labour in Germany. As in the past, such deployment will be most necessary in agriculture, but also in industry, in order to fulfil the great future tasks of peace. The formation of an integrated macro-regional European economy will serve to promote this development. Along with the importation of additional workers from the continental states to Germany, the mutual exchange of labour in the form of so-called guest workers will doubtless also gain impetus, an inter-European equalization of the labour force.[2]

Convinced that victory was around the corner, and faced with such unwelcome forecasts, the Nazis toughened their approach. Foreign workers were barred from hospitals unless their lives were in danger, and their camps were placed under constant surveillance. Local authorities ruled swimming pools out of bounds, withdrew Christmas bonuses and allowed them only to shop at certain times. One reason for these endless restrictions was that, especially in the countryside, regulations were often ignored. The friendly relations that existed between Poles and

Germans in the villages and on isolated farms worried the authorities, and they called for renewed vigilance and regimentation.[3]

After the invasion of the USSR, the capture of three million POWs, and of vast territories with huge labour reserves, raised both the economic opportunities and the risks in an entirely new way. Because the regime believed victory was imminent, and because it felt it had access to as many foreign workers as it needed, it made no plans to use Russian POWs. Indeed Hitler blocked their deployment in the Reich. After all, the end of the war was expected to bring a rapid demobilization of the Wehrmacht, easing Germany's labour shortage once and for all. Yet this was skating on thin ice, for should the war not go as predicted, Germany would quickly face enormous difficulties: the call-up for Barbarossa had eaten further into the already depleted German labour force and left a record number of unfilled vacancies in the home economy. And this was not a merely theoretical worry: coal output in the Ruhr – centre of the Reich's energy economy – dropped 15 per cent between March and August 1941. Only in October did Hitler finally relent and authorize the comprehensive exploitation of Soviet POWs inside Germany, by which time for most of them it was far too late. There was not much sympathy in Germany for their plight: on the contrary, people were so outraged by reports that the Reich was feeding millions of POWs that rations in the camps were actually cut. Those Red Army soldiers who managed to get to Germany alive were too weak to work and needed to be specially 'fattened up'.

Both Himmler and the Party hated the idea that Germany's reliance on foreign workers might become permanent. War had produced an absurd situation which they wanted ended as quickly as possible: 'The racial-political situation today is such that we no sooner get rid of 500 Jews from the area of the Reich than we immediately bring in ten times the number of racially undesired foreign races,' complained an analyst in the winter of 1941/2. Fearing a security breakdown, Himmler hoped that Germany's needs could be satisfied by 'Germanic peoples' and the assimilation of others 'fit for Germanization'. Yet this was – like all Himmler's ideas – flying in the face of the economic facts and left the Reich's growing manpower shortage still needing to be faced. Between May 1939 and May 1942 conscription led the civilian workforce to shrink by 7.8 million. With the Wehrmacht suffering substantial losses on the Eastern Front, increasing armaments production meant somehow solving the labour bottleneck.[4]

SAUCKEL'S DRIVES

In the spring of 1942, with the youthful Albert Speer put in charge, the rationalization of the war economy began which would soon lead to remarkable increases in output. But Germany clearly also needed what some were calling a 'dictator for manpower' to implement a Europe-wide labour programme. To do this, Hitler characteristically bypassed the Ministry of Labour and named Fritz Sauckel, the long-time *Gauleiter* of Thuringia, as plenipotentiary for labour. His instructions to Sauckel were to engineer a dramatic increase in the continent's contribution to the German manpower problem.

Sauckel and Speer were, in some ways, like chalk and cheese, two different generations of National Socialist man. Speer was another of those well-educated, plausible young technocrats who did not hide his contempt for the stupidity of the Party 'bosses'. Sauckel was a former sailor and manual labourer, an old-time Party leader. In fact, both men were competent organizers, and their tasks were complementary: Sauckel's job, after all, was to find the workers to fill the shortfalls in Speer's factories. Whatever he said after the war, Speer needed Sauckel – as he needed Himmler and the Wehrmacht as well – because without the forcible recruitment of Europe's labour for the Reich, boosting Germany's production of arms would have been impossible.

For a year and a half, Sauckel was extremely successful in running what a recent historian has described as 'one of the largest coercive labour programmes the world has ever seen'. In April 1943, he proudly reported to Hitler that things were functioning well: so far as labour was concerned, 'our National Socialist Reich presents a shining example compared with the methods of the capitalist and Bolshevik world'. In reality, things were much less rosy. As working conditions inside Germany became harsher, many of the volunteers left, spreading word back home about the poor diet and the brutality of their treatment. When those defined by the Germans as 'unfit' for work were sent back – as also happened in the first half of 1942 – their horrifying stories did nothing to make further recruitment easier. By late 1942, Sauckel's men were rounding people up by methods that spread terror across the General Government and the occupied Eastern territories. In 1942, he managed to bring more than one million civilian workers into the Reich from the Soviet territories alone. By mid-1943, 2.8 million new workers had been consigned to German factories, and by the end of the following year that number had risen to over 5 million. If we compare this figure – achieved in barely thirty months – with the 10–20 million Africans who were transported across the Atlantic as slaves over more than a century, we will appreciate the awesome coercive power that lay at the disposal of the modern state.[5]

The slave trade came naturally to people's minds at the time as the only conceivable parallel for the extraordinary and often random brutality of Sauckel's men. According to Rosenberg's highly critical aide, Otto Bräutigam:

We now experienced the grotesque picture of having to recruit millions of labourers from the Occupied Eastern Territories, after prisoners of war have died of hunger like flies, in order to fill the gaps that have formed within Germany . . . In the prevailing limitless abuse of Slavic humanity, 'recruiting' methods were used which probably have their origin in the blackest periods of the slave trade.[6]

In Cracow, a pro-German Ukrainian nationalist complained to the authorities:

The general nervousness is still more enhanced by the wrong methods of finding labour which have been used more and more frequently in recent months. The wild and ruthless manhunt as exercised everywhere in towns and country, in streets, squares, stations, even in churches, at night in houses, has badly shaken the feeling of security of the inhabitants. Everybody is exposed to the danger, to be seized anywhere and at any time by members of the police, suddenly and unexpectedly, and to be brought into an assembly camp. None of his relatives knows what has happened to him, and only months later one or the other gets news of his fate by a postcard.[7]

If anything, the manhunts in the countryside were worse. A graphic letter from a villager in eastern Poland described a raid in the following terms:

At our place, new things have happened. People are being taken to Germany. On 5th December, some people from the Kowkuski district were scheduled to go, but they did not want to and the village was set afire. They threatened to do the same thing in Borowytschi, as not all who were scheduled to depart wanted to go. Thereupon three truck loads of Germans arrived and set fire to their houses.

In Wrasnytschi, twelve houses and in Borowytschi, three houses were burned. On 1st October a new conscription of labour forces took place. I will describe the most important events to you. You cannot imagine the bestiality. You probably remember what we were told about the Soviets during their rule of the Poles. We did not believe it then, and now it seems just as incredible. The order came to supply 25 workers, but no one reported. All had fled. Then the German militia came and began to ignite the houses of those who had fled. The fire became very violent, since it had not rained for two months. In addition the grain stacks were in the farm yards. You can imagine what took place. The people who had hurried to the scene were forbidden to extinguish the flames and were beaten and arrested, so that seven homesteads burned down. The policemen meanwhile ignited other houses. The people fell on their knees and kissed the policemen's hands, but they beat them with rubber truncheons and threatened to burn down the whole village . . .

During the fire the militia went through the adjoining villages, seized the labourers, and put them under arrest. Wherever they did not find any labourers, they detained the parents, until the children appeared. That is how they raged throughout the night in Bielosirka. The workers who had not yet appeared by then were to be shot. All schools were closed and the married teachers were sent to work here, while the unmarried ones go to work in Germany. They are now catching humans like the dog-catchers used to catch dogs. They have already been hunting for one week and have not yet got enough. The imprisoned workers are locked in the schoolhouse. They cannot even go to perform their natural functions, but have to do it like pigs in the same room. People from many villages went on a certain day to a pilgrimage to the Monastery at Potschaew. They were all arrested, locked in, and will be sent to work. Among them there are lame, blind and aged people.[8]

In light of such events, it is not surprising that, as Sauckel himself criss-crossed the occupied territories, he encountered growing alarm and anger at the consequences among the very officials whose cooperation he needed. In pursuit of their target numbers, his men often ignored valid passes and exemption papers issued by other agencies, conscripting skilled workers whose deportation harmed other German war work. And there was the catastrophic broader social and political impact as well. Rosenberg warned Sauckel that his round-ups were fomenting partisan resistance in the eastern territories as peasants fled to the bands. Facing a choice between being sent to Germany and having their houses burned to the ground, they felt they had little to lose. The Wehrmacht's economic staff was also deeply unhappy. Worried about the harvest and the railways in particular, the army wanted to keep workers where they were. Nevertheless the needs of the Reich came first and his agents continued to plunder the former USSR: more than half the Soviet civilians working in Germany in 1944 arrived there *after* the fall of Stalingrad.

But Sauckel also turned to western Europe. In one year, the number of Belgian workers in Germany nearly doubled, while the number of French rose from 135,000 to 667,000. Ribbentrop had already alerted the Italian foreign minister to the fact that 'the Führer would have to take radical measures in the occupied territories to mobilize the local labour potential' so that Germany could combat the American rearmament drive.[9] France now experienced a milder version of the strong-arm tactics that were being used in Poland and the Ukraine. To his colleagues in March 1944, the former seaman boasted that

I even proceeded to employ and train a whole batch of French male and female agents who for good pay, just as was done in olden times for 'shanghaiing', went hunting for men and made them drunk by using liquor as well as words, in order to dispatch them to Germany. Moreover, I charged some able men with founding a special labour supply executive of our own, and this they did by training, and arming, with the help of the Higher SS and Police Führer a number of natives, but I still have to ask the Munitions Ministry for arms for the use of these men, for during the last year alone several dozens of very able labour executive officers have been shot dead. All these means I have to apply, grotesque as it sounds, to refute the allegation there was no executive to bring labour to Germany from these countries.[10]

By 1943 the costs were escalating in the form of increased unrest, breakdowns in public order and growing resistance to German rule. Sauckel's employees were being attacked, and the registers and police files that helped them select labourers through bureaucratic channels were often deliberately burned by resisters. As a result, recruiters were giving up any pretence of selectivity at all, and rounding people up indiscriminately in the streets, cinemas, market-places and train stations. Such *razzias* and *blocco*s became hard to distinguish from police operations. In Warsaw, in January 1943, 35,000 were seized in four days. The terrifying *blocco*s which took place in the 'Red' quarters of Athens in the summer of 1944 – organized by the SiPo/SD, but carried out mostly by Greek security police and informers – sent thousands to the Haidari camp and thence to the Reich: known or suspected resistance activists were simply shot on the spot.

Following the German occupation of the unoccupied zone in France, and the government's announcement of compulsory labour service STO (Service du Travail Obligatoire), there was widespread public unrest, culminating in the assassination of Sauckel's head of operations in Paris. As young men made for the hills to avoid being sent to Germany, Vichy argued that uprooting workers and forcing them into Germany was not the best way to make use of their labour. Albert Speer agreed, arguing strongly for a more differentiated policy and for keeping workers where they were when they were already producing for the German war effort. In September, Speer, who had just been appointed minister for arms and war production, began to intervene directly. In a reaffirmation of the policy of collaboration, he and the French minister for industry, Jean Bichelonne, agreed that enterprises producing for the German war effort should be immune to conscription levies. Once Hitler gave his approval, the system was extended across much of western Europe. By March 1944, a frustrated Sauckel claimed that more than 1.3 million workers were affected in France alone, preventing him from fulfilling his targets. Speer responded that while 2.7 million workers across western Europe fell into this category, this was still a relatively small proportion of its total labour force.

The manpower debate that took place in Berlin in July 1944, as the Allies pushed into northern France, was particularly acrimonious. Sauckel complained at the lack of support from the Wehrmacht, which, he claimed, 'saw in the labor recruiting program something disreputable'. He demanded more raids and greater harshness. But others reckoned that, since the Germans lacked the necessary manpower, such an approach would prove counter-productive. Even RSHA head Ernst Kaltenbrunner warned that he had only 2,400 men in France and that it was doubtful 'whether entire age classes could be seized with those weak forces'. For their part, the diplomats questioned the leverage they could apply to foreign governments; these governments were themselves badly weakened and further pressure would not help.[11]

Thanks to Speer's self-exculpatory recollections after the war, the significance of the Speer–Sauckel controversy has been exaggerated, especially as it really only applied to west European workers: in the East, Speer had less to say, and Sauckel's drives continued to herd hundreds of thousands of unfortunates into the Reich. The agreements on industrial cooperation which Speer reached with his opposite number in Vichy fitted easily into the prevailing view in Berlin of a two-track European economy, where Germany would deal one way with its industrial partners and another with the agrarian East. But doing without foreign workers was never an option, for by 1944 the German war economy had become completely dependent upon them. They made up at least one-fifth of the total working population, up from 3 per cent in 1940, and they were to be found not only in agriculture, but also in mining, construction, armaments and metalworking as well: indeed industry had become more reliant upon them than farmers. Of those working in the crucial munitions sector, 30 per cent were foreigners: more than 16,000 worked for BMW's Munich operations alone, a key supplier of Luftwaffe engines. When the Germans occupied Hungary, the country's labour was of such overriding importance to them that even Hungarian Jews were brought to work in the Reich – an unprecedented occurrence. In short, Speer, as minister of armaments, was dependent upon the success of Sauckel's efforts, and could scarcely have sought to sabotage them.[12]

FOREIGN WORKERS AND THE INTENSIFICATION OF TERROR

Nazism's policy of expelling foreign populations from the country had thus been thrown violently into reverse. Indeed, thanks to Sauckel, there were more foreigners in Germany than ever before. It was not after the war, in other words, but during it that Germany became a 'country of immigration'. A small town like Osnabrück, which scarcely had any foreigners before the war, suddenly housed 12,000 – one-fifth of its population – speaking some nineteen different languages. Lodged in barracks, dance halls, schools, vacant premises as well as private homes and specially constructed camps, the poorly fed, wretchedly clothed skeletal figures were a ubiquitous presence in city streets. It is not surprising that their arrival worsened what was already a punitive approach to the policing of relations between Germans and non-Germans, drawing the SS ever further into the German legal system and bringing terror to the lives of foreign workers themselves.[13]

The Polish Decree of March 1940 was only the start. Two years later, the judicial crisis of the summer of 1942 was exacerbated by Sauckel's success. It was above all unhappiness about the inflow of foreign workers that led Himmler to persuade the newly appointed justice minister, Otto Thierack, to grant him penal jurisdiction over what he called 'asocial elements'. This fateful decision opened the way to a far harsher line towards foreign workers. Thierack's chilling justification for his extraordinary weakening of the power of the judiciary highlighted the threatening presence of these non-Germans and showed how conditional their presence among Germans was. In the new minister's own words:

With the aim in mind of ridding the German people of Poles, Russians, Jews and Gypsies, and of opening up the Eastern territories to be added to the Reich as a settlement area for German culture, it is my intention to leave penal prosecution against Poles, Russians, Jews and Gypsies to the jurisdiction of the Reichsführer-SS. I am proceeding here on the assumption that the justice system can contribute only in a minor way to the extermination of these ethnic elements.[14]

This was now the language of the Justice Ministry itself. Thierack may have intended this arrangement to apply in the occupied territories in the East only; however, Himmler took it to mean that the SS had acquired penal powers over foreign workers inside Germany too. Yet, by the end of 1942, there was such an outcry among *Gauleiters* and Justice Ministry officials at this expansion of the SS's power that the new minister tried to backtrack. Thierack himself now claimed that 'it is impossible today to proceed on the basis of the idea that we want somehow to annihilate these people'; they had to 'be guaranteed some sort of court proceedings'. But like all those other Nazi lawyers before him, his protests came too late: the SS, the police and the Party were far too worried about keeping these racial inferiors and potential enemies of the Reich apart from Germans. SS officials explained that 'the Pole and Soviet Russian, simply by existing in the territory under German hegemony, represent a danger for the German national order'. For the SS, Greater Germany thus already existed as a quasi-legal space stretching from the Rhineland to the Soviet front: in policing the war against the racial enemy, the boundaries between domestic and foreign were dissolving, and the SS refused to accept the need to distinguish between them, whatever the implications for the legal situation inside the Reich itself.[15]

The SS not only toughened up the rules but it also enlisted ordinary Germans to keep the foreign workers in line. In this case as in others, the Gestapo relied on members of the public to inform them about suspect activities: doctors, guards, fellow workers, neighbours, Party and Hitler Youth members were all alerted to the dangers posed by the new threat in their midst and encouraged to denounce both foreign workers and those who openly sympathized with them. In late 1943, Himmler stressed that 'none of them is dangerous so long as we take severe measures at the merest trifles'. Public humiliation and punishment provided open reminders of the new rules. A man accused of having had sex with a Polish woman, for instance, was marched through his village led by eighty storm-troopers and Hitler Youths to the sound of trumpets before being publicly lectured by a Party official in front of the town hall. If arrested, foreign workers themselves faced incarceration, the camps or even public execution. Eventually public hangings took place in German towns and villages; only in the Catholic south was open disapproval reported.[16]

In the war's final months the repression intensified even further as the Wehrmacht was forced on to the defensive, and the regime started to worry seriously about subversion on the home front. Himmler underlined the need to ensure 'order and discipline among the foreign workers under all circumstances, together with the prevention of acts of sabotage, forming of resistance groups and revolutionary gatherings etc.'. It was for that purpose that works managers and supervisors were told to keep their eyes open. An indication of the tone in which such matters were discussed was provided by records of a meeting of Ruhr mine-owners who convened to talk about Russian workers. The powerful head of the German Labour Front, Robert Ley, warned his audience that getting out the coal was crucial to German victory: 'The coal must be got, whatever happens. If not with you, gentlemen, then against you.' And in a drunken tirade he laid out the apocalyptic fate that awaited them if they failed: 'After us there is nothing, everything will be over ... Germany will be destroyed. Everybody will be slaughtered, murdered, burned and destroyed. We have, after all, burned all bridges behind us, deliberately, we have. We have practically solved the Jewish question in

Germany. That alone is something awesome.' All in the room agreed that Russian workers needed to be kept in line, by beating if necessary. 'Below ground it is dark, and Berlin is a long way away,' commented Ley's co-chair Paul Pleiger, one of the Reich's most important industrial leaders.[17]

Harshness in the workplace was accompanied by some talk of improving incentives as well. Happy to cooperate with the Gestapo in dealing with trouble-makers, the 'workshy' or simply those whom 'we don't need', German managers also contemplated boosting their workers' performance through better treatment. They went on courses to learn how to optimize labour productivity and introduced bonuses, though whether incentives such as allowing workers to wear the 'Ost' badge on their sleeve rather than chest were really helpful must be open to doubt. In the final year of the war, performance-related pay was brought in, and some restrictions on the workers' movement were lifted. Nevertheless, when the air-raid sirens sounded and Allied bombers appeared overhead, it was the foreign workers who were kept out of municipal shelters so that disproportionately high numbers of them died. And by the end, with coal and food running very short, their living conditions were truly grim. A local government report from the winter of 1944/5 described a camp run by a Berlin company:

The rooms are completely dark. The gym is completely dark. In the middle an open fire is burning. Straw is lying around in heaps on the ground with foreigners lying on it ... The clothing of the inmates present is meager, dirty and partly torn ... Only 150–160 of the 320 inmates went to work today; 120 remained in the camp because they have no footwear (they have developed lumps on their feet). About forty have colds ... The camp is dirty and disorderly, the provision of clothing for the inmates is inadequate, the heating is insufficient, the inmates are covered in lice.[18]

The talk of improving the lot of the 'eastern worker' thus amounted to very little, undercut at every turn by much more fundamental and much harsher attitudes. Racial contempt was one, the product of a society which worried about ethnic interaction and had come to despise most non-German peoples. A cold-blooded business appraisal of the workers themselves was another. Like Hitler himself, German business never saw them as a scarce or valuable resource, still less as human beings to be nurtured and preserved. Rather they were cheap commodities to be worked until they were worn out. The third factor was fear of revenge. As Ley's speech suggested, many Germans – even when unclear exactly what had happened abroad – were well aware of the suppressed bitterness and hostility that Germany's behaviour had aroused among its victims. The regime itself had been talking the language of revenge and retaliation since it took power and constantly warned that these would be turned back on Germany itself in the event of Nazism's defeat. And finally, there was a kind of paranoia about 'criminals' running amok as Germany collapsed. In the war's final months, as the Nazis became more and more violent towards suspected offenders of all kinds, Himmler urged mass executions of foreign trouble-makers. Accused of plunder following a devastating bombing raid, for example, more than 200 Italian POWs were hung in batches on an improvised gallows in Düsseldorf. By the war's end, the Gestapo was killing Germans and foreign workers alike in order to get rid of 'dangerous criminals', as supposed threats to public order, or simply because they were too weak to be moved.[19]

SLAVE LABOUR AND THE SS

As the agency in charge of concentration camps, the SS had its own potentially valuable sources of labour. However, when the war broke out, the inmate population was very small: in September 1939 the main camps of Dachau, Sachsenhausen, Buchenwald, Mauthausen, Flossenbürg and Ravensbrück housed a mere 21,400 prisoners between them at a time when the Soviet Gulag contained more than 1.3 million. It was not until the great turning-point of 1941/2 that Himmler awoke to their significance. By the spring of 1942, the number of inmates had doubled, but more importantly, the SS had begun to build or expand another nine camps, including three – Auschwitz, Stutthof and Lublin-Majdanek – each of which was designed to take numbers that alone would have dwarfed the total in SS custody before the war. Although the plans upon which this expansion was based were never fully realized, the total camp population rose very fast to 110,000 (September 1942) and 200,000 (June 1943). At Auschwitz, Dachau and elsewhere, numerous satellite camps surrounded the main camps. By early 1945, there were more than 700,000 inmates, and some 40,000 guards, in twenty badly overcrowded major camps and another 165 SS-run labour camps, and the German system had mushroomed to something approaching the proportions of the Gulag.[20]

The SS Camp System: Prisoner Numbers

Camp	September 1939	April 1942	August 1943	January 1945
Dachau	4,000	8,000	17,300	57,560
Buchenwald	5,300	9,000	17,600	87,300
Sachsenhausen	6,500	10,000	26,500	60,800
Flossenbürg	1,600	4,700	4,800	40,300
Auschwitz	–	c. 20,000	72,000	67,000
Lublin	–	c. 9,500	15,400	–
Total for all concentration camps	c. 21,000	c. 75,000	224,000	714,000

Sources: TWC, v, R-129; 1468-PS; N. Wachsmann, Hitler's Prisons: Legal Terror in Nazi Germany (London, 2004), 394–5; H. Krausnick and M. Broszat, eds., Anatomy of the SS State (London, 1973), 247–8.

The catalyst for the new policy was – as we have already seen – Himmler's desire to anticipate the imminent victory by embarking immediately upon the groundwork for General Plan East. This implied using foreign labour not inside the Reich – something about which Himmler always had the deepest reservations – but further east. As a result, he started to shift the focus of the camp system eastwards to the fringes of the Reich and the General Government with the construction of the Auschwitz and Lublin mega-camps. Lublin in particular was projected to become a settlement centre, trebling in size, with a renovated city centre, new industries and a ring of settlements around it. Such a quantum leap in the use of slave labour mandated a shake-up of the moribund camp system. Himmler therefore placed it under the energetic Oswald Pohl, who was put in charge of a brand-new SS department, the Economics and Administrative Head Office (WVHA). Combining camp administration, the SS's chief building and construction unit and its business operations, the WVHA was intended to organize the peace for the SS in the East. Pohl's subordinate, the talented but cold-blooded chief SS building engineer, Hans Kammler, drew up plans for the new Lublin camp and looked forward to the deployment of peacetime 'building brigades' which would utilize 175,000 slave workers to start the construction of roads and settlements.[21]

The extraordinary ambition behind these plans lasted most of the year despite the fact that barely 30,000 Soviet POWs were actually delivered into SS care in 1941. Kammler, Pohl and Himmler saw nothing to worry about. Kammler's peacetime construction plans talked airily about exploiting 'prisoners, POWs, Jews etc.', and they saw the transport of able-bodied Slovak Jews to Auschwitz in March 1942 as just the start. General Plan East's main architect, Professor Konrad Meyer, envisaged that 850,000 workers would be needed over the next twenty-five years.[22] Thus, as Pohl put it to Himmler, 'the war has brought about a marked change in the structure of the concentration camps and has changed their duties with regard to the employment of the prisoners'. Mobilizing prisoners for the war economy and 'for purposes of construction in the forthcoming peace' now took precedence over security considerations or ideological indoctrination. Himmler agreed. In the crucially important speech he delivered to senior SS leaders that June (on the occasion of Heydrich's funeral), he emphasized that

if we do not fill our camps with slaves – in this room I mean to say things very firmly and very clearly – with worker slaves who will build our cities, our villages, our farms without regard to any losses, then even after years of war we will not have enough money to be able to equip the settlements in such a manner that real Germanic people can live there and take root in the first generation.[23]

Pohl himself was no romantic. He wanted camp commanders to start behaving like managers rather than policemen and to make sure that their camps were economically productive. Yet even more than German businessmen, the SS treated its prisoners as though there was an infinite supply of them. The new policy worked them to the limit of their endurance and beyond – cutting breaks, demanding unlimited work hours, degradation and constant surveillance. Their use, as Pohl put it, had to be 'in the true meaning of the word, exhaustive'. How great the supply – or indeed the capacity of the camps themselves – really was could not be easily answered. It had become embarrassingly clear that Richard Glücks, the inspector of the concentration camps, was not even sure how many prisoners they already held. Pohl wanted all this changed and tried to monitor performance through productivity statistics.[24]

In fact, the supply of prisoners was about to soar far beyond the capabilities of the SS management. Funnelled in huge numbers towards the camps as the Final Solution unfolded, those Jews 'unfit for work' were sent straight to the extermination camps, while the rest were 'selected' to face 'extermination through labour'. A similar fate faced foreign and German workers who fell into the hands of the police. The 1942 Thierack–Himmler agreement sent those arrested into the camps, bypassing the judicial system. The idea of 'exterminating them through labour', Goebbels remarked at that time, should apply to 'Jews and Gypsies unconditionally, Poles who have to serve three to four years of penal servitude, and Czechs and Germans who are sentenced to death or penal servitude for life'. As a result, 35,000 'eastern' workers were handed over to the Gestapo at the end of 1942 alone. The burgeoning partisan war in eastern Europe added many more, as did a decision to transfer to the camps all Poles facing prolonged prison custody in the General Government. By late 1944 the number of monthly arrests had doubled in less than two years.[25]

Pohl himself was an energetic administrator but he was also vain, dogmatic (prone, like Hans Frank, to make much of his supposed likeness to Mussolini) and, according to a former colleague, a complete dilettante in economic matters. In the second half of 1942, and following the huge numbers of new arrivals into the camps, conditions became so bad that the population of the system as a whole actually fell – from 115,000 to 83,000. 'Destruction through labour' was being taken too far, even for the SS.[26] The only mystery is why SS managers themselves were surprised when they finally got a clear overall picture of camp mortality – thanks to their new statistics – and realized how high it was. By December 1942, the military and Speer's Armaments Ministry were criticizing them for their inefficiency and arguing that it was better to send workers to Speer's factories and to keep Jews in ghettoes for the army's use.[27]

If there was one thing to which Himmler was sensitive it was the charge of inefficiency, and the fear that this might jeopardize his hold over racial policy and, at his prodding, an SS internal commission began investigating the management of the camps. It uncovered such a network of corruption, stolen property, arbitrary killings and secret slush funds that hundreds of SS men were discharged or arrested. One-third of camp commanders were replaced. 'Every means must be used to lower the death rate,' Glücks instructed his subordinates in January 1943. As a result, there was a period from the end of 1942 to early 1944 when the WVHA did bring mortality rates among its inmates down from an astonishing average of 10 per cent monthly to 2–3 per cent. But this was still astronomical. Moreover, throughout this same period, hundreds of thousands of Jews were being gassed upon arrival at Auschwitz-Birkenau, while others elsewhere were being starved to death. The camp system managers did not monitor the supply of food for the camps, curb the lethal behaviour of the guards or take other obvious measures that would have kept more prisoners alive. On the contrary, new measures helped kill people faster.

As the system expanded, Himmler tried distinguishing the different kinds of camps and their functions in order to emphasize the economic utility of the WVHA-run institutions in particular. By this time, after all, he was responsible for POW, internment, labour and transit camps as well as extermination centres and the concentration camps proper under the control of the inspector of concentration camps and the WVHA. In May 1943, he wrote revealingly that the work camp at Salaspils near Riga could only be turned into a concentration camp if it 'includes a genuine and really important armaments enterprise'. As it was, the inmates were mostly kept digging turf, quarrying, mining and making cement, work which he described as 'only done to keep them busy'. But whether or not they fell under the WVHA brought no appreciable difference in the way prisoners were treated. On the contrary, more industrialized facilities – including modern crematoria – and medical resources simply meant inmates could be murdered in greater numbers. Camp doctors killed sick inmates by injecting them with phenol; others were simply gassed or burned. Like Jews, wrote an SS officer in Lublin during the Zamość resettlement, Poles being sent to Auschwitz were to be 'liquidated' if they were mentally ill, physically disabled or unwell. The only difference was that, 'unlike Jews, Poles should die a natural death'. Meanwhile, deaths were no longer reported to local registry offices; in the camps themselves a new registration code helped to obscure the rising numbers.[28]

The resulting death toll was staggering. Of 12,658 prisoners transferred to the camps (most went to Mauthausen-Gusen) from preventative detention in the Reich at the end of 1942, 5,935 were already dead by early the following April. The overall mortality rate was even higher. Recent estimates suggest that of the 1.65 million inmates of camps who worked for the German war economy, no more than 475,000 survived the war; relatively few were actually released. The camp system had grown enormously from its modest beginnings after the Nazi seizure of power, and this growth brought with it rocketing mortality rates. In the hands of the SS, it was too lethally wasteful ever to become the major supplier of the labour that the Reich war effort desperately needed.

The numbers tell their own story, impersonal though it may be. The size of the German labour force actually shrank between 1939 and 1944 from 39 million to 29 million, entirely as a result of the conscription of men into the military, and much of that shortfall was filled by the seven million foreign workers, most of them dragooned by Sauckel's agents. Against these figures, the 475,000 starving and enfeebled survivors of Himmler's camps represented a pitiful indictment of Nazism's economic idiocy. A very different policy would have allowed the German labour force to expand not contract. After all, millions of potential workers had either been deliberately murdered (in the Final Solution) or starved (in POW camps). But in the Third Reich, and above all in the SS – as its leaders often proclaimed – some things were more important than economics.

DOING BUSINESS WITH THE SS

Where business was concerned, the SS was a lot better at destroying things than building them up. After the *Anschluss*, while Göring was turning his Reichwerke into a massive state-led industrial conglomerate, the SS too stepped tentatively into the world of production. Its early initiatives in this area had focused on quarrying and construction and it had opened camps such as Mauthausen, Flossenbürg and Gross-Rosen in anticipation of the Reich's planned great rebuilding projects. Taking advantage of privileged access to expropriated Jewish property, in particular, Pohl and the WVHA also managed to take over numerous small companies, from saw-mills to food processors. But there was little logic to their purchases – mineral water bottling plants here, cycle repair shops and ceramics producers there. His mind elsewhere, Himmler occasionally dabbled with the idea of an SS armaments industry producing anti-aircraft guns, grenade-launchers and machine-guns. But men with business experience were in short supply in the SS, and the combination of a starving and brutalized labour force, Himmler's obsession with postwar agrarian resettlement in the East and lack of investment capital prevented the SS from creating a manufacturing empire of any consequence.[29]

A particularly macabre example of its economic incompetence was the feeble business spin-off from the mass murder of Polish Jews in Operation Reinhard. In the autumn of 1942, Himmler decided to counter criticisms of the genocide – the Wehrmacht in particular was concerned at the disruption to Polish manufacturing production as the Jews were removed from their workplaces – by creating 'a few large Jewish concentration camp factories' round Lublin to produce for the war effort. Although these never materialized in the form Himmler had envisaged, Odilo Globocnik's OSTI conglomerate round Lublin did employ several tens of thousands of Polish Jewish workers in a range of operations which included a glassworks, a brush factory, carpentry shops, a bicycle assembly shop and a pharmaceuticals firm. Neither the cruel, corrupt, fun-loving Globocnik nor his men were natural managers; one remarked that 'I feel nauseated when I just hear the word industry!' The SS's own business experts were also confused: OSTI had been set up as a company in March 1943 with Pohl chairing the board of directors and 'Globus' as managing director. But was it just a policing operation, a cover for personal profit or a serious commercial venture? The answer emerged soon enough. Amateurishly and barbarically run, it was a momentary byproduct of policies of plunder and genocide rather than the nucleus of a new SS concern with industry, and its mismanagement was one of the things that got Globocnik fired for the second time in his career and sent away from Lublin to run the police in Trieste. Before his dismissal he had suggested – and Himmler had backed him – that the Łódź ghetto be transferred to OSTI management too. He was concerned that industrialists and the Wehrmacht seemed to placing orders there rather than with him. But those in charge of the Warthegau's industrial centre managed to get the idea scrapped: nothing the SS had done suggested it could match the efficiency with which the Łódź ghetto workforce under the orders of a German businessman was turning out uniforms for the Wehrmacht.[30]

In the hands of the SS, the extermination of Polish Jewry thus resulted in private enrichment on a massive scale but little economic gain for the German war effort. Globocnik claimed that Operation Reinhard produced more than 1,900 box-cars of used clothing between September 1942 and December 1943. From the killing of hundreds of thousands of Polish Jews, his men collected millions of reichsmarks' worth of assets that they said they planned to plough back into OSTI. In Globocnik's final report, the list of items upon which this calculation was based stretches for several pages and includes currency in denominations from Hungarian pengoes to Australian pounds as well as enormous piles of jewels, watches, precious metals, briefcases, pocket knives, sunglasses, cigarette cases, alarm clocks and razors. What did not go into Christmas presents for German settlers or SS members, or into the ample pockets of the officials involved, was supposed to help finance the cash-strapped OSTI conglomerate. Nevertheless, the firm did not thrive. It staggered on through most of 1943 only so long as Himmler wished to preserve a small Jewish workforce in the East; in November – following the revolts in the extermination camps of Treblinka and Sobibor – its remaining employees were murdered in the course of the bloody Operation 'Harvest Festival' that wiped out the few surviving Jews of Poland. In February 1944 many of the other SS companies were declared to be insolvent. That October, Speer claimed control of labour throughout the Reich, leaving the SS's larger economic ambitions in the dust.[31]

Speer himself later boasted he had helped to avert the danger of an SS takeover of the economy, by reminding Hitler of the importance of keeping arms production in the hands of those who knew how to run it. But Himmler's interests – occasional day-dreaming aside – had never really lain in that direction. So far as the peace was concerned, he remained committed to his postwar building programmes in the East, a vision of colonial resettlement that planned using modern governmental techniques to restore a pseudo-medieval order into which industry itself fitted awkwardly. As for the war, if duty required him to kill off Jewish workers, he would. He was therefore speaking the truth when he reassured Speer that 'I have completely different ambitions than to become a competitor in this sector [i.e. arms production].'

There had been just one brief tussle between the two men – in the autumn of 1942 – over whether to allow camp inmates to work for outside concerns, or whether factories should be founded in the camps themselves. The cause was the Gustloff armaments works at Buchenwald, an intended pilot project for the use of camp labour in arms production, where there had been delays in deliveries. But having the SS as an employer could be disconcerting. After some forceful interventions by Himmler, Gustloff's managers began to worry that the SS might start policing them as well as their slave workers. Not even Hitler thought it would be a good idea to have the SS telling Germany's industrialists how to run their operations. Once that round was over and Speer had come out on top, he found Himmler ready to cooperate: new camps were set up inside and outside the Reich, and even prohibitions on employing Jews inside Germany were eventually relaxed in the interests of war production. Concentration camp labour was channelled into the armaments economy, and in return the SS got special access to munitions and material.[32]

By the final year of the war, the focus on Germany's management of Europe's economy had narrowed to a concern with arms production in particular. Given extensive powers over the economies of all the occupied territories, Speer was finally able to contemplate centralizing European industrial production for the German war effort, gearing everything to increased arms output and focusing on productivity gains. Speer's rise showed Hitler's confidence in him: it was, after all, transparently clear that Speer was a better alternative than Himmler so far as producing weapons (or indeed anything) was concerned. Whereas the camps combined poor labour productivity with high mortality and soaring corruption, labour productivity rose in arms factories under Speer's management. Despite only modest increases in German national income, his reforms brought about an impressive growth in munitions output without requiring a major restructuring of the economy. Combat aircraft production alone nearly doubled in a year. By mid-1943, it is doubtful that Himmler could successfully have challenged Speer even had he wanted to.[33]

From the autumn of 1943, camp inmates were used in significant numbers to produce arms, and this trend accelerated during 1944, considerably worsening conditions. As the commandant of Auschwitz, Rudolf Höss, explained at the Nuremberg trials:

The main reason why the prisoners were in such bad condition towards the end of the war, why so many thousands of them were found sick and emaciated in the camps, was that every internee had to be employed in the armament industry to the extreme limit of his forces. The Reichsführer constantly and on every occasion kept this goal before our eyes, and also proclaimed it through the Chief of the Main Economic and Administrative Office, Obergruppenführer Pohl, to the concentration camp commanders and administrative leaders during the so-called commanders' meetings. Every commander was told to make every effort to achieve this. The aim was not to have as many dead as possible or to destroy as many internees as possible; the Reichsführer was constantly concerned with being able to engage all forces available in the armament industry.[34]

Perhaps 25,000 camp prisoners were working for the war economy in early 1942; by the end of 1944 that figure had risen to 400–420,000 and the SS and German industry were cooperating in their exploitation. Housed mostly in former Jewish slave labour camps (the original inmates of which were now dead), some inmates were helping construct the coal-based chemicals industry in Silesia. Elsewhere in the Reich, the camp at Oranienburg fed the Heinkel plant, Sachsenhausen supplied Daimler-Benz, and Dachau was linked with BMW. The Krupp concern turned to the camps as it ran short of manpower, its managers scouring Buchenwald for skilled workers. The largely foreign labour force at Volkswagen was producing military vehicles, aircraft parts, rockets and many other weapons: the firm gave the SS jeeps, and in return the SS built and manned a special camp near its main factory.[35]

Speer himself asked Himmler to provide him with as many workers as possible. In May, Justice Minister Thierack allowed him to use prison inmates as well. By the spring of 1945, perhaps as much as half of the camp population – roughly 5 per cent of the Reich's total workforce – was working either directly manufacturing for the war effort or for Kammler's SS Building Directorate. Through Kammler the SS lent its support to Volkswagen and to Porsche's rocket-building programme. It also supplied the 60,000 prisoners who quarried vaults out of the Harz mountains to create the tunnels for V-2 production. Management was not sophisticated: before roll-call, SS guards simply punched workers in the face: those who remained upright were counted as 'fit for work'. For Kammler, unconcerned about the thousands who died, this was an efficient way of utilizing labour reserves, and he was amply satisfied with the rate of work that resulted.[36]

In the end Hitler's gamble failed and his bid to wage a continental war in defiance of Germany's economic capabilities backfired. The USSR's continued resistance, its apparently endless reserves of manpower and the remarkable success of its own rearmament effort in the face of crippling shortages of foodstuffs condemned his entire strategy. The key phase of the struggle was in the first year and a half after the German invasion of the USSR, when the Reich's new conquests and the profound shock to the Soviet economy brought it many advantages at a time when the American economy was still gearing up for war. It was in those crucial months that the Nazi capacity for wastage and incompetence, Hitler's strategic mistakes and the regime's inability to convert resources into weapons as effectively as its enemies cost the Reich dearly.

Its mismanagement of labour – one of its scarcest commodities – was critical. Across the span of the entire war, Germany could put into the field fewer than half the 35 million men Stalin was able to muster and after the autumn of 1942 the disparity between their armies grew and grew. Germany bled dry on the Eastern Front, unable to match its opponent either in manpower (its population was about half that of the USSR), management or arms output. In the west it faced largely unscathed British and American forces, with abundant reserves of man-power and food behind them. By the war's end, it had lost more than 3.2 million men. The USSR had lost more than twice this number and suffered many more civilian deaths. But its speedy mobilization testified both to the superior Soviet will to win and to the regime's greater industrial and technological adaptability. Its ease of access to mineral resources and oil and the supply of Lend-Lease equipment helped hugely. But we should not overlook the fact that, in the case of manpower, the USSR overcame what were in some ways much greater obstacles than the Third Reich: within a year of the invasion, after all, its working population had shrunk from 85 to 53 million people. Given near-full employment, even emptying the Gulag, which happened rapidly, could not make up the shortfall. Instead, the entire population was mobilized, and existing workers were redirected very early on into war industries. Despite evacuation and swingeing losses of industrial plant, the USSR still produced more weapons in 1942 than the Germans.[37]

Unwilling to squeeze civilian living standards as ruthlessly as the Soviet regime did, and already worried about the mass bombing raids that ultimately killed hundreds of thousands of people in the Reich itself, Hitler was only able to continue the war beyond 1942 thanks to the Wehrmacht – without doubt the finest fighting force in the war – and to Germany's increasingly intense exploitation of Europe's industry, agriculture and labour. As brutally effective as this policy was, it would have helped much more if millions of workers had not been deliberately and callously killed off. Some were worked or starved to death; others were hanged, gassed or shot as racial enemies. In every case, they testified to the impossibility of fighting a race war on several fronts at once. The same sense of racial solidarity that primed the German soldier and made him such a formidable fighter served as a limitation when it came to mobilizing labour and other resources outside the country. Both liberal-ism and communism, from this point of view, were much more effective ideological motivators in a protracted war than National Socialism. Hitler's critics in the SS turned out to be right, after all: Germany could have racial purity or imperial domination, but it could not have both.[38]

I I

Ersatz Diplomacy

*Unbridled nationalist egoism being the very essence of totalitarianism, it
was inevitable that every country which went fascist, no matter how
spontaneously, had one aim: the preservation or restoration of its national
independence and integrity, which was why it was bound to turn against
German domination. This opened the unexpected vista of a totalitarian
Europe, spelling the doom for the motherland of totalitarianism . . .*

Countess Waldeck, *Athene Palace* (1942), 300–301

THE CRUSADE AGAINST BOLSHEVISM

'No illusions about allies!' This was how General Franz Halder, chief of
the army general staff, summarized Hitler's words on the subject when
he spoke to his generals on the eve of Operation Barbarossa. The Führer
made an exception for the Finns, who had already been attacked by the
Russians in the winter of 1939 and had fought back astonishingly
effectively: even he acknowledged that they were reliable and committed
opponents of the Red Army, and he had already been supplying them
with arms. But as for the Romanians, the other ally he was counting on
to provide substantial support, his views reflected the standard Austrian
contempt. ('Cowardly, corrupt, depraved' was his verdict, according to
the notes of another member of his audience.) Neither he nor his officers
believed Germans would need help from anyone else.[1]

In fact, led by General Antonescu, Romania committed 587,000
troops, making it, together with Finland, Germany's most important
military supporter. Not wanting to be outbid, the Hungarians went

along too, although they were far less enthusiastic and were calling for their troops to be withdrawn by November. As for the rest, their contribution was close to symbolic. Mussolini had something to prove after his soldiers' abject performance in Greece, France and east Africa and sent three divisions. General Franco softened the blow of keeping Spain out of the war by allowing volunteers to enlist in the so-called Blue Division. Keen to demonstrate their solidarity and to win Germany's favour for further territorial claims, the Croats and Slovaks sent token units of their own. And from across western Europe came small groups of Dutch, French, Walloon, Flemish and Norwegian anti-Bolsheviks.

Writing to Mussolini a week after the attack on the Red Army, Hitler sounded pleased: 'Large parts of Europe have been roused from a truly lethargic disinterestedness.' Apparently people now understood that Germany's 'battle against Bolshevism' was part of 'a common policy which, in the last analysis, is a truly European one'. Yet what did this actually mean? Was it all words, or did the Führer's talk of 'Europe' really imply some reward for those who gave their support? As the war ebbed and flowed, a fierce debate began in Berlin, Rome and elsewhere over what this anti-Bolshevik 'European' policy should be.[2]

Hitler's instincts were, as always, to promise as little as possible, especially given his conviction that the war would be won quickly without needing anyone else's help. So far as the eventual dispensation of former Soviet territory was concerned, he was categorical: only the Reich had the right to determine this. At the key planning meeting of 16 July he had been astonished that a Vichy newspaper had dared describe the struggle against Bolshevism as 'Europe's war and that therefore it had to be conducted for Europe as a whole'. Germany, he went on, should not make 'superfluous declarations'; even with allies like Romania – he was now an admirer of General Antonescu – one never knew how relations might suddenly evolve.[3]

It was in the following month that Roosevelt and Churchill met and issued their statement of war aims in the Atlantic Charter. German Foreign Ministry officials criticized its lack of any 'fresh conception of Europe' and saw a chance for the Third Reich to stake out its own vision of the postwar world. The declaration, they argued, demonstrated that England, by virtue of its geographical location and interests, could never act as the 'organizer and protector of a newly unified Europe', and they urged a response: 'For us there is no competition . . . The field is free to counterpose a constructive plan for Europe to England's'.[4] Hitler's closest ally felt the same way. The Duce too wanted to seize the moment to match the liberal democracies in the global war of words. People, he told his diplomatic adviser, Anfuso, would not fight for Germany simply for the honour of being 'organized' by the Reich. They had to be promised something more definite. He wanted a joint declaration that the Axis would respect 'European national and social ideals'. As Anfuso put it, they needed the reassurance that Germany was not fighting a colonial war in Europe, nor solely for the *Herrenvolk*, but for a new Europe.[5]

At the end of August, therefore, when Mussolini visited Hitler on the Eastern Front to celebrate the Wehrmacht's success against the Red Army, he came armed with policy papers drawn up by Italian diplomats for a possible 'proclamation of social and economic principles by the Axis in opposition to the Anglo-Saxon formulations'. His officials were talking about a political future for Europe which included guarantees of sovereignty and independence for member states. Mussolini himself had been kept in the dark about the invasion of the Soviet Union until the last moment and he was never as convinced as Hitler was that it would be wrapped up quickly. He was also acutely aware that entering the war had damaged Italy's freedom to manoeuvre, and reports of the maltreatment of Italian workers in the Reich had made him conscious of Germans' lack of sensitivity even to their most important ally.[6]

As they made the long journey to Hitler's mosquito-infested headquarters in the Prussian forests, Italian diplomats prayed that the Duce, often strangely silent in Hitler's presence, would be brave enough to raise the question of the continent's future. It is to the Foreign Ministry's Filippo Anfuso – 'considered to be one of the handsomest men in Rome', according to a German colleague – that we owe a vivid impression of the encounter between the two dictators. According to Anfuso, Hitler already betrayed the physical effects of living underground much of the time in his vast new bunker complex. His gaze was less mobile, and he seemed thin and worn. But he had not lost his habit of lengthy soliloquizing and he insisted triumphantly to his Italian guests that victory was at hand despite the animal-like resistance of the Asiatic *Untermenschen*. The Italians appear to have been unaware of the enormous arguments over strategy that had been going on earlier in the month between Hitler and his generals about how to force the issue against the Red Army, or about the uncertainty that had crept in as a result of the continued Soviet resistance. Mussolini himself noted that Hitler seemed obsessed with the 'almost religious desire to liberate Europe from Bolshevism, while in his speech the word "Europe" recurred often, sometimes substituting for the word "Germany"'. Yet, concluded Anfuso, 'no other hint could be detected in his words on the future of Europe'. When he repeated insistently that he was defending Europe from 'Asian Marxism', his Italian guests asked themselves *sotto voce* 'Which Europe? The Europe of the Master Race? Of Athens and Rome? Of the Pope? Of the Socialists? Of Talleyrand? Of Charles V?'[7]

Seemingly convinced that the final victory lay just around the corner, Hitler seemed euphoric as he toured the smoking ruins of the front with his ally. Mussolini could scarcely get a word in edgeways. The Duce was in a quite different mood, weighed down by the recent death of his favourite son, the twenty-three-year-old Bruno, in a flying accident and, as often in his meetings with Hitler, he seemed reluctant to press his own point of view. His true feelings – at what was perhaps the most critical of all the meetings between the two men – emerged only at odd moments and in unpredictable ways. At one point, he insisted on taking the controls of the small plane in which they were flying, alarming Hitler and his entourage; it was all they could do to persuade him not to attempt the landing. Sometimes, too, he matched the Führer's endless monologues with his own, dilating on Trajan's campaigns across the Danube. And after Hitler had compared the achievements of his armies with those of Frederick the Great, Napoleon and Alexander and conjured up future plans of conquest beyond the Urals and into Asia, Mussolini deflated him with a single line from Pascoli's poem on the Greek conqueror: 'And then?' he interjected. 'Shall we weep for the moon like Alexander the Great?'[8]

In private, the Duce told his aides that the war could not be won without an Axis declaration of political principles. He wanted Hitler to state that this was not merely a 'colonial war' for the benefit of the Master Race, but the birth of a new political order for Europe as a whole. Unwilling as always to trouble Hitler with a thorny issue, however, he delegated Anfuso to talk it over instead with Foreign Minister Ribbentrop, who had set up his headquarters in a nearby estate. But the timing was bad – one month earlier Ribbentrop had had the most violent quarrel of his career with Hitler. *Persona non grata* in the 'Wolf's Lair', he did not welcome the Italians' approach. In fact, a tussle lasting several days ensued over the drafting of the communiqué and went on right up to the very last moment: the homeward train of the Italian delegation was even brought to a stop outside Klagenfurt, shortly before it reached the frontier, so that there could be yet another discussion. In the end the original Italian proclamation – full of promises and pledges to the peoples of Europe – was hopelessly watered down, and the result merely talked feebly of 'eradicating the menace of Bolshevism and of plutocratic exploitation'. For Hitler, it was all beside the point, for there was no point in issuing lofty declarations so long as the Axis looked as though it was winning. Afterwards, they would be superfluous.

Yet despite further tremendous victories in September, with the encirclement of Kiev and the Wehrmacht pushing almost to the outskirts of Moscow in early October, the Red Army did not fold, and German losses mounted. 'The gramophone records were being changed,' was how the chief Foreign Ministry interpreter remembered those months. 'Instead of "We have won the war," foreigners now heard "We shall win the war," and finally "We cannot lose the war." ' In the Foreign Ministry itself there was much sympathy for the Italian proposals; Germany's diplomats were keen to reassert the need for a political track. 'Aggressive, disruptive and polemical propaganda must be supplemented by something more positive, especially as regards the future of Europe,' a position paper from late September warned. Ribbentrop's propaganda adviser, a journalist and Reichstag deputy called Karl Megerle, talked not only about economic cooperation but of political partnership and even freedom and independence.[9]

Between 25 and 27 November 1941, the foreign ministers of Germany, Italy and Japan were due to meet in Berlin to renew the 1936 Anti-Comintern Pact. They were to be joined by eight new signatories: Bulgaria, Croatia, Denmark, Finland, Hungary, Romania, Slovakia and Spain. Bringing together Germany's allies and well-wishers to celebrate the continent's imminent liberation from the threat of Bolshevism, the meeting seemed the obvious time to issue a declaration on Europe's future. Briefly the Führer showed signs of being more diplomatic and he publicly extolled the contribution made by Germany's faithful allies: 'in the ranks of our German soldiers, making common cause with them, march the Italians, the Finns, the Hungarians, the Romanians, the Slovaks and the Croats; the Spaniards now move into the battle; the Belgians, the Dutch, the Danes, the Norwegians, yes, even the French have joined this great front'. In mid-October, he actually gave the green light for Ribbentrop to prepare a 'European manifesto' to be issued with the expected proclamation of victory that winter. It looked as though the Italians' hopes of August were about to be realized.[10]

Yet it was another false dawn and the product perhaps only of Hitler's temporary pessimism at the course of the war. Whenever he thought victory was in sight, he forgot about diplomacy. At the end of October, Italy's Foreign Minister, Count Ciano, reported to Mussolini that the Führer was again convinced Stalin had been knocked 'out of the game'. He believed the evacuation of Soviet industry and manpower behind the Urals had no chance of success, and that such a highly centralized state (in which, so Hitler said, 'the state even distributed toothbrushes, assuming that the Russians brush their teeth') could not suddenly set up a new headquarters. Russia could no more continue to fight than the Reich could if 'it had lost the Ruhr, Upper Silesia, ninety per cent of its munitions factories, sixty per cent of its means of communication'. It was an entirely reasonable, if mistaken, assessment. But despite the great victories in the Ukraine, Ciano detected traces of uncertainty beneath the bombast: Hitler, he thought, was still wondering whether other surprises lay in store from 'the very vast region which remains under Stalin's control', surprises far worse than the delayed Soviet mines which had blown up Axis officers in newly occupied Kiev and Odessa. Ciano himself felt the real knock-out punch was still to be delivered, and he suspected the Germans thought so too.[11]

Hitler's rhetorical emphasis on the 'European' contribution to the fight continued therefore but carried no real conviction. He warned – as he would from now on for the rest of the war – that any commitments for the future would simply be construed as weakness by Germany's enemies. Ribbentrop was thus ordered to purge his speech of any references to Europe's political future. The 'European solidarity' and 'community' Hitler saw emerging in the anti-Bolshevik struggle remained primarily military in character; his vision involved non-Germans being regimented and organized under German leadership in a common crusade. It had nothing to say about what political arrangements should emerge on the continent in peacetime.[12]

At the November summit itself, Hitler failed to dispel the feeling among his guests that it was the Germans who were 'masters of the house'. He pontificated breezily but said little. 'Europe was moving towards a great period of peace,' he told the Bulgarian Foreign Minister Popov. For the laconic Danish foreign minister, Scavenius, forecasts of the continent's rosy economic prospects came wrapped in meaningless verbiage. 'Once the rich territories of eastern Europe which had hitherto always been mobilized *against* Europe would be organized *for* Europe,' Hitler assured him. 'Europe could be made self-sufficient.' To the obsequious Croatian foreign minister, he stressed Germany's 'blood sacrifice' and its right to leadership: 'if we were leaders in the fighting we had also the right to a leading role in the new organization of Europe'. His systematic opacity about the continent's political future enshrouded the fate of the occupied eastern territories in particular. It was on the eve of the Anti-Comintern conference that the Germans finally made a public announcement of the formation of civil administrations under Rosenberg's Ministry for the Occupied Areas from the Baltic to the Ukraine. Yet German propaganda was tight-lipped, and guidelines explicitly stipulated that all 'concrete statements about the German political aims would only serve the enemy in his attempt to discredit and disrupt precisely the form of the work of reconstruction which is planned in the East by a corresponding campaign operating with insinuations and distortions'. A few months later, when the Foreign Ministry brought together an assortment of exiled Caucasian princelings and tribal chieftains and put them up at the Hotel Adlon, Hitler told his diplomats sharply to 'refrain from all talk of collaboration with eastern peoples'.[13]

There was a similar lack of clarity vis-à-vis western Europe as well. When Göring met Marshal Pétain, the latter explained how hard it was to work with the Germans without a clearer sense of the future:

[Pétain] was himself, as was known, a very strong advocate of the idea of collaboration, but . . . he did have to say that so far France had not been informed how she would fit into the new order of Europe. France was, so to speak, proceeding with closed eyes into the future. She wanted to know something more about the future organization of Europe, and about the place to be occupied by her . . . Just as for military procedure, a plan was also necessary for a work of peace such as the development of the new Europe.[14]

Göring's scarcely reassuring answer was that 'this would depend on how close the two people came to one another'. Göring even recalled for Pétain that he had told the delegates at the Anti-Comintern meeting to think in terms of a 'political ledger in which Germany would set down the debits and credits for every country', and which he would open at the war's end to 'draw the balance'. Only one thing that was sure, Göring continued: someone other than Germany would have to pay for the war. Once again, a political argument had been dodged and turned into a matter of economics.

The sheer inadequacy of this kind of 'ersatz diplomacy' (as Ciano described it) struck everyone except its authors. Hitler set the tone, and his ministers followed. Even when they were forced to ask their allies for more troops, the leaders of the Third Reich remained deeply reluctant to flesh out their political vision of Europe's future. The truth was that they probably did not have one. All that mattered for them was the conquest of the USSR and the continued exploitation of the rest of Europe. Everything else could wait. 'To concoct an "Atlantic Charter" is naturally quite simple,' Hitler told the faithful at one of the last large rallies he addressed. 'This stupidity will soon be rectified by hard facts.' All the British and Americans were doing, he claimed, by talking about freedom from want and the need to guarantee work, was stealing the Nazis' own programme. The Germans did not need to talk; they acted.[15]

The Italians could scarcely believe it. According to Mario Luciolli, a member of the Berlin embassy, the Germans were simply unable to conceive of European reconstruction except in material terms. An uncomprehending 'political sterility' – in his words – blighted their chances of winning the war even more than the military threat they faced from their enemies. At the heart of German policy, with its monotonous repetition of victory after victory, lay 'an intrinsic vacuity'. Himmler's racism had been pushed to an extreme 'hard for an Italian to comprehend', leading to such 'horrors' as 'systematic massacres, killings of women and children, forced prostitution'. Whenever sincere offers of collaboration were made to the Germans, they were met with 'immediate disappointment and humiliation and rebuffs'. 'All the questions put to Germany concerning the manner in which it proposes to resolve the problems of today and tomorrow, of the war and the peace, go unanswered: Germany is mute.'[16]

It was one of the paradoxes of Italian fascism, Luciolli himself remarked after the war, that a regime sensitive to the slightest dissent allowed a junior diplomat like himself to pen such a damning prognosis of Axis failure. But in this case it was not so surprising, since Luciolli was only expressing what his superiors secretly thought. In fact it was his own minister, Ciano, who had urged him to put his thoughts down on paper and then sent them on to Mussolini himself. Nor did Mussolini disagree. '[The Germans] have no political sense,' he told another of his ministers after reading a report on the Netherlands a few days later. 'In those occupied countries they had an opportunity to create a good situation – and they let it slip. Now they are hated. I've said it, and written it, many times to the Führer. One must give a definite shape to western Europe.' Still, it was easy to criticize the Germans, and diplomats always want political solutions. How differently did their allies behave, when power fell into their hands?[17]

OTHER OCCUPATIONS

Germany's allies – like most European nationalists in the middle of the twentieth century – believed in territorial expansion. The prospect of more land, to which a claim could usually be found on historico-legal, ethnographic or civilizational grounds, was the primary reason why they were willing to sacrifice so many of their own troops. Even so, the scale and nature of their goals differed from Germany's. They were basically only interested in fighting either for security – as in the case of Finland – or to recover their historical rights to lands of which former peace settlements had deprived them. Only Italy in any way emulated the Third Reich's imperial ambitions. As for the rest, once they had achieved their goals, their concern with the war waned quickly. Thus the Hungarians were generally satisfied with the territorial gains they had made by the summer of 1941, and the Croats and Slovaks with no more than independence and preserving what German largesse had given them. The Bulgarians, without even having to declare war on the USSR, found themselves by 1943 occupying most of the territories they had claimed ever since they had emerged as a state in 1878. Only the Romanians fought on in order to win back the lands a German decision had deprived them of.

These differences of goals and ends were fairly evident when compared with Hitler's far more open-ended and inchoate dreams of mastery, but the contrasts in means and tactics were not so clear-cut. Under German hegemony, many of the Reich's allies ended up running occupation regimes of their own. Looking at these helps answer a vital question: how much of what happened under German rule reflected specifically *German* or indeed Nazi behaviour and ideology, and how much was part of a much broader set of European responses to war and occupation?

The Hungarians, for example, were in some ways following an older Habsburg model. Their slogan was 'forward to the thousand-year-old frontiers' and, once they had reached them, they almost immediately incorporated their new territories and gave them representation in the Hungarian parliament (which was unquestionably the freest such forum in wartime central Europe). Serbian and Croat politicians from prewar Yugoslavia were elected as deputies and called for the country's new minorities to become loyal Hungarian citizens. Despite the anti-Bolshevism, and growing official anti-Semitism, there was thus a less radical break with nineteenth-century political traditions than there was in the Third Reich. But then Hungary was ruled not by an anti-monarchist corporal but by a former Habsburg admiral and aide-de-camp to the Emperor Franz Josef. Horthy wrapped himself in the nationalist mysticism of the medieval Crown of Saint Stephen. Few remembered that, in the early 1920s, he had prevented the Emperor Karl from making a come-back; what everyone knew was that he styled himself 'His Serene Highness, Regent for the Kingdom of Hungary'.[18]

But in other ways Horthy's Hungary and Hitler's Germany were not so different, and the new population politics left its mark there too. Concerned as ever with Magyarization, the authorities registered populations into old and new (meaning post-1918) inhabitants in their new territories and tried to expel large numbers of the latter. Many thousands were deported both into Serbia and into Romania, freeing lands and properties that could be used for settling Hungarians, or sold to raise state revenues. When their neighbours' objections (and the threat of retaliatory expulsions in reverse) prevented them from expelling as many people as they wished, they established camps for dissenters, targeted the churches and schools of Serbs and Jews in their (formerly Yugoslav) 'Southern Territories', prohibited cultural activity in minority languages and made Hungarian mandatory. Only the ethnic Germans were protected from this intense barrage of nationalizations, thanks to the Reich's oversight and influence.[19]

In terms of brutality, too, some of the Hungarian units in the field scarcely lagged behind the Germans. Indeed, in the Ukraine, they displayed a ruthlessness towards the civilian population which surprised even the German troops they were fighting with. In January 1942, after suffering losses at the hands of the partisans, they proclaimed that they would no longer take prisoners. It was also during that winter that Hungarian soldiers and gendarmes massacred several thousand Serbs and Jews in and around Novi Sad, a town in Hungarian-occupied Yugoslavia, in a series of reprisal killings for supposed attacks by partisans. Hundreds of victims were lined up, shot and forced through broken ice in the Danube, and corpses washed up along the river's shores for weeks afterwards. (These events later became the inspiration for the writer Danilo Kiš, who survived them as a child: his father was among those waiting in line to be shot when the orders came for the operation to end.) The killings were condoned by the government in Budapest as a way of highlighting the strength of the partisan movement in the region and hence reminding the Germans of the usefulness of having the Hungarians there.[20]

Such actions were reminiscent of the bloody White Terror that Hungary's leader, Admiral Horthy, had presided over when crushing the Bolsheviks after the First World War. Going a little further back in time, they also evoked the brutality with which Hungarian units of the Habsburg army had treated Serbs in 1914. And as in the First World War the Hungarian army's violence against civilians was eventually criticized by politicians in Budapest, themselves worried at the army's influence. The Novi Sad massacres elicited an official investigation which resulted in charges against the officers responsible – something that was impossible to imagine happening in the Third Reich. But we should be cautious not to idealize the regime of Admiral Horthy: always manoeuvring between the Germans and the British and Americans, he only took the Novi Sad investigation seriously when he realized it might be a painless way of signalling to the latter that Hungary wanted peace.[21]

The Bulgarians' equally ruthless behaviour as occupiers also suggested many parallels with the past: for them, too, this was essentially a continuation of regional struggles dating back to the Balkan Wars, the Macedonian Struggle of 1904 and even earlier. In fact, Bulgaria supported the Axis for one reason only: to build the Greater Bulgaria that had first been promised by the Russians in 1878. Partnership with Nazi Germany brought them closer to this than ever before or after. In return for allowing Germany privileged access to vital raw materials, they were allowed to administer most of Yugoslav Macedonia and Kosovo; from 1942, they also policed part of Serbia proper, which was quietly annexed de facto, and tyrannized by a heavy Bulgarian military presence. Unlike the Hungarians, they had never actually ruled most of these territories in peacetime, and the precedent they had in mind was their own very brutal occupation policy in the First World War.

In northern Greece they annexed 16,000 square kilometres and 590,000 inhabitants, renaming the area the 'Aegean provinces'. Here their population policy was even more far-reaching than in former Yugoslavia. Reversing decades of Hellenization, they drove many Greeks out, made Bulgarian the official language and brought in Bulgarian teachers to teach the local (often bi-lingual) peasant children. When there was an uprising in the Greek town of Drama in reaction to these policies, the Bulgarians crushed it and killed an estimated 3,000 people. Those refusing to opt for Bulgarian nationality were told they would have to leave, and tens of thousands of Greeks were either expelled or sent into central Europe to work for the Germans. In 1943, the local Jewish communities too were rounded up and deported to Treblinka and Auschwitz. By 1944 only perhaps half the prewar population of the region were still in their homes. At the same time, an entirely new governing class arrived, attracted by land grants and other concessions. Regional directors for colonization supervised the expropriation of Greek-owned property and the settlement of tens of thousands of Bulgarians.[22]

But probably the most murderous occupation regime outside National Socialism – and that most admired by the Führer – was run by the Romanian dictator, General Ion Antonescu. Antonescu was an intensely xenophobic professional soldier – 'brutal, duplicitous, very vain, a ferocious will to succeed' was how a knowledgeable colleague had evaluated him in the 1920s. Like much of the country's political and administrative elite, he was fervently anti-Semitic. Originally Francophile, he had become a supporter of National Socialist Germany before he was made dictator – or *Conducator* as he liked to be known – by King Carol of Romania in September 1940. The country had just been humiliated by the award of northern Transylvania to Hungary; Stalin had also helped himself to chunks of the provinces of Bukovina and

Bessarabia. Antonescu forced Carol to resign in favour of his eighteen-year-old son Michael and took Romania into the war on the side of the Germans, thinking this was the likeliest way to get these territories back.

In the winter of 1940/41, having assured Hitler he would join in the attack on the USSR, Antonescu crushed an attempted *coup d'état* by the Romanian fascist Iron Guard movement, his former allies. The Iron Guard had been on the rampage, killing more than 100 Jews in a bloody pogrom, when Antonescu finally moved against them. His main concern was law and order and ridding himself of the greatest single internal threat to his own position: he had his own plans for the Jews. Tens of thousands of Romanian refugees were already fleeing into the country from Hungarian-occupied northern Transylvania, and Antonescu set up a new refugee resettlement office, funding it largely by expropriating and redistributing property belonging to Romanian Jews. After the invasion of the USSR, the office's jurisdiction was extended to Bessarabia and north Bukovina, which the Wehrmacht and the Romanian army between them quickly won back from the Soviets and reincorporated in late July.[23]

But Antonescu wanted more, and Hitler agreed. Since he was not willing to return northern Transylvania (this would have angered the Hungarians), the Führer promised the Romanians much of the southern Ukraine, including the city of Odessa. This area, between the Dniester river and the Bug, which had never been part of Romania and which most Romanians were completely uninterested in, was now baptized 'Transnistria'. A face-saver for Antonescu, Hitler's decision was of major strategic significance for, together with the handover of Galicia to the General Government, it meant no substantial independent Ukrainian state could emerge under German control. By the end of August, a Romanian civil administration had been set up in Transnistria and, in mid-October, with German help, Romanian troops forced the Red Army back and took over Odessa itself.

For Antonescu, the new lands were basically a pawn, which would strengthen his hand when the time came to demand Transylvania back, and the government's lack of long-term interest in them meant that they were treated as little more than a source of plunder. Even the Germans were shocked by the Romanians' pointless destruction of buildings, their looting, pillaging, rape and killing. 'The plunder by Rumanian soldiers

has reached such proportions,' the general commanding the German
11th Army wrote to Antonescu early on, 'that one must anticipate a
political aversion [against the Germans] on the part of the Ukrainians.'
The civilian administration that followed was a little better organized,
but it too became a by-word for corruption and venality. The gendarmerie in particular were notorious for arbitrary confiscations, getting
drunk and attacking civilians without provocation. 'Plunder and
Romanize' was how some summed up the Romanian policy. 'Take as
much as possible from Transnistria but without leaving a written record,'
Antonescu instructed his ministers.[24]

Before the war, an estimated 3.4 million people had lived in Transnistria, but by late 1941 that figure had dropped to 2.2 million; Odessa's
population alone had fallen from 620,000 to an estimated 300,000
when the Red Army withdrew; more than half the Jewish community
of 180,000 managed to flee. Despite vague plans to colonize the countryside with Romanians, Romanianization made little sense given the predominance of Ukrainians and Moldovians in the countryside, and the
heavily Russian and Jewish towns. As a result, Antonescu's nationality
policy was half-hearted and much less rigid than the Germans'. Many
Romanian officials were Russian-speaking Bessarabians who had lived
under Tsarist rule before 1917; unlike the Germans, they sympathized
with the locals and could communicate easily with them. Odessa's
mayor, Gherman Pantea, was a Russian-speaker, a graduate of Odessa
University and a former captain in the Tsarist army who was greeted
by his Russian patronymic as he wandered the market at dawn. The
Romanian governor even issued an order that his staff should learn
Russian within three months, something that would have been unimaginable in the German administration to the north. Because
Ukrainian nationalism itself was not strong, the Romanians felt relatively unthreatened and allowed Ukrainian to remain the language of
instruction in 80 per cent of the schools in the region: each village voted
for the language it wished to be taught its children, and German and
Romanian became obligatory foreign languages. In practice, even this
policy, far milder than what the Germans were doing next door, was
often ignored locally due to a lack of personnel or books. Much of the
time, the Soviet system remained in force, and the key change was the
emergence of private schools. Ukrainian auxiliary police forces were set
up, wearing coloured armbands when they lacked uniforms.

The Romanian administration's unrivalled venality did have some benefits. It allowed people to buy their way out of requisitioning, death sentences and forced labour duties. It also let people buy their way *into* business: abolishing price controls and distributing licences to anyone who paid, the Romanians simply took their cut and stood back as individual enterprise galvanized the local economy. Looted property – especially Jewish – injected capital. In Odessa itself, new hairdressers, cafés, shops, taverns and movie theatres flourished. German visitors were astonished at the availability of food, the well-stocked restaurants, snack-bars and stands selling home-made jams, sweets and bread rolls, which stood in such sharp contrast with the misery in those parts of the Ukraine under their control. Here, for a brief moment between the early 1920s and the collapse of communism in 1989, the inhabitants of Odessa – in the midst of total war and genocide – embraced capitalism.

In a way, it worked. After the spring of 1942 there was no food scarcity, and following that year's harvest there was, by the standards of the region, something approaching plenty: peasants and others with access to the market prospered. Even German journalists were impressed. 'It was known everywhere that life in Transnistria was incomparably better than anywhere else in the occupied territories in Europe,' noted a young Russian black marketeer. Wading through the mud of a dirty northern Transnistrian town, he found

something which distinguished it from all the other towns of Russia and the Ukraine under German occupation: an abundance of food in the market ... There was fat, so rare in the Ukraine. There was butter, bacon, vegetable oil, meat – which we had almost forgotten existed: pork, chicken, goose – and many other things that made our eyes pop. Moreover it was inexpensive. We bought a lot more than we needed, enough for a week.

This was certainly not the result of the sophistication of the Romanian occupation. It simply showed what could have happened across the former Soviet territories if the Germans had allowed markets to flourish and not planned to destroy the social order.[25]

In their sheer murderousness, however, the Romanian and the German occupations were not far apart at all. What the Romanian government wanted from Transnistria was to use it primarily as an ethnic dumping ground that would allow them finally to solve their minorities problem. One group singled out were the gypsies: keen to resettle nomadic Roma as far from Bucharest as possible, the regime with its characteristically cruel incompetence deported more than 25,000 to Transnistria. Typhus killed thousands over the winter of 1942/3, after which their living conditions slightly improved. Although there was no organized policy of systematic execution, a recent study estimates that more than half died.[26]

The regime's measures against the Jews were more systematic, and considerably more lethal. Romanian anti-Semitism had been a matter of international concern as far back as the nineteenth century; now, under the aegis of National Socialist Germany, the country's rulers saw the chance for radical measures of the kind the democracies had always prevented them from undertaking. The Iron Guard might have been suppressed, but their impulse to blame the Jews for the country's woes was widely shared inside the administration itself. Reports that Jews in Bessarabia and Bukovina had welcomed the arrival of Soviet troops in the summer of 1940 added fuel to the fire.

On the eve of Barbarossa, Antonescu met again with Hitler, and shortly afterwards he set up special units to instigate the ethnic cleansing of the northern part of the country. In particular, he gave specific instructions to the army and the Interior Ministry to organize the 'evacuation' of the 45,000 Jews in the border town of Jassy, and preparations, based on similar but much smaller-scale events the previous year, were soon made. The doors of Christian houses in the town were marked with a cross to distinguish them, and rumours were deliberately spread that Soviet parachutists had landed in the city. Once the pogrom erupted on the night of 28/29 June, soldiers, gendarmes, policemen and hundreds of civilians rampaged through the streets, broke into houses and brought their occupants back under arrest to police headquarters. Many Jews were raped, attacked or killed on the spot. More than 1,000 were gunned down in the grounds of the police headquarters when the Germans opened fire at random. Some of those who survived were beaten and tortured before they were herded on to airless carriages, filled to three times their intended capacity with both the living and the dead. As the trains carrying their human cargo crawled across the plains through the summer heat, more than 2,700 perished of dehydration, and their bodies were thrown out on to station platforms or into the fields. In all, between 13,000 and 15,000 people died.[27]

The Italian journalist Curzio Malaparte, who happened to be visiting Jassy at the time, woke up the next morning:

I went to the window and looked down Lapusneanu Street. Scattered about in the street were human forms lying in awkward positions. The gutters were strewn with dead bodies, heaped one upon another. Several hundred corpses were dumped in the centre of the chuchyard. Packs of dogs wandered about sniffing the dead in the frightened cowed way dogs have when they are seeking their masters; they seemed full of respect and pity; they moved about those poor, dead bodies with delicacy, as if they feared to step on those bloody faces and those rigid hands. Squads of Jews, watched over by policemen and soldiers armed with tommy-guns, were at work moving the bodies to one side, clearing the middle of the road and piling up the corpses along the walls so they would not block traffic. German and Rumanian trucks loaded with corpses kept going by. A dead child was sitting up on the sidewalk near the *lustrageria* with his back against the wall and his head drooped on one shoulder ... The road was crowded with people – squads of soldiers and policemen, groups of men and women, and bands of gypsies with their hair in long ringlets were gaily and noisily chattering with one another, as they despoiled the corpses, lifting them, rolling them over, turning them on their sides to draw off their coats, their trousers and their underclothes; feet were rammed against dead bellies to help pull off the shoes; people came running to share in the loot; others made off with arms piled high with clothing. It was a gay bustle, a merry occasion, a feast and a market-place all in one.[28]

The Jassy massacre was part of a much larger plan being worked out by the Antonescu regime, whose real target was the estimated 275,000 Jews living outside Old Romania, in the Bukovina and Bessarabian borderlands. Over the previous year these provinces had suffered an upheaval. During the Soviet occupation, the large ethnic German community had departed for the Reich, and many Romanians had fled southwards; others had been deported by the NKVD. Now that they had the provinces back, the Romanians wanted to get rid of the Jews, whom they saw as a pro-Soviet fifth column. This was to be the first step in ethnically cleansing the entire country. On 8 July, Foreign Minister Mihai Antonescu emphasized the significance of the moment to his cabinet colleagues:

Even if some traditionalists among you do not understand me, I am in favour of forced migration of the entire Jewish element from Bessarabia and Bukovina; they must be driven over the border ... In all of our history, there has never been a more appropriate, more complete, more far-reaching, freer moment for total ethnic liberation, for renewed national self-examination, for a cleansing of our nation ... Let us utilize this historic moment ... If need be, use machine guns.[29]

Special orders were issued, telling military commanders to instigate pogroms in the villages, and as soon as Romanian troops marched into the Russian-held provinces they forced the Jews from their homes and assembled them for deportation; those who were too old or sick were shot on the spot, and many women were raped. The rest were then pushed across the Dniester into territory that was still at that time under Wehrmacht control. The German military were completely taken by surprise and were appalled at the prospect of having to deal with huge numbers of Romanian Jews at a time when they were worrying about supply lines for troops at the front. Hitler might privately admire Antonescu's 'radicalism', but German commanders wanted the Romanians to slow down. Even Einsatzgruppe D itself, led by the officious Ohlendorf, was highly critical of the Romanians' lack of direction and their sadism and criticized them for pillaging and raping and for the trail of corpses they left behind them. His men pushed thousands of expellees back on to the Romanian side of the river and shot those who were unable to keep up.

'The Romanians act against the Jews without any idea of a plan,' wrote a German observer. 'No one would object to the numerous executions of Jews if the technical aspect of their preparation, as well as the manner in which they are carried out, were not wanting. The Romanians leave the executed where they fall, without burial.' What made matters more serious for the Germans was that the Romanians also seemed to be plotting to drive out the other large ethnic group in Bukovina, the Ukrainians. Thanks to their allies, the Germans were already having to look after Ukrainians who had fled across the Dniester for protection. It was bad enough that the Romanians were alienating them; worse that they expected to off-load their Jews on the Wehrmacht as well.[30]

The Wehrmacht's disapproval was quickly relayed to Bucharest. 'Proceed with the elimination of the Jewish element only in a systematic and slow manner,' the Germans instructed. But in fact the Romanians took little notice, perhaps because Antonescu was sure of Hitler's support. Moreover, their bitter rivals the Hungarians were also expelling émigré

Jews into the German-occupied Ukraine. One thousand were being pushed across the border daily and, by 10 August, 14,000 destitute and frightened refugees were crowded into the small town of Kamenets-Podolsk. With the army at a loss what to do, HSSPF Friedrich Jeckeln showed the initiative that would make him a key figure in the Holocaust by offering to 'liquidate' them: in three days, his men, helped by Hungarian units, shot more than 20,000 people in huge bomb craters outside Kamenets-Podolsk, and by the end of August, the slaughter – the largest under German rule to date – was over.[31]

Once their new province of Transnistria was fully under Romanian control, the expulsions into it from northern Romania accelerated. By mid-1942 only 14,000 Jews remained in Bukovina and Bessarabia; about 40,000 had died and more than 135,000 had been deported to makeshift labour camps, towns and villages in the southern Ukraine. As the transports disgorged their desperate and often half-dead cargo, German onlookers assumed that 'the purpose of the action is the liquidation of those Jews'. After all, the roads, tracks and bridges across the Dniester were strewn with bodies. Meanwhile, Romanian officers returned bedecked with rings, silks, jewels and other loot.[32]

Things got even worse when the Romanians finally took Odessa. On 16 October, after a hard-fought battle, nervous and trigger-happy Romanian and German troops entered the ruined and burned-out wreckage of the former Soviet port. They took hostages from among the civilians who had stayed behind and commandeered Jews to clear roads. But despite warnings from local people, they were completely taken by surprise when six days later a delayed-action Soviet mine blew up the newly established military headquarters, killing the Romanian commander and another sixty soldiers. Antonescu immediately demanded that 18,000 Jews should be killed in reprisal, and that another 100 should be hanged in town squares 'in every regimental sector'. Unaware who had given the orders, the incoming mayor of Odessa, Pantea, wrote him an appalled letter:

I awoke in the morning to a frightful sight: in all the main streets and at the intersections, groups of four to five people were hanging, and the terrified inhabitants were fleeing in all directions. Horrified, I asked who was responsible for this barbaric deed, this disgrace, of which we will never be absolved by the civilized world. The authorities to whom I turned told me they knew nothing.[33]

337

What Pantea also did not know was that this was only the start: in the coming days soldiers and gendarmes strung Jews from trolley-car cables, balconies and telegraph poles: the roads leading out of the centre were lined with gallows, and Odessa turned into a 'city of hanging corpses'. The army itself ended up killing at least 22,000 people: most were packed into warehouses in the suburb of Dalnic, doused with gasoline and burned alive. At least one warehouse full of people was blown up on Antonescu's direct orders in a macabre act of vengeance. Thousands of the survivors were marched away northwards in enormous columns which Pantea tried, but failed, to have halted. The victims, left without food or water, spent the nights in muddy fields, where their guards robbed and raped them. Over the coming weeks, other Jews were sent north by rail in unheated cattle cars. Two years later, frozen corpses and body parts were still scattered around the city outskirts. As the Red Army approached, the Romanian defence minister suggested clearing the site of the massacre to 'cover up the atrocities'. 'What are you talking about?' Antonescu inquired; none of his ministers rushed to remind the forgetful *Conducator* that he had been the instigator.[34]

Cemented by such crimes, as well as by Romania's military commitment to the Eastern Front, Hitler's relationship with Marshal Antonescu had become extremely close. At the end of 1941 he confided to him that Germany's ultimate intention was to deport all the Jews of Europe into rudimentary labour reservations in Russia. Like Hans Frank, who had discussed the matter with Hitler at about the same time, Antonescu clearly understood what this meant, and the resulting cabinet discussions make for chilling reading. On 16 December the Marshal told officials to 'get the Yids out of the city immediately', since he feared a Soviet attack from Sevastopol. Someone proposed letting them starve in a former Soviet naval barracks. Antonescu preferred the idea of drowning them all – except that it might mean losing a ship – and he went on:

The Germans want to bring the Yids from Europe to Russia and settle them in certain areas but there is still time before this plan is carried out. Meanwhile, what should we do? Shall we wait for a decision in Berlin? Shall we wait for a decision which concerns us? Shall we ensure their safety? Pack them into catacombs; throw them into the Black Sea! [As far as I am concerned] one hundred may die, one thousand may die, all of them may die, but I don't want a single Romanian official or officer to die.[35]

In the freezing winter of 1941/2, therefore, most of the Jews of southern Transnistria were uprooted along with the surviving Jews of Odessa and forced to trek to 'resettlement zones' near the river Bug. As before, the plan was clearly to try to push them across the river into German territory. But again the Germans resisted, and Eichmann criticized the Romanians' 'disorderly and indiscriminate' off-loading of the Jews into the Reich Commissariat.[36] Either side of the Bug, the Jews wandered under loose guard through the wintry Ukrainian countryside, where many died of frostbite or hunger. Often they passed through ethnic German villages, the inhabitants of which, helped by the SS, formed an Ethnic German Defence League to kill them. The first victims died near the German village of Novo America at the end of January 1942, where armed peasants took away about 200 Jews and shot them; the bodies were burned to avoid epidemics, and their clothing and belongings taken off to the village.

Occasionally, SS teams crossed the demarcation line at the river Bug and brought back thousands of Jews to work on sections of Durchgangsstrasse IV, the new highway that was planned to link Poland with the southern Ukraine. Housed in work camps, they too were killed once they were no longer useful. Others were worked to death by the Romanians themselves. Forced marches of the 'living dead' continued through 1942 and 1943 as the government in Bucharest discussed 'decongestion' measures in the region's towns and built hastily constructed camps for their 'human garbage' in forests, massacring the inmates in ravines and open graves, or handing them over to the Germans. The precise number of casualties will never be known. But a recent reliable estimate suggests that, by the end of the occupation, between 115,000 and 180,000 Ukrainian Jews had died in Transnistria (only 20,000 remained alive), as well as more than 100,000 of the 147,000 Jews from Bukovina and Bessarabia. In total between 280,000 and 300,000 Romanian and Ukrainian Jews are reckoned to have perished.[37]

No other German ally except perhaps Croatia could match the Romanian regime for sheer murderousness. And as in the Croatian case, little or none of this killing was the result of German pressure. Indeed, when the Germans really began to exert pressure on the regime, in the summer of 1942, the government reversed its course for its own reasons (to be explored below); the Germans could do nothing about it. The fact that 375,000 Jews in Old Romania survived to the end of the war is the clearest possible proof of the Romanians' freedom of action. In other words, the killings of 1941–2 were a Romanian initiative, a kind of 'parallel war' against the Jews, carried out with different means but to much the same end as that being waged to the north. So long as the Germans seemed to be winning, the government prided itself that Romania, as Mihai Antonescu put it, 'is counted among the nations prepared to cooperate resolutely in the final solution of the Jewish problem – not only the local one, but also the European one'.[38]

ITALY'S MEDITERRANEAN EMPIRE

Fascist Italy was unique among Germany's allies. Hitler himself always retained a sense of allegiance to Mussolini, and the two fascist powers cemented their ties with the Pact of Steel in 1939. Both were expansionist, and the Pact's preamble spoke of both parties' need 'to secure their living space'. The Italians openly talked about enlarging their empire on both shores of the Mediterranean and removing the French and British from the region for good. Germany's ascendancy seemed to offer the chance to achieve this.

But if the alliance clearly benefited Italy, what it gave the Germans was less clear. The mess that the Italians made of the invasion of tiny Albania in 1939 had been a warning. They also made heavy weather of the mini-campaign they launched belatedly against France in the summer of 1940 and then botched the invasion of Greece that autumn. As early as August 1941, the vacuity of fascism's imperial pretensions had been exposed, and a well-placed observer noted that only Germany could 'help the Italians erect their Mediterranean empire'. Italy's success in 1940 against the tiny garrisons the British had left behind in British Somaliland was its only unaided victory in the entire war. It cost many casualties and did not last long: in March 1941, when the British sent in Sikh troops to recapture it, most of the Italians were ill with malaria and relieved to surrender. Within two months, under pressure from the British and from Ethiopian irregulars, they had lost Addis Ababa as well, and the Ethiopian emperor, Haile Selassie, was back on the throne he had lost in 1936. The giant maps that had been put up in the main squares of Italian towns, so that people could see the progress of the war in Europe, Africa and the Middle East, soon vanished.

There was a lot more than poor generalship for the Germans to worry about. The Italian armed forces were under-equipped, poorly coordinated and over-bureaucratized, run by defensively minded career-ists with little strategic sense or administrative competence. Unlike Hitler, Mussolini had failed to impose himself on his general staff or to make them obey his commands. He was also unable to prioritize and scattered his forces over too many fronts. When he sent off the first 60,000 soldiers to the Eastern Front (on the grounds that 'I cannot do less than Slovakia'), their commander had a heart attack en route; it was an omen Mussolini would have done well to heed.[39]

At the most fundamental level, Italy could not really afford the weight of fascist ambitions. The war was even less popular there than it was in Germany, and the regime was acutely conscious of this: German generals deplored the fact that the Italians had not shaken off their 'peacetime mentality'. Their Italian counterparts hesitated to discipline their men, and Italian courts martial were in fact far less repressive than they had been in the First World War. The truth was that the country had basically been bankrupted by the costs of the Ethiopian and Spanish campaigns and would have benefited enormously from a period of recovery. Franco secured this for Spain by staying out of the war and thereby remained in power long enough to be toasted by President Nixon in 1970. But Mussolini's imperial pretensions stopped him from following a similar course. Italy's national income was smaller than that of any of the other major powers and it spent a smaller proportion of this on its armed forces – 23 per cent in 1941 compared with 52 per cent for Germany and 53 per cent for the UK. As a result, when the country did enter the war, it was only after the government presented the Germans with a shopping list of urgently needed items that – as Ciano put it – would have broken the back of a camel.[40]

Yet for Hitler, the strategic and military counter-arguments mattered little when set against the fact that Mussolini had joined him: this was his special relationship. 'Without Mussolini's friendship,' he told the Italian ambassador, 'I would be alone in the world.' Often he spoke as though the two powers' interests were perfectly compatible. 'Our inter-ests are in the north, yours in the south,' he told the Duce. They could divide Europe between them, he went on, since Germany's quest for *Lebensraum* took it east into Poland and Russia, while the Italian *spazio vitale* lay chiefly in the Balkans, the Mediterranean and the north shore of Africa. Mussolini agreed: they would fight a 'parallel war'. In fact, with the exception of naval affairs in the Mediterranean, there was remarkably little real coordination or joint planning, and Hitler himself refused to confide in the Duce. Despite four meetings in 1940, and three the following year, he kept back from his closest ally his plans to invade Scandinavia, to send a military mission to Romania or even to invade the USSR, while Mussolini got his own back by surprising the Führer with his invasion of Greece.[41]

Nor were their 'parallel wars' easy to keep apart. Initially, the Germans left north Africa and the Mediterranean to the Italians, who were generally happy for them to stay out (even when they could have done with their help). In the Balkans, the Germans' guiding principle was to get their allies to run as much of the occupation as possible. But although Hitler insisted on making Italy the predominant power in the western Balkans – eventually half a million Italian soldiers were committed there – the Germans never really trusted them to run the region properly. In north Africa, too, a small German expeditionary force had to be sent out under Rommel. When Mussolini flew there in the summer of 1942, anticipating an imminent triumphal march into Alexandria, Rommel refused to meet him; the Duce's crestfallen return to Italy, after it had become clear that Egypt would not be taken, marked the beginning of his downfall. What had started out, in the summer of 1940, as a 'parallel war' had degenerated into a much more unequal relationship.

Some historians have discerned a programme behind the Duce's territorial claims, but it is hard to avoid the impression that they were mostly thrown together at the last minute. In 1940, his wish list focused on Corsica, Tunis and other French possessions in Africa and the Middle East. Yet some months later, Italian energies were diverted across the Adriatic and Ionian seas. As it turned out, in Greece Italy enjoyed little real power despite running most of the country. A Greek government continued to exist, and German advisers counterbalanced Rome's men. The imperial policies the Italians did introduce went disastrously wrong. They tried to detach the islands from the mainland, linking the Cyclades in particular to Italy's existing possessions in the Dodecanese. The result was administrative chaos, economic breakdown and hunger which left thousands dead in the small island of Syros alone.[42]

Nationality politics in the fledgling Italian empire looked very different,

however, from Germany's. Short of settlers, or large reservoirs of minorities to repatriate, Rome placed cultural diffusion ahead of racial purity.
The basic historical myth was that of ancient Rome rather than the
Teutonic Knights; there was no serious programme of racial screening,
no equivalent of the SS, and instead lavishly funded networks of Dante
Alighieri schools to teach Greeks, Albanians and Croats the glories
of Italian literature. Weakness also made the Italians better able than
the Germans to appreciate the importance of acknowledging other
people's national aspirations. The Italians supported Albanian nationalists, for instance, and encouraged the formation of an Albanian fascist
party. As Ciano pointedly put it in 1942, 'it was not possible to export
fascism to a country and simultaneously deny it the principle of
nationhood which is the essence itself of the [fascist] doctrine . . . Our
action in Albania constitutes concrete proof before the world that in
the new order envisaged by Rome nations will not be subjugated but
valued.'[43]

To be sure, this was largely window-dressing; it said more about
Italian criticisms of the German approach to occupation than it did
about how they ran Albania, where local politicians still played second
fiddle to the Italian pro-consul. Moreover, the limitations of the model
became much clearer after it was introduced into Montenegro too. In
June 1941 an obedient 'consultative council' declared 'the restoration
of Montenegro'. But this new 'kingdom' lasted less than a day – the new
head of state had not even been nominated – before pro-Serb forces
opposed to independence organized a massive popular uprising. Taken
completely by surprise, the Italian army responded by summarily executing several thousand civilians: General Pirzio Biroli insisted that 'the
fable of the "good Italian" must cease', and it took a month before the
rebellion was crushed.[44]

In Slovenia, a region destined for outright annexation, this particular
fable had an even shorter life-span. The region had not figured at all on
Rome's initial shopping-list, and its 340,000 inhabitants – if the Italians'
own census was to be believed – included fewer than 500 Italians.
Undeterred, the Italians took over a truncated and economically hamstrung zone around Ljubljana – this was all the Germans left them after
helping themselves to the rest of the province. The new Province of
Ljubljana was supposed to become a model of 'benevolent' administration, revealing the superior merits of Italian rule to the unfortunate

German-ruled Slovenes just across the border to the north. Yugoslav civil servants were kept in post – hardly any Italians had the necessary language skills – but Italian welfare and social security legislation was brought in. There was the usual changing of street- and place-names, the demolition of Slav and Habsburg monuments and the downgrading of the Slovene language.

Soon Rome was pushing ahead with a programme of forced Italianiz-ation, repressing Slovene nationalism and spreading fascist institutions. Like Antonescu – though less murderously – Mussolini also saw war and expansion as a chance for the state 'to realize the maximum of ethnic and spiritual unity so that the three elements of race, nation and state come to coincide'. Adding a predominantly non-Italian border province might not have seemed consistent with that strategy, but, as with other nationalist regimes, fascist Italy preferred to take the land and worry about the people afterwards. While Italian statisticians mapped the ethnic-racial profile of the population, new citizenship laws charted how a fortunate few might eventually become full Italian citi-zens. As the Duce put it, 'special treatment' should be given those 'allogenes' who showed themselves to be fully loyal; as for the rest, 'when ethnicity conflicts with geography, it is the ethnic group that must be moved: population exchanges and forced exodus are providential'. Large numbers of Slovenes were arrested and interned, and the province was soon in the throes of a serious insurgency. But there was no Italian equivalent of the RKFDV, and the Italian regime does not appear to have planned the kind of forced population movements that lay at the heart of the German war.[45]

Along the Croatian coast, with its formerly Venetian port-towns in the shadow of the karst mountains, the fascist regime's policies were more far-reaching and intrusive still. Much of it was annexed and brought under a new Governorate of Dalmatia, headed by the diplomat Giuseppe Bastianini. There were public works, new roads, drainage works and public buildings. But plans to encourage colonies of hardy Italian settlers never really left the drawing-board. 'Re-Italianization' brought a thoroughgoing purge of the classroom, a heavy dose of high Italian culture and the expulsion of those inhabitants who had settled since the end of the First World War. 'Those who do not wish that their spirit drink at the fountains of Virgil, Horace and Dante . . . need but take the shortest road that leads to the frontier. Here Rome rules, its language, its science, its morality and the lion of St Mark has returned, armed,' declared Bastianini. Rome wanted to 're-establish the original beneficial flow from shore to shore of the Adriatic' and 'to restore pre-eminence to the Italian ruling class'. Dalmatian Slavs were to be offered the chance to assimilate – this marked another significant difference with German policy – and those that could not would face deportation. But local Slavs were not convinced. Opposition, both tacit and overt, grew quickly, fomented both by communists and by Croatian nationalists in Zagreb.[46]

The real problem was Italy's deeply troubled relationship with Croatia itself. Like many of the chunks of territory bequeathed them by the Germans (the Aegean islands were another example), Dalmatia alone was not a viable economic unit. If it was not to require permanent and expensive subsidies from the mainland, its former connections with its resource-rich hinterland needed to be restored. Almost unavoidably, therefore, in view of the coastal industries' reliance on raw materials and supplies from inland, the Italians found themselves drawn further into the former Yugoslavia, and into Croatia and Bosnia in particular.[47]

Croatia's emergence – something that was to cause the Axis so much trouble – was itself a last-minute affair. Until the end of March 1941, Hitler had assumed that Yugoslavia would become a reliable member of the Anti-Comintern Pact just like her Danubian neighbours. But ecstatic crowds had lined the roads as the Wehrmacht entered Zagreb, and, following the invasion of Yugoslavia, setting up an Independent State of Croatia was an obvious way of winning support for Germany among the mass of the Croatian population and reducing the number of German forces needed to occupy the country. A special Foreign Ministry emissary went to Zagreb to persuade the mainstream Peasant Party leader Vladko Maček to take over. This was SS Colonel Edmund Veesenmayer, Ribbentrop's trouble-shooter, and a man who had already been involved in the *Anschluss* and in establishing the Tiso government in Slovakia. But Maček refused to play along. It was only after he had turned down the Germans' invitation that they turned to the fanatical Ustaša, a fringe terrorist movement of extreme nationalists with only a few thousand followers. A week after its deputy leader had announced the formation of the new state – with Maček also having urged Croats to support it – the Ustaša leader, a former lawyer and deputy called Ante Pavelić, returned from his exile in Italy and was put in charge.

Like Antonescu the 'Conducator' and the Slovak priest-president Tiso, Pavelić immediately awarded himself a suitably dictatorial title – *Poglavnik*, or Headman – to align himself with the dictators who had put him in power.[48]

His 'eyes shone with deep black fire in his pale, earthen-coloured face,' noted Curzio Malaparte the first time he met Pavelić.

An undefinable air of stupidity was stamped on his face, perhaps stemming from huge ears, that, seen closely, looked even more vast, ludicrous and monstrous than his portraits . . . His hands were broad, thick, hairy; and his knuckles knotty with muscles. One realized that his hands bothered him; he did not know where to put them.

At their second meeting, a few months later, Pavelić had changed his office layout, pushing his desk close to the door to disconcert potential assassins. To Malaparte he already seemed paler and more care-worn, his face 'marked with a sorrow that was deep and sincere'. But then he noticed the wicker basket on Pavelić's desk, filled with shelled oysters 'as they are occasionally displayed in the windows of Fortnum and Mason in Piccadilly in London' – only to be told by the dictator that they contained human eyes, sent him by his loyal followers as they torched and killed their way across the country.[49]

The Italians had wanted Croatia for themselves, and the throne was actually offered to a member of the House of Savoy, the Duke of Spoleto, who duly became Tomislav II, King of Croatia, Prince of Bosnia and Hercegovina, Voivode of Dalmatia, Tuzla and Temun. But Pavelić need not have worried. This was really just the last pathetic gasp of Europe's traditional approach to Balkan state-building – each new Balkan state had been given a European monarch since Greece in 1832 – and it meant nothing any more. In fact, at the time he announced his abdication in the summer of 1943, the new king had still sensibly not set foot in his kingdom. As usual, Italy's 'predominance' was very conditional, and Germany had secured most of the country's vital economic interests before the Italians got started. German troops occupied the eastern zone of the country; and although the rest supposedly fell under the Italian sphere of influence, in fact the Croatians resisted their encroachments.

The Italian royals had been wise to keep away: the Ustaša reign of terror that now unfolded amply explained why in general the Germans carefully avoided handing over power to extreme right-wingers. Of the new state's 6.3 million inhabitants, only 3.3 millions were Croats: there were 1.9 million Serbs, 700,000 Muslims, 150,000 Germans and 40,000 Jews. Yet despite this, the Ustaše were pledged to the violent eradication of non-Croat, and particularly Serb and Jewish, influence in the country. The government forbade the use of Cyrillic, legalized the confiscation of Jewish property and passed a new nationality law. At the same time, paramilitary squads embarked on a campaign of carnage against Serbs, Jews and gypsies and for more than a month, until German protests forced a brief slowdown, Ustaša units carried out one massacre after another, sometimes targeting Serb notables, but at others, especially in eastern Hercegovina, slaughtering entire communities amid scenes of grotesque violence and sadism. When the jails became overcrowded, a group of concentration camps was built round Jasenovac, by the river Sava, that quickly became notorious killing centres. In June, prominent Croatian Serbs appealed to the Serbian government in Belgrade to get the Germans to intervene. They were not to know that Hitler had already met Pavelić at his Berchtesgaden retreat and urged him to continue his policy of 'national intolerance' for fifty years.[50]

Himmler's programme of forced deportations further north made matters worse. Hoping to expel huge numbers of Slovenes *into* Croatia, the Germans allowed the Ustaše to uproot 180,000 Serbs and to push *them* across the border into Serbia itself to make room for the incoming Catholic Slovenes. But that was only the start, and, as in Romania, killing intensified once expulsion was blocked. After Germany invaded the USSR, Hitler again advised the Ustaše to deal brutally with their internal enemies, and the killings continued through into the autumn, resulting in the deaths of well over 100,000 people. They intensified as a result of anti-partisan campaigns in the summer of 1942, and by early 1943 the German military estimated that the Ustaše had murdered at least 400,000 people.[51]

Most of the Axis representatives in Zagreb were completely appalled but could not agree what to do, especially since Pavelić was actually supported by the chief German political representative, Siegfried Kasche, a former Freikorps and SA man. Kasche had no diplomatic training or background – according to the SD man in Zagreb he barely knew where Croatia was – but the SA had never forgiven the SS for the 1934 Night of the Long Knives in which their leadership had been murdered, and German Foreign Minister Ribbentrop was so desperate to keep Himmler and the SS out of south-eastern Europe that he had begun appointing SA men like Kasche, none of them career diplomats, to ministerial posts in the region. (The ministers in Slovakia, Romania and Hungary all came into this category, with predictable consequences for German diplomacy.)

The Italians, on the other hand, were convinced that Pavelić's brutality was fuelling anti-Axis activity and driving Serbs into the hills. 'We are in Croatia exclusively to favour this hateful Ustaše regime and its excesses,' they protested. One officer was blunter still, commenting that 'the Croats are our enemies'. And indeed, when the Italian military pushed into Bosnia-Hercegovina in September 1941 to try to stem the bloodshed, they worked together with Serbian insurgent chetnik bands against Pavelić's forces.[52]

The Italians' pessimism was shared by the German secret intelligence service in Zagreb, and by the Wehrmacht. One knowledgeable Abwehr officer thought it was 'sheer utopia' for the Ustaše to dream of expelling even 250,000 Serbs; the three million Croats would have to learn to live with the Serbs, and not treat them as 'Helots', or try forcibly converting them to Catholicism. The main German military adviser to the Croatians, a world-weary former Habsburg staff officer called Edmund Glaise von-Horstenau, was also sceptical. Born in Hitler's home town of Braunau three years before the Führer, his basic attitude to nationality politics remained rooted in the imperial model. He criticized the Ustaše because its vision of Croatia had no place for minorities, and because it sought 'to govern a *Völkerstaat* (state of ethnic groups) like a homogeneous nation-state'. But this eminently Habsburg critique of Croatian ethno-nationalism left Hitler unmoved. For a time, he urged Pavelić to moderate his course; but after the Italians folded in September 1943, Hitler insisted that German officials display a 'positive attitude' towards him. The collapse of his major ally in the Balkans meant he could not afford to dispense with the smaller ones, however brutal or counterproductive their internal policies. One Wehrmacht official after another explained to him that the insane violence of the Pavelić regime was the cause of enormous instability and unrest, that it was a 'disturber of the peace' which rested only 'by the point of the German bayonet', and that it would be much better to replace it with a German military administration. Every time, thanks to energetic lobbying by Kasche from Zagreb, Hitler refused and Pavelić survived.[53]

COUNTER-INSURGENCIES

The myth of the 'good Italian' did not die in the mountains of Montenegro, as Governor Pirzio Biroli had hoped. After the war it flourished – at least in Italy – and the supposed contrast between the bumbling but humanitarian Italians and the lethally efficient Germans allowed many of the Italian army's crimes to be quietly forgotten. When lone scholars drew attention to the 50–60,000 estimated victims of the 1920s concentration camps in Cyrenaica, and uncovered the mass killings of Ethiopian civilians by shooting and mustard gas, the Italian public took little notice. Films such as *Mediterraneo* depicted Italian occupation as wartime Club Med, an erotic idyll interrupted only by the sounds of distant bombs; Hollywood did its bit too, and *Captain Corelli's Mandolin* contrasted the musical Italians in the Greek islands with the murderousness of the Wehrmacht. Roberto Benigni's film *La Vita è Bella* went a step further and turned the figure of his father, who had fought in Mussolini's army, into the ultimate victim, a Jew sent to Auschwitz. The conditions which faced the Italian soldiers sent into German captivity after September 1943 were indeed awful, and many died. But this did not alter the fact that the same soldiers had previously been fighting a dirty war of their own on the Axis side.

In Yugoslavia, in particular, the behaviour of the Italian army was often not very different from that of the Germans. General Robotti mandated that the entire Province of Ljubljana was to be considered a battlefield, and that its entire population were to be considered 'our enemies'. Hostages were to be taken and killed in the event of attacks. The troops were to take no prisoners, and officers were ordered to 'maintain the aggressive spirit of our soldier'. Robotti instructed his men to 'hate, hate them more than these brigands hate us'. His superior, General Mario Roatta, set the tone: back home, Roatta held parties on his yacht 'in the style of the ancient pagans'; but in the field, there was no more ruthless commander. His infamous 'Circular 3C' of March 1942 was supposed to show that Italian soldiers could fight just as harshly as their German allies. 'Not tooth for a tooth, but a head for a tooth!' was the watchword. Roatta confirmed the hostage policy and demanded a break with the image of Italian benevolence. It is true that the punitive destruction of entire villages was, according to him, to be undertaken rarely. Yet the tactics Roatta outlined essentially targeted the entire civilian population.[54]

The Italian army's experience of fighting counter-insurgency had been chiefly drawn from the Libyan campaigns of the early 1920s and the conquest of Ethiopia in 1935–6. In both it had used internment, the selection and shooting of hostages, scorched earth policies and bombed civilian areas as a collective punishment. Neither Mussolini nor the then head of the army, General Badoglio, had tried to mitigate these policies; on the contrary, they had encouraged them for the sake of Italian prestige. With the exception of the use of gas, which the Italians decided against using in Europe, the 2nd Army in Croatia, Montenegro and Slovenia treated the 'natives' of Yugoslavia in much the same fashion. The town of Ljubljana was surrounded by barbed-wire fences, and entire neighbourhoods were cordoned off and searched. Mussolini raised the possibility of a 'mass transfer' of the civilian population and urged Roatta to 'take numerous hostages and shoot them whenever necessary'. A vast network of camps extended down into Greece, within which tens of thousands were incarcerated; poorly supplied, they soon became sites of disease and a soaring death rate that matched those under German control. By the end of 1942, more than 30,000 Slovenes were interned in conditions bad enough for the Vatican to complain. On the island of Rab, the prisoners were so weakened by hunger that they could not be moved to ships taking them to the mainland: exiguous rations and appalling conditions meant that, of under 10,000 people who passed through – 1,000 of whom were children – more than 10 per cent died.

In Greece, things were quieter, at least until the autumn of 1942, since the Italian army was conscious of the presence of a Greek government, however weak, which it wished to support. But from early 1943, as the partisan movement spread into the Pindos mountains, the ferocity of the counter-insurgency increased there too, and the camps filled with inmates. Villages were burned down, and there were mass shootings. The Red Cross reported that there were at least seven concentration camps, with thousands of inmates who suffered from cold, malnutrition and malaria.[55]

How different was this from what the Wehrmacht was doing? Like any colonial army, both the Italian and the German military combined extreme violence with the idea that they were defenders of order. They criticized not only the partisans but also the Ustaše whose brutality, in the words of a German major, was 'in defiance of all the laws of civilization'. Both believed that under Pavelić Croatia faced social disintegration and anarchy, a 'general lawlessness' that had led to 'conditions similar to those of the Thirty Years' War'. And so far as the insurgents were concerned, neither army believed itself bound by the laws of war since their opponents did not behave like lawful combatants.

Yet there were some differences. In occupied Serbia, the Germans opened their anti-partisan campaign in the autumn of 1941 with greater ruthlessness than the Italians showed, killing more than 11,000 civilians in less than three months. Reprisal quotas were interpreted more literally than they were by the Italians, and on several occasions, hundreds and even thousands of civilians were rounded up and shot. Many senior Wehrmacht commanders in the Balkans had been in Serbia as young Habsburg officers in 1914 and could not wait to avenge the humiliation the imperial army had suffered then; the Italians were more concerned at keeping down the Croats, their nominal allies.

One of the key differences, in fact, was their attitude to Serb insurgents – nationalist chetniks and communist partisans. While the Germans targeted both, General Roatta tried to split the insurgency by enlisting anti-communist Serbs and Montenegrins in the fight against the partisans. The Ustaša government too was furious, of course, since the Serbs were its main enemy. Ignoring them entirely, Roatta (and Pirzio Biroli in Montenegro) went ahead and armed Serbian chetnik bands and fought alongside them in the mountains. Not only were the Italians far more conscious than the Germans that they lacked the numbers or resources to fight all the rebels at once, they were less inhibited about admitting the fact. Top-level Italian policy-makers openly doubted that major counter-insurgency sweeps could ever have a permanent effect; 'after fifteen days we will be back where we started,' said one. They felt it was easy to exaggerate the military threat posed by the insurgents and suggested the military aim not to eliminate them – an impossible task – but ensure they posed no threat to supply lines.[56]

The Wehrmacht did not always dismiss the idea of local collaboration and could play that game too sometimes. Around the Mitrovica iron mines in Kosovo, General Eberhard's 60th Motorized Infantry Division gave more autonomy to local Albanians than they enjoyed under the Italians in Albania proper. Eberhard created an Albanian gendarmerie, built schools and supported a local regime which attracted so many

Albanians that the Italians suspected it was all part of a campaign to make them look bad.[57] But this was an area where the local population was basically pro-German to begin with. As a counter-insurgency force, the Wehrmacht itself remained faithful to the idea of overwhelming the guerillas with numbers and firepower through highly orchestrated sweeps of the mountains using many thousands of troops. A few field commanders did question whether the reprisals policies did not simply drive recruits into the arms of the partisans. Yet German secret service suggestions for political alliances with the chetniks and others were spurned, and Glaise's criticism that the Wehrmacht was making things worse through its own 'policy of terror' fell on deaf ears.[58]

So how far can we attribute the violence of the German army to Nazi or fascist ideology? Hungarian, Bulgarian and Italian soldiers were evidently capable of brutal reprisals and mass executions too; what is more, a draconian approach to snipers and irregulars had been visible in the German and Habsburg armies in the First World War as well. All the regimes allied with Hitler were, of course, staunchly nationalistic, and soldiers' easy racial stereotyping of their enemies made it easier to blur the never very sharp distinction between combatants and civilians. In an age which talked more than ever before of the laws of war, armies had become accustomed to the idea that against those who did not fight in a 'civilized' fashion, there were few or no constraints on what they might do. The Manichean language used to describe the war against Bolshevism played its part here: communists could not, by definition, be worthy opponents; neither could racial inferiors. But well before the Russian revolution, Habsburg army officers marching into Serbia in 1914 had used the language of 'fanaticism' and 'treachery' with predictably lethal consequences: their men had arrested and interned numerous hostages, burned villages to the ground and killed several thousand civilians in cold blood in a few weeks.[59]

The use of collective punishment to cow populations into obedience was surely reinforced when field commanders felt, as clearly they did both in the occupied USSR and in the Balkans, that they were undermanned and overstretched. At this point considerations of prestige, akin to those evident in the colonial campaigns fought by the Italians and others, pushed them down the path of horrific reprisals. The Italian army was obeying orders during the Ethiopia massacres in 1937 and the 'pacification' of Montenegro in 1941. So were the Hungarians in Novi

Sad, and the Bulgarians in Drama. Germany's allies may have occasionally been shocked by the Wehrmacht's brutality in the Ukraine and Belorussia, but in the face of their own partisan threat, they did not respond very differently. The uncomfortable truth is that the counterinsurgency war was more the product of a certain European way of fighting than of Nazism itself. Technologies had changed in the previous decades, but in other respects they were fighting in much the same spirit, and according to the same rules, as they had observed in their colonial campaigns and in the First World War. Of course, there was one crucial difference: in the past civilian authorities had sometimes managed to exercise a moderating influence on the military – as they did, for instance, in occupied Serbia in 1917. Under the Nazis, it was the civilians who were the extremists, constantly urging their soldiers to lose their inhibitions and to increase the level of terror. Faced with the threat of the partisan, the Wehrmacht in particular lost sight of even those few constraints that had once inhibited its predecessors.[60]

SMALL STATES AND
GREATER GERMANY

Because Italy slipped with extraordinary speed from being a near-equal (in 1938) to junior partner (by 1940), the wartime Axis alliance system was always marked by the brute fact of Germany's overwhelming power. 'Let's try to do each other the least harm possible,' the French ambassador told the Italian foreign minister in June 1940. 'After all, we have to live in this Europe, whose new masters – as you know – are rather tough!'[61] At the heart of Germany's diplomatic situation, therefore, was what we might call the small state problem. Nazi commentators proclaimed the end of the liberal conception of sovereignty; press communiqués told small nations to get used to doing Berlin's bidding. The Germans claimed to speak for Europe, and paraded their partners – from Slovakia and Croatia, to Finland and Bulgaria – in support of this. But in practice, whatever the diplomatic smoke and mirrors, relations between Germany and its allies were bedevilled by the former's contempt and the latter's suspicion.

The question of sovereignty lay at the heart of Germany's relations with its allies. Nazis, after all, claimed that international law had been superseded by the needs of racial solidarity, a doctrine with deeply threatening implications for other states. One group of their citizens whom the Reich tried to claim during the war were Jews – Germany's largely unsuccessful efforts to get its allies to hand them over are discussed in the following chapter. But equally disruptive, and of longer standing, was Berlin's claim to the allegiance of ethnic Germans abroad.

In the spring of 1942, the Wehrmacht conscripted ethnic German men in Serbia into new units under its command. That May, it allowed Himmler's Waffen-SS to tap them instead. What had started out as Hitler's bodyguard elite had grown by 1939 to a force capable of fielding several armed regiments. Since it was excluded from recruiting among Germans in the Reich or in the annexed territories, the estimated two million ethnic Germans in Hungary, Romania, Yugoslavia and Slovakia, together with others already in resettlement camps, offered the only alternative available supply of 'German blood' if it was to grow further. Himmler seized the chance and he issued a confidential ruling that German minorities had an obligation of military service to the Reich rather than to their national government.[62]

Getting foreign governments to accept this, however, proved extremely hard for they were reluctant to cede control over this (or any other) group of their citizens. It was where these authorities were weakest – as in occupied Serbia – that the Germans had fewest difficulties. Croatia and Slovakia, despite being essentially puppet states, both bargained hard. With Romania and Hungary, negotiations never reached a conclusion, and Horthy and Antonescu rebuffed even Hitler, when he weighed in. In Hungary the Germans only got their way once they actually occupied the country; in Romania, despite the existence of a large ethnic German minority, they never did. The result was that, despite the very rapid growth of the Waffen-SS – by the autumn of 1944 its strength stood at well over half a million men – only a relatively small proportion of the ethnic Germans of central Europe were ever tapped. Given the success of the Germans in conscripting manpower elsewhere, this was a dramatic indication of its allies' ability to defend their own interests as well, perhaps, as of the minorities' reluctance to be drafted into a war they seemed increasingly likely to lose. The Third Reich might have been the most powerful state in Europe, but the limits to what it could do were reached sometimes surprisingly quickly. Success bred compliance: as defeat loomed, its friends and allies toughened their stance.

The way Germans treated non-German volunteers was another reason why relations with their allies quickly soured. Members of the Spanish Blue Division swore allegiance to Hitler personally and took many casualties in fighting on the front. Yet they were harshly condemned by their German comrades for fraternizing with Russians and often attacked when they walked around with German women while on leave in the Reich. A scandal erupted at Riga, for instance, in the summer of 1943 after German women started spending time at a beach house frequented by Spaniards convalescing from fighting on the Eastern Front. Behind the propaganda about Hitler's 'European army' was a feeling of contempt and racial arrogance that tinged the Germans' treatment of Italians, Romanians and others too.[63]

By 1942, the interests of the Germans and their allies were starting to diverge. The Germans needed help more than ever – they were running short of labour, fighting men, wheat, oil and other resources to feed the war machine: as we have seen, it was the spring and summer of that year that saw Berlin make the first serious efforts to mobilize the resources of the continent as a whole. On the other hand, by this time, Germany's allies had gained most of what they wanted. Finland had won back the territory it had lost in 1939; Bulgaria had gained north-eastern Greece, the Dobrudja and much of Yugoslav Macedonia. Romanian politicians rejected Hitler's offer to move further east across the Dnieper and were starting to question whether Transnistria was really adequate compensation for Transylvania. As for Hungary, its chief claims had been satisfied as long before as the summer of 1940, and its new government proclaimed its lack of interest in any further conquests. Italy itself was clinging on, its north African empire propped up by German arms, its new Balkan possessions in flames. Italian nationalists were disillusioned too: they had believed the war would bring a revival of Venice's maritime empire in the Adriatic and the Aegean; instead what they had got was a more assertive German nationalist version of a Habsburg drive to the Mediterranean. The time was ripe, in other words, for Germany's allies to reconsider their position. The Axis advance had been finally halted east and west as an Anglo-American force landed in Morocco, and the Red Army fought the Axis to a standstill in the ruins of Stalingrad: moreover, Romania, Hungary and Italy all took very heavy casualties when that city finally fell, further testing their loyalty to Berlin. By February 1943, Italy's General Ambrosio was categorical: 'Our enemy is the German.'[64]

It was in this atmosphere of intrigue, despondency and deep suspicion that many of Germany's allies began to call on Berlin once more to provide a sharper definition of what they might expect in a peacetime Europe under German hegemony. The autumn of 1942 saw north European collaborators such as the Dutch Nazi Anton Mussert and the Norwegian minister president Vidkun Quisling insist on the need for more thoughtful German leadership. 'You want to win the war to make Europe,' Laval told Hitler. 'But make Europe in order to win the war!' Inside the German Foreign Ministry, a small group of young activists sympathized. Many of them Nazis by conviction, they nevertheless believed Germany had been mistaken to believe it could rule Europe alone and they drew up a peace plan which would have restored international law, refrained from trying to export National Socialism outside Germany and given the Poles and Czechs back their independence. Despairing of Ribbentrop's leadership, they had little choice but to see what he could do with it. After much prodding, he submitted it to Hitler at the end of 1942. 'No such preparations for peace are necessary,' was the Führer's response. He did not need 'dry diplomats' or 'jurists' to formulate the peace; he himself could dictate it in two hours when the time came.[65]

In the Reich itself intense cultural diplomacy – prefiguring the equally wasteful campaigns of the cultural Cold War – acted as a kind of substitute for serious political commitment, and the Germans organized several international conferences at which the theme of Europe was publicized. There was, for instance, a Cultural Rally of European Youth – a kind of wartime Nazi Eurovision song contest, with groups competing for the 'Weimar Music Award' – and a European Youth Organization was founded at the opening of which Karl Böhm conducted Strauss waltzes. The ever-serious Wilhelm Stuckart brought together European civil servants to discuss modern administration, German and Italian journalists founded a new international union, and some well-known novelists and many second-rate ones attended a European Writers Congress. Alfred Rosenberg even thought of organizing a European anti-Jewish congress to help win over the 'educated class' in the rest of Europe.[66]

The Italians were especially keen on these events – as they had been since the late 1930s – since they saw them as a way of forging a unified fascist political community across the continent. Yet leading Nazis doubted their value, and in November Hitler himself urged an end to demonstrations of 'a European or international tendency'. This did not halt them all – Rosenberg was still planning his high-profile anti-Jewish congress late in 1944 – but it showed their irrelevance. Hitler's view of the situation could be judged from his decision that same month to bring the whole of France under German rule. What was collaboration for him compared with the security of occupation by the Wehrmacht? The following month, he rebuffed both his own and the Italian foreign minister when they urged him to consider liquidating the war in the East: he was 'certain of victory', he told Ciano. These were what a German observer called the Führer's 'fantasies in the dark wood at Rastenburg'. When Ribbentrop suggested approaching Stalin in order to concentrate on defeating the Anglo-American forces in the Mediterranean, Hitler reacted violently and forbade further discussion of the subject.[67]

The Allied invasion of north Africa and the subsequent occupation of France worried Germany's allies. Fearing they were next in line, the Spaniards warned the Germans they would defend themselves against invasion from any quarter. Making their disappointment in Germany's leadership evident, the Spaniards told the Germans that the Reich should 'abandon the idea of annexing the occupied areas in the East as "protectorates" or "General Governments": Germany must rather create independent national states'. The Finns, who had been saying the same thing for months, gave up and decided to withdraw from the war as soon as they could. Marshal Mannerheim announced publicly that offensive operations would cease and began negotiations with the Americans and the Soviets.[68] As for the states of central-eastern Europe, they too began diplomatic counter-moves of their own. The Hungarians and the Romanians started secret negotiations with the British, the Americans and the Russians and hoped that a 'Latin bloc', led by Mussolini's Italy, might negotiate a way out of the war, with or without the Germans. So desperate did the situation appear that they were not deterred when the Allies declared a policy of insisting on unconditional surrender at Casablanca in early 1943.

Following the debacle at Stalingrad, even the Germans temporarily showed signs of acknowledging their allies' disquiet. In February, there was an important change of direction when Goebbels instructed the press to avoid talk of colonizing the East and to refer positively to the role of east European nations in the fight against Judeo-Bolshevism. In a clear shot across Himmler's bows, and a sign that all the discussions of a German imperium in the East would have to be, at least temporarily, toned down, he went on: 'The National Socialist principle that only the soil can be Germanised, is used by the enemy as proof it is our declared intention to carry out mass expulsions.' Hitler had clearly sanctioned the new softer line, though there was still studied vagueness as to the eventual political fate of these 'small peoples' in the East.[69]

Ribbentrop's Foreign Ministry now returned to the discussions it had held with the Italians more than a year earlier. Ribbentrop was fed up with Goebbels making the running on the European issue; the enormous interest his diplomats reported from Germany's allies called for a serious diplomatic response.[70] Yet the foreign minister's manifest unfitness for the job was an open secret among all in the know. It was not just his extravagance and lavish use of secret ministry funds, nor his wife's incessant demands ('the tapestries in the Ribbentrops' house had to be changed four times because their colours were not precisely to Frau Ribbentrop's liking'). Much worse was his political ineptness. 'In his megalomania,' one said, he was 'smashing the last porcelain'. The frustration among his subordinates even led to a plot, which they hatched together with the SS, to get rid of him. Himmler was cautious, but the chief SS backer, foreign intelligence chief Walter Schellenberg, felt that bringing down Ribbentrop was essential to 'making progress with the Americans'. In the event, it was no more successful than the more ambitious and important conspiracy against Hitler himself the following year. All that happened was that the plotters in the ministry were forced out – one ended up in a concentration camp, the other on the Eastern Front – and the minister's position was strengthened.[71]

True to form, when he visited Rome at the end of February, Ribbentrop dismayed his hosts by ruling out a negotiated peace with Stalin – Mussolini had been urging this for months in order to ease the pressure in north Africa – and calling for greater harshness against the partisans and the Jews. On the idea of a declaration for Europe, however, the two sides seemed to be closer. As his adviser Megerle told the Italians, they understood that without a declaration of some kind, Germany might not be able to keep Europe with them. 'They are perfectly well aware,' reported his interlocutor, 'that they cannot envisage continuing to govern by the bayonet and violence and that it is absolutely necessary to associate the European peoples with the future of the continent in terms acceptable to them all, or at least to a majority.' But there was a catch: the German Foreign Ministry had so little influence with Hitler that it needed help: in fact, the responsibility for making this happen, Megerle underlined, was now Italy's. Only if Mussolini spoke with the Führer, he stressed, was there any chance of changing his mind. It all indicated a remarkable lack of confidence in his own boss, but in Berlin, a few days later, German diplomats continued the same refrain: Mussolini needed to act, they told Italian colleagues, and act fast. The 'small nations of Europe' were turning to Italy as the 'mother of civilization and justice'. Perhaps an announcement could even be made at the next meeting of Axis leaders to act as a counter-blast to the Casablanca conference.[72]

In March 1943, the Foreign Ministry drafted yet another declaration for a postwar European confederation that committed Germany unambiguously to preserving the rights of small states. 'I am of the opinion,' wrote Ribbentrop, 'that we should at the earliest possible date, as soon as we have scored a significant military success, proclaim the European Confederation in quite a specific form.' Imagining a glamorous multigovernmental ceremony, Ribbentrop emphasized the need to take the wind out of the sails of the United Nations. The announcement of a European Confederation by the Axis would, he noted, 'dispel the fear of our friends and allies that they might all be placed under German *Gauleiters* as soon as peace is concluded'; reassure neutrals that they would not be swallowed up by Germany after the war; and encourage people under German occupation to fight on the German side. His draft talked of the Confederation's members as 'sovereign states', guaranteeing each other's freedom and political independence. It was as though the National Socialist revolution in international law had never happened.[73]

Ailing and despondent, however, Mussolini was scarcely able to bear the weight of these expectations. Well aware of plotting in Rome to depose him, he had replaced Ciano as foreign minister; yet there was no real change of course. Ciano's de facto replacement Bastianini, fresh from service in Dalmatia (Mussolini having taken the Foreign Ministry portfolio for himself), reported that both the Romanians and the Hungarians saw Rome as spokesman for the 'small nations'. In his briefing notes for the Duce, Bastianini underlined the fundamental issue: the Axis powers, he wrote, had, above all, to give Europe a new order which guaranteed the independence of the lesser states.

Each of them has various specific interests to safeguard. But all – allies, neutrals, enemies – have one thing in common and that is the general interest of lesser states in an international regime which guarantees their preservation, an interest which they recognize not only for themselves, but in general for all small states which, however divided on other specific questions, feel themselves united in that solidarity which always links the most weak in the face of the stronger.[74]

Bastianini pointed – as so many critics were doing in Rome, Berlin and indeed Tokyo – to the example of the Japanese in east Asia, who appeared (at least from Europe) to have brilliantly combined hegemony with an appeal to the national sentiments of the other peoples of the region in a kind of anti-imperialist crusade. Why could the Axis not do the same thing? Why remain trapped in a passive, negative approach to war aims which ceded all the ground to the United Nations, and not be more energetic in proclaiming the social and economic virtues of an Axis victory, and the positive consequences of eventual liberation from the twin threats of Soviet Bolshevism and American plutocracy?

The moment of truth arrived in a cold spell in early April 1943, with the first summit of the year between the two Axis leaders. In the baroque corridors of Schloss Klessheim, the former seat of the Archbishops of Salzburg recently refurbished as a conference centre, the German diplomats were free with advice; Mussolini should speak *ganz brutal* with the Führer. But, shut out of the loop as usual, they had to ask the Italians what the two leaders had said. Very little, it turned out, regarding the matter at hand. Mussolini once again had been overwhelmed by the Führer's verbal energy. Hitler had already dismissed Mussolini's idea of a separate peace with Stalin (just as he dismissed Antonescu's plea to reach agreement with the Western allies to allow the war in the East to continue) and the Duce did not mention it again. The Führer drowned out a gaunt Mussolini in 'an interminable flow of words', in which hints of a new secret weapon that would make victory certain were combined with demands for greater brutality against the partisans in the Balkans. The feeble Ribbentrop could see which way the wind was blowing: the Nazi line was that no declaration was possible so long as it looked like an expression of German weakness.

In the castle, the Reich's press men explained to the Italians why it was all hopeless. A kind of 'counter Atlantic Charter' would simply spread confusion across Europe; 'the German experience in the occupied territories,' they went on, 'demonstrated that the only effective way of administering the territories is the military, without banking on collaborators or native helpers'. The Italians, they opined, echoing Hitler, 'still have the disease of politics [*sono ammalati di politica*] because with them thought always precedes events and action whereas in war it is not theory which gives birth to reality but on the contrary reality which gives birth to theories'. As Romanian, Hungarian and French statesmen followed the Italians to Klessheim, they received the same message: there would be no separate peace with Russia, and no declaration on Europe until the time was right. Quisling visited and managed to get a public commitment to 'a free and independent life for the nations of the European continent'. But the atmosphere was tense, for the Germans (rightly) detected defeatism in their visitors. 'They are right,' an Italian diplomat confided glumly to his diary. 'The whole of Europe revolts against Germany's attempt at hegemony, conducted with such bestiality.'[75]

THE FALL OF FASCISM

On 28 July 1943, the Italian Ministry of Interior in Rome received a report from Naples on 'the complete overthrow of internal politics' provoked by the king's dramatic dismissal of Mussolini a couple of days earlier:

The blow has completely disoriented the Fascists . . . and struck them profoundly . . . What has made the greatest impression is that the press has, from one day to the next, assumed tones the opposite of those before and that each person believes himself now at liberty to express his own ideas and to propagandise principles whether these be socialist, Catholic, liberal, communist or anarchist.[76]

The Duce's downfall and the reassertion of liberty in Italy was a truly shocking event. It was the first time a fascist regime had collapsed, and not just any regime either, but the one that had launched the fascist revolution. The news worried Nazis and delighted their opponents. 'Disorders in Italy,' a Belgian lawyer noted in his diary on 28 July 1943. 'The Fascist Party has been dissolved. Mass anti-fascist demonstrations

... The fatal end of the dictatorships'.[77] The Germans knew that their allies were looking for a way out of the war and were watching them to see how they would react. In the Foreign Ministry, Ribbentrop's advisers on Europe advocated restoring full sovereignty to Belgium, Holland and Norway. Yet Hitler's view did not change: 'our neighbours are all our enemies; we must get all we can out of them, but we cannot and must not promise them anything'. Germany still wanted a completely free hand after any eventual victory, reported the Italian ambassador in Berlin. Even Quisling bitterly remarked to German officials in Oslo that Europe was becoming united – against the Germans.[78]

In fact, Hitler had his own decisive response to what was happening in Italy. In early September, when an armistice with the Allies was suddenly announced, the Italian soldiers serving in the Balkans, France and Russia were caught by surprise, but the Germans were not. Moving in strength down the peninsula, their forces occupied as much of the country as they could. In a clear but hardly unpredictable violation of the rules of war, they disarmed their former comrades in arms and sent them into poorly supplied internment and labour camps, where many of them fell ill and died. The few who resisted – most notably in Cefallonia and Corfu – were shot. 'The Italian armed forces no longer exist,' ran the brief, angry communiqué from the German high command in a clear warning to other allies who might be tempted to follow them. An SS glider unit rescued Mussolini from captivity (how much he actually wanted to be rescued will never be known), took him and his family to Vienna and installed him at the head of a puppet government based near the small lakeside town of Salò. Far from escaping the war, much of Italy (together with formerly Italian-run zones in Greece and Yugoslavia) found itself in the iron grip of a new German occupation.

Symbolic of the weakness of the Duce's new position was the fact that he lived in a villa with German soldiers and liaison officers billeted next to him, keeping an eye on his visitors and controlling his access to the outside world. Security was tight, there was an anti-aircraft gun on the roof, and even his secretary had difficulty gaining access. His 'ministries' were scattered around the hotels of the area, and in towns across northern Italy. Rome was in the hands of the German military, who permitted the Duce to maintain nothing bigger there than a small coordination office. Although on paper the Italy he presided over extended to its existing legal borders, in practice the north-east had been placed under the control of new *Gauleiters* who drove out Italian civil servants as the prelude to annexation. This, even more than the Allied presence in the south of the country, represented a huge blow to the prestige of his government. Protests followed, and Mussolini himself remarked 'that the Germans have regretted allowing to form a government, especially one presided over by myself'. The only positive aspect of the situation from the Italian point of view was that relations among the different German agencies – the Foreign Ministry, the SS, the various branches of the armed services (none of which coordinated policy with any of the others) and Sauckel's labour recruiters – were the customary tangled mess, which allowed the Salò government to play one off against another.[79]

Through the winter of 1943/4, however, a burgeoning partisan struggle brought the prospect of civil war and increased the Germans' desire to run the region themselves. At the same time, the loss of territories in the East increased northern Italy's importance to the Reich. In March 1944 a wave of strikes swept the industrial heartlands, and Hitler ordered 20 per cent of the workforce to be deported to Germany. Wisely, this was disregarded for fear of disrupting the factories and making the partisan movement grow even faster. In the end the Germans deported more than 1,000 ringleaders, most of whom never returned, and thereby brought the strike to an end. Quite separately, Sauckel's recruiters were also combing the towns. Although Hitler muttered that three million Italians could be brought to work in the Reich, and Sauckel himself was aiming for 1.5 million, in fact, he only managed to get 66,000 in 1944. Italy's agricultural resources were attracting German attention too. 'The losses of foodstuffs from the East must be compensated by the intensified exploitation of this country,' Herbert Backe, the acting food minister, told the quartermaster-general of the army. Italy, a country where rations were among the lowest in Europe, was to be scoured for increased supplies to the Reich.[80]

As the Duce's eleventh-hour followers struggled to explain the events of the summer, plots, conspiracies and accusations swirled around Lake Garda. With what was left of the Fascist Party in disarray and in vengeful mood, fascism turned on itself, and special tribunals were set up to purge traitors. Mussolini's own son-in-law, Count Ciano, the former foreign minister, was tried and executed by a special tribunal, together with five other members of the Grand Council who had voted to depose the Duce. Mussolini did not intervene. 'For me, Ciano has been dead for some time,' he said. His daughter Edda, Ciano's wife, fired off bitter letters to her father and to Hitler, before fleeing to Switzerland to publish her husband's diaries, but the Germans seemed relieved the executions had gone ahead. 'There can be no doubt,' an Italian diplomat wrote to Mussolini from Berlin, 'that the Verona trials have revealed here that Republican Italy has cut its link with the past, and intends to be near to Germany always and in every way.'[81]

In fact, the Italian defection had merely increased the Führer's basic mistrust of all his allies. His intelligence chiefs were keeping him informed of their attempts to wriggle out of the war, and he rightly interpreted a growing general reluctance to agree to further Jewish deportations as a sign of their alienation. The Finns, now coming under heavy Soviet aerial bombardment for the first time, were the furthest advanced, having sent delegates to Moscow to discuss peace terms. But by far the worst offenders from his viewpoint were the Hungarians. In March 1944, Hitler summoned the Hungarian regent, Admiral Horthy, to Klessheim. There he berated him for treason and demanded a free hand in occupying the country lest 'a second Badoglio case come about'. Looking to follow the Italians, Hungary was disadvantaged by its geographical position in the heart of Europe. Yet the seventy-five-year-old Horthy was not the kind of man to be easily cowed, and even Hitler was embarrassed and surprised when he stormed out of their meeting, red in the face, after Hitler had threatened the safety of his family. Emergency measures had to be taken to detain him – a fake air raid, cancelling trains and blocking phone lines – and in the interim, Horthy finally agreed to stay in office to oversee a temporary military occupation and a change of government.

Thus German troops marched into Hungary, the second former ally to be occupied after Italy and not the last. The main purpose of the occupation was to bring in a more pro-German government, to exploit the country's economic resources for the benefit of the increasingly hard-pressed Reich and to shore up the country's defences. Another 40,000 Hungarian Germans were drafted into the Waffen-SS, thanks to a new treaty on military service, German economic penetration intensified, and several hundred thousand Jews were deported to Auschwitz with astonishing speed, helped by the efficiency of the Hungarian gendarmerie. Yet even so, the wily Horthy still managed to continue his negotiations with the Allies and he actually halted the deportations in July, to the Germans' fury.[82]

By the summer of 1944, with an Anglo-American force advancing from its bridgehead in the West and the Russians moving in rapidly from the East, Germany's allies were dwindling. The handful of heads of state or prime ministers who sent the Führer telegrams following his lucky escape from the 20 July bomb plot did not include the Romanians, the Finns or even the Croats. General Antonescu made his last visit two weeks later to the Wolf's Lair and was toppled shortly afterwards in a pro-Soviet coup. The Germans were completely taken by surprise. The Romanian army switched sides, jeopardizing the position of massive numbers of Wehrmacht troops in the Ukraine and adding very substantially to the Allied war effort. By the autumn of 1944, Romania had more troops fighting the Germans than the French did.

The same month saw neutral Turkey break off relations with Germany, while Finland elected Marshal Mannerheim as new head of state to make peace with the Russians. In Slovakia, the army rebelled against the Tiso government in the hope of opening the Carpathian passes to the Red Army. It failed, despite support from a heterogeneous collection of partisan units, but 40,000 German troops had to be sent in to occupy the country and it took them several months to regain control: their reprisals cost thousands of lives and sent tens of thousands more into camps in the Reich. In Denmark, already under martial law since the government's resignation in the summer of 1943, the underground Freedom Council was coordinating sabotage with the Allies and, following the Normandy landings, it launched a series of strikes and protests against German terror.

Increasingly Hitler talked as though Germany was on its own. His telegrams to Mussolini and the Japanese emperor on the fourth anniversary of the Tripartite Pact referred to his 'unshakeable confidence in the final victory over our enemies'. But this no longer rang true. That same week, he ordered the 'total deployment of all Germans' in the *Volkssturm* – an armed civil defence force made up chiefly of boys and men too old or unfit for military service; its creation had been necessitated by 'the failure of all our European allies'. In view of the fact that the Croats and Norway's Quisling were still faithful, this was hardly diplomatic. But the Führer's fearfulness and rage were growing. When Horthy announced over Hungarian radio that he had agreed a ceasefire with the Red Army, which was by that point approaching the outskirts of Budapest, Hitler kidnapped his son, forced the regent to resign and installed a government of Hungarian Arrow Cross fascists instead. Doubling the number of German divisions sent into the country, he congratulated the new prime minister, the deeply anti-Semitic Ferenc Szálasi, for assuring him of Hungary's continued belief 'in the ideals of a new and just Europe'.

Szálasi's Arrow Cross regime was – like Mussolini's Salò Republic – an example of the sharply leftwards shift which took place within fascist and Nazi movements across Europe at the very end of the war: this was indeed National Socialism, and its racialist emphasis helped define both components. Szálasi fully intended to do away with the aristocratic old guard and implement a National Socialist revolution at home. But the Germans were less interested in his ideological dreams than in keeping the country running smoothly. As the gateway to Austria and southern Germany, Hungary occupied a vital position and it was also a key source of oil, bauxite and manganese. Its one-million-strong army could be utilized against the Soviets, its ethnic Germans could be press-ganged into the Waffen-SS, and the hundreds of thousands of Hungarian Jews still there could even help meet the Reich's now acute shortage of industrial manpower. Hungarian Jewish labour battalions were, for instance, operating the Bor copper mines in eastern Serbia. (Among their members was the poet Mikloš Radnóti, whose last poems were found in the front pocket of his overcoat after he was shot.)

In fact, there was astonishingly little resistance to the Arrow Cross takeover – much less than the Germans had anticipated. Horthy's departure appeared to be no more mourned than the Habsburg Emperor Karl's had been twenty-five years earlier. While gangs of young Arrow Cross psychopaths set up the last ghetto in Europe in Budapest, foreign exchange, works of art and industrial equipment were carted off to Germany. Hungary at this point had scarcely any freedom of movement at all. Yet Szálasi acted as though he had not realized this. He made repeated demands to be allowed to appoint a diplomatic plenipotentiary in Berlin (these were ignored) and refused to allow deportations of Jews to Germany to resume (even though his own Arrow Cross men were slaughtering them in large numbers themselves). Even with his own puppet, Hitler still found himself frustrated.[83]

The Führer's sense of existential isolation and abandonment emerged in the long speech he composed for the German people in November 1944. Covering many of his habitual themes, it went on to talk about the 'betrayal after betrayal' that had befallen the Germans since the Russian breakthrough in late 1942. There were flattering references to Mussolini, Tiso, Szálasi and Pavelić – 'leaders of young nations'. But too many others had let them down, inside as well as outside the Reich. Still he threatened those who disputed his authority with 'annihilation'. 'The time for compromises and reservations is over for good.' In his lengthy New Year's Day proclamation at the start of 1945, he went further. Italy, Finland, Hungary, Romania and Bulgaria had capitulated because of 'the cowardice and lack of resolve of their leaders'.

Obstinate to the bitter end, the Führer also mocked the Allies' penchant for planning the future of Europe in the midst of a war which they had not yet won:

the theoretical appointment of ever new commissions for the treatment of European questions after the war, the foundation of societies for the regulation of food supplies after the German collapse ... the proclamation of economic agreements, the setting up of traffic networks and air bases, as well as the drafting and promulgation of sometimes truly idiotic laws on the treatment of the German *Volk*. They always acted as though they had already won the war, as though they could now already consider at their leisure all the measures necessary for those to rule Europe who have themselves set a sorry example of how not to rule people.

It was not his happiest speech, and the contrast with his own approach was hard to avoid.[84]

12

The Final Solution: the Jewish Question

DECISIONS

On 18 November 1941, Alfred Rosenberg's appointment as Minister of the Occupied Eastern Territories was finally announced. Propagandists lauded his personal achievements as well as the prospects for the 'New Order' under civilian leadership in the 'East'. Briefing German journalists on the many challenges ahead, the new minister stated forthrightly that

The Eastern territory is called upon to solve a question which is posed to the peoples of Europe; that is the Jewish question. In the East, some six million Jews still live, and this question can only be solved by the biological eradication of the entire Jewry of Europe. The Jewish question is only solved for Germany when the last Jew has left German territory, and for Europe when not a single Jew lives on the European continent up to the Urals. That is the task that fate has posed to us . . . It is necessary to expel them over the Urals or to eradicate them in some other way.[1]

The theme was nothing new for Rosenberg: the mystically inclined racist and ardent anti-Bolshevik had been preaching the need for a European crusade against the Jews since departing his native Estonia for Germany at the end of the First World War. 'One cannot unite fire and water, or Jew and Aryan,' he had written in 1918, calling on 'all European peoples' to join the Germans in fighting the Jews. One year later, he had become one of the first members of the Nazi Party. As head of its foreign policy office and editor of the Party newspaper, he had made the threat of world Jewish influence one of his main concerns. He had been a staunch advocate of the Madagascar 'reservation' idea and he was founder of the Institute for Research into the Jewish Question (the scholars of which plundered the libraries and museums of the continent for Judaica to bring back to Frankfurt). As late as July 1944, he was still obsessively planning to hold a star-studded 'scientific' International Anti-Jewish Congress that would avoid the danger of a 'third world war' by converting Britain and the United States to an awareness of the Jewish threat.[2]

As his comments indicated, by 1941 the Nazis saw at least three inter-connected aspects of the 'Jewish problem' – the German, the 'eastern' and the European. They had come to power vowing to rid Germany of its Jews, and forced emigration from the Reich and its newly conquered territories remained their preferred strategy for more than a year into the war itself. The 1940 Madagascar plan was a revised version of this, and in fact it was only in October 1941 that Heydrich made it unambiguously clear – in a message to the Foreign Ministry (after Spain had proposed deporting Spanish Jews living in France to Spanish Morocco as an alternative to handing them over to the Germans) – that the Reich was actually discouraging Jewish emigration from the European continent.

The invasion of the Soviet Union was the turning-point. Inside the newly occupied territories Jews were killed in the first days and weeks of the campaign in numbers unprecedented in any previous war or pogrom. From July and August, SS death squads, helped by local auxiliaries, systematically carried out massacres in many towns and villages. The eastern killing grounds were seen as an eventual destination for Germany's Jews too. When the Romanians and Hungarians began driving tens of thousands of Jews from their newly acquired border provinces across into former Soviet territory, they were only doing what the Nazis themselves planned on a much larger and more systematic scale: 'evacuation to the East' was meant literally before it became a German cover phrase.

By August the regime was coming under pressure from its own *Gauleiters* to use the eastern territories to make the Reich 'free of Jews' as quickly as possible. Not only was this a matter of prestige for them but it also suggested a way of easing the housing shortage created by Allied bombing. At a meeting called by Josef Goebbels (not only propaganda minister but also *Gauleiter* for Berlin) speaker after speaker complained that they could not understand why, after going through hell on the Eastern Front, they came back to find Jews enjoying such freedom in Germany. Hitler initially resisted the idea of deporting

German Jews while the war was in progress and even hesitated to decree the wearing of the yellow star, even though this had been mandatory in the General Government and the Warthegau for nearly two years. But he changed his mind with the news that Stalin had responded to the German drive deep into the Ukraine by deporting hundreds of thousands of Volga Germans. Ideas of revenge lay behind many Nazi atrocities, and Rosenberg suggested retaliating to the Soviet move by deporting 'all central European Jews' to the eastern territories. Since the logistical difficulties this would have posed were immense while the German offensive was still in full swing, Heydrich suggested starting off with the main German cities, and Hitler agreed.[3]

Where precisely the German Jews should go, however, and what should happen to them was anything but clear. The Wehrmacht was already finding it difficult to keep and feed three million Soviet POWs and it had already rebuffed Romanian and Serbian efforts to dump their Jews in German-occupied territory because it did not know what to do with them. Heydrich's fertile mind was not deterred, however. Initially, he contemplated using the POW camps themselves. But the formation of large, if already overcrowded, ghettoes in places like Minsk, Riga and Łódź suggested another answer, with fewer jurisdictional complications: surely they could house newcomers from the Old Reich, especially if some of their current inhabitants were killed off. Łódź, in the annexed lands of the Warthegau, was closest, and in mid-September Himmler asked Gauleiter Arthur Greiser to prepare the ghetto there for 'approximately sixty thousand Jews', since Hitler wanted 'the Old Reich and the Protectorate [to] be emptied and freed of Jews, progressing from the West to the East'. The following month, some 20,000 were transported from Vienna, Prague and major German cities. Within months many had frozen or starved to death, while from January 1942 onwards others were gassed at nearby Chelmno.

That autumn, Himmler journeyed further east as well. He toured the Baltic states – where massacres of Jews were sweeping across the region – and he visited Belorussia, where he witnessed a shooting. In October, he travelled to the Ukraine to meet HSSPF Friedrich Jeckeln, who had carried out the first really large mass executions in Kamenets-Podolsk some weeks earlier. Outside Kiev, in the Babi Yar ravine, tens of thousands of people had been machine-gunned to death a few days before his arrival, and in fact killings were still going on. Himmler talked with

Jeckeln and then sent him north to the Baltic, having decided that the ghettoes of Riga and Minsk should also receive German Jews. Jeckeln's arrival guaranteed they would not live long.

At this time, the killing fields in the East were still more like a gruesome public theatre than a carefully guarded secret, and many thousands of German servicemen and women witnessed – if they did not participate in – massacres everywhere from the Baltic to the southern Ukraine. In fact, Gestapo head Heinrich Müller sent a telegram to the *Einsatzgruppen* at the end of August 1941 telling them 'to prevent the crowding of spectators during the mass executions'.[4] Some onlookers were horrified and could scarcely believe what was happening. One officer – hardened, as he put it, by service in the First World War and again in Poland – protested that he had never seen anything so appalling. German administrators too were dismayed at the entry of Himmler's killing squads into their towns. They had anticipated nothing like this and they found it hard to allay the atmosphere of terror, suspicion and alienation.

A German interpreter arrived in the town of Borisov in Belorussia, for example, and learned of the impending liquidation of the town's Jews three days hence by one of the killing units from a Russian working for the SD:

To my astounded question that it would be impossible to dispatch 8,000 persons into Eternity in the course of a single night in a fairly orderly manner, he replied that it was not the first time that he had done this and he would be able to finish the job with his men; he was no longer a layman at this.

On the day itself, Belorussians working for the SS carried out the executions in woods so close to the town that the rifle-fire could easily be heard. Meanwhile, 'the women and children cried and screamed' and 'cars raced through the streets and the ghetto and kept bringing new victims – all before the eyes of the civilian population and the German military personnel that happened to come along'. By night, the killing spread to the ghetto and the town itself, where some Jews had either hidden or tried to escape.

During that night it was not advisable even for a member of the Wehrmacht to venture on the streets, in order to avoid the danger of being killed or at least wounded by the Russian policemen, due to a generally prevalent nervousness.

About ten o'clock in the evening, a fire was raging in the city and wild shooting was going on.

The following day, it continued, and cars returned from the woods carrying clothing from the victims. Isolated groups of cowering Jews awaited execution. The interpreter concluded his report by noting 'a rumour . . . that the now vacant houses of the Jews shall be prepared for Jews from Germany, who in turn shall be liquidated in the same manner as were the Jews of Borisow'.[5]

As Army Group Centre commander Fedor von Bock pressed on through the mud towards Moscow, his staff officers confronted him with news of the Borisov massacre and begged him to have the *Einsatzgruppe* withdrawn. They were furious, and some of them were deeply upset. Reports such as the above had been passed on to the Abwehr, whose leader, Admiral Wilhelm Canaris, had already been perturbed by the Wehrmacht's illegalities in Poland and seems to have been compiling a dossier of similar atrocities in the Soviet Union. But Bock refused to intervene. He was no great supporter of Hitler, and he submitted a memorandum to the Führer that criticized 'these unheard-of crimes'; but like most of his fellow generals in Russia, he would not use the army against the SS.[6]

Stories like this one – linking the deportations to systematic mass murder – inevitably reached Germany, where they prompted growing public disquiet. They came on top of very uncertain reactions to the introduction of the yellow star. In some cities there was outright opposition. 'The revival of the Jewish question by the required wearing of the Star of David has met with almost universal disapproval by the people of Berlin, and in some cases with astonishing manifestations of sympathy with the Jews in public,' reported an American diplomat in mid-October. 'This reaction has become increasingly obvious to all observers.' Round-ups of elderly Jews, weighed down with packs and suitcases, marched in long lines through suburban streets or jammed into the back of Gestapo trucks, added to the concern. Many Germans – including even the commissar for Belorussia, Wilhelm Kube – felt that German Jews were a quite different breed from the 'Easterners' and objected to the killing of ex-servicemen in particular.

Even some SS men reacted similarly: a Polish rabbi in the Konin labour camp in the Warthegau in May 1942 was astonished when a limousine came into the camp one day, and several SS officers got out, 'followed by a serious and grandly dressed old man with gold-rimmed spectacles on his nose. The chauffeur unloaded six leather suitcases each bearing a label with its owner's name. After the SS officers shook his hand, they bid him a courteous farewell and left.' The new arrival, who seemed like a visitor from another planet to the Polish Jews, was 'an Ashkenazi in the full sense of the word', a doctor and decorated ex-serviceman from Berlin. Like many German Jews, Dr Hans Knopf remained proudly attached to his country: he hung a picture of himself on horseback over his bed and would occasionally don his officer's uniform, complete with the decorations the Kaiser had awarded him. When he committed suicide, shortly before the liquidation of the camp in 1943, those entering his room found

On the doctor's desk, covered with a white tablecloth . . . innumerable family photographs, neatly arrayed . . . There were also photographs of his military past, including some at various fronts of the war in 1914–1918. They were living testimony to his grand and patriotic military past . . . Letters were also arrayed, as were medals in their original packing, in chronological order. And there on his bed, between the white sheets, lay our comrade the physician in delicate silk pajamas, the most important citations and medals pinned to his right breast.[7]

The Nazi regime was certainly not indifferent to popular opinion, which it monitored closely. Only that August, it had wound down the euthanasia campaign after stinging public criticism by Catholic bishops. 'Our intellectual and social strata have suddenly rediscovered their senti-ments of humanity for the poor Jews,' wrote the disgusted Goebbels in his diary. 'The Jews just need to send a little old lady with the Star of David badge hobbling down the Kurfürstendamm, and the plain honest German is already inclined to forget everything the Jews have inflicted on us over the past years and decades.' As one of the leading advocates of 'radical' measures, Goebbels had been told by Heydrich at the end of September of the plans to deport the German Jews and he did his best to change the public mood. On 16 November – in the midst of the deportations – he penned a hard-hitting article entitled 'The Jews are Guilty!' (Die Juden sind schuld) in which he spelled out that what lay ahead was nothing less than 'annihilation':

By unleashing this war, world Jewry completely misjudged the forces at its disposal. Now it is suffering a gradual process of annihilation that it had intended for us and that it would have unleashed against us without hesitation if it had had the power to do so. It is now perishing as a result of its own law. An eye for an eye, and a tooth for a tooth. In this historical dispute every Jew is our enemy, whether he vegetates in a Polish ghetto, or scrapes out his parasitical existence in Berlin or Hamburg, or blows the trumpets of war in New York or Washington.

German Jews were, he declared, as responsible for the war as Jews in eastern Europe or the United States. Whatever they endured, 'they have more than deserved it'. Publication in *Das Reich*, followed by a radio broadcast, could have left the German public in little doubt that the regime planned to 'finally be done with them'. Yet Goebbels' propaganda offensive was deliberately vague. For the lesson that he, Himmler and others drew after backing down over the euthanasia programme was that public feelings had been unnecessarily aroused, and 'useless uproar' had made it harder for the regime to do what it needed. The expertise of the mostly unemployed gassing personnel was available for use against the Jews; but they would be posted to the East under conditions of the strictest secrecy.[8]

This was a critical period for the regime's Jewish policy. The directives which the Eastern Ministry had issued in early September had talked of drastic measures, acts of retaliation and segregation in the context of a policy which would 'be comprehensively solved throughout Europe *after the war*' (my italics). But on 15 November Hinrich Lohse, the Reich commissar for the Ostland, was still puzzled about what was intended and inquired whether or not there was 'a directive to liquidate all Jews in the East'. He had prevented Einsatzkommando 2 killing Jews in Liepāja, in Latvia, because, like many of the civil administrators, he was worried about the implications for the local economy. Rosenberg met Himmler to discuss this. It was after their meeting, and another with the Führer which followed it, that Rosenberg – newly unveiled to the world as Minister for the Occupied Eastern Territories – gave the press briefing with which this chapter opens. Even as he could finally enjoy ministerial recognition, the Nazi ideologue who had been writing obsessionally about the Jews for more than twenty years had capitulated before something not even he had imagined – Hitler and Himmler's insistence on systematic mass murder.[9]

Having established his authority over the Jewish question in the former Soviet Union, Himmler now turned to the Reich itself. This was quite a different matter from pushing aside someone as weak as Rosenberg. There were established ministries to contend with and in particular the Interior Ministry, which jealously guarded its jurisdiction over matters of German citizenship. In a very long meeting with State Secretary Stuckart, Himmler tried to assert the primacy of the SS in the Reich as well: as he noted briefly in his appointment book, 'Jewish questions belong to me.' Yet several transports of German Jews had already been sent to Kovno and massacred, when Himmler suffered a serious embarrassment. It seems likely that news of the Kovno shootings had got back to Germany and caused enough adverse reaction to worry Himmler and Hitler, for when a transport of German Jews was sent to Riga, Himmler instructed his men there that there was to be 'no liquidation'. Unfortunately, the message arrived too late for the murderously efficient Jeckeln, his SS and police chief, who had had the deportees marched off to pits and shot as soon as they had arrived. (Their clothes, removed before the victims were killed, were as usual washed and sent back to Germany.) Fearful lest his competence be questioned, Himmler lectured Jeckeln angrily on the need to follow his instructions to the letter in future. As it was, horrified senior officials in Berlin were already making their concerns known. At the Interior Ministry, Stuckart's deputy for Jewish affairs, Bernhard Lösener – author of the standard commentary on the Nuremberg racial laws – heard first-hand reports of the massacres and was shocked. He confronted his boss, and demanded to be allowed to resign. 'Don't you know that these things happen because of orders from the highest level?' Stuckart told him. Lösener eventually quit; Stuckart, pragmatic and ambitious despite sharing his deputy's misgivings, stayed on and ended up running the Ministry under Himmler himself.[10]

When Stuckart and Lösener met, a few days before Christmas, much had already changed. The second week in December was one of the most dramatic of the entire war. Pearl Harbor was attacked on 7 December, and the following day Britain and America declared war on Japan, while Hitler finally gave up trying to take Moscow and ordered the 'transition to defence'. Germany declared war on the USA on the 11th, and on the 12th Hitler presided over a critical meeting in his private apartment. Speaking to his *Gauleiters*, he surveyed the international and domestic scene and sought to inspire them for a further year of struggle. Predicting an intensification of the U-boat war in the Atlantic, he addressed his audience's misgivings about being allied with Japan. The 'interests of the white race,' he lectured them, must yield to the interests of the German people: Germany was fighting for its life, and 'a beautiful theory' was not the issue. They should avoid sentimentality and over-theorizing, since 'in a struggle of life and death all means are justified'. Hitler reminded them that their task was to ensure morale remained solid at home, and he held out the promise of better housing once the war was won. And then he came to 'the Jewish question'. According to Goebbels, whose diary remains our sole source for his speech,

the Führer has decided to make a clean sweep [*reinen Tisch zu machen*]. He has prophesied to the Jews that, if they started another world war, it would mean their annihilation. That was not just words [*Dass ist keine Phrase gewesen*]. The world war is here, so the annihilation of Jewry must be the necessary consequence.[11]

There can be no doubt that this was the green light for organizing systematic mass murder beyond the territories of the USSR. A policy that had already been agreed among those in charge was now being communicated in person to key Party officers. Only a few days after-wards, Lohse finally received an answer to his inquiry of mid-November about the existence of a liquidation directive. 'Clarification of the Jewish question has most likely been achieved by now through verbal dis-cussion,' he was told. 'Economic considerations should fundamentally remain unconsidered in the settlement of the problem.'[12] Returning to Cracow from Berlin, Hans Frank brought his officials in the General Government into the picture:

[The Jews] must be done away with. I have entered negotiations to have them deported to the East. A great discussion concerning that question will take place in Berlin in January ... A great Jewish migration will begin, in any case. But what should be done with the Jews? Do you think they will be settled down in the 'Ostland' in settlement villages [*Siedlungsdörfer*]? This is what we were told in Berlin: why all this bother? We can do nothing with them either in the 'Ostland' or in the 'Reichskommissariat'. So, liquidate them yourself. Gentlemen, I must ask you to rid yourself of all feeling of pity. We must annihilate the Jews wherever we find them and wherever it is possible, in order to maintain the structure of the Reich as a whole. This will, naturally, be achieved by other methods than those pointed out by Bureau Chief Dr Hummel. Nor can the judges of the Special Courts be made responsible for it, because of the limitations of the framework of the legal procedure. Such outdated views cannot be applied to such gigantic and unique events. We must find at any rate a way which leads to the goal, and my thoughts are working in that direction.

The Jews represent for us also extraordinarily malignant gluttons. We have now approximately 2,500,000 of them in the General Government, perhaps with the Jewish mixtures, and everything that goes with it, 3,500,000 Jews. We cannot shoot or poison those 3,500,000 Jews but we shall nevertheless be able to take measures which will lead, somehow, to their annihilation, and this in connection with the gigantic measures to be determined in discussions from the Reich.[13]

Frank's comments are revealing. They indicate that for the first time Hitler had made it clear that what was involved was a policy of active extermination, and not only in the occupied Soviet territories. Ten times the number of German Jews or more, the Jews of the General Government had also to be killed. But how, and where? Deportation to the USSR was ruled out; there was no place for the Polish Jews to go. Evidently, Frank had at that moment no idea how to proceed with such an awesome and unprecedented task.

If the meeting with the Führer in mid-December marked the moment at which leading Party officials were admitted into the new policy, the Wannsee conference, rearranged for January, was when the civil servants were brought in to begin the serious work of planning and implementation. As usual in the Third Reich in which every policy initiative was regarded – usually with ample justification – as a power grab at someone else's expense, the imminent implementation of a sweeping new approach to the Jewish question left many bureaucrats fearing a further extension of the power of the SS. The Interior Ministry wanted to preserve its say over the legal boundaries of Jewishness in Germany; the Foreign Ministry wanted to make sure it was not bypassed in negotiations with foreign governments; the Eastern Ministry was still trying to win room for its own approach to racial policy in the post-Soviet territories, and Frank himself, whose General Government was home to the largest population of Jews outside the eastern territories, was not in a mood to allow the SS any leeway. Ranged against them all was Reinhard Heydrich, who hoped that 'coordination' of the Jewish question would open the way to establish tighter SS control over the German state in general.

Everyone who encountered Heydrich came away struck by his single-mindedness and his determination to come out on top in any encounter. At Wannsee, he did indeed get what he wanted, namely the general recognition that – as Himmler had put it earlier – 'the Jewish question belonged to' the SS. All agreed that the two men were to be 'entrusted with the official central handling of the final solution of the Jewish question without regard to borders'. For Heydrich in particular, taking charge of this issue was almost certainly a means to an end. Through its efficiency the SS would show how German administration of occupied Europe in general might be streamlined and properly managed, set beyond the babble of competing jurisdictions that bedevilled most other policy areas. Yet Wannsee was dominated by the question of deportations from the Reich. Speeding these up was the explicit priority, in view of 'the housing problem and additional social and political necessities' in the Reich; Heydrich emphasized that there were to be no 'wild' deportations, such as those that had taken place in 1939 from Vienna and in 1940 from western Germany, and Hitler had to give 'the appropriate approval in advance'. The Party *Gauleiters* would have to learn to wait. And there were complicated issues still to be resolved regarding mixed marriages and their offspring.[14]

Thus, although the meeting prepared the ground for the extension of Germany's anti-Jewish measures across the continent, of the estimated eleven million Jews involved, it was the 131,800 in the Old Reich, as well as 43,700 in Austria and 74,200 in the Protectorate, whose fate came under immediate consideration. Since the death toll of the *Einsatzgruppen* in the occupied Soviet territories was already far above this, killing on such a scale did not pose any problems for the SS. 'Selection' was the key motif. According to Heydrich, elderly German Jews would be sent to a special ghetto. On his orders (since he was also in charge of the Protectorate) the former Habsburg camp at Theresienstadt had already received its first Jewish inmates; eventually, some 50,000 would be crowded into an area formerly inhabited by fewer than 10,000 people, and many would die there or in Auschwitz. At the same time, 'able-bodied Jews' would be used for 'appropriate labour' in the East, building roads, 'in the course of which action doubtless a large portion will be eliminated by natural causes'; those who survived would have to be 'treated accordingly'.

This combination of selection, deliberate killing and 'extermination through labour' (as it would come to be known) was already part of German policy in the East, where the Jews had been placed under an obligation to carry out forced labour from the outset. But despite the calls of Frank's representative to start the 'final solution' in the General Government as quickly as possible, Heydrich merely remarked that the timing of 'evacuation actions' elsewhere would depend on military developments. There were, as yet, no resources at the disposal of the SS for mass killing sites on a scale large enough to cope with the kinds of numbers being discussed, and diplomacy was at a very preliminary stage with most countries. Nor was there any sense that the bulk of the killing should take place before the end of the war, which in the East was assumed to lie only a few months away.

It was in fact only over the next six months that the Final Solution as we understand it today took shape. Only then did the killings in the former USSR fuse with the development of a systematic extermination programme in Poland and the beginnings of a continental-wide policy of deportations to Auschwitz. At the start of this period, after all, Himmler himself was still pursuing two not easily reconciled goals – fulfilling Hitler's orders to kill the Jews, on the one hand, and on the other, building up a labour force large enough to carry out the postwar programme of General Plan East. 'Extermination through labour' of those able to work, and the immediate murder of the rest, was his way of combining them. Auschwitz, located just inside the borders of the expanded German Reich, at a convenient transit point on the rail system in Upper Silesia, grew at precisely this time into the most important labour camp in the SS system while developing the gassing facilities that made it the main destination of European Jewry between mid-1942 and mid-1944.[15]

It was not around Auschwitz, however, but inside the General Government and the Warthegau that dedicated extermination camps – detached from the forced labour programme, and run entirely outside the concentration camp system – first emerged in top secret during the winter of 1941/2. Frank might have been at a loss how to kill the Jews of Poland, but some Nazi officials had their own ideas. The SS, even more than the Wehrmacht and the Party itself, was an organization which liked its men to show initiative. Just as HSSPF Jeckeln had pushed forward the killing by showing that Jews could be massacred in previously unimaginable numbers at Kamenets-Podolsk in August 1941, and others had made Jews targets of mass reprisals in the context of the anti-partisan war, so now SS officers in Poland brought in the gassing experts of the T-4 euthanasia staff to solve their own local and regional problems. In the process, they demonstrated the crucial role played by mid-level Nazi functionaries in pushing the genocide forward. The slowly emerging Final Solution, in Ian Kershaw's words, 'formed a unity out of a number of organizationally separate "programmes"'.[16]

In the Warthegau, the initiative lay in the hands of Arthur Greiser and the security chiefs of the province. As the Łódź ghetto became crowded with arrivals from elsewhere, they were feeling the pressure, for it was dawning on them that the old idea that they could deport them further east was no longer a possibility. Yet they too had vowed to make their region 'free of Jews', and they were particularly anxious to keep Łódź, its most important industrial centre, productive and free of disease. One idea was to gather together all the Jews in the Warthegau into a giant labour camp. But this raised the question of what to do with those unable to work. As early as 16 July 1941, the SD had warned of hunger inside the ghetto in the coming winter and suggested 'whether the most humanitarian solution would not be to finish off those Jews who are not fit for work by some other means'. (This official also wanted to sterilize the women 'so that the Jewish problem would be fully solved to all intents and purposes with this generation'.)[17]

In October 1941, mass executions took place in the Kazimierz forest, suggesting that the SS were still thinking in terms of killing off Jews in the Warthegau the same way as in Russia. Yet gas vans may have been used on Jewish men, women and children then and even earlier – the information is sparse. Such vehicles had certainly been deployed in the area the previous summer to kill mentally ill and elderly Polish patients, probably in order to clear hospitals for German military use. Operating within the framework of the euthanasia campaign, some of the men involved in this secret unit expanded their operations at the request of the Warthegau authorities and established a permanent base for their work.

The site they chose was a deserted manor house surrounded by a fence and trees outside the village of Chelmno, about thirty-five miles away from Łódź. In December, this Sonderkommando began to kill Jews living locally, and from January they started transporting people from the city too. The transports increased after the arrival of a new Gestapo chief, Otto Bradfisch, from the killing fields of the East, and more than 150,000 people were eventually murdered there. The arrivals were told that they were being sent to Germany to work but would need to bathe first: the trucks were supposedly to take them to the bath-houses. Once 50–70 people had climbed inside, the doors were closed, and carbon monoxide was pumped in. The truck would then dump the bodies in the forest near by, and any still alive would be shot.

Despite heavy security and intense secrecy, operations on this scale could not be kept completely quiet. Near the start, for instance, a local German forestry official, Heinz May, was driving with his son along a road between Chelmno and Kolo when they were forced to stop for a truck that had come off the road:

My son got out of our truck and walked over to a group of men in police uniforms who were bustling about the vehicle. I was soon to hear those officials rebuking my son; I too got out and walked over . . . The truck in the ditch was about four meters in length and about two meters high. Its rear door was closed with an iron bolt from which a padlock hung. A definitely unpleasant smell came from the truck and from the men standing around it.

When I asked whether the road was soon to be clear, I was told impolitely that they would pull the truck a little to the side and that I should try to make it past. My son was in Kolo a few days later. On his return, he told me that the police officials were assembling groups of Jews there and taking them away by truck. I . . . no longer had any doubt that a terrible thing was happening in the Ladorudz forest, something that I had at first been unable to believe. I immediately tele-phoned Forest Constable Stagemeir and asked him what was going on in his forest district. He replied that Precinct 77 had been entirely surrounded by military police. When during his official rounds he had approached the sentries, he was told to turn around and leave the area immediately otherwise he could count on being shot . . .

Stagemeir explained to me that a large detachment of military police was stationed in Chelmno. The palace on the western side of Chelmno had been enclosed by a high wooden fence . . . I passed by there on my way back to the forest and confirmed that what Stagemeir had said . . . was true. There were rows upon rows of trucks with improvised canvas tops in Chelmno. Women, men and even children had been crammed into those trucks . . . During the short time

I was there, I saw the first truck drive up to the wooden fence. The sentries opened the gates. The truck vanished into the palace courtyard and immediately afterwards another closed truck came out of the courtyard and headed for the forest. And then both sentries closed the gates. There was no longer the slightest doubt that terrible things, things never before known in human history, were being played out there.[18]

Working along similar lines as the Warthegau SS, but responsible ultimately for almost ten times as many deaths, were their counterparts in the eastern Polish province of Lublin. The chief organizer, Odilo Globocnik, was one of those men – numerous in Nazi ranks – who had not so much failed at civilian life as turned away from it in search of adventure and commitment, their heads filled with fantasies of national revenge and racial annihilation. Himmler had rescued his career in 1939 after he had been sacked for corruption as *Gauleiter* of Vienna and he had brought him to Poland to run the SS in Lublin. 'Globus' was thus a man with something to prove and utterly loyal to Himmler, whose counsel he sought even when contemplating whom to marry. But he was abrasive, fanatical and violent towards those who angered him and widely regarded as an incompetent bully. His good friend and fellow *Gauleiter*, Friedrich Rainer, a much more self-possessed and capable administrator, remarked on Globocnik's 'aggressive personal methods' and his lack of attention to the words he used. (His Austrian mentor more slyly described him as combining 'the freshness of a young maiden and the acuteness of a peasant'.)[19]

Accompanied by a coterie of thuggish fellow-Carinthians and adoring secretaries, Globocnik ensconced himself in a smart modernist villa and began churning out ideas to bring the race war to the Polish frontier. As early as the end of 1939, Frank had had to step in to block his proposal to turn Lublin into a 'Jewish reservation'. Then he rounded up thousands of Jews (and also gypsies deported from Germany) in order to build massive military fortifications along the Nazi–Soviet border. By the time the 'border wall' idea was also abandoned, he had established a network of labour camps centred on a village called Belzec – crowded death-traps guarded by trigger-happy ethnic Germans who had been 'trained' by his men. Plundering sadists, their arbitrary terror against both Jews and Poles brought angry complaints from Frank and civilian administrators, who tried several times to get him removed.

But Himmler valued 'Globus' for his initiative and his ruthlessness and later he described him as 'a man made like no other for the tasks of colonization in the East'. In July 1941, he put him in charge of planning a string of police strong points 'in the new *Ostraum*'. As a result Globocnik hatched wild schemes for a colonial security system of 'bases stretching all the way to the Urals'; those Jews not needed to build them would be killed 'on the spot'. Bringing in planners and racial experts, he saw Lublin as a laboratory for General Plan East, a launching pad against the Slavs. In his mind, this would replay – successfully this time – the nationality wars that the German nationalists he had admired as a boy had fought against the Slovenes on Austria's southern border: Lublin would become the first purely German settlement in eastern Poland and a crucial link in a 'noose of new settlements' stretching from the Baltic to Transylvania which would encircle the Poles, 'gradually throttling them both economically and biologically'.[20]

But first the area had to be rid of Jews. Alongside the very public construction of large new camps and mass executions, Globocnik been among the small number of officials – they included Arthur Greiser, Wetzel in Rosenberg's Eastern Ministry and others – who had been discussing secretly how to exploit the euthanasia team's gassing expertise. In Riga these discussions led to the use of mobile gas vans, later deployed elsewhere throughout the eastern territories. In Minsk, they experimented with exhaust gas (and tried blowing mental patients up, with even more horrible results). Heydrich's men brought a gas van to the camp at Sachsenhausen and pushed forty naked Soviet POWs inside, after which the RSHA ordered thirty more vans to be converted. But it was Lublin which marked the most lethal development of this approach. Under Himmler's direct orders – and quite independently of Eichmann and his Jewish experts – Globocnik himself organized the construction, and selected the personnel to man the new secret extermination camps in which more than 1.2 million Polish Jews were to be killed. The code name for the whole operation – bestowed shortly after the assassination of Heydrich, in his memory – was Operation Reinhard.[21]

OPERATION REINHARD AND THE
ACCELERATION OF THE GENOCIDE

Among the German radio decrypts recently declassified and released by the Public Record Office in London is a brief top secret message that was intercepted en route from Lublin on 11 January 1943. This contained the fortnightly report from SS Major Hermann Höfle, head of Jewish affairs at Globocnik's Operation Reinhard headquarters, to the deputy commander of the SiPo/SD in the General Government. In just three lines it summarized what it described elliptically as 'recorded arrivals up to December 31, 1942' as follows: 'L 12761, B 0, S 515, T 10335, together 23611. Sum total . . . 31.12.42, L 24733, B 434508, S 101370, T 71355, together 1274166.'

Once we realize that the initials refer to camps in the Lublin district – L for Lublin-Majdanek, B for Belzec, T for Treblinka and S for Sobibor – then it becomes clear, as the authors of a recent commentary on the document have demonstrated, that what we have here are first-hand statistics from Globocnik's headquarters of the numbers of people murdered up to the end of 1942 under Operation Reinhard. According to the figures, a total of more than 1.2 million people had 'arrived' on transports, almost all of them to the three extermination camps. Of these no fewer than 713,550 (a zero has evidently dropped off the end of the relevant total in the document) had been killed at Treblinka alone. Majdanek was a very large combined labour and extermination camp only a few miles from the centre of Lublin itself; its existence could scarcely be kept quiet. But the other three were very small camps – Belzec measured barely 200 metres by 250 – located in sparsely populated areas with good rail access. Apart from the living quarters for the guards, they contained only the disguised gas chambers together with a reception area, undressing rooms and rudimentary quarters for the Jewish labourers who disposed of the corpses, either burying them in large pits or, later, burning them on pyres. They were supposed to remain shrouded in secrecy. But they were certainly not secret to the locals, who were employed briefly to help build them, and later scavenged the sites for valuables. Rumours quickly spread too to nearby towns, and passengers on the Lviv–Lublin railway could smell the Belzec camp hidden behind the pine trees and talked to one another openly about the bodies starting to rot.[22]

Like the SS in the Warthegau, Globocnik and his men had started off using 'eastern' methods on the local Jewish population; in the autumn of 1941, they had lined them up in old anti-tank ditches in their hundreds and shot them. Thanks to Himmler, who stayed with him in September, Globocnik was well informed about the first experiments with Zyklon B at Auschwitz that had taken place at the start of the month and he was also in close touch with the euthanasia gassing experts about establishing a mechanized killing centre in the General Government.[23] On 17 October, he met with Hans Frank, and they agreed on 'evacuations' of Jews from Lublin across the Bug river; but because Rosenberg had already made it clear to Frank that actual deportations across the border would not be allowed, 'evacuation' was clearly nothing but a euphemism for murder. It was on the evening of the same day that Hitler told his guests that the only task in the East was Germanization of the land, and that the natives would be treated like 'Red Indians'. 'In this matter, I am as cold as ice,' he continued. 'We eat Canadian corn and don't think of the Indians.'[24]

By early November, work had begun on turning the former Belzec labour camp into a gassing facility. Himmler and Globocnik remained in close contact over the winter, and, on 14 March 1942, the two men dined together. Three days after that the first transports arrived at Belzec – 40–60 goods wagons carrying Jews from Lublin. Soon others arrived from the district of Lviv and Cracow. Nearly 58,000 Jews were gassed there before the end of the month, by which point it was obvious to the organizers that they had found a means of mass murder that would ease the strain on the execution squads. With further input from the euthanasia experts, a second extermination camp was built at Sobibor, east of Lublin (beginning operations at the end of April) and a third, at Treblinka, in the vicinity of Warsaw, in the early summer. In the vicinity of the main camps were smaller transit camps – squalid, poorly guarded and overcrowded – the 'starved, stinking, gesticulating, insane' inmates of which could be held, and robbed, before being sent on. All were staffed by personnel assigned from the Reich euthanasia team and guarded by Ukrainians who had passed through the training camp set up by Globocnik. But the organization was poor, and Globocnik, no manager, often lost touch with the men actually running the camps. When the euthanasia team's brutal boss, a former career policeman called Christian Wirth, suddenly left Belzec for Berlin to report back after the first killings, Globocnik had no idea he had gone.[25]

An entry in Goebbels' diary at the end of March gives the sense of something new and awful afoot: Globocnik, he wrote, was 'evacuating' the Jews of the General Government to the East, starting with Lublin, by 'rather barbaric methods not to be described here more precisely; not much is left of the Jews'. These methods involved 'procedures which do not attract too much attention'. According to Goebbels, 'sixty percent of them must be liquidated, whereas only forty percent can be put to work'. Hitler was given the credit as 'the undismayed champion of a radical solution'. And what particularly interested Goebbels, as *Gauleiter* of Berlin, was that 'the ghettoes which become free in the cities of the General Government will be filled with Jews evacuated from the Reich; then the operation will be renewed from time to time'.[26]

A sense of excitement and urgency coursed among those charged with the secret killing, and they felt under constant pressure to accelerate it and finish before the news leaked out. Globocnik believed that 'the whole Jewish action should be carried out as quickly as possible to avoid the danger of one day finding ourselves stuck in the middle of it in the event of difficulties forcing us to halt the action'. Victor Brack, a leading figure in the programme, noted that Himmler himself wanted them to 'work as fast as possible if only for reasons of concealment'. The Reichsführer, however, showed no interest in Brack's suggestion that it made more sense to sterilize the '2–3 million' Jews in Europe capable of working rather than killing them. Anxieties about the Reich's growing labour shortage had led Himmler to slightly relax his selection policy in early 1942, but it went against the grain, especially as he was optimistic that the war would finish that summer.[27]

By mid-June 1942, an estimated 280,000 Polish Jews had already been murdered. Most had been killed at Belzec, Chelmno and Sobibor, though some had perished in the new gas chambers in Auschwitz-Birkenau. Yet for Himmler this was not nearly fast enough, for there were still more than two million Jews in former Poland alone. To make matters worse, the Reich's labour shortage was raising complaints that the elimination of the Jews was creating economic problems, while in the middle of June, preparations for the new summer offensive in the East led to a complete ban on non-military transports, throwing the deportation schedule into disarray. Himmler's response was to order new and larger gas chambers to be built in Belzec. In July, he manifested his impatience with those trying to retain Jewish workers in the General Government on economic grounds, informing the munitions inspectors there that henceforth only the SS would be allowed to supervise Jewish workers in its own camps; the rest would have to be handed over.

On 16 July, after meeting with Hitler, he contacted the Transportation Ministry to urge them to make more trains available for Sobibor. One of the reasons for the meeting may have been Globocnik's desire for the reassurance of a formal order covering the killings that had already taken place. Having witnessed a gassing at Auschwitz, it was now that Himmler gave Globocnik's superior, HSSPF Friedrich Krüger, the explicit instructions to complete 'the resettlement of the entire Jewish population of the General Government' by the end of the year. At the end of this fateful month – the same month that he won Hitler's approval for a preliminary draft of General Plan East – Himmler wrote to an aide that 'the occupied eastern territories will be free of Jews. The carrying out of this very difficult order has been laid on my shoulders by the Führer.'[28] Others understood this too. In the General Government, battling that August to meet its supply quotas to send the Reich from the harvest, Hans Frank told his cabinet that the 'order for the complete annihilation of the Jews', which had made his life easier in some ways (by reducing the demand for food inside the General Government), but harder in others (by increasing the shortage of skilled labour), had come 'from higher quarters' and could not be disputed. The lethal consequences of Himmler's bureaucratic triumph over Frank now became apparent: so far as the Jews were concerned (and unlike the situation two years earlier), racial considerations now trumped economic ones. Frank had wanted Globocnik dismissed because of his constant run-ins with the civil administration; but Himmler had defended his wayward young protégé in order to protect the Final Solution.[29]

In the General Government, where his power was at its height, Himmler missed his own deadline by only a month or so. But the summer of 1942 also saw the decision taken to push ahead with deportations from across Europe, turning what had largely been till then an internal German matter into a question of international diplomacy. France and Slovakia had already proved willing to send some of their Jews to the

Germans, for work as they may have believed briefly, and now the Germans increased the pressure.

In mid-August, the well-informed Hungarian ambassador to Berlin, László Sztójay reported 'a radical change of attitude here towards the settlement of the Jewish question ... While the Chancellor, and in consequence the National Socialist Party, previously held the view that the solution of the Jewish problem in countries other than Germany would have to be postponed until after the end of the war, this now no longer holds good and the Führer has issued categoric instructions to the effect that the question must be settled immediately ... According to absolutely reliable information, Reichsleiter Himmler has informed a meeting of SS leaders that it is the wish of the German Government to complete these deportations within a year.'[30]

Soon the news, and in greater detail, travelled further afield, exactly as Himmler had feared. The *Gauleiter* of Upper Silesia, Fritz Bracht, toured Auschwitz with him on 17 July. He was with Himmler as he watched the selection and killing of a transport of Jews from Holland, and he hosted a party for him that evening. A week later, a German businessman called Eduard Schulte, whose deputy had good contacts with Bracht, travelled by train to Switzerland, carrying with him important information which he passed on, via intermediaries, to Gerhart Riegner of the World Jewish Congress. The famous Riegner telegram, which was sent in early August from Geneva to prominent American Jews, summarized the change in policy with considerable accuracy:

RECEIVED ALARMING REPORT STATING THAT IN FUEHRERS HEADQUARTERS A PLAN HAS BEEN DISCUSSED AND BEING UNDER CONSIDERATION ACCORDING TO WHICH TOTAL OF JEWS IN COUNTRIES OCCUPIED CONTROLLED BY GERMANY NUMBERING THREE-AND-HALF TO FOUR MILLIONS SHOULD AFTER DEPORTATION AND CONCENTRATED IN EAST BE AT ONE BLOW EXTERMINATED IN ORDER RESOLVE ONCE FOR ALL JEWISH QUESTION IN EUROPE STOP ACTION IS REPORTED TO BE PLANNED FOR AUTUMN WAYS OF EXECUTION STILL DISCUSSED STOP IT HAS BEEN SPOKEN OF PRUSSIC ACID STOP ...[31]

As this news was received and evaluated by Allied politicians, culminating in their public warning in December 1942 that Nazi war crimes would not go unpunished at the end of the war, the architects of the

Final Solution now had a new factor to take into account. There was unease inside Germany itself, fed by reports of Allied propaganda and by soldiers returning from the East. The Party Chancellery felt obliged to issue confidential guidelines on how to respond to anxiety about the 'very hard operations' being taken against the Jews in the East. Germans were reminded why 'ruthless severity' was desirable in such measures, told they would now be extended throughout Europe and reassured that elderly Jews and decorated veterans would be resettled separately in Theresienstadt.[32]

Even as the Führer opened the New Year of 1943 predicting imminent victory, the German offensive towards the oil fields of the Caucasus finally failed, doomed by the Soviet victory at Stalingrad and the encirclement of the German 6th Army. It was at this time that Himmler commissioned his chief statistician, Richard Korherr, to collate the available data on the 'Final Solution of the Jewish Question in Europe'; a final draft of the resulting report was eventually completed in April. Himmler declared it 'excellent' – although with typical punctiliousness he directed that the phrase 'special handling of the Jews' be replaced by 'transportation of Jews from the eastern provinces to the Russian East' – and he requested that a summary be made for Hitler himself.

Korherr, a shy but ardent nationalist, was proud of his expertise as a statistician and of his objectivity; he was one of the many such technical experts upon whose skills the Final Solution depended, and in response to Himmler's request, he spent two weeks poring over documents in Eichmann's office.[33] He eventually estimated that the Jewish population of the territories earmarked for German *Lebensraum* – Germany itself, Austria, the Sudetenland, the Protectorate and former Poland – had dropped from 3.1 million in March 1939 to 606,103 at the end of 1942. The entire area was well on the way to becoming *judenrein*.

Looking at each territory from the time Nazi rule had begun, and asking how far the decline in the number of Jews was due to 'evacuation' (i.e. deportation and killing), Korherr arrived at some important findings. In Germany itself, where the drop was greatest – not surprisingly since the Nazis had been in power since 1933 – many more Jews had emigrated than had been deported. The same applied to Austria – testimony to the cruel efficiency of Eichmann's office for Jewish emigration – and to the annexed Polish territories, where many Jews had fled

The Decline of the Jewish Population in Central Europe

Country: Time Period	Emigration	'Evacuation'	Total Decrease	Remaining
Old Reich + Sudetenland (since 1/33 and 9/38) Austria (since 3/38)	382 (71%)	100 (19%)	540	51
Austria (since 3/38)	149 (70%)	48 (23%)	212	8
PBM (since 3/39)	26 (25%)	70 (69%)	102	16
Annexed Eastern Territory (since 9/39)	335 (60%)	222 (40%)	557	233
General Government (since 9/39 and 6/40)	428 (25%)	1,274 (75%)	1,702	298

Notes

PBM = Protectorate of Bohemia and Moravia. Numbers rounded to nearest 000. Total decrease = emigration + 'evacuation' + 'other decrease' (chiefly due to what Korherr termed 'excess mortality'). This last category has been omitted. Percentages indicate proportion of total decrease of the Jewish population (which included natural deaths and suicides).[34]

German rule. But in the Czech lands and the General Government the huge drop in the overall Jewish population – by the end of 1942 Korherr reckoned that there were only 15,550 Jews alive in the Protectorate; only 297,914 in the General Government, compared with more than two million at the start of the war – was overwhelmingly the result of 'evacuation' to the death camps during 1942. Further deportations in the first three months of 1943 accounted for more than 113,000 more. The Jewish population in Germany itself was, in his words, 'approaching its end'.

What stands out at this stage is the decisive role played by the Reinhard camps, where more than 1.2 million had already been killed – well over half of all the Jewish victims until that point. Korherr also estimated that 633,300 Jews had been killed in the occupied Soviet territories. (In fact, this certainly underestimated the death toll following Barbarossa.) Although he reckoned that some 308,159 Jews were still 'at liberty' (mostly in former Poland and USSR), most of those left alive throughout the German *Lebensraum* were concentrated in ghettoes (297,914), special work camps (185,776) and the concentration camps (9,127): they were primarily those who had survived the constant selections and now faced 'extermination through work'. One might have expected Himmler to be satisfied for there was no historical parallel for the organized killing of civilians on this scale in such a brief period. In fact, his reaction on reading Korherr's report was to urge his men on. 'What is of primary importance to me at the moment,' he wrote on 9 April 1943, 'is that as many Jews be transported to the East as is humanly possible.'[35]

But the death camps had done their work, and the signs of resistance were growing. When the Germans tried to clear the Warsaw and Bialystok ghettoes, they met with armed opposition; in Vilna, many Jews escaped the ghetto to join the partisans. Hundreds of thousands of Polish and Belorussian Jews had been killed at Treblinka, but after May only occasional transports arrived, and the Jewish workers who were made to systematically exhume bodies and burn them knew soon this meant it would be their turn to be shot. In August there was a break-out; the main gates were stormed, and, although most of those involved were shot by the guards, several hundred managed to escape, and a few evaded the subsequent dragnet. Those in Sobibor followed two months later, completely taking their guards by surprise and killing twelve of them; several hundred more prisoners got away.

At this point, Himmler decided to bring Reinhard to an end. The remaining ghettoes were liquidated in the grimly named Operation 'Harvest Festival' and the death camps were closed. Apart from workers in Auschwitz and in the Łódź ghetto, there were few major concentrations of Jews left. As for Globocnik, he was transferred south to the Adriatic coast, back to his birthplace, Trieste, where he astonished the town's inhabitants by making a speech in Italian and Slovene on Hitler's birthday in April 1944. He had lost much of his power but none of his instincts. Taking his killing squads with him, he established a camp for Jews in a disused rice-mill in the city, the only one with a gas chamber on Italian soil, and collected Jews and partisans there before sending them north to Auschwitz. His work was almost done.

THE JEWISH QUESTION IN EUROPE

From the start, the regime was thinking on a continental scale, and by the end of 1941, at the very latest, its approach to the Jewish question too encompassed the whole of Europe. Korherr noted that, whereas in 1880 Europe accounted for 85 per cent of the world's Jews, this had fallen to 60 per cent by 1937 and would – he predicted – drop further so that, by 1943, 'Europe should not account for more than ⅓ of the world's Jewish population'. Yet his reports also highlighted the regime's focus upon 'cleansing' the lands of the future Greater Germany and its extension into the former USSR. According to Korherr, by the end of 1942, only 8.5 per cent of those 'evacuated' had come from other European countries, chiefly from Slovakia (56,691), France (41,911), the Netherlands (38,571) and Belgium (16,866). This was a relatively small proportion of the total Jewish population in western, central and southern Europe, and outside Slovakia by no means a majority of the Jews even in the countries concerned. Somewhere in the region of 175,000 Jews had been deported to Auschwitz in 1942 – a huge number, but one that should be compared with the 1.2 million mostly Polish Jews who had already perished in the extermination camps in the General Government. If 1942 was the year in which the Germans annihilated the largest Jewish community in Europe (the Polish), it was only between April and June of that year that Nazi officials seriously turned their attention to the rest of Europe. This, however, turned out to be rather harder to push through than they expected.[36]

In its intensified anti-Semitism, Nazi Germany was scarcely alone. Through the 1930s, as Europe moved to the right, many countries had turned their back on the emancipatory liberalism of the nineteenth century and introduced anti-Semitic legislation of their own, designed to curb Jewish rights and often to force Jews to emigrate as well. In eastern Europe, in particular, the formation of national states had fanned the flames of anti-Semitism by creating a sense of competition – for university places, control of business and professional opportunities – between Jews and non-Jews. Quotas, boycotts and migration schemes followed, and violence against Jews became more common. From 1938, anti-Jewish laws were tightened up in Romania and introduced into Hungary and Italy. They were introduced in Slovakia too once it gained independence in 1939; the Germans posted Eichmann's Austrian aide, Dieter Wisliceny, there as special counsellor for Jewish affairs. Even in Bulgaria, a new law 'for the protection of the nation' discriminated against the civil rights of Jews.[37]

Yet the Third Reich was unique for two reasons. In the first place, it was the rising power in Europe, turning the Jewish question into a test of international solidarity and commitment. In addition, it was a country where the political leadership's view on 'the Jewish question' lay far to the right of mainstream public opinion. Even within the government, Hitler was outflanked in the violence of his feeling on the subject only by Goebbels. This could not be said of Pétain, Mussolini, Tiso or Horthy, all of whom espoused what one might call traditionally conservative anti-Semitic views which put them at odds with the racialist hardliners in their own countries. It is therefore not surprising that Heydrich should have begun mass killing in areas where there was no political authority to block him and where the SS enjoyed greatest influence – the occupied eastern territories. Only then, and armed with the prestige gained there, was the SS able to extend the killing policy into the General Government and the Reich itself. And if preventing their own colleagues – in the Interior Ministry, for instance – from raising endless jurisdictional and definitional issues was hard enough, how much harder were the challenges posed by dealing with foreign governments and collaborating administrations. From the moment that the Foreign Ministry's man at Wannsee reminded Heydrich of the need to consult the diplomats in dealings over the Jewish question abroad, the Final Solution entered a different phase, moving from the area of German *Lebensraum* and Greater Germany itself to the countries beyond its borders.

Early warnings of the difficulties that lay ahead were provided by the tortuous negotiations on the question of foreign Jews who were still to be found inside Germany. In late 1941 as it embarked on the first systematic deportations of German Jews, the regime got the Foreign Ministry to approach sympathetic governments to see whether they objected to their own nationals being included. In November, the Bulgarians suggested a common policy towards Jews 'among all European countries'; Luther, the Foreign Ministry official in charge, liked the idea and proposed making all countries introduce German anti-Jewish legislation, effectively stripping foreign Jews of their nationality. If, he suggested, the countries in the Anti-Comintern Pact went ahead with this, it would pressure countries like Hungary where, 'due to the influence of Jewry and Catholic opinion', he foresaw reluctance. His own colleagues, however, in the Legal Office were not so sure: would not such legislation – 'theoretically possible but *unusual* in international usage' – be resisted by other states as an infringement of their national sovereignty? This was precisely the kind of legalistic argument that made

Heydrich and Himmler furious; but in fact, it identified what would become one of the chief obstacles to the extension of the Final Solution: the reluctance of many of Germany's most important allies to do anything which might be construed as diminishing their own sovereignty.[38]

Initially, several countries did seem willing and even eager to cooperate with the Reich. At the Wannsee conference Croatia, Romania, Slovakia and France had been singled out as countries unlikely to prove problematic. All these countries had brought in anti-Jewish laws on the German model, and in France, where public opinion had increasingly blamed the Jews for food shortages and wartime hardships, the regime had introduced anti-Jewish measures as part of its own National Revolution, without any German prompting. Anxious about German plans to use the unoccupied zone as a dumping ground for Jews, Vichy said nothing when the Germans deported a trainload to Auschwitz in March 1942, supposedly in reprisal for resistance attacks. Meanwhile the Romanians and the Croats were busy slaughtering Jews without needing to be told. Both seemed open to the idea of deporting those remaining to German camps. As for Slovakia, this was the source of the first major transportations. The highly anti-Semitic government of Monsignor Josef Tiso responded 'eagerly' in February 1942 when Himmler requested they send 20,000 young able-bodied Jews. Keen for some time to bring back 120,000 Slovak workers from the Reich, the Slovak government believed offering Jews might be a way of negotiating their return. For Himmler this was a godsend: his plan to expand the slave labour population under his control in Auschwitz for the great 'peacetime building projects' had been complicated by delays in organizing the transports from Germany. Slovak enthusiasm suggested an alternative.

Some Slovak Jews were indeed sent to the rapidly expanding Auschwitz camp, thinking that they were part of the previous forced labour programme. 'They went on believing naively, even during the transport, that they were going to work in some factory within the Reich as they had been told,' recollected a survivor of the second women's transport, Margita Schwalbova. Instead arrival brought 'incredible humiliation and shock' as they were stripped, shaven, dressed in old Russian uniforms and put to work demolishing houses, draining ponds and building roads until 'exhausted to death', beaten, gassed or injected with phenol following visits from the SS doctors. In Auschwitz, the news that the Slovak government also wanted to get rid of the families of the initial deportees – at least another 50,000 people – prompted the building of two new gassing rooms at Birkenau that spring. The first selection and gassing of 638 Slovak Jews took place on 4 July.

But Auschwitz was not the Slovaks' only destination. Between late March and mid-June another thirty-eight trains, carrying roughly 40,000 people, including entire families, were sent to the Lublin region to be handed over to the tender mercies of the Einsatz Reinhard staff. Local German officials could not cope with the numbers, and while those transports which reached Lublin were subjected to selection, others were unloaded in transit ghettoes or dispersed in the surrounding villages. Often lodging in the homes of Jews who had already been deported, they were left to their own devices for days and weeks, unfed, or put to work in the fields or in local forced labour camps. It was one of these holding camps – at Izbica, halfway between Lublin and Belzec – that the fearless Polish resistance emissary, Jan Karski, visited disguised as a Ukrainian guard.[39]

That summer, Himmler's plans suffered a serious blow with the assassination of his deputy, Heydrich, in Prague. Himmler responded by pushing Eichmann to accelerate the Final Solution across Europe. Himmler himself had temporarily taken over as head of the RSHA and evidently wanted to demonstrate there would be no slackening of the pace. Visiting Auschwitz on 17 July, he told the commandant, Höss, that the camp would become the destination for Europe's Jews. 'Eichmann's programme will continue,' he told him. 'and will be accelerated every month from now on. See to it you move ahead with the completion of Birkenau. The Gypsies are to be exterminated. With the same relentlessness you will exterminate those Jews who are unable to work.'[40]

The efficient Eichmann did his best to obey. In June, he engineered the Foreign Ministry's agreement to the transportation of 40,000 Jews from France and the Netherlands, as well as 10,000 from Belgium 'to the camp at Auschwitz for labour service': the trains were to begin rolling in mid-July. Yet as news and rumours spread of the death camps, and as it became clear that the Germans' 1942 offensive had failed to knock out the Russians, unease, reservations and even outright opposition to German policy began to make itself felt.

The Slovak channel was the first to close. Thanks to the disarray in the Lublin region, some deportees escaped, and one or two even returned to Slovakia with letters smuggled out of the ghettoes. Knowledge of conditions around Auschwitz started to spread. When the Vatican protested, the government responded with defiance. 'There is no foreign intervention which would stop us on the road to the liberation of Slovakia from Jewry,' insisted President Tiso. 'Is it Christian what happens to the Jews, is it human?' he asked in the course of a speech that August. 'It would have been much worse if we did not clear ourselves of them in time. And we did so according to God's order: "Slovak, throw them away, get rid of your pest." ' But in fact he was paying heed, and the past tense in his speech was significant. Church pressure and public anger resulted in perhaps 20,000 Jews being granted exemptions, effectively bringing the deportations there to an end. 'Evacuation of Jews from Slovakia has reached a deadlock,' the German minister reported in June. Despite strong words from Berlin, only another 4,000 Jews left the country before the final train departed at the end of September.[41]

In France the new administration of Pierre Laval was also torn: was the pursuit of sovereignty better served by obeying German wishes or resisting them? In the summer of 1942 French prestige had apparently been reinforced by agreeing to deportations; they were the quid pro quo for preserving the authority of the French police. But when Laval was informed that the Germans wanted to deport more Jews to Auschwitz 'for labour service', Vichy reacted cautiously, emphasizing that it regarded French nationals very differently from foreign or stateless Jews: the Germans were forced to agree, and the summer's deportations started with the latter. The same policy had to be followed in Belgium and the Netherlands.[42]

As the summer proceeded, things went from bad to worse from Eichmann's point of view. An agreement with the Romanians that he had brokered behind the back of the Foreign Ministry unravelled when the Romanian commissar on Jewish affairs was deliberately snubbed on a visit to the Ministry. The Romanians, as we have seen, yielded nothing to the Germans in the fervour of their anti-Semitism; yet German diplomacy in Romania – in the hands of an utterly incompetent Nazi placeman – was a disaster. Moreover the Romanian government, like the Slovaks, was becoming conscious of many reasons why they should treat the Germans' demands with reserve. In the first place, the Jews' economic importance in the country could not be overlooked. Secondly, reports of what had been happening in the border provinces had disturbed many Romanians who were far less shy of voicing their criticisms than their counterparts in Germany. Even the Antonescu government was feeling disillusioned: it had committed the Romanian army to the German war effort, but it had come no closer to getting northern Transylvania back. Yet open defiance would not help either. It therefore played for time, sounding sympathetic to the German viewpoint but doing nothing.[43]

The sense of frustration in Berlin was palpable. At the end of September, Ribbentrop ordered the Foreign Ministry to 'hurry as much as possible the evacuation of Jews from the various countries of Europe'. It was easier in occupied areas that lay under direct German control, especially those with a well-run civil service. The Dutch, who were pioneers in the use of data registration and identity technology, had created a central registry for Jews which impressed even the German police. Some 45,000 were transported by mid-October, with the help of the Dutch authorities; the population were reportedly 'making no trouble whatsoever'. The Norwegian police proved similarly compliant. But all of this simply made the German Foreign Ministry look worse, since it was precisely in the countries from which they were excluded that deportations were going ahead.[44] The Danes, for instance, made it clear that German demands for the introduction of anti-Jewish discriminatory measures would pose severe constitutional problems and force the government to resign. Unwilling to push things to such a point, given the country's extensive economic value to the Reich and the relatively small Jewish population, the Germans decided on a gradual approach that would not force the issue. But that was perhaps because Denmark was a side-issue: the Hungarians and the Italians were causing far more of a problem.[45]

Hungary had a very large Jewish population (around 700,000); Italy was the Reich's chief ally in Europe. Both were evidently opposed to the policy of deporting Jews to the East. The Hungarians had not initially shown such scruples, forcing thousands of Galician and Slovak Jews across the ex-Soviet border in August 1941 to be shot. Hungarian Jews had been removed from the army and put into special frontline labour battalions (where many died). But when German diplomats told the Hungarians in 1942 to introduce further anti-Jewish legislation before sending them east, Prime Minister Miklos Kallay explicitly warned the Germans that this was 'an internal Hungarian matter'. This was the nub of the issue for the Hungarians – and not only for them. It was not a question primarily of anti-Semites versus pro-Semites (though this sometimes entered into it too) but rather of the dynamics of an alliance of unequals, in which one side tries to force the issue and the other resists for the sake of asserting its own freedom of manoeuvre. For both, the Jewish question had turned into a test of the nature of their relationship.

This led to a series of increasingly exasperated and increasingly high-level diplomatic duels. In December 1942, Budapest told the Germans they would not introduce the yellow star or agree to the deportation of Hungarian Jews to the East. The following month, a number of Hungarian Jewish families were repatriated from Brussels and Amsterdam for their own safety. Hungary, Germany's ally, was actually turning into a Jewish refuge as the tides of war turned against the Reich, and Budapest searched vainly for a way to extricate itself. In January 1943 an exasperated German Foreign Ministry official struck a very undiplomatic note with the Hungarian ambassador, Sztójay, telling him that 'the Führer is determined under all circumstances to remove all Jews from Europe during the war' and that 'it fills us with very great alarm, that one country alone in the middle of Europe, friendly to us, shelters some one million Jews. We could not view this danger passively in the long run.'

Hitler himself launched a violent attack on Hungarian policy when he met the regent, Horthy, that April. For his part, Horthy reminded the Führer that there were many baptized Jews in Hungary, many of them 'estimable people'. He had done all one could against Jews but 'one could scarcely murder them or otherwise do away with them'. Hitler cannot have been used to such plain speaking and responded with passion. Why had the Hungarians not done as the Slovaks had done? Ridding the country of Jews would open up opportunities for Hungarians. And people who talked about Jews being murdered forgot 'there was only one murderer – the Jew'. The following day, when they were joined by Ribbentrop, the subject came up again, this time even less ambiguously. Ribbentrop, who was less guarded in his words than Hitler, told the Hungarian point-blank that 'the Jews must either be annihilated [vernichtet] or sent to a concentration camp. There is no other possibility.' Hitler himself then weighed in. 'They are simply parasites. We have put Poland properly in order. If the Jews there did not wish to work, they were shot. They are like tubercular bacilli infecting a healthy body.' For the Germans, as the Hungarian ambassador lost no time in pointing out, Hungary's stance on the Jewish question had become a test of its commitment to the alliance with Germany. The Hungarians passed a new Jewish law which made many Jews unemployed. But they did little more, refusing either to issue markings or to cut back Jewish rations.[46]

Even more troubling for the Germans – because harder to deal with – was the uncooperative attitude of their leading allies, the Italians. Like the Hungarians and the Romanians, the prewar Italian regime had brought in racial legislation which discriminated against Jews. Yet the country's Jewish population was small and highly assimilated, and there was little understanding or tradition of the racial animus which prompted Nazi policy. Through 1942 internal rivalries in the German Foreign Ministry meant that there was relatively little diplomatic pressure exerted on Rome. Ribbentrop himself insisted on handling relations. But since he did not get round to raising the Jewish issue until 1943, for a long time the evident resistance and foot-dragging by Italian officials in the Balkans went largely unchallenged. In the summer of 1942, the Italian plenipotentiary in Greece had refused an RSHA proposal to introduce the marking of Jews in Italian-controlled territory; indeed, he added that, if the Germans went ahead in their zone, Italian Jews must be exempted. When the German military authorities in Greece began conscripting Jews for road building in their zone, many fled south to Italian protection.[47]

Nor were the Italians any more obliging in Yugoslavia. On the contrary, since 1941 many senior administrators had been so horrified by the genocidal violence of the Ustaše, that they had been doing their best to shield the potential victims. When the Croat government incarcerated more than two-thirds of the Croatian Jews in concentration camps, others sought refuge in the Italian zone. Bastianini, the governor of Dalmatia, sent some back and others into internment in Italy. But his colleagues were more sympathetic. Informed of Ustaše massacres against the Jews in the town of Mostar, the diplomat Pietromarchi was outraged: 'For this regression, which dishonours humanity, we are indebted to our friend, Germany.' And he remonstrated with Bastianini that handing 'undesirable' Jews back to the Croats meant 'to condemn them to extermination. Italy and the Army must avoid the shame of making themselves accomplices in such wickedness.' Senior army officers agreed. Facilitating such massacres would besmirch their reputation. Learning that the Italians were supposed to help round up Jews and hand them over to the Germans, General Paride Negri protested: 'That is totally impossible, because the deportation of Jews goes against the honour of the Italian army.'[48]

In August 1942, Ribbentrop officially requested Italian help, and Mussolini appeared to assent, scrawling the phrase 'nulla osta' (no objection) on the memo he had been sent. But the main civil and military commanders in Croatia were perfectly ready to go round the Duce. Delivery of the Jews was 'out of the question', General Roatta told Pietromarchi. Humanitarianism was involved (it is evident that, for senior Italian officials like Roatta, this concept encompassed Yugoslav Jews but not, say, the Ethiopians or the Senussi). But Roatta was concerned as well for Italian prestige. Blocking the Croats and the Germans reminded both that this was supposed to be an area where the Italians had primacy. The more Pavelić assured the Germans he would sort out the Jewish issue wherever he had power, the more incentive the Italians had to prevent him.[49]

By late 1942, high-level Italians were well aware of the fate that awaited the Jews. Mussolini himself was told by one of his key aides, the Carabinieri general Giuseppe Pièche, that Croatian Jews delivered to the Germans had been ' "liquidated" by poisonous gas in the railroad cars in which they were locked'. Reluctant to refuse the Germans outright, the commanders of the Italian 2nd Army announced publicly that, while Italian Jews in Croatia would be placed under their protection, they would round up the Croatian Jews and deliver them to Zagreb. This news prompted many Jewish refugees under their control to commit suicide. What they did not know was that the 2nd Army had no desire to hand them over. Playing for time, it kept them in Italian camps on the mainland until the spring of 1943, when they were sent to the island of Rab. Unlike the Slovenes already held there, who were dying from lack of food, the Jews received enough to keep them alive. Liberated by the partisans when Italy surrendered in 1943, they were among the many Balkan Jewish beneficiaries of Italian policy.

That such an extraordinary outcome could take place owed little to the Duce's own inclinations; rather, it reflected his relatively weak grip over the Italian state. He listened attentively as Göring, Ribbentrop and Himmler all visited him to urge him to hand Jews over in Croatia (and, later, France). But although he seemed to agree with them that 'Italy must not become the protector of Jews', and blamed the 'sentimental humanitarianism' of his generals, he was swayed when his underlings argued the contrary. His generals warned him that, if Italy handed over the Jews to the Ustaše, then it would lose the trust of the Orthodox population as well, undermining its whole Yugoslav policy. And even Bastianini, who had been promoted to the number two job in the Foreign Ministry, had changed his mind and now spelled out the extermination policy in definite terms. 'We know the fate that awaits the Jews who are deported by the Germans,' he reminded the Duce. 'They are gassed. All of them – women, old men, and children. We will have no part in such atrocities. And you, Duce, must not allow it. Are you prepared to take this responsibility on yourself?'[50]

There is no evidence that the Duce felt strongly either way. He liked to sound tough when speaking with the Germans but in practice generally threw the burden of decision back on his underlings. He had allowed his prefects on the Yugoslav border to turn Jewish refugees away well after it had become clear what their fate would be. But keeping refugees out was one thing; becoming complicit in extermination quite another. Here he tried to avoid making decisions of his own, especially those which would reduce his room for manoeuvre and tie him ever more closely to the Germans. Roatta did manage to convince him in December 1942 that the Croatian Jews should not be immediately handed back to the Croats. On the other hand, he also had the cynical advice of his confidant, General Pièche, which was to make sure, if he felt 'the handing over, and therefore the extermination' must go ahead, to get the Croats to do their own dirty work and keep the Italian army out of it. In Mussolini's mind, at least, interning the Croatian Jews was the perfect solution because it kept all his options open.[51]

In March 1943, the Germans became fed up with the Italians dragging their heels in Greece as well and deported the large Jewish community of Thessaloniki. They also got the Bulgarians to deport the Greek Jews under their control. The Bulgarians agreed to this while insisting that they would decide separately what to do with Jews who were Bulgarian citizens. The Greek government, in a much weaker position, had privately protested; but local officials in Thessaloniki cooperated readily for fear that the Germans would otherwise hand the city over to Bulgarian rule. In both cases, Italian consular officials shielded Jews with Italian passports and did their best to extend their protection to others.

Here too the humanitarian impulse which unquestionably prompted the officials themselves, who, after all, could see with their own eyes what was happening, has to be set alongside the political aspect. By early 1943, with the war moving decisively against the Axis, and the Hungarians and others pressuring Italy to push for a negotiated peace, the Jewish question took on a new significance. Showing that Italy still had the power to block German wishes was now even more valuable diplomatically than it had been the previous summer. And there were economic motives, too – namely, protecting a prosperous community with traditionally pro-Italian feelings. As the Italian plenipotentiary in Athens put it, 'there were a thousand reasons ranging from our humanity to our prestige' for refusing to intern Jews in the Italian zone. Very similar considerations explain Italian policy in south-eastern France when it occupied that part of the country in November 1942: Rome protested when Vichy police carried out round-ups and insisted racial policy was purely a matter for the occupying power. What mattered above all was upholding Italian prestige: some Jews were fortunate enough to benefit. Although one need not entirely dismiss the idea of the humanitarian Italian – the *brava gente* which is so easily contrasted with the brutal Germans – as a self-serving postwar myth, there can be little doubt that Italy's diplomats and generals saw perfectly strong and self-interested political reasons for doing what they could to chart their own course on Europe's Jewish Question.[52]

The comparison between the 'sense of high justice and humanity' of Italian fascism and the 'brutality and rapaciousness' of their Nazi allies actually started with Italian fascist officials themselves. If their analysis of the bankruptcy of German modes of rule was astute it was also self-serving for it rescued, for the realm of ideals, a purer and more politically sophisticated notion of fascism from the genocidal grime of the war's reality. 'This is one of the darkest ages of human history, perhaps the darkest – never has there been such slaughter', the Pope told an Italian diplomat in January 1943. 'And yet,' Pietromarchi replied, 'amid so much wickedness the Italians have been immune to the fever . . . The instinct by which our soldiers are repelled by atrocity has been bred by Christianity.' And he confided to his diary his belief that 'one day account would be taken of our people's humanitarianism'. A few months later, General Pièche made the same point. 'The German authorities reproach us for protecting the Jews and for not supporting them in their racial campaign, as Bulgaria has done. Yet I believe that our behaviour, inspired as it is by the principles of humanity, will one day be recognized as the most opportune at the present time.' Already convinced that the war was lost, much of fascism's elite hoped that prudence and humanitarianism might eventually converge.[53]

Thus the longer the war went on, the less inclined Germany's allies were to consider handing over their own nationals – even Jews – into German hands. The Bulgarians and the Romanians played along and bluffed their way through the rest of the war. Having consigned Greek Jews to Treblinka, the Bulgarians formed Jewish labour battalions, which they sent out into the countryside, as much to protect Bulgarian Jews from the Germans as anything else. As for the Antonescu government, this was now worrying that the prestige of the government was being damaged by the deportations. Was it not looking like a German puppet since other allied governments – notably Hungary – had not stooped to deportations or ghettoization? In October 1942, transports of Jews across the Dniester were suspended. The strong opposition of the Romanian Queen Mother helped, though strategic and diplomatic calculations probably weighed as much. The government simply ignored the Germans' objections, and Marshal Antonescu's conversations on the subject with Hitler did not conceal their disagreement. 'The Führer was of the opinion, different to the Marshal, that the more radically one treats the Jews the better,' the minutes of their discussion record. When Antonescu was asked by Ribbentrop whether Romanian Jews could not be sent to Russia, he said he wanted to move 100,000 to work in mines in the Crimea. 'He requests, however,' we read, 'that they should not be murdered, since on a previous occasion he found himself forced to stop the deportation of Jews to Russia when it was revealed that they had been purely and simply murdered there.' It was hard to believe this was the same man who had ordered more than 18,000 Jews in Odessa to be killed. But Antonescu could see which way the wind was blowing.[54]

Bulgaria and Romania switched sides before the Germans could stop them. But even when the Germans forestalled defections by marching in and occupying their former allies – as they did in Italy and Hungary – they quickly found that this did not necessarily bring greater control. In France, they overran the previously unoccupied zone in November 1942: yet the number of Jews deported in 1943 and 1944 was less than those deported in 1942. Eichmann's henchman Dannecker, who had initiated the deportations previously in France, did not do much better after he was sent to Rome in 1943. His squad organized the transport of Italian Jews to Auschwitz within a few days of its arrival. From Trieste, Globocnik sent more than 1,100 Jews northwards right up until February 1945. Yet probably some 40,000 Italian Jews survived the war (out of a prewar population of 50,000), whether in hiding or with the resistance. The Germans had more success in mainland Greece, which they took over from the Italians at the same time, but there too far more Jews survived in hiding than had done earlier in northern Greece.

The country they were most concerned about was Hungary, home to the largest Jewish community left in Europe. This was, of course, immediately endangered by the Wehrmacht's takeover in March 1944, and up to July 1944 more than 435,000 Hungarian Jews were sent to Auschwitz, far more than from any other country: never before or after, as the authors of a recent history of the camp make clear, was it 'less efficient as a labour exchange' or 'more efficient as a killing center'. Approximately 175,000 Jews had arrived at the camp in 1942; nearly 105,000 between January and March 1943, and 160,000 between April 1943 and March 1944. The Hungarian transports thus marked the apogee of its murderous career. In May and June 1944 no fewer than one-third of the entire total of approximately one million people murdered there were killed. The fivefold rise in the monthly death toll outstripped even the new incinerators' official capacity of 132,000 corpses monthly.[55]

Yet Hungary was not only the moment of Eichmann's greatest triumph but also the effective end of his career in genocide, for at this point something unprecedented occurred and Admiral Horthy, who still remained the regent of a nominally sovereign country, decided to halt the deportations in mid-flow. The Pope, Roosevelt and the King of Sweden, among others, were clamouring for him to act, and news of the Normandy landings and the Red Army's thrusting advance westwards convinced him of the need to find a way out of the war. By this point, both the Germans and their allies understood that complicity in the Final Solution demonstrated loyalty, and that conversely rebuffing it was a way of signalling the desire to disengage from the Axis. By intervening in the Ministry of the Interior and replacing gendarmerie units with loyal army regiments, the seventy-five-year-old Horthy stopped Eichmann's plans in their tracks and prevented Budapest's Jews in particular from being deported. Eichmann was astounded. 'This won't do at all,' he exclaimed. Yet without Hungarian cooperation, he could not proceed, and indeed in September Himmler ordered his unit to be wound up. The following month, Horthy was removed by the Germans and replaced by the extreme rightist and former Habsburg army officer Ferenc Szálasi. Yet Szálasi too was unwilling to hand Hungarian Jews over to the Germans, and by the end of 1944 the deportations had effectively been halted. Instead, his anti-Semitic Arrow Cross movement expanded the Hungarians' own forced labour programme, and, as public order broke down, its members went on a killing spree. Under siege and shelled by the Red Army from December, the Szálasi government left the capital and retreated to the west of the country, leaving Budapest to endure some of the worst violence of the war as local death squads rampaged through the streets massacring Jews.

The halt in deportations from Hungary and the abrupt deterioration in the German strategic position in the summer of 1944 opened up the possibility of something much more radical – a return to the emigration policy that the Germans had abandoned in 1941. Inside Budapest and in neutral venues abroad, Jewish and German agents embarked upon secret discussions to buy the release of Hungarian Jews for money or goods. The motives of the Jews concerned were easy enough to understand – whether acting as individuals or as members of political or relief organizations, their goal was to save as many Jews as possible from certain death. The real historical controversy surrounds the German side. How serious were these negotiations and what were they designed to achieve?

We should note in the first place that the idea of making exceptions to the killing policy had been built into the system from the start. As the war went on, Himmler in particular saw the Jews as a useful lever of influence with the British and the Americans. Convinced of their extensive power over Allied policy, and worried by the Red Army's rapid advances into Poland, Romania and Bulgaria, he hoped that negotiations over Jews might serve as a kind of peace feeler to the West. In 1943, he had already set up a small section inside the camp at Bergen-Belsen for 'privileged Jews' with relatives abroad. The idea was that they would both publicize their friendly treatment in German hands and be hostages for any unfavourable turn in Allied policy. Similar reasoning now led him to bless efforts to strike a deal in which Jews would be freed in return for deliveries of war materiel. Yet none of this could go very far. Himmler's anti-Semitism greatly exaggerated the degree of influence that Jewish organizations wielded over British or American policy: in fact, they could do little in the face of clear instructions from their governments not to pursue negotiations with a 'political' content. For Churchill and Roosevelt, the key was the policy of unconditional surrender – which meant no separate negotiations with the Germans – and the alliance with the USSR.[56]

Above all Hitler, to whom Himmler remained loyal, had no intention of allowing large numbers of Jews to escape. Thus there were only small gestures. Members of the Hungarian industrialist clan the Weiss family, for example, were flown to Portugal in return for control of their armaments factory, which Himmler wanted for the Waffen-SS. Himmler himself remained committed to the Final Solution, and through the summer and autumn of 1944 he battled against first the Wehrmacht and then Speer's requests for Jewish labourers: 100,000 Hungarian Jews were, exceptionally, sent to work in arms factories. The Łódź ghetto – the last surviving Jewish centre in former Poland – was liquidated, and the Chelmno death camp was reactivated for that purpose. In fact, as camps on the fringes of the Reich were emptied in the face of enemy advance, their inmates were either killed, allowed to die on pointless death marches or herded into other camps inside the Reich, where overcrowding, overwork, the lack of supplies, disease and the brutality of the guards soon caused the mortality rate to soar.

In the spring of 1945, Himmler did discreetly entertain renewed efforts by neutrals to intervene and save some inmates. Discussions with Jean-Marie Musy, a former president of Switzerland, to liberate the camps collapsed after Hitler got to hear about the release of 1,200 Jews and furiously forbade further contact. In February, Count Bernadotte, vice-chairman of the Swedish Red Cross, proposed bringing all Danish and Norwegian prisoners to Sweden; eventually thousands of prisoners were saved in this way. For Himmler, who involved himself in these negotiations despite Hitler's unambiguous prohibition, they represented a means of opening a dialogue that could perhaps be extended to the much larger question of negotiating Germany's exit from the war. [57]

This was surely the reasoning behind Himmler's most extraordinary encounter – the secret talks that he held in Berlin with Norbert Masur, a German Jewish émigré whose rescue mission was conducted in the name of the World Jewish Congress. Accompanied by Himmler's Finnish masseur, Felix Kersten, Masur flew in from Stockholm on 19 April on a flight loaded with Red Cross packages. Germany's capitulation was only a few weeks away. Driven in a Gestapo car with dimmed lights through 'the ghost-like ruins, past endless piles of rubble', they arrived – after several nerve-racking stops – at Kersten's estate, about forty miles outside Berlin, not far from the Ravensbrück women's camp. The next day Himmler was delayed by Hitler's birthday celebrations – his relations with Hitler, which had already deteriorated badly, would have taken a sharp turn for the worse if the latter had known about Masur's visit – and Masur spent the morning talking with Walter Schellenberg, Himmler's youthful head of foreign intelligence, whom he found deeply depressed and convinced Germany's defeat was not far off. Schellenberg warned Masur that, although he supported his mission, Hitler was totally opposed to any rescue bids and had completely lost his temper after hearing about the earlier Swiss negotiations. In the afternoon, Masur wandered around the estate. Finally, at 2.30 in the morning, a car pulled up and Himmler arrived.

We sat at a table, which was set up for coffee for five persons. Himmler was dressed impeccably in his uniform with the insignias of rank and shiny decorations. He looked well groomed, seemed fresh and lively in spite of the late hour, outwardly quiet, and in control. He looked better in person than in photographs. Perhaps his errant and piercing gaze was an expression of sadism and harshness; however, had I not known his past, I would never have believed that this man was singularly responsible for the most extensive mass murders in history.

As they sipped their drinks, with sugar and cakes brought from Sweden, Himmler launched into a lengthy monologue. He defended German policy against the Jews and blamed them for the country's ills. He claimed he had always wanted a policy of expulsion, but that this had failed because of the world's refusal to accept Jewish refugees. The war then brought Germany into contact with 'the Jewish masses of the East', who were proletarians, partisans and diseased. To Masur's question how Jews could have helped the partisans when they were in ghettoes, Himmler responded that they had been shooting at German troops from *inside*. The crematoria were solely a health measure; the war against the

Russians purely preventive. As for the camps, he now wished he had called them 'education camps', as the name would not have produced the same unfavourable reactions. Keen to defend himself, the Reichführer was aggrieved at the bad publicity and 'hate propaganda' that had greeted the discovery of Bergen-Belsen and Buchenwald. Masur responded by asking what practical measures might be taken to change things and managed to get him to agree – after a brief private discussion with Schellenberg and his adjutant Brandt – to release 1,000 Jewish women inmates from Ravensbrück. They were, Himmler insisted, to be described as 'Polish'. After two and a half hours, the talks finished. Masur was struck by Himmler's calmness, his cynicism regarding the fate of the Germans ('the best part of them will be destroyed with us; what happens to the rest is immaterial') and his lack of personal passion (unlike Hitler) regarding the Jews.

Later that morning, Masur drove back through the devastated suburbs to Tempelhof airport. He passed endless carts of German refugees, loaded with their possessions, fleeing the front and the fighter planes, and long columns of prisoners from the nearby Oranienburg camp being marched north. And there was Berlin itself – 'a field of ruins of unbelievable dimensions' – the façades of bombed-out houses looming over the deserted streets. At the airport he was seen off by the rumble of Soviet artillery, an SS honour guard and a 'Heil Hitler', and landed only two hours later, safely, in Copenhagen; 'it was a wonderful feeling to be again in a city where there were no damaged houses and people were calm and well dressed'. Some 7,500 women from Ravensbrück eventually arrived in Sweden, having been driven on trucks through Denmark.[58]

They were the lucky ones. In Ravensbrück itself, the site of medical experiments, forced sterilizations and unspeakable acts of sadism, systematic gassings and other killing had been going on for several months: only 40,000 of the approximately 130,000 women who were interned there survived. Those executed included women members of Britain's SOE, and of the Polish resistance: it was not a camp specifically for Jews. An important centre of labour for the armaments industries near by (Siemens was one of the main employers), by early 1945 it had become seriously overcrowded with arrivals from Auschwitz and other camps to the East. For most of these inmates, the intervention of Masur and the Swedish Red Cross was too late. Even babies and pregnant women had been gassed – more than 2,000 by April – and after the last transport left, 15,000 survivors were marched away into the countryside, shot by SS guards when they could not keep up; only a few thousand sick and dying inmates, mostly women, were still there when the Red Army liberated the camp a week later.[59]

COVERING UP: THE ENDGAME

When reports of the first massacres in the occupied Eastern territories in 1941 had reached Germany, the Nazi regime, as we have seen, had been forced to acknowledge the disquiet. Thus at the same time as it intensified its propaganda drive, blaming the Jews for their own fate, it also increased secrecy, especially regarding involvement of the gassing specialists. From the winter of 1941/2, the Operation Reinhard extermination camps in particular were constructed in an atmosphere of the utmost confidentiality. When the SS officer Max Täubner was tried – in a most unusual case – by an SS court in Munich, it was not his unauthorized murder of thousands of Jews which was punished but his bragging, his boasts that he had gone east to 'get rid of at least 20,000 Jews', and his habit of showing off his grisly collection of photographs. Täubner appealed in his defence to the existence of a Führer order to kill Jews. But he was reminded that extermination was a state secret, then sentenced to ten years' imprisonment, expelled from the SS and deprived of his civil rights for behaviour that was 'unworthy of an honorable and decent German man'. The guilty verdict against him fulfilled two functions: by making it clear that it was permissible to kill Jews 'for purely political motives' as opposed to 'self-seeking, sadistic or sexual' ones, it showed once again the absence of legal obstacles to mass murder. And simultaneously, it reaffirmed the highly confidential character of the Final Solution and the duty upon those involved not to talk about it.[60]

Even before the Täubner case, in which he took a close interest, Himmler had been concerned about secrecy. As the first denunciations of German mass murder appeared in the Allied press in the autumn and winter of 1942, he ordered Gestapo chief Heinrich Müller to make sure that all the bodies were either buried or burned. Murder on such a vast scale had already created embarrassing environmental problems. Unlike the Romanians, who had merely left corpses by the roadside in the killings of 1941, or floating down the river Bug, the Germans had buried them in pits. Yet at the Chelmno death camp, the spring thaw left defrosted bodies floating in large pools, spreading such a stench that complaints came in from surrounding villages. Threats to local health and drinking supplies were also reported around the Reinhard death camps. The German military governor near Treblinka reported to his superiors that autumn that 'the Jews in Treblinka were not covered properly with earth. Due to this, the air is saturated with an unbearable stench of bodies.' With the rapid expansion of the Final Solution the pressure grew to find an answer.[61]

Standartenführer Paul Blobel, who had served in the First World War as a military engineer and had more recently been responsible for the SS death squad which organized the Babi Yar massacres outside Kiev, was the man Himmler chose for the job. Starting with Auschwitz and Chelmno, Blobel ordered that the huge burial pits be uncovered and their remains burned, either in special crematoria or on huge bonfires. He issued similar instructions for Belzec, Sobibor and Treblinka, and his underlings visited the camps to make sure the burning of the hundreds of thousands of bodies proceeded according to instructions.

In 1943, they also began to tackle dozens of the more dispersed killing sites in the former USSR. Small units from his Operation 1005 staff, a group of SiPo/SD men sworn to secrecy, visited these sites and organized groups of Jewish prisoners to do the physical work of uncovering the bodies and burning them. In August 1943, two years after his last visit, Blobel returned to the Babi Yar ravine. By now, the corpses of his Jewish victims – more than 30,000 – lay under newer layers, of executed Soviet prisoners of war, partisans and civilians. The prisoner details were usually Jews who were executed upon the completion of their task, often being burned upon the same pyres they had been working on. In at least one case, they were transported to work in a gas van in which they were then killed. By the winter of 1943/4, Blobel's men had also traversed the killing fields of the Baltic and Belorussia. Yet although they burned a huge number of bodies, the speed of the Red Army's advance caught them by surprise. In Estonia, Soviet troops found the bonfires still burning when they arrived.

Limited to the last two years of the war, and primarily concerned with the General Government and the occupied eastern territories, 'Operation 1005' thus failed to destroy all the evidence. The task itself was an impossible one. The Reinhard death-camps had been razed to the ground in 1943; only traces survived for late twentieth-century archaeologists and forensic scientists to tell where they had once stood. And following the Soviet publicity of their gruesome finds at the liberation of Lublin-Majdanek in the summer of 1944, Himmler tried to speed up the removal of mass graves. Camps were closed down, and their inmates were forced to trek away from the front, or shot. But the genocide had simply been on too wide a scale, and the Red Army's advance was much too fast, to allow for a complete cover-up. In late 1944, Himmler ordered the gas chambers and crematoria at Auschwitz-Birkenau to be demolished. Gangs of prisoners were commanded to dynamite the walls, strew the human ash remains in the Vistula and level the old burning pits themselves and plant them with trees. But it was all too little, too late. The prisoners themselves were determined that evidence of the crime should remain. As it was, when the Russians reached Auschwitz, at the end of January 1945, they found ailing prisoners, buildings and documents. Frozen corpses lay in the snow, or piled up inside sheds. The camp's warehouses contained mountains of suitcases, sacks of hair, prayer-shawls and the other remains of the camp's million victims.

As the boundaries of Greater Germany shrank, and the Red Army pressed ever closer to Berlin, came the final reversal in German policy. From the start, the overriding goal had been to rid Germany of Jews, by any means. Now, however, as camp after camp was evacuated, the prisoners – or those at least able to survive the long train journeys in unheated cattle-cars, or the marches on foot through the freezing cold – were sent into Germany proper. SS orders mandated that none should be allowed to fall into enemy hands alive. Sick prisoners were to be shot, and the camps themselves dismantled or blown up before departure. Eichmann himself appears to have encouraged camp commanders to kill as many Jews as possible. By the spring of 1945 the policy of 'mass liquidation of prisoners' seems to have been more widely discussed. Germany now became the centre of the killing. Death marches wound their way aimlessly through country towns, while trainloads of frozen corpses stood in station sidings. An astonishing 35–40,000 people died of disease and starvation in Bergen-Belsen alone in the final weeks before liberation. It is estimated that of the 600,000 prisoners liberated from the camps by the Allies in 1945 approximately 100,000 were Jewish; 80–100,000 had died in the preceding few months.[62]

GENOCIDE AND THE NAZI EMPIRE

The Final Solution was driven by Nazi ideology and by Hitler's personal animus. Nevertheless, what happened to the Jews of Europe grew out of the circumstances of the war and fluctuated according to its fortunes. Despite most countries' reluctance to accept Jewish refugees, forced emigration – the policy until early 1941 – had sharply reduced the Jewish population in prewar Germany; but this ceased to be politically practicable once the Germans conquered Poland and its far larger Jewish population fell into their hands. The way Himmler described it to Masur, the Germans had somehow stumbled into the great centres of east European Jewry and it certainly seems that, whatever memoranda the specialists had been drawing up, the leaders of the Third Reich had given very little advance thought to the problem.

Only with the invasion of the USSR did a very new policy emerge against the backdrop of ever more ambitious plans to solve Europe's ethnic problems generally through wholesale forced population movements. The 'war of annihilation' against Judeo-Bolshevism launched genocide against the Jews living inside the Soviet Union's 1941 borders. This then provided a murderous precedent for how to treat Jews inside the Greater German Reich, and they were transported in their turn to the Eastern killing-fields. Now thinking about Europe as a whole, Hitler for the first time envisaged the extinction of Jewish life on the continent. At first with no clear end date in view, things changed rapidly as the new death camps of Operation Reinhard demonstrated that the largest Jewish population in Europe could actually be killed inside a year. Relying on the vastly expanded camp at Auschwitz rather than on the much smaller Reinhard camps, in the summer of 1942 Hitler and Himmler decided to kill Europe's Jews as quickly as they could while exploiting the labour of those capable of working. But the diplomatic and logistical challenges of a continentally coordinated policy of mass murder were substantial to begin with and grew harder with time as Germany's position in the war deteriorated. Approximately 1.1 million Jews were killed in 1941 in the East (more than ten times the number the previous year), and with the extermination of Polish Jewry the following year the death toll soared to 2.7 million. But quantitatively, these two years represented the climax of the genocide. The number of victims fell to 500,000 in 1943 and to 600,000 in 1944. These were still huge numbers, reflecting the destruction of venerable European Jewish communities. But, from the Nazi standpoint, they also reflected growing resistance to a policy that they had thought would unite the whole of the continent behind them.[63]

Attitudes to Jews certainly affected the life chances of those fleeing the slaughter. Little is sadder in the whole grim story than the accounts of Jewish women and children emerging out of the Polish woods to give themselves up at gendarmerie posts asking to be shot. Their certainty that they were doomed if they relied on local Christians is chilling. Elsewhere – in the Italian, French or Greek countryside, for instance – attitudes were very different and allowed many more to hide. Yet the view outlined here suggests that, if we turn to the international level and ask what affected policy, what really counted was not so much attitudes to Jews per se but where the Jewish question fitted into the war aims and political relations of Germany and her allies. If we want to understand the scale and intensity of deportation, it is timing and politics that are of critical importance.

Vichy provided the classic case: Laval and his police chief René Bousquet, for instance, were less anti-Semitic men than Pétain and Xavier Vallat, but it was they who were really responsible for sending France's Jews east. So long as Germany seemed to be winning the war, it was easier for Berlin to get the vital cooperation of local police forces, railway authorities and others. But as it became clearer that the Jews were not primarily being deported for labour, and as the Allies denounced German policy, so the Germans found it harder to get their own way. Popular opinion was frequently shocked as more and more became known. And for elites, deporting Jews raised issues of sovereignty to which the Germans had not been sensitive in the past. Refusing to help was a relatively straightforward way for the Hungarians, Italians and others to signal their desire to escape their alliance with Berlin in exactly the same way that helping them had been a marker of their loyalty earlier. That most of the politicians involved were anti-Semites with inflated expectations of Jewish influence over Allied policy made them all the keener to distance themselves from Himmler and his men. This is why the Final Solution was most successful in 1941 and 1942 and ran into stiffer resistance thereafter. Hitler's will to annihilation was undaunted, but the costs rose steadily.

And there is one final point to bear in mind: because the Final Solution of the Jewish Question emerged out of even more ambitious Nazi plans for a racial reorganization of much of eastern Europe – plans which were never clearly defined and constantly changed – the boundaries of the killing were always unclear. In Germany the sensitivity of this issue could be seen in the lengthy discussions among lawyers and civil servants over who qualified for exemption for deportation. The Jews certainly occupied a special place in the political demonology of the Third Reich. But there were disquieting indications that the Jews constituted only one – albeit the most urgent – of the regime's ethnic targets. It had already embarked on the killing of the mentally and physically handicapped – those 'lives unworthy of life'. And during the war, instructions were issued in many areas of occupied Europe to treat gypsies 'like the Jews'. Indeed many *were* murdered, for there were long-standing policies that targeted gypsies not only in Germany but also in Hungary, Romania and Slovakia, and a separate 'gypsy camp' was established in Auschwitz. In the Baltic states, both native and German police registered and rounded up gypsies, killing many of them and deporting others to labour camps. Policy towards the gypsies was less consistent, however, and they were clearly not such a priority for Hitler himself. On the other hand, Justice Minister Thierack ordered unambiguously in September 1942 that 'Gypsies [in police custody] should be exterminated unconditionally.' Perhaps quarter of a million – and maybe more – were killed, many of them gassed in Belzec and Auschwitz.[64]

There were also indications that once the SS was done with the Jews it planned to turn on some of the Slavs. Heydrich had predicted eventual exile to Siberia for those millions of Czechs who could not be assimilated. That clearly meant their death. Germany's leading racial scientists were already discussing 'the extermination of the Russian people', and the brutality of Globocnik's Zamosc evictions aroused foreboding in the Polish countryside: rumours circulated widely that once the Jews had been gassed, the Poles would be next. The territorial commander in the General Government warned that one of the key catalysts for resistance in Poland was that the Poles saw 'an atrocious picture of their own destiny' in what had been done to the Jews. Warsaw's sanitary officer, Wilhelm Hagen, actually lost his job when he sent Hitler a letter protesting at plans to treat 70,000 of the 200,000 Poles facing resettlement – old people and children – 'in the same manner as the Jews'. If this was what a middle-ranking member of the German administration believed, it is not surprising that many Poles anticipated something similar.[65]

Nor was this entirely fantasy. As we have seen, Globocnik's genocidal initiatives were primarily impelled by the desire to extinguish both Jewish and Polish life in the region, and he did indeed send many Polish families to the camps, selecting – as he did with the Jews – between those able to work and the rest. In this sense, the fate of the Jews – so closely bound up as it was with Hitler's own political vision – perhaps gestured towards the even wider horizons of annihilation that lay ahead in the event of a Nazi victory.

13
Collaboration

We find ourselves today in this appalling situation – that the fate of France no longer depends upon the French.

Marc Bloch, *Strange Defeat:*
A Statement of Evidence Written in 1940 (1968), 174

The French, as the only Great Power to fall under German domination, were always a special case – special in the extent of their hopes and illusions, in their resources and in the freedom the Germans gave them to prove themselves reliable partners. For Marshal Pétain, collaboration was the only way to preserve France's standing as a major imperial power. His was an ambition on a very different scale from that of those Slovak, Croat or Baltic politicians who aspired merely to independence, and it made for a far tenser relationship with Berlin. For collaboration depended not only upon the desire to collaborate but also upon being given the opportunity, and it was the Germans who had to make the offer.[1]

Domestically, France's defeat led to sudden political transformation. Pétain presented his regime as a sharp break with France's parliamentary past, and he promised an authoritarian revolution. But in reality strong currents of continuity with the Third Republic also ran beneath the surface. It was not so much the fact that he himself had been elected by its last assembly: that was never something he liked to draw attention to, and his decision to put leading figures from the prewar governments on trial was intended not only to fix the blame for defeat on them but more generally to demonstrate the bankruptcy of the old order. (The trial itself – at Riom in 1942 – became an embarrassment and had to be wound up quickly.) Much more important was the hidden continuity that was provided by France's mayors, gendarmes, ministries and prefects. Although Vichy purged some of its civil servants, it relied heavily on those that were left; indeed occupation gave them more power than they had enjoyed before, because both the Germans and Pétain needed bureaucrats, whereas they could easily dispense with politicians and their parties. Collaboration, in short, is about a gamble on change that failed, but it is also a story of the continuities that a powerful sense of national tradition and administrative *esprit de corps* made possible, continuities that led both into Vichy from the Third Republic and out of it into the Fourth and Fifth.

The idea of collaboration directs attention to France's relationship with the Germans. But this only raises the question of who stood for France. For the conflicts among the different German agencies in Paris – intense though these were – paled in comparison with France's own disunity. Had the country not been so bitterly divided when it was invaded, the occupation would probably have taken a very different course, as the example of Norway shows. In fact, many on the French right welcomed the collapse of parliamentary democracy and saw occupation as the chance to settle scores with the left that went back decades – to the time of the Dreyfus Affair and perhaps even to the Revolution. Yet only vis-à-vis the Popular Front was this in any sense a unified group. Some opponents of the Third Republic admired and adored the occupiers while others hated them. Many backed Pétain, at least for a time, but there were others who detested him and hoped that the Germans would get rid of him in favour of a more radical right-wing alternative. The story of collaboration was like one of those horribly complicated family quarrels which Germany's war of conquest exposed and made much worse, and explains why occupation posed such a threat to national unity and remains such a sensitive issue to this day.[2]

IN THE PATH OF COLLABORATION

'A collaboration has been envisaged between our two countries. I have accepted it in principle.' With these words, Marshal Philippe Pétain, the eighty-four-year-old hero of the Battle of Verdun, left his meeting with Hitler at Montoire in October 1940 and announced his government's willingness to work with Berlin. Some Frenchmen were dismayed. 'The only right we have left is to comment upon the messages and extol the wisdom of a marshal of the last war who can hardly even count his decorations, an old army pensioner who repeats the words of his prompters,' wrote Jean Guéhenno after Pétain took power in July. But this was a minority view. Charles Maurras, the long-time leader of the French anti-republican right and a key ideological influence both on Pétain himself and on many of his later ultra-right critics, hailed 'the Marshal's masterpiece'. Writing in *L'Action Française* after Montoire, he went on:

'Are you in favour of what the Marshal calls "collaboration"?'
'It is not for me to be in favour of it.'
'Are you against it.'
'No.'
'Neutral?'
'No.'
'So you allow it?'
'It is not for me to allow it, still less to discuss it.'

For Maurras, what counted was less what Pétain said than the fact that it inaugurated a new era in French history. The 'regime of discussion' was over; the reign of obedience, discipline and authority had begun.[3]

Was there another country in Europe more sharply polarized in 1940 than France? Guéhenno and Maurras, for all their differences, agreed that defeat represented not only the victory of the Germans over the French, but the triumph of the right over the Popular Front and the Third Republic. And they agreed on more than that, for both saw – one despondently, the other gladly – that this shift in power was accepted by the mass of ordinary French men and women. That it had happened under the shock of German occupation pleased neither – they were, both of them, instinctively anti-German. But for many on the right, in those first days and months, German domination was the price that had to be paid for restoring France to greatness.

Collaboration thus involved a balancing act of enormous delicacy. It was a way for conservatives like Pétain to push through an authoritarian National Revolution and to effect a sweeping transformation of French life. But it was simultaneously an effort to preserve French autonomy and sovereignty in the face of overwhelming German power. National Socialism had facilitated the turn to the right inside France – this was why Laval, for example, announced in June 1942 that he wished for a German victory – but too sweeping a Nazi domination would have left no room for collaboration at all. Vichy's politicians were French nationalists, gambling on whether German National Socialism was prepared to trust them sufficiently to grant them the power they sought.

At first, many people believed the gamble was worth taking for the sake of the country's stability. In less than two years, Pétain would find himself under attack from all sides, accused of selling out to the Germans by the Gaullists, of 'Gaullism' by hard-line fascists. But in the traumatic summer of 1940 all this lay in the future, and he seemed to embody unity. Battered and stunned, scarred by the chaos, criminality and astonishingly swift social disintegration that millions had experienced during the panicky exodus away from the advancing Germans, the country embraced the reassuring figure of the Marshal who had brought an end to the fighting and restored calm. A personality cult sprang up, and gifts flooded the foyer of the Hôtel du Parc in Vichy; hundreds of towns and villages named streets and squares after him. It was an adulation Pétain did nothing to deter. With no clear doctrine, no party and no constitution, nothing embodied the New Order in France more tangibly than his own person.

As Pétain buried the Third Republic, there were few mourners. Only later did the central political and ethical question become one of choosing between collaboration and resistance. In 1940, the issue was rather what kind of collaboration would best secure the country's future. Catholics who favoured an 'organic' state had little in common with racist street-fighters who wanted to abolish the Church. Pro-fascist businessmen hoping to repress Marxist unions wondered if they could trust former socialists with their anti-capitalist rhetoric and their calls for a racially purified society of equals spending heavily on housing and welfare policy. As Europe shifted to the right, so the right itself revealed its many faces.

Like Tiso in Slovakia, Franco in Spain, Horthy in Hungary or Salazar in Portugal, Pétain was above all a rightist who looked backwards, a representative of an older conservative order, a revolutionary despite himself. He disliked the term 'revolution' – it had all the wrong connotations – and he preferred talking about 'renovation' instead. He was not interested in political parties and refused to found a new one of his own. What he wanted was to purge France of Jews, communists and freemasons, police society against trouble-makers and return to the putative values of peasant France – obedience, paternalism, family and hard work. The prewar cult of motherhood and sexual conservatism was beefed up with new laws targeting abortionists and homosexuality. Businessmen welcomed Vichy's abolition of independent trade unions, and, although employers' unions were also dissolved, the balance of power tilted decisively in their favour, as it had done under fascist regimes previously in Italy and Germany. Local notables and the Church welcomed the regime's stress on deference to authority. At the same time, Vichy had its own modernizers as well – a younger crowd of technocrats and administrators, fresh out of France's elite administrative training colleges, who planned to push ahead with an overhaul of the country's industrial and institutional infrastructure without political parties and labour organizers getting in the way.[4]

That was Vichy, the sleepy, small spa town that suddenly found itself at the centre of France's New Order. The nation's capital, by contrast, became the centre of a certain kind of opposition. While Paris was no longer the seat of government, it remained a hot-bed of French politics and home in particular to some of Pétain's most violent critics. Here, close to the Germans in more than one sense, one found France's *ultras* – all those for whom Pétain was too conservative, too timid and insufficiently *political*. This was the base of the Parti Populaire Français, a prewar party of the right, led by Jacques Doriot, a former communist and metal-worker who spent part of the war on the Eastern Front leading a unit of French volunteers. The more professorial Marcel Déat was there too, hoping to create a single pro-German fascist party that would evict Pétain from power. When Pétain unexpectedly fired his deputy, the wily Pierre Laval, because he feared he was plotting against him, Déat was the man Laval ended up with. Behind them, ideologically and financially, stood the German ambassador in Paris, Otto Abetz, a former art teacher and an ardent Francophile since the 1920s. (Abetz was married to a Frenchwoman, and he had done so well looting Jewish art works in Paris in the first months after the occupation that he had been promoted to ambassador.) 'King Otto', as he was known after the lavish parties he threw at the embassy, thought Pétain was too old-fashioned, out of touch and elitist and he supported Déat and Laval because he wanted to make collaboration genuinely popular and dynamic. Like Nazi officials stationed in the Netherlands, Slovenia and elsewhere, he believed a new party might help solidify pro-German sentiment – it had, after all, been vital to the Nazi revolution in Germany itself – and so the Rassemblement National Populaire (RNP) was born.

Déat himself detested Pétain because he thought he was taking France backwards and squandering the opportunity for the *real* national revival that would restore its former glory. He might have been right but he was hopelessly mistaken in thinking the Germans would therefore back *him*: there was nothing Hitler wanted less than a resurgent France, and Otto Abetz was regarded as something of a light-weight in Berlin and was not in fact the arbiter of the country's politics. Collaboration, Göring commented dismissively, was something 'Mr Abetz' did, as though the real business of running France had nothing to do with his kind of politicking at all. For Göring the priority was plundering the country of its produce. For Hitler and for the Wehrmacht military commander, it was public order not ideological convergence. France was certainly not the only place where the Germans preferred to support reliable conservatives rather than headstrong and airy-fairy radicals with no power base. The real significance of the *ultras* was the implied threat they constituted: the RNP was a sword the Germans could hold over Pétain's head.

For Pétain was certainly too independent and too cautious for Hitler to trust him. The Maréchal might have felt that only a German victory would allow him to carry through his National Revolution but he certainly saw no reason to rush to enter the war on Germany's side. He did not change his mind even after the British – desperate to stop any accretion of the Axis's naval strength – sank the French fleet, killing 1,300 sailors in the Algerian port of Mers-el-Kébir in July 1940, causing a wave of anti-British outrage in his entourage. Entry into the war was the commitment Hitler had hoped to extract from him at their Montoire meeting that October, but he had been disappointed. Another war like that of 1914–18, thought Pétain, would cost the country too dearly, a view he held to the bitter end. Vichy would do what it could to defend its colonial possessions against British attack, and it did this actively in 1940–41 – even bombing Gibraltar. However, it guarded its de facto neutrality as the most prudent option, and its ability to keep the country at peace was one of the sources of the regime's domestic popularity, especially in the unoccupied zone.

Not even the intensely anti-British feelings of Admiral Darlan, who became Pétain's deputy in early 1941, were enough to bring the French in on the German side, though at one stage he came close. In Darlan's view, a British victory would probably have had the effect of leaving France a 'second-class Dominion, a continental Ireland'. But fortunately no doubt for the French, his proposals for a Grand Design, a partnership with the Reich which would have turned France into the leading power in the Mediterranean, were rebuffed in Berlin. The Germans were as greedy with the French as they were with the Spaniards and as unwilling to contemplate their terms for help: it was thus ironically the Third Reich and its refusal to envisage 'turning the Armistice into collaboration' that saved Vichy's neutrality. As a result, many governments accepted the legitimacy of Pétain's regime and maintained cordial diplomatic relations with it, at least until the Germans occupied the entire country in November 1942. Vichy broke off relations with Britain after Mers-el-Kébir, but both Australia and Canada still recognized it.

So did the USA. In 1940, the American ambassador, Admiral Leahy, had been instructed by Roosevelt that Pétain 'occupies a unique position in the hearts of the French people'. Leahy stayed in Vichy for two years, seeking to prevent it from joining the German side. Only after the Allied invasion of north Africa were relations between the two powers broken off by Laval, a step which Roosevelt publicly regretted. As it was, the system of government established by Vichy continued for some months under Allied rule in Algeria: the concentration camps in the south of the country remained in operation, and the anti-Jewish laws continued in force.[5]

For the Germans, a neutral France could still serve their interests; what really mattered for them were deliveries of goods, labour and stability both inside metropolitan France and also within its possessions abroad. With the war being fought chiefly in the East, the military priority so far as France was concerned was to keep the number of troops deployed there to the minimum. The kind of domestic changes Pétain hoped to make did not threaten them; on the contrary, provided he remained reasonably popular, and loyal – and the POWs in German hands helped to ensure the latter – his drive to create a more centralized, authoritarian state could only make the occupation easier. The Germans thus had little reason – especially in 1940–41, when they believed the war was all but over – to press for more military assistance than France wished to give. As the Gaullists gathered strength overseas, taking French

Equatorial Africa in the autumn of 1940 and helping the Allies invade Syria and Lebanon the following summer, Pétain was driven into a more pro-German position. Not that he resisted very hard: he clearly believed in the probability of a German victory long after the invasion of the USSR and the anti-Bolshevism which he shared with Hitler cemented their unlikely tie more firmly.

Yet there was no real trust between the two countries, and each partner mounted an intense spying effort on the other. The Germans organized a massive intelligence operation against Vichy, trebling the numbers of their spies there in the first year of occupation. But Vichy's counter-espionage service was their equal: it tracked German agents, arresting nearly 2,000 in two years and actually executing several dozen. Like the Spaniards, the French were especially vigilant against German agents in north Africa. Vichy agents even did deals with anti-German resistance networks on the mainland, permitting them to continue communicating with London once they had established that they were not animated by 'anti-French' feelings. Both animated by patriotism (as they saw it), these resisters and many within Vichy shared a common antipathy to the Germans.[6]

After the invasion of the USSR, and the spate of attacks on German military personnel in France, the balancing act of collaboration became harder to maintain, and support drained away from the regime. As the tally of French victims of German executions soared from only eight in 1940 and fifty-one in the first nine months of 1941 to more than 500 in the next six months, Pétain's popularity plummeted. In early 1941, France still favoured collaboration, remarked a supportive notable, but by the following year Pétain's supporters could no longer speak openly. 'Loyal Frenchmen,' in his gloomy words, 'have entered the night'; the rest would have to be made to 'obey by force'.[7] The middle ground disappeared, Pétain's legitimacy dwindled, and his rivals in Paris, sensing (mistakenly) that their moment was near, started fighting among themselves. At a send-off for volunteers to the Eastern Front, Déat – Laval's ally – was shot and nearly killed. Déat himself, a man whom Léon Blum had once regarded as his natural successor in the French socialist movement, was becoming impatient and even contemplated a Mussolini-style March on Vichy to seize power for French fascism.

The *ultras* were stirring – especially as Heydrich and the SS started to turn their attention to France – and there were far more extreme men than Déat. Eugène Deloncle was a decorated artillery officer, a shady, unstable character from the violent fringes of prewar French fascism, whose paramilitary, anti-republican Cagoule organization had been backed in the 1930s by right-wing business executives in the cosmetics giant L'Oréal. The German military commander in Paris had cautiously 'tolerated' but not 'authorized' his successor to the Cagoule, the Mouvement Social Révolutionnaire (MSR), which was committed to 'constructing a new Europe together with National-Socialist Germany and all the other European countries liberated from liberal capitalism, Judaism, Bolshevism and Freemasonry'. The MSR – as keen on proclamations as all the other political groupings of the occupation – sought to regenerate France 'racially', to prevent Jews from 'polluting' the French race and to create a socialist economy. Looting Jewish property helped, as – despite the supposed commitment to socialism – did L'Oréal's continued backing, but when Deloncle tried to take over Déat's RNP, both men were weakened by the infighting.

Infighting among the German agencies in Paris was just as bad. Deloncle was also being backed by the SiPo/SD. Equipped with explosives they supplied, his men tried to dynamite seven synagogues in Paris during the night of 2/3 October 1941. Six of the buildings were damaged, along with others around them; two German soldiers and numerous French residents were among those wounded. When the military police investigated the explosions, the SD tried to cover up its involvement, saying it was probably a 'purely Jewish story', and there was a head-on collision with the Wehrmacht military commander who quickly uncovered the facts after Deloncle's handler boasted drunkenly of the affair in a Paris night-club. General von Stülpnagel demanded the recall of the two senior SS officers in Paris and blocked Deloncle from going to the Eastern Front to join his men. The affair drove a breach between the Wehrmacht and the SS that eventually gave Heydrich the opening to take over policing in France and to appoint his own HSSPF there the following spring. As for Deloncle, he lost control even of the MSR, drifted into secret contacts with Allied agents, and ended up being killed by the Gestapo in a shoot-out in January 1944. It was not an uncharacteristic end in the tortured world of French extremism.[8]

Yet some of the younger and more prudent of his Cagoulard comrades navigated the war more successfully: André Bettencourt, who wrote numerous nasty pro-German articles in 1941, ended up a decorated hero of the resistance. After the war, he married into the L'Oréal family dynasty, helping to whitewash the company's rather dirty record, and became a government minister. One of Bettencourt's associates on the fringes of the Cagoule rose even higher. Like others on the right, François Mitterrand served Vichy – in his case, helping run the office dealing with French POWs – before moving into resistance as his faith in Pétain waned.[9]

Pétain, Déat, Deloncle – collaboration covered a vast spectrum of possibilities, many of which mirrored and intensified the bitter rivalries among the various German agencies themselves. When someone remarked to Laval that Nazi Germany was an authoritarian state, he replied: 'Yes, and what a lot of authorities.' As elsewhere, in Paris they were fighting a war within a war of their own. The military commander headquartered in the Hotel Majestic was pitted against the SS; Abetz's embassy against Goebbels' Propaganda-Staffel: it was a situation that presented endless opportunities for French machination and gave ample scope for French initiative.

GOOD GERMANS AND BAD FRENCHMEN: COCTEAU'S WAR

Collaboration's ambiguities emerge even more sharply in the realm of the arts, for here the Germans allowed the French enormous leeway. Occupied Paris was not only a place of queues, rationing and anxiety, it was also – especially in the early years of the war – a booming centre of publishing, fashion shows, film premieres and galleries. Through its very permissiveness, the German occupation raised the stakes for the identity of French national culture and triggered off ferocious battles between conservatives and modernists over the nature of art and the power of censorship. The Germans themselves turned into protectors of painters and poets as much as oppressors – at least for those not excluded from their protection on racial grounds.

Jean Cocteau's war illustrates many of these paradoxes. The renowned Surrealist, homosexual and opium addict symbolized the decadence and corruption Vichy had in its sights. Paris's racist right-wing *ultras*, too, had many reasons to loathe him, for he had signed a petition organized by the International League against Anti-Semitism on the eve of the war, and before that he had made the headlines managing the boxing exploits of Panama Al Brown, a brilliant bantamweight who was the first Hispanic world champion in boxing history. We might therefore expect the story of Cocteau's war to be a story of modernist resistance against the philistines of collaboration. And so in many ways it was, as he struggled hard to resist Vichy and its thuggish chorus of Parisian fascists, except that, in doing so, he actually found some of his staunchest allies among the Germans. But what was so surprising about that? In Cocteau's mind, Germans could be artists, too, and only petty souls could fail to understand that some things were higher than the Nation.

Occupation and Vichy between them posed enormous challenges to any ambitious French artist's career. In late August 1941, even as the first round-ups sent thousands of Parisian Jews to the Drancy internment camp in the north-eastern suburbs, Cocteau seemed about to fall foul of Vichy's censoriousness. When their cultural overseers banned his new play, *The Writing Machine*, the writer responded in the same way he had always done in the past, by seeking patrons and protection. Who better for him to turn to against the authorities of Vichy than the Germans themselves, especially when their officials in Paris were as congenial as the novelist Ernst Jünger, a well-known icon of the right turned critic of Nazism? And in fact, through Jünger, and his colleague Gerhard Heller, a keen student of French literature, Cocteau succeeded in getting Vichy's ban removed. His French critics were outraged. After the production of another of his plays was also authorized, they took matters into their own hands: Deloncle's fascists, fresh from trying to blow up Parisian synagogues, burst into the theatre and attacked the cast.

The struggle with the *ultras* continued even after Deloncle's men were reined in. When Vichy's education minister dismissed one of his works as 'inopportune', Cocteau gave a private reading to his German friends to see what they thought: they loved it. It seemed easier, the publisher Gaston Gallimard wrote, to communicate with 'good Germans' than with 'bad Frenchmen'. Otto Abetz, the German ambassador, and his French wife were much more appreciative than the right-wing French novelist Céline, the violence of whose vituperative attacks on his countrymen left Germans stunned. Having enjoyed his conversations with Cocteau, and visited Picasso in his studio, Ernst Jünger – no liberal – had been shocked by Céline's 'astonishment that we, soldiers, are not shooting the Jews, that we don't hang or exterminate them, his astonishment that someone with bayonets refuses to use them to the end'.

Céline was not the only prominent writer to make a cult of fascism. The journalist and critic Lucien Rebatet published the violently anti-Semitic *Les Décombres* (The Ruins), a diatribe against those responsible for France's downfall, praised German culture, and discerned 'profound political meaning' in the disciplined style of the Berlin Chamber Orchestra. Put in charge of the prestigious *Nouvelle Revue Française*, the novelist Drieu la Rochelle hewed to an anti-democratic and pro-German line and dreamed of a fascist European third way between America and the threat of Bolshevism. So did Robert Brasillach, another brilliant young literary extremist, who felt that the French were 'an absurd and mediocre people' and insisted on praising the youthful Germans and criticizing the senile office-holders of Vichy. His infatuation with a handsome young German lecturer at the German Institute took a tragic turn when the latter was killed in action on the Eastern Front. Visiting the Katyn forest as a journalist, he recalled his friend and hailed their friendship as the expression of a rejuvenated Europe that would defeat both bourgeois complacency and the 'forces out of the East'. Pétain and Vichy struck Brasillach as a dead end, and, as collaboration collapsed, he put his faith solely in the Germans themselves. Mussolini's fall shocked him deeply and seemed to spell the end of his ideal of a fascist Europe: 'Fascist France in a fascist Europe, what a beautiful dream! Since there is no longer a fascist Europe.' But unlike many other *ultras*, he refused to give up his beliefs. Even in the dark days of late 1944, when he saw the winds blowing towards 'the temple of universal peace, the enforced brotherhood of all races and creeds', Brasillach still felt that fascism had been 'the most exciting truth of the twentieth century'.[10]

This was the *ultra* outlook, but it was emphatically not Cocteau's: he was not an extremist and he valued society and sociability above ideology. 'Events bore me,' the poet Valéry confided to Gerhard Heller at this time. 'Events are the froth of things. It is the sea which interests me.' So far as politics were concerned, Cocteau felt much the same. Shadows fell over him as friends fled abroad, or went into hiding. Some wrote him anguished letters before arrest and deportation, and one or two committed suicide. Together with Picasso, he attended the burial of the émigré Jewish painter Chaim Soutine in 1943, an act of solidarity with a man who had died on the run from the Gestapo. But his social life continued its habitual hectic whirl. He was struck, as so often, by Paris's 'prodigious beauty' – the Germans coming to pay homage, the visitors from the Free Zone who were 'stupefied by the city', the restaurants 'which sell everything that is supposedly prohibited'; autograph hunters still pursued film-stars and actors through the streets. 'How the Germans must be astonished by this spring-time Paris,' he mused in May 1942. 'these flowers, these women's hats, these small carts pulled by teams of cyclists, by the unbelievable grace of the air's resistance! Paris digests everything and assimilates nothing. A spectacle of profound lightness . . .'[11]

Cocteau had a particularly close relationship with Hitler's favourite sculptor, Arno Breker, whose monumentally bombastic nudes – giant symbols of 'a race renewed and splendid' – had won acclaim in the Third Reich. Breker was a Francophile and had known the Parisian arts scene since the 1920s: it was he who, together with Albert Speer, had shown Hitler round Paris at dawn in June 1940, shortly after the city had fallen. In May 1942, in the same month that French Jews in the German zone were obliged to wear the yellow star, an exhibition devoted to Breker's work opened at the Orangerie, sponsored by the Germans. To mark the occasion, Cocteau penned an affectionate tribute entitled 'Salute to Breker', a document that was to cause him considerable trouble. 'I salute you, Breker,' he wrote. 'I salute you from the lofty fatherland of poets, a fatherland where fatherlands do not exist except to the extent that each of them brings with it the treasure of its nation's labour.' A shocked disapproval greeted this, and friends wrote to him to protest and ask for an explanation. Cocteau was upset that his critics had misunderstood him; what he valued with Breker was friendship, and it was this personal bond that had impelled him to write, not some intervention in the political game of collaboration.

It was not as if he was unaware of Breker's politics, though, or of his close relationship with Hitler. During their conversations at the time of the latter's visit to the exhibition, Breker had told Cocteau that what really mattered was victory in the East; 'in France we have only bureau-crats who want to demonstrate their zeal and bolster their prestige'. Victory over Russia, Breker went on, would bring happiness to France. The two friends talked about Hitler – who supposedly regarded Breker as tenderly as a son – Pétain's fraility and the problem of the Jews. 'No exception is possible,' Breker sternly warned Cocteau, who had numerous Jewish friends, on this theme. 'It is a duel to the death.' Where Hitler was concerned, their views were closer. Influenced perhaps by Breker's praise for the Führer, Cocteau persisted in seeing the German leader as an improvement on the old parliamentarians, a mythical figure who should not be stopped from 'carrying out his task fully'. Hitler, he wrote, was 'a poet beyond the comprehension of the soul of drudges', and he criticized his own countrymen – in the privacy of his diary – for treating him with 'lack of respect and absolute ingratitude'.[12]

Cocteau himself had much to feel grateful for. It was German patronage that protected him from French extremists. Not especially interested in politics, he showed how easy it could be for an independently minded myth-maker to pursue the arts under German occupation – indeed with German backing. With the censors' approval, the war saw his career as film director take off. When an article denouncing him appeared in a right-wing magazine, he noted that 'all the Germans laughed at it'. The *ultras* apart, Cocteau's busy career had a place for almost everyone, even the Maréchal, whose regime had tormented him. In 1942, he contributed to a luxurious piece of Vichyite idol-worship, a book of tribute entitled *De Jeanne d'Arc à Philippe Pétain*. Subtitled *Five Hundred Years of French History*, the lavishly illustrated book appeared just in time for the Maréchal's visit to Paris. The occupation was nearing its end by then, but Pétain was still popular and received a warm welcome. As a wartime theme, Joan of Arc was highly appropriate – given the ambiguity of her associations – for Cocteau's own war: a symbol initially of anti-British sentiment, especially after the disaster of Mers-el-Kébir, by the time the book appeared in 1944, Joan herself had flitted over to the Gaullist side as an example of resistance to the occupier. Cocteau was not far behind.[13]

But his case was in no way untypical. German agencies in Paris were pursuing cultural diplomacy with enormous energy, and ambiguity and opportunity characterized the art world of wartime France. For the ambitious and unconcerned, it was a time to found newspapers and publishing houses. And while hard-line critics like Lucien Rebatet might have seen the occupation as a chance to rid France of Jewish cosmopolitanism and decadent modernism, modernism was not so easily banished. In the privacy of his studio, Picasso continued to paint; Braque himself continued to exhibit publicly. Vichy itself was resolutely old-fashioned and preferred commissioning tapestries of French harvesters amid idyllic landscapes. But in Paris, 'patriotic abstraction' – in red, white and blue – enjoyed the approval of Gaullists and the Germans alike. After the war, Manhattan's Museum of Modern Art propagated the myth that Nazism had evicted modernism from Europe and allowed New York to take over from Paris. But this was not strictly true. A few artists fled: some – like Soutine and Krémègne – hid, or holed up like Fautrier and Matisse. But under the surprisingly uninterested eye of the occupation authorities, Paris remained hospitable to art of many kinds.

This was because the German management of the wartime Paris arts scene aimed, as far as possible, to ensure a kind of normality amid the deprivation, the censorship and the propaganda, and it provided numerous incentives to the French to comply with the new regime as a result. Apart from the prohibition on showing the works of Jewish artists and émigrés, there were few bars. Picasso could not exhibit publicly because the Spanish government had requested this, but the ban did not stop a new wartime arts publisher, Éditions du Chêne, from bringing out an attractive wartime edition of his latest still lives, complete with mounted colour plates – at a time when paper was in short supply everywhere in Europe. With nearly twice as many galleries open in 1943 as there had been two years earlier, entry into the French art world was arguably easier than before. Booksellers and publishers hastened to comply with the new rules laid down by German censors in order to take advantage of the favourable climate. The French were more desperate than ever to read, and sales of Simenon and other best-sellers soared.[14]

German cultural diplomacy targeted well-known painters and writers, promoted lectures and mounted exhibitions. During the war, the Foreign Ministry built up a network of cultural institutes across Europe – from Lisbon to Sofia – but they were more active in France than anywhere else. Ambassador Otto Abetz, whose efforts in the cause of Franco-German reconciliation went back to the 1920s, revived his old Cercle France-Allemagne, – renaming it the Groupe Collaboration – and attracted a circle of writers, publishers and journalists. Not unlike after 1945, Franco-German rapprochement was presented as a European ideal, a means of bringing peace to the continent as a whole. Abetz himself saw 'the idea of Europe' more cynically as something that could be 'usurped by the Reich without prejudice to the demand for continental primacy anchored by National Socialism in the German people'.[15]

Abetz's 'active propaganda' led to a series of huge public exhibitions. The first of these, 'La France européenne', opened in Paris in the summer of 1941, eventually attracting 635,000 visitors. Others quickly followed – on labour-saving home improvements, on 'the Jews and France' and on the danger of Bolshevism for Europe. Falling off rapidly in popularity after 1942, when the public mood turned hostile, these exhibitions nevertheless attracted between them more than three million visitors. But there were plenty of other cultural highlights too. Herbert von Karajan conducted the Mozart requiem, and the Berlin Philharmonic performed Wagner and Strauss. There were also lectures by eminent intellectuals such as Carl Schmitt and Heidegger's student Hans-Georg Gadamer, who spoke at the Institut Allemand about Herder, the failings of democracy and the power of the idea of the *Volk*. For Gadamer, as for so many German intellectuals, strolling along the Seine in wartime Paris was the perfect location in which to imagine a future of peace, high seriousness and national reconciliation under the leadership of the Reich.[16]

Nor was the travel all one-way. The Germans rewarded sympathetic French artists and writers by inviting them to the Reich on high-profile junkets. A delegation of French painters – including Vlaminck, Derain and de Segonzac – visited Germany in early 1942. French singers toured the POW camps in the Reich – among them Maurice Chevalier, who had declared his faith in Pétain and whose wartime career had flourished as a result. There were the Mozart celebrations in Vienna at the end of 1941, and conferences in Weimar organized by Goebbels' Propaganda Ministry which brought Brasillach and Drieu together with an uninspired list of second-rate hacks to attend the annual German writers' convention. The second of these, in 1942, turned into a meeting of the new German-controlled European Writers Union, where German and French *littérateurs* mixed with representatives of the 'New Europe'. (Among the guests was the elderly Nobel laureate Knut Hamsun, who later enraged Hitler at a private interview in Berchtesgaden by complaining about the destructiveness of German policy in Norway and demanding the recall of the Reich commissioner from Oslo. Another, much younger, delegate, already known for his Europeanism and his love of German literature, was the brilliant Italian Giaime Pintor, who was to die less than two years later as an anti-fascist partisan outside Rome.)

Nowhere else in Europe was cultural diplomacy so heavily promoted by the Germans as in occupied France. The Nazis associated the country with the arts and they both admired and despised it for this. Once it had dominated Europe. But that was before it had allowed itself to degenerate, thanks to its outmoded attachment to parliamentarianism, its reliance on colonial troops and its encouragement of Jewish, Arab and east European immigrants. Hitler believed that the pursuit of taste in music, books, food and fashion had made the French soft; their interests could be safely encouraged, especially as this showed German rule in a rather more tolerant light than anywhere else. His visit to Paris in 1940 remained a vivid memory and he was very glad not to have had to destroy the city – a 'European document of culture': it would have been much more painful, he remarked the following year, than ordering the destruction of Moscow and Leningrad. (Three years later, of course, he overcame these scruples and did order the last German commander of the French capital to leave it in ruins.) Paris, after all, provided the standard against which his future Berlin would be judged.[17]

ADMINISTRATORS

Who was actually running France? Certainly not 'King Otto' Abetz and his coterie of intellectuals. And not the SS either, whose presence even after the establishment of Carl Oberg as HSSPF in May 1942 remained rather small. In fact, Werner Best's theory of the 'supervisory administration' provides a largely accurate guide to how the occupation was actually organized. Overseen by Wehrmacht officials, the country lay in the hands of French civil servants.

The continuity of the state through the most violent ideological upheavals is one of the major unwritten themes of modern European history, and nowhere was this more evident than during the Second World War. In France – unlike in the East – the Germans had no immediate goals apart from running an efficient and orderly occupation, and this made the civil servants more important even than the politicians. Politics was basically distraction, whereas administration was the essence of a military occupation. And because the bureaucrats could only function in this way if they could be relied upon, the Germans were more sensitive than we might imagine to public opinion, monitoring it carefully and trying to shape it, not least through the propaganda campaigns mentioned above.[18]

Vichy had its own interest in preserving a strong administrative machine too. Without it, the regime might easily become a mere figure-head for German influence, unable to reach the French grass-roots. Just as some German intellectuals schemed to break France up, so Vichy was determined to hold it together, and the civil service was far and away the most important instrument for doing this. As for the civil servants themselves, occupation was far less troubling in some ways for them than it was for the politicians. Indeed, with the political class badly weakened, German rule offered them an opportunity to push ahead with policies to centralize and streamline the administration of the country that the politicians had been blocking for years.

At the start, they had been caught badly off guard. So sure were they that the war would not end quickly that unlike, say, their Dutch counterparts they had hardly prepared at all for what to do in the event of defeat. In the summer of 1940, as Paris emptied in panic, the Ministry of Education was still sending out circulars reminding teachers how to apply for their annual spa retreat. Yet once Pétain was installed, the forces of continuity quickly asserted themselves. Fears for the country's national security had already led to centralization, purges and repression at the start of the war in September 1939: Vichy merely intensified the trend.

This continuity was in some ways quite unexpected. After all, Vichy was not a country run by civil servants like Belgium and the Netherlands; in France there was a legitimate government with a clear political pro-gramme of breaking with the past. Yet Pétain (like de Gaulle four years later) had every reason to preserve the existing state institutions if he wished to rule effectively. Purges therefore produced less change than might have been expected, and the extremists of the right com-plained bitterly as a result; in 1944, Marcel Déat criticized the 'reaction-ary commune' of the capital, claiming its members were 'profoundly *attentiste*', not to say Gaullists. Whether or not they were Gaullists, nearly 80 per cent of the mayors in the wartime Paris suburbs were prewar republicans. As for the countryside, change-over on purely politi-cal grounds was generally discouraged; the Germans too feared the impact on efficiency and continuity. In Aquitaine and Charente, for instance, fully half of the local government officials who had been in post in 1939 were still there when the occupation ended.[19]

Vichy's promise of a new authoritarian revolution thus masked the reality of its dependence on the country's civil service. Of course, the bureaucrats could – and did – serve as instruments of repression, notably in round-ups of Jews and political opponents. But in general they had no intention of offering the revolutionary dynamism demanded by France's extreme right. The cult of Pétain disguised the political vacuum at the heart of his government, and his refusal to allow the formation of a single political party meant that ironically French civil servants never encountered anything close to the radicalizing competition the Nazi *Gauleiters* inflicted on their German counterparts, or that the Dutch NSB used – much less successfully – in its effort to take over the civil service in the Netherlands. Having the conservative Pétain in power thus safeguarded France from the kind of Nazification that threatened other countries, at least until it was too late in the war to make much difference. Increasing their grip over the provinces, creating a new rung of super-prefects, preventing most of the regime's new specially formed commissariats from having much influence, France's senior civil servants presided over a wartime expansion of the bureaucracy and a consolidation of state power that Wilhelm Stuckart in the Reich Ministry of the Interior would have envied. The Germans might have conquered France, but the French state survived more or less intact.

As they saw it, the civil servants played a vital role in preserving a France that occupation had already dismembered, and that might face further fragmentation in the peace should Germany's support for regional separatists ever amount to anything. But while meeting these wartime challenges, they were also pursuing an older agenda of rationalization and modernization of the state that many of them had been actively proposing since the 1920s. Admiral Darlan, who ran the government after Laval was dismissed, was a reformer in this mould: he was against any 'politicization' of the administration, entirely unimpressed by the stodgy, 600,000-strong veterans' Legionary movement that Pétain had imagined might stand in for a political party, and keen to exploit the shock of defeat to ram through a 'new administration'. When the Legion's leader boasted that it '*was* the State', Darlan made sure it was not. Disillusioned with parliaments and parties, he and his technocrats churned out proposals for bureaucratic reform and placed their trust in the civil servants.[20]

There were, naturally, dangers in this course – chiefly the danger of losing touch with sentiment in the country itself. Some of the civil service elite despised and mistrusted public opinion. 'Opinion is just an enormous female!' according to one. Yet wiser heads fretted that the regime – like any authoritarian and overly bureaucratized government with no political wing – risked isolation. One prefect warned of the danger of creating 'veritable governors, as in our distant colonies'. Without political parties to mediate popular concerns, Xavier Vallat, Vichy's first anti-Jewish supremo, feared the emergence of 'a gap that could become an abyss of incomprehension'.[21] 'There is, for your government,' a veteran senator warned Pétain, 'an extreme danger of lacking any contact with the country except via civil servants, whose antennae and vision are professionally deformed'. Such fears pushed Pétain to open his doors to local notables, though this was scarcely enough and opened him to accusations from the right that the trouble with his regime was its lack of energy and its inability to mobilize the French behind it.[22]

Reliance on the civil servants carried a further risk for an increasingly jittery and indeed paranoid government. Vichy followed public opinion and monitored its own cadres for any signs of disloyalty: the Gestapo could scarcely compare with the extraordinarily effective French security services when it came to checking up on the political views of café owners or school teachers. Yet when it tried to purge the civil servants themselves, it found the service fought hard to protect its own. From the very first purges of 1940, following laws which targeted Jews, communists and freemasons in particular, senior administrators proved extremely reluctant to fire their staff, preferring to issue warnings, or to move them to less sensitive posts. There were great disparities in the impact of the purges across ministries – Interior and War, not surprisingly, being especially punctilious, Labour and Foreign Affairs far more resistant. As the war went from bad to worse, Vichy felt less and less able to trust them. This necessitated organizing constant reassertions of loyalty. In July 1941, Pétain ordered all civil servants to *repeat* an earlier compulsory denial that they were freemasons, and he followed this with a spate of public oath-taking ceremonies. 'One is with me, or against me,' he insisted, 'and this thought is above all true for the servants of the State.' An 'inflation of oaths' followed, and this necessitated the absurd law of April 1942 which actually spelled out when an oath could legally be demanded.[23]

*

Laval's return to power the same month meant the end of Darlan's projects for administrative reform but did nothing to curb the power of the state. On the contrary, as a man of the Third Republic, Laval was much happier than Darlan had been working with the old institutions and its functionaries and had less desire to change them. 'Back to the Third Republic' was the angry complaint of disillusioned Pétainists, who saw their hopes of a domestic revolution fading. Focusing on foreign policy, however, Laval wanted subordinates who would run France's affairs without fuss, efficiently and smoothly enough to win the Germans' respect.

But the civil servants, who had managed so adroitly to maintain and even increase their power through the early months of the occupation, now found that the price of preserving that achievement was rising sharply. It started before Laval's return to power with the spate of attacks on German personnel that followed the invasion of the Soviet Union. The hostage crisis of autumn 1941 would have affected French–German relations much less had Hitler himself not got involved. It was his insistence on inflicting massive reprisals on the French that provoked the first serious breach with Vichy. Yet from the point of view of the government, what mattered was to restore French control over the judicial process. If anyone, to put it bluntly, was going to try to shoot Frenchmen, it should be other Frenchmen. This was why Vichy was so keen to do the Germans' dirty work for them, by establishing special courts to find and try communists and other suspects.

Once embarked on this course, there was no knowing where it would lead. The Franco–German policing agreement of the following summer was even more revealing about how far the civil servants would go for the sake of preserving French sovereignty. Policing was the most vital part of the French state for the Germans to control, especially as the largely republican police force had turned out to be a solidly reliable partner. By the same token, it was vital for Vichy to keep it in French hands. The French negotiator securing this was a brilliant rising star, René Bousquet, once the youngest prefect in France and installed by Laval as secretary general of the police. It was a mark of his supreme self-confidence that he handled the French side alone; the HSSPF Carl Oberg, along with his SiPo/SD colleagues Knochen, Lischka and Hagen, presented the Germans' demands. No ideologue of the right, Bousquet's political roots lay instead in the radical-socialist tradition of the interwar

Third Republic. What really mattered for Bousquet and Laval was reaching a deal with the SS that would regain autonomy for the French police – 'the most striking sign of the sovereignty of its government' as he put it – and marginalize dangerous incoming amateurs, like the self-styled Darquier de Pellepoix, the new general commissary for Jewish affairs.[24]

For this he was prepared to gamble. Assured and self-confident, Bousquet managed to get Oberg to agree that the French police would not have to hand over prisoners or provide the Germans with hostages. In exchange he went well beyond the instructions Laval had given him on the question of deporting Jews. He cooperated in the big round-up of foreign-born Jews in Paris in mid-July and in the unoccupied zone the following month. Pétain's instructions had been to ensure that the French police would play no part in their arrest; Bousquet offered their help anyway and shrugged off the protests of French churchmen with a classic bureaucrat's dismissal, saying that 'the role of public opinion is to stir itself up; the role of the government is to choose'. Concerned, as ever, with the question of sovereignty, the government made a sharp distinction between French and foreign Jews. Thanks to Bousquet's insistent orders, the police did the Germans' work for them and rounded up the latter. Keen to ensure the French side delivered the agreed numbers, Bousquet reminded prefects of the need to deport children as well as adults. The Germans had discussed the matter and determined that they could be sent too: as a result, more than 2,600 between the ages of two and sixteen were among those deported to Auschwitz.

Eichmann's SD representatives were disappointed. In June his office had planned on deporting 100,000 from France, but had scaled back these figures when they realized Vichy would only start with foreign-born Jews. In July, Eichmann himself was furious when the first transport from Bordeaux had to be cancelled because only 150 stateless Jews had been found there; he berated his deputy in Paris about this 'disgraceful' business. By early September, the Germans calculated that no more than 27,000 Jews had been deported from France.

Yet Oberg, the head of the SS in France, was much more realistic than the 'Jewish specialists' and he congratulated Bousquet that the 'French police has realized till now a task worthy of praise': the round-ups demonstrated that they could still be relied upon. Oberg himself was aware that, thanks to the demands of the new offensive on the Eastern

Front, German manpower in France was stretched to the very limit. The number of troops available for occupation duties had dropped from 100,000 to 40,000 in a few months, and there were fewer than 3,000 German policemen in France under Oberg's direct command; since Bousquet controlled 47,000 men, cooperation was obviously a good idea. In fact, as events the following year were to prove, without the collaboration of the French police, targeted mass deportations were virtually impossible to achieve. Pessimistic but ever the realist, Bousquet himself saw actively helping Oberg as the only alternative to the slide into 'total subordination'.[25]

Step by step, this intelligent civil servant was being led down the path of ever-intensified repression. Although Oberg was in fact resisting his superiors – Himmler and Hitler – in order not to further weaken Pétain, the German policy of mass executions and round-ups continued, angering French popular opinion. Things got a lot worse at the start of November 1942, when the Germans responded to the Allied landings in north Africa by moving into the unoccupied zone and stepping up their surveillance of the entire country. Bousquet's response, as the German demands increased, was to negotiate and then to insist that the French police be allowed to execute operations themselves. Oberg himself was not the protector he had once been; he was under fire in Berlin for spending too much time in Paris, and Himmler criticized him for being too much the 'diplomat' and insufficiently tough. In fact, it was the direct intervention of both Himmler and Hitler that pushed Bousquet to new extremes during the so-called Battle of Marseille.[26]

In reality this was not a battle so much as the first massive operation of urban destruction carried out in Europe. Speaking with Norbert Masur more than two years later, Himmler had sounded proud of what had happened there. 'During our occupation there was law and order in France, even though I only had 2,000 German police there,' he had told him. 'Everybody had work, and everybody had enough to eat. Only *we* managed to clean up the harbour area of Marseille, institute healthy conditions and establish law and order, something that no French government ever achieved.' And it was true that neither Vichy nor the Germans ever liked the city, especially not the labyrinthine and uncontrollable alleys around its Vieux-Port, which were home to German deserters, Jewish refugees and *résistants*. One evening early in December 1942, a small bomb went off in front of the Hôtel Astoria, between La Canabière and the boulevard Garibaldi; a few hours later, another exploded beside a German car outside the Hôtel de Rome et Saint-Pierre. Both were used by the Germans, but there were no casualties apart from a couple of passers-by who were wounded. Nevertheless, the Germans imposed a curfew, and started searches for resistance cells. On 3 January, there was a third explosion outside a German military brothel, which wounded several of those inside, and another outside the Hôtel Splendid, which wounded two, one fatally, and which led to martial law being declared by the German military commander. When Himmler heard the news, he blamed Oberg for not clamping down. Hitler himself was said to be 'extremely troubled and unhappy' and wanted the entire Vieux-Port to be evacuated immediately and then levelled. Kurt Daluege, the German head of police, was flown out, and an SS police regiment sent in to take charge; meantime, the military informed Vichy that the French police and gendarmerie would be placed under German orders. A few days later, despite Laval's protests, the regional *préfet*, M. Rivalland, was replaced, and the SS regiment, numbering several thousand men, arrived in Marseille.[27]

Laval and Bousquet were desperate to regain control of the situation because these new developments made a mockery of Vichy's claims to sovereignty. Dramatic and tense negotiations therefore took place in Paris in a forbidding atmosphere – the French civil servants, led by Bousquet on one side and Oberg and the other German SS and police officials on the other. Oberg read out a letter from Himmler which stated that Hitler wanted Marseille 'cleansed' for the sake of 'the health of the Europe of the future': it was the 'cancer of Europe, a refuge for the international underworld [*la pègre internationale*]', and the *quartiers* around the Vieux-Port must be destroyed. The French could hardly believe it, nor that some 40,000 people were to be sent north to be screened in a concentration camp. There was no precedent for collective punishment on the scale anywhere in western Europe, especially given the relative insignificance of the explosions themselves. Yet although the orders sounded unambiguous, Bousquet negotiated. He pointed out the unpredictable repercussions of such an event, the difficulty of guaranteeing the security of the German troops themselves, the difficulties, too, that the Germans might have organizing the transportation of such a large group across the country. His request for a month's delay was refused. But in the end he and Laval decided to insist that if the operation was to go ahead, it should be carried out by the French police themselves, and the question of who was deported or arrested should be left up to them. Three days later, on 16 January, Berlin gave its consent, and in less than a week 12,000 French police arrived in Marseille to carry out the largest such operation ever seen in France. For a day and a half, they combed the streets house by house, checked the identity cards of 40,000 locals and arrested nearly 6,000. Halfway through, Oberg told Bousquet that, because of another bomb blast, all 40,000 people would have to be deported north to the camp at Compiègne as originally planned. When Bousquet protested, one more round of discussions ended in agreement that all foreigners without proper papers, as well as Germans and Italians found in the round-up, would be handed over. Most of those who were deported – nearly 1,600 in all – were central European Jewish refugees, who were jammed into the wagon cars by Oberg's SS men. He and Bousquet inspected the train personally before it left, and Bousquet allowed a handful of people off. For those who were not so fortunate, the journey north took nearly a day and a half; by the time the train arrived, some of them had already died. The rest of the Vieux-Port's population was dumped in an old French military camp while their apartments were ransacked and systematically demolished by a private contractor. Then the destruction of the entire quarter began. It took more than two weeks, only ending on 17 February, by which time more than 1,400 buildings had been blown up in an area of 14 hectares.[28]

One can scarcely imagine a greater test of Vichy's willingness to carry out German orders than this completely gratuitous and colossal act of vandalism and murder. It is not surprising that, when he met Bousquet in April, Himmler described him as a 'precious collaborator in the framework of police collaboration'. But in fact by this point, the morale of the French police was already starting to collapse, and the SS were seriously losing confidence in Bousquet himself. He was only being kept in office, some said, for want of an alternative. One basic problem was working conditions. For while Vichy relied heavily on the police – to hunt down its enemies (real and imagined), to monitor public opinion, and even to keep an eye on the Germans themselves – it had failed to do anything to compensate them for the vastly increased workloads they faced. Many of their stations remained poorly furnished, underfunded flea-pits that were all too vulnerable to attack as the resistance began to emerge. On top of these worries, the German takeover of the unoccupied zone made it harder for policemen to claim they were not acting on the Germans' behalf. Oberg himself now frequently issued orders directly to French gendarmerie officers, and there were weekly meetings between them and the SS.

Above all, Sauckel's new labour drives tested the loyalty of public servants to the limit. Reliable when ordered to arrest foreign Jews and communists, the police reacted more hesitantly when they had to chase up *réfractaires* following the imposition of compulsory labour service in February 1943. It was about this time that news arrived of the Allied landings in north Africa and the Soviet victory at Stalingrad, and by now many 'Pétainists of the first hour' were having second thoughts. The former tennis star and Wimbledon champion Jean Borotra, who had served as Vichy's sports chief, dedicating himself to turning France back into a nation of athletes, was arrested by the Gestapo trying to flee abroad and sent to a camp in Germany (where he survived the war). The youthful François Mitterrand, despite winning a Vichy decoration, was already turning away towards resistance.

In fact many of France's civil servants were well aware that an alternative source of legitimacy had been emerging in Algiers, where the Committee for National Liberation was recognized by the Allies and was starting to organize purges of 'unworthy' bureaucrats in north Africa and Corsica. De Gaulle was now based just across the Mediterranean. That June, Laval referred ironically in a radio broadcast to civil servants who were 'examining their consciences'. More and more of them were. In October, the writer Georges Bernanos scornfully described how

over the past six months we have witnessed a veritable epidemic of conversions among the Vichyist functionaries . . . If the servants of the Roman empire had thus been converted en masse to Christianity, the Cross would have flown above the Capitol long before Constantine, and Nero, instructed in our saintly religion by the pious Agrippina, might perhaps have finished his days in a monastery. But for the civil servants I am talking about, martyrdom is not a vocation; it is the worst of all possible solutions . . . Their civil servants' consciences crossed oceans to hasten to aid liberty under threat, but their civil servants' bodies remained where they were . . .[29]

THE MILICIEN STATE

As the Germans lost confidence in the French police, they looked else-where for support. They were worried by the rise of the Maquis and by the gendarmerie's weak response to these 'terrorists' and they were reneging on previous agreements with Bousquet that limited their own involvement in French police affairs. In 1943, for instance, they arrested nearly 35,000 people on political grounds, the French police fewer than 10,000. Calling for Vichy to act more energetically to weed out those who were 'insufficiently collaborationist', they demanded that their own candidates be put in charge. From Paris came Philippe Henriot as minis-ter of information and propaganda. As for Bousquet's police, they faced rivals in the shape of the paramilitary *miliciens* of Joseph Darnand, a former member of Deloncle's Cagoule, a close associate of Pétain and an ardent pro-German who had become an officer in the Waffen-SS in the summer of 1943.[30]

Darnand had won his reputation as a man of action, and the motto of his Service d'Ordre Légionnaire (SOL), which he founded in 1941, was 'against Apathy, for Enthusiasm'. Like the SS, he favoured an elitism of nationalists – against the nation, if it came to that. 'We are determined to save France despite public opinion,' he proclaimed, 'and against it if necessary.' He would have gone off to fight on the Eastern Front, if Oberg had not told him he was needed in France. Together with Laval, he had set up the Milice – an organization modelled after the Nazi Party – to inject some dynamism in Vichy after Pétain vetoed the idea of a mass party; it grew out of the old SOL, but soon became used by the Germans in anti-resistance operations.

With its endless calls for action, its mistrust of the authorities, its haste, brutality and sheer stupidity, the Milice itself was a classic paramilitary response to emergency. In June 1943, it had some 30,000 members, of whom only about half were on active full-time service. Wearing brown shirts, a blue coat and a wide beret, most of them were very young and generally of modest means. If some were believers, others were convicted felons looking for a way out, or had joined up simply to avoid being sent to Germany as labourers. The police saw them as no better than criminals; reportedly, they were waiting for 'the first opportunity to strangle the Milice'. For their part, the *miliciens* felt the career civil

servants were no longer ideologically trustworthy and ought to be dismissed. In early December 1943, a group of them killed Bousquet's
former political patron, Maurice Sarraut, and thus precipitated the final
rift between Bousquet and the regime. Bousquet resigned, and Darnand
was appointed secretary-general for the maintenance of order at the end
of the month. At his first meeting with the head of the gendarmerie, he
complained of their passivity and urged that they become 'ardent, hot,
revolutionary like the Milice'.[31]

The state's monopoly of force – always strained under occupation –
now disintegrated, and France faced anarchy and civil war. It was the
same story elsewhere in Europe – in Italy, for example, or Greece
– where German arms flowed into the hands of death squads and
anti-communist bands. Robberies multiplied because enterprising criminals dressed themselves up as policemen, and it was impossible to tell
the real ones from the false. The sudden rise of the resistance also scared
many conservatives. Charles Maurras himself – the apostle of order and
discipline – wrote in February 1944 that 'the best response to the threats
of terrorists is to subject them to a legitimate counter-terror'. After a
resistance unit, disguised as *miliciens*, killed Information Minister
Henriot and his wife in their Paris apartment, the Milice responded by
assassinating several well-known French Jewish politicians and intellectuals, including Victor Basch, the president of the League for the Rights
of Man, and the former minister Georges Mandel. They moved into the
former occupied zone, setting up their headquarters in Paris, and worked
alongside the Germans for their own protection – in Dijon, the town
unit was known as the 'Milice SD'. Through the first half of 1944, they
hunted down deserters and *réfractaires* and ordered French prefects to
stop complaining about their crimes.

Darnand's rise thus prompted a real crisis of the state, especially after
new legislation in April 1944 placed police power in his hands and
allowed him to bypass normal judicial channels. He appealed to the
police to serve 'without after-thoughts or mental restrictions'. But
despite his success in appointing reliable *miliciens* to senior posts, such
calls fell on deaf ears. On the week following D-Day, nearly one-third
of the gendarmes in the Auvergne abandoned their posts, most of them
joining the *maquis*. The Milice were increasingly isolated and detested
and feared the vengeance that Liberation would bring. Hence, when
the Germans finally quit France in the autumn of 1944, they were

accompanied by several thousand *miliciens* and their families who made the long trek to Sigmaringen, the small town on the upper Danube which became the last seat of Pétain's government. Many of them were conscripted into the Waffen-SS Charlemagne Division and ended up fighting the Red Army in Poland. A few were among the last troops in Berlin to surrender at the end of April 1945.[32]

What characterized the *miliciens* was their impetuous intransigence, their cruelty and their lack of political realism. More prudent and far-sighted, France's policemen and civil servants had by this point generally moved into an attitude of *attentisme*, which allowed them to share their countrymen's joy at the ending of an occupation they had served more or less faithfully. Although large numbers of unfortunate women were publicly humiliated and had their heads shaved for the crime of con-sorting with German soldiers, and although some notable politicians and cultural icons faced investigation and trial at Liberation, the purges of the civil service allowed many Vichy figures to escape unscathed. René Bousquet received a minimal penalty, was congratulated for his role in the resistance and enjoyed a profitable career in banking and newspapers. Maurice Papon, secretary-general of the prefecture of the Gironde, became a highly controversial chief of police in Paris during the Algerian War, a politician and minister: only in 1997–8 was he convicted for his role in deporting Jews from Bordeaux.

Their longevity offers a clue to the dynamics underlying wartime collaboration in France. The French were not a nation of collaborators, though they had initially been drawn in large numbers to the idea. Pétain's government was initially popular because it appeared to promise to restore order after the chaos of defeat. Those most impatient with it were those on the extreme right who suspected his National Revolution was really a conservative restoration in disguise rather than the fascist break with the past they wanted. But by late 1941 at the very latest – the hostages crisis was a turning-point, but food shortages accentuated the rift – the French public had turned away from Vichy. 'The general opinion appears to be very unfavourable to the government', reported the prefect of the Puy de Dôme that October. Increasingly detached from French opinion, the administration remained true to the ideals of collaboration and responded positively even after the Germans signifi-cantly stepped up their demands. Meanwhile large numbers of Pétain's supporters entered the resistance in one form or another and thus ensured a smooth passage into the postwar Fourth Republic.[33]

Vichy's last-ditch defence of French sovereignty depended increasingly upon its hold over the police. Yet as the Germans themselves understood very well, the police – like civil servants generally – depended for their effectiveness on public support, and this was draining away amid the growing violence. By the spring of 1944, the regime needed the assistance of the Milice to cling to power while the gendarmerie faced a 'veritable conspiracy of silence' whenever they tried tracking down 'terrorists'. Most civil servants were simply looking forward to the inevitable, and Pétain – still viewed sympathetically in much of the country – had lost all credibility as a national leader. Legitimacy had long since accumulated instead around those figures in north Africa who made their triumphant return to the mainland with the Anglo-American armies in the summer of 1944.[34]

14
Eastern Helpers

Was collaboration an illusion born of German indifference? Was it ever possible in those regions that the Nazis were determined to wipe off the map and to turn into zones of German settlement? Some Poles claimed that theirs was the only European country without collaborators. They pointed out that, unlike the Czechs, they had fought back against the Germans and if they had suffered for it at least they had remained on the path of virtue. In January 1945, the resistance Home Army boasted that 'Poland is an organically anti-Fascist country. In our country there is no Hacha, Quisling [or] Vlasov [and] no pro-Fascist party.' The same year, a Polish journalist described it as 'the most purely moral among all the nations that had to live under [Nazi] occupation'.[1]

In fact, morality was not really the issue, and it is hard to say whether Poles behaved better or worse than anyone else would have done under comparably awful conditions. As it is, recent revelations about Polish participation in anti-Jewish massacres in 1941 have complicated the discussion of wartime ethics there. The point was that, as in the French case, it was German policy that defined the options – and in the Polish case there was really no opportunity to collaborate given Hitler's decision to destroy Poland's very identity. In addition, General Sikorski's government-in-exile was recognized abroad as early as the end of 1939. Sikorski's government commanded more than 80,000 soldiers in France alone, as well as a large air force, three destroyers and a much-respected intelligence service. It also established an underground presence in occupied Poland itself – the Government Delegacy – and many officials, like Warsaw's deputy mayor, who did work alongside the Germans, secured the Delegacy's permission before doing so precisely in order to avoid the stigma of collaboration.[2]

There was actually a very brief indication – how serious it is hard to say – that the Germans were thinking of installing a Polish puppet government. In mid-September, before Hitler had made his final decision about Poland's fate, the Gestapo arrested the veteran Peasant Party chief and three-time prime minister, Wincenty Witos, and offered to release him if he would collaborate. Witos refused, as he did on several other occasions. But although German policy changed sharply after this, other Poles certainly continued to feel drawn to Berlin, just as they had through the 1930s, and even earlier – the pro-German tendency in Polish politics went back too far to disappear overnight. Many people remembered the First World War, when the Central Powers had proclaimed an independent Poland. Władysław Studnicki, a follower of the great First World War advocate of Polish–German cooperation, Jósef Piłsudski, had been involved in the 1916 German–Austrian proclamation and now he pressed the Germans to set up a Polish government once again so that it could use the Polish army against the Soviets.[3] More ambiguous was the case of another former Piłsudskiite, Leon Kozłowski. After being jailed and tortured in the Lubyanka prison in Moscow, he then fled *west* and, at a press conference the Germans organized in January 1942, he predicted that the Soviets would lose the war. He deliberately avoided making pro-German comments, but even so, there was speculation that the Germans had lined him up to head a collaborationist government.[4]

In fact, in 1942 almost no one in Berlin was thinking of such a thing: the Reich's intentions for Poland pointed in a very different direction. Typically, it was only after Stalingrad – and even then only haltingly and without the slightest real conviction – that the idea of promoting a common Polish–German crusade against Bolshevism started attracting the Germans. Goebbels and Hans Frank in particular wanted to exploit the shock that was felt throughout Poland when the graves of Polish army officers murdered by the NKVD were discovered in the Katyn forest and members of the Polish Red Cross were included among the foreign forensic scientists, journalists and others who were taken to the site. Even as the remaining Jews in the Warsaw ghetto were being hunted down, Hans Frank was trying to shift course in this direction. The Polish Central Welfare Council was officially recognized in the General Government, and Frank wanted its president, Adam Ronikier, to serve as his intermediary with Polish politicians. Ronikier refused, but Frank was not deterred. In June 1943, he told Hitler that Germany should give up 'useless ideology and falsely construed supremacies' and should instead raise rations, improve conditions for Polish workers in the Reich, end the public executions of women and children and rein in the use of terror.[5]

In the General Government, Frank made several public gestures in the direction of a more pro-Polish policy. A keen amateur pianist himself, he opened a new Chopin museum in Cracow. (Only afterwards did he learn that the young prodigy who had been given the great honour of performing for him on Chopin's original piano was herself half-Jewish.) He publicly thanked Polish peasants for their hard work, opened a theatre and published leaflets urging the Poles to support the Germans against the Russians. The governor of Cracow actually took part in a ceremony commemorating the Polish soldiers who had died in the 1939 campaign. But Hitler himself was not convinced, and more importantly neither were the Poles. Their hatred of Frank by this point was far too great for them to believe anything he said, and, at the end of January 1944, he had a narrow escape when his train was blown up just outside Cracow.[6]

As we know, Germany had not only annexed the western parts of the country but also envisaged eventually taking over the General Government as well. In such circumstances, there was no way a Polish Pétain could possibly have emerged. And yet there were good reasons why the Nazis might have taken the model of a collaborative occupation (like that the Germans had followed in Poland in the First World War) much more seriously than they did. For the same economic and administrative pressures that forced the Reich to rely heavily on civil servants to run the occupations in western Europe applied in Poland as well. Indeed the Polish administration in the General Government grew very rapidly after 1939: Frank estimated after the war that at one point there were approximately 250,000 Polish civil servants taking orders from some 40,000 German officials. Excluding the rail and post personnel, the number of Germans ranged between a mere 7,300 in 1940 and 14,753 four years later, together with 50–80,000 SS and police, and anything up to half a million troops. Since a disproportionate number of the Germans were based in major towns – and concentrated there more and more as insurgency spread through the countryside – Frank's civilian administrators relied even more on Poles in many areas than these figures suggest. They did so even though their own regulations mandated the use of German for government business and discriminated against 'all non-Germans'. They were discovering too late that, like most imperial powers, they simply lacked the manpower to do everything by themselves.[7]

In the Polish countryside, the very brutality of Frank's regime reflected its precarious grip. In the rural county of Janow, for instance, only fifty German civil servants, backed up by around 500 policemen, ran an area the wartime population of which fluctuated between 150,000 and 200,000. Helping them were approximately 1,500 Polish government employees – mostly teachers, municipal and village officials, foresters and members of the food administration. Poles collected the taxes, supervised the harvest, distributed food and mail, issued identity papers, ran the railways, maintained public roads and looked after refugees. (This is not to mention the tens of thousands of Poles and Jews who built roads, dug irrigation canals and anti-tank ditches and quarried stone in appalling conditions.)[8]

Unlike in western Europe, the Germans relied on terror from the start to keep the Poles in line. Polish civil servants could be shot as hostages or sent to the camps in the event of partisan attacks. Meanwhile, elective posts and self-governing institutions like cooperatives were scrapped or run by German appointees, and the nobility, in particular, were closely watched and their estates placed under direct German supervision or simply confiscated. Subjected to periodic purges, the bureaucracy absorbed German-speaking refugees from the annexed territories of western Poland, as well as a few Ukrainians and ethnic Germans. At first these measures seem to have worked satisfactorily for the Germans: a recent in-depth study describes a situation of 'widespread compliance' – at least until 1942. Many Polish civil servants obediently returned to work after the invasion, while a stream of new recruits were attracted by official rations or by the hope of evading labour deportation or other duties.[9]

So miserable was the state of the country, so few the alternatives, that such jobs remained attractive well after the Germans' harshness towards those holding them became evident. Officials responsible for bringing in the harvest were especially vulnerable. 'I remember how in Krasnik the *Kreislandwirt* yelled, "You Polish pigs, forget Poland. He who does not surrender the quota will be sent to [the concentration camp at] Majdanek!",' recalled a member of one food quota committee. 'Before our eyes, five hamlet heads were arrested because their villages failed to turn in the quota. They all died within a week.' Fearing such treatment if they failed, village mayors became violent and abusive towards the peasants, and fear spread among the latter. 'Today is the last day for the delivery of the grain quota,' a Polish doctor noted in November 1940. 'Throughout the whole day, horse-drawn wagons full of grain have been coming to town. Farmers are fearful of arrest so they are bringing their quotas on time.'[10]

But in 1943, the turning tide of the war and the rise of criminal gangs and armed resistance units in the woods marked a new mood. 'No mayor, secretary, hamlet head or his deputy should come to tell me that the people do not listen to him,' warned one county official in January 1943. 'I demand of them to be able to impose their will under all circumstances.' This was no longer possible for the same post-holders now had others to worry about besides the Germans. Violence was spreading through the countryside – formerly far safer and more peaceful (unless one was Jewish) than the towns, and far less touched by the Germans themselves. Numerous partisan attacks brought German 'pacification' raids in retaliation, which left dozens of villages smouldering and thousands of their inhabitants dead. As in France, the brutality of the occupation escalated as it ended, undermining the morale and effectiveness of civil servants, dooming what little was left of Hans Frank's 'flexible line' and forcing the Germans to rely more and more heavily on the SD, the police and the Wehrmacht itself.

POLICING THE EAST

Ensuring the collaboration of local police and auxiliaries was important to the Germans in the occupied eastern territories for one main reason: the Final Solution. Tasked with the murder of hundreds of thousands of people, many of them living in scattered and remote settlements across vast areas, Himmler's troops – and above all the few thousand men in the SS *Einsatzgruppen* – depended upon others for help, and they were recruiting locally even before official permission came through in the second half of July 1941. Not that it proved difficult to find them, for volunteers soon presented themselves. Some were criminals or former communists anxious to prove their reliability to the Germans. Others had suffered at the Bolsheviks' hands – especially policemen, who were keen on revenge. 'Latvian policemen almost all have a bit of sadism in their blood,' noted the German official running the provincial town of Daugavpils (shortly before he was dismissed for corruption, fur coats and silver spoons (from murdered Jews), dozens of bars of soap, flying jackets and hundreds of cigarettes having been found in his possession). But many others joined in too, some willingly, others to escape starvation, captivity or labour service. In Poland, those used in anti-Jewish operations included young men who had been conscripted into the Baudienst labour organization.[11]

Members of Baltic fascist groups were a key source of enthusiastic recruits, and many of these rivalled the Nazis in their blending of anti-Semitism and anti-communism. Their murderous handiwork was evident, for instance, in the city of Vilnius – one of the great centres of Jewish learning – where thousands of Jews were murdered in a nearby former beauty-spot by young men belonging to a well-known prewar paramilitary organization. Aged mostly between seventeen and twenty-five, these riflemen escorted convoys of their victims through police checkpoints into the forest at Ponary, where they shot them in giant storage pits that the Soviets had dug for aircraft fuel. Those who tried to escape through the pine woods were hunted down. To curious German servicemen who turned up to watch, they justified their actions by telling them what the *Bolsheviks* had done to them.

Yet high-minded race idealism was not the only motivation; there were considerable material rewards as well. The Polish journalist Kazimierz Sakowicz witnessed men bargaining over the corpses under the pine trees. 'For the Germans 300 Jews are 300 enemies of humanity,' Sakowicz notes, 'for the Lithuanians they are 300 pairs of shoes, trousers and the like.' Nor was it just the riflemen who took advantage of these pickings. One day silk stockings were sold in the nearby village; the next it was furs, nightshirts or gold extracted from the victims' teeth. As tens of thousands of corpses filled the sandpits and goods and violence spread across the countryside – drunken guardsmen occasionally started shooting Poles and other Lithuanians – there were quarrels and fights, and, in at least one case, one of the executioners was himself forced to wear the star of David and then shot because he had taken some watches which 'belonged to someone else'. When villagers turned up hoping to buy clothes, the guards offered to shoot Jews of the 'right' size from the next convoy to appear.[12]

Scholars have recently suggested that Aryanization across western and central Europe helped to buy public compliance in the Final Solution. The argument has been overstated for in most of western Europe there were simply not very many Jews, but it is much more plausible in the case of eastern Europe, where the Jewish population was much larger and more highly urbanized, where assimilation had not gone so far or been regarded as so integral a part of political identity, and where the overall standard of living was much lower. In Hungary, the local ethnic Germans welcomed the assault on the Jews that took place in the spring of 1944, after the Wehrmacht had moved in: 'the process of purification,' according to a report, 'proved to be very beneficial for the ethnic German group'.

In the Ukraine, clothes from groups of gypsies and Jews murdered by German forces were similarly offered to local *Volksdeutsche*. In the former Pale of Settlement, in eastern Poland and western Belorussia, largely Jewish *shtetls* still existed in 1941 as islands of urban life in a sea of Christian peasants. Many Poles ignored the instructions of the exile government and profited from Jewish property. 'Cases of mass robbery of former Jewish property bear eloquent witness to the ongoing moral decay,' an underground newspaper warned in 1942. In towns, 'in the departments and offices, everyone traded'. In rural areas, many peasants robbed Jewish survivors before denouncing or killing them. Resistance leaders were deeply worried at their 'demoralisation and running wild'.[13]

'A mob of peasants descended on the town, seeking bargains, asking for property, promising in the name of the Holy Trinity to return them after the war,' one survivor recalled of the day when the Jews were expelled from one small town. 'Soon they were driving off the goats and cows that the Jews could not take with them.' The peasantry gathered with their carts outside the *shtetls* in anticipation of the massacre or expulsion of their Jewish inhabitants; in larger towns, the wartime ghettoes were gutted by looters in the aftermath of their abandonment. Across the Ukraine and Belorussia, entire streets, quarters and even whole towns and villages stood empty for months on end, the buildings ransacked or used as stores.[14]

Yet peasants were an unsentimental and suspicious lot, and taking goods from those who could no longer use them did not translate automatically into support for the Germans or their views. 'It was not a question of straightforward hatred or traditional anti-Semitism; Nazi propaganda of the usual bizarre type hardly ever reached these far-flung isolated hamlets. It was rather a question of total estrangement,' wrote Michael Zylberberg, a Jewish survivor, about the Polish villagers he lived among briefly.

To them the Jews seemed beneath contempt, an odd, strange group from another planet . . . It was as if the Jews had been gone for centuries. The general reaction was indifference and it was hard to imagine that any amicable cooperation had ever existed. The villagers did not know in detail what had happened to the Jews but they wondered if they would ever come back, since many of them owed the Jews money. This last troubled them greatly.

Although the first wave of Jewish killings had not been greeted with mass unease, by 1942 a new question was emerging in Christian minds. 'It's the Jews now, when will our turn come?' some asked. By the end of that year, rumours circulated round Brest that, 'after the Jewish actions', the turn of the Poles, Russians and Ukrainians would follow. Encouraged to participate in the plunder of Jewish property – which many of them did – local populations nevertheless felt increasingly uncertain about the Germans and the wave of lawlessness in which they themselves took part.[15]

The Germans preferred to try to channel Jewish goods into the hands of local authorities directly. Apart from anything else, this made it easier to pay for administration and for raising additional police and auxiliary forces against partisans. In Belorussia, in particular, where nationalists were allowed to enlist in such German-approved bodies as the People's Self-Help Organization and the Union of Belorussian Youth, revenues from the sale of Jewish houses became the single largest source of income for the local authorities. As in Poland, the Germans relied on native mayors, and control of the newly formed Jewish ghettoes and their resources provided them with a major source of funds.

Although the killing slowed during the winter of 1941/2, there were more massacres the following year, and it was now that the real build-up of local police forces – the *Schutzmannschaft* and ethnic German *Hilfspolizei* – took place, especially after Hitler approved the expansion of local units to help fight the partisans. The new recruits swore 'to be true, brave and obedient, and to carry out their duties conscientiously in the struggle against murderous Bolshevism'. Under only patchy German supervision, these policemen were effectively the masters of the local communities they ran and became notorious for their corruption, drunk-enness and cruelty. They were mostly very young Belorussian and Ukrainian village men and they rounded up and killed Jews, Poles and gypsies without qualms. By 1943, no fewer than 45,000 Belorussians were serving as auxiliary policemen; outnumbered by the partisans, they were nevertheless killing Jews and villagers targeted in anti-partisan raids as efficiently as the Germans themselves until they were transported west to escape the advancing Red Army and conscripted into the Waffen-SS.[16]

THE END OF GERMANIZATION

Berlin needed non-Germans for much more than killing Jews. Germaniz-ation itself always existed in two dimensions. One – the priority for Himmler in 1939–42, when he believed the end of the war was imminent – was directed towards the future. General Plan East was its primary expression; the colonies established at Zamość and Hegewald were first steps along this path. This vision of Europe's new elite was exclusive, proud and unaccommodating. But the other dimension was oriented towards the needs of the war itself, and, as the struggle dragged on, and the future of the General Plan East receded, this increased in importance and urgency. The Germans could not now afford to be quite so selective over whom they counted within the fold; in fact, even as they relaxed the criteria for Germanness, they also came to abandon the principle that only Germans could fight for the Reich and to such an extent that Slavs – even Russians – entered the ranks of the German armed forces. There was no real change of heart at the top of the Third Reich, but the needs of the war allowed the promise of collaboration to flicker briefly in the East.

In the summer of 1942, Hitler entrusted Himmler with the task of deciding how the 'Germanic' peoples should contribute to the New Order. Norway and the Low Countries had been targeted by SS recruiters since 1940 and there was an immediate propaganda offensive hailing the coming union between the Reich and the other 'Germanic peoples' of northern and north-western Europe. Himmler established a 'Working-Group for the Germanic *Raum*' and opened a 'Germanic House' in Hanover: representatives of west European SS groups attended the opening ceremony.

All of this was really designed to find 'Germanic' recruits to fight on the Eastern Front, and thousands of volunteers signed on and left. After Stalingrad, the effort was stepped up. The Belgian fascist Léon Degrelle converted his Légion Wallonie into the SS Freiwillige Sturmbrigade 'Wallonien', hoping that Himmler's support would bring him closer to power in Belgium itself. The Flemish nationalist VNV's Flemish Legion became the SS-Freiwilligen Legion 'Flandern'. 'Charlemagne' and 'Nordland' divisions also grew out of these smaller national legions, intended to be kernels of a future European SS. Never reaching full divisional strength, their volunteers fought to the very end with the desperation of men who had nothing to return to. The SS even formed a small Britische Freikorps (BFK), whose members – a few hundred British POWs who were a mix of former Mosley men and adventurers – wore the Union Jack on their Waffen-SS uniforms; they never saw combat service, though a tiny number of British soldiers did serve in other SS units. No fewer than 125,000 west Europeans eventually served in the ranks of the Waffen-SS – about 50,000 Dutch, 40,000 Belgians (divided between Walloons and Flemings) and 20,000 from France. These were not insignificant numbers, but they were hardly evidence that Europe was burning to volunteer.[17]

If the numbers of 'Germanic' recruits were never enough for Himmler, the Wehrmacht saw to it that neither were those of his purely German units. He had formed the first Waffen-SS divisions – Adolf Hitler, Das Reich and Totenkopf – in order to show that the SS too could play a role as a military force, and they were largely responsible between them for the brutal and fanatical reputation that the Waffen-SS gained. But the Waffen-SS was initially only a small fraction of the size of the Wehrmacht, and attracting German volunteers into it was becoming harder and harder. Recruiters in the Reich itself, scouring the Hitler Youth and the Labour Service, reported that 'the young men are not only anti-Waffen-SS but basically opposed to any form of military service'. The SS tried press-ganging 'volunteers' for front service, but their officers were often critical of the new recruits' motivation and training.[18]

It was therefore as German war losses mounted, and the ideological barriers to conscripting non-Germans became less important, that Himmler realized that confining himself to western Europe would be self-defeating: it was obviously much more sensible to exploit the fears and anxieties of those most directly in the path of the Red Army. Once the initial decision had been taken to look more widely for recruits the Waffen-SS expanded incredibly fast. Of the 170,000 men serving in its ranks in early 1942, only 18,200 were not Reich Germans; yet by the war's end, nineteen of its thirty-eight divisions were basically made up of foreigners, nearly half a million of them, mostly from eastern Europe. By 1944, it had become an enormous bureaucratically bloated army with no real claim to racial exclusivity, and its troops were increasingly either ethnic Germans from south-eastern Europe or other nationalities entirely.[19]

The ethnic German 'Prinz Eugen' Division was the forerunner, formed to help the hard-pressed Wehrmacht combat the partisans in Yugoslavia. Himmler's recruiters also began press-ganging ethnic Germans from the Serbian Banat region, and when people protested, he responded dismissively: 'Nobody cares what we do down there with our racial Germans.' Hungary, Yugoslavia, Romania and even Poland eventually contributed more men to the Waffen-SS than western Europe. Racial guidelines were quickly relaxed, and complaints reached Himmler that his recruiters were taking almost anyone: 'entirely unsuitable replacements' from Hungary included men 'with epilepsy, severe tuberculosis and other serious physical disabilities'. Some were not even ethnic Germans at all. One divisional officer regarded it as 'perfectly possible that many of the racial German volunteers do not regard this war as their own nor consider service in the Waffen-SS as their duty to the German people'. In fact, many of these 'Germans' later deserted or surrendered when the opportunity arose to American or British troops declaring themselves to be Poles or Hungarians. As early as December 1942, the SS angrily noted the behaviour of some *Volksdeutsche* soldiers from Upper Silesia who were spotted 'in Polish bars in uniform conversing with the Poles in Polish' and engaging in defeatist talk about the Eastern Front.[20]

Himmler was also rethinking his racial theories in order to take advantage of the intense anti-communism in the Baltic states. By the end of 1942, they were providing the Germans with almost as many volunteers as the Low Countries, and numerous Latvians were serving in the German armed forces, police units, labour battalions and SS death squads. By 1943 he had conscripted more than 30,000 'Germanizable' men into the Latvian and Estonian SS Legions, and high-ranking Baltic army officers held senior SS grades. Once he had barred the French and Walloons from serving in the Waffen-SS because they were not 'Germanic' enough; yet, having inspected some Estonians undergoing training, Himmler now found that 'racially they could not be distinguished from Germans . . . The Estonians really belong to the few races that can, after the segregation of only a few elements, be merged with us without any harm to our people.'[21]

In fact, Himmler even came round to the idea of giving Estonians and Latvians greater political autonomy because he could see that the Germans' refusal to grant this was jeopardizing his recruiting efforts. After Stalingrad, the youthful prewar finance minister, Alfred Valdmanis, a member of the Latvian Self-Administration, told the Germans that the Administration would only cooperate in recruiting volunteers for the Eastern Front if the Germans pledged to privatize property – till this point much Soviet-era legislation still remained in force – stopped arresting Latvian patriots and, above all, moved towards recognizing Latvian independence. The outspoken Latvian was sent to Germany for the rest of the war, watched by the SD. (After 1945 he fled to Canada, where he became the country's director general of economic development before his wartime career was unearthed.) From then on, the Germans continued their usual game – promising concessions in the future, while the list of their demands got longer and longer. Hitler definitively ruled out political autonomy for the Baltic peoples in November 1943; but this decision was not made public, in order not to staunch the flow of recruits.[22]

Once Hitler lifted his ban on forming SS 'national legions', Himmler also started recruiting in areas where the population had never been considered 'Germanizable' in any sense but which had some kind of historical association with Germany or the Habsburgs. One of these was Bosnia, where Muslim regiments had acquired a legendary status fighting for the Emperor Franz Joseph in the First World War. Himmler repeated the experiment, recruiting thousands of Muslims – many of whom had been attacked both by the Croatian Ustaše and the Serbian chetniks – into the SS 'Handschar' Division in 1943. The local Bosnian *ulama* warned people not to collaborate, but the Mufti of Jerusalem was flown in to give his blessing, and Himmler himself, who had decided that the Bosnian Muslims were not Slavs but Aryans, inspected the new division in Sarajevo. Their fezzes adorned with SS runes, and their flag emblazoned with the scimitar which gave their unit its name, they enjoyed similar privileges to those of their Habsburg predecessors, including special rations and concessions to their religious practices. But those – and they were many – who joined thinking that they would be behaving much like the old Habsburg units had done, guarding their own homes and carrying out gendarmerie duties, were soon disillusioned. After training in France – where some of them mutinied – they were mostly deployed in anti-partisan operations in Yugoslavia and acquired a grim reputation for atrocities.

With the Habsburg model in mind, other ethnic groups beckoned as well, notably the Ukrainians. They were anti-Bolshevik and pro-German, yet bringing *them* in meant reversing well-established Nazi policy and coping with another of Hitler's numerous prejudices. The Führer thought the Habsburgs had erred in insisting on Ukrainian independence in the First World War and he could never forgive the Ukrainians themselves for the killing of the German military governor there in 1918.[23] Nor did Ukrainian activists help their own cause; within the fascistic Organization of Ukrainian Nationalists (OUN), the two main factions, OUN-B (led by Stepan Bandera) and OUN-M (led by a former Austrian officer called Andrei Melnyk), spent much of the time fighting one another. After the invasion of the USSR, Hitler's contempt for what they stood for was reflected by award of the south-west Ukraine to the Romanians and of Galicia to the General Government. Rosenberg's hopes of an independent Ukraine vanished, and when the Abwehr's OUN-B units mutinied in protest they were sent to Sachsenhausen concentration camp. In Koch's Reich Commissariat all Ukrainian activism was driven underground. 'No German soldier will ever die for that nigger people,' Koch declared, adding that whenever he met an intelligent Ukrainian he felt obliged to shoot him.[24]

In Galicia, the Ukrainians could be more hopeful, however, because the governor there, SS-Brigadeführer Otto Wächter, was supportive. At the same time that he was helping to organize the killing of the region's Jews (a policy of which he was a hardline proponent), Wächter permitted the formation of a Ukrainian national committee and allowed Ukrainians to carry out social and welfare work. The number of

Ukrainian-language schools in the General Government, for example, rose from 2,510 in 1939 to over 4,000 in 1942, and Poles began to worry openly about this resurgence.[25] Levying a Ukrainian armed division for the Waffen-SS was the natural next step, and Wächter approached Himmler, who approved the idea on condition there was no mention of the word 'Ukraine'. As a result, on 28 April 1943, Wächter announced the formation of the SS 'Galicia' division, and his chief Ukrainian collaborators called for volunteers. The response was overwhelming. Nearly 100,000 men volunteered, almost all from the western Ukraine, showing what an opportunity the Germans had squandered by Koch's brutality in the Ukraine itself.

Many of the older men among the 30,000 who were eventually accepted had fought for the Austrians in the First World War; for them, as for German officers involved too, memories of their earlier comradeship were never far away, and the Habsburg army's official marching tune was adopted by the division. The Germans themselves were taken aback by the intensity of their response. Their training was accompanied by lectures on Ukrainian history, frequent religious services and concerts as well as considerable drinking, especially when their relatives visited. In May 1944, Himmler inspected the division, and the following month it was assigned to the Eastern Front, where it was placed under the operational command of a former Habsburg officer.[26]

In three years, German policy had apparently swung round nearly 180 degrees. Yet despite the recruiting posters, which showed German and Ukrainian soldiers fighting together through the cornfields, neither Himmler nor the Ukrainians really had much more confidence in each other than before. The Germans were still making no promises about a future Ukrainian state; all they wanted was cannon fodder. As for the Ukrainians, they knew they had little reason to trust Himmler. The SS Galicia Division itself did not last long: it was smashed within days by the Red Army near the town of Brody, losing most of its 14,000 men and regrouping with barely 1,500 survivors.

Its sacrifices had not been completely in vain. Himmler was impressed by its performance and ordered that it be built up again. It was now allowed to call itself 'Ukrainian', and its propaganda took on a more overtly nationalistic character. But the war was driving it further away from the Ukraine and German and Ukrainian interests were ceasing to converge. After being employed in savage anti-partisan operations in

Slovakia, many of its men deserted when the Germans retreated across the Carpathians. Staying near their homes and fighting a vain last-ditch struggle to save Galicia from communism, they continued their resistance against both Soviets and Poles long after the war had ended everywhere else.[27]

The Führer's own doubtful verdict on them emerged from a surreal conversation in the Berlin bunker, in late March 1945. It was harsh and unromantic and entirely consistent with his political attitudes all along:

HITLER: One never knows what is floating around. I've just heard, to my surprise, that a Ukrainian SS division has suddenly turned up. I know absolutely nothing about this SS division.

GÖHLER: [SS liaison officer] It has been in existence for a long time.

HITLER: But it has never been mentioned at any of our conferences. Or do you recall otherwise?

GÖHLER: No, I don't remember.

. . .

HITLER: [Referring to foreign units in general, and the Ukrainian Division in particular] Either the unit is reliable or it isn't reliable. At the moment, I can't even create new formations in Germany because I have no weapons. Therefore it is idiocy to give weapons to a Ukrainian division which is not completely reliable . . . If it composed of [former] Austrian Ruthenians, one can do nothing other than immediately take away their weapons. The Austrian Ruthenians were pacifists. They were lambs not wolves. They were miserable even in the Austrian army. The whole business is a delusion . . . I don't want to maintain that nothing can be done with these foreigners. Something can indeed be made of them. But it requires time. If one had them for six, or ten years and controlled their homelands as the old monarchy did, they would naturally become good soldiers. But if one gets them when their homeland lies somewhere over there [in enemy territory] – why should they be expected to fight?[28]

LOOKING FOR THE RUSSIAN
DE GAULLE

In recruiting non-Germans for the Nazi cause, Himmler was following where the Wehrmacht had led: indeed the SS never matched the army in the number of non-Germans it conscripted. For some time, army commanders had been improvising wherever it was necessary to find collaborators locally and combing the POW camps for so-called 'Hiwis' (*Hilfswillige* = auxiliary volunteers). To keep them away from Hitler's eyes, they were not formally listed on the Wehrmacht strength until well after Stalingrad. But plenty of Russians and Ukrainians were working as translators, drivers, cooks, servants and guards even before the winter of 1941. 'Many NCOs and lieutenants had "their own Ivans",' recollected an observer, and their growing reliance upon them – by the spring of 1943, there were half a million of these auxiliaries – helped German officers get used to the idea of working with 'Eastern units' more systematically.[29]

As German manpower needs grew, the arguments for levying 'eastern troops' became harder to resist, and in the late summer of 1942, their position was regularized under new army regulations governing their conditions of service. By the end of the year, almost half the troops of the front-line 134th Infantry Division were former Soviet POWs. Much of this shift was due to the extraordinary head of the organization section of the army high command, Claus von Stauffenberg. Inspired by his neo-Bismarckian vision of a Germany united in partnership with a post-Bolshevik Russia – until he lost faith in the Nazis' ability to bring this about – Stauffenberg is better known, of course, as the man whose despair at the way Hitler was conducting the war led him to plant the bomb in Hitler's bunker in July 1944.

Stauffenberg had plenty of reasons to feel frastrated. Getting the Führer to agree to make use of Russian anti-communism was, of course, even harder than overcoming his prejudices against Ukrainians. His objections to Russians were well known, and he tried to get the army to confine its use of Soviet volunteers to small anti-guerilla units. It proved easier to change his mind where non-Russians were concerned, and a visit by a Turkish general pleading for Turkic prisoners to be released paved the way for separate 'legions' for Turkestanis, Caucasian Muslims, as well – incongruously – as for Georgians and Armenians. A Cossack Corps, accompanied by its women and herds, fought alongside the Germans, before its unreliability and high desertion rates led it to be transferred west. There was also a Kalmuck cavalry corps and Tatar units. Scattered across Europe, by the spring of 1945 some ended up in Brittany, where they terrified the local population. Overall, according to one estimate, at least 650,000 former Soviet citizens wore German uniform. The Wehrmacht was turning into a multi-national army despite itself.[30]

Yet the clearest indication that policy was being driven not by the SS but by the more pragmatic Wehrmacht was the decision to look for military collaborators among the Russians themselves. For Hitler this was the bitterest pill of all to swallow. Apart from his anti-Russian prejudices, his reluctance may have been influenced by the fiasco that took place in November 1942, when some 2,500 Russian volunteers in a secret anti-partisan unit had killed their German liaison officers, kidnapped their own commander and handed him over to the partisans. As late as mid-1943 Hitler was still insisting that 'we shall never build up a Russian army'. Yet in January 1942, Rosenberg's adviser Otto Bräutigam had already proposed the idea of setting up a 'Russian counter-government' led by a 'de Gaulle' figure, ideally to be chosen from among the captured Red Army generals. Rosenberg was too timid to endorse such a bold suggestion, and Hitler, unsurprisingly, ruled it out. When some captive Russian generals were interviewed, they made it clear that Germany needed to make more definite political commitments than Hitler was willing to do. But officers in the East were aware that the Germans could not afford to be so aloof. As the situation at Stalingrad deteriorated, the army's intelligence chief in the East, General Gehlen, called for 'the fictitious formation of a national Russian sham government', utilizing 'personalities with impressive names' from among the captive generals to front a 'National Committee for the Liberation of the Homeland.' By the Christmas of 1942, the army, Rosenberg's Eastern Ministry and Goebbels' Propaganda Ministry all basically agreed that a more political approach to the region's future was needed.[31]

One possible candidate for the past of 'Russian de Gaulle' was a well-known Soviet general, Andrei Vlasov, who had been captured that summer after the failure of an attempt to lift the siege of Leningrad. The tall, gaunt Vlasov was an impressive figure who had played a major role in the defence of Moscow, and the Wehrmacht were interested not only in his military experiences but also in using him politically. In captivity, he told the Germans straight out that, while many in the Soviet military were ready to overthrow Stalin, they were unsure whether to count on the Germans or the Anglo-Americans. Underlining the durability of the Soviet regime, Vlasov emphasized that the Germans would fail to topple it without Russian help; only an alternative Russian army held any chance of defeating it. He himself inclined to the Germans, he admitted; nevertheless, the question remained of what future they envisaged for Russia.

Because they knew Hitler and Bormann in particular would be violently opposed to any suggestion of political warfare with Russian help, Vlasov's Wehrmacht backers tried to enlist the support of Alfred Rosenberg and his Eastern Ministry. Rosenberg agreed, provided that Vlasov's programme did not contradict his policy of appealing to the non-Russian nationalities. He also insisted that any propaganda effort should be directed to the Soviet side of the front. But when German planes began flying over the Soviet lines, distributing millions of leaflets from Vlasov calling for the end to Stalinism, an honourable peace and a Russian place in the New Europe 'without Bolsheviks and capitalists', they 'accidentally' dropped them over German-held territory as well. The Wehrmacht reported huge interest among the Russians under their control, and Vlasov's cause was greatly enhanced. In the spring of 1943 he was allowed to tour the occupied territories in order to publicize his 'Russian Army of Liberation' (as the *Osttruppen* were now called). Speaking in Smolensk, with German officers standing next to him, Vlasov declared he did not want to bring back Tsarism, capitalism or Bolshevism. The message was straight Russian nationalism. 'The Russian people lived, lives and shall live,' he declared, with German officers near by. 'It will never be possible to reduce it to the status of a colonial people.' He denounced German atrocities against the civilian population and predicted that Germany's war in the East would fail unless it made its long-term plans for the USSR clear.[32]

All of this, one hardly need say, ran directly counter to Hitler's thinking. In June 1943, he explicitly ruled out promoting indigenous collaborators at all in the former Soviet territories; the most he was willing to tolerate was a purely propaganda effort. According to him, following the Japanese strategy – 'something like the so-called free or national China in East Asia' – was simply too dangerous, since any large Russian armed force might eventually turn against its German backers. As so often, he returned to the supposed experiences of the First World War, in this case with the consequences of Germany's efforts to raise a Polish army. 'We already had a tragic lesson with the Poles in the World War,' he objected.

Ludendorff said later: 'People told me I would get 500,000 men.' Any sensible person should have immediately said: 'Those 500,000 Poles won't fight against Russia, rather they are setting up an army to take on Germany and Austria if necessary and to liberate Poland. Each nation thinks of its own interest or not at all [oder sonst gar nichts] . . . This is all theorizing in cloud-cuckoo-land, to imagine that our goal is to set up independent, autonomous states.'

For the Nazi hardliners like Hitler or Erich Koch, real support for Russians, Ukrainians or any other nationalists was anathema. Here, at the very top, was the basic stumbling-block to any effort to recruit collaborators in the west European sense.[33]

Even the idea of a proclamation to 'all the peoples of the East' was more than the Führer was willing to countenance, and Goebbels himself could not bring him round. When Hitler learned some of the Osttruppen had defected to the partisans, the remaining units were transferred to western Europe and the Balkans, and it seemed as though the idea of a 'Vlasov army' was gone for good. Himmler himself was at this time still one of Vlasov's strongest opponents. In October 1943, he reaffirmed his contempt for the whole idea of recruiting Untermenschen and explicitly criticized the thought of establishing 'an army of liberation under General Vlasov'. Indeed he could not believe that Vlasov had had the temerity to lecture German officers on the way they treated the Russians, nor that none of the Germans had protested.[34]

Yet Himmler's racial objections were by now being tempered by Germany's growing manpower shortage in the East, and at the very last minute his own SS was becoming the last hope of the easterners. The Waffen-SS itself was nearly thirty divisions strong and included, as we have seen, large numbers of former Soviet citizens. The Cossack Corps had just transferred to the SS to secure better equipment, and at the same time the new SS-Generalkommissar for Belorussia was supporting nationalist circles there even more than his civilian predecessor had done. In the spring of 1944 Himmler came round to the idea of recruiting among Soviet Muslims in an 'East Turkic Corps', expanding the Turkic regiment which was then actively fighting partisans in Belorussia. The proposed leader of the new SS Osttürkischer Waffenverband was Wilhelm Hintersatz, better known as 'Harun-el-Raschid' Bey, a former Austrian officer who had converted to Islam and once worked with Enver Pacha on the Turkish General Staff. Although Himmler himself was still dreaming of a German advance to the Urals, his fantasies had an increasingly pronounced Habsburg tinge and he spoke about building – before the German *Ostwall* – 'a defensive frontier in the East of neo-Cossacks, after the great models of the Austro-Hungarian frontier and the Russian model of Cossacks and soldier settlers'.[35]

A particularly nasty collaborator who joined the SS at this time was a psychopathic adventurer called Bronislav Kaminsky. The antithesis of Vlasov's disciplined and high-minded brand of political activism, Kaminsky was an engineer from the small town of Lokot in Belorussia who had fallen foul of the NKVD before 1939 and ruled the region as his own personal 'empire' for nearly two years after the Germans invaded. His rough and ready so-called Russian National Liberation Army had been built up with Wehrmacht help and numbered more than 10,000 men. It was kept in line by Kaminsky's own Kurtz-like penchant for violence; German liaison officers visiting his camp in the Briansk forest got used to seeing the bodies of his former aides swinging outside the main entrance. 'Clever Hans' von Kluge, the commander of Army Group Centre, tolerated the thieving, pillaging and rape of the 'famous' Kaminsky's men because he helped run anti-partisan operations from his self-proclaimed Republic of Lokot, and Kaminsky himself was awarded the 'Iron Cross of the Eastern Peoples – First Class'.[36]

But what went on out of sight in the remote marshes and woodlands of Belorussia struck even the Germans rather differently when transported hundreds of miles to the west. In the summer of 1944, Kaminsky's men retreated in disarray from Belorussia and as the newly rebranded 29th Waffen-SS Division they were sent to help crush the Warsaw uprising. There, in the working-class district of Ochota, they distinguished themselves by a series of crimes so horrific they shocked their German superiors. Killing an estimated 30,000 people in barely a day, they left cellars full of machine-gunned corpses behind them and robbed and raped the staff and patients of a local cancer hospital. Even the SS officers in charge were disgusted and pulled them out. Slowed down by loot and incapacitated by alcohol, their brutality had merely prolonged the resistance of the desperate Polish residents and made the Germans' task harder. On his way to Łódź – loaded down with watches and jewellery – Kaminsky himself was arrested and shot, probably by the Gestapo. Offered the remaining men from Kaminsky's brigade, Vlasov himself contemptuously described them as 'mercenaries' and refused to take most of them.[37]

The Russian general himself was clearly of a very different calibre from a dissolute opportunist like Kaminsky. By the autumn of 1944, with the Red Army smashing through the lines of Army Group Centre and advancing to the borders of Poland and Romania, Himmler was coming to rethink the Vlasov option – the V-100, as wags called it, after the regime's obsession with 'secret weapons'. This was, in Hitler's words, 'a time of what we can do, not what we want to do'. Still convinced that the Germans would eventually manage to turn the tide and push the Russians back east to the Urals, Himmler met Vlasov and agreed to back him in launching a Committee for the Liberation of the Peoples of Russia' (KONR), whose first meeting took place at the Hradčany castle in Prague in November. Himmler had had to override his security men's fears about the location in order to allow Vlasov to hold it in an occupied Slav country.[38]

But what did such a quixotic enterprise really signify at a time when the Red Army was advancing rapidly westwards and about to invade German soil? An expression of the bankruptcy of German efforts at political warfare in the East, the new Committee was just one one of several pathetic and totally fictitious governments set up well past their sell-by date: Pétain's French government reformed in Sigmaringen, and there were, or would shortly be, Albanian, Croatian, Serbian and Greek national committees as well: Austria's spas and ski resorts were filling up with collaborators nervously waiting for their exile to end. KONR itself was purely a propaganda spectacle, laid on for the benefit of the Russians themselves. None of Hitler's ministers were present in Prague, and not even Himmler showed up. Plans to treat KONR as a sovereign government were scrapped. Instead, the Germans sent a special train from Berlin to convey the 'delegates' – many of them were in fact eastern workers who had been plucked from camps and dressed up for the occasion. Vlasov himself had drawn up a manifesto that made no mention of Hitler or National Socialism and itemized fourteen points in a clear signal to the Western Powers that he was thinking of Woodrow Wilson and 1918. But this was nothing more than 'cabaret', as a German observer described it; had Hitler thought there was the slightest chance of its being realized, Vlasov would never have been allowed to issue it.[39]

It did not matter that all these schemes existed only as fantasy options; at this late hour, Berlin's turf wars retained a life of their own, and Vlasov was still a plaything. Alfred Rosenberg, Himmler's long-standing enemy, could not keep from getting involved even though he now headed a ministry without any meaning. (When Himmler's man there, Gottlob Berger, finally resigned in December 1944, he started his report to Himmler with the words: 'Subject: Reich Ministry for the No Longer Occupied Eastern Territories'.) The fact that the only German soldiers on Russian soil were POWs did not stop Rosenberg devoting his last months in office to making trouble for Vlasov and his backers in the SS. Furious at being shunned by Hitler – who had not seen him since November 1943 – Rosenberg warned of the danger of Russian nationalism and encouraged representatives of the non-Russian nationalities to hold rival congresses: tiny 'national committees' of Azerbaijanis, Tatars, 'Turkestanis' and 'Caucasians' thus waged a paper war on the 'Greater Russians' around Vlasov. In early 1945 came the last farcical act with a constituent conference of Ukrainian nationalists in Weimar and the formation of a Ukrainian national army. Rosenberg's Eastern Ministry and Himmler's SS were fighting, even when there was nothing of substance left to fight about: Vlasov and these other increasingly pathetic groups of anti-communist nationalists were merely the pawns in their by now meaningless rivalry. The East remained what it had always been for the Nazis – a place in which the imagination ran wild and reality could be ignored.

Most of the Russians contemplating the Vlasov option were, of course, more realistic men. Monitored by the SD, their anxious discussions of what it all added up to gave an acute sense of the grim alternatives they faced:

The minority maintains that Germany has lost the war one way or the other and will be occupied by the Anglo-Americans ... Among these Russians the view prevails that after their victory England and America will destroy Bolshevism in

Russia and establish 'genuine democracy'. 'If today we go with Vlasov,' these Russians say, 'the Anglo-Americans will not forgive us this.'

The other part of the Russians feels that . . . victory over Bolshevism in Russia is only possible with the help of a real Russian army. The Russians also say: 'We often expressed the wish to join the Vlasov Army, but it has always been turned down. Instead we were told to join the Waffen-SS. This we haven't wanted because it isn't a genuine Russian force.'[40]

Prompted by similar feelings, and despite Himmler's support, Vlasov himself refused to allow troops under his command to form part of the Waffen-SS. After an angry exchange, it was actually the SS who capitulated, and the Russian *Untermenschen* who prevailed. Himmler thus allowed the first Vlasov division to be formed in December 1944 as an independent unit; the following month, another was authorized as well, and Vlasov was given the power of direct command, independently either of the Wehrmacht or of Hitler, as its commander-in-chief. It was the finest hour for his 'Russian Liberation Army': yet two years of discussion had produced no more than 50,000 troops, a poor return from the millions of Soviet citizens who had worked for the Wehrmacht and the millions more who had been murdered or allowed to starve.

But the Nazi leadership had drifted off into a dream world. What reason was there for Himmler to make any greater effort to win the Russians' support when as late as January 1945 he still apparently seriously believed that Russia could be forcibly oriented east and south – turned into an 'East-Russian Siberian state' with its western border running down past Moscow? Supremely confident when this was not warranted, the Reichsführer-SS saw dangers where they did not exist and even took minor Serbian and Slovak initiatives to recognize Vlasov as signs that a dangerous anti-German pan-Slav front was opening up. None of the other Nazi leaders were any better at facing the truth. Goebbels regarded Vlasov as a puppet, while Göring, when he met him, talked about nothing more substantial than Red Army ranks, uniforms and questions of military protocol. Finance Minister von Krosigk wanted to intensify 'Vlasov propaganda against the Bolsheviks' to hammer home the contrast in living standards between Germany and Russia – according to him, this was (absurdly) 'the trumpet under whose blasts the Soviet Jericho will fall'. Only Hitler was more realistic, seeing the Vlasov troops not as the source of an effective psychological weapon that would bring down the Red Army but merely as extra cannon fodder, to be pushed into the front line to save German lives. Vlasov and his staff were packed off to the Hotel Richmond in Karlsbad, where the Sudeten *Gauleiter* Konrad Henlein was outraged at the prospect of Russians staying in such luxury and threatened to kick them out.

What was likely to happen to them had already become all too clear in February after the fall of Budapest. Amid the debris of the ruined city – a mass of rubble after one of the grimmest sieges in Europe – Red Army men had searched out 'Vlasovists' and shot most on the spot. Anyone who admitted to speaking Russian or failed to answer in German while wearing German uniform faced instant execution. In fact none of Vlasov's men had been sent to Budapest; but his name was now applied to all former Soviet citizens who had changed sides.[41]

It was only at the very end of the war in Prague that the Vlasov army saw its first and last real fighting, and this was ironically *against* the Germans. In early May, several days after Hitler's suicide, the First Vlasov Division, stationed outside Prague, did something remarkable: in response to a request by Czech insurgents it switched sides and helped the Czechs, who were trying to expel the SS from the Hradčany citadel. It was keen to demonstrate its anti-German attitude to the Allies and believed it had done so. But the Americans refused to enter the city, honouring their boundary agreement with Stalin, and with the Red Army about to move in from the east, the Czechs turned on the Vlasov men and ordered them to leave. Most made their way to American lines, from where they were then handed over to the Soviets: as for Vlasov and his senior officers, they were executed for treason in 1946.[42]

On the whole, the fate of Germany's 'eastern helpers' after the war was not a happy one. The Cossacks were delivered to the Russians, and Croatian and Slovene collaborationist units were handed over to Tito's men, who murdered most of them. But once they realized that this fate was likely to await others who had also fought for the Germans, the Allies abandoned their mandatory repatriation policy and things started to look up for the survivors. Granted the status of Displaced Persons, once they proved they had not been members of the SS (which some had in fact been), many Ukrainians and Balts eventually resettled in the USA, Canada, Australia and Britain, or remained in West Germany. With the help of Reinhard Gehlen's intelligence contacts – the well-connected Gehlen had been a not noticeably effective head of the

German army's military intelligence service in the East during the war – US intelligence chiefs bypassed Congressional barriers to the recruitment of Nazi war criminals and financed émigré anti-communists through the 1950s in the hope that they would help the Americans to build up a viable anti-Soviet resistance movement in the western USSR. This was yet another failure; the phantom army was no match for Soviet counter-intelligence. Nevertheless, their CIA backers – fully informed of, but indifferent to, their protégés' horrendous wartime crimes – helped a number of leading collaborators to find new homes, thereby ensuring that Belorussian National Day was celebrated each year around the barbecues in South River, New Jersey.[43]

15
Opposition

'*Yet wars and rebellions are not only a curse and misfortune; they also spawn hope and creativity . . . In opting for war, we came to understand who we were. Only in armed conflict could we affirm ourselves and force the enemy to understand us and grant us recognition.*'

Milovan Djilas, *Wartime* (New York, 1977), 22

'POLISH METHODS'

When they marched into Poland in 1939, the Germans encountered fierce resistance from the outset, and a few Polish soldiers were still in the woods fighting when the Wehrmacht handed over control to civilian rule. By the spring of the following year, these had been hunted down and killed. But pacification did not bring acceptance, and the population's hostility to the Germans was unmistakable. 'Polish children especially treat Germans on the street most impolitely,' complained one incoming administrator. Faced with 'passive resistance' on a large scale, others were struck by the fact that 'the Pole feels himself master of the street'. There was no 'open resistance', the Kreishauptmann of Biłgoraj wrote, but German orders were only obeyed when they were enforced. The occupiers seized hostages, withheld rations and executed notables in order to show the Poles, 'who are experienced in revolutionary affairs', that the Third Reich would be tougher than the Russian tsars had been.[1]

For opposition to the invaders had certainly not been eradicated by the murderous 'ethnic housecleaning' that Heydrich's men had carried out in the first days of the occupation. On the contrary, as one activist recalled, 'secret societies were springing up all over the place, like mushrooms after the rain'. The Gestapo thought this was too uncoordinated

– and the Poles were too disunited – to pose a significant threat. And it was true that, after the defeat, most of the established political parties had formed their own underground sections alongside hundreds of other smaller groups. But within a month of the German invasion, the pre-1939 parties of opposition had formed the Main Council of National Defence, and the main wartime armed resistance organization, the Union for Armed Struggle (ZWZ), known later as the Home Army (AK), had also emerged.[2]

Despite this ferment, there was little overt armed resistance. Major Henryk Dobrzanski 'Hubal' – the 'crazy major' as the Germans called the former Olympic equestrian – was the officer who had refused to disarm and led a small group of his soldiers into the early months of 1940, anticipating the opening of a new front in the West. His unit had inflicted heavy casualties on several German units, but the cost had also been heavy: the Germans had burned several villages and killed an estimated 700 people. Local sentiment had turned against Hubal for this reason, and the underground feared the impact on its own recruitment more generally. But when the ZWZ told him to quit, he refused, and he continued his raids until he was eventually cornered and killed by the Germans at the end of April. Almost immediately there followed the round-ups that were supposed to prevent a unified resistance movement emerging at all. As a result of the so-called AB (Extraordinary Pacification) Action, around 30,000 Poles were arrested and sent to concentration camps, including the new camp at Auschwitz; 3,500 were shot in the execution ground outside Warsaw. Coming after the internment of the professors of Cracow University, and coinciding with the Soviet mass murder of Polish army officers, the AB Action indicated that it would be suicidal to openly oppose the Germans unaided.[3]

These events confirmed the already prevailing view among the reserve army officers involved in clandestine activity: they believed they should build up an underground organization that would emerge in the open only at the point when it seemed possible to evict the Germans. This was exactly the strategy they had followed with some success during the First World War, when several years of careful underground preparation had eventually culminated in the Polish uprising of October 1918. Now they aimed to repeat the same tactics. Resistance, wrote the commander of the underground in November 1939, should reveal itself only when Germany seemed close to defeat 'or at least when one leg buckled. Then

20. Looking for shelter in the ghetto, Kovno, 1941.

21. Roma deported from Germany are held in the camp at Belzec, 1940.

22. Marshal Antonescu and his wife at home, March 1942.

23. Hitler and Mussolini inspect Italian troops in the Ukraine, 28 August 1941.

24. Removing the Royal Yugoslav eagle from army helmets, Croatia, May 1941.

25. Painting on the Ustasha 'U', Croatia, May 1941.

OPPOSITION

26. German troops set fire to a Serbian village, 1941.

27. Commissars of the Molotov partisan brigade, Belarus, 1942.

28. Jews captured during the Warsaw ghetto uprising, April–May 1943.

29. Corpses unloaded from the Jassy death train under the supervision of a Romanian policeman, 1 July 1941.

30. Hungarian Jewish deportees are marched through Kamenets-Podolsk to the execution site, Ukraine, 27 August 1941.

31. Auschwitz personnel at a weekend retreat, 1944.

32. Forced labourers in the Plaszow concentration camp, 1943–4.

33. Survivors, the day after the liberation of Dachau, 30 April 1945.

34. Soviet troops enter Budapest, January–February 1945.

35. Danzig, 1945.

36. Shaving the head of a woman accused of sleeping with a German: note the portrait of Hitler on the left, France 1944.

37. The Nazi elite in captivity, Mondorf-les-Bains, summer 1945. Göring presides. Ribbentrop is standing in the first row far left behind the seated Lammers; Walter Funk stands next to him; Seyss-Inquart is between them. Robert Ley stares off to the right; Alfred Rosenberg stands behind his right shoulder, Frick behind his left shoulder. Among the assortment of military men, Party officials and bureaucrats, von Krosigk, Dönitz, Frank, Jodl and Keitel may also be found.

we should be able to cut through veins and tendons in the other leg and bring down the German colossus.' Initially they were thinking in terms of months, and expecting Poland's ally, France, to help. But France's collapse in the summer of 1940 catastrophically belied this prognosis, and many people were so disheartened that they left the resistance in the second half of 1940, realizing the occupation was not going to end soon.[4]

Thus Poland became the first, and most patient, exponent of the secret army approach to resistance. Many other countries – Norway, Yugoslavia, Denmark, Holland, Belgium and France – later followed the same strategy: fear of provoking pointless civilian casualties, and the desire not to draw the Germans' attention to the smaller-scale strategically valuable sabotage and intelligence-gathering activities that resistance groups could also carry out, were its chief – and completely understandable – justifications. Things would have been much the same in Britain, too, if we may judge from the record of the Channel Islands, where resistance was similarly discouraged by the local authorities.

From the summer of 1940, therefore, the Poles concentrated on building what became the most remarkable underground state on the continent – complete with its own educational, judicial, welfare and propaganda wings. Its purpose was to preserve Polish society from disintegrating under the pressure of Nazi occupation policies, while preparing for the moment when the Germans could be driven out.[5] The lack of armed incidents before 1942 in the General Government was thus no indication of the country's state of mind. Gestapo arrests did badly disrupt the Home Army. Nevertheless, it soon had tens of thousands of men in training for a general rising. The SiPo/SD, always anxious that the police were not being tough enough, could not understand the Wehrmacht's sanguine assessment; *they* feared, as early as January 1941, that they were standing 'on the edge of a volcano'.[6]

WESTERN EUROPE

In Poland, resistance was a response to deliberate denationalization. But in western Europe, where the German occupation had no such radical purpose, the Wehrmacht was less harsh, and against the backdrop of widespread unemployment and dissatisfaction with the old interwar order, the promise of a New Order seemed initially worth pursuing. The Belgian socialist Henri de Man did not speak for himself alone when he proclaimed: 'For the working classes and for socialism, this collapse of a decrepit world, far from being a disaster, is a deliverance.' Yet the Germans proved completely incapable of exploiting this powerful desire for a new beginning and soon helped sow the seeds of opposition there too.

Even where the invading troops behaved 'correctly', public opinion turned very quickly against them. The German army's traditionally draconian approach to occupation did not help, nor the battery of threats and prohibitions they immediately issued: unauthorized public demonstrations, breaking curfew, listening to British radio or circulating 'German-hostile' books and pamphlets all became serious offences. The replacement of military by civil occupation authorities brought no improvement – quite the reverse. Popular frustration grew once it became clear that there was no end in sight to the shortages and cuts, that German rule meant isolation from the rest of the world and that there would be no early peace settlement.

In western Europe, however, popular anger was directed initially as much against local officials as it was against the German military. In April 1941, the American diplomat George Kennan noted the way the Wehrmacht had striven to preserve a non-political approach to occupation, and 'outwardly a correct and impartial attitude throughout towards the civilian population, regardless of race, class or nationality'. This was often appreciated, especially after the chaos and panic of the invasion itself. The French in the Eure, for example, recognized that 'the most absolute discipline reigned in the ranks of the invaders' and that 'acts of vandalism, demands, and assaults were the exception'. But if the French acknowledged the efforts made by German officers to help bring in the harvest and to feed refugees, they also resented the arrogance, high-handedness and requisitioning that sent crops and commodities across the Rhine, and the rationing that made transport increasingly expensive. Some of this was the hostility which occupation always brings in its train. But whether or not the military behaved properly, the fact was that politically they also embodied the threat of a sweeping and entirely unwanted Nazification of people's way of life. It is this prospect that explains why in Belgium, for instance, alongside the widespread anger people felt towards the French, their contempt for their own politicians and their deeply ambiguous attitude (in the early days) towards the British, an observer could detect the swift emergence of 'almost general hatred' towards the Germans.[7]

One expression of this was in an almost instantaneous hostility directed against women who fraternized with the invader. Defeat was a failure for the men of the nation, and a blow to masculine pride, above all in countries where soldiers had been seized as prisoners of war, so it is scarcely surprising that sexuality and morals became a lightning-rod for attitudes towards the Germans. One of the first fliers to be posted on the walls of Warsaw alerted Polish women not to consort with Germans. In the spring of 1940, Hitler ordered that 'Danish women are to be approached with caution'. When German soldiers took no notice, waiters refused to serve their companions, and people spat at them in the street: a diplomatic brouhaha quickly followed. In France, the problem was even worse because so many French POWs were absent, and a police commissioner warned that the combination of alcohol and women was fuelling fights between Frenchmen and German soldiers. At stake was the honour of all sides. 'We are the victors! You have been beaten! The women, even the children, of your country are no longer yours!' a German territorial commander in a French town told a French magistrate. Taunted that 'your daughter is the Boches' whore', one neighbour reported another to the German authorities. In fact, withholding sexual favours from Germans could be seen as an act of resistance, just as taking a German lover was assumed to reflect a desire for self-advancement and selfishness. (At Liberation, French courts treated prostitutes more lightly than other women, since they regarded them as motivated by professional rather than political motives.)[8]

Occupation thus often began with an intense discussion about ethics, about how people should behave towards the occupiers, especially since no one knew how long they might be around. The prospect of indefinite foreign rule was disarming, and such exhortations as emerged tended to be highly prescriptive efforts to reorient a public badly bewildered by the shock of defeat and (at least in the minds of the authors of these works) in danger of letting the nation down. 'They are the conquerors. Be correct with them . . . but don't exaggerate,' advised Jean Texcier's *Conseils à l'occupé*. At a time when there was still much criticism of the Norwegian king for fleeing to England, his supporters circulated 'Ten Commandments for Norwegians'. Article 1 ran: 'You shall obey King

Haakon for whom you yourself have voted.' It was followed by: 'You shall hate Hitler and never forget that with no declaration of war he allowed his fellow-murderers to attack a peace-loving people.' It went on to denounce as traitors not only those who associated with Germans or Quislings but any member of parliament who voted to depose the King. In all, it was not a document that conveyed confidence in the unguided judgement of the average Norwegian.[9]

There were, however, plenty of other early indicators of opposition to the Germans' presence. People boycotted German-language newspapers and moved when a German sat next to them: in Norway this actually became a punishable offence. They clapped in cinemas when newsreels showed British soldiers and they applauded Allied POWs themselves when they were marched through the streets. Dress also expressed dissent: in the Italian-occupied districts of France, a piece of macaroni conveyed the inhabitants' contempt. In the Netherlands, where the Germans banned flags, people wore carnations for Prince Bernhard. Royal birthdays and public holidays celebrating the First World War dead or national independence became rallying points and triggered new bans. 'Long live England!' and 'Dirty Germans!' were heard on 11 November 1940 during marches in Brussels and Paris. Students protested against the dismissal of Jewish faculty in Delft University the same month, and there was a large strike over the round-ups that took place in the Jewish quarter of Amsterdam the following February.[10]

The first clandestine newspapers, pamphlets and tracts appeared early on, some of them carrying news gleaned from the BBC, others denunciations or satires on the Germans. 'Underground newspapers are multiplying,' the Belgian lawyer Paul Struye noted in his diary in October 1940. Modest in appearance though they were, he nevertheless found that they were, 'as a symptom, comforting.' The following month, it was forbidden to sell stencils or duplicating paper in Clermont-Ferrand without authorization.[11] Graffiti on walls and bridges was another way of striking back. In Warsaw, 'Poland will be Victorious' was painted along a street wall; the BBC's 'V for Victory' campaign resulted in a rash of such signs, alarming Goebbels. King Haakon's own 'H-7' sign became ubiquitous in Norway, for the occupation had quickly restored his popularity, despite (or because of) German propaganda attacking him personally. In April 1941, new graffiti in Brussels celebrated the Greeks and the Yugoslavs, and the following month ironic slogans –

'Heil Hess!' – embarrassed members of the occupation forces. When the inscription 'Only for Germans' was painted on benches in Cracow, it was accompanied within days by the reminder: 'The benches are ours, the arses are yours.' And even the occupiers' propaganda was often turned on itself. The SS got worried when the Poles circulated a spoof pamphlet at the end of 1941: entitled 'Learn German!', it differed from the genuine article by offering useful phrases for members of the resistance: 'Halt! Hands up, face to the ground! Were you a member of the Party, SA or SS? Whoever lies, will be shot. We will deal with you as the Germans dealt with us. Hands behind the head, face the wall. Take a shovel and dig a grave!'[12]

Even joining the new mass political organizations allowed by the Germans could constitute an act of opposition. In the Protectorate, almost all eligible Czechs joined National Solidarity (Národní Sourou-čenství) in order to demonstrate their sense of national unity and their defiance of the Czech fascist movement. 800,000 Dutch joined the Nederlandse Unie before it was banned in December 1941, prompted above all by the desire to block the Dutch Nazis. The organization's ambiguous purpose allowed it to serve as a symbol of national solidarity and a possible vehicle for opposition to the Germans, which is exactly why it was eventually shut down.[13]

The disintegration of the very bodies which the Germans had hoped would drive forward the Nazification of the occupied countries of north-western Europe led Himmler to conclude even before the end of 1940 that the policy of the 'gentle hand' had failed. But that was a self-serving conclusion designed to justify an SS takeover. In fact, Himmler's power was still limited outside the East – in Belgium and France, for instance, the SiPo/SD could not make arrests without the authorization of the military commander – and the military and civilians in charge disagreed with his analysis. Prioritizing public order and tranquillity rather than political change and Nazification, they were not overly alarmed by public resentment nor by Nazi failures at building new pro-German mass parties. They absorbed the evidence of their political unpopularity and focused instead on building up reliable administrations. They monitored opinion closely, censored the press and discouraged large groups and demonstrations. Aware of people's unhappiness at the occupation, they were chiefly concerned that it should not turn violent – whether in acts of sabotage or in assaults on their own troops.

But when events did threaten to escape their control, their reaction was harsh and frequently made things worse. In the Netherlands, they responded to demonstrations for Prince Bernhard by dismissing the mayor of The Hague and interning General Henri Winkelman, the Dutch commander in chief. In Norway, the badly mishandled political transition at the start of the occupation, and the emergence of the deeply unpopular Vidkun Quisling, prompted uproar and protest from the start, and, as civil disobedience spread, mass arrests followed, pushing overt resistance underground. Unions, churches, professional bodies and the universities came together to prevent the Nazification of the country: by 1941 a coordinating committee representing forty-three member organizations had nearly three-quarters of a million people behind it. Norway's clandestine 'Milorg' army was formed in late 1940 and recognized by the government in exile: like the Poles, it planned to avoid action until nearer the moment of liberation. 'Lie low, go slow' was its motto as it sought to avoid German attention and minimize attacks on civilians.[14]

In many areas, prominent notables were seized as hostages by Wehrmacht officials at the start of the occupation to guarantee the peaceful behaviour of the inhabitants, but in fact there were very few direct assaults on German military personnel or property, and many of them were soon released. In any case, some military commanders doubted their efficacy and preferred to respond to unrest in a more graduated way. In Belgium and northern France, for example, General von Falkenhausen was anxious to allay bitter memories of the German occupation in 1914–18. He regarded hostage-taking as a blunt instrument of order – nothing, he later wrote, was more enduring than hatred – and he preferred to reduce attacks by making the local police responsible for helping to guard military installations. Until the summer of 1941, he regarded these measures as working well and described the internal situation to army high command as 'peaceful'. Small acts of sabotage had not, in his view, been able to disrupt the continued exploitation of the Belgian economy or the recruitment of more than 200,000 Belgian workers for the Reich. Between the start of the occupation and the end of May 1941, there were only seven death sentences issued under his jurisdiction, and none of them was carried out. Only one German soldier was killed in the entire time, shot in a brawl over a Belgian girl. Despite the tiny police forces at his disposal, von Falkenhausen seemed sanguine, a view largely shared in France by his old friends, Field Marshal von Witzleben and General Streccius; Streccius' successor in Paris, Otto von Stülpnagel, did not see things very differently. Recent scholars have rightly questioned the contrast drawn between a 'bad' Wehrmacht in eastern Europe and a 'good' Wehrmacht in the West. By 1943, the distinction makes no sense. But at this stage it was certainly behaving much less repressively and more rationally than the police and the SS who were running their occupation regime in the General Government.[15]

With tightly organized national resistance networks avoiding direct confrontation, the biggest headache for the Germans was initially strikes, labour unrest and spontaneous surges of popular anger triggered off by food and housing shortages and lagging real wages. Industrial stoppages occurred in north-western Europe through the autumn of 1940, mostly over food, clothing and soap rations. During the winter, there were also food riots, often led by angry housewives. These were chiefly directed against local authorities but when such stoppages threatened their economic interests, the Germans clamped down harshly. They did so in Amsterdam in February 1941, when strikers protested the persecution of Dutch Jews, and again in the working-class mining towns of Belgium and northern France during strikes in May. On the anniversary of the German invasion, a major stoppage – the so-called 'strike of the 100,000' – broke out around Liège, Hainaut and the Limburg basin, which only ended when the employers conceded substantial wage rises and embarked upon secret negotiations with the workers' leaders. In northern France, when the French police failed to break the picket lines, the Germans brought in soldiers and declared a state of siege. The military commander in Lille ordered the miners back to work, suspended the distribution of meat and arrested 400 ring-leaders, most of whom were sent to the Reich as forced labourers. By the second week in June the strike was over.[16]

A strike that long was a substantial achievement in the face of the Germans' overwhelming power. But General Falkenhausen did not want to bring 'Polish methods' to northern France and Belgium, and, had he done so, the strikers might have hesitated. In the General Government, stoppages faced far more draconian punishment. When workers in the main Warsaw tram garage downed tools in December 1940, the Germans threatened to kill them all, and they quickly returned. Many German police officials in Poland felt terror worked. 'Not a single Pole

... really works for the benefit of the German government,' wrote one; it was thus useless to try appealing to them, still less to look for collaborators.[17]

THE REVERBERATIONS
OF BARBAROSSA

From the outset, resistance had a vital geopolitical dimension. Without foreign backing, providing sanctuary (for those able to reach it), money, supplies, training and, above all, hope, resistance in occupied Europe would have been even more limited than it was. The first Great Power to offer support were the British, who had been considering waging an unconventional war against the Germans even before the actual outbreak of hostilities. A military intelligence officer from London had visited eastern Europe in the summer of 1939 to investigate the possibilities of cooperation in the event of a German invasion. Contacts with the extremely efficient Czech and Polish intelligence services proved invaluable to the British war effort, and after September, discussions began in London about how to use Europe's underground opposition to help defeat the Germans.[18]

After Dunkirk, the British government needed a new strategy and believed it had found one in the idea of backing popular uprisings against Nazi rule. In July 1940 it established Special Operations Executive (SOE) with the mandate – provided by Churchill – to 'set Europe ablaze'. Without any likelihood of being able to take on Germany directly, the British planned to exploit the enemy's weaknesses through their traditional weapon of economic warfare (chiefly via the sea blockade). But stirring up unrest behind enemy lines was seen as a supplementary nuisance, one whose value it was believed the Germans themselves had demonstrated through their own 'Fifth Columns'. Hugh Dalton, the minister of economic warfare, talked about creating organizations behind enemy lines

comparable to the Sinn Fein movement in Ireland, to the Chinese guerillas now operating against Japan, to the Spanish irregulars who played a notable part in Wellington's campaign, or – one might as well admit it – to the organizations which the Nazis themselves have developed so remarkably in almost every country in the world. This 'democratic international' must use many different methods, including industrial and military sabotage, labour agitation and strikes, continuous propaganda, terrorist acts against traitors and German leaders, boycotts and riots.[19]

In fact, neither Dalton nor anyone else in the British cabinet had a firm grasp of the immense difficulties and deterrents facing the Nazis' victims in occupied Europe, nor had they come to appreciate how complicated it was to conduct small-scale sabotage operations and large-scale political action at the same time. They saw German occupation in old-fashioned terms and failed to appreciate the efficiency of its police forces or the scope of its propaganda. They simply imagined that the desire for liberty on the part of those living under occupation would explode into insurrection given the right spark. The Czechs and the Poles in exile in Putney and Kensington were more realistic. They were unwilling to jeopardize their intelligence networks by organizing ambitious mass uprisings that could only fail, and they understood that resistance could accompany military operations but not act as a substitute for them. Fortunately for all concerned, SOE's rhetoric was not matched by its funding, nor by its access to military resources. By the time, some two or three years later, that it had grown into a major factor behind enemy lines, its role in Allied war strategy – and that of the European resistance itself – had been scaled back, thanks to American involvement, and to Eisenhower's preference for taking the Germans on directly at a time of the Allies' choosing.[20]

This change of heart regarding SOE was also because the British had come to realize the uncontrollable and often undesirable political dimensions of the *levée en masse*. For with the German invasion of the Soviet Union, the geopolitics of resistance were completely transformed. The invasion gave Europe hope, and everyone recalled Napoleon's disaster in the snows of Russia. A new Great Power had now been brought actively into the war against the Third Reich – one desperate for relief from the German onslaught, and hoping that armed insurrection in the Wehrmacht's rear might blunt its power. As we have seen, the Wehrmacht's drive into the Russian interior was accompanied from the start by fears of partisan resistance. Mostly imaginary at first, this underground war soon became all too real as Stalin urged Soviet citizens to rise up behind the enemy lines. The idea of a guerilla campaign coordinated from Moscow and stretching not only into the occupied eastern territories but even across much of the continent of Europe gave the Nazis nightmares. But gradually it became something more than fantasy.

In fact, well before the emergence of bands in Belorussia, the largest and earliest uprisings had already occurred far to the south, in Yugoslavia, which had been occupied in April. By the summer the Ustaše regime's bloody massacres of Serbs had created turmoil, and in this chaos the Yugoslav communists spotted their chance. On a train in Montenegro in July, Serb survivors told a young communist horrifying stories of villages being surrounded, and of everyone being clubbed to death or driven over nearby ravines. His message to them, and to the provincial Party organizers, was to prepare for armed struggle. He was only spreading the Party line. When Tito informed Moscow that he was planning a partisan war, Georgi Dimitrov, the Comintern's general secretary, was enthusiastic. 'Communists should rouse the people to open the struggle against the occupier,' he told him. The Comintern gave prominent coverage to the Yugoslav partisans, and by 1942 was describing them as a model for others to follow.[21]

That summer – just as the partisan war was being centralized in the USSR itself and finally receiving Stalin's full backing – Dimitrov praised the insurrections in the Balkans. He insisted that what counted was not terrain but spirit: 'The source of partisan strength is not nature but the people.' Only the Yugoslavs' sectarianism worried Moscow. The Communist Party there had decided even before the invasion of the USSR that a war might be their route to power, one which allowed them to take advantage of the political vacuum caused by the German occupation and bypass the stage of 'bourgeois-democratic' revolution. As orthodox Leninists, they were convinced the Red Army would quickly defeat the Germans and that proletarian revolutions would then erupt across Europe. But for the Soviets, who were anxious to foster their new and still fragile relationship with the British, this was a stupid and dangerous illusion. 'The issue is liberation from fascist oppression not socialist revolution,' they told Tito.[22]

For the Yugoslav communists did not have the field to themselves. The Serbian nationalist chetnik movement, led by royalist army officers, had also mobilized against the Ustaše. By August, western Serbia was up in arms: Tito's partisans numbered about 8,000, and Mihailovic's chetniks even more. The two sides made an effort to cooperate, but while the partisans wanted to use the war to transform Yugoslavia into a federal, communist state, the chetniks were traditionalists fighting to bring back the Serbian king and to restore a Greater Serbia inside Yugoslavia. Arguments about the country's future thus plagued resistance cooperation from the very start. Nowhere would such arguments be more bitter or lethal than in Yugoslavia, where several hundred thousand people may have perished as a result.

The other thing that drove the partisans and the chetniks apart was their reaction to German reprisals. Like the Poles, Mihailovic and the chetnik leadership were cautious about acting prematurely. They had vivid recollections of 1917, when an uprising against the Bulgarian military occupation had been crushed at the cost of thousands of lives. Mihailovic himself basically wanted to unify all resistance forces under his personal command, and to avoid a general insurrection that could, in his view, lead only to disaster. His worst fears were confirmed by German reprisals on a previously unimagined scale on 20–21 October 1941. What Milovan Djilas describes as a 'deathly horror' gripped Serbia as news spread that a joint partisan-chetnik attack on a German unit had prompted the Germans to round up nearly 10,000 men in the town of Kragujevac and to shoot 2,300 of them in batches; another 1,736 were executed in Kraljevo. In Djilas's words,

The tragedy gave to Nedić [the quisling Serbian prime minister] 'convincing proof' that the Serbs would be biologically exterminated if they were not submissive and loyal, and to the Chetniks 'proof' that the Partisans were prematurely provoking the Germans and thus causing the decimation of Serbs and the destruction of Serbian culture. As for the Communists, they were given the needed stimulus to call the population to armed struggle as the only salvation . . . The massacres in Kragujevac and Kraljevo were, by their calculated total horror, beyond the comprehension of both Germany's collaborators and its opponents, and could be resisted only by a movement to which its enemies offered death as the only alternative.[23]

The chetniks were so shocked in fact that they seriously doubted whether the Serbs could survive years of such repression and saw no point in further attacks on Germans unless they were likely to lead to liberation. On the other hand, the partisans remained faithful to Moscow's demand for constant struggle. The alliance between the two collapsed and after German offensives drove the partisans out of Serbia, the chetniks slowly rebuilt their organization. For the first six months of 1942, they caused the Germans little trouble, anxious to avoid inflicting further reprisals on the civilian population.

For Tito, however, the winter of 1941/2 was a desperate time. On the run from the Germans, partisan spirits were buoyed only by the news of the successful Soviet counter-offensive outside Moscow. The following spring, the Kozara offensive in north-western Bosnia in June 1942 saw over 30,000 German and Croatian forces deployed against 3,500 partisans, many of whom were killed. But Tito's movement had not been crushed, and their very survival was a kind of victory. As they criss-crossed the country to evade the Axis's increasingly ambitious anti-guerilla operations, they changed from being a predominantly Serbian force to one that more closely reflected their ideology of 'unity and brotherhood', with substantial followings of Croatian, Bosnian, Slovene and Macedonian fighters. By the end of 1942, there were roughly 11,000 partisans in Bosnia and perhaps 40,000 across the fomer Yugoslavia.[24]

Elsewhere in the Balkans, the partisan movement was also spreading. In Greece, the first food protests, riots and strikes had broken out in towns and cities in the winter of 1941/2. But by 1942 the Greek Communist Party had come round to understanding the importance of the mountains, and their minds were concentrated by the arrival of a British military mission, tasked with cutting off the German supply route to north Africa which ran down the vulnerable railway line between Thessaloniki and Athens. The Gorgapotamos viaduct was successfully blown up by a combined team of British and Greek saboteurs, and afterwards the British stayed on, and their Military Mission became a factor of key importance in the development of the second major partisan movement in the Balkans. Helped by Italy's weakness in central Greece, EAM/ELAS – the main armed resistance movement, led mostly by Greek communists – grew rapidly, especially during 1943, until it became one of the largest in Europe and posed a major threat to the German strategic position in the Balkans.

Yet if we were to pause the clock momentarily in the winter of 1941/2, it would have been very hard to predict the later success of these two guerilla movements from their rather limited and precarious situation at that time. In Yugoslavia Tito's forces were on the run (as were the chetniks); in Greece, there were only small isolated pockets of armed men, short of food, clothes and boots. The Germans' draconian counter-insurgency measures had borne out Mihailovic's fears and seemed to confirm the prudence of his low-key approach. In western Europe, armed resistance to the Germans was even more limited. In France, communist attacks on German soldiers triggered off not mass uprising but public shock at German reprisals. And in the Protectorate, Heydrich's campaign of terror ripped through the underground organization that the British had rated as 'one of the best in Europe'. When Beneš became worried and sent in agents to assassinate him, the German response was even more draconian – culminating in the notorious massacre at Lidice. Hitler's open threat to President Hácha that he would deport a huge number of Czechs 'to the East' in the event of further trouble ensured there would be virtually no resistance in the Protectorate until the very end of the war. 'A trip to Prague at the end of 1942 was a trip to tranquillity,' wrote a visiting German. 'Surrounded by war ... The Protectorate was the only Central European land living in peace.' As for charmed Denmark, as late as the spring of 1943 there had still not been a single serious assault on a German soldier reported there; even after the great strike wave of August, the Germans remained sanguine. Visiting in October, a military intelligence officer summed up their attitude as 'somewhat stubborn but not unreachable', adding that 'one can hardly describe the comfort-loving Danes as fanatical freedom-fighters or partisans.' Over much of occupied Europe, it seemed as though the Germans' targeted terror had managed to prevent opposition surfacing, and had broken it up where it had become visible.[25]

THE SOVIET PARTISAN MOVEMENT

Only in the USSR did German counter-terror fail. It was, to be sure, not for lack of effort – not even in the Balkans did German army units cause such devastation as in the occupied eastern territories. Yet small bands of partisans survived the first winter, helped by the success of the Soviet counter-offensive in December 1941. And as they renewed their attacks on the German-appointed village *starostas* and armed guards, the Wehrmacht responded in force. In Operation Bamberg, the first of a series of large-scale operations, German soldiers, policemen and Slovak

auxiliaries rampaged through the countryside, burning and killing anyone they found. By the end they had lost the grand total of seven men,
captured forty-seven guns, torched numerous villages and killed several
thousand peasants. But the partisans, estimated at more than 1,000, had
slipped away and as an effort in large-scale encirclement, with a ring of
armed men gradually drawn tighter and tighter, it was a complete failure.
Few civilians remained alive in the zones that were 'cleared' by these
methods, but the troops – under pressure to meet daily targets set
centrally – rarely achieved either the surprise or coordination required.
The partisans themselves hid in impenetrable marshes or slipped through
gaps in the German lines. Himmler's main coordinator of anti-partisan
operations bitterly criticized such 'so-called mopping up operations' for
'annihilating the population sympathizing with the Bolsheviks' rather
than the partisans themselves.[26]

Not every operation misfired so spectacularly. To the north-east,
round Smolensk, where the Third Panzer Army was clearing the areas
immediately behind the front, 35–40,000 troops outnumbered a partisan force of some 20,000, and, after bitter fighting, the bands suffered
heavy casualties. Nearly half of them were killed, for over 2,200 German
losses. But success like this required huge numbers of troops, frequent
patrolling of the areas after they were cleared and some effort to distinguish between partisan sympathizers and the rest of the civilian population. In the much larger rear areas, where available troops were tied
up guarding long lines of communication, it was impossible to reproduce
these factors.[27]

It did not help that Hitler was intervening directly, pushing for ever
greater 'radicalism'. He was angry that Wehrmacht soldiers were being
held to account for wrong-doing during anti-partisan sweeps and he
demanded use of the 'most brutal means possible'. The Geneva conventions were to be forgotten, 'military chivalry' too – yet somehow the
troops were to try not to kill innocents. Himmler was becoming more
closely involved as well. Charged with overall responsibility for the
anti-partisan campaign, he chose the ruthless HSSPF of Central Russia,
General von dem Bach-Zelewski, to be in charge. The SS general had
overcome the not inconsiderable twin handicaps of Polish ancestry and
Jewish brothers-in-law to rise high in the SS (by this point he had
dropped the Polish-sounding Żelewski) and he was a favourite of Hitler,
too, who regarded him as 'one of the cleverest people'.[28]

Following von dem Bach's appointment, the Germans continued to attempt large-scale encirclements and they continued to kill civilians in large numbers when they could not trap the partisans themselves. There were nearly twenty such operations in 1942 alone and more the following year. The death toll soared, and often hundreds would be shot at a time, leaving heaps of corpses amid the burning villages. This culminated in the horrors of Operation 'Cottbus' in May and June 1943, when one notorious SS unit alone killed over 10,000 people, prompting protests from German civilian administrators. In fact, the only real change that was introduced was that innocent civilians were increasingly being sent off to labour camps rather than murdered. In Belorussia, which would later strike an American journalist as 'the most devastated country in Europe', the average ratio of Belorussians to Germans killed was – on the basis of the *German* figures – 73 to 1, which gives some indication of the scale of the violence that the civilian population suffered. In total, some 345,000 civilians are reckoned to have died as a result of such operations, together with perhaps 30,000 partisans.[29]

It need hardly be said that, by driving civilians into the woods, the Wehrmacht served the partisans well. Their numbers grew steadily – from some 30,000 in January 1942 to 93,000 by August. Using rumours to create 'the illusion of great power', bands of former Red Army escapees and villagers built well-hidden bases in the forests and made the undermanned German units feel increasingly insecure. Winning over the villagers was another matter. In many areas, their belief in the likelihood of a German victory did not collapse until some time in 1943. Farmers did not like armed 'looters' whether they wore German uniforms or called themselves 'partisans', and fear of being punished by the Germans also led them to hand many partisans over to the occupier. Thus – as in all such wars – it was imperative from the start for the partisans to remind those whose food, acquiescence and shelter they needed that Bolshevism had not been completely vanquished.[30]

The first step was to demonstrate their power. On 9 June 1942, a group ambushed a SiPo/SD unit from Baranovitch at the village of Naliboki and killed fifteen men. According to the subsequent German investigation,

All those who had fallen had had their boots taken off, the SS men had also been undressed down to their underpants and all their identity documents and identifying marks had been stolen. One *SS-Obersturmführer* had had a swastika and a Soviet star burned into his chest. From an interrogation of villagers, it was established that 4 Germans, probably two *SS-Unterführers* and the two gendarmerie officers, had been captured and taken through Naliboki on a lorry stolen by the partisans. They had placed red flags in their bound hands. In addition, the partisans had scornfully shouted: 'Look! These are your masters!' The bands of partisans consisted of 90–100 Russians, including parachutists wearing Russian uniform. They were armed with heavy equipment and had radio equipment.[31]

In other areas, around Smolensk for example, partisans re-established the institutions of Soviet local government, appointing new officials, rebuilding the Komsomol and the collective farms, and sowing the fields. They shot some collaborators, and pressed others into the partisans. Proudly they sent a letter, with 15,000 signatures, to Stalin describing their achievement in killing 'Fascist barbarians' and ending the occupation. To the population, they highlighted the Germans' unpredictability and they warned their appointees that even they would likely end up being accused of being partisans, and shot or sent 'to Germany where they will perish'. 'The bandit, bloodsucker and cannibal Hitler' had a programme for destroying 'all Slavic peoples', and the 'German Fascist band' was simply carrying out his orders. 'The Commander of the Partisan Movement in the Territories Temporarily Occupied by the Germans', on the other hand, gave collaborators a chance, offering them an amnesty if they quit working for the Germans immediately. After all, the proclamation ran: 'Many of you were deceived and misled in various ways by the German cannibals.'[32]

Gradually the partisans' resilience overcame not only the Wehrmacht, but also the scepticism of the political elite in Moscow. At the end of May 1942, the Central Staff of the Partisan Movement was established, led by a young Belorussian communist official, Panteleimon Ponomarenko. Panicked by the initial success of the German offensive that summer, Stalin overrode the military's objections and came round to accepting Ponomarenko's view that a properly supplied partisan movement could cause real trouble in the Germans' rear. At the start of September he gave a reception in the Kremlin for some partisans. Praising his guests, Stalin told them, having already been informed by Churchill that no second front could be opened in 1942: 'You must open the second front, the partisans, the people, and we will help.' 'Fan the Flames of the All-People's Movement,' urged *Pravda* that November: Stalin's orders, it went on, signified 'the transfer of the partisan movement to a new higher level'. By the end of the year, there were an estimated 102,500 men and women under arms, and despite the German sweeps, the movement was spreading rapidly through eastern Belorussia and Russia.[33]

As a result of recent research, we know much more than we did about who the partisans were and how they lived. They were mostly Russians and Belorussians, for the movement was much weaker in the Baltic states, the plains of the Ukraine and the area of Army Group North. It was above all a product of the pre-1939 USSR and never emerged so strongly in the regions it had annexed in that year. There were approximately 20–30,000 Jewish partisans as well, and even some Jewish partisan units, but in general the Wehrmacht's assumption that Jews were synonymous with partisans was wide of the mark; on the contrary, many partisan commanders had a deeply ambiguous view of the Jews who came to them for help.

In general, the bands formed around Red Army men, or local villagers whose knowledge of the paths through the forests and swamps was indispensable. Hidden in almost impenetrable woods, they built dispersed camps defended by bunkers and gun emplacements. But conditions were harsh: they could not light fires during the day, and their dug-outs were often damp and muddy, freezing in winter, infested with mosquitoes in summer. Winter exposed the bands – especially to attack from the air – and food became scarce. On the other hand, from mid-1942 onwards, primitive air-strips allowed supplies to be brought in from the Soviet side. A report of the Jewish Bielski partisans to the Kirov Brigade gives a good indication of the scale of their activities. Tasked with looking after survivors of massacres as well as with partisans, the Bielski group – several hundred strong – had stockpiled potatoes, cabbages, beet, grain and meat, some of which was stored secretly. In the camp they built a makeshift bakery and mill since the Germans had burned down those in the area. There was a sausage-making unit, shoemakers, tailors, gunsmiths, saddlers and carpenters; there was a common kitchen and a 'hospital', with a doctor and two nurses.[34]

By the autumn of 1942, Moscow's impact was evident in the growing standardization of groups into brigades and detachments, based on the

Red Army model, with a military commander and a political commissar as adviser. Many partisans who had survived on their own wits for more than a year openly doubted the value of military training and formal planning. Impetuous and brave, though also prone to panic, they often questioned Moscow's orders, preferring costly direct attacks on enemy garrisons to sabotage operations of greater military significance. Politically as well as militarily, they were an unknown quantity. Thus, the partisan experience introduced volatile new elements into a Bolshevik system already under enormous strain – an ethos of freedom, vengeance and individual responsibility, and a patriotism that reflected local and regional pride as much as anything wider. Clashes were not uncommon among different pro-Bolshevik units, often requiring the intervention of the Central Staff. In the early days Moscow was in direct radio contact with only a handful of groups, and such control was hard. But helped by cheaply produced radio sets and a network of stations, Central Staff was able to contact 42 per cent of its units by August 1942 and 87 per cent by the following May.

The result of these improvements was that, from the spring of 1943, the Soviet partisans' sabotage operations tied up increasing numbers of troops, slowed communications with the front and had an increasing impact on the course of the war itself. That summer, two major operations, involving between 90,000 and 120,000 partisans, demolished miles of railway tracks behind the lines of Army Group Centre. More spectacular if less immediately useful, other units undertook highly dangerous forced marches deep into the western Ukraine to help the Party rebuild itself in these areas. One column, four miles long, reached the foothills of the Carpathians, suffering heavy losses after being strafed from the air, but alarming the SS at the possibility that the partisan war was spreading far to the west. Such raiders saw themselves as an elite, believing – much like their Yugoslav counterparts – that 'movement is the mother of partisan strategy and tactics'. By the time the bulk of Russian territory had been liberated in early 1944, and the Central Staff was permanently disbanded, a large and sophisticated Soviet guerilla movement – well equipped with crude but effective arms – had emerged. While western Europe was crushed into sullen silence, with resistance mostly confined to illicit activities that did not assault the Germans directly, Stalin's support allowed the partisans in the occupied eastern territories to survive the winter of 1941/2 and grow. The costs were horrific – hundreds of thousands of civilians killed, and thousands of villages burned down – but the Germans never felt secure.[35]

RÉFRACTAIRES

If there was one man who could be said to have stirred up things in western Europe it was Reich Labour Plenipotentiary Fritz Sauckel. At meetings of the Central Planning Board in Berlin in 1943 and 1944, his forced labour drives were accused of being 'responsible for the European partisan nuisance'. France, where there was very little armed activity before mid-1942, provided a dramatic confirmation. When Sauckel's conscription decree was published in August, Vichy's popularity began the nose-dive from which it never recovered: there were strikes in Lyon and Nantes in October, stoppages and riots. In February 1943, after Sauckel demanded another half a million workers, Laval's Compulsory Labour Service (STO = Service du Travail Obligatoire) made work in the Reich an alternative to military service, and local officials warned that unprecedented hostility was being caused by young men having to register. 'There is no doubt that the name "Sauckel" sounds pretty bad to French ears,' warned a German observer in Paris. 'The mere announcement of an impending visit of the Gauleiter is sufficient for one to see for days hundreds of young people hurrying to the various Paris stations with their little suitcases.'[36]

It was thus thanks to Sauckel that the idea of 'taking to the Maquis' emerged. To be sure, not all – indeed often only a small minority – of the *réfractaires* in hiding took up arms. Young men arrested near Cahors in July 1943, were being 'fed by the people of the village, who have looked after them well' and were engaged in nothing more insurrectionary than 'smoking locally-produced tobacco'.[37] Yet even if those fleeing conscription did not necessarily intend to actively resist the Germans, their initial act of disobedience pushed them beyond the law and spawned new forms of illegality as well. Those who hid them were concealing outlaws; others supplied them with false papers or mounted raids on town halls to destroy local registers. As the police, collaborators and Sauckel's own units hunted them down, there were fights and shoot-outs. The constant hunt for *réfractaires* was forcing young men into the arms of the resistance, and Vichy's gendarmes were aware of the danger. 'Treat *réfractaires* as those who have gone astray, not as criminals,' the Languedoc gendarmerie were instructed in August 1943. But by the autumn, an estimated 15–20,000 young men had enrolled in resistance formations that were much more tightly organized than a year earlier: thanks to the efforts of the major movements, the three leading groups in the south – Combat, Franc-Tireur and Libération – had united, and the main groups in the north joined them under the prompting of de Gaulle's representative, Jean Moulin, to form the National Resistance Council.[38]

While many areas of France remained quiet, others – like the Auvergne – witnessed almost daily attacks on prisons, banks and town halls as well as numerous acts of sabotage on military targets. In the Eure, a crude opinion survey carried out by the prefect showed that, while Pétain was still respected (if 'less loved'), his government was loathed as a puppet of the Germans, and the STO was 'more and more unpopular' and making everyone look forward to Liberation. By early 1944, the owners of village garages were even being advised to guard their petrol pumps: Vichy had lost control of much of the countryside.[39] Three hundred Maquisards took over the town of Oyonnax in November 1943 – there were no Germans – where they organized a military parade and sang the 'Marseillaise' before withdrawing. There were similar, if smaller, demonstrations elsewhere. For Field Marshal von Rundstedt, the Wehrmacht's supreme commander west, 1943 was 'a serious turning-point in the internal situation'.[40]

The disruption was even greater elsewhere. In Norway, the Oslo Labour Registration Board offices were blown up. In Greece, a protest strike in Athens actually prevented workers being sent out of the country. As for Poland, Sauckel's deputy described growing chaos and conflict:

Especially in Poland the situation at the moment is extraordinarily serious. It is well known that violent battles occurred just because of these actions. The resistance against the administration established by us is very strong. Quite a number of our men have been exposed to increased dangers, and it was only in the last two or three weeks that some of them were shot dead, e.g., the head of the Labour Office of Warsaw who was shot in his office, and yesterday again, another man. This is how matters stand at present, and the recruiting itself, even if done with the best will, remains extremely difficult unless police reinforcements are at hand.

In the Netherlands, where the Germans tried to make entire age cohorts register, many men went into hiding and a vast underground relief network emerged to provide them with shelter, food and false papers. It came on top of an ill-advised announcement by the German military commander – that all former Dutch POWs must return to Germany – that triggered uproar and strikes which at their peak involved half a million people. For the first time, rural areas were also being drawn in. The SS imposed martial law, and more than 100 people were executed before the strike was ended. Armed resistance did not yet worry the authorities there. But as in France, 1943 was a turning-point, and Sauckel's men delivered only 7 per cent of the numbers of Dutch workers that had been planned.[41] In Belgium, where there were traumatic memories of the Germans' deportations of Belgian workers in the First World War, the forced labour programme was, if anything, more sensitive. 'We've returned to the deportations of 1916–17' was one commentator's reaction to the compulsory labour orders. Despite strikes, nearly 150,000 were sent to the Reich. Communist and Catholic relief organizations – the latter funded by employers and by the government-in-exile – helped those who went into hiding.[42]

The labour shortage influenced how the Germans responded to resistance too. This became evident from October 1942, when Göring ordered the evacuation of areas in the occupied eastern territories that were of no economic value to the Germans and the screening of the inhabitants: those capable of work were to be sent to the Reich or put to work locally. As we have already seen in the case of Belorussia, army and SS commanders started conducting anti-partisan operations according to the spirit of this order as well: Operation 'Franz' in January 1943 was the first to result in large numbers of civilians being arrested and sent west. Eventually, tens of thousands of civilians were herded into labour and concentration camps and put to work by the army, civilian agencies or handed over to Sauckel's men. Behind these 'evacuations', the army left 'dead zones' of burned villages and rotting fields which civilians entered at their peril. The rural population was being screened and selected as the Jews had been before them. Those not capable of being put to work were sent to camps like the 'Russian Family Camp' in Auschwitz, where some were gassed.[43]

In Poland, in particular, a new 'spirit of resistance' began to emerge in late 1942. Laconically the causes were summed up by the German territorial commander in the General Government as: 'increasing hunger; increasing tangible burden of the war; mental dejection; increasing curbs on freedom; a psychologically mistaken policy; harshness counter-productive to the point of crass injustice; complete neglect together with inadequate care [which] eliminate the last residue of belief in the good will of the Germans'. He identified two key catalysts: the *Fangaktionen* – or labour raids – and the mass murder of the Jews, in which the Poles saw 'an atrocious picture of their own destiny'. He was certainly not alone in seeing how Himmler's and Globocnik's resettlement actions around Zamość had driven many farmers to become outlaws and turned the Lublin region into the epicentre of Polish partisan activity. It took Frank, Goebbels and anti-partisan commissar von dem Bach-Zelewski six months to get the forced evictions halted, and Globocnik reassigned, but by that time the damage had been done.[44]

And by then an example of armed resistance had already erupted in the heart of Warsaw among the last Jews left in the ghetto. The Home Army lent them a little support but was deeply uncertain about whether it wished to support an uprising that could easily spread to the rest of the city before it was ready. The Jewish uprising was essentially an autonomous act by people with nothing more to lose. By early 1943 there were only 50–70,000 left in a ghetto which had numbered around 450,000 two years earlier; most of the rest had died in Treblinka in the preceding months. Inspired by reports of Jewish resistance in towns further east, the multi-party Jewish Fighting Organization (ZOB) killed Gestapo informers, Jewish policemen and collaborators, bought up arms and disrupted a deportation in January.

The cost was heavy: four-fifths of the ZOB members (most of whom were unarmed, since arms were scarce) were arrested and killed for a handful of German casualties. But the event itself was enough for Himmler to order the ghetto to be emptied completely. In February, he instructed HSSPF Krüger to tear it down so as to root out 'criminal disorder'. In the longer run, the demolition would help reduce the size of a city, which had 'always been a dangerous centre of decomposition and of rebellion'. After leisurely preparations, the Germans moved in, not anticipating much resistance. In fact, they were taken by surprise by ZOB's carefully prepared plans, and several weeks of tough fighting followed before the revolt was finally defeated. Their initial disarray made an impression on the Poles, who watched from the outside as the smoke rose above the ghetto walls. A few even went inside: both the Home Army and Polish communists made raids to support the ZOB fighters. Driven by his German guards into the Gestapo's Pawiak prison, which was located inside the ghetto, a Polish Home Army officer heard the grenades and glimpsed the corpses in the deserted streets as gendarmes and SS men cowered under fire from Jewish snipers.[45]

If this was one example to rouse the Home Army to greater action, there was more outside Warsaw, for resistance activity was now spreading into the central Polish countryside. One year after Hitler had approved his General Plan East, Himmler's priorities had changed dramatically. In the summer of 1943 he declared the entire General Government a 'partisan war zone' (*Bandenkampfgebiet*). Urged on by him to 'burn down entire villages if necessary', the SS and police responded with the usual terror tactics, leaving thousands dead. But inside the SS, there was serious disagreement, and von dem Bach-Zelewski insisted that 'no country can be ruled with the use of police and troops alone' and pushed for a more astute policy (much as others were doing in the Balkans) that would exploit the Poles' anti-communism and bring them in under the Germans. The SS hoped to appeal to the Home Army, whose commander, 'Grot', they had captured in June; but his refusal to cooperate (which led to his own death) meant that they had to settle for working – behind the scenes, and intermittently – with the smaller, far-right NSZ.

One way or the other, Himmler wanted the burgeoning resistance in Poland crushed and he brought SS-Brigadeführer Franz Kutschera into Warsaw as SSPF to do this. As the Germans carried out highly public executions in the city's streets, the Poles, who had been excited by news of the summer's events in Italy, were horrified and thrown back into a state of deep pessimism. 'The mood is dreadful,' noted one Warsaw resident in his diary. 'No one believes in a quick end to the war. More and more people keep returning to what the Germans have done to the Jews: does not the same fate await us?' Exceptionally – because the fear of German reprisals meant that targeted killings of senior German personnel were rare during the war – the Home Army decided to assassinate Kutschera to demonstrate that the Poles remained unbowed. After two attempts failed, a hit squad succeeded in shooting him dead in the middle of Warsaw in an operation that lasted barely a minute.

The Germans executed 300 people in retaliation, but his death did at least succeed in bringing public executions to an end.[46]

THE WEHRMACHT IN
SOUTHERN EUROPE

But in the summer of 1943 it was not in Poland – where the Wehrmacht was remarkably sanguine about the growing unrest – that the Germans felt most exposed, but in southern Europe, where they faced the threat of an Allied invasion. As the latter consolidated their position in north Africa, the Germans tried to anticipate where they would land next. There were contingency plans for a pre-emptive invasion of the Iberian peninsula, and Hitler himself remembered Churchill's obsession with the Balkans in the First World War and worried about landings on the coast of Greece. The Wehrmacht therefore moved troops out of the Eastern Front and south through the Balkans and was well prepared either to shore up the Italians or to take over from them. Nevertheless, when Mussolini's ouster in July forced their hand, their already depleted forces were stretched over a vastly increased area. The growth of partisan bands in Yugoslavia, Greece and Italy itself, the Italian army's disintegration and the Allied landing in Sicily all complicated their task. With much of southern Europe declared a war zone, it was the Wehrmacht, not the SS, that led the German counter-insurgency effort in the final two years of the war.

Not that this meant any lessening in brutality: the Wehrmacht was if anything more murderous in defence than it was in attack. Back in December 1942, Hitler had already mandated the destruction of 'bandits' as part of the preparations against an attempted Allied landing, and the day after Mussolini's overthrow, he issued new orders. To protect rear areas behind vulnerable coastal defences, the Wehrmacht was to crush the 'gangs of bandits' it encountered with 'the utmost intensity' in order to 'annihilate' them. In August, as German fears of an Allied invasion of Greece peaked, General Löhr, the overall Wehrmacht commander in the Balkans, issued an extraordinary order: 'It may be necessary [in areas occupied by the guerillas] to seize the entire male population, insofar as it does not have to be shot or hanged on account of participation in or support for the bandits, and insofar as it is not incapable of work, and bring it to the prisoner collecting points for further transport into the Reich.' If it was impossible to distinguish guerillas from other civilians, the German army's answer was to empty the territory completely. As previously in Belorussia, the dividing line between fighting the partisans and labour recruitment was starting to blur.[47]

Even as Löhr issued this command, Greek volunteers were flocking to the hills. In Athens, Italian soldiers were selling their uniforms and equipment. In the Pindos mountains, *andartes* (partisans) successfully disarmed the Italian Pinerolo division. German forces were rushed into the country from Yugoslavia and the Soviet territories, and soon the 'dead zones' that had scarred the Belorussian countryside were blighting central Greece and the Peloponnese as well. In July and August, for instance, men of the elite 1st Mountain Division – back from fighting the Red Army in the heights of the Caucasus – pushed down the mountain roads to clear the west of Greece before the expected Allied attack. This never came, but behind the coastal fringe they shot hundreds of villagers and burned down their homes. They then crossed to the Ionian islands to disarm Italian troops that were holding out; and massacred these too after they surrendered. Eastern Front rules had come to Greece, and Italian and Greek civilians were now being treated much like the Russians had been.

Other units fanned out across the Peloponnese. In the space of only a few days at the end of 1943, the war diary for the Wehrmacht in the Peloponnese records: 4 December: 50 hostages shot in Aighion following an attack on a truck; 5 December: 50 hostages hanged at the Andritsa railway station; 7 December: 25 hostages shot at Gythion. Some days later, troops entered the mountain town of Kalavryta, rounded up all the men they found there, more than 500, and shot them; this was by way of a reprisal after *andartes* had kidnapped and killed German soldiers near by. In other atrocities the following spring in central Greece, young Waffen-SS soldiers did not even spare women and children. Germany's diplomatic plenipotentiary in the Balkans was furious; after a massacre at the village of Klissoura, he wrote: 'The wonderful result of this heroic deed is that babies are dead; but the partisans continue to live.' There was even an internal Wehrmacht inquiry. But his protests did little to change the troops' behaviour. The partisan movement went from strength to strength, hundreds of villages were destroyed, and tens of thousands of people were killed or made homeless.

Thanks to the Wehrmacht's conduct of the anti-partisan war and its reliance on indiscriminate collective punishment, Greece faced a colossal relief and refugee crisis that Swedish and Swiss Red Cross workers struggled to tackle.[48]

Events in Italy over the summer of 1943 lay at the heart of these developments. The collapse of Mussolini's regime had left the country divided and created a political vacuum. In the south, the advancing Allies established a military occupation of their own on the first parts of European soil to be liberated; figures from the fascist *ancien régime* like Marshal Badoglio – the 'Duke of Addis Ababa' – tried to ensure a smooth political transition, while die-hard pro-Duce loyalists went underground and even briefly contemplated resistance. North of the slowly retreating German lines, Italy fell under Wehrmacht control, although there was the customary tangle of German officials (the Foreign Ministry plenipotentiary and Himmler's HSSPF being the most important). Rescued by Hitler, the Duce was propped up and re-established a figurehead fascist government.

As yesterday's allies turned into masters and the Germans tightened their grip on the country, opposition took shape very fast, propelled by the rapid revival of party politics after two decades of fascism. Politically, the resistance to the Germans (and to Mussolini's new government) was organized by a cross-party committee for national liberation which formed in Rome the day after the armistice and then metastasized into a network of regional affiliates under the German occupation. At the same time, as the Italian army broke up, the country was awash with guns. Most soldiers went underground to avoid internment, and the spontaneous help they, and the Allied POWs freed from Italian jails, received from the rest of Italian society could be seen as the first collective act of resistance to the country's new rulers. A few took to the hills, but initially the tightly organized communist sabotage and assassination squads in the cities were much more lethal to the occupiers. But the partisans' numbers grew in the spring of 1944 – conscription drives were having the same effect as elsewhere – and a huge and politically diverse range of groups emerged: 'Garibaldi' brigades organized on the Soviet system; 'Justice and Freedom' units from the Action Party; Catholic 'Green Flames' and many others.[49]

Hamstrung by lack of training, poor cover and a shortage of arms, their political significance was greater than their military capability. Politically, they represented the new Italy that was emerging from the rubble of fascism, with all its divisions and uncertainties, and it was natural that there should be clashes between these different groups – as yet outside any central control. The Italian state had collapsed, and this was the battle for renewal, a second *Risorgimento*. The historian Claudio Pavone, who himself took part in the resistance, has distinguished three separate yet related wars that were going on within the partisans' struggle. For some of them this was a class war for socialism: they were hoping to return to the 'revolutionary' situation that had gripped the country in 1919–21 but this time to force Italian history down a new path. Many were simply fighting against Mussolini's *repubblichini* for a democratic future to demonstrate to Italy and the world the vitality of the anti-fascist tradition that had been crushed for twenty years. And for everyone, there was the struggle to drive out the Germans.

The Germans themselves were taking no chances and clamped down hard. In north-eastern Italy, brought under civilian rule as a preliminary to its eventual annexation, Odilo Globocnik – the architect of Operation Reinhard and the Zamość resettlements – was assigned to police his birthplace, Trieste. In the south, Field Marshal Kesselring fought skilfully throughout much of September in a vain attempt to prevent the Allies establishing a bridgehead. Many small towns had already been flattened by an Allied campaign of massive bombing raids intended – redundantly – to rouse the Italian population against the fascist regime. When the Wehrmacht came in, lacking the reserves that Kesselring believed he needed, it rounded up thousands of men for labour and requisitioned farm animals and food. Their troops spread thinly across the parched mountains of Campania and Basilicata, the Germans retaliated violently to the slightest sign of disobedience, and there were dozens of executions and massacres in small south Italian villages and towns as the front stabilized. The main reason for this indiscriminate killing was the Wehrmacht's characteristic desire to achieve absolute security in its rear. The German troops felt furious with their former allies for their 'betrayal' and took their revenge on civilians at the slightest provocation. Kesselring himself was a superb general, surprising Hitler with his success in slowing the Allied advance up in the peninsula; but his brilliance as a commander went hand-in-hand with an utterly ruthless attitude towards the local population.

Nor did the region's suffering end when the Allies arrived. General Mark Clark's liberal use of heavy artillery fire saved soldiers' lives but devastated built-up areas on the front line. Several thousand women were raped by French and north African troops. The Italians' homes were plundered, rations plummeted to starvation levels, and there were German bombing raids as well. By early 1944, much of southern Italy resembled a moonscape of devastated towns through which homeless, starving and demoralized women and children searched for safety and shelter.[50]

German reprisals and massacres were responsible for the deaths of hundreds of civilians in the rest of Italy as well. In March 1944, for example, a partisan attack on a German column marching through Rome caused many casualties and Hitler ordered that 100 Italians be executed for every dead German. After the Rome head of the SD decided a lower ratio would be sufficient, his men, their nerves calmed with drink, shot 335 hostages in a nearby abandoned quarry – the so-called Fosse Ardeatine – in a massacre that still provokes heated debates today. But the Wehrmacht was behaving very similarly in the countryside. Frustrated at his inability to locate the partisans, whose members had been growing through the spring, Kesselring was coming to regard the civilian population in its entirety as part of the problem. 'The struggle against the bands must be waged with all the means at our disposal and with the maximum harshness,' ran his most notorious order, issued in the critical weeks after Rome fell on 4 June. 'I will back any officer who in his choice and harshness of means goes beyond our customary limits.' On 28 June he threatened the Italian population in a radio broadcast that the troops' struggle with the partisans would become 'more ruthless and tougher'. He meant what he said, and in the days that followed, the worst massacres in the entire occupation took place: 245 were killed in the village of Civitella della Chiana on 29 June; 71 the same day at San Pracazio di Bucine; 176 on 4 July at Castelnuovo dei Sabbioni; an astonishing 560 at Sant'Anna di Stazzema on 12 August, where the piles of bodies were so badly disfigured by flame-throwers that identification became impossible. By this point, the sadism of the troops was comparable to that displayed by the *Einsatzgruppen* in the East in 1941.[51]

Mussolini had been complaining since March about the Wehrmacht's 'criminal behaviour', and Kesselring reminded his men to preserve their discipline. But nothing changed. On 15 September Mussolini complained a third time, warning the German ambassador that the Wehrmacht was becoming hated in Italy and insisting that 'as man and Fascist, I can no longer carry the responsibility – however indirect – for these massacres of women and children'. Precisely two weeks later, however, the 16. SS-Panzergrenadier-Division 'Reichsführer SS', which had perpetrated the Sant'Anna bloodbath, went on the rampage in the village of Marzabotto in the Apennines, about sixteen kilometres south of Bologna, and killed at least 770 people. It was one of the worst German atrocities of the war in western Europe. The village had been looted and partly burned by the Germans in May, and they had shot some men then because no one would give them information about the partisans. Now, Sturmbannführer Walter Reder reported that he had wiped out the 'bandits' there. In fact, the victims included more than 150 children under ten years old, and about the same number of elderly villagers.[52]

Reder was a courageous and highly decorated Waffen-SS officer and in many ways an exemplary product of Hitler's army. He had participated in the invasion of Poland, taken part in the advance on Leningrad in 1941 and fought his way through the last battle for Kharkov, before losing part of his arm; afterwards he had helped clear the Warsaw Ghetto. For him – and his superiors – the *Vernichtungskrieg* in the East had simply reinforced his suspicion of civilians (the way the Italians had 'betrayed' the Germans merely confirmed their inherent duplicity) and anyway he regarded reprisals as entirely lawful. After months on the retreat, military necessity dictated securing the Apennines – the last line of defence before the Po valley – and in the summer of 1944 this was far from assured. It was scarcely a coincidence that the Marzabotto massacre occurred at the very moment when the Germans defending the central section of the Gothic Line came under pressure from the advancing Allied forces.

On the other hand, none of this explains the troops' targeting of women and children and their sadistic zest in killing, something which appears to have fed on itself over the preceding weeks, as one crime followed another, nourished by a mixture of fear, contempt, impunity and psychopathic pleasure. The life of one German, an officer informed an Italian priest, was worth that of fifty Italians. By this point, none of the German army's previous ethical boundaries functioned any longer: priests would be shot as they tried to mediate, numerous women and babies were killed along with the men.[53]

Or was this kind of indiscriminate killing more rational – at least as far as the German military saw it – than we like to think? After all, in purely functional terms, these massacres had not lost their terrifying effectiveness. In the winter of 1944/5, there was a noticeable falling-away in partisan activity as the Wehrmacht, the SS and their Italian allies – together vastly outnumbering the insurgents – continued their drives. Deporting tens of thousands of 'bandit suspects' north to camps in Poland and Germany, they successfully cleared several areas in the mountains of northern Italy that the partisans had declared 'free zones'. As the weather worsened, many partisans were disappointed by the Allies' failure to break through. Even more discouragingly, the Allies urged them to disband for the winter. The SD knew that many of those who had fled to the bands had only done so to escape the German round-ups, and Mussolini's regime tried – rather unsuccessfully – to take advantage of this, and to pose as a more moderate force, by offering an amnesty to all those 'bandits' who gave themselves up. A mere 2,000 did so. Nevertheless, at the beginning of 1945, the partisan movement was on the defensive and it only re-emerged as a significant force in Italy in the very last month of the occupation. From the Wehrmacht's viewpoint, deterrence and terror worked and allowed it to retain control of the north until the end of the war.[54]

TOWARDS CIVIL WAR

In Nazi Europe, opposition and hatred was always directed at least as much against collaborators as against the Germans. It was the Quislings, Musserts and Degrelles who threatened to turn their country towards Nazism; and where collaborationist parties assisted the Germans, they were regarded as the enemy by much of the population from the moment of their appearance. In France, after Vichy's initial legitimacy wore off, there was a similar polarization. Even though Pétain himself remained popular, or at least respected, until the very end, this was not true of those who served him. Smiling tousle-haired Legionnaires might pose for celebratory photographs as they departed for the Eastern Front, their railway carriages scrawled with 'Vive le Maréchal!', 'Vive Hitler!' and 'A bas les Juifs!', but in the cinemas, pictures of Laval, Henriot and Déat were greeted with whistles, cat-calls and shouts of 'Sell-out!' and

'Death!'[55] Seen as traitors, collaborators became prime targets for attack and assassination; for them, on the other hand, the resistance were 'terrorists', 'communists' and 'criminals' trying to disrupt public order and fragment the nation. As weapons became more plentiful and the end of the war – with all its political uncertainties – beckoned, this violence intensified in many countries to the point of civil war.

In November 1942, three of Degrelle's Rexist mayors were shot in Belgium, prompting his party to demand better protection. But the police's reluctance to get drawn in led them to take the law into their own hands. By mid-1944, Rex, the Flemish SS and the right-wing VNV were killing opponents in the vicious struggle between them and the underground. 'It is a veritable civil war,' was how the lawyer Paul Struye summed up his analysis of public opinion in the final months of the occupation.

Numerous collaborators with the occupier are attacked in their homes, in the street or in the countryside. Women figure in rather large numbers among them. Apparently, they are informers who handed over *réfractaires* to the occupier . . . The 'reprisals' are even more violent . . . The succession of the bloody dramas has created in much of the country, especially in villages and small towns, a veritable atmosphere of terror . . . The hatred which some Belgians manifest towards others at present is implacable and truly ferocious. It is infinitely more violent than that shown towards the occupiers.[56]

In Italy, emerging fitfully from more than two decades of fascism, there were scores to settle that went back not just two or three years but twenty. The anti-fascist left was keen to avenge its bitter memories of the years of the fascist militias. At the same time, what remained of the Fascist Party was more radicalized than it had been before the collapse, and there was a conscious return to the violent *squadrismo* of fascism's first hour. A new wave of violence coursed through the towns and villages of the Po valley. Mussolini himself was greeted by cheering crowds when he first reappeared in public near Bolzano in April 1944: there were many people, especially in the border areas and the staunchly Catholic north-east, who feared Italy falling to the Bolsheviks. His new Black Brigades (*Brigate nere*) were not the only force at fascism's disposal: there was also the Republican National Guard and a host of small, more or less voluntary forces, death squads and warlords, some of whom preferred to take orders from the SS rather than from Mussolini.

Gradually, his regime became no more than an arm of the German anti-partisan campaign, and its adherents saw themselves in a war in which 'there is no difference between the external and the internal enemy'. In the summer of 1944, after all, the partisans were assassinating fascist notables and killing hundreds of Mussolini's men monthly. The following winter, the latter fought back alongside the Germans and took their revenge, publicly hanging partisans and anyone else they wished.[57]

The Catholic Church tried to calm both sides and preached moderation, for its leadership was deeply suspicious of both Nazism and communism. The Vatican feared a postwar takeover by the left in Italy; but it also refused to establish diplomatic relations with Mussolini's Salò regime. Yet the pressures towards civil war were strong, and the Church was too weak for it to be able to do much: both fascists and anti-fascists criticized it for fence-sitting. At Easter in 1944 bishops were advised to 'stigmatise every form of hatred, of vendetta, reprisal and violence, from wherever it comes', but the pro-Duce *Piemonte repubblicano* immediately rounded on the Church for not realizing that 'we are in times of exception, in a time of war, and there is no doubt that "between the two belligerent parties", every Italian – bishop or not – has the obligation to note that one of them is stained, and daily, by horrible crimes'. As it was, priests were caught up in the violence: 191 were killed by fascists, 125 by the Germans, and 109 by the partisans themselves. There were priests who fought in pro-fascist bands, and others – the so-called 'partisan chaplains' and 'red priests' – who fought as anti-fascists. (These last were actually backed by the Vatican, which was worried at the lack of religious guidance available to partisans who would otherwise be exposed to communist propaganda without any spiritual support.)[58]

But the resistance was not only fighting a civil war against collaborators; there were also tensions within the resistance itself, tensions which reflected the multiplicity of tiny groups from which resistance had emerged and the very different conceptions of the ideal postwar order that existed among them. In western Europe, these differences were containable. Except perhaps in France, where the resistance did occasionally turn on itself, none of these disagreements spilled over into open violence, and groups either tolerated each other's existence or accepted the authority of overarching coordinating bodies. In the Balkans, it was different. The Greek and Yugoslav governments in exile lacked legitimacy, and attempts to unify resistance forces failed. As a result, the latter fought openly not only with collaborators but also with one another. In Yugoslavia, the war between the partisans and the chetniks left a trail of blood across the country. Greece was spared violence on this scale, but only because the main movement – EAM/ELAS – broke up smaller groups by force in order to establish itself as the dominant authority in the mountains.

As the end of the war approached, the main battle lines in the incipient civil war were not between resistance and collaborators but between communists and their opponents. Croatian Ustaše and Nedić gendarmes in Belgrade both saw themselves as their country's last defence against Bolshevization, and this fear allowed them to appeal to members of the non- or anti-communist resistance as well. In Greece, such coalitions of anti-communist forces – bringing together collaborators and resisters – were organized by the quisling government with German support. In fact, fomenting civil war there was something the Germans were deliberately trying to do. SS-Standartenführer Walter Blume, an educated lawyer and former Gestapo official, had progressed from killing Jews on the Eastern Front via killing partisans in Slovenia to becoming the head of the Athens SiPo/SD. According to his so-called 'chaos thesis', the Germans ought to kill off Greece's leadership class and get the Greeks to fight one another so fiercely that they could withdraw undisturbed. Hence he armed thuggish anti-communists in security battalions and unofficial death squads and gave them carte blanche in the war with the 'communists' and 'bandits'. The final months of occupation were thus punctuated by a series of horrific massacres perpetrated by Greeks on Greeks in which the Germans themselves played little direct role. In the final months of occupation, the seeds of the Greek civil war were already being sown.

The shadow of communism meant that the decline in Germany's fortunes had an enormous impact on the partisan war in eastern Europe as well. Poles, Ukrainians and the Baltic peoples all asked themselves what a German collapse would mean, and insurgents increasingly acted with an eye to the future rather than the present. In Poland, where the development of armed resistance had been deliberately held back, the Home Army established its Directorate of Underground Resistance only in late 1942, and by late 1943 one estimate suggests it controlled approximately 3,000 men across the country – not a large number. By this point, others were already in the field. There was a well-equipped communist movement, also attracting Poles in the East who were frustrated by the Home Army's absence; there were numerous Peasant Battalions (associated with the Peasant Party) and Jewish bands, made up of survivors of the massacres in eastern Poland; there were the Soviet partisans in the east of the country; and on the right, there was the NSZ. Clashes were common between these groups, but for obvious reasons the real split was emerging as that between those sympathetic to the Soviets and the rest. The tension grew with the formation of the Civic Anti-Communist Committee, uniting all the main non-communist political parties. For their part, the communists had already established the National Council of the Homeland as an alternative to the government in exile. 'One thing is certain,' ran an OSS report on the Polish resistance, 'the Germans are helped by the lack of unity in the underground and by the fact that each side has other aims than fighting the Germans.'[59]

One of the catalysts for the development of armed resistance among the Poles was the sudden eruption of a war inside the war – between Poles and Ukrainians in eastern Poland and the western Ukraine. The entire zone between Vilnius and Lviv was already the site of some of Europe's most violent experiments in ethnic cleansing. In a few months in 1943, things got even worse and infinitely more complicated. The first Soviet partisans had appeared in Volhynia the previous year, and Ukrainian nationalists wanted to prevent peasants from supporting them; in their words, they sought an alternative for 'elements of the Ukrainian nation who might otherwise seek shelter from German imperialism in Moscow'. Ukrainian policemen working for the Germans were defecting to the forests in large numbers, and the nationalist OUN-B encouraged them to form a new Ukrainian Insurgent Army (UPA).

By April 1943, UPA had 10–20,000 members and, prompted by news of Stalingrad, they embarked on a campaign of ethnic cleansing to make room for a future independent Ukrainian state before the Russians arrived. First they attacked Himmler's ethnic German settlements and burned many of them down. Next they turned on the Poles, killing an estimated 50,000; many more fled westwards. Thanks to well-planned massacres and expulsions they had virtually succeeded by December in bringing Volhynia under Ukrainian control, helped by thousands of peasants who coveted land controlled by Poles. 'Liquidate all Polish traces,' ran an OUN order from early 1944. 'Destroy all walls in the Catholic Church and other Polish prayer houses. Destroy orchards and trees in the courtyards so that there will be no trace that someone lived there . . . Pay attention to the fact that when something remains that is Polish, then the Poles will have pretensions to our land.'[60]

The repercussions were immediate and long-lasting. The violence persuaded Stalin that Poles and Ukrainians could not live together, and Moscow began to plan the series of forced population exchanges between Poland and the Ukraine which uprooted hundreds of thousands of people between 1944 and 1947. In neighbouring Galicia, Poles now turned on Ukrainians in revenge, and the embryonic Polish partisan movement was swollen by the refugees from Volhynia. This movement then spread not only west into central Poland but also northwards towards Vilna into the other regions of prewar eastern Poland where Poles were in a minority and needed defending. At the same time, the Home Army's failure in Volhynia itself encouraged many Poles to look to the Soviet partisans instead. Like the Ukrainians, the Poles were now caught between the Russians and the Germans, and compromises were hard to avoid. Both the extreme right NSZ and Home Army commanders negotiated temporary agreements with German SS and Wehrmacht officers to prevent the 're-Sovietization' of the area. (Although Himmler forbade such agreements, they happened anyway on a small scale.) But other Home Army commanders cooperated with the Soviet partisans, recognizing the futility of opposing them. Both the Poles and the Ukrainians hoped to see a world in which they could carve out a space of their own, independently of both the great totalitarian powers. But such a world would need much longer than just a couple of years to materialize.[61]

TIMING THE UPRISING

On 28 September 1943, Naples became the first European city to rise up against the Germans. The *Quattro giornate* – the famous 'Four Days' – were prompted by Field Marshal Kesselring's attempt to deport 20,000 men. When German lorries pulled up in Piazza Dante, in the heart of the city, to take them away, women tried to stop them from leaving. At the same time, young men armed themselves and began to patrol the streets. The next day, as news spread that 8,000 men had already been driven off, people overturned buses, threw up barricades and set up machine-gun posts to prevent the Germans bringing in reinforcements. Over the following days, intense street fighting in the city's labyrinthine alleys and lanes was punctuated by negotiations (the Neapolitans captured several German soldiers and surrounded others, including the commandant of the city), lynchings (of fascist collaborators) and mass executions by the Germans. The Allied armies were approaching the city's outskirts, and their boats had scouted the bay. But in fact, the inhabitants fought very effectively without Allied help, especially in the steep old streets around Vomero, and the Germans, having realized that they lacked the forces to regain control, withdrew at the beginning of October as the first Allied troops arrived. Behind them they left at least 663 Italians dead and many more wounded. Already half-destroyed by months of Allied aerial bombing, the historic centre and port were barely recognizable. Entering the city, British soldiers found 'charred wood, with ruins everywhere, sometimes completely blocking the streets, bomb craters and abandoned trams'. There was no drinking water or food and there were rumours that lasted for days that a secret SS squad remained hidden in the catacombs.[62]

The insurrection itself was a rare example of a popular uprising that had not been planned in advance (one reason perhaps why it is not much remembered in Italy today). It took local anti-fascists by surprise as much as the Germans, and the swift spread of the fighting reflected more than anything else the powerful community spirit for which the city's neighbourhoods were well known, fuelled by fury at both the remnants of the disintegrating fascist state and the newly arriving, trigger-happy Germans. Elsewhere in Europe, however, resistance movements had based their entire strategy on preparing to rise up against the occupier, and for them the chief challenge was to tell when the right moment had arrived. As 1943 came and went without the Second Front that so many had expected, many of them were combating disappointment and impatience in their own ranks.

It was the following year – with the simultaneous invasion of France and the Soviet thrust west through Belorussia into Poland – that became the year of truth. Strikes, sabotage and armed attacks on German troops reached unprecedented levels, and the Germans themselves, fighting in both front and rear, brought mass terror and reprisals into areas that had so far been spared them. In some of the smaller countries of north-western Europe, where by the summer of 1944 resistance movements had become relatively centralized, exile governments, together with SOE and General Eisenhower's SHAEF command, did their best to put the brakes on. The Dutch discouraged a mass rising, though a rail strike in September led the Germans to declare a state of siege. In Norway, the Milorg resistance movement warned against insurrection and tried to divert its members' energies into increased sabotage and to trying to obstruct the scorched earth policy pursued by the retreating Germans in the north of the country. In Denmark, where resistance developed rapidly after the collapse of *collaboration d'état* in the summer of 1943, London and the new Freedom Council promoted sabotage by small bands of professionals and tried to avoid turning the underground army into a military force for use against the Germans. In all these cases, the British and the exile governments were not solely concerned about avoiding casualties. They also had eminently political reasons for avoiding mass action since they basically wanted to restore the existing political class after Liberation and realized a large armed resistance movement might hinder those plans.

Resistance leaders in many countries were also influenced by events in France, where the costs of getting the timing wrong became horribly visible. In June, on the eve of the Normandy landings, sabotage attacks increased sharply, and rail lines were cut in many places. But some leaders of the Maquis wanted to go beyond this, to take the Germans on in open battle and to win the glory of liberation for themselves. In the Auvergne, they dusted off older plans to turn the mountains into a central redoubt of resistance and, heartened by Allied arms drops, they issued a mobilization order which brought several thousand workers and students into the area of Mont Mouchet. The local Wehrmacht kept an eye on this activity and in early June decided to crush it. Within a few days, after brief resistance, they had regained control, killing dozens of Maquisards for relatively low losses of their own. Field Marshal Sperrle had reacted to the Normandy landings by commanding 'extreme severity . . . and the most ruthless methods' to crush resistance, and it was in accordance with these orders that the troops simply shot or deported anyone they encountered on their way into the mountains. The Mont Mouchet episode demonstrated how costly it could be to abandon the guerillas' basic weapons of surprise and mobility, and how exposed the resistance was to effective German counter-attack when it revealed itself too early. There was a similar debacle on the Vercors plateau, and in several small towns and villages across France premature acts of 'liberation' led to bloodbaths. One understands why communist calls for insurrection fell on deaf ears: 85 per cent of communes in France prudently preferred to wait for the Allies.[63]

The uprising was later, and more successful, in Paris itself. In mid-August, the approach of Allied forces, including a Free French division, led the French police to go on strike. By 18 August, the stoppage had become total, paralysing the city, and the French Forces of the Interior ordered a general mobilization. Police vans and commandeered cars sported 'FFI' painted in large white letters and the Cross of Lorraine. As German troops evacuated the city they came under fire, and barricades were thrown up. Fighting with them lasted until 25 August, when the German commander, General Dietrich von Choltitz, ignored Hitler's orders to destroy the city and surrendered to General Leclerc, commander of the French 2nd Armoured Division: about 3,200 Germans died, and another 12,800 were taken prisoner. On the same day, General de Gaulle arrived as president of the provisional government and hailed the jubilant crowds from the Hôtel de Ville with words which immediately became famous:

Paris! Outraged Paris! Broken Paris! Martyred Paris! But liberated Paris!

Liberated by itself, liberated by its people with the help of the French armies, with the support and the help of the whole of France, of the fighting France, of the only France, of the real France, of the eternal France!

Thanks to de Gaulle's flamboyant rhetoric, the liberation of Paris provided the origins for the founding myth of postwar France – a country that had supposedly been united in resistance to the Germans and liberated itself. Paris was really in the process of being evacuated by the Germans anyway, and its liberation had nearly not happened at all, since Eisenhower had planned to bypass the city, aware of its strategic unimportance and worried at the possible costs of an extended siege. But for de Gaulle this was unacceptable. Paris had to be liberated, for the sake of France, and liberated by the French themselves.

And there was another reason as well for de Gaulle's insistence. For at that very moment, all eyes were turned to the far more bitter and bloody struggle that was going on for the fate of another great European city. In Paris, about 1,500 Frenchmen lost their lives in the space of a week; but in Warsaw, where the Polish resistance had been fighting for nearly a month, more than 40,000 people had already been killed, and the struggle was still not over. It was Warsaw that had been on Hitler's mind when he ordered von Choltitz to hold on to Paris at all costs, to blow up its bridges and to crush the French uprising as ruthlessly as the SS were fighting the Poles. It had been on General von Choltitz's mind too when he first tried to broker an informal armistice, and then deliberately ignored the orders the Führer had given him. As for de Gaulle – who had been posted there during the Russo-Polish war of 1919–20 – one reason that he diverted Leclerc's armoured division to Paris to aid the resistance was because he knew what was happening in Poland, where they had been left to struggle alone.[64]

In Poland, there were compelling arguments in favour of a mass uprising – arguments that became more compelling with time. Unlike west Europeans, the Poles faced liberation by the Red Army, and for most of them that scarcely meant liberation at all. By 1944, relations had broken down between the London government in exile and Stalin, and the British and Americans were clearly neither prepared nor willing to disregard Soviet wishes where Poland was concerned: SOE arms drops were a fraction of those delivered to France, for instance. Because much of the contention between the Poles and the Soviets concerned the fate of the eastern territories that the latter had occupied in 1939, the Home Army changed its plans in 1943 to focus on successful uprisings there that would allow the Poles to greet the Red Army 'as hosts'. But this assumed that the Germans were weaker than in fact they were, that the Poles were stronger, and that the Red Army would simply acknowledge the Poles' claims if they rose in time. In fact, what happened as the Red Army advanced on the cities of Volhynia and Galicia did not follow the blueprint. Home Army units helped take on the Germans, Ukrainians and Lithuanians, often cooperating with the Soviet troops. But they were too weak to liberate cities like Vilnius, Lviv and Lublin by themselves, despite their mostly Polish population, and they were completely deprived of any element of surprise. Red Army commanders initially treated the Poles like allies. But not for long. On 14 July, Moscow ordered Home Army units to be disarmed in Lithuania, west Belorussia and west Ukraine, and many Polish officers were arrested. The Polish government in exile had hoped that the sight of Poles liberating these towns would make a splash in the West and boost the Polish cause. But the press in England and America barely noticed.

It is against this background that the Home Army's decision to begin the Warsaw uprising at the end of July needs to be understood. Events in eastern Poland had shown, firstly, that the Wehrmacht generally remained too strong for the Poles, and secondly, that the only source of outside support they could count on – the Red Army – saw the Home Army as the instrument of an illegimate government. Yet the one reasonably firm conclusion that could have been drawn from this – that any uprising was militarily doomed without outside backing, and probably politically doomed in any case – would have gone against the strategy upon which the Polish resistance had built its hopes for five years. Having built up an extremely effective underground organization, at enormous human cost, throughout the occupation, it was unimaginable to the leaders of the Home Army that they would not use it. They remembered the triumphant end of the First World War and did not want to think that the Second might not end the same way.[65]

By the end of July, the Red Army's tanks had covered hundreds of miles and pushed the Germans back to the outskirts of Warsaw at the end of perhaps the most extraordinarily effective offensive of the entire war; it was understandable that the Poles believed an assault across the Vistula to be imminent. In fact, the Soviet troops were exhausted, out of fuel and supplies and needed to regroup and they had been brought to a halt by a determined German defensive line. But believing that they were about to attack the city itself, the Home Army's commander gave the order for the uprising to begin. It was a last-minute decision which astonished many of his comrades. Stocks of food and water were low. So were arms, as Warsaw had been supplying Home Army units in the East in the previous weeks. The Germans, on the other hand, had been expecting an uprising for some time; they were bringing in reinforcements and strengthening their police patrols. They did not have enough men to crush the rebellion quickly. But even so, some 20,000 poorly armed Poles confronted 13–20,000 well-armed German police and army units, dug into fortified positions around the city. It was – on the Poles' part – a fatal misjudgement.[66]

It is a tribute to both the heroism and the desperation of Warsaw's defenders that the insurrection lasted a full two months before it was

defeated. But it was also a reflection of the Germans' own misjudge-
ments. In the first place, as the Naples uprising had already shown, their
troops coped much less well with street fighting in old and crowded
cities than with operations in open country. Few places in Europe were
more densely inhabited than Warsaw, especially in its centre, and this
nullified some of the Germans' overwhelming superiority in arms and
manpower. But the Poles also kept fighting because of the indiscriminate
terror that the troops, acting on Himmler's explicit orders, meted out
to the city's inhabitants, especially in the first few days.

Hans Frank and Himmler had both seen the uprising as a blessing
in disguise since it would allow them to destroy Warsaw permanently,
as Hitler had demanded. 'When I heard the news of the uprising in
Warsaw,' Himmler said later,

I went immediately to the *Führer*. I said: 'My *Führer*, the time is not right.
Historically, it is a blessing that the Poles do that. We'll get it over in five or six
weeks. But then Warsaw, the capital, the head, the intelligence of this sixteen or
seventeen million people of Poland, is extinguished, this nation that has blocked
our way to the East for seven hundred years and has been in our way ever since
the first battle of Tannenberg. Then the Polish problem historically for our
children and for all who come after us, even for us, will no longer be a big
problem.'[67]

The 'war of extermination' that had first arisen in the occupied USSR
and then been brought by the Wehrmacht to the Balkans and Italy now
came to Warsaw as well. According to the orders issued to the troops,
all captured rebels were to be shot; non-combatants were also to be
massacred; and the whole city was ultimately to be razed. Several hundred people were killed in the first couple of days. But with the arrival
of special SS units on 5 August, the death toll soared: 30–40,000 people
were probably killed in one suburb on that day alone before von dem
Bach-Zelewski, who had been brought in to oversee the operations,
pulled out the worst offenders and forbade the indiscriminate shooting
of women and children. But tens of thousands of people had already
fled into the areas of the city under Home Army control, and the uprising
assumed a new character: a defence of the city's inhabitants against
massacre and terror. Even the Germans noticed the shift. According to
the propaganda company of the SS 'Viking' Tank Division, the public
had initially 'turned away' from the rebels and criticized them for their

lack of preparation. Yet after seeing the Germans 'mercilessly destroy-ing the life and property of the inhabitants and razing all Warsaw, whether guilty or innocent, the mood changed completely'. In this way the Germans themselves contributed to turning the insurrection into a popular revolt.[68]

By the time the uprising came to an end, the rebels had accomplished several things by their extraordinary endurance. They managed to get the Home Army recognized as part of the regular forces of the government in exile with the result that the Germans ultimately acknowledged their rights as combatants in the negotiations that led to the final surrender on 2 October. Moreover, by early September the Soviets had been shamed into sending fighter planes over the city which largely eliminated the Germans' advantage in the air. The Red Army also attacked the suburb of Praga on the east bank of the Vistula, though did not move beyond there. But Stalin was unwilling to do more, and the Allies too did little apart from send over B-17s to drop supplies. None of this could change the outcome and the costs were higher than anywhere else in Europe. After the capitulation, the Germans took about 15,000 fighters prisoner. Another 15,000 had died – of hunger, thirst and disease as well as from combat – together with more than 185,000 civilians. 48,000 civilians, many of them openly unhappy with the Home Army, emerged from the devastated city on 3 October; another 130,000 left in the following three days for transit camps from which many were trans-ported to labour camps inside Germany, or sent to concentration camps, in a violation of the surrender terms. While Paris celebrated liberation, Warsaw itself was ruined and deserted.

It was at this point that the Germans resolved to demonstrate once and for all to the Poles the futility of resistance. Their longer-term plans to destroy the major cities of the East – Moscow, Leningrad and Warsaw itself – had never been fully effected. The defeat of the uprising gave the Nazis their chance to show that resistance meant annihilation not only of the physical enemy but of his very civilization. This lesson had already been applied to the Jews: for more than a year, several thousand concen-tration camp workers had been systematically demolishing what was left of the old ghetto, some 445 acres in all, carting away rubble on twelve miles of specially laid track before the summer's events brought their work to a halt. Now it was to be rammed home for the Poles as well. Thirty per cent of Warsaw had been destroyed during the uprising.

Himmler instructed von dem Bach-Zelewski to blow up the rest, sparing only the railroad and its buildings. Warsaw SSPF Paul Geibel led the operation. His men blew up libraries – the last one only a few hours before the Soviet and Polish armies entered Warsaw in January 1945 – mined palaces, museums and public buildings and shipped their contents to the Reich or blew them up. In Lublin, where the new Soviet-backed regime had established its provisional capital in the city that Globocnik had once seen as the headquarters of the German East, the National Assembly resolved to rebuild Warsaw as the 'capital of an independent Polish state'.[69]

This destruction was, of course, an expression of the Nazis' deep and abiding hatred of Polish nationalism and devoid of any strategic rationale. The failure of the uprising and subsequent German drives against Home Army fighters in the nearby forests were enough by themselves to destroy Polish morale in the final months of the occupation. 'The Home Army resistance movement . . . has suffered a serious blow from which it will not succeed in recovering in the near future,' reckoned a Wehrmacht staff officer in the General Government. There were no uprisings elsewhere in the country – as had been envisaged in the Home Army's original plans and as von dem Bach-Zelewski had feared. No doubt this was just as well. At the height of the fighting in Warsaw, the SiPo in central Poland had been warned to expect unrest in the country-side 'at any moment' and to arrest 10,000 people in towns who were to be shot as soon as it started. But after the fall of Warsaw, partisan activity declined, and when the Germans pulled back in January 1945 they faced only negligible resistance in their rear.[70]

THE VALUE OF RESISTANCE

During the war, the British and American governments often expressed reservations about the military value of Europe's partisans. For them, after all, what counted was the extent to which they contributed to their war against the Germans. SOE itself was regarded with deep suspicion by other branches of the armed forces and had to justify its activities in those terms. Ever since then there has been a debate among British historians about what the military value of the resistance really was. Some go so far as to say that it had little or none, that strategic bombing and the naval blockade were more important, that lack of precise information prevented saboteurs identifying the best targets. 'Almost all sabotage,' writes Alan Milward, 'was from a German standpoint, economically insignificant'. After the war, German officials were similarly dismissive. 'What French resistance?' Speer scoffed. Falkenhausen was no more complimentary about the Belgians. The implication, not always unspoken, is that given the heavy toll in reprisals, much resistance activity was not only a waste of resources but far too costly in human life. It is a viewpoint sometimes echoed, understandably enough by the survivors of German reprisals, and – in a rather more *parti pris* spirit – by anti-communist politicians in Italy and elsewhere.[71]

It seems clear that, with the exception of the Eastern Front, where extensive partisan activity really did worry the Germans, there were few places or moments in the occupation of Europe when the Germans were seriously troubled for very long. Even if we accept that strikes and deliberate go-slows in the workplace affected productivity and that rail sabotage did cause them trouble near the end of the war, the Wehrmacht's brutal response showed that it was only then that they really worried about having to secure their rear whilst guarding against invasion. And even then, in most cases, their draconian response proved sufficient to quell opposition or to turn it against collaborators rather than against themselves. There were many instances of the resistance abandoning plans to assassinate German figures for fear of the consequences, and the communist strategy of armed insurrection at all costs proved too unpopular to sustain outside the Balkans.[72]

Yet it will not do to reduce resistance to a question of military accounting. For most of those involved it was a question of pride, and a demonstration that the rule of force had not succeeded in crushing the spirit of freedom. It involved enormous courage, and for those engaged from the start a refusal to accept the 'realities' of 1940, when German domination of the continent seemed unassailable. Hundreds of thousands were ultimately involved in active opposition, many of whom paid a heavy price. Perhaps 30,000 were shot in mass executions in France alone; 20,000 Free French were killed and 60,000 were deported. Tens of thousands died in Italy and Greece as a result of the anti-partisan war, hundreds of thousands in the occupied eastern territories. The kind of commitment this demanded could only be sustained by ideals both ethical and political. In other words, we should look beyond the question of how opposition to the Germans affected the outcome of the war, and ask what it envisaged for the peace. This was a critical dimension of resistance and one that left lasting traces on the course of events.

The political character of resistance was evident to everyone involved. For exile governments, anxious about their postwar standing, a record – however brief – of national resistance to Nazi rule was inestimably valuable. It allowed Denmark to be recognized as a member of the United Nations and led France to be treated as a Great Power, reducing Vichy to the status of an embarrassing interlude; German reprisals in the Protectorate after Heydrich's assassination bolstered the often shaky standing of the Beneš government, and the Slovak national uprising wiped out the memory of Tiso's collaboration.

Internally, resistance used violence for political goals. By pushing the occupier into repression, it undermined the mainstream appeal of collaboration and delegitimized it, making governments like Vichy's seem more and more like German puppets. People might reproach the resistance for the disruption and suffering that came in its train, but they invariably hated the Germans more for their reprisals, and collaborators more still. And while some simply wanted nothing more than to drive the occupiers out, others had specific goals in mind for what should follow. The Soviet partisans stood for the re-Bolshevization of territories that the USSR had lost: much of their energy was therefore devoted to rebuilding Party organization and promoting Bolshevism. The Home Army represented the determination of Polish nationalists to defend their society from the assault that German occupation represented, and to defend as far as possible the gains of 1919. The Danish Freedom Council constituted an implicit indictment of the entire political system that had collaborated with the Germans so smoothly until 1943.

Some did not even wait for the war to end. The partisans who founded short-lived 'partisan republics' in northern Italy – or EAM/ELAS's 'Free Greece' in the mountains – aimed to create alternative self-governing political structures in the midst of the war. These were experiments in democracy, with parliaments, elections and welfare and educational services. They policed the areas under their control, intercepted enemy infiltrators and dispensed justice against thieves and black marketeers – none activities with an obvious military purpose but all of them essential to assert the power and political ambitions of the partisans themselves. 'Wash your clothing!' 'Cut your hair!'; 'No lice means no typhus!' were some of the slogans that appeared around Foča under the Yugoslav partisans in the spring of 1941. ('Long live communism!' was written next to them in Esperanto.) Communist-led resistance movements wanted to break with the past and turn wartime mobilization into the force that would replace bankrupted prewar 'bourgeois' regimes with postwar communist ones. It was natural for them to try to build proto-states in the territories under their control.

After Liberation, therefore, one of the most pressing problems was reconciling these versions of the state with other ideas being brought back by politicians returning from wartime exile abroad. For the latter the problem boiled down to one of how to control the resistance, or to be more precise, the various resistance groups that had sprung up in the vacuum of power. This was first seen in the USSR itself, where partisan units were swiftly disbanded and the NKVD was brought in to clear areas in the rear of the rapidly advancing Red Army of resistance from Poles and Ukrainians. By the time the Soviet troops reached central Poland its task was much harder, and although more than 50,000 Home Army members were arrested by the NKVD and many were deported to the Gulag, anti-communist resistance to communist rule continued in parts of Poland even after the official amnesty of 1947. In Cracow – once Hans Frank's capital – Peasant Party supporters outnumbered communists and openly criticized the latter. People saw the Warsaw government as 'an agent of a foreign power' and they took the view that 'we have lived through five years of German occupation and shall also live through these few months to independence'.[73]

Yugoslavia was the only place in Europe where a partisan movement seized control: Tito's partisans, helped by the Red Army, took over the country and settled scores with wartime collaborators as well as with Mihailovic's chetniks. There was a similarly bloody reckoning in Greece, although there the outcome was reversed. The left-wing EAM/ELAS had emerged at Liberation as the dominant force in the country, but in Greece, unlike Yugoslavia, Churchill felt the British had a strategic interest, and when fighting broke out in the winter of 1944 between EAM/ELAS and the returning unity government of George Papandreou, Churchill threw British support behind the latter. British troops and RAF planes attacked ELAS positions in the capital and eventually forced them to withdraw. British dead and wounded numbered more than 1,000. Many more Greeks were dead, including hundreds of hostages executed by the communists. The King of Greece was eventually brought back, and a new government was formed with the support of numerous collaborators in the police and armed forces.

For the rest of Europe, and especially for returning politicians seeking to re-establish their authority, Greece provided a warning of what could go horribly wrong. The immediate cause of the breakdown there had been an inability among the political parties to agree the terms on which resistance fighters would be brought into the new armed forces. In France, de Gaulle had moved very swiftly to avoid this and immediately incorporated groups into the Free French units, reckoning that this was the best way to bring them under the control of the state. A similar policy was adopted in the Netherlands, where the Binnenlandse Strijdkrachten (NBS) eventually attracted no fewer than 120,000 volunteers into its ranks. In Denmark, SHAEF worked hard in the spring of 1945 to reconcile the politicians and the resistance, which had nearly 50,000 armed men in the underground. Only the Belgian government botched the disarmament of the resistance badly by brusquely insisting all arms be handed over to the police within weeks of liberation. There were dire threats of punishment if the decree were not obeyed – and when police opened fire on demonstrators marching towards parliament, there was nearly civil war. Churchill claimed a communist uprising had been narrowly averted. But this was pure fantasy, and fortunately for the Belgians the resistance eventually disarmed itself. The Belgian resistance was far more divided than EAM/ELAS and had never planned to take power. On the contrary, as in other countries – and perhaps indeed as in Greece itself – most members of the Belgian resistance basically felt their work was done once the Germans had left.

The other country where events in Greece left a deep impression was Italy. Here many in the resistance wanted to make sure that the break with fascism was a permanent one: *this* was the real legacy they hoped to leave to the peace. It was as much to ensure this as to drive out the Germans that uprisings had occurred in one city after another in the North in April 1945, often with tremendous loss of life. The partisans were well aware that, although the Duce would not return – his corpse with fourteen other fascists had been displayed in Milan – many members of the old regime had profited from the confusion of 1943–5 to preserve their power. Nevertheless, events in Greece made a big impression on Togliatti, the leader of the Italian Communist Party. They reinforced the view he had taken since returning to Italy from Moscow in 1943 of the importance of cooperating peacefully with other parties. The Allies feared the strength of the communists even so and were determined to prevent a takeover there. As a result, former partisans on the Italian left suffered a version of what their Greek counterparts endured in the late 1940s, with even less cause – persecution, judicial repression and the bitter sight of numerous civil servants who had once served Mussolini loyally now transferring their allegiances to the new democracy. The new state might proclaim it was built on the values of the resistance: but for many who had actually fought in it, it did not feel like that.

Controlling those who had fought in the resistance was one thing; controlling the memory and meaning of resistance itself was another and no less important. The blind violence of the war's final year had confirmed two things in the memory of Europe. One was the image of nations united in resistance to German oppression, and the other was the equation of the German occupation with extreme brutality against civilians. Most people joined the resistance in the war's closing stages, and it was in this phase that the Germans – in both the SS and the Wehrmacht – had perpetrated many of the really horrific massacres of civilians in places that had been designated as 'battle zones' or in order to secure rear areas as the noose tightened sharply around their forces. Oradour, Marzabotto, Kalavryta and Distomo had all been hit at times when the Wehrmacht was overstretched, and young field officers were empowered to make up for short numbers by draconian action. The impression of pointless barbarism was compounded by memories of last-minute labour round-ups, emergency measures and the kinds of scorched earth policies that turned northern Norway into a barren waste and left Warsaw in ruins.

But these memories were even more partial than memories usually are. As we have seen, there was generally little unity within the resistance, and by its nature it tended to fragmentation, anarchism and disputatiousness. It relied on solidarity, but the idea of national unity was often less important in cementing this – especially in western Europe – than party affiliation, ideology or the kind of local pride that lay behind the Naples insurrection. Indeed localism and regionalism were one of the resistance's defining characteristics, though not, for obvious reasons, ones that postwar national governments highlighted in their acts of commemorative piety. Some localities came to stand in for the national suffering – they became, in effect, sites of national martyrdom – while others were soon forgotten. The politicians and commentators imposed their meanings on what had happened, and often not much was said – except through silence – about the very mixed local reactions that had often greeted acts of resistance and the reprisals that had come in their train. The complex feelings they had left behind them waited for a later and more distanced generation, for whom Europe was a *fait accompli* and the nation-states that made it up had proven themselves again through several decades. But in the immediate aftermath of the German occupation, such complexities could only undermine the fragile feeling of national solidarity that postwar governments worked hard to build up, and what emerged instead was a picture of the war in which the only response of Europe's peoples to occupation had been opposition.

16

Hitler Kaputt!

A victory of our enemies will undoubtedly lead to Bolshevism in Europe. Everyone must and will understand what this Bolshevisation would mean for Germany. This is not a question of a change in the state, as in the past. State changes have taken place innumerable times in the life of the people; these changes come and go. But this concerns the existence of the essence itself. Essences are either preserved or eliminated. Preservation is our aim. Elimination could destroy a race like this, possibly for ever.
Hitler before the Ardennes offensive, 28 December 1944[1]

BAGRATION, 1944

Three years to the day after the Wehrmacht swept into the USSR, the Red Army launched Operation Bagration – not only the most effective Soviet offensive of the war but perhaps the most overwhelming and devastating single military assault in history. That it is scarcely remembered in Europe today is no reflection of its strategic significance. Thanks to extensive preliminary deception plans, two and a half million Soviet troops caught the Wehrmacht completely by surprise and smashed into the much smaller German force – less than half the size – that was defending the central section of the Belorussian front. Shocked by the most intense artillery barrage they had ever experienced, soldiers panicked and fled, and within days many were encircled in the same cities – Vitebsk, Bobruisk and Minsk – where the Red Army had been trapped three years earlier. Hitler's 'no retreat' policy contributed to the disarray, and reinforcements were slow to plug the gaps. German losses soared from 48,363 in May to 169,881 in July and 277,465 in August: they eventually numbered well over half a million killed and wounded, higher even than at the toll at Verdun in 1916. The Soviets brushed aside their efforts to rebuild their lines, and in only a few weeks Russian tank detachments covered more than 300 miles to reach the Gulf of Riga and the edge of Warsaw. In Moscow, Stalin ordered a Roman-style triumphal march, and 57,600 German prisoners of war were paraded through the streets. Designed to take the pressure off the Allies as they opened the Second Front, Bagration overshadowed the landings in Normandy – there were fifty German divisions in Belorussia and nine in Normandy – and dwarfed even the impact of Stalingrad. The great forgotten offensive of the war, it showed that the Russians had mastered the principles of the *Blitzkrieg* and it left Stalin, much to his relief, poised to dictate the postwar order in eastern Europe.[2]

In East Prussia, the Reich's most exposed province, came the first signs of panic. At the 400th anniversary celebrations of the University of Königsberg in July the regime showered praise on its 'Prussian bastion against Asiatic influence'. Yet despite the Party's insistence that everything was under control, refugees were packing up to head west in overcrowded trains and Party bosses argued angrily about whether to allow them to leave. Gauleiter Erich Koch sent thousands of pensioners and Hitler Youth to the border to build a defensive 'eastern wall'. But who would defend it? The Wehrmacht had already lost more men in three months than it had in the whole of 1942. The retreating German survivors of the fighting were exhausted, worn out and disoriented by the speed of the Soviet advance; their units had disintegrated and they had been forced to march for miles in the summer heat with scarcely any supplies. 'They were no longer soldiers, but moving human tatters,' according to a Polish onlooker, 'exhausted, horrified, inert, in a state of visible physical and moral decline. Perspiring, emaciated and covered in mud ... they wore long beards and had dispirited faces and sunken eyes.' To the Poles, the sight was 'heavenly'; to the Germans it was chilling.[3]

Since American and British forces had managed to secure the Normandy bridgehead in the face of stiff resistance, by the summer of 1944 Germany faced a gruelling land war on several fronts. Aware of how many troops it had lost in the southern Ukraine because they had not been allowed to pull back in time, the Wehrmacht wanted to withdraw systematically to new lines. Yet Hitler angrily insisted upon defence at all costs and railed against the defeatism of his own generals. The

Wehrmacht Supreme Command had become Hitler's personal fiefdom rather than a professional guide to war strategy, and the Reich's most senior commanders were not the men to get the Führer to respond realistically to the new situation, least of all after the failure of the bomb plot in July. For the Germans themselves, the war's continuation was an unmitigated disaster, and they entered the most violent stage of the conflict. Before July 1944, they had suffered some 2.8 million war dead – already far in excess of their casualties in the previous world war. But these figures were dwarfed by the number – 4.8 million – of those killed in the nine and a half months that followed.[4]

Hitler's vengeful purge of the army after his attempted assassination and the failed military coup did nothing to halt the Allies' momentum. The Red Army followed up Bagration with another offensive, this time into the northern Ukraine, and by August the Wehrmacht's Army Group North Ukraine had also been smashed, and the Romanian king had switched sides so suddenly that Baron Manfred von Killinger, the former SA man who was German minister there, committed suicide to avoid falling into Soviet hands. For the Reich, the loss of the Romanian oil fields was devastating and increased the significance of its last accessible oil reserves in Hungary, tiny though these were. In the West, Florence and Paris were liberated; Antwerp fell on 3 September, Athens and Belgrade the following month. By the time the fronts stabilized and the Germans were able to temporarily consolidate their position, they had lost much of their empire. The line from Riga and Warsaw in the north to Budapest and Belgrade in the south marked the new limit of the territory under their control in the East.

Yet despite the overwhelming odds against it, the Wehrmacht had certainly not given up. It was still a substantial force, twice the size it had been in 1939, and more than two million men were positioned to defend the Reich between Norway and Italy. It successfully blocked the Allied advance across the Apennines and kept the Red Army out of most of East Prussia through 1944. The coup that toppled Horthy and brought in Szálasi's Arrow Cross regime led to fierce tank battles on the Hungarian plains that halted the Russian advance there. At the same time, hundreds of thousands of civilians were dragooned to dig anti-tank trenches and to construct new defensive fortifications in a vast arc ringing the Reich.

Inside Germany, the Party played an increasingly active role in home defence, especially in levying the new *Volkssturm* militias; the members of this last-ditch Dad's Army were given minimal training, black armbands and a rifle before being pressed into duty. Goebbels became plenipotentiary for the total war effort, and his propaganda demanded ever more intense levels of commitment. 'We know that an idea lives on even if all its bearers have fallen,' he told the first *Volkssturm* swearing-in ceremony. 'The enemy that does not have more than it can deploy will eventually capitulate before the massed strength of a fanatically fighting people.' But the regime did not rely only on propaganda. Internal dissent was suppressed by special courts, SS execution units and summary killings. Ruthless disciplinarians like Himmler and General 'Bloody' Ferdinand Schörner now rose to the fore. More than 30,000 death sentences were issued in the final months – and many more Germans were shot or hanged on the spot.

Schörner, whose men held out longer than any others, was named last commander-in-chief of the German army by Hitler and would eventually face trial in postwar West Germany for his draconian punishment of deserters. But the Germans' will to resist was motivated by fear of another kind of punishment as well. The Reich had the blood of millions on its hands – Jews, political opponents, the victims of so-called 'atonement actions' (*Sühnemassnahmen*) and 'revenge actions' (*Vergeltungsmassnahmen*) – and the regime had always emphasized that the enemy planned to do the same thing to the Germans if they surrendered. Hitler's orders to Field Marshal Kesselring at the start of 1944 commanded his men to fight 'in a spirit of holy hatred for an enemy who is conducting a pitiless war of extermination against the German people'. As the year ended, it publicized news of Red Army atrocities to drive the point home and to stiffen the will to fight inside Germany itself.[5]

As a result, although the Wehrmacht had rapidly overrun much of eastern Europe earlier in the war, once the momentum of Bagration was broken it took months for the Red Army to push it back. Poland, for instance, which had been defeated in a few weeks in October 1939, experienced nine months of fighting in 1944–5. In March 1944, Hitler first called on the troops to turn German-held towns in the East into fortresses that would break the enemy's advance. Surrender was not an option. When American troops crossed into the Reich in September 1944, he insisted that 'every bunker, every housing block in German towns and every German village must become a fortification where the enemy either bleeds to death or the occupying forces bury man upon man in its ruins'. And despite the diversion of troops to the Ardennes and the Hungarian oil fields, the conquest of German cities was protracted and bloody. Königsberg held out for seventy-seven days, having been cut off twice, slowing the advance on Berlin. Breslau fought on from the time it was encircled on 13 February until the final surrender on 6 May – after Hitler's death. By the end little remained of the old East Prussian and Silesian capitals: ferocious Soviet bombing and fires left them in ruins, together with the remains of tens of thousands of civilians who had been trapped in them. In Budapest, which Hitler had also declared a 'fortress city', more than 40,000 German and Hungarian soldiers died, alongside another 38,000 civilians and 80,000 Soviet and Romanian troops. In Berlin, although the actual siege was over in two weeks, the death toll was even higher.[6]

Finally, in March 1945, faced with the Allies' inexorable advance, the scorched earth policy that Hitler had ordered for the occupied territories was mandated for the Reich as well. The German army had used this means of slowing the enemy's advance in the First World War; retreating to the Hindenburg Line, they had created 'dead land, which, ten, twelve to fifteen kilometres broad, stretches in front of the whole length of our new positions and offers a ghastly wall of emptiness for every enemy who designs to get at them'.[7] The Red Army used similar tactics very effectively in 1941, and the retreating Wehrmacht did so too, first in European Russia, and then leaving swathes of northern Finland and Norway uninhabitable: they burned numerous bridges, mined the roads and left the towns in ruins. But the increasingly obvious outcome made the policy seem pointless. German officials in the Netherlands and Denmark simply ignored their orders. And when the Führer issued the so-called 'Nero Decree' to lay waste to those parts of the Reich threatened by the enemy, Armaments Minister Albert Speer confronted him and pointed out the practical difficulties of knowing when to carry this out. Hitler did not withdraw the decree, but fortunately for the Germans it was often disregarded in practice.[8]

THE FLIGHT OF HANS FRANK

Hitler was not alone in regarding suicide alongside falling in battle as the only honourable exit from the coming defeat. 'Many are coming round to the idea of doing away with themselves,' reported the SD in one of its last analyses of German morale. 'The demand for poison, for a pistol or some other method of putting an end to one's life, is high everywhere. Suicide in sheer despair at the certainty of the approaching catastrophe is the order of the day.' The *Reichskommissar* of Norway, Josef Terboven, after drinking his way through the Hotel Adlon in Berlin, cracking 'macabre jokes about the impending end', returned to Oslo and blew himself up in his bunker at Skaugum; next to him, his SS police chief had already shot himself. ('That seems to be the classic pattern for an Old Fighter,' Speer noted later. 'Taking to drink out of a feeling that the Idea had been betrayed, and then explosives.') Fritz Bracht, the *Gauleiter* of Upper Silesia, poisoned himself and his wife; Odilo Globocnik – the architect of Operation Reinhard – killed himself after hiding out in the Austrian Alps; and Konrad Henlein slit his wrists in captivity. There were in fact tens of thousands of suicides, mostly in the eastern territories, and by the war's end people in Berlin were carrying around potassium cyanide capsules or razor-blades in terrified anticipation of the Red Army's arrival.[9]

Hitler had decided, according to General Alfred Jodl, chief of the Armed Forces General Staff, to 'fight to the death' as early as 1942; now, he resolved to take the rest of the country with him, for the alternative – as he warned – was that 'men and children are murdered, women and girls are humiliated as whores, the rest marched to Siberia'. 'The war will decide if the German people shall continue to exist or perish,' he had predicted. Since he equated the nation's salvation with the continuation of National Socialism, this was perhaps not – from his point of view – as peculiar as it sounds today. Yet this desire to fight to the finish for fear of the alternative was, in Michael Geyer's words, the expression of 'a catastrophic nationalism that led into real-life disaster in order to avoid mythical catastrophe'.[10]

The result was that, in the eastern provinces, perhaps half a million people died in late 1944 and early 1945 thanks to orders that held back evacuations and turned civilians, whether they liked it or not, into last-ditch defenders of the Reich. Nevertheless, millions more simply ignored the regime and fled, and over two million were ferried across the Baltic by the navy. The war's final months saw the German equivalent of the French *exode* of 1940 – a desperate mass flight away from the invading armies into the heart of the homeland, among them many of the very Party bosses who were loudly ordering fellow Germans to stay where they were. This atmosphere of *sauve qui peut* exposed the seamy underside of the regime's imperial pretensions and finally unmasked the greed and selfishness of those it had empowered to realize them. Hinrich Lohse, the Reich commissar of the Ostland, left Riga to its fate, and Karl Hanke, the former *Gauleiter* of Lower Silesia, whose brutal reign had earned him the nickname 'Hangman of Breslau', flew out of the burning city and was in Prague disguised as a Waffen-SS soldier the day it surrendered. (Hitler had named him the new Reichsführer-SS in his final testament, but Hanke had prudently not let that stop him going into hiding.) Gauleiter Erich Koch abandoned Königsberg for the safety of the port of Pillau as early as January, spent most of the intervening months in Berlin and finally fled East Prussia, the province he had run since 1928, on a commandeered ice-breaker in April, leaving thousands of angry refugees by the dockside to face the Russians' vengeance.

Yet no one exemplified the inglorious retreat from the New Order better than Poland's Nazi ruler, Hans Frank. It was Frank who had pledged to turn the General Government into a model colony for the Reich and for more than four years, surrounded by his wife, relatives and entourage, had presided with extravagant pomp over a programme of racial extermination, cultural repression and Germanization. While Cracow's Jewish population fell from 68,000 to 500, and brutal *razzias* sent thousands of Poles to the camps or the Reich, Frank had patronized artists, architects, writers and singers, received dignitaries and attended weekly concerts of lieder and opera. There were feasts in the Wawel castle, where 'even the short-hand typists led a life such as one reads about in the Arabian Nights'; Frank's court had been 'an oasis where no one notices the war'. But on 17 January 1945, as the Red Army advanced on the city, Frank himself pulled the swastika down from the castle masthead, rounded up his staff, and fled.[11]

It was a bright wintry afternoon when they drove in a convoy of lorries and Mercedes tourers more than halfway back to Berlin, installing themselves temporarily at Count Manfred von Richthofen's castle at

Seichau in Silesia. This was the General Government's designated evacuation headquarters, and they spent several days burning official papers and sorting through packing cases – Frank had been storing art treasures, food and spirits there since August. Frank himself visited one of his favourite novelists, the elderly Nobel prize-winner Gerhart Hauptmann, who lived near by, while two trucks loaded with valuables were sent onwards to his wife for safekeeping. On 23 January, after a riotous farewell party in the castle, he joined them, detouring only to visit his mistress before ending up at his country house in Bavaria. When the last headquarters of the Government General was set up near by in a café in the small resort town of Neuhaus am Schliersee, its staff numbered just five people. The Alpine scenery was spectacular and peaceful – the war must have seemed very far away – and although nothing like the urban sophistication of Cracow there was the odd reminder of what had been left behind. The Café-Pension Bergfrieden was a simple wooden chalet with a rockery garden and a terrace overlooking the mountains. Frank's few visitors could scarcely believe their eyes when they looked around the walls and saw the works that he had hung 'for safe-keeping' – Leonardo's 'Lady with an Ermine', a Rembrandt self-portrait and a Rubens Crucifixion, not to mention the Dürer, the Guardi and the Cranach.[12]

Back in the castle at Seichau, the local Party officials listed with shocked precision everything that had been left behind: a room full of paintings, four cases of books, fourteen typewriters, 'innumerable' empty filing cabinets, confidential documents, three sets of cutlery, personal toiletries, twenty car rugs, silver, linen, a deck-chair and even a savings book. A luxury Mercedes eight cylinder had simply been abandoned in the castle courtyard – for the use of the armed forces, Frank's adjutant had called out as they drove away. 'The rooms were in the greatest disorder,' reported a maid. 'Wine and schnapps bottles, cigarette ends, bread and sausage lay around everywhere. In the large kitchen we found opened cans of meat, the contents of which had already gone bad, opened cases of butter and eggs.' To the villagers, the waste confirmed all their worst stereotypes of the Party bosses. 'In the village these matters were much discussed' – not surprisingly, since Frank's entourage had still been drunk when they left, colliding with a gateway, and leaving large cases of rationed foodstuffs and hundreds of cigars in the mud behind them.

But soon the fleeing leader of the General Government was forgotten. Upper Silesia was in the line of the Russian advance, and a mass of new and less distinguished refugees arrived in Count von Richthofen's ancestral home. A wild band of 'Eastern volunteers' – no German officer in sight – helped themselves to the alcohol that was lying around and broke into the locked store-room containing Frank's possessions. Only a few cases of tinned food were left for the German refugees who followed behind them. No doubt the collapse of empire is never a pretty sight. And after all, the turmoil Frank had left behind him in Seichau was only a microcosm of the infinitely greater destruction he had wreaked on Poland and its inhabitants.[13]

Astonishingly, that was not how it seemed to him or his wife. The fur-draped former 'Queen of Poland', whose lover, Lasch, had been killed by the Gestapo and who had once enjoyed 'shopping' in the ghetto, welcomed the arrival of the Americans, looked forward to a 'normal life' and felt confident she had done nothing wrong. Frank himself – self-pitying, deluded and theatrical to the last – proudly sipped his coffee each morning in the Café Bergfrieden with his aides, boasting, as he read about Hitler's suicide in the Swiss newspapers that he liked to peruse, that he was the last of his ministers to enjoy his morning coffee in freedom. When he was finally arrested – Lieutenant Walter Stein of the US 7th Army drove up for him on 4 May – he got up from the table, making sure he brought the forty-two volumes of his diaries along with him. As he tucked them next to him on his way into captivity, he believed they would confirm his innocence. Instead, they were to be a key documentary source for his prosecution at Nuremberg, as they have been for historians of Nazi genocide ever since.

THE LAST FÜHRER

Despite the Allies' policy of unconditional surrender, Germany's transition from Nazism was anything but clear. In Hitler's political testament, dictated in the bunker in Berlin on 29 April while his entourage celebrated his marriage to Eva Braun with champagne and sandwiches, he named Grand-Admiral Dönitz as president of the Reich and supreme commander of the armed forces. He also made Goebbels prime minister and Bormann head of the Nazi Party. In a gesture which ensured a break with the old system of power, he expelled both Himmler and Göring from the Nazi Party for treachery. The next afternoon, he and Eva Braun committed suicide, and their bodies were burned in the garden of the bunker.[14]

Thanks to an intrepid pilot, the news that Hitler had ordered Himmler's dismissal reached Dönitz on 29 April itself. The next day he learned the even more astonishing news that the Führer had appointed him *Reichspräsident* and charged him to continue the war. (Hitler had not designated him as Führer, unwilling that anyone else should claim the title.) Yet at his headquarters at the Plön naval base, with only a small detachment of U-Boat men to protect him, Dönitz was hardly in a strong or uncontested position. Himmler was widely regarded as Hitler's natural successor – neither his dismissal nor Hitler's death immediately became public knowledge – and he was visiting Dönitz daily, escorted by an intimidating group of battle-hardened SS veterans. With Albert Speer, Himmler discussed how, despite Hitler's wishes, he and Göring would rule Germany between them. 'Europe cannot manage without me in the future,' he told Speer confidently. As Speer left, he saw Field Marshal Keitel arrive and pledge loyalty to Himmler as he had once done to the Führer.[15]

The same evening that he learned of his appointment, therefore, Dönitz asked Himmler to visit and confronted him with Hitler's instructions while SS men in armoured troop carriers and the admiral's sailors squared off in the streets outside. According to the dramatic but unreliable portrayal of this meeting in Dönitz's memoirs, Himmler, although angry, backed down wordlessly when Dönitz told him an appointment in his new government was out of the question. In fact, there was probably no showdown, for the two men continued to cooperate and the question of Himmler's precise role was shelved. His intelligence and police network would have been indispensable to the new government, and it would have been hard for it to continue the war, as it initially intended to do, without the assistance of the SS. Himmler himself appears to have been confident that the time would come when, as he had long been plotting, he could lead a German government alongside the British and the Americans to continue the fight against Stalin.[16]

Thus National Socialism lived on after Hitler's suicide. Even more than the long-imagined Alpine redoubt (which never materialized), Plön and Flensburg – the port by the Danish border where Dönitz moved his headquarters on 3 May – were magnets for senior Nazis. Those of Hitler's ministers who had headed north included Ribbentrop, Alfred Rosenberg and Herbert Backe. With the exception of Himmler and Ribbentrop, they met together regularly in the small town of Eutin in eastern Holstein; most of them had apparently expected Himmler to become Hitler's successor and were as surprised as he was by the news of Dönitz's appointment. The erstwhile ruler of the Ukraine, Erich Koch, showed up and tried to commandeer a submarine to take him to Latin America; Lohse, who had run the Baltic, wanted the same thing. (Dönitz refused them both.) The SS officials who materialized included the former Auschwitz commandant, Rudolf Höss, and Hans Prützmann, who was supposed to be organizing last-ditch resistance to the Allies. But alongside the SS hard men there were also the long-time members of the SS intelligentsia, like Himmler's foreign intelligence chief, Walter Schellenberg, and the economist (and former *Einsatzgruppe* commander) Otto Ohlendorf, who were in the thick of the discussions about what to do next. Ohlendorf in particular – 'the Galahad of National Socialism' to the bitter end – was still hoping to rescue the SD's reputation and make it a partner in the reconstruction of postwar Germany 'along National Socialist lines'.[17]

Ohlendorf's idea that a reformed National Socialism might be able to play a leading role in Germany after Hitler indicates how hard it was to imagine a future without Nazism. There was no more fervent believer in National Socialism than Ohlendorf, but Dönitz himself did not see things very differently from him. 'We may ourselves abolish many of the trappings of National Socialism,' he wrote. 'Others may be abolished by the enemy; but the best aspect of National Socialism, the community of our people, must under all circumstances be preserved.' His very conception of a break with the past reflected this outlook. Starting on 2 May, Dönitz reshuffled his cabinet. He dismissed the now redundant Alfred Rosenberg – after all, there were no more Occupied eastern territories to rule – who was turned away, drunk, from the government building, sprained his ankle and ended up in hospital. Unaware of the deaths of Goebbels and Bormann, Dönitz ordered their dismissals too, as well as that of the justice minister, Thierack, who had effectively handed the courts over to the SS in 1942. But he kept Herbert Backe, the architect of the 'hunger plan' in the occupied eastern territories, as minister of agriculture and Franz Seldte, founder of the right-wing paramilitary Stahlhelm, as the new labour minister. Ohlendorf was given the economics portfolio. Wilhelm Stuckart, the bureaucratic genius behind Germany's expansion, finally became minister of the interior. Remaining in office were two dependable technocrats, Julius Dorpmüller, the long-serving transport minister, and the ever adaptable conservative Count Schwerin von Krosigk, who had been finance minister since 1932 and who now became foreign minister.[18]

Himmler was still a force to be reckoned with and, on 3 May, the Reichsführer-SS moved his entourage to Flensburg to be closer to the new government. Caught on the road in an air raid, most of his staff officers and their secretaries abandoned their vehicles and dived for shelter as the planes attacked, leaving only Himmler at the wheel of his Mercedes shouting for discipline. Next to him was Werner Best, the Reich plenipotentiary for Denmark, who had just arrived from Copenhagen. Himmler told him that 'Hitler had not been himself' in the last days – a reference to his dismissal – and explained how hard it had been to advance his peace feelers to the Allies when surrounded by enemies. He assured Best that two hours' conversation with Eisenhower would suffice to persuade him to join forces with Germany against Russia. To the incredulous Best, Himmler seemed nervous, crushed in spirits, hardly any longer believing the phrases he had repeated for so long.[19]

At first Dönitz – like Himmler – clung to the hope that they could split the wartime Big Three and surrender to the British and Americans alone, while continuing to fight the Russians. On 4 May, after some prevarication, he arranged the surrender of German forces in north-western Germany, Denmark and the Netherlands to Field Marshal Montgomery. But the speed of events and Montgomery's firmness changed Dönitz's mind. At a cabinet meeting the same day, he overruled Himmler, who still wanted to use Scandinavia and the Netherlands as bargaining chips. Three days later, on Dönitz's orders, OKW chief of staff Alfred Jodl surrendered unconditionally to the Allies in Rheims, and Field Marshal Keitel repeated the ceremony the following day at the Red Army headquarters in Berlin, officially bringing the war in Europe to an end.[20]

Dönitz's switch to the surrender camp meant there was no place any longer for Himmler in his administration. On 5 May, the two men bargained over a loose form of words that would not imply any specific post in the new government; the following day, Dönitz told Himmler personally that he was severing his connections with him and ordered him not to visit the government headquarters in future. Himmler had no fight left in him. After a few days spent in a farmhouse outside Flensburg with a group of loyal aides, he started to make his way south, disguised as 'ex-Sergeant Heinrich Hitzinger' supposedly attached to the Secret Field Police. (The real Hitzinger had been executed as a deserter.) But Himmler had not realized that this organization too was on the Allies' automatic arrest list, and he and his companions were picked up at a checkpoint. In a camp south of Lüneberg, the former Reichführer-SS calmly admitted his identity to the British captain in charge but committed suicide by swallowing a cyanide capsule before he could be stopped.[21]

As for Dönitz, what kind of government did he and his staff of 350 really represent? Among the Allies, no one wanted to give him full recognition, especially since even at the highest levels they were still not completely sure that Hitler and other senior Nazis were really dead. The reactionaries of Flensburg were an embarrassment, as were the soldiers and sailors who milled outside the Marine and Signal School – the seat of the 'government' – singing the Horst Wessel Song or 'Wir fahren gegen Engeland'. They resented being told to give up the Hitler salute, and Dönitz kicked up a fuss when told to get rid of military decorations and insignia. He refused to order the official dissolution of the NSDAP and only lowered the old flag outside his headquarters when forced to do so.[22] Churchill and local British army officers saw advantages in temporarily keeping alive a central German administration operating under Allied orders. 'There are two million German troops and swollen numbers of civilians into the bargain,' they noted. 'To discipline, feed and administer the German troops it may well be necessary to continue provisionally the German chain of command and to allow it to requisition foodstuffs from the population.'[23] But it became clear very quickly that the continued existence of the Dönitz government was making the Russians nervous. And not only the Russians; there was a row after local British officers allowed his officials to make radio broadcasts ordering Germans to obey them, and the BBC carried an interview with von Krosigk, in which he referred to the admiral as the new Führer. Allied political advisors increasingly disliked the authoritarian instincts of this self-styled 'Acting Government of the Reich'. When Dönitz's arrest was ordered, the Russians were relieved, and so was almost everyone else.

Only Churchill muttered crossly that it seemed 'a notable step in making sure we have no one to deal with in Germany'.[24]

On 23 May, the Admiral and the other members of his 'government' were arrested by men of the 11th Armoured Division. They were strip-searched and humiliatingly lined up in a courtyard with machine-guns trained on them and photographed by more than sixty reporters who had been invited by SHAEF for the occasion. Suitcases in hand, they were then spirited away to Luxembourg and a welcoming committee of heavily armed soldiers and angry, jeering villagers. In the faded elegance of the four-storey Palace Hotel in the leafy spa-town of Mondorf-les-Bains, on the French border, they were reunited with the other leading members of the regime who had fallen into Allied hands. The hotel, built in the 1920s, had once been an elegant retreat for those taking the waters. Now, however, its tightly guarded grounds were surrounded by a fifteen-foot-high barbed-wire fence, screened with canvas and camouflage netting, with watch-towers in each corner. To the GIs in charge it was known as Central Continental Prisoner of War Enclosure 32, or more colloquially as 'Ashcan'.

An American military interrogator, John Dolibois, has left a vivid record of his own arrival there:

I climbed up the stairs, located room 30 and let myself in . . . It was an ordinary hotel room, with rather noisy wallpaper. A table and two chairs, and a folding army cot made up the furnishings. I started to unpack my duffel bag when I heard a knock on the door. Thinking this might be Captain Sensenig or one of the guard officers, I opened the door and got the surprise of my life. Before me stood a stout man, about five foot ten inches, dressed in a natty pearl-gray uniform, gold braids on the collars, gold insignia of rank on the shoulders. He clicked his heels, bobbed his head once, and said, 'Goering, Reichsmarschall!' I gave a damn poor impression of an intelligence officer. My mouth fell open. Quickly, I gathered my wits and asked the man to step inside. He came to the point at once. On his arm he held a pair of uniform trousers which he handed to me. Then he explained that this was a pair he had 'overlooked' when told the day before that he could have only one suit and one extra pair of trousers. 'Since I am determined to be a model prisoner,' he explained, 'I thought I should bring this surplus item to you.' I think I detected a note of sarcasm.[25]

They were almost all there. Seyss-Inquart had arrived first, along with Frick and Keitel. Hans Frank, who had tried to commit suicide, was carried in in his silk pajamas. Göring himself, his hands shaking badly from his paracodeine addiction, had brought so much luggage it took an entire afternoon to search it. Franz Ritter von Epp, nearly eighty years old, was held in his capacity as long-time governor of Bavaria: this was the end to a career that had taken him from the Boxer Rebellion in China and the massacres in German South West Africa, through the First World War and right-wing politics in Weimar before becoming the Third Reich's leading colonial activist. Soon the hotel contained virtually every surviving Reich minister – Ribbentrop, Dönitz, Rosenberg, Funk, Robert Ley, von Krosigk, Darré; Admiral Horthy, together with a select upper crust – mostly former ambassadors – were housed in a separate villa known as the 'von Annex'. Made to watch films of the camps, the inmates also gave lectures for one another – von Krosigk on Shakespeare; Robert Ley on the economics of Germany's postwar recovery, one of Keitel's aides on fish-breeding. At mealtimes they were only allowed to use spoons so as to rule out suicide attempts.

Gradually they split into cliques, and their true characters emerged once more. The military men kept to themselves; as did the Nazi 'Old Fighters', and the bureaucrats like Stuckart, Lammers and von Krosigk. Frick turned out to be a quiet, softly spoken, officious yes-man. Keitel spent most of his time acquiring a tan. Von Ribbentrop was nervous, aloof, hurt at having been excluded from Hitler's last testament, and unable to keep his room tidy. Göring, despite turning out to be afraid of thunderstorms, was in many ways the outstanding figure – alert, witty and sarcastic with his captors, a raconteur who liked laughing at himself, forthright about admitting responsibility for the camps. He regarded himself as the leader of them all but was in fact shunned and sat alone most mealtimes. Dönitz, his rival, remained stoically calm and arrogant. The two men fired off complaints to Eisenhower that they were not being treated as befitted heads of state, but they were simply ignored. (Indeed Dönitz continued to insist as late as 1953, by which time he was in prison as a war criminal, that he remained Germany's legal head of state.)[26]

Eventually, Mondorf's secret leaked out and the world press began to gather. To appease them, it was decided to arrange a one-off photo shoot and the hotel's inmates were asked to gather together for a group picture on the front steps: the result was eventually published in the American press with the caption: 'The Class of 1945'. On 10 August they were sent into Germany in preparation for the forthcoming trials. As they crossed the border and caught sight of the bombed-out ruins around Trier, they were visibly shocked and one of them burst into tears.

For those guarding them, the return journey back to Mondorf brought a much more disturbing reminder of what National Socialism had been responsible for. Their convoy had only been driving a short distance when it passed a group of five 2½-ton cargo trucks and a broken-down jeep by the side of the road. Stopping to help, they were immediately hit by an overpowering sickly stench that made some of the men retch. 'What in God's name are you hauling?' Dolibois asked the captain in charge. Wordlessly, he drew back the tarpaulin on one of the trucks to reveal corpses stacked like firewood, some naked, some still in rotting camp uniforms. They were being moved from one mass grave to another.[27]

The brief rise and fall of Germany's last Führer had never really threatened to drive a wedge between the Big Three, but it had done nothing to improve their relations either. From the outset, the Russians had refused to deal with Dönitz and confined their interactions to the German general staff. The British and the Americans, on the other hand, had vacillated and – in the words of one British civil servant – 'bungled the Doenitz business quite unnecessarily'. They had neither satisfied Moscow nor established a reliable central German administration.

Yet among the victors neither side at this point wanted a break. The fighting was scarcely over, and everyone remembered Germany's resurgence after the First World War. The desire to find a workable solution to the German problem – and to the European balance of power in general – continued to unite them. At the crucial conference held in Potsdam that summer, this urge for unity remained. Stalin now met President Truman (Roosevelt had died in April) for the first time, and Clement Attlee took over halfway through from Churchill. Yet despite the departure of two of the wartime Big Three, their successors established a Council of Foreign Ministers, with a permanent secretariat based in London, to prepare peace treaties and offer solutions to territorial disputes in postwar Europe. Most urgently and importantly, they also outlined the basis of an agreement on a highly interventionist strategy for the occupation of Germany.

The original plan proposed in 1944 by US Treasury Secretary Hans Morgenthau had called for Germany to be partitioned, stripped of its heavy industry and turned into a 'primarily agricultural and pastoral country'. It was ironic, Albert Speer commented in prison some time later, that Morgenthau and Himmler wanted much the same thing. In fact, Morgenthau's ideas had aroused huge controversy and been much modified by the spring of 1945. According to the Potsdam Agreement, the country was to be demilitarized, de-Nazified (through purges and prosecutions of war criminals; propaganda and the repeal of Nazi-era laws) and democratized (especially through educational reform and the re-establishment of political parties). Cartels and monopolies were to be broken up. Following earlier agreements at Yalta, four occupation zones were to be established in both Germany and Austria, and in their respective capitals. But permanent partition was certainly not envisaged; on the contrary, the Agreement stressed the importance of establishing 'uniformity of treatment of the German population throughout Germany' and talked of treating the country 'as a single economic unit'. Reparations from the Soviet zone were accepted, as was the idea that the German standard of living should be maintained at levels not exceeding the European average. The country's economy was to be tightly controlled, and there were still echoes of a watered-down Morgenthau Plan in the recommendation that it was to be turned away from heavy industry and armaments production and towards agricultural goods and light manufacturing.[28]

But most striking were the border changes and population movements that the Agreement approved: not only did it reverse all border changes and annexations made since the *Anschluss*, but Germany's eastern border with Poland was to be moved sharply westwards, reducing the size of the prewar Reich by nearly one-quarter. At the same time, the conference also approved the expulsion westwards of millions of Germans who lived east of the new borders. The only stipulation was that such expulsions – or 'transfers' as the document called them – should take place 'in an orderly and humane manner'. Since the Polish, Czech and Hungarian authorities were already expelling Germans from their countries, the Powers requested them to suspend these temporarily so that refugees could be properly looked after and resettled on arrival in Germany.

Nothing changed the long-term map of eastern Europe as much as the expulsion of the Germans. It was a response both to Nazi policies of turning ethnic Germans into tools of the Reich, and to their own forced population transfers. The idea had been peddled by the Soviets and the Czechs since 1942, but by 1945 it had hardened into a much more sweeping agreement in effect to eradicate centuries of German life east of the country's new borders. But this was not all the diplomats' doing and the idea that the Powers could turn expulsions on and off at will takes little account of the real driving force behind them – the immense popular hatred towards the Germans that existed in the regions they had occupied as the war came to an end. To understand what was happening, in other words, it is not enough to listen to the conference chambers and the pronouncements of the politicians. We have, above all at this chaotic time when power and authority were still scattered and fragmented across much of Europe, to look at what was happening on the ground.

EXPULSION: THE END OF THE GERMAN QUESTION

'The Russians are in the neighbourhood!' 'Everyone for himself. The Russians will be here in half an hour!' What had begun with the drive to the East ended from the East too. When it came, after weeks of panic, the moment arrived astonishingly quickly for one young German medical student. As she later recalled:

Suddenly the shooting stopped, the panzer rolled up and on all sides there were Russian soldiers in snowshirts. The confusion was so great that one at first did not know whether they were German or Russian soldiers, but then we saw German soldiers with their hands up ... The panzer rushed through the row of carts. Carts were hurled into ditches where there were entrails of horses, and men, women and children were fighting with death. Wounded people were screaming for help ... Then came an officer on horseback. Some German soldiers were brought to him. He took his revolver; I shut my eyes, shots fell and the poor fellows lay in front of us shot in the head, an expression of horror on their faces. The corpses remained there, no one dared to touch them.

The panzer kept rolling up with soldiers. That is the Russian Army, which as we were told was nearly famished to death and in rags. These strong and strapping fellows, and gun-women in the full bloom of health were sitting next to the soldiers, all in new uniforms and with felt boots and fur caps. We stood on the edge of the road looking at the panzer rolling past and at the soldiers. Most of them had primitive faces, round heads and expressions of unbounded joy. They waved to us and shouted out 'Hitler kaputt'.[29]

The Slavic *Untermenschen* shocked the Germans with more than their 'primitive faces' and the sound of their unfamiliar language. The frontline troops drank and looted their way through the towns and villages they passed through. Watches – 'Uri, Uri!' – were a favourite of theirs (a weakness they shared with the Belorussians in the SS Kaminsky Brigade), and some soldiers ended up with their arms covered in them. Boots were even more important: the first thing one of the Jewish partisans emerging from the Briansk forest did on liberation was to take the leather riding boots of a captured German soldier. But 'trophy collecting' of all kinds was endemic among men who found themselves battling their way through a world where the enemy appeared to live with a degree of comfort and luxury that they had not even dreamed existed. 'Now I am sitting in the estate of a rich German,' one young soldier wrote to his parents. 'There are divans, sofas, silk everywhere and the floor shines like a mirror.'[30]

Cognac, sheep, down pillows, cigars – a new world of commodities was theirs, ready to be seized from the fascists and capitalists who had turned their own country into a wasteland. But their immediate response was not so much desire as hatred. 'It's obvious from everything we see that Hitler robbed the whole of Europe to please his bloodstained Fritzes,' one soldier wrote home. 'In the near future, these goods will appear in Russian shops as our trophies.' Fuelling their rage, too, as they battled west was news of what had been found at Lublin-Majdanek in July 1944, or the still-smouldering pyres of torched corpses in Estonia: details of these horrors spread through the Red Army's ranks and intensified their desire for revenge. 'Our soldiers have not dealt with East Prussia any worse than the Germans did with Smolensk,' wrote another. 'We hate Germany and the Germans deeply . . . But the Germans deserve the atrocities that they unleashed. You have only to think about Majdanek.'[31]

The desire for revenge manifested itself above all in the rapes for which the Red Army's troops soon became notorious. It is true that not much has been written on *German* soldiers and rape in the East during their occupation; it was probably more widespread than is generally believed and it certainly featured prominently in wartime Soviet propaganda. But racial ideology meant that military courts often punished sexual crimes by German soldiers severely. In any case, desire for vengeance was only one cause of the orgy of rape, plunder and looting that Soviet troops embarked upon. It began from the moment Soviet units passed into Romania in August 1944 and even allies like Tito's partisans, who liberated Belgrade together with the Russians, were horrified. In Budapest, thousands of women were violated; the same thing happened in Poland, forcing even the Polish communists to protest. But it was worst when the Red Army crossed into Germany itself. In East Prussia and Upper Silesia, the troops picked out women from the crowds of refugees and raped them in rows by the roadside, surrounded by 'a raucous armada of men with their trousers down'. Officers watched and encouraged their men to take part. Estimates of the number of women attacked in what was almost certainly the largest case of mass rape in history vary enormously: figures range up to nearly two million for German women alone.[32]

Belatedly, having been told to hate, the Russian troops were now lectured against behaving like 'robbers and marauders'. In January 1945, Marshal Rokossovski issued an order warning that rapists would be shot on the spot. It had little effect, and some officers who protested were arrested and later imprisoned for 'bourgeois humanism propaganda and sympathy with the enemy'. When Stalin himself became worried that his men's lawlessness was actually making the Germans resist more fiercely, his strictures were also ignored. 'To my amazement,' wrote Grigori Pomerants, 'neither officers nor Communists could give a damn about the letter from Stalin himself! It would take more than Stalin to stop the army.'[33]

For the now defenceless Germans, the rapes were a terrifying reminder that the Reich's formidable fighting machine had been overwhelmed. Putting Himmler in charge of Army Group Vistula, as Hitler had done in January 1945, the day after Soviet troops had cut off Poznań, only made matters worse thanks to 'Reichsheini's' ignorance of generalship; he was replaced within weeks, but the damage had been done. The perils of evacuation by sea were highlighted by the sinking of the *Wilhelm Gustloff* at the end of January. Leaving Gdynia with more than 10,000 refugees and wounded soldiers on board, it was torpedoed by a Soviet submarine and sank in the freezing waters of the Baltic in one of the greatest losses of life in maritime history. As the army withdrew from Poland, a civil servant's wife noticed that its formerly mechanized units were relying on horse-drawn carts or retreated on foot. It was the Red Army – moving rapidly thanks to its ZIS-5 trucks and its American-made Lend-Lease Studebakers – which now stood for mobility and modernity.[34]

As soon as Liberation came, the Germans found that it was not only the Russians who were determined to exact their revenge. The punitive measures they had forced on the *Untermenschen* of eastern Europe during the years of occupation were now turned back on them. 'We will deal with the German population in these areas, which have been Polish since the beginning of time, just as the Germans taught us,' proclaimed the new Polish governor when he took over Katowice county in February 1945. Making Germans dig up the remains of the victims of their violence was often the first step – echoing what they themselves had done when they marched into Poland and the Soviet Union. In western Germany, townsfolk were forced to file past the piles of emaciated corpses from the liberated camps. In one Upper Silesian town, in contrast, Germans were forced to dig up a recent mass grave with their hands – it contained the remains of prisoners of war tossed out of railway cars in the winter of 1944/5 – so that the bodies could be photographed and reburied properly. 'Despite the fact that they washed their hands with Lysol and other disinfectants,' one recalled, 'the "grave-diggers" could not get rid of the stench of the corpses for days.' At least they were not then massacred themselves, as had happened to their own victims during the invasion of the USSR four years earlier.[35]

In many parts of Poland and Czechoslovakia, Germans were made to wear white armbands with a large black letter N (Niemiec = German), or large swastikas were simply painted on their backs. In some places, they were not allowed to use the pavements, trains or shops except at certain times; they were made liable for labour service and not allowed to speak German in public. German institutions and property were swiftly confiscated by the state. Terezin in Czechoslovakia and Auschwitz were only two of the former camps that now confronted German inmates with the terrors of a new regime.

These were not the only lessons that the victims had learned from their years of suffering. Polish officials also established what they openly referred to as ghettoes. 'During the night of August 7th to 8th,' recalled a resident of one Upper Silesian town, 'notices containing the following instructions were affixed to all the buildings in the town: "All Germans must line up outside their houses, immediately. Fifty-five pounds of luggage maximum."' Soon afterwards Polish militia arrived and forced the people into the so-called German ghetto, 'beating and whipping them to make them hurry'. Three streets were sealed off and placed under guard, and familiar problems of overcrowding and hunger quickly emerged. Elsewhere, German farmers were thrown off their land to make way for Polish settlers, and their property was confiscated: if they were lucky, they could remain for a time as labourers serving either the Russians or the Polish settlers. Thrown out of eastern Galicia by the Russians, many Poles were being moved by the communist authorities into western Poland. 'They introduced themselves to the German farmers, owners of smallholdings and cottagers, as the new owners, with the words: "I now farmer, you Hitler, work."'[36]

Many of these forms of persecution – which some Polish officials themselves criticized as 'Nazi' methods – emerged spontaneously and temporarily and were accompanied by lawlessness, plundering and violence. 'The German is not subject to the law anymore,' complained a German priest from Görlitz. 'His honour, his body, his life and his property are at the merciless disposal of an insolent victor.' But this was all preliminary to a much more radical and permanent solution to the 'German problem' – expulsion. Pushed by President Beneš, wartime plans had been approved in Washington, London and Moscow for the eventual expulsion of the German minorities in Czechoslovakia and Poland. The Beneš government had been whipping up the Czechs' already fierce anti-German hatred. 'When the day comes, our nation will take up the old battle cry again: Cut them! Beat them! Spare nobody! Everyone has to find a useful weapon to hit the nearest German,' an officer screamed on the BBC in late 1944. The Polish case was different, because it was prompted chiefly by Stalin's plans to shift the country's borders westwards into the Reich. The Allies skated over the issue at Yalta, but this only increased the incentive for the Poles and Czechs to create facts on the ground. 'We ... will carry out the whole thing ourselves,' Beneš declared in 1945.[37]

In western Poland, 'wild deportations' began early in 1945. Agreements for a Polish–Ukrainian population exchange between Poland and the USSR had already brought several hundred thousand Polish refugees from the western Ukraine, Lithuania and Belorussia and they were directed towards the German lands that the Red Army was gradually handing over to the Polish authorities. However, once the Third Reich officially surrendered, many Germans who had fled began returning to their homes in this same region. It was at this point that the Poles began systematically driving them away again to make room for the incoming Polish settlers and 'to purify the border strip of land of Germans'. The old Bismarckian conception was being turned back on the Germans. The ruling communists in the Polish Workers' Party decided on expulsion at the end of May, and, by the end of June, more than a quarter of a million people had already been forced out.[38]

In the towns, especially those that had been German before 1939, the reckoning took longer because the Soviets had greater control and greater interest in keeping enough Germans there to allow them to function. In August 1945, Breslau, for instance, had 189,500 German and only 16–17,000 Polish inhabitants. The Red Army had handed over power to local German 'anti-fascists' whose anti-fascism was often only skin-deep: that summer, for instance, they tried to mobilize 'all Jews, half-Jews, Poles and citizens of any nationality whatever' for labour duties. The Poles wanted *all* the Germans gone but, as so often, military needs bred pragmatism, and in the short term the Soviets told the factory workers and civil servants to stay where they were. There were even clashes between Soviet soldiers and Poles when the former defended and protected Germans, 'saying they were their friends and worked for them'. But by the winter of 1945/6, the Poles were curtailing the Germans' access to apartments and food to force them out. Gradually Polish policy became clearer. On the one hand, a relatively loose nationality law ensured that many Germans could qualify to stay as Poles – an important consideration for the government, which was worried about depopulating its newly acquired western territories. But at the same time, the deportations proper started: the trains began running regularly westwards from the start of 1946, and by the end of the following year only a few thousand Germans were left.[39]

In Prague, the struggle between Czechs and Germans simply continued right through May, from occupation into the Liberation. The final days of the battle there had been marked by desperate acts of violence by the SS: it had rounded up prisoners at Terezin and shot them, marched civilians as human shields in front of their tanks and executed many captured fighters. In all, 3,700 Czechs had been killed. Once Soviet troops entered, the tables were turned with a vengeance: captured Germans were rounded up and shot in stadiums and hospitals and some were hanged or burned alive. Outside the capital, law and order broke down completely, and the revenge that many Germans had been fearing for months was not slow in coming. The prisons were filled not only with known Nazis, but with those described as 'doubtful' cases or people simply denounced as friends of friends of collaborators. Some partners in mixed marriages were arrested for the crime of having married a German. As late as August, the government had no clear information about how many prisoners were interned, why or under what conditions. The Hanke camp in Ostrava acquired a particularly bad reputation for beatings, rape, torture and random killings of inmates by the guards which they invited their friends to watch. Czech women accused of having fraternized with Germans were at risk of being hauled out, stripped and beaten. Even the Red Army was shocked by the Czechs' humiliation of the Germans – the violent killings, the torching of their homes and farms. Some Germans came to see Soviet soldiers as their only defenders; they begged them to stay and tried to remain under their protection.[40]

The Beneš regime initially did nothing to curb this outpouring of hatred. On the contrary, on 12 May, the newly returned president told the inhabitants of Brno that 'the German people . . . behaved like a monster . . . We must liquidate the German problem definitively.' As he spoke, 1,000 suspected German collaborators were interned in the town. Within a few days demonstrators began demanding more radical measures and complaining that the German community itself was to blame for the lack of shelter or food. Eventually the police evicted 20,000 Germans from their homes and marched them towards the Austrian border; the column was said to stretch for miles. This 'wild deportation' took the government by surprise, and the interior minister tried to block the border crossing and demanded instead that they be interned. But in fact, in the chaos, two-thirds did cross into Austria before the remainder were lodged in a small village brickworks on the Czech side of the line. More than 1,700 of them died on what they remembered as the 'March of Death', mostly from hunger, illness and neglect.

It was the local Brno Czechs who had been primarily responsible for this, though their own national leaders had – as they saw it – given their approval. In fact, when informed about the deportation, the national government was worried about the impression it would create at a time when the Big Three were preparing to meet. So can we say that popular anger at the local level drove national policy? Expulsion was certainly *not* just the product of Stalin or Churchill's decrees; it was precisely what many people who had endured years of humiliation at the Germans' hands wanted. But it was facilitated by an intensely volatile and uncertain political situation: weak national governments, new political parties competing for votes, and large numbers of angry armed men jostling for power in provincial towns and villages ratcheted up the violence. Some of these so-called Revolutionary Guards, noted an observer, were really 'thieves and prostitutes, armed to the teeth, who walked the streets in the light of day, shooting out German language signs and stealing whatever they could'.[41]

One other factor that should not be overlooked also contributed to the violence – the fear that the Germans were only temporarily defeated and were preparing to launch their revenge. The memory of German power did not die easily, and many Czechs believed that Nazi 'Werewolves' were mobilizing and preparing to attack. Remembering the vicious fighting that had accompanied the aftermath of the German defeat in the last war, they could not imagine the end of this one would bring peace. In 1944, the Germans had in fact set up such an organization, and the former HSSPF of Russia-North, Hans-Adolf Prützmann, began training small stay-behind units for sabotage and partisan operations. Goebbels himself played up the 'Werewolves' successfully enough for the Allies to take the threat seriously. But although caches of explosives were buried for future use, the organization itself was tiny and collapsed with the end of the Reich; Prützmann committed suicide and only a few die-hards remained holed up in the woods of the Harz mountains.

Yet while there was never any threat to the Czech lands, the 'Werewolf' hysteria lived on there precisely because it was so difficult, especially in the west of the country, for the Czechs to imagine a world in which the Germans were no longer dominant. In Ústí nad Labem (Aussig) a small industrial town in northern Bohemia, there was an arms depot at which German POWs sorted through ammunition left behind at the end of the war. On the afternoon of 30 July, this exploded, killing and wounding local residents, both Czech and German. Convinced the blast was the work of Werewolf terrorists, Czechs armed with fence-posts and crowbars attacked Germans crossing the town's central bridge – identifying them by their white armbands – and threw them into the Elbe, where Revolutionary Guards shot at them. Several hundred Germans may have been killed or drowned. In Prague, the government was horrified at the news. But it also concluded that there was only one way to ensure that 'the streets will not rule': that was to speed up the deportations and to 'liquidate the Werewolves'. Recent estimates are that between 19,000 and 30,000 Germans died during the 'wild' phase of the expulsions in Czechoslovakia as a whole: 5,000 committed suicide, and 6,000 were directly murdered; the rest died of starvation or disease. By August, around three-quarters of a million people had been driven out of the country.[42]

After Potsdam, the so-called 'wild' phase of the expulsions gave way as it did in Poland to a more sustained and systematic policy that – at least in theory – linked the pace of deportation to the capacity of the authorities in Germany to receive the new refugees. It was thus from late 1945 onwards, well after the immediate reverberations of Liberation had died away – and conveniently too after the harvest had been brought in – that most of the Germans were actually deported from the Czech lands. The result was that, by the late 1940s, innumerable Habsburg and medieval German settlements had ceased to exist. Individuals and indeed communities with little or no connection to Nazism had been forced to leave purely because they were Germans. There was virtually no effort made to establish the political record of those they deported. Anti-fascists and social democrats were thrown out of their homes just like Nazis. Even many German-speaking Czech Jews were made to leave, as the Czechs were keen to seize the opportunity to force the surviving Jews out as well. Some families evaded deportation only by hanging themselves or taking poison. By 1948, no more than 200,000 Germans remained in the Czech republic.[43]

For the Great Powers, this 'transfer' of the Germans promised to bring Europe's German question to a close. After all, the Nazis had exploited the German minorities across eastern Europe and turned them into a fifth column for their foreign policy. Deportation was a way of making sure that this could never be repeated. 'Bitter experience for a hundred years shows that these European *irredenta* are a constant source of war,' wrote former US president Herbert Hoover in 1942. 'Consideration should be given even to the heroic remedy of transfer of population. The hardship of moving is great, but it is less than the constant suffering of minorities and the constant recurrence of war.' Churchill agreed. The 'total expulsion of the Germans ... will be the most satisfactory and lasting guarantee of stability after the war,' he stated in December 1944. 'There will be no mixture of populations to cause endless trouble ... A clean sweep will be made.'[44]

But there were other reasons for the expulsions too. For the Poles, in particular, the country's economic prospects were vastly improved by what was, in effect, the swap of poor agricultural land in the western Ukraine for wealthier regions in the west and especially the industrial belt of Upper Silesia. The likelihood was that Poland's standard of living would thereby be raised closer to Germany's – a consideration for those who believed the German–Polish antagonism had primarily economic origins. A sweeping land reform was proclaimed as early as January 1945, allowing all German farms to be expropriated. While the Red Army retained some of these for several years for its own use, the rest lay at the disposal of the Polish state. It distributed much of the land to colonists and smallholders, and in several border regions it turned large estates into state farms – Bismarck's Varzin was one – thereby increasing the state's control over the country's economic resources.[45]

The rapidity of Poland's resettlement contrasted with that the Germans had carried out during the war. Himmler had, with difficulty, settled perhaps half a million ethnic Germans in the occupied Polish territories in the five years that he ran the Nazi resettlement programme. By contrast, the Poles settled one and a half million colonists on former German land in only a couple of years and eventually brought in no fewer than four million. Admittedly, they were helped by the fact that there was no war going on at the same time. Nevertheless, the disparity points to another factor as well: the Nazis' complete lack of political reality. They had gone to war in pursuit of an unrealizable ideal, for Himmler's resettlement ambitions vastly outran the number of Germans actually available to him; even for those in his power, his cumbersome racial screening slowed down the passage from expropriation to handover. For the Poles, on the other hand, the colonization of the new western territories simply meant accelerating the long-term westwards drift of populations, and putting to use the large number of Poles who had been forced to leave their homes in the East. It was only somewhat later that the limitations of communist control of the land would become apparent, as peasants fought back against the collectivization of the land and Party bosses turned fallow land to forest.

Ironically, although the Polish communists had more people to settle – thanks to Stalin's forced transfers from eastern Poland – they were ultimately no more able to dictate the settlers' life decisions than the Nazis had been. In postwar Poland and Czechoslovakia, settlers did what they had already been doing under the Germans – they left the remote border regions for the towns and deserted the frontier farms. By the early 1950s, both countries had become dependent on Russian grain, and the Party was drumming up shock troops of young people to reverse the trend. But although the Party itself was worried, it also knew that its championing of the expulsions and resettlement had already served its purpose. It had helped communism come to power and identified it with the national cause.

For this was the final aspect of the expulsions: they represented the triumph of nationality politics across eastern Europe. The Germans were the largest ethnic group to be targeted for displacement but they were not the only ones. Polish agreements with the USSR meant that in return for receiving nearly 2.1 million Poles, it was able to deport 482,000 Ukrainians in 1945–6. The following year, most of the remaining Ukrainians in south-eastern Poland were targeted in a punitive military operation called Akcja Wisła and forced to move to western Poland, dealing a heavy blow to what was left of the Ukrainian resistance that was still battling both Poles and the Soviets. At the same time, there was a wave of popular anti-Semitic riots – over 350 Jews were killed by the end of 1945 alone – that revealed the limited reach of the new government's authority in many areas and drove out many of Poland's Jewish survivors. Like the Czechs, the Poles wanted the Jews out too. Hungarians and Italians were forced out of Yugoslavia, and there was a de facto exchange of Hungarians and Slovaks. In this way, Stalin took over the role at the end of the 1940s that Hitler had played at the start – the arbiter of territorial and minority issues in east-central Europe, mediating between Poles and Czechs, and Hungarians, Slovaks and Romanians.[46]

By 1950, eastern Europe's minority populations had shrunk to a very small proportion of what they had been two decades earlier, and communities of ethnic Germans existed only in isolated pockets. Germany itself was divided and occupied and unable to intervene internationally on their behalf, even had its politicians wanted to. Under the firm eye of Washington and Moscow, politicians in either half of the divided country entered alliances with their neighbours. Bonn tried to defang well-funded refugee movements and prevent any repetition of the *revanchist* wave of the Weimar years. These movements spearheaded calls for a return to 'the German East', and under their pressure even Adenauer publicly demanded a return to the Reich's 1937 borders. Translating their claims into the language of the Free World, they called for 'human rights' for the expellees – including the right to return to their homes – and 'liberation'. Across the border, their deserted villages in western Czechoslovakia crumbled into ruins, and their once-great cities like Breslau remained underpopulated for decades. Yet most refugees were integrated astonishingly quickly, their paths eased by postwar prosperity. West German coffee tables groaned under the weight of nostalgic photo-albums of the lost East; but long before the 1990 Treaty by which the two Germanies finally acknowledged the country's postwar borders most people knew it had gone for good.[47]

PART 3

Perspectives

17

We Europeans

Germany will not be occupied by its enemies in the year 2000. The German nation will be the intellectual leader of civilized humanity. We are earning that right in this war. This world struggle with our enemies will live on only as a bad dream in people's memories. Our children will erect monuments to their fathers and mothers for the pain they suffered, for the stoic steadfastness with which they bore all, for the bravery they showed, for the heroism with which they fought, for the loyalty with which they held to their Führer *and his ideals in difficult times. Our hopes will come true in their world and our ideals will be reality.*

Joseph Goebbels, 'Das Jahr 2000', *Das Reich*, 25 February 1945[1]

THE YEAR 2000

It was surely one of the most bizarre and revealing articles Goebbels ever published. On 11 February 1945, the Big Three issued the Yalta Declaration of Liberated Europe and reaffirmed their commitment to bringing democracy back to the continent. They pledged to restore stability in Europe and to help eradicate 'the last vestiges of Nazism and fascism', and they looked forward to the downfall of the Third Reich and its ruling party. 'Nazi Germany,' they predicted confidently, 'is doomed.' A fortnight later, Goebbels fired off a blistering reply – a piece of apocalyptic futurology entitled 'Das Jahr 2000' that appeared in his favourite propaganda vehicle, the mass weekly *Das Reich*.

'What will the world look like in the year 2000?' the Reich's propaganda minister asked. Some of his answers were unremarkable: 'our children's children will have had children, and . . . the events of this war will have sunk into myth'. He predicted accurately that Europe would be united, and – only slightly less accurately – that 'one will fly from Berlin to Paris for breakfast in fifteen minutes'. But he thought it was absurd to imagine that – as Yalta suggested – the British and the Americans could still be occupying Germany and training its people in democracy years into the future. His own prognosis was far more alarming. Yalta was 'an occupation program that will destroy and exterminate the German people'. Churchill and Roosevelt had fallen into Stalin's trap and would quickly find themselves helpless against his plans for world domination.

It was not only the Germans who would suffer. An 'iron curtain' – Goebbels deployed this phrase a year before Churchill popularized it – would fall across Europe, and behind it 'nations would be slaughtered' while the world's 'Jewish press' cheered. Leaderless, the inhabitants of eastern Europe would become 'a stupid fermenting mass of millions of desperately proletarianized working animals' who would – like robots – simply carry out the Kremlin's will. Isolationism would sweep the USA, and it would withdraw its troops from Europe. The British, their population in rapid decline, would find themselves overstretched and undermined from within by Bolshevism. There would be a short 'so-called Third World War' which the USSR would win easily, leaving Europe 'at the feet of the mechanized robots from the steppes'. Within five years, they would be ready to move across the Atlantic and attack the US itself. 'The Western Hemisphere, which despite lying accusations, we have never threatened, would then be in the gravest danger. One day those in the USA will curse the day in which a long-forgotten American president released a communiqué at a conference at Yalta, which will long since have sunk into legend.' He scoffed at the thought of the British and the Americans laying plans for the next fifty years. 'They will be happy if they survive until 1950.'[2]

Goebbels' intention was clear enough: as plenipotentiary for the total war effort his job was to persuade the Germans to fight on and to ignore Yalta's call for them to capitulate. But what was striking was the way he couched this in terms of making them understand that they had 'a European mission'. Never was the connection between Europe and National Socialism made more clearly: only the Reich could now save Europe from Bolshevism, and only faith in National Socialism could save the Germans and give them the strength to fight on. 'Either Greater Germany will be Europe's leader [*Führer*], or Europe will cease to exist,' was how an elderly historian had put it, and this was exactly Goebbels' view.[3]

If – and it is a big if – one ignores the Bosch-like hell-fire, Goebbels got many things right – above all, the world divided by the Cold War, with Europe helpless as America and Russia tussled for world supremacy. He got the Iron Curtain right too – even though he thought it would soon be brushed aside by the Kremlin's hordes – and many Americans in 1945 would have backed his assessment of US isolationism as well. It was clear to him that the British were spent as a world power, and the only mystery – as it had been all along to the Nazis – was why they had so obstinately refused the idea of the partnership with the Third Reich that might have saved their empire. Even his fears of population decline, exaggerated though they were, have acquired a new relevance in a world where many countries – including almost all of Europe – suffer from declining fertility (although it is ironic, in view of his fear of Bolshevism, that one of the fastest cases of population decline is to be found today in Russia).

Yet, although Goebbels stressed the Reich's European mission and had indeed been singing the European tune ever since Stalingrad, it was equally striking that he had nothing at all to say about what Europe would actually look like if the Germans won. This silence was not new. When he had broached the subject two years earlier, he had done little more than rebut accusations that the Reich saw other Europeans as its inferiors. 'Germany's one object,' he had written, was 'to set up a Europe united in the spirit of comradeship and mutual self-respect'. The BBC's German-language service had a good laugh at his expense and told him to try preaching his message of brotherly love to the 'Poles and Czechs who today are being treated worse than cattle', and to the Norwegians, Dutch, Greeks and Yugoslavs: 'You have been breaking their skulls – and now you say you "only want to be their brother".'[4]

The more the Nazis talked about Europe, the less they actually seemed to be saying. But this was not really Goebbels' fault. Hitler was in some ways the most European of the leading statesmen of the Second World War; unlike Roosevelt, Churchill and Stalin, after all, he did have a conception of Europe as a single entity, pitted against the USSR on the one hand, and the USA on the other. But when British Eurosceptics teasingly suggested after 1990 that the European Union was nothing more than a Nazi dream come true they got things badly wrong. At the heart of Hitler's idea of Europe was a gaping hole, and in saying as little as he did on the subject, Goebbels was doing no more than following his Führer. If we want to understand how the Nazis saw Europe, what they planned for it, and what alternatives they pushed their opponents into proposing in their place, then it is really with Hitler's strident yet oddly vacuous formulations of the European problem that we should begin.

THE NAZI CONCEPTION OF EUROPE

In the 1920s, the immediate concerns of the Nazi Party were domestic. But expansion – beyond the borders of 1914 – in order to bring all Germans within the borders of one state was already the key to its programme. This implied doing away with the League of Nations, the Entente powers who stood behind it and the 'small state mess' (*Kleinstaaten-Gerümpel*) in eastern Europe that they had created. And it also meant taking on Russia. Hitler's vision of *Lebensraum* was fuelled both by anti-Bolshevism and by the idea that Germans and Slavs were locked in an economic and geopolitical struggle for control of the Eurasian heartland. Land itself was needed not only to bring all ethnic Germans under the political authority of the Reich, but also to resettle the surplus German population supposedly crowded inside the existing borders.

While his anti-Russian orientation never went away, Hitler started talking much more about Europe as such in the unpublished Second Book he put together in 1928. Stalin's forced industrialization of the USSR was still some years away. Henry Ford and Charlie Chaplin, on the other hand, were making headlines as a wave of American capital threatened to swamp a continent still struggling to recover from the Great War. What made the USA so uniquely powerful in Hitler's eyes was not merely its land and abundant resources but its human stock; a 'true European colony', it had attracted the 'best Nordic forces' as immigrants from across the Atlantic and was taking steps – in the shape of immigration controls – to prevent them being adulterated with inferior racial types from southern and eastern Europe. In short, it demonstrated the geopolitical potency of a state that had overcome both food scarcity and threats to its racial purity.

How should Europe respond? Not, Hitler insisted, by an association of nation-states – any attempt to set up a United States of Europe (as many others were then urging) he swiftly dismissed. A 'formal union of European peoples', he wrote, was bound to fail if pursued through peaceful, democratic means; for no political development could last unless it was brought about through struggle and war. Moreover, without a racial policy to rival America's, Europe would simply produce an enfeebled 'pan-European mish-mash'. He felt nothing but contempt for the pan-European movement the founder of which, Count Richard Nikolaus Eijiro Graf Coudenhove-Kalergi, the Tokyo-born son of an Austrian-Hungarian count and a Japanese mother, welcomed racial diversity and saw the Jews as 'the spiritual nobility of Europe'. For Hitler, Coudenhove-Kalergi was a rootless cosmopolitan and elitist half-breed trying to repeat the mistakes of his Habsburg forebears on a continental scale.

In the 1920s, Hitler still paid lip-service to the idea of a Europe of 'free and independent nation-states whose areas of interest are kept apart and precisely defined'. But as time went on and Germany became stronger, Nazi rhetoric shifted into a more imperialistic and authoritarian mode. And even in that earlier conception of a system of states under German hegemony one detects an anxiety about boundaries and ethnic interaction. Hitler fretted that any power willing to assume the role of continental leader would condemn itself to 'racial decline': he wanted to run Europe but not to be contaminated by it. Thus he was, from the outset, deeply suspicious of Germany's neighbours and unwilling to depend on them or see them as partners in any real sense: the talk of 'free and independent nation-states' was only a sham. Because Nazism was opposed to both American plutocracy and Soviet Bolshevism, it was easy for him to talk European, but in fact his real commitment was to the German people alone.[5]

All of this became very clear in the summer of 1940 once the Reich was transformed unexpectedly into arbiter of the continent as a whole. Most .of the discussion at that time was about economics and thus did not greatly interest Hitler. There was nothing especially National Socialist about German calls to rationalize Europe's economy on the German model in order to pull it out of depression, to divide labour between its agricultural south-east and industrial north-west or to make Berlin the centre of planning, finance and trade. These ideas came mostly out of business circles, and represented an updating of schemes and blueprints that had been around since the First World War. More characteristically Nazi was the tone of brutal 'realism' that surfaced when Goebbels spoke with Czech journalists in September 1940. He started off talking vaguely about reorganizing and unifying Europe 'on principles corresponding to the social, economic and technical possibilities of the twentieth century'. The model would be Germany, which had itself come together and formed a unity out of fragmentation. Technological change was making a nonsense of boundaries, and railways, radio and air travel were bringing people closer together. But then he went on to remind his listeners that force too would be required from time to time to overcome the 'pecularities of individual states, prejudices, limitations and parochial ideas'. Goebbels denied that Germany wanted to 'stifle' other peoples; even so, the latter had best recognize who was now in charge: 'It makes no difference whether you approve this state of things or not. Whether or not you welcome it from your hearts, you cannot do anything to alter the facts.'[6]

The invasion of the Soviet Union reinforced this emphasis on leadership and gave Europe a warrior-like ring: now it was something to be fought for rather than traded over, and hierarchy made more sense. The drive to the East handed influence from the businessmen around Göring to Himmler and the resettlement ideologues, and turned Hitler into the *Heerführer Europas* – the Military Leader of Europe – in the fight to push back the racial boundary between Europe and Asia.[7] 'Collaboration' now seemed like an amusing delusion of the French rather than a goal for the Germans to take seriously. To his ambassador to France, Otto Abetz, in September 1941, Hitler talked about the future in terms which suggested how little had changed in his mind since the mid-1920s:

The Asiatics and Bolsheviks had to be driven out of Europe; the episode of 250 years of 'Asiatics' [*Asiatentum*] had come to an end ... Once the Asiatics had been driven out, Europe would no longer be dependent on any outside power; America, too, could 'get lost' as far as we were concerned. Europe would itself provide all the raw materials it needed and have its own markets in the Russian area, so that we would no longer have any need of other world trade. The new Russia, as far as the Urals, would become 'our India', but one more favourably situated than that of the British. The new Greater German Reich would comprise 135 million people and rule over an additional 150 million.[8]

Hitler was confident that unified under German leadership, the continent would eventually be able to take on the United States and prevail. The one element that had changed in his thinking since the 1920s was that his opinion of the Americans and the threat they posed had fallen. But the precondition was victory against Stalin and control of the riches of European Russia, and the fighting itself was desirable because it created a sense of Europeanness. He told Ciano, the Italian foreign minister, that:

Noteworthy in the fighting in the East was the fact that for the first time a feeling of European solidarity had developed. This was of great importance for the future. A later generation would have to cope with the problem of Europe-America. It would no longer be a matter of Germany, or England, of Fascism, of National Socialism, or antagonistic systems, but of the common interests of Pan-Europe within the European economic area with her African supplements. The feeling of European solidarity, which at the moment was distinctly tangible ... would gradually have to change generally into a great recognition of the European community ... The future did not belong to the ridiculously half-civilized America, but to the newly arisen Europe that would definitely also prevail with her people, her economy and her intellectual and cultural values, on condition that the East was placed in the service of the European idea and did not work against Europe.[9]

Perhaps it is his confidence that German leadership could help Europe see off the transatlantic challenge that explains why Hitler cared so little for what other Europeans themselves might want. For what is striking about the Nazis' plans for postwar Europe – it is the major difference with both Anglo-American and Soviet thinking on the same subject – is how exclusively they were oriented towards *German* needs alone. Dozens of German towns – Hamburg, Linz, Munich, Klagenfurt – were to be beautified or rebuilt, along with the new 'garrison towns' in the colonized East that would become German centres of government or industry. These were the schemes that set Hitler's imagination on fire. Afterwards Albert Speer reflected ruefully that the war was a time of endless unfulfilled plans and noted that those for the East in particular 'would have kept us occupied for the rest of our lives'. Housing estates, cinemas, motorways, giant railways, memorials, parks and sport-centres were all designed in enormous detail. In places such as Cracow, Zamość and Auschwitz, camp commandants would have relaxed after work in the gardens of their new villas, while their wives and servants went shopping in the arcaded streets of neo-medieval town centres. It was ensuring this kind of life for their hard-fighting soldiers in the postwar German *Lebensraum* that preoccupied Hitler and Himmler.[10]

As for worrying about the rest, that was left to businessmen, backroom offices in the Economics Ministry or Foreign Ministry dissidents. The SS would wipe out the Jews and later sort out the Slavs as well. In the West, Hitler was fundamentally uninterested. He was happy so long as Belgian and Danish industrial magnates and civil servants made sure their factories supplied the Reich, and many of them obliged efficiently and even enthusiastically. But the need to safeguard Fortress Europe's western flank meant Berlin could never allow the French, Belgians or Norwegians to go their own way politically or become in any sense the Reich's partners, however ideologically aligned. Hitler himself was only really concerned about the possible contribution the Dutch and other 'Germanic' peoples might make to the colonial settlement of the East. For it was already starting to dawn on some on the fringes of the Nazi leadership that they might have actually conquered too *much* land, and that the mythically overcrowded Reich might turn out to be short of people after all.

This ruthless pursuit of a demographic chimera, with its unashamedly exploitative nationalism and its indifference to everyone else, made a mockery of Germany's claims to be leading Europe. The Germans, Mussolini fumed, were 'bad psychologists and worse politicians'. 'The remarkable thing is this,' commented an experienced Panzer general in a lecture to fellow POWs shortly after the war had ended, 'how is it that a country like Germany, which is situated in the middle of the continent, has not developed politics to an *art*, in order to maintain . . . a sensible peace.' This was not just hindsight. In a conversation secretly tapped by British intelligence in a POW camp in 1943, another officer had insisted to his comrades that: 'We have shown that if it's possible for anyone to have leadership in Europe, it must in no circumstances be us.'[11] Not even in western Europe would Hitler acknowledge that non-Germans had legitimate political aspirations of their own. Concessions, in Hitler's understanding of politics, could indicate only weakness: other countries could only be rivals or competitors. He told his comrades they should be glad Japan was not a European power; as it was, they only had to deal with the Italians, who were scarcely 'serious competitors for the future organization of Europe'. It was, to put it mildly, a bizarre conception of European unity.

NATIONALISM: THE CURSE

The Nazi diagnosis of Europe's problem, however, was much more persuasive than their cure. In their view, the Versailles settlement, by setting up numerous small nation-states, had badly botched the problem of creating a new order and had sown the seeds of its own destruction. 'Until the beginning of the war,' Goebbels advised his propaganda team in December 1940, 'Britain had the absolute power to reorganize Europe. The question should be asked what Britain did to reorganize Europe along sensible lines after her victorious war of 1914–1918. Nothing was done then. Europe was atomized at Versailles according to the laws of political reason.'[12]

Germany's opponents in Washington and London were reaching a surprisingly similar conclusion. On both sides of the Atlantic, endemic nationalism – especially in its east European variant – was widely seen as a dangerous and inherently belligerent phenomenon of modern mass psychology, and the question arose whether the peace of the continent – and of the world – could be secured without in some way curbing its capacity for violence. Even many anti-Nazi commentators regarded Germany's triumph as opening the path to something better. If sovereignty could be so easily infringed, if it offered so little protection in the real world, was there much point in making a fetish of it rather than trying to work out forms of political organization that would do a better job of guaranteeing peace and security?

The British – who did not repudiate the Czech–German borders fixed at Munich until surprisingly late in the war – were worried about restoring the Versailles settlement in eastern Europe, though for a quite different reason from the Germans. Their anxiety was that it had failed to produce an adequate counterweight to Germany itself. The Czech president, Beneš, suggested keeping the states of eastern Europe as they were but expelling their German minorities while breaking Germany itself up into a 'decentralized federation' that effectively turned the clock back to the old nineteenth-century confederation of the Rhine. But even Beneš accepted that many of the small new states had failed to get along, and so, together with the dismemberment of Germany, he advocated creating a series of 'larger federal blocs' across much of Europe.[13]

In fact, federalist solutions seemed for a time to many of Hitler's opponents to be the best way to make states get along and to defuse arguments over boundaries. There was the Federal Union movement, which proposed a United States of Europe on precisely the grounds that Hitler rejected it – that it was the only means to secure a democratic, liberal order across the continent. The American journalist Clarence Streit, in his 1939 best-seller *Union Now*, argued for a democratic-federal union between the USA and the UK as the first step towards a federal world government. And an elderly fan of Streit's, Lionel Curtis, the veteran architect of both the British Commonwealth and the League of Nations, pushed for a global 'Commonwealth of God' – since globalization had, he argued, undermined arguments for national sovereignty. Inside occupied Europe, some resistance groups were thinking along similar lines, and small groups of intellectuals in Italy, France and the Netherlands drew up blueprints for overcoming the problems of nationalism and creating a new European community that would be treasured decades later by historians seeking to identify postwar Europe's anti-Nazi roots.[14]

Such schemes were highly fashionable for a year or two, and were even taken up by British and American policy-makers. The US State Department's Advisory Committee recommended in 1940 that 'there must be in Europe such derogation to the sovereignty of states that quick and decisive action' by a future supranational authority would be facilitated. Sumner Welles, the under-secretary of state, returned from a tour of Europe that spring suggesting far-reaching alterations to the Versailles order. Apart from the major states (France, Britain, Germany, Italy and an expanded Poland), he proposed four federations of small states – Iberian, Scandinavian, Danubian and Balkan. Even George Kennan, certainly no starry-eyed enthusiast for federalist solutions, wrote in June 1944 that 'some degree of federation for Central and West Europe . . . seems to offer the only way out of the labyrinth of conflict which is Europe today'.[15]

Many exiled European governments were keen to secure American and British support not merely for the war, but into the postwar era as well, and they took up the language of 'solidarity' themselves, with varying degrees of conviction. In November 1940, the Czechs and Poles pledged as 'independent and sovereign states' to enter 'into a closer political and economic association'. The Polish prime minister in exile, General Sikorski, issued a declaration in favour of all-European federation while the Czechs wanted to include all of eastern Europe and to reach agreement with the USSR as well. The Greeks and Yugoslavs signed treaties designed to lead to the same end; the Low Countries signed the Benelux agreement, which provided the earliest fully functioning regional integration scheme on the continent. Yet with the exception of this last, the agreements themselves were still-born and paid nothing more than lip-service to federationist fashion; they envisaged only very loose confederations and basically offered warmed-up versions of prewar arrangements that had already failed.[16]

It is not hard to see how the debate could lead some people towards the idea of a continental European confederation. In his 1942 discussion of Europe's future, the Austrian émigré Egon Ranshofen-Wertheimer, a former League of Nations official, suggested that the destructiveness of Hitler's New Order had actually been helpful in making Europeans see themselves differently. Since Hitler had destroyed 'the myth of sovereignty', it should not be resurrected. He had accustomed Europeans to think beyond their national borders, and they should go on doing so. 'Perhaps Hitler has been riding on the wave of the future, after all. Only not quite in the manner he originally intended.' From this it was a short step to arguing – as the author went on to do – for the emergence of a European confederation with compulsory membership and a monopoly of pooled military power that could benefit from the wartime experience of the United Nations. Yet as the author went into further details, he revealed the drawbacks and dilemmas involved in this kind of armchair theorizing. In the first place, he admitted that democracy could not be made a requirement for membership. He also imagined that the Soviet Union could be kept outside the proposed Union while looking benignly on its emergence. And no less implausibly, he too joined the bandwagon of those calling for the amalgamation of small countries in regional federations – Scandinavia, the Low Countries and the all-important 'great Central European Federation', which would act as a counter-weight to Germany.[17]

Such schemes had one major failing: they ignored the considerable opposition that faced them in the very region they wished to remake. In fact, life under Nazi occupation had made most Europeans appreciate the benefits of national independence more rather than less. In Belgium, for instance, where the German-run Radio Bruxelles had signed off each night with a tune beginning 'For the New Europe . . .', schemes for European federation were regarded as Nazi propaganda. Some critics abroad also thought the new federalism was nothing more than disguised geo-politics – little better than what the Germans themselves were doing. How could one simply ignore differences in national cultures and traditions? Was not this obsession with 'viable spaces' and grand strategy a sign of the kind of insensitivity to the sheer untidiness of human life that was responsible for the New Order itself? The émigré sociologist Sigmund Neumann was scathing. 'One cannot simply dismember Switzerland, Belgium, Portugal and Hungary simply in order to set up nine large European blocs (and incidentally create a Greater Germany, a Greater Italy and a Greater Spain!),' he wrote in a 1943 article in *Foreign Affairs*. 'To do that may satisfy a technician's view of a well-balanced Europe, but it shows an utter disregard of Europe as a living body.'[18]

Many European politicians – including de Gaulle, the Dutch and the Norwegians – were equally unenthusiastic. Even those who were supposedly pioneering the confederationist idea often disagreed on what they wanted: the (anti-Soviet) Poles, for instance, wanted something very different from their (pro-Soviet) Czech partners. But it was in Moscow that the most consequential opposition emerged. This became clear in 1943 when the British Foreign Office dusted off old plans from the First World War and proposed 'the question of a confederation of the smaller European states with special reference to the Danubian area'. Churchill had taken the idea up with Stalin, suggesting carving off chunks of Germany – Bavaria, Baden, Württemberg and the Palatinate – to increase the new confederation's impact. Stalin turned out to be completely opposed. He had no wish to acquiesce in the formation of a potentially powerful new east European state. He was perfectly well aware of the anti-Soviet tenor of much federalist thinking, from Count Coudenhove-Kalergi in the 1920s onwards: back in 1930 he had described moves towards European federation as 'a bourgeois movement for intervention against the Soviet Union'.[19] Most crucially, he doubted whether these confederations would really guarantee the USSR against a German revival. Would it not be better for the Soviet Union to retain direct control over eastern Europe and to seek agreement with Britain and the

USA to that end? In other words, his preferred alternative to some kind of central European federation was a Great Power agreement over spheres of influence to succeed his now obviously defunct agreement with the Germans. Stalin's allies did not resist. The British, in particular, were not completely sure the Americans would stay in Europe after the war, and they were therefore inclined to allow the Russians to have their say. Whitehall's bottom line was summarized by Sir William Strang at the Foreign Office: 'It is better for us that Russia should dominate eastern Europe than that Germany should dominate western Europe.'[20]

In fact, it was not only Soviet opposition that was responsible for the collapse of the federalist balloon. A restorationist drive had been implicit in British and American policy ever since the 1941 Atlantic Charter had pledged them to 'see sovereign rights and self government restored to those who have been forcibly deprived of them'. The 1945 Yalta Declaration continued in the same vein: it announced the formation of a new world organization to be based on the wartime coalition of the United Nations, pledged 'the restoration of sovereign rights and self-government to those peoples who have been forcibly deprived of them by the aggressor nations', and announced the dismemberment of Germany itself under the control of the Big Three. This was tantamount to the complete reversal of the Nazi programme: Greater Germany – the imperial nation – was to be broken up into different zones of occupation, and the captive nation-states of Europe were to be restored to political life.[21]

Stalin drove the final nail into the coffin of European federalism around the time of the Yalta conference. The Yugoslav communist leader Tito was Europe's last committed federalist. Leading the single home-grown communist mass movement to have survived the Nazi occupation and emerged victorious, Tito planned to replicate the Soviet experience and to transform Yugoslavia into the core of a much larger Balkan federation that would bring socialism to the entire region. Already dominating Albania, and with an eye on northern Greece, he tried to get the Bulgarians to sign a treaty of federation between the two states. But the Bulgarians did not like the idea at all. They saw this as a Yugoslav bid to reduce them to subordination, and Stalin was inclined to agree. Angered by Tito's unwillingness to heed his advice, he told the Yugoslavs in no uncertain terms to abandon the scheme, which very reluctantly they did.[22]

Dreams of federalism certainly did not die and they remained powerful enough in the late 1940s to help bring new kinds of European organizations into being. Yet Europeans came out of the war too attached to their nation-states to allow federalist ideas to get very far. The Americans had been the prime movers in schemes to supersede the nation-state in Europe, and the British had gone along with them, but continental Europe itself was lukewarm. Reversing the course of German history by turning the centralized Reich back into a confederation was one thing; but amalgamating existing nation-states into larger entities had little support locally either west or east. And the United States was nowhere near strong, knowledgeable or committed to Europe enough to force its ideas on the Europeans in the teeth of Soviet opposition. Thus the wartime glimpse of a federalist alternative to the Nazi New Order proved short-lived.

STALIN'S ALTERNATIVE

In May 1945, Churchill ordered British military planners to think the unthinkable and to work out how – should it prove necessary – to 'impose upon Russia the will of the United States and the British Empire'. He was particularly anxious about Poland, and those working on Operation Unthinkable were told to make the beginning of July their hypothetical starting-date. The planners took only a few days to reach the obvious deeply pessimistic conclusions: an Allied campaign against the Red Army could not lead to a lasting result without 'total war', and a much deeper and more successful invasion of the USSR itself than the Germans had managed. The tattered German forces would not be much use, and, if the Americans lost interest, the whole enterprise would become completely hopeless. In fact, the conclusion drawn by the chief of the Imperial General Staff, Sir Alan Brooke – and by Churchill himself – was that it was hopeless anyway. In Brooke's words: 'There is no doubt that from now onwards Russia is all powerful in Europe.'[23]

Yet Soviet intentions were hard to fathom (so hard in fact that Churchill immediately commissioned another staff investigation of the consequences for Britain of a complete Soviet takeover of the Continent). That eastern Europe would come under Moscow's influence was obvious. Goebbels himself, as we have seen, fantasized about a Bolshevik steamroller crushing the region. But others thought it might run out of steam rather quickly and highlighted the more traditional and circumscribed nature of *Russian* security concerns rather than the threat of universal revolution. In May 1945, for example, the young American diplomat George Kennan predicted that the Russians would be unable to absorb even eastern Europe into the Soviet system: 'It should not be forgotten that the absorption of areas in the west beyond the Great Russian, White Russian and Ukrainian ethnological boundaries (Poland, Finland and the Baltic states) is something at which Russia has already tried and failed.'[24]

There was much to be said for Kennan's prognosis, for the USSR faced an immense challenge in taking over the diverse states of postwar eastern Europe. Not only was the Soviet Union itself more devastated than any other country in Europe by the German occupation. In eastern Europe, communism had failed between the world wars and in almost every case, the right had swept the board; Communist Party organizations, where they had managed to survive the Stalinist terror, were tiny. This was no obstacle in the minds of the orthodox Leninists running them, but Stalin knew it was a major problem: creating a political machine powerful and reliable enough to hold power would take time and could not be achieved overnight. The Germans might have proved unable to exploit the wave of anti-communism that swept over the parts of eastern Europe occupied by the Red Army in 1939, but Stalin did not fail to notice it. By 1945, despite the prestige the Red Army had won and the widespread hatred of the Germans, the region as a whole remained staunchly anti-Bolshevik, above all in the areas of key concern to Soviet security – Poland and Romania.

There was the economic aspect of the region's prospects to take into account as well. In eastern Europe, interwar capitalism had scarcely been a great success: fast population growth and the sluggish performance of the region's peasant economies, hit by cheap transatlantic grain imports, had produced stagnant national income and unemployment. The Czech, Hungarian, Romanian and Bulgarian economies had boomed during the war, yet there was no guarantee of this continuing into the peace. And yet from the Russians' viewpoint, an unstable eastern Europe could not be allowed to become the jumping-off point for another invasion from the West. Imposing some form of control was therefore necessary.

Neither of the two obvious alternatives appealed to the Kremlin.

Hitler's New Order had eviscerated the Versailles settlement and subjected areas destined for Germanization to harsh rule and denationalization. The federalist alternative espoused by the Americans and the British proposed substituting a few large regional confederations for Versailles' unstable jumble of states; the logic of spheres of influence would be replaced by that of the balance of power. In effect, they turned the clock back to the nineteenth century, to a kind of Habsburg polity reworked for a democratic age. Stalin liked neither the Nazis' repudiation of Versailles nor the American. He ruled out federalism, but also any Soviet equivalent of the kind of permanent land grab that had been envisaged in General Plan East. In fact, as he made clear from an early date, he had no desire to extend the USSR territorially beyond the lands it claimed on historic grounds from Tsarist times. For the rest of eastern Europe, he saw an agreement over spheres of influence as the best way to get the British and the Americans to acknowledge peacetime Soviet hegemony, and instead of federalist schemes he preferred to deal on a bilateral basis with individual states, since this made it easier to enforce Soviet wishes. In this way, Stalin paradoxically emerged as the protector of the Versailles order, and Czechoslovakia, Poland and Yugoslavia were restored. Insofar as the new postwar Europe was one dominated by the USSR, it was therefore going to look – at least on the map – very much like the old one had done, its borders modified only to take account of the enormous increase in Soviet power between 1919 and 1945.

THE MEANING OF EUROPE

A week after Hitler's death, Admiral Dönitz did something the Führer had never done: he personally convened a meeting of as many of the senior German officials running the empire's last remaining territories as he could. The Reich Protector of Bohemia and Moravia, Karl Hermann Frank, flew in from Prague; Werner Best came from Copenhagen, Terboven from Norway and Seyss-Inquart from the Netherlands. As they sat there in the Flensburg schoolroom discussing the problems of whether to surrender or fight on in Hungary, Moravia, northern Italy and Scandinavia, their meeting reflected the European scale of Nazi rule even in its final days. Thanks to them and their now-dead master, Europe had indeed become – in the propaganda phrase – a 'community of fate' (*Schicksalsgemeinschaft*).

Precisely because Nazi conquest linked together the peoples of Europe more tightly than they had ever been connected before, those fighting the Germans also found it necessary to plan in European terms. As early as 1942, American policy-makers had recommended taking advantage of the partial unification that the Nazis had created and going beyond it. After all, defeating Hitler was also a kind of invitation to think ahead. 'The Nazis are challenging the Allies to improve on Hitler's New Order,' commented the *Observer* in March 1945, 'the Allies have to show that free men can do far better.' As the war wound down, their troops were dealing with displaced persons everywhere from Nantes to Minsk, and their officials were estimating the continent's food, health, housing and energy needs, as well as starting to plan for its longer-term economic development. SHAEF's 'Solid Fuels Division' turned into the European Coal Organization while the European Central Inland Transportation Organization and the Emergency Economic Committee for Europe also tried to tackle the continent's needs by building on wartime operational planning experience. The Allies established the European Advisory Commission in 1943 to think through political strategy; later, the UN approved the creation of an Economic Commission for Europe to coordinate recovery.[25]

Cold War suspicions stopped these first genuinely pan-European organizations living up to their original practical mandates, and some of them were never intended to outlast the war and were quickly wound up. The European Advisory Commission was soon confined to working out the details of the occupation of Germany and Austria, while the UN's Economic Commission for Europe – which still exists today – ended up reporting on reconstruction rather than guiding it. The USSR in fact regarded any effort to organize Europe permanently on a regional basis as a threat against it. Radio Moscow denounced Léon Blum in September 1945 for proposing a scheme for European unity since this could only be 'a union directed against the USSR'. By the time the Kremlin barred its satellites from participating in Washington's European Recovery Program (better known as the Marshall Plan) in 1947, this hostility was already well established.

Yet if Stalin was against Europe, Churchill and others were for it. They wanted in particular to prevent Germany's defeat creating a power vacuum that would have facilitated the spread of Bolshevism. And so, as Goebbels' Iron Curtain descended, 'European' organizations of a slightly different kind started to emerge. In 1946, Churchill called for a United States of Europe, and although he claimed to hope that the USSR would support the idea, he can scarcely have expected it to, not least because, six months earlier, he had made his famous Iron Curtain speech in Missouri. He believed it was important that Europeans come together to form a confederation that could speak for the continent and act as a partner to the British Commonwealth. The following year he founded a Provisional United Europe Committee in London – a European Federalist Union had already been established in Paris – and thanks to the pressure of such lobby groups the Council of Europe was established in 1949. Its main achievement – the European Convention on Human Rights and the associated European Court – articulated an idea of Europe as a law-bound and rights-governed community that was defined both against the still vivid memory of Nazi occupation *and* against the threat posed by Soviet totalitarianism.[26]

This Cold War Europeanism inspired both federalists and nationalists, but it was the latter who prevailed. National governments in western Europe were convinced Europeans in the sense of supporting the new regional bodies but they kept as much control of the process of cross-national integration and cooperation as they could. They rejected efforts to found a European Political Community, and the French assembly voted against a European army; instead what emerged was NATO, an organization which pooled the resources of nationally controlled armies. Washington had hoped that its European Recovery Program would force West Europeans to coordinate their economic planning through the new Organization for European Economic Cooperation (OEEC). Instead, Robert Marjolin, the French civil servant who had wanted to turn the OEEC into a dynamo for integration, ended quitting early in frustration. Today, the OEEC's successor is best known for its economic surveys. European integration took an entirely different course.[27]

Politically, postwar Europe was thus emerging through nation-states rather than over their heads. The most effective forms of integration exploited converging national interests and operated via relatively dull economic institutions rather than through headline-grabbing attempts to reshape political or military ones. Continuities with wartime concerns and policies too were much stronger in these areas than they were in the political and legal realm, where the break with Nazism was more emphatic. After Robert Schuman, the French foreign minister, proposed in 1950 that France and West Germany pool their coal and steel resources, the European Coal and Steel Community under the presidency of his adviser Jean Monnet kept both sides happy (its members also included Italy, Belgium, Luxembourg and the Netherlands) and eased industrialists' and mine-owners' ability to trade across Germany's borders. Many of those involved had taken part in similar negotiations a decade earlier when the German Economics Ministry had talked about organizing European cartels and output planning. And one could trace a similar line in the case of food – from wartime concerns about self-sufficiency in occupied Europe to the highly interventionist Common Agricultural Policy.

Thus the Nazi New Order had played its part in bringing about the new postwar Europeanism. The architects of the Common Market had impeccable Gaullist, anti-fascist and anti-Nazi records. Nevertheless, some of the key figures and advisers behind the scenes were not anti-fascists but wartime insiders – French, Belgian and above all German – who had served the Nazis but grown deeply disillusioned with them. Typical of them was a man like Hans-Peter Ipsen, the young jurist who served with the military occupation authority in wartime Brussels and then became West Germany's foremost expert on European Community law. The continuities were even more striking in the case of the small wartime German team in the Reich Ministry of Economics that had, despite Hitler's veto on such activities, been discussing plans for a postwar European economic community dedicated to full employment and self-sufficiency. Meeting in the Esplanade Hotel in Berlin, the members of this 'European Circle' (*Europakreis*) had included not only leading Nazi economists and businessmen but also men who would play a very prominent role in postwar West German affairs – Ludwig Erhard, the father of the economic 'miracle', the banker Hermann Abs, and the future Bundesbank president Karl Blessing.[28]

No longer believing that the Reich could win the war, these men argued in the early 1940s that any postwar European economic recovery would nevertheless still require German leadership. They followed the Anglo-American debate about postwar aims, discussed Dumbarton Oaks and Bretton Woods, read the *Economist* and applauded Britain's new commitment to full employment, but they pointed out that the

Third Reich had been pursuing such policies for some time with great success: it was thus Germany, not Britain, that had the experience best suited to ensure a postwar model of high living standards and social security. If Europe was to find a third way between Soviet-style central planning and British laissez-faire, it would surely need German guidance. Germany, in other words, would lose the war but could still win the peace.[29]

The fact that some policy-makers in the Third Reich talked in such terms no doubt confirms the worst fears of Euro-sceptics and makes the Common Market look as though it was something dreamed up by the Nazis. And indeed these men did identify many of the concerns that also worried postwar Europeanists – the threat of cheap competition from abroad, the need to prevent any repeat of the prewar slump by moving away from laissez-faire while reducing barriers to trade within the European 'community', as well as the importance of guaranteeing a continental food supply by protecting farm producers. A glance at the treaty establishing the European Economic Community in March 1957 confirms the striking similarity between its goals and theirs. But as Keynes had already remarked in 1940, the question where economics was concerned was not whether the Nazis had the right ideas, but whether they could be trusted to carry them out. With Hitler and the Nazi Party in charge the answer was obvious. It took Germany's defeat and American hegemony to create the conditions within which a real community of nation-states could emerge, and when it did, Berlin was no longer at its centre and Europe was not alone. Most of these businessmen, bankers and economists understood that America's power was irresistible; just as the Americans would need Germany to get postwar recovery going in Europe, so the Germans needed the Americans too.

To get things in perspective it may be useful to remember how things looked to the marginal cadres of Nazis who refused to compromise. After the war, small, generally short-lived fringe groups denounced both the Americans and the Soviets and recycled ideas drawn from Hitler's writings of thirty years earlier. They reacted violently, too, against the Europeanist stirrings that were becoming visible in postwar western Europe. Karl-Heinz Priester, a former SS officer who had become active on the extreme right, appeared at the first meeting of European neo-fascists in Rome in 1950 and warned that the more some yes-men hasten to turn not only our motherland, Germany, but also our fatherland, Europe, into a colony . . . through such devices as the Council of Europe and 'European Union' . . . the more quickly will grow the determination of all honest and independent Germans to accompany us on our way from nationalism to Nation Europa.[30]

Even Nazis like Priester could see that, in the age of the Superpowers, Germany was not powerful enough to regain its independence without regional support. 'Nation Europa' was thus the extremists' alternative to Brussels and Strasbourg, a kind of peacetime version of Himmler's 'European' Waffen-SS. Yet such men regarded parliamentary democracy as a sham 'democratatorship' (*Demokratur*), believed the multi-party system had to be abolished and wanted somehow to reunify the country with the assistance of like-minded fascists abroad. Ignored by the voters, they were constantly quarrelling among themselves, accusing one another of selling out or compromising on the question of race. Some founded a New European Order movement the following year to wage war on 'mongoloid Bolshevism' and 'negroid capitalism' in the name of the white man. Others thought about appealing to African nationalists and forging a new Eurafrica that would allow Europe to regain its position at the centre of world affairs.[31]

They were much too stupid, backward-looking and loud to gain more than a precarious foothold in the Europe of the Free World. Others were ideologically more flexible and made the transition much more smoothly. The American war against the USSR might, unlike the Nazis' previous version, have been increasingly global in its ambition, but that certainly did not mean that German expertise was suddenly irrelevant. Reinhard Gehlen, the Wehrmacht's spy-master in the East, established an intelligence-gathering network in eastern Europe with American backing and drew on this when he founded the West German Federal Intelligence Service. Otto Bräutigam, Alfred Rosenberg's outspoken critic of SS policy in European Russia, became West Germany's chief Soviet expert, and a host of so-called 'East-researchers' clawed their way back into prestigious academic careers. Few were as prominent as Theodor Oberländer, former *Freikorps* fighter and 'political adviser' to various unsavoury anti-partisan units in the occupied eastern territories, who served in Bonn as minister for refugees and expellees for much of the 1950s and gave posts to numerous other ex-Nazis, including the former wartime mayor of Łódź and a former SA newspaper editor. Chancellor Adenauer's government was constantly being embarrassed by nasty revelations of this kind. Nearly sixty of Ribbentrop's former officials were employed in the West German Foreign Ministry when the Allies finally allowed it to open in 1951 and most diplomats and many judges and prosecutors were former Nazi Party members.[32]

It was a similar story across much of Free World Europe. René Bousquet shrugged off a minor punishment at the end of the war, and his deputy, Jean Leguay, prospered in pharmaceuticals. Maurice Papon, the wartime civil servant from Bordeaux, became chief of police in Paris and eventually a minister. L'Oréal and Louis Vuitton were among the many large firms that kept quiet about their wartime past. In Italy, while the new political elite emerged out of anti-fascist Catholic and left-wing circles, the judiciary, intelligence services and police were mostly staffed with former fascists. In Greece, too, the civil war in the late 1940s allowed many wartime collaborators to return to positions of power. Eventually even Franco's Spain was admitted to the United Nations.

Because the right had been so powerful in many countries in Europe, the transition back towards a more democratic world could probably not have happened without such compromises. They certainly did not signify that the fascist or Nazis regimes themselves had managed to survive their emphatic defeat. Once the dictators were gone, things could never be the same. Albert Speer tells how at the end of July 1943, shortly after Mussolini's government collapsed, Hitler was sitting in the teahouse at his East Prussian headquarters with a group of his political advisers and senior generals when suddenly General Alfred Jodl interjected: 'Come to think of it, Fascism simply burst like a soap bubble.' The appalled silence that followed showed how the thought weighed on those present. Mussolini himself had been reminded by a nervous Italian fascist at exactly this time that 'the state is fascist only because You want it to be such, because You have issued decrees which transformed it into a fascist state and above all because YOU are at its centre.' This was true of Nazism too, of course, although in 1945, and for some years afterwards, there were a few Nazis who did not believe it, and who thought that they could continue to fight for National Socialism – perhaps even improve it – without the Führer. Eventually most of them too realized that the New Order had collapsed beyond repair with

Germany's defeat. But no political order begins from nothing. And postwar Europe – so keen to proclaim its break with the past – was bound to it in more ways than it liked to admit.[33]

18

The New Order in World History

'The century of German predominance in Europe had reached its term. So, too, had the supremacy of Europe in the world.'   Lewis Namier[1]

THE NOMOS OF THE EARTH

Over the period of time which stretched roughly from 1750 to 1950, the repercussions of Europe's own internal rivalries were felt around the world. As the nineteenth century began, Napoleon's bid to forge a European empire loosened Spain's grip over South America; as it ended, a frenzied colonial carve-up in Africa, Asia and the Pacific was producing flashpoints and stand-offs everywhere from Venezuela to Fashoda. The new imperialism, closely linked to the struggle for mastery in Europe, had created an interconnected system of states competing for land, resources and prestige. The 'civilized world', wrote an American author in 1900, was engaged in an 'economic conquest . . . of the natural resources of the globe'.[2]

Idealists like the US president, Woodrow Wilson, were determined that things must change. At Paris in 1919, the victors in the First World War proclaimed that this unseemly competition had ended with the establishment of the League of Nations and they heralded this as the start of a new legal order for the world. But the defeated powers disagreed: for them the competition for colonies was not over and they saw the League as nothing more than a device invented by the winners to bank their gains. That the British and French had in fact gained could not be denied – the British empire was never as large as between the wars, swollen by its League mandates. It took an American geologist to point out the awkward truth that by the 1930s England and the United States between them controlled nearly three-quarters of the world's mineral output; in his words, 'the defence of democracy and the defence of the mineral position more or less coincide'.[3]

In April 1939, with the League's reputation in tatters, the German jurist Carl Schmitt outlined a completely different model for managing the international system. Prague had fallen a fortnight earlier, and the Third Reich's star was in the ascendant. In a hard-hitting talk, Schmitt argued that the League had been a bad idea from the start, and had actually made the world more unstable by erecting a supposedly universal system of law on the shaky foundations of the post-1918 settlement. Nazi Germany's rise provided the opportunity to reconstruct international relations on a sounder footing. What he proposed was to follow the example of the United States of America by replacing Geneva with a system of regional power blocs. The USA, after all, might proclaim its commitment to general principles of world government but in fact it saw no incompatibility between this and the Monroe Doctrine – a regionally bounded arrangement between a greater and lesser powers that excluded non-American states from its affairs. Here – in a system of law grounded in control of territory – Schmitt saw a new model for Germany and everyone else. Universalism was a fiction, he insisted, a hypocrisy to be abandoned in favour of the recognition that some states were stronger than others. Order could best be secured by splitting up the globe into regions, each governed by a single hegemon with the duty of enforcing stability on the basis of its ruling 'political idea' and precluding outside intervention in its domain. That task, in Europe, now fell to Germany.[4]

Schmitt's speech was widely reported in the press, and the basic idea of a German Monroe Doctrine was soon being discussed. In the wake of the German takeover in Czechoslovakia only days earlier, British newspapers gave it prominence: 'Hitherto no German statesman has given a precise definition of his aims in eastern Europe,' wrote The Times, 'but perhaps a recent statement by Professor Carl Schmitt, a Nazi expert on constitutional law, may be taken as a trustworthy guide.' The Daily Mail identified Schmitt as 'Herr Hitler's "key" man in this policy'. Schmitt certainly was not that; he was politically, at this point, a relatively marginal figure in the Nazi firmament with many powerful enemies. Nevertheless, he articulated more clearly than anyone else in the Third Reich the way the regime saw its place in the world at this time. Indeed Hitler himself started using what sounded very much like Schmittian language. At the end of April, he responded to a speech of Roosevelt by mentioning the Monroe Doctrine and saying that 'we Germans support a similar doctrine for Europe – and above all, for the territory and the interests of the Greater German Reich'. He came back to the idea after the conquest of Poland. In March 1940, Ribbentrop told Sumner Welles, the US deputy secretary of state – visiting Europe to assess the chances of peace – that 'Germany too has its Monroe Doctrine'. The dizzying German successes of the months that followed saw such talk – initially meant to refer only to central and eastern Europe – extended to form a kind of claim on the continent as a whole. 'America for the Americans, Europe for the Europeans', was Hitler's pithy formulation for an American journalist, adding that he felt the need for a 'fundamental, mutually compatible Monroe Doctrine' between the Old and New Worlds.[5]

Yet, as Hitler quickly found, turning Germany into the arbiter of the continent, and trying to rule Europe as though it could be detached from the rest of the world, raised more questions than it answered. One pressing problem for Berlin was to explain exactly what future this implied to their main European ally, Italy. The Italians were understandably upset, fearing that a Monroe Doctrine for Europe would leave them playing Mexico to the Third Reich's USA. Allaying those fears (which were fully justified) was not really possible, especially since the boundaries between the German and Italian 'living spaces' were always blurred, and Italy's military weakness meant the Germans were being pulled into areas that the Italians regarded as in their own sphere of influence.

A bigger question-mark concerned Europe's colonies, with their invaluable raw materials and minerals. Hitler was acutely aware of the importance of these and had built up stockpiles of key commodities before the war. He also invaded Norway to secure his access to Swedish iron ore, expanded nickel production at Petsamo in Finland, grabbed the Bor copper mines in Yugoslavia and the manganese deposits in the Ukraine. But outside Europe it was a different story. When Chad and Cameroon backed de Gaulle in 1940, giving the Allies access to gold, oil, tungsten and titanium, the Germans were helpless. As for the riches of Belgian Congo, the Reich scarcely stood a chance. It managed to seize the refined uranium stored in Belgium itself but the Union Minière de Katanga had already moved most of its mineral stockpiles beyond Germany's reach before the invasion. Once the Belgian governor-general in the Congo declared for the Allies and American engineers arrived to reopen the Shinkolobwe mines, there was nothing Hitler could do. Overall, Africa is estimated to have supplied half the world's gold during the war, nearly 90 per cent of the cobalt and virtually all its diamonds and uranium, but the Third Reich got next to none of it.[6]

Events in the western hemisphere offered a further reminder of the Reich's lack of transcontinental reach. In 1940 Hitler could only fume when the Havana Conference invoked the Monroe Doctrine to claim a mandate over all those European colonies in the Americas whose metropoles had been conquered by the Germans. In fact, the USA tolerated Vichy's rule in the Caribbean (including the establishment of nasty authoritarian regimes in places like Martinique), but it kept a close eye on Surinam's vital bauxite mines and the oil refineries in the Dutch Antilles as its own rapid rearmament got underway. Even Nazi espionage operations in the Americas achieved little that was of any operational significance despite the existence of large supportive German colonies in places like Argentina, Paraguay and Chile; extensive covert involvement in the 1940 presidential campaign in the USA failed to prevent Roosevelt's re-election and was, if anything, counter-productive. When Germany tried to get a foothold in Brazil, it was easily fended off by the Americans, who developed their own hemispheric air base system through Pan-Am and the Airport Development Program, a programme that enormously increased their ability to project their power across the Atlantic and Pacific oceans. In short, while Germany failed to make headway in Africa or the Americas, the *threat* posed by its rapid conquest of Europe allowed the USA to do so.[7]

For here was the basic problem. Just when the Germans started talking about the Monroe Doctrine, the Americans were looking far beyond it and starting to imagine themselves as a world military power. The actual state of US preparedness was lamentable – in the summer of 1940, its army could put only one-third the number of divisions into the field that the Belgians managed – but for this very reason, Roosevelt was determined on a rapid build-up. Hitler's answer to the Havana Conference had been to insist that the Americans stay out of European affairs. But there was little chance of that. Roosevelt had already explained to Congress that the USA could not accept an Allied defeat since that 'would leave the western hemisphere between the jaws of a victorious German Empire in a conquered Europe and a triumphant Japanese Empire in a subjected Asia'.[8]

The parallels between what was happening in Europe and Asia were certainly striking. The Japanese government, proposing a Monroe Doctrine of its own, had already proclaimed in 1934 that it had 'special responsibilities in East Asia'. Naturally, the Americans had been dismissive. 'There is no more resemblance between our Monroe Doctrine and the so-called Monroe Doctrine of Japan than there is between black and white,' stated Roosevelt's secretary of state in April 1940. But the idea itself became much more compelling in Japan in the following months thanks to the Germans' victories in western Europe. French Indochina and the Dutch East Indies suddenly seemed vulnerable, and there were calls to introduce a one-party state in Tokyo on the German model. Conservatives and the palace successfully resisted these, but the idea of founding a Japanese New Order got much further. Hoping, much as the Germans themselves did, that conquest would bring self-sufficiency and blunt the growing global power of the USA – whose sanctions already revealed Japan's acute dependence on imported energy supplies – Tokyo poured troops into French Indochina to offer Vichy its 'protection', blocking vital supply-lines into China. As they moved the following year into Hong Kong, the Dutch East Indies, Malaya and Singapore, bauxite, iron ore, rice and rubber were shipped back in such quantities that the Americans became alarmed. In fact, even more ambitious plans were being drawn up to expand Japan's empire into Alaska, and down the western coastline of the Americas.[9]

The Tripartite Pact which Japan signed with Germany and Italy in September 1940 was nothing less than the international diplomatic expression of Schmitt's *Grossraum* concept and the apotheosis of his idea of regionally defined autarky. According to the Pact, Japan recognized 'the leadership of Germany and Italy in the establishment of a New Order in Europe', while the latter acknowledged Japan's leading role in the coming New Order in 'Greater East Asia'. With its talk of 'leadership', of each nation's 'proper place' in the world, the Pact spoke of power, region and hierarchy, not of equality, universality and sovereignty. On paper, at any rate, the Pact appeared to realize Schmitt's idea that a legal order is rooted in the very act of parcelling out territory.

In reality there was little that these three powers shared, beyond their hatred of the League of Nations, their resentment and fear at having been excluded from the 1919 division of the world and their determination to avoid further isolation by banding together. Since they could not bring the fighting to an end in 1940, this lack of coordination mattered more than appeared at the time; once the USA entered the war, and it became a truly global 'world war' for the first time, their lack of communication contrasted sharply with the partnership forged by their enemies. Among the members of the Tripartite Pact there was no institutional framework for consultation, and the only common bodies were purely ceremonial. No joint military strategy emerged during the war: true to the Schmittian conception, what counted was how each power ruled within its regional sphere, not what went on between them.[10]

IMPERIALISM: BEYOND THE LIBERAL VARIANT?

Hitler would have much preferred to have Britain instead of Japan as his partner in Asia. As a colonial power, the British had few greater admirers than the Führer and he often emphasized the harmony of their and German interests. 'If today the globe has an English world empire,' he had written in 1928, 'then for the time being there is also no *Volk* which, on the grounds of its overall governing qualities as well as its political clear-headedness, would be more fitted for it ... There is no reason why England's enmity against Germany should last forever.'[11]

His admiration had been shared by others in Germany before him. The mighty British empire had long set the bar for German imperialists, and their view of the causes of its rise to world power was basically the one articulated by many historians today. Access through its colonies to overseas land and energy supplies in the Americas and the Pacific and control of vibrant markets in south Asia had allowed the British to escape the Malthusian constraints of the limited resources available in their own little island and to embark on the specialization of production that fuelled the industrial revolution and world power.[12]

Would-be German imperialists were also inclined to emphasize a third factor – the character, energy and ruthlessness of the colonizers themselves. The British takeover of India, for instance, had depended upon the initiative shown by a relatively small number of individuals. Their domination of North America and Australia highlighted the importance of self-reliant bands of white settlers who had not shied away from expelling, enslaving or eradicating the 'savages' they found living there in order to colonize the land for themselves. Even at the time, after all, these massacres had seemed inevitable, part of the march of progress. Had not Victorian anthropologists themselves charted the astonishing rates of 'decrease and extermination' of native tribes as a result of the coming of the white man? Some actually advised that 'the natives must be exterminated or reduced to such numbers as to be readily controlled' when they failed to produce profits. Darwinian popularizers criticized the ignorance of people who protested 'the elimination of inferior races'. Killing native peoples seemed to be a price many Europeans were willing to pay in order to claim land overseas.[13]

As the British built a new empire in Africa and consolidated their white settler colonies, the colonial lobby in the Kaiser's Germany feared being left behind. Germans were emigrating in colossal numbers, but, as observers at the time noticed, they were scarcely serving the interests of *German* colonialism in so doing. Left to themselves, extraordinary numbers of emigrants had made their way to the Americas, outnumbering the Irish or English for much of the nineteenth century. More than half a million Germans arrived there in the mid-1850s alone, more than five million in the century after 1815. Indeed, they made up over 40 per cent of *all* immigrants to the US (by far the largest single group) between the 1850s and the early 1890s. German colonialists bemoaned their loss. According to the manifesto issued in 1884 by Carl Peters' Gesellschaft für Deutsche Kolonisation:

The German nation has come away empty-handed from the partition of the earth as it has proceeded from the 15th century until now ... The German Empire – great and strong through unification, achieved by blood, stands as the leading power on the continent of Europe [but] the great stream of German emigration flows into foreign races and disappears within them ... *Deutschtum* abroad is doomed to constant national ruin.[14]

The USA itself, on the other hand, stood out as the world's leading example of modern colonial settlement – exactly what the lobbyists wanted for their country. 'Could Germany maintain its power and status in the world if the Anglo-Saxons and Russians continued to double their population while Germany was prevented by lack of space,' asked one enthusiast in 1879. 'Shouldn't Germany be a queen among nations, ruling widely over endless territories, like the English, the Americans and the Russians?'[15]

'A queen among nations': the phrase conveys perfectly the wounded national pride, the desire to be taken seriously, that animated much of Europe's imperial competition. Expansion was thus seen not only as necessary for increased growth and prosperity, but also as providing a renewed sense of national purpose. Lobbyists sought support from their government, insisting that the Germans were 'a state- not people-colonisers'.[16] But if they had to plead, it was because Bismarck himself was unmoved by the pioneer spirit. Neither he nor his successors paid much heed to those who argued that the scale of German emigration to South America justified colonial claims in the Western hemisphere – in Brazil, perhaps, or Argentina. They were more concerned about the Reich's eastern border.[17]

Hitler and the Nazis agreed with the old prewar colonial lobby: Germany could not build an empire without sustained backing by the state. They also agreed with Bismarck: colonization must focus on the East. In the sheer scale of their ambitions, however, they had no peers. In the winter of 1944, Hitler referred to the transatlantic emigrants when he complained that only Germany's political disunity had led to the American continent 'being English instead of German'. The demo-graphic drift westwards, according to one wartime population expert, was 'the worst enemy of our settlement work' and needed to be reversed. 'Go East, Young Man!' ran the title of a wartime article in the *Deutsche Zeitung im Ostland*. The deployment of modern state power, and exploiting the will of individual colonists to serve the interests of the nation, were their basic policy tools. Whether the numbers of potential settlers actually existed to realize a policy that dwarfed the scale of the Oregon and California settlements was not a question that bothered the Nazis. In the mid-nineteenth century, it had taken twenty years to get half a million Americans to make the trek to the West Coast; the Nazis, using the power of modern wartime bureaucracy, moved more than that in just three. What mattered for them was that Europe's future lay not across the Atlantic but in the 'vast area which begins beyond Vienna, Breslau and Danzig and reaches to the depths of the

Asiatic continent'; mass emigration and settlement would satisfy 'the economic requirements of Europe for an era of peace that shall last for centuries'.[18]

If the USA provided the settlement model, it was the pre-1914 colonies that provided what little administrative expertise existed in the Third Reich. From 1939 onwards, therefore, veterans of Germany's earlier forays into colonial policy were drafted in to help. Viktor Böttcher, the provincial governor of wartime Posen, had served in the administration of the German Cameroons before 1914, and one of his colleagues had set up branches of the Nazi Party in southern Africa. Some of the Germans settled on former Polish estates had come from as far away as Cape Town, Angola and Brazil. Ethnographers, anthropologists and racial scientists all quickly lent their expertise to the 'colonial calling in the East'. As one 'colonial pioneer' put it in 1941, Germany's old Africa-hands would 'have to perform now in the East of the Reich, the constructive work that they had once carried out in Africa'.[19]

Much more important than actual personnel, though, was the repertoire of ideas and practices that the Nazis drew upon. In prewar German colonies, for instance, race laws had criminalized native/non-native sexual relations, and similar trends – whether formalized in law or not – were clearly visible in other colonial regimes as well. Like the Nazis, many European colonial administrators had established dual systems of law and employment that distinguished (white) citizens from (non-white) subjects, and made it all but impossible to pass from the latter category to the former. Inside the USA (whose racial laws and eugenics movement had earned Hitler's praise in the 1920s) native Americans were viewed up to 1924 as 'nationals' but not citizens – a distinction that late nineteenth-century American commentators acknowledged to be the prerogative of 'a great colonial power'; Puerto Ricans were defined constitutionally much as the Germans later did the Czechs – they were 'foreign to the United States in a domestic sense'.[20]

In other cases, of course, natives were ruled without law at all, on the basis of disciplinary regulations and administrative fiat, as in the case of the French *indigénat*. Forced labour and many of the other impositions that shocked Europeans when they were subjected to them by the Germans were also commonplace. Just before the war, the League of Nations sponsored a conference to compare the way different colonial authorities treated their 'native populations'. When Margery Perham, a

British colonial expert, tried to defend her country's record, a liberal critic reminded her of

the question of the colour bar in South Africa, the confiscation of the political rights of the Cape natives during the last two or three years, the forced labour which was still a part of British policy in certain African territories and also the loss of the best territory in Kenya by the natives so that white settlers should be supplied . . .[21]

What, then, *was* the difference between what other imperial powers did abroad, and what the Nazis were doing in Europe? Some thought very little. The standard communist line – at least until the USSR was attacked in 1941 – was that the war, far from being a struggle for freedom, was really nothing more than a competition among rival imperialist blocs. 'As long as England and France plunder and oppress millions of people in their colonies, that is nothing but a species of "freedom and humanity",' wrote the Austrian communist émigré Ernst Fischer in 1940. 'But as soon as other imperialists claim a share in the booty, that is a blow at the harmony of the continents.' 'The declared slogans about democracy and liberty,' declared the Communist Party of Ireland in October 1939, calling for the return of the six counties in the north, 'are smokescreens concealing the imperialist aims of the ruling circles . . . [who] are waging war to defend their colonial plunder . . . Any fight for liberty or a better life abroad is a sham while these are denied at home.'[22]

In the colonies themselves, the key issue was not so much capitalism as race. After the war, the writer Aimé Césaire wrote that the problem all along had been the Europeans' lack of understanding and their limited imaginative sympathy. They had needed Nazism, in a sense, to bring home to them what racial prejudice produced. They had failed to grasp the true nature of colonialism because racism had prevented them sympathizing with the plight of those they oppressed. They tolerated 'Nazism before it was inflicted on them . . . they absolved it, shut their eyes to it, legitimized it, because, until then, it had been applied only to non-European peoples.'[23]

Césaire's point was confirmed by the fact that such anti-imperialists as could be found in the metropole were much more likely to be concerned about the corrupting effect of empire on civil liberties at home than they were about racial equality. In the words of the nineteenth-century radical British lawyer Frederick Harrison, 'We cannot make rules for negroes without baiting traps for Europeans.' Harrison formed part of a venerable, if minority, chorus who warned of the danger of treating people one way abroad and another at home. However, the deeply ambiguous concept of 'civilization' offered mainstream opinion in Europe a justification for doing exactly this. For while Victorian international law legitimized colonial rule, it did so by holding out the promise of liberation: in a theory that was generally honoured only in the breach, the closer a people came to being able to form a state in accordance with the so-called 'standard of civilization', the greater their autonomy and the likelier they were to gain independence. Freedom had to be earned. Legal and political theorists talked about tiers of sovereignty and they distinguished between 'civilized', 'barbarian' and 'savage' peoples. It was a way of talking about racial hierarchies without having to mention race, and implying that racial differences could at some unspecified point in the future be ignored.[24]

This was the view of the world that underpinned the 1919 peace settlement. At Versailles the victor powers had bestowed sovereignty upon the 'civilized' peoples of eastern Europe and created a set of 'New States' there, subjected only to the conditional oversight of the minority rights regime. In the Middle East, they had established League mandates to usher the Arab peoples towards independence and full statehood, a process that brought freedom (of a kind) to Egypt and Iraq before the outbreak of the war (though not to Syria or Lebanon). Only among the 'savages' of Africa and the Pacific did they justify colonial rule into the indefinite future.

It was this promise of eventual (if always tenuous) political redemption that Nazism decisively rejected. If the Italian conquest of Ethiopia had violently reduced a sovereign state – and member of the League – to colonial status, the Nazi conquest of eastern Europe was a further, and even more dramatic, assault on these liberal assumptions. Based upon the immutable truths of racial hierarchy, Nazism was a doctrine of perpetual empire for the only alternative it envisaged to domination was oppression and national death. In his Reichstag speech of 6 October 1939, Hitler justified Poland's dismemberment on the grounds that it had proved itself 'incapable of existence'. 'It is not possible to treat European countries like colonies,' Mussolini complained to the Italian industrialist Pirelli in June 1941, but this was what the Germans intended to do.[25]

The Nazis were thus tearing down the whole noble façade of nine-teenth-century international law. As Werner Best put it in 1939, 'the relations between states, hitherto called international law, cannot be called "law"'. The key difference between them and other European imperialists from this point of view was simply that they set the fault line that divided rulers from ruled inside Europe not outside it. In the British-dominated Raj, a civil servant had once dismissed the protests of an Indian princely state on the grounds that 'the maxims of inter-national law' only regulated 'the relations of independent and co-equal European States'. In effect, central and eastern Europe were now Germany's India. By proclaiming the Protectorate of Bohemia-Moravia in March 1939, the Germans imported the colonial model for imagining ties between advanced and backward peoples to the continent of Europe itself. Wiping out the independent states of Czechoslovakia and Poland, the Nazis reversed the progressivist assumption that sovereignty, once gained, could not, as an aspect of civilized life, be abolished or whittled down.[26]

An empire that threatened its subjects with denationalization was obviously reliant on very different means of keeping itself in power than one based on liberal premises. Hitler's reading of how the British ruled India showed that what counted for him at bottom was force. A ruling power, according to him, should not even pretend that what it was doing was in anyone's interest but its own:

It would never have occurred to an Englishman at the time England's colonies were founded to justify his actions otherwise than by the very real and sober advantages which they might bring with them . . . The less thought the English-man ever gave to, say, imposing English culture or English breeding on savages, the more sympathetic did such a form of government necessarily seem to savages who were certainly not hungry for culture. On top of this, to be sure, there was also the whip which one likewise could use all the more readily if one did not run the danger of contradicting a cultural mission.[27]

A stance of such crudity was certainly not unknown among the British themselves. At the time of the 1865 Jamaica uprising, for instance, expressions of a new racial authoritarianism had emerged in the Victorian press. According to the editor of the medical journal *The Lancet*, small groups of white men could only safeguard themselves in the colonies by the most coercive methods; natives had either 'to be constantly kept down with a rod of iron or be slowly exterminated'. Such ideas expressed a possibility inherent in the practice of empire itself and the British were becoming uneasily aware that the 'power of numbers' was against them. Virginia Woolf's uncle, Fitzjames Stephen, wrote in a famous letter to *The Times* in 1883 that 'an absolute government, founded not on consent but on conquest' – like the British in India – represented 'a belligerent civilisation' that should not 'shrink from the open, uncompromising, straightforward assertion of [its own] superiority'. Nevertheless, this was not the customary line in England, and it was always subjected to criticism. This is ultimately where Hitler's empire stood out. As brutal and murderous as they often were, neither the British nor any other European colonial power ever dealt with the problem of 'the power of numbers' as violently or as hastily as the Nazis. Their approach was generally gradualist and experimental, driven by a political imagination that was constrained from extremism of the Nazi variety by factors that included a more law-bound culture and surprisingly unmotivated state bureaucracies. If they lacked the ideology and the resources to systematize mass killing on the scale of the New Order, they also lacked the fundamental sense of urgency. Having carried out their revolution at home, the Nazis were in a hurry to reap the benefits abroad. 'We wanted to establish a world empire only four years after we had introduced general conscription,' was how a captured German officer summed it up in 1943. As the war itself created shortages, bottlenecks and enormous new problems, the cult of force and the racial geopolitics that the Nazis took so seriously turned into a programme of extermination on a scale which had no precedent.[28]

One reason why Hitler's brutal 'realism' in fact served him poorly was that it deprived the Germans of the chance of exploiting nationalism as a tool of political warfare. Contrast the Japanese, who successfully enlisted Asian nationalists to work with them. They followed the Allies' postwar propaganda and tried to trump it with conferences and declarations of their own in which Asia's 'liberated nations' pledged cooperation and respect for one another's sovereignty and independence. At the Greater East Asia Conference which they organized in 1943, they brought together representatives of China, Manchukuo, Thailand, Burma and the Philippines as well as the leader of the Free India movement. There was talk of a 'new internationalism', and the Foreign Ministry presented the conference's Declaration as an Asian liberationist counterblast to the Atlantic Charter. Of course, the Japanese profited from the fact that they were toppling unpopular European colonial regimes whereas the Germans were marching into states which had already gained independence. Still, there were many places where the Germans could have played a similar game, but refused to do so.[29]

One was the Middle East. Near the end of the war, Hitler apparently regretted his lack of interest in political warfare there. 'All Islam vibrated at the news of our victories [in 1940],' he told Bormann in the Berlin bunker. 'The Egyptians, the Iraqis and the whole of the Near East were all ready to rise in revolt. Just think what we could have done to help them, even to incite them, as would have been both our duty and our interest.' But his memory betrayed him. To Bormann, writing it all down, the Führer blamed his diplomats for having misled him, but in fact the truth was the reverse: they had been urging *him* to issue a Declaration on Arab Independence, and he had refused. Preoccupied by the impending invasion of Russia, and convinced his troops would soon control the Caspian, he had neglected to take the opportunities in Iraq and Iran seriously. He had disappointed the Grand Mufti of Jerusalem and the Indian nationalist Subha Chandra Bose, hindering Germany from exploiting the disturbances which swept the Indian sub-continent in the summer of 1942. When Axis forces did cross into Egypt, the declaration they issued on Egyptian independence was so feeble and so far short of what Arab politicians had called for that it won Berlin no credit. The reality was that, outside Europe, Hitler remained a believer in the racial superiority of the Anglo-Saxon peoples and did not want to do anything that might hasten Britain's demise as 'a dominant race'.[30]

As for the far more important occupied Soviet territories, a series of proposals to back nationalists there had been presented to the Führer and dismissed. The German Foreign Ministry dusted off many of its old schemes for political warfare in the Middle East, India and central Asia and then had to shelve them again. The army and Rosenberg's Eastern Ministry had tried supporting Ukrainian and Baltic nationalists, and even Goebbels eventually came round to the idea, if only for propaganda purposes. When the Japanese foreign minister made a speech strongly supporting Indian independence, Goebbels noted the 'exceptional wisdom' of the move and commented that 'we could learn a lot from them'.[31]

The Japanese themselves were in a remarkably good position to see how badly their ally was miscalculating, not least because they were the one power that had observers on either side of the German–Russian lines and thus had a sense of the impressive speed of the Soviet armaments recovery. After Stalingrad, the Japanese ambassador, Oshima, discussed the situation with Ribbentrop and with Hitler in an effort to get them to change course. Bluntly he warned the Führer that, thanks to German policy, Bolshevism was back in charge:

the [Soviet] war aims have been well driven home and the determination of the people may be called unshakeable. All the people cry: 'Let us slay the German invader!' You get the impression that the whole Soviet nation in its fury is welcoming another attempt by Germany to come back.

Arguing for a change of strategy, the Japanese ambassador was polite but unambiguous:

In view of the diversity of nationalities within Russia, the emancipation of these people should be made our leading slogan. On the basis of Germany's policy in the occupied eastern territories, wouldn't it be possible for Germany to consider its political strategy towards Russia from this viewpoint?[32]

'Your idea sounds plausible enough,' Hitler responded. 'However, the fact is that the most effective way is to weaken morale on the battlefield by military offensive. There is a danger that political schemes would have just opposite results.' A couple of months later, Oshima was still trying to get Ribbentrop to 'lose no time in giving guarantees of independence to the Ukraine and the three Baltic nations'. Yet the problem was – as always – the Führer. He resisted all calls to cooperate with nationalists in eastern Europe on the basis of their common anti-Bolshevism, and even in western Europe, he preferred to work through bureaucrats. In Nazi Europe there was thus no German equivalent of the Japanese slogan of 'Asia for the Asiatics' and no German version of indirect rule. Not only did Hitler remain a German nationalist to the end; he remained one unable to see how Germany's interests might require some accommodation with other people's national sentiments as well. Astute in his understanding of German politics, he displayed a fatal provincialism when it came to the aspirations of those beyond its borders.[33]

ENDING EUROPEAN IMPERIALISM

In his 1939 article 'Not Counting Niggers', George Orwell prefigured Césaire's criticisms and denounced the vogue for sweeping the problem of empire under the carpet. How, he wondered, could people seriously say that the fight against Nazism in Europe had no implications for British, Dutch, Belgian or French rule in Africa and Asia? How could this seriously be described as a struggle between democracy and fascism as though the democracies themselves were not also imperial masters ruling the lives of millions of non-voting subjects? 'What meaning would there be,' he wrote, 'in bringing down Hitler's system in order to stabilize something that is far bigger and in its different way just as bad?'[34]

Orwell was, as so often, ahead of his time, for most people still refused to see the connection. During the war, the British Ministry of Information even mounted an Empire Crusade to whip enthusiasm for the war, fatuously highlighting the difference between the tyrannical Nazi 'slave empire' and Britain's utterly different 'family of free nations'. It was an utter waste of time and money. But the idea that Europeans should be treated differently from the rest was not one that would disappear overnight simply because the Nazis had brought home the realities of colonialism. The informal colour bar in the British Empire remained in force, even though the more far-sighted officials worried at the collapse of 'white prestige' and the prospect of a 'race revolt' if things did not change. One Colonial Office civil servant responded to the loss of Singapore by warning that people in the colonies 'cannot be certain that this is a black as well as a white man's war, unless they are persuaded beyond of a shadow of a doubt that the peace which follows it will be a black as well as a white man's peace'.[35]

Such an outcome was exactly what Churchill in particular was determined to avoid. The Americans were already proclaiming that 'the age of imperialism' was over. Yet while Churchill had signed up to the Atlantic Charter, he made it clear that in his view its pledge of liberation did not apply outside Europe. The Gaullists, Belgians and Dutch felt the same. 'Imperialism' might be over, but that did not mean that the European powers were planning to pack up and leave. Even as the war ended, the postwar French colonial minister was explaining that a record of wartime resistance to Vichy in the colonies did not entitle activists to affiliate with the prestigious mainland French Conseil National de la Résistance, not least since there was the risk that Guadeloupean resisters – who were in no way comparable 'with our heroes of the *maquis*' – might exploit such membership to publicize their desire for another liberation – from French colonial rule altogether.[36]

A bitter global clash over empire was thus preordained. In 1945, colonial nationalists everywhere from Algeria to Indochina hailed the defeat of Nazism as the start of their own liberation. But the European powers were determined to fight their way back into the colonies they had lost and to cling to those they had kept for as long as they could. They wanted, at most, to reshape their empires, certainly not to discard them. One reason was that the German occupation itself had highlighted and even increased the colonies' political importance. Another was that the dollar-strapped economies of war-torn Europe, facing what Keynes described as a 'financial Dunkirk', badly needed colonial exports to shore up their balance of payments and pay for American goods. And at a deeper level, too, the humiliation they had all suffered at the hands of the Germans or Japanese only increased their determination to demonstrate their power. In November 1945, the British got the Dutch back into the East Indies by sending in 24,000 troops and putting down the Indonesian independence movement in Surabaya with the help of a massive naval and air bombardment that caused thousands of extra casualties. Although they pulled out of India and Palestine, there was no overall winding-up of empire, and the Middle East in fact became the new centre of the postwar British imperial system. As for the French, in the late 1940s they could be as murderous in their extended empire as the Germans had been in France itself. In May 1945, thousands of Algerians died in massacres following VE-Day celebrations that got out of hand. The same month, between 600 and 2,000 (estimates vary) inhabitants of Damascus died when the French shelled the city in a futile attempt to shore up their rule. In Indochina they simply ignored the Viet Minh's declaration of independence and sent the troops to reoccupy the country; about 6,000 people were killed when a French cruiser shelled Haiphong the following year. Bloodiest of all was the repression on Madagascar: approximately 80,000 Malagasy died in 1947–8 as French troops quashed an uprising on the island that had once been earmarked as a home for the Jews.[37]

But as Europeans held grimly on to their colonies, the impact of

Nazism made itself felt in other ways. Its defeat had certainly not led to ideas of racial superiority being completely abandoned – this took much longer – but a change of vocabulary signalled new anxieties about how they sounded. Colonial powers now generally gave up talking about their racial or even civilizational superiority – they dropped references to 'backwardness' and 'savages', and replaced 'native' with 'autochthons' – and tried to justify their rule in terms of economic development, political participation and social welfare. The British talked about 'partnerships' instead of 'trusteeships', since, as one civil servant put it in 1942, 'we must avoid any reproach that when we blamed Hitler for his poisonous doctrine of the *Herrenvolk*, we had a similar doctrine in our own hearts'. 'British "Imperialism" is dead,' asserted a Labour government pamphlet in 1946, heralding a new colonial policy that was supposed to be 'both liberal and dynamic'. Civil servants came up with ingenious new constitutional arrangements to replace empire with commonwealths, confederations and other more consensual-sounding entities. The French officially abolished their empire and replaced it with a 'French Union'. (It lasted twelve years, and its successor, the 'French Commonwealth', lasted just two.)[38]

These schemes were taken seriously in the late 1940s, but they stood no real chance of shoring up the rotting edifice of European imperialism, for much greater disintegrative forces were at work at the same time. The war had led to a resurgence of nationalism not only in Europe, but in the colonies as well. Rapid wartime urbanization had facilitated the rise of new African and Asian political elites; the humiliation and disarray of colonial administrations had undermined European prestige. These forces could be resisted and were, as we saw above. Nevertheless, in the longer term, the costs of keeping their armed forces abroad in expensive policing and counter-insurgency duties were not popular either economically or politically with Europeans. It was one thing where white settlers had killed off native opposition long before, or so weakened it that it could be easily ignored, but it was quite another where their presence and brutality triggered off large and well-organized armed resistance, as in Algeria, Kenya and Angola (where the number of Portuguese settlers doubled after the war). In such cases, the old settler order came under attack. As attitudes in the colonies themselves became polarized, and the settlers moved sharply to the right, European metropoles quickly lost their appetite for financing confrontation.[39]

The international environment itself had completely changed as a result of Hitler's defeat as well. Before the Second World War, the world had been run by imperial powers. After it, it was run by anti-imperial superpowers. The influential American journalist Walter Lippmann launched a blistering attack against any attempt to revive 'a dead or dying imperialism' after the war; 'white imperialism' was finished, he wrote, and the war was being fought to enlarge the sphere of human freedom and bring peace through the creation of 'equal, self-respecting nations'. Even though the British disagreed, the Americans were simply too powerful to ignore. Moreover the Cold War, while it tempered Washington's anti-colonialism in some cases, strengthened it in others, for the USA did not want Europeans keeping their military forces tied up in the colonies when they needed them against communism nearer home. And they did not want colonial nationalist movements allowing communism a foothold in the Third World, especially as the leaders of these movements were often astute in playing on the Americans' fear of the USSR. Moscow itself had started playing the anti-imperialist card in 1947, when the ideologue Andrei Zhdanov declared the Soviet Union to be 'the only true defender of freedom and independence for all nations'.[40]

Squeezed, therefore, between growing opposition in the colonies themselves and intense pressure from Washington, Europe's powers withdrew, reluctantly and often only after immense bloodshed. Within two or three decades, the process was essentially over and marked a major turning-point in world history. Insofar as both the fascist and the Japanese New Orders had been responses to the challenge posed by existing European empires, the disappearance of the latter eradicated many of the justifications for fascist empire-building too. In short, the geopolitical rivalries that had motivated Nazism disappeared, and the whole nineteenth-century edifice collapsed. Hitler had been right: the struggle between Germany and Britain had ended the imperial age.[41]

In the 1950s Europe found itself on an entirely new growth path. For the first time in its history, and quite unexpectedly, this banished the fear of famine from the continent and allowed food – perhaps the single most important economic and social policy concern of the Nazi regime – to slip off the political agenda almost unnoticed. According to Nazi logic, this should never have happened. The Iron Curtain had cut off the food-deficit areas in the West from the producers of eastern Europe and made the problem of supplying the continent's industrial heartlands on the face of it much harder than before. To make the challenge even more forbidding, in 1947 Europe's population was at least twenty million bigger than in 1938. A divided Germany itself was struggling to cope with an enormous refugee problem, far worse in 1950 than in 1920.[42]

Yet despite these pressures and the additional tensions of the Cold War, there was no resurgence of radical nationalism inside the former Reich, as many well-placed observers had feared. Nor did it prove necessary to settle millions of Germans in West African colonies, as a worried Hjalmar Schacht – still anxious about overpopulation in central Europe – had helpfully suggested while in captivity in 1945. On the contrary, soon there was a shortage of labour that pulled villagers into towns and then started to attract Turks, Portuguese, Yugoslavs and Greeks to West Germany, and north Africans, Caribbeans and Indians elsewhere.[43]

Astonishingly, Europe proved able to feed them all easily, and living standards rose steadily from the end of the 1940s. By 1953 food intake was already close to prewar levels in much of western Europe; by the 1960s, the problem was surpluses not deficits. It was an extraordinary turn-around. Part of this was the new Common Market. Guaranteed high buy-in prices for farmers and improvements in agricultural technology helped to achieve the old Nazi goal of continental self-sufficiency much more effectively than their wars of conquest: from this point of view, the Common Agricultural Policy marked the triumph of democracy over dictatorship. Reintegration into a global trading system lubricated by American dollars brought more benefits. Cooperation by independent but increasingly coordinated nation-states under American hegemony guaranteed far higher rates of growth than the Nazis' model of continental autarky, bilateral clearings and highly centralized resource extraction had been able to do.[44]

To some observers, these developments looked epochal in their significance: land itself – the source of sustenance, the basis of political and economic power for centuries, the central obsession of the Nazis themselves, as it had been of generations of European nationalists – was finally losing its significance. In a brilliant article published in 1957, an

American political scientist called John Herz reflected on what it all meant. He argued that the shift from a basically nineteenth-century model of control through empires to a mid-twentieth-century model of power through markets signalled the final demise of the European territorial state – in other words a state that defined itself by its control of a certain land mass and its ability to extend its sovereignty over this territory. Herz believed the war had finally made the territorial state obsolete because it showed that boundaries mattered much less than in the past. Powers could now ignore them by bombarding hostile populations with propaganda or by bombing them from the air. Missile technology mocked the pretensions of the state to be able to defend its subjects. The British and the Americans – the war's victors – had seemed to be particularly attracted to such modes of warfare: they had heavily bombed the cities of Germany, Italy and France and they had tried to use the shipping blockade to starve them too. Anticipating this, Hitler had tried to enlarge the area under Germany's control in order to become self-sufficient and withstand enemy pressure. He had thus remained faithful to the nineteenth-century idea of expanding borders to guarantee security. But Germany's devastation had shown that this was not the answer.[45]

Herz suggested that in the nuclear age sovereignty meant less than it did. Like many of the wartime advocates of federalism, he saw the nation-state as outmoded. Anticipating many more recent theorists, he saw that a new empire was emerging – the American – that projected its power not through formal conquest and control of land, but more invisibly – through its penetration of markets, its culture and its flexibly deployed naval and air power. He might have added in support of his argument the equally striking disappearance of Europe's peasant classes that took place at this time, bringing with it the collapse of the very way of life the Nazis had been dedicated to preserving.[46]

Yet perhaps this obituary for land (and farewell to the state) was premature, and more a matter of perspective than anything else. After all, both the USA and the USSR still behaved very much like old-fashioned territorial powers. Indeed, in another article published a decade later, Herz accepted that the territorial state turned out to have had more life left in it than he thought. Not only had the war left nationalism strengthened, not weakened; it had helped to turn it into a global phenomenon. Decolonization, he wrote in 1968, had produced a 'new territoriality' across the globe, and the number of sovereign nations had exploded as a result. Massive superiority in airpower – on which he had laid so much stress – while useful fighting another state, was much less useful when countering guerilla insurgencies and national liberation movements. The war in Vietnam was clearly relevant to this new line of thought. But it was another new nation-state whose experience was uppermost in his mind – Israel. As events there suggested, the mystique of land remained alive and well.[47]

THE JEWISH QUESTION: FROM EUROPE TO THE MIDDLE EAST

Nazism aimed to renew Germany's strength by creating a classless, racially pure community in which there would be no minorities. Later, it offered ethnic purification as the solution for regional instability in eastern Europe as well. In Hitler's speech of 6 October 1939, he had talked about adjusting 'the disposition of the entire living space according to the various nationalities, that is to say, the solution of the problems affecting the minorities'. The Nazis did not invent this approach, which had first emerged in the Balkans. It also continued after them, and more people were expelled from eastern Europe between 1945 and 1949 than during the war itself. With decolonization, the ideal of the nation-state was exported overseas, just as Herz came to appreciate. But this simply globalized the struggle for land and the problem of minorities as well. In 1947 came the first move in this direction with the partitions in the Indian sub-continent, accompanied by extraordinary loss of life as millions of Hindus, Muslims and Sikhs moved across the newly created national borders of India and Pakistan. The following year brought war and ethnic expulsion in Palestine and the establishment of a Jewish national state there. Thus the end of Europe's Jewish question turned out to be the start of the Middle East's.

That Europe and the Middle East were so closely connected should have come as no surprise. Zionism had been a European national movement from the start, and a response to the anti-Semitism at the heart of many other European national movements. In outlook and vocabulary, it partook with them of a common European intellectual tradition.

597

Between the wars, to take a particularly striking example, it was not only German racial theorists whose 'research' provided an imprimatur of scientific respectability to the Third Reich's policy of forcing the Jews to emigrate; some Jewish scholars and commentators justified Zionism on similar grounds. The German-born Zionist Arthur Ruppin, for instance, was close in many of his theoretical views to Hans Günther, the 'Nordic race' expert who acted as mentor to Himmler. Both men – they met in 1933 to discuss the 'Jewish question' – believed the Jews were a racially distinct people who should not assimilate and did not belong in Europe. (Günther regarded them as 'a wedge driven by Asia into the European structure', while Ruppin believed that the Jews and Arabs were 'racial brothers' and that both belonged in Palestine.)[48]

But Europe's impact upon Zionism was not just a matter of ideas, and Ruppin's real significance does not lie in his views on race. As the first head of the Palestine Bureau he had been buying up property and land on behalf of Jewish colonists since before the First World War. A Prussian Jew who had grown up near Posen before emigrating to Palestine, he was familiar with the experience of the Prussian Coloniz-ation Commission and its resettlement activity. 'I see the work of the Jewish National Fund (JNF) as being similar to that of the Colonization Commission working in Prussia and Western Poland,' he wrote in 1907 after just two weeks in the country. 'The JNF will buy land whenever it is offered by non-Jews and will offer it for resale either partly or wholly to Jews.' Thus the struggle between Germans and Poles in the Prussian borderlands framed Ruppin's approach to Zionist settlement among Arabs. In Ottoman Palestine, to be sure, the odds were even tougher on Zionists than they were on Prussian nationalists in Posen: more than 88 per cent of the land's inhabitants were Arabs compared with 60 per cent Poles in the Prussian province. Faced with such an overwhelming challenge, Ruppin planned to establish small Jewish settlement 'islands' which could eventually be joined up – a rather different goal from those of his Prussian precursors. Nevertheless, he sought to apply the lessons of his homeland to Palestine and brought in a Prussian adviser to help him.[49]

The minorities situation in eastern Europe was a constant point of reference for many people and not only for Ruppin. Austrian Zionists who warned that Jews were in danger of being swamped by Arabs explained that 'if things continue thus, we shall fall victim to the same fate as the Germans in certain Slavic lands'. In the 1920s, advocates of a bi-national state criticized Ruppin for being too wedded to a 'German' approach, too much of a eugenicist, too committed to keeping the Jewish people separate and to making them a political majority in their own state. According to Martin Buber, 'we appear to have scarcely made any more progress [regarding the Arabs] than the Poles have made relative to us'. Ruppin's colleague, Samuel Bergman, sarcastically wrote off his obsession with land as simply more of the same old European disease:

Just as the Italians are hastening to constitute the majority in the South Tyrol so as to ensure their rule over the Germans, just as the Czechs are hastening to ensure their own majority, and the Germans vis-à-vis the Poles, and the Poles vis-à-vis the Ukrainians, and so on and so forth, so let Israel . . . begin from the very beginning: let there be a majority for us in Eretz Israel![50]

Prague-born Hans Kohn was equally critical, contrasting the 'German' idea of a mono-ethnic state, territorial control and national separation with the Habsburg empire in which different peoples had shared the same state. (Kohn increasingly believed that the Zionists were simply repeating the mistakes of other European nationalists and he left Palestine after the 1929 riots.)[51]

Ruppin, 'the father of Zionist settlement', died in 1943 and did not live long enough to see the dénouement. But he had laid the foundations upon which others built. Unlike Ruppin, they were not bothered by eugenic considerations; they used the Jewish National Fund Land Authority to settle as many Jews as possible on the land and tried to co-ordinate this with large-scale transfers of populations. Not surprisingly, perhaps, the German influence on Israeli settlement strategy remained strong after independence. In few countries after the war, for instance, was spatial planning as important as it was in the new Jewish state, and the first Israeli national plans for population distribution were strongly influenced by the interwar German school of economic geography, especially by the ideas of Walter Christaller, whose theories about the optimal location of settlements had been deployed in Himmler's colonization of wartime Poland and in General Plan East. To be sure, the Israeli use of such ideas in the new postwar conquest of the land was far from unique. Indeed Christaller's Central Place Theory, which had been worked up for the SS to replace the Slavs' ancient hamlets with a geometrically perfect system of new towns and villages, ended up becoming a staple of development planning across the postwar world, a sign in itself of that new global concern with land which Herz discerned in the 1960s.

Israel's emergence also pointed to another key feature of this expanded territoriality – the worsened position of minorities. After the First World War, Jewish lobby groups had been among the most ardent supporters of minority rights. But after the Second, they abandoned this completely. In the face of the genocide, many of them had turned to Zionism, and very few saw a long-term future for the Jews in eastern Europe at all. Demographically and politically, the Nazi New Order had wrought a shattering transformation: the great east European centres of *shtetl* life – notably Poland, Ukraine, the Baltic states and Belorussia – were wiped out, and in Hungary, the Czech lands and Romania, too, provincial Jewish life did not recover. Many Jewish survivors were driven out of their homes even after Liberation, confirming what the Final Solution itself had suggested, that many east Europeans were generally sympathetic to the Nazis' basic goal of getting rid of the Jews. Some survivors moved to western Europe. Nevertheless, after the war, Europe as a whole ceased to be the heartland of a severely depleted world Jewry. Instead the world's largest community emerged on the American continent, while Israel's own Jewish population jumped from 445,000 in prewar Palestine to 2.6 million by 1970.[52]

Table: Percentage of World Jewish Population by Region[53]

	1900	1939	1951	2005
in Europe	81	58	24	12
in Americas	11	32	53	46
in Palestine/Israel	0.3	3	12	41
Total Jewish Population (millions)	10.6	16.7	11.6	13

In Palestine itself, Zionist leaders were concerned not only to help the survivors of the genocide but to assess their potential for assisting the national cause and their representatives visited many of the camps of Jewish Displaced Persons. David Ben Gurion, the leader of the Jewish Agency for Palestine, was dismayed by the inmates' state of mind – their factionalism, selfishness and incessant demands – and he anticipated great difficulty teaching them how to become 'citizens of the Jewish state'. Even so, in March 1945 he reckoned on a million Jews arriving over the following year and a half in order to push the British into a more pro-Zionist stance. The figures were much too ambitious. When the British upheld immigration restrictions instead and turned back Mossad ships carrying illegal immigrants, Ben Gurion compared their policy with that of the Nazis. But in fact only a small proportion of the survivors actually wanted to go to the Middle East at all, and there were no more than 220,000 in Palestine when the 1948 war broke out.[54]

As Ben Gurion understood very well, Israel's emergence – while intimately connected to the experience of the war – depended much less on the influx of survivors from Europe than it did on the political impact of the Holocaust and on American backing in particular. In the massive immigration wave of the first years of the new state, the crucial source of youthful arrivals was not eastern Europe (migrants from there tended to be older) but the Middle East and North Africa. Europe's Jewish population started to grow again after 1950, but that in the Arab lands did not. In short, the central European practice of ethnic homogenization was spreading – and being spread – to the Arab lands as well. The motor was Israel's single-minded pursuit of an organized, state-led 'homecoming' which saw the existence of Jews abroad as a source of national weakness and their 'return' as essential for national survival (another way perhaps in which the influence of German nationalism continued to exert itself). In 1953, Jacques Vernant, a scholar of refugee flows, noted that Israel had accepted a larger number of refugees than any other country in the world – both relatively and absolutely. Whether in some cases it actually tried to force Jews to leave their homes in order to immigrate – from Iraq, for example – remains shrouded in controversy. But this too was a policy which could be found in the longer European history of forced population movements. As we have seen throughout this book, in the minds of politicians keen to build up their national strength, 'rescuing' co-nationals abroad was often hard to distinguish from deliberately uprooting them.[55]

MINORITIES, REFUGEES
AND RIGHTS

Minority rights had been a vestige of an older conception of international governance, in which the League, run by (west) European Great Powers, confident in the values of 'civilization', had exercised an intrusively paternalistic oversight over new states and the mandates. But after Europe's internecine war, confidence in 'international civilization' was shattered and defending sovereignty appeared more necessary than before. There was deep resistance to any restoration of the old minority rights regime after the war and it was quietly buried while the world celebrated the United Nations' new commitment to individual human rights instead. At the same time, as the global extension of the model of the ethnically homogeneous nation-state produced wave after wave of refugees, what emerged in the rebuilt international institutions around the United Nations was an entirely new regime of refugee protection.[56]

The trigger was the question of finding homes quickly for Europe's stateless persons, the problem that Europe itself had singularly failed to tackle between 1938 and 1942. In early 1946, there were still some 576,000 of them left over from *before* the war. To this figure, over-stretched relief agencies added at least another 850,000 'non-repatriables' – Displaced Persons – and then several hundred thousands more – many of them Jews – fleeing eastern Europe *after* 1945. Their care became a key concern of the new postwar international organizations – first the United Nations Relief and Rehabilitation Administration, and then the new permanent welfare and refugee agencies established by the UN. But the international dimension was not the only one. Today, some radical thinkers seek to decouple the figure of the 'refugee' from that of 'human rights' and the 'nation-state'. But in the early 1950s, commentators such as Hannah Arendt saw things very differently: for her the point was to force states to grant rights and to solve the problem of statelessness that way. Hence the sheer scale of the postwar refugee problem itself not only bolstered international cooperation among agencies and relief workers; it also constituted a powerful argument for rebuilding strong states with the capacity to take in and care for those people who needed their help.[57]

In the early twenty-first century, amid the perhaps momentary demise of American internationalism, it became tempting to look back to 1945 and the war against Hitler as a kind of Golden Age in which the far-sighted architects of a new and mutually beneficial world order learned the lessons of the Nazi New Order and resolved to revive liberalism on a new basis. As history this is questionable. Human rights talk in the 1940s was mostly just that, and took a long time to become politically influential – perhaps not until the 1970s. Its function in 1945 was to allow the burial of the old minority rights system, clearing the way for a globalization of the ethnically purified model of the nation-state which the Nazis had done more than anyone to push through. The new regime of refugee protection was not intended to confront a permanent large-scale phenomenon but rather to ease the plight of the very specific populations stranded or evicted during and immediately after the war itself.[58]

In another sense, however, 1945 did mark a turning-point. Designed to create an empire in Europe, the Nazi New Order had also been intended, at least in Hitler's mind, to mark Germany's rise to the kind of world prominence enjoyed by her enemies, and to inaugurate a new world system run along the lines and according to the political conceptions defined by Berlin. Directed against the victors in the European scramble for empire, it was also the last stage of that process. Germany lacked either the forces to prevail alone or the political vision to win enough allies to help. By the time leading Nazis saw the need for pragmatism and compromise, it was already much too late. A Greater Germany in the Wilhelmine sense or the continental hegemon envisaged by Schmitt might have endured, but not the all-mastering Reich which was all Hitler was willing to consider. The result was not only Germany's downfall but the end of the two-centuries-long span in which Europe dominated the world.

With both Germany and Europe divided, the new postwar world order could only survive on the basis of the balance of power – and the understanding – between the two powers lurking on its margins – Soviet Russia and the USA. The two countries which Hitler had feared above all others thus came to determine Europe's fate. Europe itself turned into a laboratory for a new struggle – the Cold War – that would be fought out over the entire world. Within only a few years, the brand-new techniques of political, economic and psychological warfare that were deployed either side of the Berlin Wall were being recalibrated for use further afield. As one Marshall Plan administrator put it in 1951, 'We have learned in Europe what to do in Asia, for under the Marshall Plan we have developed the essential instruments of a successful policy in the arena of world politics.' This was not, as some disconsolate Germans feared in 1945, the 'end of Europe'. But it was the end of Europe as the maker of norms and world policeman, and the sociologist Alfred Weber was right in more than one sense when he talked in 1946 about 'a farewell to our former history' (*Abschied von der bisherigen Geschichte*). Henceforth, international order would emerge on a different basis, guided by different hands.[59]

Notes

Preface: The View from Varzin

1. C. von Krockow, *Hour of the Women: Based on an Oral Narrative by Libussa Fritz-Krockow* (New York, 1991), 27–30; on the death marches, Y. Bauer, 'The Death Marches, January–May 1945', *Modern Judaism*, 3:1 (1983), 1–21.
2. M. Dönhoff, *Before the Storm: Memories of My Youth in Old Prussia* (New York, 1990), 197–9; T. Dönhoff and J. Roettger, *Weit ist der Weg nach Westen: Auf der Fluchtroute von Marion Gräfin Dönhoff* (Berlin, 2004), 186–90.
3. L. Machtan, 'Bismarcks Varzin–Warcino heute: Betrachtungen zu einem Symbol politischer Kultur aus Preußen-Deutschland,' *Zeitschrift für Geschichtswissenschaft* 38:9, (1990), 771–86.
4. B. Ankermann, in foreword to R. Parkinson, *Thirty Years in the South Seas: Land and People, Customs and Traditions in the Bismarck Archipelago and on the German Solomon Islands*, trans. J. Dennison (Honolulu, 1999), xxxv–xxxvi.
5. Ibid., xxii, 24; K. Neumann, *Not the Way It Really Was: Constructing the Tolai Past* (Honolulu, 1992), 19.
6. T. Kaminski, 'Bismarck and the Polish Question: The "Huldigungsfahrten" to Varzin in 1894', *Canadian Journal of History*, 22 (August, 1988), 235–50.
7. L. Snyder, *The Blood and Iron Chancellor: A Documentary-Biography of Otto von Bismarck* (Princeton, 1967), 376–8.
8. C. Winter, 'The Long Arm of the Third Reich: Internment of New Guinea Germans in Tatura', *Journal of Pacific History*, 38:1 (2003), 85–124, here 105.

Introduction

1. S. Neitzel, ed., *Tapping Hitler's Generals: Transcripts of Secret Conversations 1942–1945* (Barnsley, 2007), 159.
2. W. Boelcke, ed., *'Wollt Ihr den totalen Krieg?' Die geheimen Goebbels-Konferenzen 1939–1943* (Stuttgart, 1967), 189–91. The original reference is to India's 'north-eastern' frontier – clearly an error.
3. H. Arendt, *The Origins of Totalitarianism* (New York, 1951) was ahead of her time in linking European imperialism and totalitarianism. A recent synthesis that brings Nazi Germany into the broader history of empire is J. Darwin, *After Tamerlane: The Global History of Empire* (London, 2007), esp. 417–18 for the idea of interwar world history as a bloody sequel to the 'new imperialism' of the late nineteenth century. The recent debate may be followed in U. Poiger, 'Imperialism and Empire in Twentieth Century Germany', *History and Memory*, 17:1 (2005), 117–43. I. Hull, *Absolute Destruction: Military Culture and the Practices of War in Imperial Germany* (Ithaca, 2006) powerfully cautions against assuming that influences between the colonial world and continental Europe only

travelled in one direction. W. D. Smith, *The Ideological Origins of Nazi Imperialism* (Oxford, 1986) remains fundamental.

4. Hitler as opportunist in A. J. P. Taylor, *The Origins of the Second World War* (London, 1961) and E. M. Robertson, *Hitler's Prewar Policy and Military Plans, 1933–1939* (London, 1963). On the programme, K. Hildebrand, *Deutsche Aussenpolitik 1933–1945: Kalkül oder Dogma?* (Stuttgart, 1971). Versions of the 'Atlanticist' Hitler are also to be found in G. Weinberg, *A World at Arms: A Global History of World War II* (Cambridge, 2005) and (in a rather different spirit) by A. Tooze, *Wages of Destruction: The Making and Breaking of the Nazi Economy* (London, 2006). The argument that Hitler's aims were essentially European was first made by H. Trevor-Roper, 'Hitlers Kriegsziele', *Vierteljahrshefte für Zeitgeschichte*, 8 (1960). The war aims literature is summarized in N. W. Goda, *Tomorrow the World: Hitler, Northwest Africa and the Path toward America* (College Station, TX, 1998), in M. Hauner, 'Did Hitler Want World Dominion?' *Journal of Contemporary History*, 13:1 (January 1978), 15–32, and G. Schreiber, 'Der Zweite Weltkrieg in der internationalen Forschung. Konzeptionen, Thesen und Kontroversen', in W. Michalka, ed., *Der Zweite Weltkrieg: Analysen, Grundzüge, Forschungsbilanz* (Munich, 1989), 3–25.

5. On Hitler and the US, see the very sensible comments of E. May, 'Nazi Germany and the United States: A Review Essay', *Journal of Modern History*, 41:2 (June, 1969), 207–14; Seward in E. N. Paolino, *The Foundations of the American Empire: William Henry Seward and US Foreign Policy* (Ithaca, 1973), 7–8; W. Jochmann, ed., *Adolf Hitler: Monologe im Führer-Hauptquartier, 1941–1944* (Hamburg, 1980), 110.

6. H. Mackinder, 'The Geographical Pivot of History', *Geographical Journal*, 23:4 (April 1904), 436; G. Stoakes, *Hitler and the Quest for World Dominion: Nazi Ideology and Foreign Policy in the 1920s* (New York, 1986) and N. Rich, *Hitler's War Aims*, vol. 2: *The Establishment of the New Order* (London, 1974); see also D. Aigner, 'Hitler und die Weltherrschaft', in W. Michalka, ed., *Nationalsozialistische Aussenpolitik* (Darmstadt, 1978), 49–69.

7. The Rosenberg quotation is from G. Stroble, *The Germanic Isle: Nazi Perceptions of Britain* (Cambridge, 2000), 93.

8. On the question of proximity and racial threat see D. Furber, 'Going East: Colonialism and German Life in Nazi-Occupied Poland', D. Phil., Pennsylvania State University, 2003, pages 45–9; quotation from A. Polonsky, 'The German Occupation of Poland during the First and Second World Wars: A Comparison', in R. A. Prete and A. H. Ion, eds., *Armies of Occupation* (Ontario, 1981), 133. *Ostrausch* in D. Blackbourn, *The Conquest of Nature: Water, Landscape and the Making of Modern Germany* (London, 2006), 250. See also A. Steinweis, 'Eastern Europe and the Notion of the Frontier in Germany to 1945', in K. Bullivant et al., eds., *Germany and Eastern Europe: Cultural Identities and Cultural Differences* (Amsterdam, 1999).

9. German losses from R. Overmans, *Deutsche militärische Verluste im Zweiten Weltkrieg* (Munich, 1999), 265; other figures from data in E. M. Kulischer, *Europe on the Move: War and Population Changes, 1917–1947* (New York, 1948), 278–9, 305; G. Frumkin, *Population Changes in Europe since 1939* (New York, 1951), 174–82. Soviet figures based upon M. Ellman and S. Maksudov, 'Soviet Deaths in the Great Patriotic War: A Note', *Europe-Asia Studies*, 46:4 (1994), 671–80. Some of these figures are particularly hard to verify and the estimates for civilian casualties in Poland, Yugoslavia and the USSR in particular stand in urgent need of re-examination; French figures have recently been persuasively revised downwards by Pieter Lagrou. Little has been written to date on the political dimension of wartime and early postwar statistics.

10. L. Smith, *The Embattled Self: French Soldiers' Testimony of the Great War* (Ithaca, 2007), 184.

11. H. Heiber, ed., *Hitler and His Generals: Military Conferences, 1942–45* (New York, 2003), 533–4.

12. Ute Frevert makes the point about war as a Europeanizing process in 'Europeanising

Germany's Twentieth Century', *History and Memory*, 17:1–2 (2005), 87–116. Drieu is cited in Smith, *The Embattled Self*, 184; The journey of the Gestapo official Gerhard Bast is described by his son in M. Pollack, *The Dead Man in the Bunker* (London, 2006); M. Harrison, 'Resource Mobilisation for World War II', *Economic History Review*, 2 (1988).

13. There is a striking lack of up-to-date syntheses of the Nazi New Order in European perspective. The indispensable English-language accounts include Rich, *Hitler's War Aims*, vol. 2 and A. and V. Toynbee, eds., *Survey of International Affairs: Hitler's Europe, 1939–1946* (London, 1954). One should also mention three still useful works by G. Reitlinger: *The Final Solution* (London, 1953), *The SS, Alibi of a Nation* (London, 1956) and *The House Built on Sand: The Conflicts of German Policy in Russia, 1939–1945* (London, 1960). The major collaborative collections are W. Schumann et al., eds., *Europa unterm Hakenkreuz (1938–1945)*, 10 vols. (Berlin, 1988–94), and W. Benz et al., eds., *Nationalsozialistische Besatzungspolitik in Europa, 1939–1945*, 9 vols. (Berlin, 1996–9). The eight volumes to date of the Militärgeschichtliches Forschungsamt series *Das Deutsche Reich und der Zweite Weltkrieg* (Stuttgart, 1979–2004) are also invaluable. An excellent recent synthesis is G. Corni, *Il sogno del 'grande spazio': le politiche d'occupazione nell'Europa nazista* (Rome, 2005). E. Collotti, *L'Europa nazista: il progetto di un nuovo ordine europeo, 1939–1945* (Florence, 2002) is a collection of essays. The Polish historian Czeslaw Madajczyk has written important articles not only on his specialism, Poland, but also on Nazi occupation policies in Europe as a whole.

14. P. Geyl, 'Hitler's Europe', *Encounters in History* (New York, 1961), 264.

15. 'Report of deputy chief of police Jozsef Sombor-Schweinitzer', 29 January 1943, in M. Horthy, *Confidential Papers*, ed. M. Szinai and L. Szucs (Budapest, 1965), 204.

16. F. Bacon, 'Of the True Greatness of Kingdoms and Estates', in *Selected Writings of Francis Bacon* (New York, 1955), 80–81.

17. J. Colton, *Léon Blum: Humanist in Politics* (Durham, NC, 1987), 430.

18. G. Aly, *Hitler's Beneficiaries: Plunder, Racial War and the Nazi Welfare State* (New York, 2006); an extended critique is A. Tooze, 'Economics, Ideology and Cohesion in the Third Reich: A Critique of Götz Aly's *Hitlers Volksstaat*', unpublished paper available online at http://www.hist.cam.ac.uk/academic_staff/further_details/tooze-aly.pdf; on soldiers, see O. Bartov, *Hitler's Army: Soldiers, Nazis and War in the Third Reich* (New York, 1991).

19. Gross cited in Kum'a N'dumbe III Alexandre, 'Fascisme colonial et culture', in C. Madajczyk, ed., *Inter arma non silent musae: The War and Culture, 1939–1945* (Warsaw, 1977), 17–149, here 119.

20. Hitler to Budak, 18 February 1942, in A. Hillgruber, ed., *Staatsmänner und Diplomaten bei Hitler*, vol. 2 (1942–4) (Frankfurt, 1970), 62–3; see also Z. Klukowski, *Diary from the Years of Occupation, 1939–1944* (Urbana, IL, 1993), 173, 227.

21. R. Overmans, 'Die Toten des Zweiten Weltkriegs in Deutschland. Bilanz der Forschung inter besonderer Berücksichtigung der Wehrmacht-und Vertreibungsverluste', in Michalka, ed., *Der Zweite Weltkrieg*, 858–75. The estimates Overmans considers range from between 3.35 and 9.4 million deaths in all. The variation is mostly explained by the difficulty of determining the numbers killed during the expulsions from 1945 onwards. The most plausible estimates lie in the region of 5.2 to 5.65 million people. Estimates of the Wehrmacht dead and missing alone range mostly between 3 and 4 million.

Chapter 1: Germans and Slavs: 1848–1918

1. See A. Graziosi, 'Il mondo in Europa: Namier e il "Medio oriente europeo", 1815–1948', *Contemporanea*, 10:2 (April 2007), 193–229.

2. L. Namier, *1848: The Revolt of the Intellectuals* (Oxford, 1992), 88; see also his 'Nationality and Liberty', in his *Vanished Supremacies: Essays on European History, 1812–1918* (London, 1962), 46–73. See, too, G. Wollstein, *Das 'Grossdeutschland' der Paulskirche: Nationale Ziele der bürgerlichen Revolution 1848/49* (Düsseldorf, 1977) and H. J. Hahn,

The 1848 Revolutions in German-speaking Europe (London, 2001), esp. 147–51. B. Vick, *Defining Germany: The 1848 Frankfurt Parliamentarians and National Identity* (Cambridge, MA, 2002), makes a spirited effort to criticize this interpretation and to emphasize the inclusive character of German nationalism at this time, something more persuasive where the Habsburg lands are concerned than with the Poles.

3. R. Höhn, *Verfassungskampf und Heereseid; Der Kampf des Bürgertums um das Heer (1815–1850)* (Leipzig, 1938); J. Goebbels, *The Goebbels Diaries, 1939–1941*, ed. F. Taylor (London, 1982), 114. In general, R. Zitelmann, *Hitler: The Policies of Seduction* (London, 1999), 60–61. Contesting the meanings of 1848 was a feature of Italian fascism as well: see C. Pavone, 'Le idee della Resistenza', in Pavone, ed., *Alle origini della Repubblica: Scritti su fascismo, antifascismo e continuità dello Stato* (Turin, 1995), 7.

4. P. Judson, 'Changing meanings of "German" in Habsburg Central Europe', in Charles Ingrao and Franz Szabo, eds., *The Germans and the East* (West Lafayette, IN, 2007) 109–28, here 116.

5. F. Epstein, 'Friedrich Meinecke on Eastern Europe', in Epstein, ed., *Germany and the East: Selected Essays* (Bloomington, IN, 1973), 37.

6. J. Remak, 'The Healthy Invalid: How Doomed was the Habsburg Empire?', *Journal of Modern History*, 41:2 (June 1969), 127–43; A. Kogan, 'Social Democracy and the Conflict of Nationalities in the Habsburg Monarchy', *Journal of Modern History*, 21:3 (September 1949), 204–11.

7. M. Cornwall, 'The Struggle on the Czech–German Language Border, 1880–1940', *English Historical Review* 109:433 (September 1994), 914–51; D. Low, *The Anschluss Movement, 1918–1919 and the Paris Peace Conference* (Philadelphia, 1974), 15.

8. W. D. Smith, 'Friedrich Ratzel and the Origins of Lebensraum', *German Studies Review*, 3:1 (February 1980), 51–68; G. Kiss, 'Political Geography into Geopolitics: Recent Trends in Germany', *Geographical Review*, 32:4 (October 1942), 632–45; K. Lange, 'Der terminus "Lebensraum" in Hitlers "Mein Kampf"', *Vierteljahrshefte für Zeitgeschichte*, 13:4 (1965), 426–37.

9. W. F. Reddaway, 'Prussian Poland: 1850–1914', in W. F. Reddaway, J. H. Penson, O. Halecki and R. Dyboski, eds., *The Cambridge History of Poland: From Augustus II to Pilsudski (1697–1935)* (Cambridge, 1951), 409–22.

10. R. L. Koehl, 'Colonialism inside Germany, 1886–1918', *Journal of Modern History*, 25:3 (September 1953), 255–72; R. W. Tims, *Germanizing Prussian Poland: The H-K-T Society and the Struggle for the Eastern Marches in the German Empire, 1894–1919* (New York, 1941), 54.

11. Cited in J. M. Winiewicz, *Aims and Failures of the German New Order* (London, 1943), 19.

12. J.-R. Pare, 'Les "Ecrits de jeunesse" du Max Weber: l'histoire agraire, le nationalisme et les paysans', *Canadian Journal of Political Science*, 28:3 (1995), 437–54; W. Mommsen, *Max Weber and German Politics, 1890–1920* (Chicago, 1984), ch. 2; Höhn, in *Festgabe für Heinrich Himmler* (Darmstadt, 1941).

13. Kaminski, 'Bismarck and the Polish Question', 235–50; Tims, *Germanizing Prussian Poland*, 244.

14. Winiewicz, *Aims and Failures*, 20; Tims, *Germanizing Prussian Poland*, 34.

15. Ibid., 142, 269; W. Hagen, *Germans, Poles and Jews: The Nationality Conflict in the Prussian East, 1772–1914* (Chicago, 1980), 307.

16. Cited by W. Hagen, ibid., 283–4.

17. F. Epstein, 'East Central Europe as a Power Vacuum between East and West during the German Empire', in Epstein, ed., *Germany and the East*, 56–7.

18. O. Fedyshyn, *Germany's Drive to the East and the Ukrainian Revolution, 1917–1918* (New Brunswick, 1971), 23.

19. A. Polonsky, 'The German Occupation of Poland during the First and Second World Wars: A Comparison,' in Prete and Ion, eds., *Armies of Occupation*, 97–142; M. Handelsman, *La Pologne: sa vie économique et sociale pendant la guerre* (Paris, 1933), 83–99, 124–7.

20. Ibid., 170–71; I. Geiss, *Der polnische Grenzstreifen, 1914–1918: Ein Beitrag zur deutschen Kriegszielpolitik im Ersten Weltkrieg* (Lübeck, 1960), 172.
21. Hull, *Absolute Destruction*, 256–7;, 259; D. G. Rempel, 'The Expropriation of the German Colonists in Southern Russia during the Great War', *Journal of Modern History*, 4:1 (March 1932), 49–67; P. Gatrell, *A Whole Empire Walking: Refugees in Russia during World War 1* (Bloomington, IN, 2005), ch.1; E. Lohr, *Nationalizing the Russian Empire: The Campaign against Enemy Aliens during World War 1* (Cambridge, MA, 2003).
22. Polonsky, 'The German Occupation of Poland', 127–8.
23. F. Fischer, *Germany's Aims in the First World War* (New York, 1967), 103–42; Hull, *Absolute Destruction*, 206–11, 234–40.
24. V. G. Liulevicius, *War Land on the Eastern Front: Culture, National Identity and German Occupation in World War I* (Cambridge, 2000); Hull, *Absolute Destruction*, 247–8, 259–62.
25. G. Fong, 'The Movement of German Divisions to the Western Front, Winter 1917–1918', *War in History*, 7:2 (2000); Liulevicius, *War Land*, 205.
26. Fischer, *Germany's Aims*, 546–9; R. Koehl, 'A Prelude to Hitler's Greater Germany', *American Historical Review*, 59:1 (October 1953), 43–65; H. Herwig, 'Tunes of Glory at the Twilight Stage: The Bad Homburg Crown Council and the Evolution of German Statecraft, 1917/1918', *German Studies Review*, 6:3 (October 1983), 475–94.
27. R. Waite, *Vanguard of Nazism: The Free Corps Movement in Postwar Germany, 1918–1923* (New York, 1952), 118; R. Höss, *Death Dealer: The Memoirs of the SS Kommandant at Auschwitz* (New York, 1996), 60.
28. Von Salomon, cited by R. Waite, *Vanguard of Nazism*, 108, 129.
29. Ibid., appendix.
30. Herwig, 'Tunes of Glory', 478.
31. J. Goebbels, *The Goebbels Diaries, 1942–43*, ed. L. Lochner (New York, 1948), 126.

Chapter 2: Versailles to Vienna

1. M. Burleigh, *Germany Turns Eastwards: A Study of Ostforschung in the Third Reich* (Cambridge 1988), 145.
2. Cited by M. Dockrill and J. D. Goold, *Peace without Promise: Britain and the Peace Conferences, 1919–1923* (London, 1981), 24.
3. Ibid., 3; J. W. Headlam, *A Memoir of the Paris Peace Conference, 1919* (London, 1972), 127–8.
4. T. Bottomore and P. Goode, eds., *Austro-Marxism* (Oxford, 1978), 31; R. Steininger, '12 November 1918–12 March 1938: The Road to the Anschluss', in R. Steininger, G. Bischof and M. Gehler, eds., *Austria in the 20th Century* (New Brunswick, 2002), 85–114, here 85–7; F. Carsten, *The First Austrian Republic, 1918–1938: A Study Based on British and Austrian Documents* (Aldershot, 1986).
5. S. W. Gould, 'Austrian Attitudes toward Anschluss: October 1918–September 1919', *Journal of Modern History*, 22:3 (September 1950), 220–31; D. P. Myers, 'Berlin *versus* Vienna: Disagreements about *Anschluss* in the Winter of 1918–1919', *Central European History*, 5:2 (June, 1972), 150–75.
6. P. R. Sweet, 'Seipel's Views on Anschluss in 1928: An Unpublished Exchange of Letters', *Journal of Modern History*, 19:4 (December 1947), 320–323.
7. F. G. Campbell, 'The Struggle for Upper Silesia, 1919–1922', *Journal of Modern History*, 42:3 (September 1970), 361–85; M. Housden, 'Ewalde Ammende and the Organization of National Minorities in Interwar Europe', *German History*, 18:4 (2000), 439–60, 449. Basic data from J. P. Schechtman, *European Population Transfers, 1939–1945* (New York, 1946), 29; interwar census data in R. P. Magocsi, *Historical Atlas of East Central Europe* (Seattle, 1993).
8. J. Hiden, *The Baltic States and Weimar Ostpolitik* (Cambridge, 1987).

9. Housden, 'Ewald Ammende and the Organization of National Minorities'.
10. J. Koralka, 'Germany's Attitude to the National Disintegration of Cisleithania', *Journal of Contemporary History*, 4:2 (April 1969), 85–95; F. G. Campbell, *Confrontation in Central Europe: Weimar Germany and Czechoslovakia* (Chicago, 1975), 76.
11. Ibid., 82–3; J. W. Bruegel, 'The Germans in Prewar Czechoslovakia', in V. Mamatey and R. Luza, eds., *A History of the Czechoslovak Republic, 1918–1948* (Princeton, 1973), 175; E. Wiskemann, *Czechs and Germans* (Oxford, 1938); D. Miller, 'Colonising the Hungarian and German Border Areas during the Czech Land Reform, 1918–1938', *Austrian History Yearbook*, 34 (2003), 303–17.
12. H. van Rieckhoff, *German–Polish Relations, 1918–1933* (Baltimore, 1971), 18; H. Stern, 'The Organisation Consul', *Journal of Modern History*, 35:1 (March 1963), 20–32.
13. R. Blanke, *Orphans of Versailles: The Germans in Western Poland, 1918–1939* (Lexington, KY, 1993), ch. 2.
14. R.Blanke, 'The German Minority in Interwar Poland and German Foreign Policy: Some Reconsiderations', *Journal of Contemporary History*, 25 (1990), 87–102; E. Wiskemann, *Germany's Eastern Neighbours* (Oxford, 1956), 20; C. Raitz von Frentz, *A Lesson Forgotten: Minority Protection under the League of Nations: The Case of the German Minority in Poland, 1920–1934* (New York, 1999), 213–16.
15. The January 1925 memo, cited in R. Steininger, '12 Nov. 1918–12 March 1938: The Road to the Anschluss', in Steininger et al., eds., *Austria in the 20th Century*, 98; C. Fink, *Defending the Rights of Others: The Great Powers, the Jews and International Minority Protection, 1878–1938* (Cambridge, 2004), 298; Raitz von Frentz, *A Lesson Forgotten*, 160.
16. H. B. Calderwood, 'International Affairs: Should the Council of the League of Nations Establish a Permanent Minorities Commission?', *American Political Science Review*, 27:2 (April 1933), 250–59; H. B. Calderwood, 'International Affairs: The Proposed Generalization of the Minorities Regime', *American Political Science Review*, 28:6 (December 1934), 1088–98; Fink, 'Stresemann's Minority Policies, 1924–1929', *Journal of Contemporary History* (1979), 403–22, at 420 n. 37.
17. K. Fiedor, 'Attitude of German Rightwing Organisations to Poland in the Years 1918–1933', *Polish Western Affairs*, 14:2 (1973), 247–67.
18. A. Komjathy and R. Stockwell, *German Minorities and the Third Reich: Ethnic Germans of East Central Europe between the Wars* (New York, 1980), 3; Burleigh, *Germany Turns Eastward*.
19. S. Suval, 'Overcoming *Kleindeutschland*: The Politics of Historical Mythmaking in the Weimar Republic', *Central European History*, 3 (1969), 312–30, Lach cited pp. 326–7.
20. P. R. Sweet, 'The Historical Writing of Heinrich von Srbik', *History and Theory*, 9:1 (1970), 37–58, 48.
21. O. Hammen, 'German Historians and the Advent of the National Socialist State', *Journal of Modern History*, 13:2 (June 1941), 161–88; R. Ross, 'Heinrich Ritter von Srbik and "Gesamtdeutsch" History', *Review of Politics*, 31:1 (January 1969), 88–107; M. Ruehl, 'In This Time Without Emperors: The Politics of Ernst Kantorowicz's *Kaiser Friedrich der Zweite* Reconsidered', *Journal of the Warburg and Courtauld Institutes*, 63 (2000), 187–242.
22. Hammen, 'German Historians', 187–8.
23. Goebbels, *The Goebbels Diaries, 1939–1941*, 114.
24. Komjathy and Stockwell, *German Minorities and the Third Reich*, 8.
25. I. Kershaw, *Hitler, 1889–1936: Hubris* (New York, 1999), 330.
26. V. Lumans, *Himmler's Auxiliaries: The Volksdeutsche Mittelstelle and the German National Minorities of Europe, 1933–1945* (Chapel Hill, NC, 1993).
27. Burleigh, *Germany Turns Eastwards*, 145; I. Haar, 'German *Ostforschung* and Anti-Semitism', in I. Haar and M. Fahlbusch, eds., *German Scholars and Ethnic Cleansing, 1920–1945* (Oxford, 2005), 14.
28. V. Gott, 'The National Socialist Theory of International Law', *American Journal of International Law*, 32:4 (October 1938), 704–18; L. Preuss, 'National Socialist Concep-

tions of International Law', *American Political Science Review*, 29:4 (August 1935), 594–609.

29. R. Murphy et al., eds., *National Socialism: Basic Principles, Their Application by the Nazi Party's Foreign Organization and the Use of Germans Abroad for Nazi Aims* (Washington, 1943), 69.

30. Komjathy and Stockwell, *German Minorities and the Third Reich*, 85.

31. Hossbach memorandum in J. Noakes and G. Pridham, eds., *Nazism, 1919–1945: A Documentary Reader*, vol. 3: *Foreign Policy, War and Racial Extermination* (Exeter, 1991), 68–9; Göring and Mussolini, ibid., 699–700.

32. G. Botz, *Die Eingliederung Österreichs in das Deutsches Reich* (Linz, 1976), 41–4.

33. Ibid., 82–100; J. K. Pollock, *The Government of Greater Germany* (New York, 1938), 150–51.

34. J. von Lang, ed., *Eichmann Interrogated: Transcripts from the Archives of the Israeli Police* (New York, 1999), 56–62.

35. H. Safrian, *Eichmann und seine Gehilfen* (Frankfurt, 1995), 28–31; F. Bajohr, 'The Holocaust and Corruption', in G. Feldman and W. Seibel, eds., *Networks of Nazi Persecution: Bureaucracy, Business and the Organization of the Holocaust* (New York, 2005), 121.

36. Safrian, *Eichmann und seine Gehilfen*, 44–5.

37. Steininger, 'The Road to Anschluss', 112–13.

38. R. Schwarz, 'Bürckel and Innitzer', in F. Parkinson, ed., *Conquering the Past: Austrian Nazism Yesterday and Today* (Detroit, 1989), 143.

39. M. Williams, 'German Imperialism and Austria, 1938', *Journal of Contemporary History*, 14:1 (January 1979), 139–53; E. Bukey, 'Popular Opinion in Vienna after the Anschluss', in Parkinson, ed., *Conquering the Past*, 151–65.

Chapter 3: Expansion and Escalation: 1938–40

1. From *Gemeinschaftslieder. Lieder für Frauengruppen* (1940) cited and translated (with adaptations) in N. Frei, *National Socialist Rule in Germany: The Führer State, 1933–1945* (Oxford, 1993), 192.

2. Noakes and Pridham, eds., *Nazism, 1919–1945*, 629.

3. Best's comment on imperialism is described in H. Höhne, *The Order of the Death's Head: The Story of Hitler's SS* (New York, 1970); U. von Hassell, *The von Hassell Diaries, 1938–1944* (London 1948), 71, 75, 86; figures for the Polish campaign from C. Madajczyk, *Die Okkupationspolitik Nazideutschlands in Polen, 1939–1945* (Berlin, 1987), 312.

4. K. Robbins, 'Konrad Henlein, the Sudeten Question and British Foreign Policy', *Historical Journal*, 12:4 (December 1969), 674–97, here 696.

5. W. Murray, *The Change in the European Balance of Power, 1938–1939: The Path to Ruin* (Princeton, 1984); R. J. Young, 'The Aftermath of Munich', *French Historical Studies*, 8:2 (Autumn 1973), 305–22.

6. H. Groscurth, *Tagebücher eines Abwehroffiziers, 1938–1940* (Stuttgart, 1970), 140–47; H. Umbreit, 'Structures of German Occupation Policy during the Initial Phase of the German–Soviet War', in B. Wegner, ed., *From Peace to War: Germany, Soviet Russia and the World, 1939–1941* (Oxford, 1997), 244.

7. R. Gebel, *'Heim ins Reich!' Konrad Henlein und der Reichsgau Sudetenland (1938–1945)* (Munich, 1999), 222–33.

8. T. Prochaska, 'The Second Republic, 1938–1939', in Mamatey and Luza, eds., *A History of the Czechoslovak Republic*, 255–61.

9. V. Mastny, *The Czechs under Nazi Rule: The Failure of National Resistance, 1939–1942* (New York, 1972), 47–50.

10. E. Erdely, *Germany's First European Protectorate: The Fate of the Czechs and the Slovaks* (London, 1942), 40–41.

11. Mastny, *The Czechs under Nazi Rule*, 51; M. Moskowitz, 'Three Years of the Protectorate of Bohemia and Moravia', *Political Science Quarterly*, 57:3 (September 1942), 353–75; Militärgeschichtliches Forschungsamt, ed., *Germany and the Second World War* vol. 5: *Organization and Mobilizations of the German Sphere of Power*, ed. B. Kroener et al. (Oxford, 2000), 39–40.

12. J. Milotova, 'Die NS-Pläne zur Lösung der "tschechischen Frage"', in D. Brandes, E. Ivanickova and J. Pesek, eds., *Erzwungene Trennung: Vertreibungen und Aussiedlungen in und aus der Tschechoslowakei 1938–1947 in Vergleich mit Polen, Ungarn und Jugoslawien* (Tübingen, 1999), 23–37, here 24.

13. A. Speer, *Inside the Third Reich* (London, 1970), 147; Mastny, *The Czechs under Nazi Rule*, 54; G. Kennan, *From Prague after Munich: Diplomatic Papers, 1938–1940* (Princeton, 1968), 146–7.

14. James Ward's Stanford University doctoral thesis on Tiso should provide the definitive study of his career.

15. J. Hoensch, 'The Slovak Republic, 1939–1945', in Mamatey and Luza, eds., *A History of the Czechoslovak Republic*, 271–95.

16. G. Ciano, *Ciano's Diary, 1939–1943*, ed. M. Muggeridge (London, 1947), 45; A. Hitler, *Hitler: Speeches and Proclamations, 1932–1945*, ed. M. Domarus, vol. 3 (1939–1940) (Wauconda, IL, 1997), 1523–35.

17. Ciano, *Ciano's Diary*, 124.

18. Cited in Noakes and Pridham, eds., *Nazism, 1919–1945*, 743.

19. A. Rossino, *Hitler Strikes Poland: Blitzkrieg, Ideology and Atrocity* (Lawrence, KS, 2003), 196–7.

20. Ibid., 27.

21. M. Broszat, *Nationalsozialistische Polenpolitik, 1939–1945* (Stuttgart, 1961), 19–20; Rossino, *Hitler Strikes Poland*, 13–15.

22. Ibid., 77, 159.

23. E. B. Westermann, ' "Friend and Helper": German Uniformed Police Operations in Poland and the General Government, 1939–1941', *Journal of Military History*, 58:4 (October 1994), 643–62; A. de Zayas, *Wehrmacht War Crimes Bureau, 1939–1945* (Lincoln, NE, 1989), 141.

24. C. Jansen and A. Weckbecker, 'Eine Miliz im "Weltanschauungskrieg": der "Volksdeutsche Selbstschutz" in Polen, 1939/40', in Michalka, ed., *Der Zweite Weltkrieg*, 482–501. My thanks too to Catherine Epstein for allowing to me to read relevant sections of her forthcoming study of Arthur Greiser.

25. Estimates for the numbers of ethnic German fatalities from de Zayas, *The Wehrmacht War Crimes Bureau*, 139–40, a fascinating book but one to be used with care. 2,000 is a postwar Polish estimate; 6,000 the figure reached at the time by Wehrmacht investigators.

26. Rossino, *Hitler Strikes Poland*, 69–73.

27. Ibid., 175.

28. C. Browning, *The Origins of the Final Solution: The Evolution of Nazi Jewish Policy, September 1939–March 1942; With Contributions by Jürgen Matthäus* (Lincoln, NE, 2004), 17; H. Umbreit, *Deutsche Militärverwaltungen 1938/39: Die militärische Besetzung der Tschechoslowakei und Polens* (Stuttgart, 1977), 154–5; Rossino, *Hitler Strikes Poland*, 116–17; G. Engel, *At the Heart of the Reich: The Secret Diary of Hitler's Army Adjutant* (London, 2005), 79 (entries for 15/10 and 18/11/39).

29. Umbreit, *Deutsche Militärverwaltungen 1938/39*, 91–3.

30. Noakes and Pridham, eds., *Nazism, 1919–1945*, vol. 3, 927.

31. Engel, *At the Heart of the Reich*, 75.

32. Madajczyk, *Die Okkupationspolitik Nazideutschlands*, 30–35.

33. Engel, *At the Heart of the Reich*, 76.

34. Hitler, *Hitler: Speeches and Proclamations*, 1840–46.

35. Ciano, *Ciano's Diary* 166–70; Goebbels, *The Goebbels Diaries, 1939–1941*, 15.

36. Ibid., 16.

37. *Krakauer Zeitung*, 24 April 1941, cited in Polish Ministry of Information, *The German New Order in Poland* (London, 1942), 8.
38. Frank, cited in J. Connelly, 'Nazis and Slavs: From Racial Theory to Racist Practice', *Central European History*, 32:1 (1999), 1–33, here 8.
39. D. Rebentisch, *Führerstaat und Verwaltung im Zweiten Weltkrieg: Verfassungsentwicklung und Verwaltungspolitik, 1939–1945* (Stuttgart, 1989), 172–3.
40. W. Präg and W. Jacobmeyer, eds., *Das Diensttagebuch des deutschen Generalgouverneurs in Polen, 1939–1945* (Stuttgart, 1975), 113–17; International Military Tribunal, *Trial of the Major War Criminals before the Nuernberg Military Tribunal under Control Council Law No. 10*, 14 vols. (Washington, DC, 1949–53) (hereafter *TWC*), vol. 5 (Washington, DC, 1951), 20–21 ('The significance of the collapse of the Polish state from the point of view of international law', 15 May 1940).
41. C. Madajczyk, 'Legal Conceptions in the Third Reich and Its Conquests', *Michael*, 13 (1993), 131–59, here 135–6; T. Szarota, *Warschau unter dem Hakenkreuz* (Paderborn, 1978), 48–9; Präg and Jacobmeyer, *Das Diensttagebuch des deutschen Generalgouverneurs*, 247.

Chapter 4: The Partition of Poland

1. Cited in the excellent new study by P. T. Rutherford, *Prelude to the Final Solution: The Nazi Program for Deporting Ethnic Poles, 1939–1941* (Lawrence, KS, 2007), 30.
2. I. Haar, 'German *Ostforschung* and Anti-Semitism', in Haar and Fahlbusch, eds., *German Scholars and Ethnic Cleansing*, 1–28.
3. Schechtman, *European Population Transfers*, 53–5; note that there was also a transfer clause in the settlement with Czechoslovakia over the Sudetenland, though this was never brought into effect.
4. Reitlinger, *The House Built on Sand*, 44–5; P. Lossowski, 'The Resettlement of the Germans from the Baltic States in 1939/41', *Acta Poloniae Historica*, 92 (2005), 79–98.
5. M. Carlyle, ed., *Documents on International Affairs, 1939–1946*, vol. 2: *Hitler's Europe* (London, 1954), 23.
6. Winiewicz, *Aims and Failures*, 4; Schechtman, *European Population Transfers*, 171.
7. Lossowski, 'The Resettlement of the Germans from the Baltic States', passim; V. Lumans, 'A Reassessment of *Volksdeutsche* and Jews in the Volhynia-Galicia-Narew Resettlement', in A. Steinweis and D. E. Rogers, eds., *The Impact of Nazism* (Lincoln, NE, 2003), 87–100.
8. Polish Ministry of Information, *The German New Order in Poland* (London, 1942), 181.
9. Klukowski, *Diary from the Years of Occupation*, 41.
10. Estimates of Jewish emigration discussed in Kulischer, *Europe on the Move*, 190–91.
11. Rutherford, *Prelude to the Final Solution*, 48–53.
12. Von Lang, ed., *Eichmann Interrogated*, 59–61.
13. C. Browning, 'Nazi Resettlement Policy and the Search for a Solution to the Jewish Question, 1939–1941', in his *The Path to Genocide: Essays on Launching the Final Solution* (Cambridge, 1992), 3–27.
14. H. S. Levine, 'Local Authority and the SS State: The Conflict over Population Policy in Danzig-West Prussia, 1939–1945', *Central European History*, 3 (1969), 331–55; on the fate of Gdynia, see Polish Ministry of Information, *The German New Order in Poland*, 207.
15. P. Rutherford, ' "Absolute Organizational Deficiency": The *1. Nahplan* of December 1939 (Logistics, Limitations, and Lessons)', *Central European History*, 36:2 (2003), 235–72, here 241.
16. Rutherford, *Prelude to the Final Solution*, 258.
17. Ibid., 246–8, 248.
18. Noakes and Pridham, eds., *Nazism, 1919–1945*, 937–40.
19. Browning, *The Origins of the Final Solution*, 114–15.
20. Ibid., 169–72. Further details of the Madagascar Plan in the next chapter.

21. M. Housden, *Hans Frank: Lebensraum and the Holocaust* (New York, 2003), 132–7.
22. Rutherford, *Prelude to the Final Solution*, 174–5.
23. Ibid., 164.
24. Ibid., 159–64.
25. E. Harvey, 'Management and Manipulation: Nazi Settlement Planners and Ethnic German Settlers in Occupied Poland', in C. Elkins and S. Pedersen, eds., *Settler Colonialism in the Twentieth Century* (New York, 2005), 95–113.
26. Noakes and Pridham, eds., *Nazism, 1919–1945*, 962–5.
27. Polish Ministry of Information, *The German New Order in Poland*, passim; Präg and Jacobmeyer, eds., *Das Diensttagebuch des deutschen Generalgouverneurs*, 220.
28. Ibid., 119–20, 178.
29. F. Bajohr, 'The Holocaust and Corruption', in Feldman and Seibel, eds., *Networks of Nazi Persecution*, 118–41.
30. Madajczyk, *Die Okkupationspolitik Nazideutschlands*, 42.
31. Präg and Jacobmeyer, eds., *Das Diensttagebuch des deutschen Generalgouverneurs*, 178–9; D. Mejer, *'Non-Germans' under the Third Reich: The Nazi Judicial and Administrative System in Germany and Occupied Eastern Europe with Special Regard to Occupied Poland, 1939–1945* (Baltimore, 2003), 210.
32. H. Harten, *De-Kulturation und Germanisierung: Die Nazionalsozialistische Rassen- und Erziehungspolitik in Polen 1939–1945* (Frankfurt, 1996), 88–92; Mejer, *'Non-Germans' under the Third Reich*, 208.
33. On Jäger, see C. Epstein's forthcoming biography of Arthur Greiser, ch. 5. I am indebted to Professor Epstein for allowing me to see a draft of this.
34. Polish Ministry of Information, *The German New Order in Poland*, 408–9; Schechtman, *European Population Transfers*, 337–8.
35. Polish Ministry of Information, *The German New Order in Poland*, 156–8, 165; Harten, *De-Kulturation und Germanisierung*, 86–7; C. Luczak, 'Nazi Spatial Plans in Occupied Poland (1939–1945)', *Studia Historiae Oeconomicae*, 12 (1978), 156.
36. J. Heydecker, *Un soldat allemand dans le ghetto de Varsovie 1941* (Paris, 1986), 45–6, 88–90.
37. A. Rieber, 'Civil Wars in the Soviet Union,' *Kritika*, 4:1 (Winter 2003), 129–62.
38. J. Erickson, 'The Soviet March into Poland, Sept. 1939', and R. Szawlowski, 'The Polish-Soviet War of September 1939', both in K. Sword, ed., *The Soviet Takeover of the Polish Eastern Provinces* (London, 1991), 21–2, 28–44.
39. N. S. Lebedeva, 'The Deportation of the Polish Population to the USSR, 1939–1941', *Journal of Communist Studies and Transition Politics*, 16:12 (2000), 28–45; Rieber, 'Civil Wars in the Soviet Union'.
40. D. Engel, 'An Early Account of Polish Jewry under Nazi and Soviet Occupation Presented to the Polish Government-in-Exile, February 1940', *Jewish Social Studies*, 45:1 (1983), 1–16.
41. B. Pinchuk, *Shtetl Jews under Soviet Rule: Eastern Poland on the Eve of the Holocaust* (Oxford, 1990), 5.
42. Z. Sobieski, 'Reminiscences from Lwow, 1939–1946', *Journal of Central European Affairs*, 6:4 (January 1947), 351–74.
43. V. Riismandel, 'Soviet Law in Occupied Estonia', *Baltic Review*, 5 (June 1955), 23–42; D. Marples, 'Western Ukraine and Western Belorussia under Soviet Occupation: The Development of Socialist Farming, 1939–1941', *Revue Canadienne des Slavistes*, 27:2 (June 1985), 158–77; W. Bonusiak, 'Die Landwirtschaftspolitik der sowjetischen Besatzungsmacht auf dem Gebiet des sog. westlichen Weissrusslands in den Jahren 1939–1949', *Studia Historicae Oeconomicae*, 24 (2001), 149–63.
44. G. Swain, *Between Stalin and Hitler: Class War and Race War on the Dvina, 1940–1946* (London, 2004), 55; A. Rossino, 'Polish "Neighbours" and German Invaders: Anti-Jewish Violence in the Bialystok District during the Opening Weeks of Operation Barbarossa', *Polin*, 16 (2003), 431–52.

45. Germany, Auswärtiges Amt, *Amtliches Material zum Massenmord von Katyn* (Berlin, 1943).

Chapter 5: Summer 1940

1. Germany, Auswärtiges Amt, *Documents on German Foreign Policy, 1918–1945*, series D (1937–1945), 13 vols. (1937–45) (hereafter *DGFP*), vol. 9 (Washington, DC, 1956), 7.
2. R. J. Overy, *Goering: The 'Iron Man'* (London, 1984), ch. 4.
3. H. A. Jacobsen, 'Formen nationalsozialistischer Bündnispolitik', in H. Kling, ed., *Der nationalsozialistische Krieg* (Frankfurt, 1990), 231–8; July naval memo cited in Militärgeschichtliches Forschungsamt, ed., *Germany and the Second World War*, vol. 3: *The Mediterranean, South-east Europe and North Africa, 1939–1941*, ed. G. Schreiber et al. (Oxford, 1995), 291.
4. Ibid., vol. 5:1, 66.
5. K. Kwiet, 'Vorbereitung und Auflösung der deutschen Militärverwaltung in den Niederlanden', *Militärgeschichtliche Mitteilungen*, 1 (1969), 121–53.
6. W. Warmbrunn, *The Dutch under German Occupation, 1940–1945* (Stanford, 1963), 27–8, 131–2; J. Goebbels, *Tagebücher*, ed. R. Reuth (Munich, 1999), vol. 4 (1940–1942), 1424.
7. *DGFP*, vol. 11 (Washington, DC, 1960), 612–19; Goering cited in W. Lipgens, ed., *Documents on the History of European Integration*, vol. 1 (Berlin, 1984), 57.
8. W. Warmbrunn, *The German Occupation of Belgium, 1940–1944* (New York, 1993), 110–13; J. H. Geller, 'The Role of Military Administration in German-occupied Belgium, 1940–1944', *Journal of Military History*, 63:1 (1999), 99–125.
9. J. Jackson, *The Fall of France: The Nazi Invasion of 1940* (Oxford, 2003), 174–82.
10. J. David, *A Square of Sky: Memories of a Wartime Childhood* (London, 1992), 109.
11. Noakes and Pridham, eds., *Nazism, 1919–1945*, 882.
12. I. Hueck, ' "Spheres of Influence" and "*Völkisch*" Legal Thought: Reinhard Höhn's Notion of Europe', in C. Joerges and N. S. Ghaleigh, eds., *Darker Legacies of Law: The Shadow of National Socialism and Fascism over Europe and Its Legal Traditions* (Oxford, 2003), 71–87; Best's ideas in U. Herbert, *Best: Biographische Studien über Radikalismus, Weltanschauung und Vernunft, 1903–1989* (Bonn, 2001), 268–9.
13. J. Jackson, *France. The Dark Years, 1940–1944* (Oxford, 2001), 126–36.
14. N. Wylie, 'Switzerland', in Wylie, ed., *European Neutrals and Non-Belligerents during the Second World War* (Cambridge, 2002), 331–54.
15. H. A. DeWeerd, 'Hitler's Plans for Invading Britain', *Military Affairs*, 12:3 (1948), 147–8; A. Hillgruber, 'England's Place in Hitler's Plans for World Dominion', *Journal of Contemporary History*, 9:1 (January 1974), 5–22.
16. W. Schellenberg, *Invasion 1940: The Nazi Invasion Plan for Britain*, intro. J. Erickson (London, 2000).
17. G. O. Kent, 'Britain in the Winter of 1940 as Seen from the Wilhelmstrasse', *The Historical Journal*, 6:1 (1963), 120–30.
18. N. J. W. Goda, 'The Reluctant Belligerent: Franco's Spain and Hitler's War', in C. Kent et al., eds., *The Lion and the Eagle: Interdisciplinary Essays on German–Spanish Relations over the Centuries* (London, 2000), 383–96.
19. W. Bowen, *Spaniards and Nazi Germany: Collaboration in the New Order* (Columbia, MO), 77–9; C. Burdick, *Germany's Military Strategy and Spain in World War II* (Syracuse, 1968), 119–88.
20. W. Schmokel, *Dreams of Empire: German Colonialism, 1919–1945* (New Haven, 1964), 128.
21. *DGFP*, vol. 11, 484; D. Eichholtz, 'Unfreie Arbeit-Zwangsarbeit', in Eichholtz, ed., *Krieg und Wirtschaft* (Berlin, 1999), 129–57, here 145; K. Linne, ' "New Labour Policy" in Nazi Colonial Planning for Africa', *International Review of Social History*, 49:2 (2004), 197–224.

22. G. Weinberg, 'German Colonial Plans and Policies, 1938–1942', in his *World in the Balance: Behind the Scenes of World War II* (Hanover, NH, 1981), 96–136; Schmokel, *Dreams of Empire*; 50–52.

23. Ibid.; K. Hildebrand, *Vom Reich zum Weltreich: Hitler, NSDAP und koloniale Frage, 1919–1945* (Munich, 1969); R. Herzstein, *When Nazi Dreams Come True: The Third Reich's Internal Struggle over the Future of Europe after a German Victory: A Look at the Nazi Mentality, 1939–45* (London, 1982), 25; R. W. Kestling, 'Blacks under the Swastika: A Research Note', *Journal of Negro History*, 83:1 (Winter 1998), 84–99.

24. *DGFP*, vol. 11, 171.

25. G. Anderl, 'Die "Zentralstellen für jüdische Auswanderung" in Wien, Berlin und Prag: Ein Vergleich', *Tel Aviver Jahrbuch für Deutsche Geschichte*, 23 (1994), 275–99; *DGFP*, vol. 10 (Washington, DC, 1958), 111–13; xi, 491; G. Hahn, *Grundfragen europäischer Ordnung: Ein Beitrag zur Neugestalung der Völkerrechtslehre* (Berlin, 1939); C. Browning, *The Final Solution and the German Foreign Office* (New York, 1978), 36–7; Präg and Jacobmeyer, eds., *Das Diensttagebuch des deutschen Generalgouverneurs*, 247–8.

26. C. Tonnini, *Operazione Madagascar: La questione ebraica in Polonia, 1918–1968* (Bologna, 1999), 17–135; also M. Brechtken, ' "La géographie demeure": Frankreich, Polen und die Kolonial- und Judenfrage am Vorabend des Zweiten Weltkrieges', *Francia*, 25:3 (1998), 25–60.

27. *DGFP*, vol. 10, 112–13.

28. Ibid. 305, 484; Gigurtu in *Time*, 5 August 1940; G. Aly and S. Heims, *Architects of Annihilation: Auschwitz and the Logic of Destruction* (Princeton, 2003), 164–5.

29. E. T. Jennings, *Vichy in the Tropics: Pétain's National Revolution in Madagascar, Guadeloupe, and Indochina, 1940–1944* (Stanford, 2001), 96.

30. Browning, *The Final Solution and the German Foreign Office*, 38, 42, 79; Noakes and Pridham, eds., *Nazism, 1919–1945*, 1077 (RSHA memo of 15 August 1940); Engel, *At the Heart of the Reich*, 103 [2/2/41].

31. Goebbels in Noakes and Pridham, eds., *Nazism, 1919–1945*, 900.

32. W. Warlimont, *Inside Hitler's Headquarters, 1939–1945* (London, 1964), 101; E. Weizsäcker, *Die Weizsäcker-Papiere, 1933–1950*, ed. L. E. Hill (Frankfurt, 1974), 205; von Hassell, *The von Hassell Diaries*, 139.

33. Predöhl cited in P. Fonzi, 'Nazionalsocialismo e nuovo ordine europeo: La discussione sulla "Grossraumwirtschaft" ', *Studi Storici*, 45:2 (2004), 313–65.

34. Noakes and Pridham, eds., *Nazism, 1919–1945*, 884–8.

35. Y. Jelinek, 'Slovakia's Internal Policy and the Third Reich, August 1940–Feb. 1941', *Central European History*, 4:3 (1971), 242–70; *DGFP*, vol. 9, 685; ibid., vol. 10, 16.

36. Herzstein, *When Nazi Dreams Come True*, 105.

37. W. Lipgens, ed., *Documents on the History of European Integration*, vol. 1, 55–71; R.-O. Mueller, 'The Mobilisation of the German War Economy for Hitler's War Aims', in Kroener, Mueller and Umbreit, *Germany and the Second World War*, 572; German discussion of Keynes in Fonzi, 'Nazionalsocialismo', 326–7.

38. Speer, *Inside the Third Reich*, 132–5; A. Speer, *Spandau: The Secret Diaries* (New York, 1976), 45, 80n.

39. Speer, *Inside the Third Reich*, 181.

40. J. Thies, 'Hitler's European Building Programme', *Journal of Contemporary History*, 13 (1978), 413–31; on Rügen, see W. Cook, 'Inside the Holiday Camp Hitler Built', *Observer*, 12 August 2001.

41. Thies, 'Hitler's European Building Programme', 426; Speer, *Inside the Third Reich*, 144, 181.

42. Ibid., 416.

43. *DGFP*, vol. 9, 507.

44. Italy, Ministero d'Affari Esteri, *I Documenti Diplomatici*, 9 (1939–1943) (hereafter *DDI*), vol. 5 (Rome, 1987) 9–10; vol. 6 (Rome, 1987), 399–400.

45. P. Schmidt, *Hitler's Interpreter* (London, 1951), 185.

46. *DGFP*, vol. 10, 440.

47. Benjamin Martin, 'German–Italian Cultural Initiatives and the Idea of a New Order in Europe, 1936–1945', D.Phil. thesis, Columbia University, 2006. My thanks to Benjamin Martin for discussing these issues with me and allowing me to quote from his dissertation.

48. Warlimont, *Inside Hitler's Headquarters*, 114.

49. I am extremely grateful to Holly Case for discussing her forthcoming work on this subject.

50. G. Weinberg, *Germany and the Soviet Union, 1939–1941* (Leiden, 1954), 106–25.

51. Reitlinger, *The House Built on Sand*, 47–9.

52. Ciano, *Ciano's Diary*, 388; on the Italian Balkan bloc, see Schreiber et al., *Germany and the Second World War*, 381.

53. *DGFP*, vol. 11, 639–41.

54. W. Manoschek, *'Serbien ist judenfrei': Militärische Besatzungspolitik und Judenvernichtung in Serbien, 1941/42* (Munich, 1993), 18–19.

55. Goebbels cited in H. Umbreit, 'Towards Continental Domination', in Militärgeschichtliches Forschungsamt, eds., *Germany and the Second World War*, vol. 5:1, 99.

56. See Hitler's letter to Mussolini, R. J. Sontag and J. S. Beddie, eds., *Nazi–Soviet Relations, 1939–1941* (Washington, DC, 1948), 347–53; Weizsäcker, *Weizsäcker-Papiere*, 222; Reitlinger, *The House Built on Sand*, 62.

Chapter 6: War of Annihilation: Into the Soviet Union

1. USA, Office of the United States Chief of Counsel for Prosecution of Axis Criminality, *Nazi Conspiracy and Aggression*, 8 vols. and supplements (Washington, DC, 1946–7) (hereafter *NCA*), Supplement A (Washington, DC, 1947), 331.

2. 'Weisung Nr 21. Fall Barbarossa vom 18. 12. 1940', in G. R. Überschär and W. Wette, eds., *'Unternehmen Barbarossa': Der deutsche Überfall auf die Sowjetunion 1941: Berichte, Analysen, Dokumente* (Paderborn, 1984), 298–300; K. J. Arnold, *Die Wehrmacht und die Besatzungspolitik in den besetzten Gebieten der Sowjetunion: Kriegsführung und Radikalisierung im 'Unternehmen Barbarossa'* (Berlin, 2005), 80–83. See also A. Kay, *Exploitation, Resettlement, Mass Murder: Political and Economic Planning for German Occupation Policy in the Soviet Union, 1940–1941* (New York, 2006), ch. 3.

3. Engel, *At the Heart of the Reich*, 96.

4. I. Maisky, *Memoirs of a Soviet Ambassador: The War, 1939–1943* (London: Hutchinson, 1967), 234–5.

5. G. R. Überschär, 'Das Scheitern des Unternehmens "Barbarossa"', in Überschär and Wette, *'Unternehmen Barbarossa'*, 151; 'Auszug aus Hitlers Ausführungen vom 30. 3. 1941 [Halder]', in ibid., 302–3; Bartov, *Hitler's Army*.

6. O. Bartov, *The Eastern Front, 1941–1945: German Troops and the Barbarization of Warfare* (New York, 1986).

7. H. Heer and K. Naumann, eds., *War of Extermination: The German Military in World War II, 1941–1944* (New York, 2000).

8. A. Hillgruber, 'The German Military Leaders' View of Russia', in Wegner, ed., *From Peace to War*, 169–87, here 179–80.

9. Ibid., 176–80; cf. the discussion in Arnold, *Die Wehrmacht und die Besatzungspolitik*, 52–5.

10. K. Schüler, 'The Eastern Campaign as a Transportation and Supply Problem', in Wegner, ed., *From Peace to War*, 206–19; 'Anordnung des ObH', 3 April 1941, in N. Müller, ed., *Deutsche Besatzungspolitik in der UdSSR, 1941–1944: Dokumente*, 35; Engel, *At the Heart of the Reich*, 105, 108.

11. Ben Shepherd, *War in the Wild East: The German Army and Soviet Partisans* (Cambridge, MA, 2004), 53; A. Dallin, *German Rule in Russia, 1941–1945: A Case Study of Occupation Politics* (Boulder, CO, 1981), 32–3.

12. J. Foerster, 'The German Army and the Ideological War against the Soviet Union', in

G. Hirschfeld, ed., *Policies of Genocide: Jews and Soviet Prisoners of War in Nazi Germany* (Boston, 1986), 18.

13. C. Streit, *Keine Kameraden: Die Wehrmacht und die sowjetischen Kriegsgefangenen, 1941–1945* (Bonn, 1997), 55–6; Foerster, 'The German Army and the Ideological War against the Soviet Union', 17.

14. C. Streit, 'The German Army and the Policies of Genocide', in Hirschfeld, ed., *Policies of Genocide*, 5–6.

15. C. Hartmann, 'Verbrecherischer Krieg – verbrecherische Wehrmacht?', *Vierteljahrshefte für Zeitgeschichte*, 21 (2004); N. Rich, *Hitler's War Aims*, vol. 2, 333.

16. Kay, *Exploitation*, 190–91.

17. Goebbels cited by J. Steinberg, 'The Third Reich Reflected: German Civil Administration in the Occupied Soviet Union, 1941–1944', *English Historical Review*, 110:437 (June 1995), 626; J. Billig, *Alfred Rosenberg dans l'action idéologique, politique et administrative du Reich hitlérien* (Paris, 1963), 197; J. Fest, *The Face of the Third Reich: Portraits of the Nazi Leadership* (London, 1979), 250.

18. Dallin, *German Rule*, 50–51; Kay, *Exploitation*, chs. 3–4.

19. G. Aly, *'The Final Solution': Nazi Population Policy and the Murder of the European Jews* (London, 1999), 161.

20. Göring cited in Shepherd, *War in the Wild East*, 25.

21. A. Dallin, *German Rule*, 39–40; Kay, *Exploitation*, 50–51.

22. Dallin, *German Rule*, 52–3; Arnold, *Die Wehrmacht und die Besatzungspolitik*, 85–7.

23. Dallin, *German Rule*, 54.

24. Ibid., 56.

25. Ibid., 76; H. Trevor-Roper, ed., *Hitler's Table Talk* (Oxford, 1988), 3–5.

26. 'Auszug aus einem Aktenvermerk von Reichsleiter M. Bormann vom 16. 7. 1941', Überschär and Wette, '*Unternehmen Barbarossa*', 330–31.

27. Rich, *Hitler's War Aims*, vol. 2, 326 seq.

28. Dallin, *German Rule*, 128; Göring, 31 July 1941, in Müller, *Deutsche Besatzungspolitik in der UdSSR*, 181; O. Bräutigam, *So hat es sich zugetragen ... Ein Leben als Soldat und Diplomat* (Würzburg, 1968), 343.

29. Rosenberg, in Überschär and Wette, '*Unternehmen Barbarossa*', 332; Reitlinger, *The House Built on Sand* 143; Kay, *Exploitation*, 193.

30. Steinberg, 'The Third Reich Reflected', 621; B. Chiari, *Alltag hinter der Front: Besatzung, Kollaboration und Widerstand in Weissrussland, 1941–1944* (Düsseldorf, 1998), 59–60.

31. Bräutigam, *So hat es sich zugetragen*, 366–71.

32. Rich, *Hitler's War Aims*, vol. 2, 378; *NCA*, Supplement A, 331.

33. A. Prusin, 'A Community of Violence: The SiPo/SD and its Role in the Nazi Terror System in Generalbezirk Kiew', *Holocaust and Genocide Studies*, 21:1 (Spring 2007), 1–30.

34. On Hans Koch, see A. Kappeler, 'Ukrainian History from a German Perspective', *Slavic Review*, 54:3 (Autumn 1995), 691–701.

35. T. Anderson, 'Germans, Ukrainians and Jews: Ethnic Politics in Heeresgebiet Süd June–December 1941', *War in History* 7:3 (2000), 321–51, here 336–46.

36. V. Lumans, *Latvia in World War Two* (New York, 2006), 175.

37. Rich, *Hitler's War Aims*, 358; Bräutigam, *So hat es sich zugetragen*, 355–6.

38. Rich, *Hitler's War Aims*, vol. 2, 360–62.

39. Ibid., 366; C. Gerlach, *Kalkulierte Morde: Die deutsche Wirtschafts- und Vernichtungspolitik in Weissrussland, 1941 bis 1944* (Hamburg, 1999), 196–9.

40. A. Rosenberg, *Letzte Aufzeichnungen: Ideale und Idole der nationalsozialistischen Revolution* (Göttingen, 1955), 166.

41. M. Broekmeyer, *Stalin, the Russians and their War, 1941–1945* (Madison, WI, 2004), 56–7; K. Berkhoff, *Harvest of Despair: Life and Death in Ukraine under Nazi Rule* (Cambridge, MA, 2004), 14–20.

42. Dallin, *German Rule*, 65; Anderson, 'Germans, Ukrainians and Jews', 337.

43. Dallin, *German Rule*, 64.
44. Ibid., 63.
45. Ibid., 57, 65.
46. Überschär and Wette, eds., '*Unternehmen Barbarossa*', 312, 316–18.
47. Dallin, *German Rule*, 66–9.
48. S. P. Mackenzie, 'The Treatment of Prisoners of War in World War II', *Journal of Modern History*, 66:3 (September 1994), 487–520.
49. M. Balfour, *Helmuth von Moltke: A Leader against Hitler* (London, 1972), 170, 175; G. van Roon, 'Graf Moltke als Völkerrechtler im OKW', *Vierteljahrshefte für Zeitgeschichte*, 18:1 (1970), 12–61.
50. Arnold, *Die Wehrmacht und die Besatzungspolitik*, 328–9; Mackenzie, 'The Treatment of Prisoners of War in World War II', 507. On Keitel and Jodl, International Military Tribunal, *Trial of the Major War Criminals before the International Military Tribunal, Nuremberg, 14 November 1945–1 October 1946*, 42 vols. (Nuremberg, 1947–9) (hereafter *TWCI*, vol. II (1947), 56; vol. 15 (1948), 360–61.
51. Arnold, *Die Wehrmacht und die Besatzungspolitik*, 336–7.
52. W. Lotnik, *Nine Lives: Ethnic Conflict in the Polish–Ukrainian Borderlands* (London, 1999), 26; Arnold, *Die Wehrmacht und die Besatzungspolitik*, 355–6.
53. Rich, *Hitler's War Aims*, vol. 2, 375.
54. Hartmann, 'Verbrecherischer Krieg'; Berkhoff, *Harvest of Despair*, ch. 4; Arnold, *Die Wehrmacht und die Besatzungspolitik*, 353.
55. C. Hartmann, ' "Massensterben oder Massenvernichtung": Sowjetische Kriegsgefangene im "Unternehmen Barbarossa" ', *Vierteljahrshefte für Zeitgeschichte*, 21 (2001), 102–58; Arnold, *Die Wehrmacht und die Besatzungspolitik*, 357.
56. Ibid., 372, 407; Mackenzie, 'The Treatment of Prisoners of War in World War II', 510–11; Gerlach, *Kalkulierte Morde*, 811; C. Streit, 'Soviet Prisoners of War in the Hands of the Wehrmacht', in Heer and Naumann, eds., *War of Extermination*, 80–91.
57. Gerlach, *Kalkulierte Morde*, 797–802; Streit, 'Soviet Prisoners of War', 82.
58. Müller, ed. *Deutsche Besatzungspolitik*, 195; Berkhoff, *Harvest of Despair*, 99, 164–8; Überschär and Wette, eds., '*Unternehmen Barbarossa*', 335; Militärgeschichtliches Forschungsamt, ed., *Germany and the Second World War*, vol. 5:1, 1166; K. J. Arnold, 'Die Eroberung und Behandlung der Stadt Kiev durch die Wehrmacht im September 1941: Zur Radikalisierung der Besatzungspolitik', *Militärgeschichtliche Mitteilungen*, 58:1 (1999), 23–63.
59. Rosenberg-Keitel, 28 February 1942, Überschär and Wette, eds., '*Unternehmen Barbarossa*', 399–400.
60. C. Hartmann, 'Massensterben oder Massenvernichtung?', citation 158.
61. Ibid.; Gerlach, *Kalkulierte Morde*, 814–17; U. Herbert, 'Labour and Extermination: Economic Interest and the Primacy of *Weltanschauung* in National Socialism', *Past and Present*, 138:2 (1993), 144–95.
62. A. Hill, *The War behind the Eastern Front: The Soviet Partisan Movement in North-west Russia, 1941–1944* (Abingdon, 2005), 69–70, 82–7; Hartman, 'Verbrecherische Krieg', 300.
63. Hill, *War behind the Eastern Front*, 55, 60; Shepherd, *War in the Wild East*, 60–62; Anderson, 'Germans, Ukrainians and Jews', 338–9.
64. Hill, *War behind the Eastern Front*, 47–8.
65. Shepherd, *War in the Wild East*, 95–8.
66. Ibid., 104–5.
67. S. Friedländer, *The Years of Extermination: Nazi Germany and the Jews, 1939–1945* (New York, 2007), 215–17.
68. Foerster, 'The German Army and Ideological War', 20; Anderson, 'Germans, Ukranians and Jews'; K. J. Arnold, 'Die Eroberung und Behandlung der Stadt Kiev durch die Wehrmacht in September 1941: Zur Radikalisierung der Besatzungspolitik', *Militärgeschichtliche Mitteilungen*, 58:1 (1999), 23–63.

69. Nebe cited in R. B. Birn, *Die höheren SS- und Polizeiführer: Himmlers Vertreter im Reich und in den besetzten Gebieten* (Düsseldorf, c. 1986) 286; Überschär and Wette, eds., '*Unternehmen Barbarossa*', 339–40, 344–5.

70. T. Anderson, 'Incident at Baranivka: German Reprisals and the Soviet Partisan Movement in Ukraine, October–December 1941', *Journal of Modern History*, 71:3 (September 1999), 585–623, here 602.

71. H. Heer, 'Killing Fields: The Wehrmacht and the Holocaust in Belorussia, 1941–1942', in Heer and Naumann, eds., *War of Extermination*, 55–80; also, W. Manoschek, ' "Coming along to Shoot some Jews?" The Destruction of the Jews in Serbia', ibid., 39–55; PS-3428, in S. Krieger, *Nazi Germany's War against the Jews* (New York, 1947).

72. L. Smilovitsky, 'Righteous Gentiles, the Partisans and Jewish Survival in Belorussia, 1941–1944', *Holocaust and Genocide Studies*, 11:3 (Winter 1997), 301–29.

73. M. Vestermanis, in Heer and Naumann, eds., *War of Extermination*, 'Local headquarters Liepaja: two months of German occupation in the summer of 1941', ibid., 219–36.

74. Müller, *Deutsche Besatzungspolitik in der UdSSR*, 72.

75. G. Swain, *Between Stalin and Hitler: Class War and Race War on the Dvina, 1940–1946* (London, 2004), 70.

76. P. Longerich, 'From Mass Murder to the "Final Solution": The Shooting of Jewish Civilians during the First Months of the Eastern Campaign within the Context of Nazi Jewish Genocide', in Heer and Naumann, eds., *War of Extermination*, 253–74.

77. Ibid.

78. W. Benz, ed., *Einsatz im Reichskommissariat Ostland: Dokumente zum Völkermord im Baltikum und in Weissrussland, 1941–1944* (Berlin, 1998), 33–5, 43.

79. Krieger, *Nazi Germany's War against the Jews*, 355–6; A. Strauga, 'The Holocaust in occupied Latvia, 1941–1945', in Symposium of the Commission of the Historians of Latvia, vol. 14, *The Hidden and Forbidden History of Latvia under Soviet and Nazi Occupation, 1940–1991* (Riga, 2005), 161–74; D. Erglis, 'A Few Episodes of the Holocaust in Kustpils: A Microcosm of the Holocaust in Occupied Latvia', ibid., 175–87.

80. P. Longerich, 'From Mass Murder to the "Final Solution" '.

81. Aly, '*The Final Solution*', 137–48; Rich, *Hitler's War Aims*, vol. 2, 352.

82. E. Haberer, 'The German Police and Genocide in Belorussia, 1941–1944. Part 1: Police Deployment and Nazi Genocidal Directives', *Journal of Genocide Research*, 3:1 (2001), 13–29.

83. Berkhoff, *Harvest of Despair*, 48; H. Buchheim, 'Die höheren SS- und Polizeiführer', *Vierteljahrshefte für Zeitgeschichte*, 11 (1963), 368–71; Haberer, 'The German Police and Genocide', 26–7.

84. L. Smilovitsky, 'A Demographic Profile of the Jews in Belorussia from the Prewar Time to the Postwar Time', *Journal of Genocide Research*, 5:1 (2003), 117–29.

Chapter 7: Make This Land German for Me Again!

1. C. Bryant, *Prague in Black: Nazi Rule and Czech Nationalism* (Cambridge, MA, 2007), 117.

2. A. Hohenstein [Franz Heinrich Bock], *Wartheländisches Tagebuch aus den Jahren 1941/42* (Stuttgart, 1961), 39.

3. Ibid., 174–5. This is a source to be used with care: see Furber, 'Going East', ch. 5.

4. Cited in Ferenc, *Quellen*, 51.

5. H. Pringle, *The Master Plan: Himmler's Scholars and the Holocaust* (New York, 2006).

6. Himmler in the June–July 1942 issue of *Deutsche Arbeiterpartei*, cited by C. Madajcyk, 'Deportations in the Zamosc Region in 1942 and 1943 in the Light of German Documents', *Acta Poloniae Historica*, 1 (1958), 78.

7. Taylor, *The Origins of the Second World War*.

8. See C. M. Hutton, *Race and the Third Reich: Linguistics, Racial Anthropology and Genetics in the Dialectic of Volk* (Cambridge, 2005) for a fascinating discussion.

9. I. Heinemann, '*Rasse, Siedlung, deutsches Blut*': *Das Rasse- und Siedlungshauptamt der SS und die rassepolitische Neuordnung Europas* (Göttingen, 2003), 119–22; I. Haar, 'German *Ostforschung* and Anti-Semitism', 15; E. Ehrenreich, 'Ottmar von Verschuer and the "Scientific" Legitimization of Nazi Anti-Jewish Policy', *Holocaust and Genocide Studies*, 21:1 (Spring 2007), 58–60; O. von Verschuer, 'Rassenbiologie der Juden', *Forschungen zur Judenfrage*, 3 (1938).

10. G. Aly and K. H. Roth, *The Nazi Census: Identification and Control in the Third Reich* (Philadelphia, 2004).

11. Gebel, '*Heim ins Reich!*', 222–7, 288; R. Koehl, *RKFDV: German Resettlement and Population Policy 1939–1945: A History of the Reich Commission for the Strengthening of Germandom* (Cambridge, MA, 1957), 40–41.

12. G. Köckenhoff, 'Grossraumgedanke und Völkische Idee im Recht', *Zeitschrift für Ausländisches öffentliches Recht und Völkerrecht*, 12 (1944), 34–82, here 34; J. Milotova, 'Die NS-Pläne zur Lösung der "tschechischen Frage" ', in Brandes et al., eds., *Erzwungene Trennung*, here 24; Connelly, 'Nazis and Slavs', here 5–6.

13. Heinemann, '*Rasse, Siedlung, deutsches Blut*', 127–49; Koehl, *RKFDV*, 42–3.

14. Cited by T. Zahra, *Kidnapped Souls: National Indifference and the Battle for Children in the Bohemian Lands, 1900–1945* (Ithaca, 2008), ch. 6. See also Ziemke-Foreign Ministry, 5 October 1940, in L. Poliakov and J. Wulf, eds., *Das Dritte Reich und seine Denker* (Wiesbaden, 1989), 492–3.

15. C. Bryant, 'Either German or Czech: Fixing Nationality in Bohemia and Moravia, 1939–1946', *Slavic Review*, 61:4 (Winter 2002), 683–706, here 688; Zahra, *Kidnapped Souls*, ch. 6, 289. My thanks to Tara Zahra for her help with this issue.

16. Bryant, 'Either German or Czech', 686–7.

17. 143,000 of these sought to reverse that decision after 1945. T. Zahra, 'Reclaiming Children for the Nation: Germanization, National Ascription and Democracy in the Bohemian Lands, 1900–1945', *Central European History*, 37:4 (2004), 501–43, here 529–30.

18. Ibid., 501, 530, 533.

19. Zahra, *Kidnapped Souls*, chs. 6, 8.

20. *TWC*, vol. 5, 91–4; Noakes and Pridham, eds., *Nazism, 1919–1945*, 951. Polish estimates gave 92 per cent Polish population and 6 per cent German, Schechtman, *European Population Transfers*, 264.

21. Noakes and Pridham, eds., *Nazism, 1919–1945*, 932–4.

22. *TWC*, vol. 5, 102–3; Heinemann, '*Rasse, Siedlung, deutsches Blut*', 193; Meyer memo of January 1940, W. Röhr and E. Heckert, eds., *Die faschistische Okkupationspolitik in Polen (1939–1945)* (Berlin, 1989), 159–60.

23. Heinemann, '*Rasse, Siedlung, deutsches Blut*', 228–30; Koehl, *RKFDV*, 117.

24. Noakes and Pridham, eds., *Nazism, 1919–1945*, 942–4.

25. *TWC*, vol. 4 (Washington, DC, 1949), 980–85; N. Goda, 'Black Marks: Hitler's Bribery of his Senior Officers during World War II', *Journal of Modern History*, 72:2 (June 2000), 413–52, here 447. Manstein himself was receiving significant gifts of money from Hitler.

26. Harten, *De-Kulturation und Germanisierung*, 86–7; V. O. Lumans, 'A Reassessment of Volksdeutsche and Jews in the Volhynia-Galicia-Narew Resettlement', in Steinweis and Rogers, eds., *The Impact of Nazism*, 81–100.

27. Präg and Jacobmeyer, eds., *Das Diensttagebuch des deutschen Generalgouverneurs*, 165, 210, 339.

28. Heinemann, '*Rasse, Siedlung, deutsches Blut*', 195; *TWC*, vol. 5, 102–5.

29. H. Himmler, *Heinrich Himmler: Geheimreden 1933 bis 1945*, ed. B. Smith and A. F. Peterson (Berlin, 1974), 142–3 (speech of February 1940).

30. *TWC*, vol. 4, 714–15; Schechtman, *European Population Transfers*, 343–6.

31. D. Bergen, 'The *Volksdeutsche* of Eastern Europe and the Collapse of the Nazi Empire, 1944–1945', in Steinweis and Rogers, eds., *The Impact of Nazism*, 101–28.
32. C. Luczak, 'Die Ansiedlung der deutschen Bevölkerung im besetzten Polen (1939–1945)', *Studia Historiae Oeconomicae*, 13 (1978), 193–205.
33. Noakes and Pridham, eds., *Nazism, 1919–1945*, 948; Koehl, *RKFDV*, 121; Levine, 'Local Authority and the SS State', 344.
34. Noakes and Pridham, eds., *Nazism, 1919–1945*, 949; Levine, 'Local Authority and the SS State', 340.
35. Koehl, *RKFDV*, 120; NO-5432, *TWC*, vol. 4, 819.
36. Connelly, 'Nazis and Slavs', 15–17.
37. 'Aufzeichnung über eine geheime Rede Hitlers vor Reichs-und Gauleitern in der Reichskanzlei', in Groscurth, *Tagebücher eines Abwehroffiziers*, 385; Rosenberg cited in Warlimont, *Inside Hitler's Headquarters*, 68; Militärgeschichtliches Forschungsamt, ed., *Germany and the Second World War*, vol. 5, 72.
38. C. Grohmann, 'From Lothringen to Lorraine: Expulsion and Voluntary Repatriation', *Diplomacy and Statecraft*, 16 (2005), 571–87; D. Harvey, 'Lost Children or Enemy Aliens? Classifying the Population of Alsace after the First World War', *Journal of Contemporary History*, 34:4 (October 1999), 537–54 gives a figure of 150,000 (p. 550); P. Maugue, *Le Particularisme Alsacien, 1918–1967* (Paris, 1970), 103.
39. Ibid., 107; A. Irjud, 'La Germanisation des noms en Alsace entre 1940 et 1944', *Revue d'Alsace*, 113 (1984), 239–61.
40. Heinemann, '*Rasse, Siedlung, deutsches Blut*', 309–15; Rich, *Hitler's War Aims*, vol. 2, 234–7.
41. *DGFP*, vol. 9 265–8; Warmbrunn, *The Dutch under German Occupation*, 85; Hirschfeld, *Nazi Rule and Dutch Collaboration*, 273–4; the basic article is H.-D. Loock, 'Zur "Grossgermanischen Politik" des Dritten Reiches', *Vierteljahrshefte für Zeitgeschichte*, 8 (1960), 37–64.
42. Rich, *Hitler's War Aims*, vol. 2, 137–8; Loock, 'Zur "Grossgermanischen Politik"', 56–7.
43. T. Ferenc, 'The Austrians and Slovenia during the Second World War', in Parkinson, ed., *Conquering the Past*, 207–24.
44. T. Dulic, *Utopias of Nation: Local Mass Killing in Bosnia and Hercegovina, 1941–1942* (Stockholm, 2005).
45. H. Harriman, *Slovenia under Nazi Occupation, 1941–1945* (New York, 1977), 38–46.
46. P. Witte et al., eds., *Der Dienstkalendar Heinrich Himmlers 1941/42* (Hamburg, 1999), 473–93.
47. F. Kersten, *The Kersten Memoirs, 1940–1945* (London, 1956), 132–7.
48. Speer, *Spandau*, 47–50.
49. On Christaller, see K. Bosma, 'Verbindungen zwischen Ost- und West-Kolonization', in M. Rössler and S. Schleiermacher, eds., *Der 'Generalplan Ost': Hauptlinien der nationalsozialistischen Planungs-und Vernichtungspolitik* (Berlin, 1993), 198–215; also M. Rössler, 'Applied Geography and Area Research in Nazi Society: Central Place Theory and Planning, 1933 to 1945', *Environment and Planning*, 7 (1989), 419–31.
50. C. Madajczyk, 'Introduction to General Plan East', *Polish Western Affairs*, 3:2 (1962).
51. M. Karny, J. Milotova and M. Karna, eds., *Deutsche Politik im 'Protektorat Böhmen und Mähren' unter Reinhard Heydrich, 1941–1942: Eine Dokumentation* (Berlin, 1997), 110–15; H. Trevor-Roper, ed., *Hitler's Table Talk*, 621 (8 August 1942).
52. Aly, *Architects of Annihilation*, 219–21.
53. H. Heiber, 'Der Generalplan Ost: Dokumentation', *Vierteljahrshefte für Zeitgeschichte*, 6 (1958), 280–326; Noakes and Pridham, eds., *Nazism, 1919–1945*, 977–9.
54. K. H. Roth, ' "Generalplan Ost"-"Gesamtplan Ost". Forschungsstand, Quellenprobleme, neue Ergebnisse', in Rössler and Schleiermacher, eds., *Der 'Generalplan Ost'*, 25–117.
55. Heinemann, '*Rasse, Siedlung, deutsches Blut*', 372–3; Rössler and Schleiermacher, eds., *Der 'Generalplan Ost'* 136–7.

56. Witte et al., ed., *Der Dienstkalendar Heinrich Himmlers*, 214; R. Hilbrecht, 'Litauen im Reichskommissariat Ostland 1941–1943/44', in R. Bohn, ed., *Die deutsche Herrschaft in den 'germanischen' Ländern 1940–1945* (Stuttgart, 1997), 187–209.

57. K. Brown, *A Biography of No Place: From Ethnic Borderland to Soviet Heartland* (Cambridge, MA, 2004), 192–205; W. Lower, 'Hitler's "Garden of Eden": Nazi Colonialism, *Volksdeutsche* and the Holocaust, 1941–1944', in J. Petropoulos and J. K. Roth, eds., *Grey Zones: Ambiguity and Compromise in the Holocaust and Its Aftermath* (New York, 2005), 185–204.

58. Trevor-Roper, ed., *Hitler's Table Talk*, 557 (4 July 1942).

59. B. Rieger, *Creator of the Nazi Death Camps: The Life of Odilo Globocnik* (London, 2007), 98.

60. Madajcyk, 'Deportations in the Zamosc Region', 75–106.

61. Ibid., 85.

62. B. Wasser, 'Die "Germanisierung" im Distrikt Lublin als Generalprobe und erst Realisierungsphase der GPO', in Rössler and Schleiermacher, eds., *Der 'Generalplan Ost'* 271–94; *TWC*, vol. 5, 128–9; *Polish Fortnightly Review*, 77 (1 October 1943), 6.

63. *TWC*, vol. 4, 737–9.

64. Röhr and Heckert, eds., *Die Faschistische Okkupationspolitik*, 203–4.

65. *TWC*, vol. 4, 951.

66. Harvey, 'Management and Manipulation', 105–8.

67. 'Die Bereitstellung von Menschen für die Eindeutschung neuer Siedlungsräume im Osten' (June 1942), in C. Madajczyk, ed., *Vom Generalplan Ost zum Generalsiedlungsplan* (Munich, 1994), 138–50.

68. U. Mai, *'Rasse und Raum': Agrarpolitik, Sozial und Raumplanung im NS-Staat* (Paderborn, 2002), 334–5.

69. Madajczyk, ed., *Vom Generalplan Ost zum Generalsiedlungsplan*, 168–70 (Berger), 172 (Himmler speech, 16 September 1942), 284 (Himmler speech of 3 August 1944).

70. Bergen, 'The *Volksdeutsche* of Eastern Europe', 112–14.

71. My thanks to Kiran Patel for his insights. His forthcoming work on food policy in postwar West Germany will provide a much fuller treatment of this and related issues.

72. A. Sauvy and S. Ledermann, 'La Guerre biologique (1933–1945): Population de l'Allemagne et des pays voisins', *Population*, 1:3 (July–September 1946); E. Kulischer, *Europe on the Move*, 315–24.

Chapter 8: Organizing Disorder: 1941–2

1. Figures from H. P. Ipsen, 'Reichsaussenverwaltung' (*Brüsseler Zeitung*, 3 April 1943), in H. W. Neulen, ed., *Europa und das 3. Reich: Einigungsbestrebungen im deutschen Machtbereich, 1939–1945* (Munich, 1987), 112–13. On Ipsen, see C. Joerges, 'Continuities and Discontinuities in German Legal Thought', *Law and Critique*, 14 (2003), 297–308. The parallel with Napoleon is discussed by P. Geyl, 'The Historical Background of the Idea of European Unity', in his *Encounters in History*, 291–321.

2. Trevor-Roper, ed., *Hitler's Table Talk*, 87, 279, 373; J. Noakes, '"Viceroys of the Reich"? Gauleiters, 1925–1945', in A. McElligott and T. Kirk, eds., *Working towards the Führer: Essays in Honour of Sir Ian Kershaw* (Munich, 2003), 118–53. The fundamental work is P. Hüttenberger, *Die Gauleiter: Studie zum Wandel des Machtgefüges in der NSDAP* (Stuttgart, 1969).

3. On Göring, Fest, *The Face of the Third Reich*, 123.

4. H. N. Gisevius, *To the Bitter End* (London, 1948), 210.

5. H.-U. Thamer, *Verführung und Gewalt: Deutschland, 1933–45* (Berlin, 1986).

6. On Forster and Greiser, see H. S. Levine, *Hitler's Free City: A History of the Nazi Party in Danzig, 1925–1939* (Chicago, 1973); C. Child, 'Administration', in Toynbee and Toynbee, eds., *Survey of International Affairs*, 99.

7. Hüttenberger, *Die Gauleiter*, 138–45.

8. Rebentisch, *Führerstaat und Verwaltung im Zweiten Weltkrieg*, 328; R. J. Overy, *The Dictators: Hitler's Germany, Stalin's Russia* (London, 2004), 71.
9. Rieger, *Creator of the Nazi Death Camps*, 44.
10. Levine, *Hitler's Free City*, 158; H. Kehrl, *Krisenmanager im Dritten Reich: 6 Jahre Frieden, 6 Jahre Krieg: Erinnerungen* (Düsseldorf, 1973), 205.
11. E. Peterson, *The Limits to Hitler's Power* (Princeton, 1969), 116–17.
12. On Stuckart's involvement in the West, see P. Schöttler, 'Eine Art "Generalplan West"': Die Stuckart-Denkschrift vom 14. Juni 1940 und die Planungen für eine neue deutsch-französische Grenze im Zweiten Weltkrieg', *Sozial Geschichte*, 18:3 (2003), 83–131; on the June 1940 verdict, D. Rebentisch, 'Hitlers Reichskanzlei zwischen Politik und Verwaltung', in D. Rebentisch and K. Teppe, eds., *Verwaltung contra Menschenführung im Staat Hitlers: Studien zum politisch-administrativen System* (Göttingen, 1986), 92 and, especially, L. Kettenacker, 'Die Chefs der Zivilverwaltung im Zweiten Weltkrieg', ibid., 397–402.
13. Jochmann, *Adolf Hitler*, 139, 158.
14. J. Caplan, *Government without Administration: State and Civil Service in Weimar and Nazi Germany* (Oxford, 1988), 266–73; Trevor-Roper, ed., *Hitler's Table Talk*, 85–6, 106, 423–33.
15. Kay, *Exploitation*, 190–91; Peterson, *Limits*, 121.
16. Quoted in Caplan, *Government without Administration*, 307.
17. Peterson, *Limits*, 78; Rebentisch, 'Hitlers Reichskanzlei', 91; Kay, *Exploitation*, 191.
18. Quoted in Caplan, *Government without Administration*, 309.
19. Ibid., 283–4.
20. Peterson, *Limits*, 117.
21. Ibid., 126; S. Aronson, *Beginnings of the Gestapo System: The Bavaria Model in 1933* (Jerusalem, 1969), 25, 35.
22. Levine, *Hitler's Free City*, 159; von Hassell, *The von Hassell Diaries*, 164.
23. M. Wildt, ed., *Nachrichtendienst, politische Elite und Mordeinheit: Der Sicherheitsdienst des Reichsführers-SS* (Hamburg, 2003), 15–37; M. Wildt, 'The Spirit of the Reich Security Main Office [RSHA]', *Totalitarian Movements and Political Religions*, 6:3 (December 2005), 333–49; S. Aronson, 'Heydrich und die Anfänge des SD und der Gestapo (1931–1935)', dissertation, Freie Universität Berlin, 1967, 190 seq.
24. G. Browder, *Hitler's Enforcers: The Gestapo and the SS Security Service in the Nazi Revolution* (Oxford, 1996), 193–5; On Höhn postwar, see L. Hachmeister, 'Die Rolle des SD-Personals in der Nachkriegszeit: Zur nationalsozialistischen Durchdringung der Bundesrepublik', in Wildt, ed., *Nachrichtendienst, politische Elite und Mordeinheit*, 347–55. There is also a good discussion of Höhn in J. A. Katz, 'The Concept of Overcoming the Political: An Intellectual Biography of SS-Standartenführer and Professor Dr Reinhard Höhn, 1904–1944', MA thesis, Virginia Commonwealth University, May 1995.
25. C. Klingemann, 'Ursachenanalyse und ethnopolitische Gegenstrategien zum Landarbeitermangel in den Ostgebieten: Max Weber, das Institut für Staatsforschung und der Reichsführer SS', *Jahrbuch für Soziologiegeschichte* (1994), 191–203.
26. U. Herbert, 'Ideological Legitimization and Political Practice of the Leadership of the National Socialist Secret Police', in H. Mommsen, ed., *The Third Reich between Vision and Reality: New Perspectives on German History, 1918–1945* (Oxford, 2001), 95–108.
27. H. Höhne, *The Order of the Death's Head*, 288–9.
28. P. Romijn, 'Die Nazifizierung der lokalen Verwaltung in den besetzen Niederlanden als Instrument bürokratischer Kontrolle', in W. Benz et al., eds., *Die Bürokratie der Okkupation: Strukturen der Herrschaft und Verwaltung in besetzten Europa* (Berlin, 1998), 93–121.
29. Herbert, *Best*, 281–3.
30. On Hitler's indifference, N. in't Veld, 'Höhere SS- und Polizeiführer und Volkstumspolitik: Ein Vergleich zwischen Belgien und den Niederlanden', in Benz et al., eds., *Die Bürokratie der Okkupation*, 121–39; on the HSSPFs, see H. Buchheim, 'Die höheren SS- und Polizeiführer', in *Vierteljahrshefte für Zeitgeschichte*, 11 (1963), 362–91.

31. Browning, *The Final Solution and the German Foreign Office*, 61.
32. J. Tomasevich, *War and Revolution in Yugoslavia, 1941–1945: Occupation and Collaboration* (Stanford, 2001), 68–9, 74–5.
33. C. Browning, 'Harald Turner und die Militärverwaltung in Serbien, 1941–1942', in Rebentisch and Teppe, eds., *Verwaltung contra Menschenführung im Staat Hitlers*, 367.
34. Browning, *The Final Solution and the German Foreign Office*, 56–65 goes into some of the twists and turns of this complicated and horrible story.
35. Ibid.; W. Manoschek, 'The Extermination of the Jews in Serbia', in U. Herbert, ed., *National Socialist Extermination Policies: Contemporary German Perspectives and Controversies* (New York, 2000), 163–86.
36. H. Buchheim, 'Die SS – das Herrschaftsinstrument: Befehl und Gehorsam', in H. Buchheim et al., eds., *Anatomie des SS-Staates*, vol. 1 (Munich, 1967), 90; G. Deschner, *Reinhard Heydrich: Statthalter der totalen Macht* (Erslagen, 1977), 212–38; C. MacDonald, *The Killing of SS Obergruppenführer Reinhard Heydrich, 27 May 1942* (London, 1989), esp. 131–6.
37. Hitler's comments reported in H. D. Heilmann, 'Das Kriegstagebuch des Diplomaten Otto Bräutigam', in G. Aly et al., eds., *Biedermann und Schreibtischtäter: Materialien zur deutschen Täter-Biographie* (Berlin, 1987), 146–7 (entry for 30 September 1941).
38. MacDonald, *Killing*, 165–6; cf. Schellenberg, *Hitler's Secret Service*, 286–7.
39. U. Herbert, *Best*, 237; Höhne, *The Order of the Death's Head*, 554; on opposition views of war aims, H. Mommsen, 'Beyond the Nation State', in McElligott and Kirk, eds., *Working towards the Führer*, 248–9.
40. Best's account of the founding of *RVL* in S. Matlok, ed., *Dänemark in Hitlers Hand: Der Bericht des Reichsbevollmächtigten Werner Best über seine Besatzungspolitik in Dänemark mit Studien über Hitler, Göring, Himmler, Heydrich, Ribbentrop, Canaris u. a.* (Husum, 1988), 188; on 'Führung' and 'Herrschaft', see C. Bilfinger, 'Streit um das Völkerrecht', in *Zeitschrift für ausländisches öffentliches Recht und Völkerrecht* 12 (1944), 1–34.
41. Cited by C. Joerges, 'Europe a *Grossraum*? Rupture, Continuity and Re-configuration in the Legal Conceptualization of the Integration Project', *EUI Working Paper, Law no.* 2002/2, 13; Herbert, *Best*, 283; Himmler to Krueger, in H. Himmler, *Reichsführer! . . . Briefe an und von Himmler*, ed. H. Heiber (Stuttgart, 1968), 131.
42. NO-2585 ('Bericht über die Sitzung am 4. 2. 1942 bei Dr Kleist über die Fragen der Eindeutschung, insbesondere in den baltischen Ländern'), in H. Heiber, 'Der Generalplan Ost', 296; on the rise of the HSSPF, see Buchheim, 'Die höheren SS- und Polizeiführer'.
43. Herbert, *Best*, 288–9; on dictatorship and leadership, G. Kuchenhoff, 'Grossraumgedanke und völkische Idee im Recht', in *Zeitschrift für ausländisches öffentliches Recht- und Völkerrecht* 12 (1944), 48–9.
44. A. Meyer, 'Grossraumpolitik und Kollaboration im Westen', in *Modelle für ein deutsches Europe* (Beiträge zur NS Gesundheits- und Sozialpolitik: 10) (Berlin, 1992), 29–77; E. Jäckel, *Frankreich in Hitlers Europa* (Stuttgart, 1966), 186–98.
45. Präg and Jacobmeyer, eds., *Das Diensttagebuch des deutschen Generalgouverneurs*, 113, 151.
46. Trevor-Roper, ed., *Hitler's Table Talk*, 111–17; Childs, 'Administration', in Toynbee and Toynbee, eds., *Survey of International Affairs*, 117.
47. Housden, *Hans Frank*, 62; Präg and Jacobmeyer, eds., *Das Diensttagebuch des deutschen Generalgouverneurs*, 160; C. Klessmann, 'Hans Frank', in R. Smelser and R. Zitelman, eds., *The Nazi Elite* (London, 1993), 41.
48. Jochmann, ed., *Adolf Hitler*, 140.
49. H. Frank, *Die Technik des Staates* (Berlin, 1942), 20–22, 28–9. Housden, *Hans Frank*, 160–61.
50. On corruption in general, see F. Bajohr, 'The Nazis and Corruption', in Feldman and Seibel, eds., *Networks of Nazi Persecution*, 118–41.
51. 'Interview with the Former Governor, Dr Lasch', 25 April 1942, 3814-PS, *NCA*, vol. 6 (Washington, DC, 1946), 745–7.

52. A good account of the whole affair is Höhne, *The Order of the Death's Head*, 359–66.

53. Housden, *Hans Frank*, 171–2.

54. 'Dokumentation: Rechtssicherheit und richterliche Unabhängigkeit aus der Sicht des SD,' *Vierteljahrshefte für Zeitgeschichte*, 4 (1956), 398–422.

55. On Ohlendorf and his relations with Himmler, see Kersten, *The Kersten Memoirs*, 206–20.

56. Von Hassell, *The von Hassell Diaries*, 16 March 1942.

57. H. W. Koch, *In the Name of the Volk: Political Justice in Hitler's Germany* (London, 1997), ch. 7.

58. A. McElligott, ' "Sentencing towards the Führer"? The Judiciary in the Third Reich', in McElligott and Kirk, eds., *Working towards the Führer*, 153–86; Himmler, in Buchheim, 'Die höheren SS- und Polizeiführer', 370; N. Wachsmann, *Hitler's Prisons: Legal Terror in Nazi Germany* (London, 2004), 208–18.

59. Childs, 'Administration', 117.

Chapter 9: Making Occupation Pay

1. Noakes and Pridham, eds., *Nazism, 1919–1945*, 681–3.

2. Funk cited in H.-E. Volkmann, 'Landwirtschaft und Ernährung in Hitlers Europa, 1939–45', *Militärgeschichtliche Mitteilungen*, 35 (1984), 37; Tooze, *Wages of Destruction*, 386.

3. Overy, *The Dictators*, 503–4.

4. Tooze, *Wages of Destruction*, 419.

5. J. Krejci, 'The Bohemian-Moravian War Economy', in M. Kaser, ed., *The Economic History of Eastern Europe, 1919–1975*, vol. 2 (Oxford, 1986), 452–72; P. Liberman, *Does Occupation Pay? The Exploitation of Occupied Industrial Societies* (Princeton, 1996).

6. J. Gillingham, 'The Politics of Business in the German *Grossraum*: The Example of Belgium', *Studia Historiae Oeconomicae*, 14 (1979), 23–4; C. Buchheim, 'Die besetzten Länder im Dienste der Deutschen Kriegswirtschaft während des Zweiten Weltkriegs', *Vierteljahrshefte für Zeitgeschichte*, 34:1 (1986), 117–45, here 119.

7. Radice in Kaser, *Economic History*, 340–42; Tooze, *Wages of Destruction*, 385.

8. D. Veillon, *Fashion under the Occupation* (Oxford, 2002), 22; D. Veillon, 'The Black Market', in M. Gijsen, ed., *Belgium under Occupation* (Washington, DC, 1947), 76.

9. H. Bell, 'Monetary Problems of Military Occupation', *Military Affairs*, 6:2 (Summer 1942), 77–88.

10. O. Hayes, *Industry and Ideology: I. G. Farben in the Nazi Era* (Cambridge, 1989).

11. R. Overy, 'German Multi-nationals and the Nazi state in Nazi-occupied Europe', in Overy, ed., *War and Economy in the Third Reich* (Oxford, 1994), 318.

12. Noakes and Pridham, eds., *Nazism, 1919–1945*, 959.

13. See P. Giltner, *'In the Friendliest Manner': German–Danish Economic Cooperation during the Nazi Occupation, 1940–1945* (New York, 1998), 33 seq.; Hayes, *Industry and Ideology*, 263. M. Nissen, 'Danish Food Production in the German War Economy', in F. Trentmann and F. Just, eds., *Food and Conflict in Europe in the Age of the Two World Wars* (Basingstoke, 2006), 172–93.

14. J. Gillingham, *Industry and Politics in the Third Reich: Ruhr Coal, Hitler and Europe* (London, 1985), 147, and 'The Baron de Launoit: A Case Study in the "Politics of Production" of Belgian Industry during Nazi Occupation' (Parts I and II), *Revue Belge d'Histoire Contemporaine*, 5 (1974), 1–59.

15. Hayes, *Industry and Ideology*, 276; G. Aalders, 'Three Ways of German Economic Penetration in the Netherlands', in R. J. Overy, G. Otto and J. H. van Cate, eds., *Die 'Neuordnung' Europas: NS-Wirtschaftspolitik in den besetzten Gebieten* (Berlin, 1997), 273–99. A. Milward, *The New Order and the French Economy* (Oxford, 1970), 47–50; 73.

16. P. Burrin, *France under the Germans: Collaboration and Compromise* (New York, 1996), 236–41; Gillingham, *Industry and Politics*, 159.

17. Overy, 'The Reichswerke "Hermann Göring": A Study in German Economic Imperialism', in Overy, ed., *War and Economy*, 144–75, here 167–8.

18. Hirschfeld, *Nazi Rule and Dutch Collaboration*, 186–90.

19. Ibid., 194.

20. Veillon, *Fashion*, 72–82; R. Kaczmarek, 'Die deutsche wirtschaftliche Penetration in Polen (Oberschlesien)', in Overy et al., eds., *Die 'Neuordnung'*, 257–73.

21. R. J. Overy, 'The Economy of the German "New Order" ', in Overy et al., eds., *Die 'Neuordnung'*, 22–3; Milward, *The New Order*, 55.

22. C. Buchheim, 'Die besetzten Länder', 117–45; P. Liberman, 'The Spoils of Conquest', *International Security*, 18:2 (Autumn 1993), 141; Tooze, *Wages of Destruction*, 391; von Krosigk, *NCA*, vol. 8 (Washington, DC, 1946), 21.

23. Milward, *The New Order*, 283.

24. Jäckel, *Frankreich in Hitlers Europa*, 94.

25. R. W. Lindholm, 'German Finances in Wartime', *American Economic Review*, 37:1 (March 1947), 121–34; Cathala in Hoover Institution, *France during the German Occupation, 1940–1944*, vol. 1 (Stanford, 1958), 108.

26. G. A. Makinen, 'The Greek Hyper-Inflation and Stabilization of 1943–46', *Journal of Economic History*, 46:3 (1986), 795–805; *Nazi Conspiracy and Aggression*, vol. 7 (Washington, DC, 1948), 692–4; G. Etmektsoglou, 'Changes in the Civilian Economy as a Factor in the Radicalization of Popular Opposition in Greece, 1941–1944', in Overy et al., eds., *Die 'Neuordnung'*, 223.

27. Rost von Tonningen, cited in Hirschfeld, *Nazi Rule and Dutch Collaboration*, 240.

28. A. Hitler, *Hitler's Second Book: The Unpublished Sequel to Mein Kampf*, ed. G. Weinberg (New York, 2006), 23; G. Corni, *Hitler and the Peasants: Agrarian Policy of the Third Reich, 1930–1939* (New York, 1990), 162–4. The argument may be followed in H. Backe, *Das Ende des Liberalismus in der Wirtschaft* (Berlin, 1938).

29. J. H. Richter, 'Continental Europe's Prewar Food Balance', *Foreign Agriculture*, 6 (1942), 300–301; Volkmann, 'Landwirtschaft und Ernährung', 13–14; U. Spiekermann, 'Brown Bread for Victory: German and British Wholemeal Politics in the Inter-war Period', in Trentmann and Just, eds., *Food and Conflict in Europe*.

30. C. Luczak, 'Die Agrarpolitik des Dritten Reiches', *Studia Historiae Oeconomicae*, 17 (1982), 197.

31. M. Chodakiewicz, *Between Nazis and Soviets: Occupation Politics in Poland, 1939–1947* (Lanham, MD, 2004), 108; K. Brandt, *Management of Agriculture and Food in the German-Occupied and Other Areas of Fortress Europe: A Study in Military Government* (Stanford, 1953), 290.

32. Z. Mankowski, 'Die Agrarpolitik des Okkupanten im Generalgouvernement, 1939–1945', *Studia Historiae Oeconomicae*, 23 (1998), 255–68.

33. P. Hansen, 'The Danish Economy during War and Occupation', in Overy et al., eds., *Die 'Neuordnung'*, 72.

34. P. Pétain, *Discours aux Français: 17 juin 1940–20 août 1944*, ed. J.-C. Barbas (Paris, 1989), 84.

35. A. Milward, *The Fascist Economy in Norway* (Oxford, 1972), 297; H. R. Kedward, *Resistance in France: A Study of Ideas and Motivation in the Southern Zone 1940–1942* (Oxford, 1978), 222–3.

36. C. Pilichowski, 'Verbrauch von Nahrungsmitteln durch jüdische Bevölkerung und Häftlinge der Okkupationslager in besetzten Polen', *Studia Historiae Oeconomicae*, 17 (1982), 209.

37. J. Gross, *Polish Society under German Occupation: The Generalgouvernement, 1939–1944* (Princeton, 1979), 156; Noakes and Pridham, eds., *Nazism, 1919–1945*, 994.

38. Brandt, *Management*, 118; *TWC*, vol. 11 (Washington, DC, 1946), 427–8.

39. V. Hionidou, *Famine and Death in Occupied Greece, 1941–1944* (Cambridge, 2006); Etmektsoglou, 'Changes in the Civilian Economy', 199, 214.

40. J. Breunis 'The Food Supply', in *Annals of the American Academy of Political and Social Science*, 245 (May 1946), 87–92, and C. Banning, 'Food Shortage and Public Health, First Half of 1945', ibid., 93–110.

41. 'The Food Rationing System in Poland', *Polish Fortnightly Review*, 55 (1 November 1942), 7; M. Brzeska, *Through a Woman's Eyes* (London, nd [1945]).

42. H. Backe, *Um die Nahrungsfreiheit Europas: Weltwirtschaft oder Grossraum* (Leipzig, 1942), 170 seq.; for prewar figures, see L. Volin, 'The Russian Food Situation', *Annals of the American Academy of Political and Social Scientists*, 225 (January 1943), 89–91.

43. Cited in Brandt, *Management*, 622–30; Aly and Heims, *Architects of Annihilation*, 246. On Backe, see Tooze, *Wages of Destruction*, 478–9.

44. Brandt, *Management*, 124.

45. 'A Citizen of Kharkiv', 'Lest We Forget: Hunger in Kharkiv in the Winter of 1941–42', *Ukrainian Quarterly*, 4 (Winter 1948), 72–9.

46. Bräutigam, in Noakes and Pridham, eds., *Nazism, 1919–1945*, 913–14; also, T. Mulligan, *The Politics of Illusion and Empire: German Occupation Policy in the Soviet Union, 1942–43* (New York, 1988), 47–8.

47. W. Boelcke, ed., *The Secret Conferences of Dr Goebbels, the Nazi Propaganda War, 1939–1943* (New York, 1970), 222–3.

48. J. Lehmann, 'Herbert Backe', in R. Smelser and R. Zitelmann, eds., *Die braune Elite* (Darmstadt, 1993), 1–13.

49. B. Smith and A. Peterson, eds., *Heinrich Himmler: Geheimreden 1933 bis 1945* (Frankfurt, 1974), 159; Tooze, *Wages of Destruction*, 547–8.

50. Noakes and Pridham, eds., *Nazism, 1919–1945*, 901; also *TWC*, vol. 8 (Washington, DC, 1952), 797 seq.

51. Also ibid., 803.

52. Trevor-Roper, ed., *Hitler's Table Talk*, 615–24.

53. Boelcke, ed., *The Secret Conferences*, 270, 276, 284; Tooze, *Wages of Destruction*, 548; Trevor-Roper, ed., *Hitler's Table Talk*, 658–9 (25 August 1942).

54. Brandt, *Management*, 125, 563; D. Eichholtz, 'Die Ausbeutung der Landwirtschaft der faschistisch besetzten Gebiete durch die Okkupanten und die Taktik der materiellen Korrumpierung in Deutschland während des Zweiten Weltkrieges', *Studia Historiae Oeconomicae*, 14 (1982), 153–71; Reicke v. Göring, *TWC*, vol. 13 (Washington, DC, 1952), 807.

55. N. Goodman, 'Health in Europe', *International Affairs*, 20:4 (1944), 473–80; Spiekermann, 'Brown Bread for Victory', 150–59; Sauvy and Ledermann, 'La Guerre biologique', 477; Brandt, *Management*, 610–13.

56. P. Vincent, 'Consequences de six années de guerre sur la population française', *Population*, 1:3 (July–September 1946), 436; J. Daric, 'Quelques aspects de l'évolution démographique aux Pays-Bas', ibid., 501–9.

57. J. Valin, F. Mesle, S. Adamets and S. Pyrozhov, 'A New Estimate of Ukrainian Population Losses during the Crises of the 1930s and 1940s', *Population Studies*, 56:3 (November 2002), 249–64.

58. J.-L. Charles and P. Dasnoy, eds., *Les Dossiers secrets de la Police Allemande en Belgique: La Geheime Feldpolizei en Belgique et dans le Nord de la France*, 2 vols. (Brussels, 1972–3), passim, esp. vol. 1: 45, 82–4, 155, 192–3, 205; vol. 2: 46.

59. G. Hill, *Trends in the Oil Industry in 1944* (Washington, DC, 1944), 10–12. My thanks to Alison Frank for this reference; W. G. Jensen, 'The Importance of Energy in the First and Second World Wars', *Historical Journal*, 11:3 (1968), 538–54.

60. D. Eichholtz, 'Öl, Krieg, Politik: Deutscher Ölimperialismus (1933–1942/43), *Zeitschrift für Geschichtsgewissenschaft*, 51:6 (2003), 493–511.

61. Tooze, *Wages of Destruction*, 445–6.

62. Ibid., 574, 598.

63. Jensen, 'The Importance of Energy', 550; Milward, *The New Order*, 288.

64. Liberman, *Does Conquest Pay?*

Chapter 10: Workers

1. U. Herbert, *Hitler's Foreign Workers: Enforced Foreign Labor in Germany under the Third Reich* (Cambridge, 1997), 35.

2. Ibid., 100–103, 107.

3. Ibid., 110–11.

4. Ibid., 146–62; Wetzel, in Heiber, 'Der Generalplan Ost', 312.

5. *NCA*, Supplement B (Washington, DC, 1946), 373, Sauckel-Hitler, 14 April 1943; *NCA*, vol. 7 (Washington, DC, 1946), 'Stenographic transcript of the 17th conference of Central Planning', R-124, 196; Tooze, *Wages of Destruction*, 517.

6. Nüremberg Document (hereafter ND), 294-PS/USA 185; ibid., 304.

7. ND, 1526-PS/USA 178, cited in *TWCI*, vol. 3 (Nuremberg, 1947), 12 December 1945, 299.

8. ND, 018-PS, Rosenberg-Sauckel, 21 December 1942, in ibid., 304–5.

9. Memorandum of Ribbentrop-Alfieri discussions', 22 February 1943 in *NCA*, vol. 7, 196–7; M. Eikel, ' "Weil die Menschen fehlen": Die deutschen Zwangsarbeitsrekruitierungen und -deportationen in den besetzten Gebieten der Ukraine, 1941–1944', *Vierteljahrshefte für Zeitgeschichte*, 53:5 (2005), 405–34.

10. R-124, minutes of the Central Planning Board, 1 March 1944, *TWCI*, 312.

11. 3819-PS, Sauckel and Speer's correspondence with Hitler, in *NCA*, vol. 6, 760–65; Manpower Executive Conference, 12 July 1944, ibid., 766–72.

12. Tooze, *Wages of Destruction*, 519; C. Gerlach and G. Aly, *Das letzte Kapitel: Realpolitik, Ideologie und der Mord an den ungarischen Juden, 1944/45* (Stuttgart, 2002); B. Kroner, ' "Soldaten der Arbeit": Menschenpotential und Menschenmangel in Wehrmacht und Kriegswirtschaft', in Eichholtz, ed., *Krieg und Wirtschaft*, 109–29.

13. P. Panayi, 'Exploitation, Criminality, Resistance: The Everyday Life of Foreign Workers and Prisoners of War in the German Town of Osnabrück, 1939-1949', *Journal of Contemporary History*, 40, 3 (2005), 483–502.

14. Herbert, *Hitler's Foreign Workers*, 265–6.

15. Ibid., 267–8; N. Wachsmann, *Hitler's Prisons: Legal Terror in Nazi Germany* (London, 2004), 284–306.

16. 'Extracts from Posen meeting', 4 October 1943, *NCA*, vol. 8, 318–22; R. Gellately, *Backing Hitler: Consent and Coercion in Nazi Germany* (Oxford, 2001), 174–5.

17. 'Decree for Ensuring the Discipline and Output of Foreign Workers', 25 September 1944 'D-226', in *NCA*, vol. 6, 1089–90; Tooze, *Wages of Destruction*, 529–30.

18. Cited in Panayi, 'Exploitation, Criminality, Resistance', 489–90; also Herbert, *Hitler's Foreign Workers*, 293–5.

19. Gallately, *Backing Hitler*, 239–57.

20. Figures for the Gulag from A. Nove, 'How Many Victims in the 1930s? II', *Soviet Studies*, 42:4 (October 1990), 811–14; 1939–42 figures in *NCA*, vol. 7, R-124, Pohl-Himmler, 30 April 1942.

21. J. E. Schulte, *Zwangsarbeit und Vernichtung: Das Wirtschaftsimperium der SS: Oswald Pohl und das SS-Wirtschafts-Verwaltungshauptamt, 1933–1945* (Paderborn, 2001).

22. Ibid., 335–60; M. T. Allen, *Hitler's Slave Lords: The Business of Forced Labour in Occupied Europe* (London, 2002), 198–9.

23. Himmler, *Geheimreden 1933 bis 1945*, 159.

24. Allen, *Hitler's Slave Lords*.

25. PS-682 in S. Krakowski, 'The Satellite Camps', in Y. Gutman and M. Berenbaum, eds., *Anatomy of the Auschwitz Death Camp* (Bloomington, IN, 1994), 51; M. Broszat, 'The Concentration Camps, 1933–1945', in H. Krausnick and M. Broszat, *Anatomy of the SS State* (London, 1973), 243; Wachsmann, *Hitler's Prisons*, ch. 8.

26. W. Naasner, ed., *SS-Wirtschaft und SS-Verwaltung: 'Das SS-Wirtschafts-Verwaltungs-hauptamt und die unter seiner Dienstaufsicht stehenden wirtschaftlichen Unternehmungen' und weitere Dokumente* (Düsseldorf, 1998), 93–9; F. Piper, 'The System of Prisoner Exploitation', in Gutman and Berenbaum, eds., *Anatomy of the Auschwitz Death Camp*, 34–50, here 38.
27. Engel, *At the Heart of the Reich*, 145.
28. Ibid., ch. 5; Glücks-camp commanders, 20 January 1943, Eicke comment in *TWC*, vol. 5, 383, Pohl-Himmler, 5 April 1944 (NO-020(a)); mortality rates in *TWC*, vol. 5, 379–81, Pohl-Himmler, 30 September 1943 (1469–PS). Overall calculations in Tooze, *Wages of Destruction*, 523, 526–7; Broszat, 'The Concentration Camps', 222–3, 244–5.
29. Schulte, *Zwangsarbeit und Vernichtung*, 208–32.
30. Ibid., 246–7; L. Dobroszycki, ed., *The Chronicle of the Lodz Ghetto, 1941–1944* (New Haven, 1984), lxi–lxiii; H. Krausnick, 'The Persecution of the Jews', in Krausnick and Broszat, eds., *Anatomy of the SS State*, 136–7.
31. Ibid., 250, 260–61.
32. Allen, *Hitler's Slave Lords*, 194–6.
33. See A. C. Mierzejewski, *The Collapse of the German War Economy, 1944–1945* (Chapel Hill, NC, 1988), ch. 1, for the rise of Speer. Also W. Schumann, 'Probleme der Deutschen Aussenwirtschaft und einer "Europäischen Wirtschaftsplanung"', *Studia Historiae Oeconomicae*, 14 (1979), 142–60.
34. *TWC*, vol. 11, 402–3.
35. K. J. Siegfried, 'Racial Discrimination at Work: Forced Labour in the Volkswagen Factory, 1939–1945', in M. Burleigh, ed., *Confronting the Nazi Past: New Debates on Modern German History* (London, 1996), 37–51.
36. Allen, *Hitler's Slave Lords*, 194, 225.
37. S. Kotkin, 'World War Two and Labor: A Lost Cause?', *International Labor and Working-Class History*, 58 (Fall 2000), 181–91.
38. Ibid.; also R. J. Overy, *Why the Allies Won* (London, 1995).

Chapter 11: Ersatz Diplomacy

1. J. Foerster and E. Mawdsley, 'Hitler and Stalin in Perspective: Secret Speeches on the Eve of Barbarossa', *War in History*, 11:1 (2004), 61–103, here 77.
2. *DGFP*, vol. 13 (Washington, DC, 1954), 55.
3. Ibid., 28–9, 42–3.
4. 'Gegnerische Kriegsziele', in *Zeitschrift für ausländisches öffentliches Recht und Völkerrecht*, 11 (1942–3), 11.
5. F. Anfuso, *Da Palazzo Venezia al Lago di Garda (1936–1945)* (n.p., 1957), 196–210, 226–7.
6. *DDI* 1, vol. 7 (Rome, 1987), 470.
7. Ibid., 509–10; see also Anfuso, *Da Palazzo Venezia al Lago di Garda*, 209.
8. E. Dollmann, *The Interpreter: Memoirs of Doktor Eugen Dollmann* (London, 1967), 192–3.
9. Schmidt, *Hitler's Interpreter*, 258; Lipgens, ed., *Documents on the History of European Integration*, vol. 1 (New York, 1984), 86–9.
10. M. Bloch, *Ribbentrop* (London, 1992), 340–41.
11. *DDI*, vol. 7, Ciano–Mussolini, 26 October 1941, 690–94.
12. Bloch, *Ribbentrop*, 342–3; L. Simoni, *Berlino, Ambasciata d'Italia 1939–1943* (Rome, 1947), 262.
13. *DGFP*, vol. 13 (Washington, DC, 1964), 858–9, 861, 867, 911; Bloch, *Ribbentrop*, 351.
14. *DGFP*, vol. 13, 920–21.
15. Hitler, *Speeches and Proclamations, 1932–1945*, vol. 4 (1941–1945) (Wauconda, IL, 2004), 2672, 30 September 1942.

16. *DDI*, vol. 8 (Rome, 1988), 409–12.

17. M. Luciolli, *Palazzo Chigi: Anni roventi, ricordi di vita diplomatica italiana dal 1933 al 1948* (Milan, 1976), 99–101; G. Bottai, *Diario, 1935–1944* (Milan, 1982), 300.

18. Tomasevich, *War and Revolution in Yugoslavia*, 168–71.

19. *The Confidential Papers of Admiral Horthy* (Budapest, 1965), 193, 224.

20. T. Anderson, 'A Hungarian *Vernichtungskrieg*? Hungarian Troops and the Soviet Partisan War in Ukraine, 1942', *Militärgeschichtliche Mitteilungen*, 58:2 (1999), 345–66; N. Kallay, *Hungarian Premier: A Personal Account of a Nation's Struggle in the Second World War* (London, 1954), 107–11 on Novi Sad.

21. Horthy, *Confidential Papers*, 269–72.

22. Tomasevich, *War and Revolution in Yugoslavia*, 156–68; R. Lemkin, *Axis Rule in Occupied Europe: Laws of Occupation, Analysis of Government, Proposals for Redress* (Washington, DC, 1944), 187–90; Schechtman, *European Population Transfers*, 415–24.

23. D. Deletant, *Hitler's Forgotten Ally: Ion Antonescu and His Regime, Romania 1940–1944* (London, 2006), 38.

24. J. Ancel, *Transnistria 1941–1942: The Romanian Mass Murder Campaigns*, vol. 1 (Tel Aviv, 2003), 24–5.

25. V. Petrov, *Escape from the Future: The Incredible Adventures of a Young Russian* (Bloomington, IN, 1973), 394–6.

26. Deletant, *Hitler's Forgotten Ally*, 187–96.

27. Ibid., 130–41; A. Angrick, 'The Escalation of German-Rumanian Anti-Jewish Policy after the Attack on the Soviet Union', *Yad Vashem Studies*, 26 (1998), 203–39, gives a higher figure for Jassy casualties. See now 'The Report of the International Commission on the Holocaust in Romania', Bucharest, 11 November 2004, available online at http://www.yadvashem.org/about_yad/what_new/index_whats_new-report.html.

28. K. Malaparte, *Kaputt* (London, 1989), 142.

29. J. Ancel, 'The German–Rumanian Relationship and the Final Solution', *Holocaust and Genocide Studies*, 19:2 (Fall 2005), 252–75, here 258; for the original, see L. Benjamin, ed., *Problema evreiasca in stenogramele Consiliului de Ministri* (Bucharest, 1996), 264–9.

30. Angrick, 'The Escalation of German-Rumanian Anti-Jewish policy', 213–15.

31. Ibid., 224–9.

32. R. Hilberg, *The Destruction of the European Jews* (New York, 1985), vol. 2, 758–83; Deletant, *Hitler's Forgotten Ally*, 146.

33. Ancel, *Transnistria 1941–1942*, 193.

34. Ibid., 193–203.

35. Ancel, 'The German–Rumanian Relationship and the Final Solution', 259.

36. 'The Report of the International Commission on the Holocaust in Romania'.

37. A. Dallin, *Odessa 1941–1944: A Case Study of Soviet Territory under Foreign Rule* (Santa Monica, CA, 1957), 68–78; a thorough discussion of estimates of the death toll may be found in 'The Holocaust in Romania' in 'The Report of the International Commission on the Holocaust in Romania'.

38. 'Rezolvarea problemei evreiesti' (Solution of the Jewish Problem), in *Unirea*, 10 October 1941; copy in J. Ancel, *Documents Concerning the Fate of Romanian Jewry during the Holocaust* (New York, 1987), vol. 3: no. 208, p. 318 cited in 'The Report of the International Commission on the Holocaust in Romania'.

39. M. Knox, *Hitler's Italian Allies: Royal Armed Forces, Fascist Regime and the War of 1940–1943* (Cambridge, 2000), 24–71.

40. R. DiNardo, *Germany and the Axis Powers: From Coalition to Collapse* (Lawrence, KS, 2005), 28–36.

41. Bottai, *Diario, 1935–1944*, 216.

42. D. Rodogno, *Fascism's European Empire: Italian Occupation during the Second World War* (Cambridge, 2006), 284–7; see also S. Lecoeur, 'The Italian Occupation of Syros and its Socio-Economic Impact, 1941–43', Ph.D. thesis, University of London, 2006.

43. Rodogno, *Fascism's European Empire*, 59.

44. H. J. Burgwyn, *Empire in the Adriatic: Mussolini's Conquest of Yugoslavia, 1941–1943* (New York, 2005), 96.
45. Rodogno, *Fascism's European Empire*, 82–4, 264–5.
46. F. P. Verna, 'Notes on Italian Rule in Dalmatia under Bastianini, 1941–1943', *International History Review*, 12:3 (1990), 441–60.
47. Rodogno, *Fascism's European Empire*, 73.
48. Tomasevich, *War and Revolution in Yugoslavia*, 49–53.
49. Malaparte, *Kaputt*, 264–6.
50. M. A. Hoare, *Genocide and Resistance in Hitler's Bosnia: the Partisans and the Chetniks, 1941–1943* (Oxford, 2006), 22–3.
51. T. Dulic, *Utopias of Nation: Local Mass Killing in Bosnia and Hercegovina, 1941–1942* (Stockholm, 2005).
52. Burgwyn, *Empire in the Adriatic*, 164–6.
53. Rich, *Hitler's War Aims*, vol. 2, 280–81; Glaise in J. E. Gumz, '*Wehrmacht* Perceptions of Mass Violence in Croatia, 1941–1942', *Historical Journal*, 44:4 (2001), 1015–38, here 1028; Dulic, *Utopias of Nation*, 146; J. Gumz, 'German Counter-insurgency Policy in Independent Croatia, 1941–1944', *The Historian*, 61 (1998), 33–50.
54. M. Legnani, 'Il "ginger" del generale Roatta: le direttive della 2a armata sulla repressione antipartigiana in Slovenia e Croazia', *Italia contemporanea*, 209–10 (December 1997–March 1998), 155–74; Burgwyn, *Empire in the Adriatic*, 270–74.
55. Rodogno, *Fascism's European Empire*, 336–61.
56. For Italian objections, *DDI*, vol. 10 (Rome, 1990), 86, 547.
57. B. Fischer, *Albania at War, 1939–1945* (West Lafayette, IN, 1999), 85–7.
58. Gumz, '*Wehrmacht* Perceptions of Mass Violence', 1032; on spurned chances for negotiations, see W. Hoettl, *The Secret Front: The Story of Nazi Espionage* (New York, 1954), 154–5.
59. J. Gumz, 'Stepping Back from Destruction: Invasion, Occupation and Empire in Habsburg Serbia, 1914–1918', Ph.D. thesis, University of Chicago, 2006.
60. See Hull, *Absolute Destruction*; A. Kramer, *Dynamics of Destruction: Culture and Mass Killing in the First World War* (Oxford, 2007); and especially Gumz, 'Stepping Back from Destruction'.
61. Bottai, *Diario*, entry for 11 June 1940.
62. Lumans, *Himmler's Auxiliaries*, 215.
63. Bowen, *Spaniards and Nazi Germany*, 170.
64. Burgwyn, *Empire in the Adriatic*, 277.
65. Schmidt, *Hitler's Interpreter*, 259–60; C. Browning, 'Unterstaatssekretär Martin Luther and the Ribbentrop Foreign Office', *Journal of Contemporary History*, 12:2 (April 1977), 313–44.
66. Herzstein, *When Nazi Dreams Come True*, ch. 6; Martin, 'German–Italian Cultural Initiatives'.
67. Lipgens, ed., *Documents on the History of European Integration*, vol. 1, 98–109; Simoni, *Berlino, Ambasciata d'Italia*, 299; Schmidt, *Hitler's Interpreter*, 261; J. von Ribbentrop, *The Ribbentrop Memoirs* (London, 1954), 169.
68. Mulligan, *The Politics of Illusion and Empire*, 39–40.
69. Lipgens, ed., *Documents on the History of European Integration*, vol. 1, 118–22.
70. Bloch, *Ribbentrop*, 365–7.
71. Browning, 'Unterstaatssekretär Martin Luther', 334.
72. *DDI*, vol. 10, 91–2, 103–4.
73. Lipgens, ed., *Documents on the History of European Integration*, vol. 1, 123–4.
74. *DDI*, vol. 10, 232–4.
75. Ibid. 278–9; Bloch, *Ribbentrop*, 378; Simoni, *Berlino, Ambasciata d'Italia*, 333.
76. G. de Antonellis, *Le Quattro Giornate di Napoli* (Milan, 1973), 65.
77. P. Struye, *Journal de guerre, 1940–1945* (Brussels, 2004), 411.
78. Herzstein, *When Nazi Dreams Come True*, 206.

79. F. W. Deakin, *The Last Days of Mussolini* (London, 1962), 112–13.
80. E. Collotti, *L'amministrazione tedesca dell' Italia occupata* (Milan, 1963), 290–91; L. Klinkhammer, *Zwischen Bündnis und Besatzung: Das nationalsozialistische Deutschland und die Republik von Salò, 1943–45* (Tübingen, 1993), 291–301, 494.
81. Deakin, *The Last Days of Mussolini*, 141, 149.
82. Gerlach and Aly, *Das letzte Kapitel*, 117–21; Lumans, *Himmler's Auxiliaries*, 226.
83. P. Sipos, 'The Fascist Arrow Cross Government in Hungary (October 1944–April 1945)', in Benz et al., eds., *Die Bürokratie der Okkupation*, 49–63.
84. Hitler, *Speeches and Proclamations*, vol. 4, 1 January 1945.

Chapter 12: The Final Solution: the Jewish Question

1. Cited in C. Browning, *Nazi Policy, Jewish Workers, German Killers* (Cambridge, 2000), 48; see also Boelcke, ed., *The Secret Conferences*, 190.
2. R. Cecil, *The Myth of the Master Race: Alfred Rosenberg and Nazi Ideology* (London, 1972), 20; 'Eine ernste Frage', in A. Rosenberg, *Schriften und Reden*, vol. 1 (Munich, 1943), 75–9; Billig, *Alfred Rosenberg*, 194–7, 209–11.
3. B. Lösener, 'Das Reichsministerium des Innern und die Judengesetzgebung', *Vierteljahrshefte für Zeitgeschichte*, 9:3 (1961), 303; P. Witte, 'Two Decisions Concerning the "Final Solution to the Jewish Question": Deportations to Lodz and Mass Murder in Chelmno', *Holocaust and Genocide Studies*, 9:2 (1995), 318–45.
4. L. Rein, 'Local Collaboration in the Execution of the "Final Solution" in Nazi-Occupied Belorussia', *Holocaust and Genocide Studies*, 20:3 (Winter 2006), 381–409, here 395.
5. 'Report on the Execution of Jews in Borrisow', 24 October 1941, ND 3047-PS, in American Jewish Conference, *Nazi Germany's War against the Jews* (New York, 1947).
6. Reitlinger, *The House Built on Sand*, 85.
7. Morris-State, 14 October 1941, in J. Mendelsohn, ed., *The Holocaust in Selected Documents in Eighteen Volumes*, vol. 8 (New York, 1982), 18–19; E. Farbstein, 'Diaries and Memoirs as a Historical Source – The Diary and Memoir of a Rabbi at the "Konin House of Bondage" ', *Yad Vashem Studies*, 26 (1998), 87–129, here 106.
8. J. Herf, 'The "Jewish War": Goebbels and the Anti-Semitic Campaigns of the Nazi Propaganda Ministry', *Holocaust and Genocide Studies*, 19:1 (Spring 2005), 51–80, here 67; B. Musial, 'The Origins of "Operation Reinhard": The Decision-Making Process for the Mass Murder of the Jews in the Generalgovernment', *Yad Vashem Studies*, 28 (2000), 113–53, here 136 (citing *Tagebücher*, 2, 132, entry for 28 October 1941).
9. Y. Arad, 'Alfred Rosenberg and the "Final Solution" in the Occupied Soviet Territories', *Yad Vashem Studies*, 13 (1979), 263–86.
10. Witte et al., eds., *Der Dienstkalender Heinrich Himmlers*, 258–84; Lösener, 'Das Reichsministerium', 311.
11. Goebbels, *Die Tagebücher von Josef Goebbels*, ed. E. Froehlich, vol. 2:2 (October–December 1941) (Munich, 1996), 487–500.
12. Arad, 'Alfred Rosenberg', 281.
13. Frank Diary, 16 December 1941, NG 2233D-PS (USA 281) in American Jewish Conference, *Nazi Germany's War against the Jews*.
14. M. Roseman, 'Shoot First and Ask Questions Afterwards? Wannsee and the Unfolding of the Final Solution', in N. Gregor, ed., *Nazism, War and Genocide: Essays in Honour of Jeremy Noakes* (Exeter, 2005), 130–46.
15. See chapter 10 for more details.
16. I. Kershaw, 'Improvised Genocide? The Emergence of the "Final Solution" in the "Warthegau" ', *Transactions of the Royal Historical Society* (1994), 51–78, here 76.
17. Dobroszycki, ed., *The Chronicle of the Lodz Ghetto*, liv; Kershaw, 'Improvised Genocide?'
18. Dobroszycki, ed., *The Chronicle of the Lodz Ghetto*, lvi. May's memoir was written in February 1945.

19. M. Williams, 'Friedrich Rainer and Odilo Globocnik. L'amicizia insolita e i ruoli sinistri di due nazisti tipici', *Qualestoria*, 1 (June 1997), 141–75. See Rieger, *Creator of the Nazi Death Camps*.

20. P. Black, 'Rehearsal for "Reinhard": Odilo Globocnik and the Lublin *Selbstschutz*', *Central European History*, 25:2 (1992), 204–26; Musial, 'The Origins of "Operation Reinhard"', 119–20, 122.

21. Himmler–Globocnik, 27 March 1942, on the termination of his charge preparing, planning and implementing police *Stützpunkte* in the East, in H. Friedlander and S. Milton, eds., *Archives of the Holocaust*, vol. 11:1 (New York, 1992), 254; on the background, Browning, *The Origins of the Final Solution*, 354–6.

22. P. Witte and S. Tyas, 'A New Document on the Deportation and Murder of Jews during "Einsatz Reinhardt" 1942', *Holocaust and Genocide Studies*, 15:3 (Winter 2001), 468–86. Note the lack of agreement on the spelling, which is sometimes rendered as 'Reinhard' and sometimes 'Reinhardt'; Rieger, *Creator of the Nazi Death Camps*, 114.

23. Musial, 'The Origins of "Operation Reinhard"', 127.

24. Jochmann, ed., *Adolf Hitler*, 91.

25. E. T. Wood, *Karski: How One Man Tried to Stop the Holocaust* (New York, 1994), 125–9; J. Karski, *Story of a Secret State* (Boston, 1944).

26. Goebbels, *The Goebbels Diaries, 1942–1943*, ed. Lochner, 148.

27. Noakes and Pridham, eds., *Nazism, 1919–1945*, 1147–8.

28. Witte, ed., *Der Dienstkalender Heinrich Himmlers*, 483, 493; C. Browning, 'A Final Hitler Decision for the "Final Solution": The Riegner Telegram Reconsidered', *Holocaust and Genocide Studies*, 10:1 (Spring 1996), 3–10; A. C. Mierzejewski, 'A Public Enterprise in the Service of Mass Murder: The Deutsche Reichsbahn and the Holocaust', *Holocaust and Genocide Studies*, 15:1 (Spring 2001), 33–46, here 38.

29. Frank, 24 August 1942, USA 283 reprinted in American Jewish Conference, *Nazi Germany's War against the Jews*, 350–51.

30. E. Levai, *Black Book on the Martyrdom of Hungarian Jewry* (Zurich and Vienna, 1948), 26–7.

31. Browning, 'A Final Hitler Decision', 7.

32. J. Billig, 'The Launching of the Final Solution', in S. Klarsfeld, ed., *The Holocaust and the Neo-Nazi Mythomania* (New York, 1978), 63–6.

33. Aly and Roth, *The Nazi Census*, 29–30, 90–91.

34. G. Wellers, 'The Number of Victims and the Korherr Report', in Klarsfeld, ed., *The Holocaust and the Neo-Nazi Mythomania*, appendices.

35. Himmler–Chief of SiPo/SD, Berlin, 9 April 1943 reproduced in Klarsfeld, *Holocaust and the Neo-Nazi Mythomania*, appendices.

36. Gutman and Berenbaum, *Anatomy of the Auschwitz Death Camp*, 86.

37. A. Cohen, 'La Politique antijuive en Europe (Allemagne exclue) de 1938 à 1941', *Guerres mondiales*, 150 (1988), 45–59.

38. *TWC*, vol. 8, 195–206.

39. M. Schwalbova, 'Slovak Jewish Women in Auschwitz II-Birkenau', in W. Długoborski et al., eds., *The Tragedy of the Jews of Slovakia: 1938–1945: Slovakia and the 'Final Solution of the Jewish Question'* (Oswiecim, 2002), 201–12; Y. Buechler, 'The Deportation of Slovakian Jews to the Lublin District of Poland in 1942', *Holocaust and Genocide Studies*, 6:2 (1991), 151–66; D. Dwork and R. Jan van Pelt, *Auschwitz: 1270 to the Present* (New York, 1996), 299–306.

40. Ibid., 320.

41. L. Rothkirchen, 'A Few Considerations on the Historiography of the Holocaust', in Długoborski et al., eds., *The Tragedy of the Jews of Slovakia*, 83; I. Kamanec, 'The Deportation of Jewish Citizens from Slovakia in 1942', ibid., 111–39; J. Ward, '"People Who Deserve It": Jozef Tiso and the Presidential Exemption', *Nationalities Papers*, 30:4 (2002), 571–601.

42. Browning, *The Final Solution and the German Foreign Office*, 103–4; *TWC*, vol. 8, 231; M. Marrus and R. Paxton, *Vichy France and the Jews* (New York, 1981).
43. Browning, *The Final Solution and the German Foreign Office*, 115–17, 125–6.
44. Aly and Roth, *The Nazi Census*, 66–8.
45. *TWC*, vol. 8, 255.
46. Hillgruber, ed., *Staatsmänner und Diplomaten bei Hitler*, vol. 2, 233, 245, 257.
47. Browning, *The Final Solution and the German Foreign Office*, 136–7.
48. Burgwyn, *Empire on the Adriatic*, 186–7.
49. Ibid., 188–9.
50. Ibid., 192–3; Rodogno, *Fascism's European Empire*, 397.
51. Ibid., 383–4.
52. Ibid., 390.
53. Ibid., 403–5.
54. Deletant, *Hitler's Forgotten Ally*, 212–14.
55. Gutman and Berenbaum, *Anatomy of the Auschwitz Death Camp*, 86, 89; Dwork and van Pelt, *Auschwitz, 1270 to the Present*, 342.
56. M. Hindley, 'Negotiating the Boundary of Unconditional Surrender: The War Refugee Board in Sweden and Nazi Proposals to Ransom Jews, 1944–45', *Holocaust and Genocide Studies*, 10:1 (Spring 1996), 52–77.
57. L. Rothkirchen, 'The Final Solution in Its Last Stages', *Yad Vashem Studies*, 8 (1970), 7–28.
58. N. Masur, *En jude talar med Himmler* (Stockholm, 1945); the text of Masur's report to the World Jewish Congress is available online at http://ux.brookdalecc.edu/fac/tlt/wwz/memoir_details.php?id=53; Schellenberg, *Hitler's Secret Service*, 386–7.
59. R. Breitman and S. Aronson, 'The End of the "Final Solution": Nazi Plans to Ransom Jews in 1944', *Central European History*, 25 (1992), 177–203.
60. Y. Buechler, ' "Unworthy Behavior": The Case of SS Officer Max Täubner', *Holocaust and Genocide Studies*, 17:3 (Winter 2003), 409–29.
61. S. Spector, '*Aktion 1005* – Effacing the Murder of Millions', *Holocaust and Genocide Studies*, 5:2 (1990), 157–73.
62. Rothkirchen,. 'The "Final Solution" in Its Last Stages', 7–29.
63. Hilberg, *The Destruction of the European Jews*, 1220.
64. A. Weiss-Wendt, 'Extermination of the Gypsies in Estonia during World War II: Popular Images and Official Policies', *Holocaust and Genocide Studies*, 17:1 (Spring 2003), 31–61; M. Zimmermann, 'Die nationalsozialistische Lösung der Ziegeunerfrage', in U. Herbert, ed., *Nationalsozialistische Vernichtungspolitik, 1939–1945* (Frankfurt, 1998).
65. Jacobmeyer, 'Die polnische Widerstandsbewegung im General Gouvernement und ihre Beurteilung durch deutsche Dienststellen', *Vierteljahrshefte für Zeitgeschichte*, 25:4 (1977), 655–81, here 677; R. Hilberg, *The Destruction of the European Jews*, 3rd edn (New Haven, 2003), vol. 2, 547–8.

Chapter 13: Collaboration

1. On this way of formulating the problem of collaboration see J. Gross, 'Themes for a Social History of War: Experience and Collaboration', in I. Deak et al., eds., *The Politics of Retribution in Europe* (Princeton, 2000), 15–37.
2. S. Hoffmann, 'Collaboration in France during World War II', *Journal of Modern History*, 40:3 (September 1968), 375–95; Y. Durand, 'Collaboration French-style: A European Perspective', in S. Fishman et al., eds., *France at War: Vichy and the Historians* (New York, 2000), 61–76.
3. Guéhenno and Maurras translated in G. Bree and G. Bernauer, eds., *Defeat and Beyond: An Anthology of French Wartime Writing, 1940–1945* (New York, 1970), 95–9, 101–3.

4. R. Paxton, *Vichy France: Old Guard, New Order, 1940–1944* (New York, 1972), parts 1–2; R. Vinen, *The Unfree French: Life under the Occupation* (New Haven, 2006), chs. 1–2.

5. R. Paxton, 'Le Régime de Vichy était-il neutre?', *Guerres mondiales et conflits contemporaines*, 194 (1999), 149–62.

6. P. Burrin, *Living with Defeat: France under the German Occupation, 1940–1944* (London, 1996), 109–11; S. Kitson, 'Spying for Germany in Vichy France', *History Today*, 56:1 (January 2006), 38–45 and especially his *Vichy et la chasse aux éspions nazis, 1940–1942: Complexités de la politique de collaboration* (Paris, 2005).

7. Burrin, *Living with Defeat*, 437–8.

8. H. Umbreit, *Der Militärbefehlshaber in Frankreich 1940–1944* (Boppard am Rhein, 1968), 109; B. Gordon, 'The Condottieri of the Collaboration: *Mouvement Social Révolutionnaire*', *Journal of Contemporary History*, 10:2 (April 1975), 261–82.

9. On Mitterrand, see P. Péan, *Une jeunesse française: François Mitterrand, 1934–1947* (Paris, 1994); on the L'Oréal connection there is the muck-raking M. Bar-Zohar, *Bitter Scent: The Case of L'Oréal, Nazis and the Arab Boycott* (New York, 1996).

10. A. Betz, 'Céline entre le IIIe République et la France occupée', in A. Betz and S. Martens, eds., *Les Intellectuels et l'Occupation: Collaborer, partir, resister, 1940–1944* (Paris, 2004), 90–105; W. R. Tucker, *The Fascist Ego: A Political Biography of Robert Brasillach* (Los Angeles, 1975), 253–70; Smith, *The Embattled Self*, 181–2.

11. J. Cocteau, *Journal, 1942–45* (Paris, 1989), 34, 114.

12. Ibid., 173; Burrin, *Living with Defeat*, 348.

13. The key source for Cocteau is C. Arnaud, *Jean Cocteau* (Paris, 2003), 543–87.

14. M. Cone, *Artists under Vichy: A Case of Prejudice and Persecution* (Princeton, 1992); Y. Menager, 'Aspects de la vie culturelle en France sous l'occupation allemande (1940–1944)', in Madajczyk, ed., *Inter arma non silent musae*, 367–421.

15. G. Sapiro, 'La Collaboration littéraire', in A. Betz and S. Martens, eds., *Les Intellectuels et l'Occupation*, 39–63; E. Michels, 'Die deutschen Kulturinstitute im besetzten Europa', in W. Benz et al., eds., *Kultur-Propaganda-Öffentlichkeit: Intentionen deutscher Besatzungspolitik und Reaktionen auf die Okkupation* (Berlin, 1998), 11–35.

16. B. Lambauer, 'Otto Abetz, inspirateur et catalysateur de la collaboration culturelle', in Benz et al., eds., *Kultur-Propaganda-Öffentlichkeit*, 64–90; J. Grondin, *Hans-Georg Gadamer: A Biography* (New Haven, 2003), 212–13.

17. Jochmann, ed., *Adolf Hitler*, 116.

18. On the continuity of the state, the classic statement is C. Pavone, 'La continuità dello stato,' in Pavone, *Alle origine della Repubblica*.

19. G. Le Begnec and D. Peschanski, eds., *Les Elites locales dans la tourmente* (Paris, 2000).

20. The key source is M.-O. Baruch, *Servir l'Etat Français: L'Administration en France de 1940 à 1944* (Paris, 1997), esp. 36–209.

21. Ibid., 242; Vinen, *The Unfree French*, 85.

22. Baruch, *Servir l'Etat Français*, 256; Vinen, *The Unfree French*, 94.

23. Baruch, *Servir l'Etat Français*, 298–313.

24. Ibid., 398; Marrus and Paxton, *Vichy France and the Jews*, 245; J.-M. Berlière, 'L'Impossible Pérennité de la police républicaine sous l'Occupation', in *Vingtième Siècle*, 94 (April–June 2007), 183–96.

25. Baruch, *Servir l'Etat Français*, 400–403; U. Lappenküper, 'Der "Schlächter von Paris": Carl-Albrecht Oberg als HHSPF in Frankreich, 1942–44', in S. Martens and M. Vaïsse, eds., *Frankreich und Deutschland im Krieg (Nov. 1942–Herbst 1944): Okkupation, Kollaboration, Resistance* (Bonn, 2000), 129–43; Umbreit, *Der Militärbefehlshaber*, 112; Vinen, *The Unfree French*, 109.

26. J. Delarue, *Trafics et crimes sous l'occupation* (Paris, 1968), 248.

27. Ibid., 249–51.

28. Ibid., 258–62.

29. S. Kitson, 'From Enthusiasm to Disenchantment: The French Police and the Vichy

Regime, 1940–1944', *Contemporary European History*, 11:3 (2002), 371–90; Baruch, *Servir l'Etat Français*, 449–465, 515.

30. Numbers of arrests in Umbreit, *Der Militärbefehlshaber*, 116.

31. Baruch, *Servir l'Etat Français*, 548; E. Alary, 'Les Années noires du maintien de l'ordre: L'Exemple de la gendarmerie nationale, entre omnipotence allemande et emprise de la Milice', in Martens and Vaïsse eds., *Frankreich und Deutschland im Krieg*, 567.

32. Baruch, *Servir l'Etat Français*, 580; Burrin, *Living with Defeat*, 451; J. Sweets, 'Hold that Pendulum! Redefining Fascism, Collaborationism and Resistance in France', *French Historical Studies*, 15:4 (Autumn 1988), 731–58, here 751.

33. On the so-called 'Vichyite-resisters', see J. Barasz, 'Un vichyste en Résistance, le général de la Laurencie', *Vingtième Siècle*, 94 (April – June 2007), 167–81 and bibliography.

34. Sweets, 'Hold that Pendulum!', 754.

Chapter 14: Eastern Helpers

1. K.-P. Friedrich, 'Collaboration in a "Land without a Quisling": Patterns of Collaboration with the Nazi German Occupation Regime in Poland during World War II', *Slavic Review*, 64:4 (Winter 2005), 712–46, here 714, 719.

2. The trigger for debates into wartime Polish anti-Jewish violence was J. Gross, *Neighbors: The Destruction of the Jewish Community in Jedwabne* (Princeton, 2002).

3. M. Kunicki, 'Unwanted Collaborators: Leon Kozłowski, Wladyslaw Studnicki and the Problem of Collaboration among Polish Conservative Politicians in World War II', *European Review of History*, 8:2 (2001) 203–20; R. Lukas, *Forgotten Holocaust: The Poles under German Occupation, 1939–1944* (New York, 1990), 111.

4. Ibid. Kozłowski himself died in a bombing raid in Germany in the spring of 1944.

5. See the discussion in W. Borodziej, *Terror und Politik: Die deutsche Polizei und die polnische Widerstandsbewegung im Generalgouvernement, 1939–1944* (Mainz, 1999).

6. Lukas, *Forgotten Holocaust*, 114–15.

7. D. Furber, 'Going East', 150; Sobieski, 'Reminiscences from Lwow', 361.

8. These and the paragraphs that follow are based on Chodakiewicz's pioneering *Between Nazis and Soviets*.

9. Ibid., 81.

10. Ibid., 84; Klukowski, *Diary from the Years of Occupation*, 123.

11. Swain, *Between Stalin and Hitler*, 91.

12. K. Sakowicz, *Ponary Diary, 1941–1943: A Bystander's Account of a Mass Murder* (New Haven, 2005).

13. Aly, *Hitler Beneficiaries*; Friedrich, 'Collaboration in a "Land without a Quisling"', 733; Klukowski, *Diary from the Years of Occupation*, 227.

14. O. Pinkus, *The House of Ashes* (London, 1991), 109; D. Bergen, 'The *Volksdeutsche* of Eastern Europe and the Collapse of the Nazi Empire, 1944–1945', in Steinweis and Rogers, eds., *The Impact of Nazism*, 110.

15. Ibid., 16, 30, 40; M. Zylberberg, *A Warsaw Diary* (London, 1969), 201; L. Rein, 'Local Collaboration', 381–409.

16. M. Dean, *Collaboration in the Holocaust: Crimes of the Local Police in Belorussia and Ukraine, 1941–44* (Basingstoke, 2004), 68.

17. G. Stein, *The Waffen-SS: Hitler's Elite Guard at War, 1939–1945* (Ithaca, 1966), 138–9; C. Childs, 'The Political Structure of Hitler's Europe', in A and V. Toynbee, eds., *Survey of International Affairs*, 75–9; Reitlinger, *The SS, Alibi of a Nation*, 158–60; B. de Wever, 'Military Collaboration in Belgium', in Benz et al., eds., *Die Bürokratie der Okkupation*, 153–73.

18. Höhne, *The Order of the Death's Head*, 535.

19. Reitlinger, *The SS, Alibi of a Nation*, 194–5; Militärgeschichtliches Forschungsamt, ed., *Germany and the Second World War*, vol. 5, 1027.

20. Stein, *The Waffen-SS*, 171–3; Höhne, *Order of the Death's Head*, 537; Bergen, 'The Volksdeutsche of Eastern Europe', 112.
21. Stein, *The Waffen-SS*, 178–9.
22. G. Bassler, *Alfred Valdmanis and the Politics of Survival* (Toronto, 2000).
23. Reitlinger, *The House Built on Sand*, 160–64.
24. Ibid.
25. J. A. Armstrong, *Ukrainian Nationalism*, rev. edn (Littleton, CO, 1980), 34–7.
26. W. D. Heike, *The Ukrainian Division 'Galicia', 1943–45: A Memoir* (Toronto, 1988), 4–5, 19, 28–9.
27. For more on this, see the discussion in the next chapter on the politics of the Ukrainian nationalist resistance in West Ukraine in 1943–4.
28. Quoted in Stein, *The Waffen-SS*, 194–5.
29. Dallin, *German Rule*, 534–6.
30. Reitlinger, *The SS, Alibi of a Nation*, 200–201; Dallin, *German Rule*, 534.
31. P. Biddiscombe, '*Unternehmen* Zeppelin: The Deployment of SS Saboteurs and Spies in the Soviet Union, 1942–1945', *Europe-Asia Studies*, 52:6 (2000), 1115–42; Dallin, *German Rule*, 546.
32. Ibid., 564–6.
33. Ibid., 574; Hitler cited in Borodziej, *Terror und Politik*, 116.
34. Dallin, *German Rule*, 593–4.
35. Ibid., 601, 616.
36. Heiber, ed., *Hitler and his Generals*, 259–60.
37. T. Schulte, *German Army and Nazi Policies in Occupied Russia* (New York, 1989), 172–7; J. Hanson, *The Civilian Population and the Warsaw Uprising of 1944* (Cambridge, 1978), 85; Lukas, *Forgotten Holocaust*, 205–7.
38. Hitler–Szalasi, in Hillgruber, ed., *Staatmänner und Diplomaten*, 525.
39. Reitlinger, *The House Built on Sand*, 368–9.
40. Dallin, *German Rule*, 636.
41. K. Ungvary, *Battle for Budapest: One Hundred Days in World War II* (London, 2003), 274.
42. Dallin, *German Rule*, 646; C. Andreyev, *Vlasov and the Russian Liberation Movement: Soviet Reality and Emigré Theories* (Cambridge, 1987), 76–9.
43. A gripping but unverifiable account is J. Loftus, *The Belarus Secret* (New York, 1982).

Chapter 15: Opposition

1. On Polish resistance into 1940, L. Dobroszycki and M. Getter, 'The Gestapo and the Polish Resistance Movement', *Acta Poloniae Historica*, 4 (1961), 88; other quotations from Jacobmeyer, 'Die polnische Widerstandsbewegung', 655–81.
2. K. Lanckoronska, *Michelangelo in Ravensbrück: One Woman's War against the Nazis* (New York, 2007), 20.
3. G. von Frijtag Drabbe Künzel, 'Resistance, Reprisals, Reactions', in R. Gildea, O. Wieviorka and A. Warring, eds., *Surviving Hitler and Mussolini: Daily Life in Occupied Europe* (Oxford, 2006), 190–91.
4. W. Borodziej, *The Warsaw Uprising of 1944* (Madison, WI, 2006), 6–8, 38–9.
5. E. D. R. Harrison, 'The British Special Operations Executive and Poland', *Historical Journal*, 43:4 (2000), 1071–91.
6. Jacobmeyer, 'Die polnische Widerstandsbewegung', 674–5.
7. G. Kennan, 'The Technique of German Imperialism in Europe' (April 1941), p. 5, in George E. Kennan Papers, Mudd Library, Princeton University. (My thanks to Anders Stephanson for pointing me to this document.) M. Baudot, *L'Opinion publique sous l'Occupation: L'Example d'un département français (1939-1945)* (Paris, 1960), 15; P. Struye, *L'Evolution du sentiment publique en Belgique sous l'occupation allemande* (Brussels, 1945), 54.

8. On the Poles, see Szarota, *Warschau unter dem Hakenkreuz*, 283; A. Warring, 'Intimate and Sexual Relations', in Gildea, Wieviorka and Warring, eds., *Surviving Hitler and Mussolini*, 108–13; F. Virgili, *Shorn Women: Gender and Punishment in Liberation France* (New York, 2002), 11, 22–6.

9. Szarota, *Warschau unter dem Hakenkreuz*, 282–3; K. Stokker, 'Hurry Home, Haakon: The Impact of Anti-Nazi Humour on the Image of the Norwegian Monarch', *Journal of American Folklore*, 109:433 (Summer 1996), 289–307.

10. J. Haestrup, *European Resistance Movements, 1939–1945: A Complete History* (London, 1981), ch. 3.

11. Struye, *Journal de guerre*, 143; J. Sweets, *Choices in Vichy France: The French under Nazi Occupation* (Oxford, 1986), 203.

12. Brzeska, *Through a Woman's Eyes*, 34–40; Struye, *Journal de guerre*, 194, 203; Jacobmeyer, 'Die polnische Widerstandsbewegung', 670.

13. Hirschfeld, *Nazi Rule and Dutch Collaboration*, 35.

14. A. Moland, 'Norway', in B. Moore, ed., *Resistance in Western Europe* (Oxford, 2000), 223–37.

15. W. Weber, *Die innere Sicherheit im besetzten Belgien und Nordfrankreich, 1940–1944* (Düsseldorf, 1978), 54–5; Alexander von Falkenhausen, *Mémoires d'outre-guerre* (Brussels, 1974), 135–6, 153–5, 198.

16. L. Taylor, *Between Resistance and Collaboration: Popular Protest in Northern France, 1940–1945* (Basingstoke, 2000), 70–80; R. Gildea, D. Luyten and J. Fürst, 'To Work or Not to Work?', in Gildea, Wieviorka and Warring, eds., *Surviving Hitler and Mussolini*, 43–4; D. Luyten and R. Hemmerijckx, 'Belgian Labour in World War II: Strategies of Survival, Organisations and Labour Relation', *European Review of History*, 7:2 (Autumn 2000), 207–27.

17. W. Borodziej, *Terror und Politik*, 93–4.

18. G. Schulz, 'Zur englischen Planung des Partisanenkriegs am Vorabend des Zweiten Weltkrieges', *Vierteljahrshefte für Zeitgeschichte*, 30:2 (1982), 322–39.

19. M. R. D. Foot, 'Was SOE Any Good?', *Journal of Contemporary History*, 16:1 (January 1981), 167–81, here 169.

20. D. Stafford, 'The Detonator Concept: British Strategy, SOE and European Resistance after the Fall of France', *Journal of Contemporary History*, 10:2 (April 1975), 185–217.

21. M. Djilas, *Wartime* (New York, 1977), 12–13; G. Swain, 'The Comintern and Southern Europe, 1938–1943', in T. Judt, ed., *Resistance and Revolution in Mediterranean Europe, 1939–1948* (London, 1989), 29–53, here 38–40.

22. Djilas, *Wartime*, 12–13.

23. Ibid., 94; S. Trew, *Britain, Mihailovic and the Chetniks, 1941–42* (London, 1998), 61.

24. M. Wheeler, 'Pariahs to Partisans to Power: The CPY', in Judt, ed., *Resistance and Revolution*, 110–56; Trew, *Britain, Mihailovic and the Chetniks*, 149–50; M. A. Hoare, *Genocide and Resistance in Hitler's Bosnia: The Partisans and the Chetniks, 1941–1943* (Oxford, 2006), chs. 4–5.

25. On the impact in France, see R. Gildea, 'Resistance, Reprisals and Community in Occupied France', *Transactions of the Royal Historical Society*, 13 (2003), 163–85; MacDonald, *Killing*, 77–80; Bryant, *Prague in Black*, 179; F. Petrick, ed., *Die Okkupationspolitik des deutschen Faschismus in Dänemark und Norwegen (1940–1945)* (Berlin, 1992), 176, 190.

26. Gerlach, *Kalkulierte Morde*, 884 seq.

27. J. Armstrong, ed., *Soviet Partisans in World War II* (Madison, WI, 1964), 438–9.

28. Heiber, ed., *Hitler and His Generals*, 17, 771.

29. Gerlach, *Kalkulierte Morde*, 946–73.

30. Hill, *The War behind the Eastern Front*, 138–45.

31. J. Kagan and D. Cohen, *Surviving the Holocaust with the Russian Jewish Partisans* (London, 1997), 153–4; Dean, *Collaboration in the Holocaust*, 122–4.

32. Armstrong, ed., *Soviet Partisans*, 430–31, 672–3.
33. K. Slepyan, *Stalin's Guerillas: Soviet Partisans in World War Two* (Lawrence, KS, 2006), 27–46.
34. Cited in Kagan and Cohen, *Surviving the Holocaust*, 194.
35. Slepyan, *Stalin's Guerillas*, passim, esp. 91–101.
36. Ambassador Hemmen, 1764-PS in *NCA*, Supplement B (Washington, 1946), 402–3; Sauckel in '54th Conference of the Central Planning Board', R-124, *NCA*, vol. 8, 150.
37. H. R. Kedward, *In Search of the Maquis: Rural Resistance in Southern France, 1942–1944* (Oxford, 1993), 31.
38. Ibid., 42–3, 53; O. Wieviorka, 'France', in Moore, ed., *Resistance in Western Europe*, 125–55.
39. Baudot, *L'Opinion publique*, 233.
40. N. In'T Veld, 'Die Wehrmacht und die Widerstandsbekämpfung in Westeuropa', in G. Otto and J. H. ten Cate, eds., *Das organisierte Chaos: 'Ämterdarwinismus' und 'Gesinnungsethik': Determinanten nationalsozialistischer Besatzungsherrschaft* (Berlin, 1999), 279–301.
41. D. van Galen Lost, 'The Netherlands', in Moore, ed., *Resistance in Western Europe*, 189–221, here 199–201.
42. R. Gildea, D. Luyten and J. Fürst, 'To Work or Not to Work?', in Gildea et al., eds., *Surviving Hitler and Mussolini*, 64–66; Struye, *Journal de guerre*, 330.
43. Gerlach, *Kalkulierte Morde*, 996–8, 1011–35, 1141.
44. Jacobmeyer, 'Die polnische Widerstandsbewegung', 677; Hilberg, *The Destruction of the European Jews*, 3rd edn, vol. 2, 547–8.
45. *TWC*, vol. 5 (Pohl case), 622, Himmler-Krüger, 16 February 1943; T. Szarota, *The Warsaw Ghetto: The 45th Anniversary of the Uprising* (Warsaw, 1987); J. Garliński, *The Survival of Love: Memoirs of a Resistance Officer* (Cambridge, 1991), 112; Hilberg, *The Destruction of the European Jews*, 3rd edn, 534–40.
46. Szarota, *Warschau unter dem Hakenkreuz*, 279; Dobroszycki and Getter, 'The Gestapo and the Polish Resistance Movement', 118; Jacobmeyer, 'Die polnische Widerstandsbewegung', 677; W. Borodziej, *Terror und Politik*, 117–25, 174.
47. H. Trevor-Roper, ed., *Hitler's War Directives, 1939–1945* (London, 1966), 204–14; NOKW-159, 'Treatment of Prisoners and Deserters in Bandit Fighting, Reprisal and Evacuation Measures', *TWC*, vol. 11 (The Hostage Case), 1027–8; 'Proclamation to Norwegian Population' (n.d.), 1117.
48. Neubacher comment in NOKW-469, 'The Blood Bath of Klissura', 15 May 1944, *TWC*, vol. 11 ('The Hostage Case'), 1034–6; J. Hondros, *Occupation and Resistance: The Greek Agony, 1941–1944* (New York, 1983).
49. G. Corni, 'Italy', in Moore, ed., *Resistance in Western Europe*, 160–64.
50. G. Gribaudi, *Guerra totale: tra bombe alleate e violenze naziste. Napoli e il fronte meridionale 1940–1944* (Turin, 2005).
51. A. Portelli, *The Order Has Been Carried Out: History, Memory and the Meaning of a Nazi Massacre in Rome* (London, 2003); G. Schreiber, *Deutsche Kriegsverbrechen in Italien* (Munich, 1996), 95–109; 167–83. Numbers of casualties from Schreiber or E. Collotti and T. Matta, 'Rappresaglie, stragi, eccidi', in E. Collotti et al., eds., *Dizionario della Resistenza*, vol. 1 (Turin, 2000), 261–3.
52. Schreiber, *Deutsche Kriegsverbrechen in Italien*, 108–11.
53. Ibid., 195. In Tuscany, massacres took place far from the front lines: M. Battini and P. Pezzino, *Guerra ai civili: occupazione tedesca e politica del massacro. Toscana 1944* (Venice, 1997).
54. Klinkhammer, *Zwischen Bündnis und Besatzung*, 521.
55. B. Bowles, 'Newsreels, Ideology and Public Opinion under Vichy: The Case of *La France en Marche*', *French Historical Studies*, 27:2 (Spring 2004), 419–63, here 454.
56. Paxton, *Vichy France*, 293; Struye, *L'Evolution du sentiment publique*, 178–9.
57. P. P. Poggio, 'Reppublica sociale italiana', in Collotti et al., eds., *Dizionario della*

Resistenza, vol. 1, 66–77, here 73; R. Lamb, *War in Italy, 1943–45: A Brutal Story* (London, 1993), 99–101.

58. M. Franzinelli, 'Chiesa e clero cattolico', in Collotti et al., eds., *Dizionario della Resistenza*, vol. 1, 300–322.

59. Lukas, *Forgotten Holocaust*, 76.

60. T. Snyder, 'The Causes of Ukrainian-Polish Ethnic Cleansing 1943', *Past and Present*, 179 (May 2003), 197–235; Brown, *A Biography of No Place*, 221; Armstrong, *Ukrainian Nationalism*.

61. B. Chiari, 'Reichsführer-SS: Kein Pakt mit Slawen: Deutsch-polnische Kontakte im Wilna-Gebiet 1944', *Osteuropa Archiv* (April 2000), A134–A153.

62. N. Lewis, *Naples '44* (London, 1978), 26–33; Gribaudi, *Guerra totale*, 174–98.

63. Sweets, *Choices in Vichy France*, 221–3; Gildea, 'Resistance, Reprisals and Community', 163–85; see also T. Todorov, *A French Tragedy: Scenes of Civil War, Summer 1944* (Hanover, NH, 1996).

64. K. J. Müller, 'Le Développement des opérations du groupe d'armées B fin juillet-août 1944', in C. Levisse-Touzé, ed., *Paris 1944: Les Enjeux de la Libération* (Paris, 1994), 102–25; H. Umbreit, 'La Libération de Paris et la grande stratégie du IIIe Reich', in ibid., 327–43.

65. This summarizes a much more complex and confused series of decisions described by Borodziej, *The Warsaw Uprising of 1944*, chs. 3–4.

66. Ibid., 74–5; Hanson, *The Civilian Population*, 68.

67. Himmler cited in Borodziej, *The Warsaw Uprising*, 79.

68. Ibid., 81.

69. Hilberg, *The Destruction of the European Jews*, 3rd edn, 539; Szarota, *Warschau unter dem Hakenkreuz*, 319.

70. Corni, *Il sogno del 'grande spazio'*, 253; Dobroszycki and Getter, 'Gestapo and the Polish Resistance Movement', 117–18.

71. A. Milward, 'The Economic and Strategic Significance of Resistance', in S. Hawes and R. White, eds., *Resistance in Europe, 1939–1945* (Salford, 1973), 186–203; von Falkenhausen, 'Quatre ans', in *Mémoires*, 198.

72. On non-violent resistance, see J. Semelin, *Unarmed against Hitler: Civilian Resistance in Europe* (London, 1993).

73. B. Goldyn, 'Disenchanted Voices: Public Opinion in Cracow, 1945–46', *East European Quarterly*, 32:2 (June 1998), 139–65.

Chapter 16: Hitler Kaputt!

1. Heiber, ed., *Hitler and His Generals*, 554.

2. R.-D. Müller, *Der letzte deutsche Krieg, 1939–1945* (Stuttgart, 2005), 276–8, 285; F. de Lannoy, *La Ruée de l'Armée Rouge: Opération Bagration* (Bayeux, 2002); S. Zaloga, *Bagration 1944: The Destruction of Army Group Centre* (London, 1996).

3. Cited in Hanson, *The Civilian Population*, 68; A. Noble, 'The First *Frontgau*: East Prussia, July 1944', *War and History*, 13 (April 2006), 200–216; losses from Overmans, *Deutsche militärische Verluste*, 277.

4. Noble, 'The First *Frontgau*', 216.

5. H. Mommsen, 'The Dissolution of the Third Reich: Crisis Management and Collapse, 1943–45', *German Historical Institute (Washington): Bulletin*, 27 (Fall 2000), 9–23, here 18–19; Trevor-Roper, ed., *Hitler's War Directives*, 233; On the Nemmersdorf controversy, see G. Überschär, ed., *Orte des Grauens* (Darmstadt, 2003).

6. Ungvary, *Battle for Budapest*, xi; K. Ungvary, 'The "Second Stalingrad": The Destruction of Axis Forces in Budapest (February 1945)', in N. Dreisziger, ed., *Hungary in the Age of Total War* (New York, 1998), 151–67.

7. Karl Rosner on the 1917 retreat to the Hindenburg Line, in C. F. Horne, ed., *Source Records of the Great War*, vol. 5 (New York, 1923).

8. Trevor-Roper, ed., *Hitler's War Directives*, 234–6, 288; Hitler's order of 16 September 1944 in H. Schwendemann, 'Strategie der Selbstvernichtung: die Wehrmachtführung im "Endkampf" um das Dritte Reich', in R.-D. Müller and H.-E. Volkmann, eds., *Die Wehrmacht. Mythos und Realität* (Munich, 1999), 224–44, and his ' "Drastic Measures to Defend the Reich at the Oder and the Rhine": A Forgotten Memorandum of Albert Speer of 18 March 1945', *Journal of Contemporary History*, 38:4 (2003), 597–614.
9. C. Goeschel, 'Suicide at the End of the Third Reich', *Journal of Contemporary History*, 41:1 (2006), 153–73; M. Steinert, *Capitulation 1945: The Story of the Dönitz Regime* (London, 1969), 4; on Terboven, see Speer, *Spandau*, 239.
10. Trevor-Roper, ed., *Hitler's War Directives*, 293–4; M. Geyer, ' "There Is a Land Where Everything is Pure: Its Name is Land of Death": Some Observations on Catastrophic Nationalism', in G. Eghigian and M. P. Berg, eds., *Sacrifice and National Belonging in Twentieth Century Germany* (College Station, TX, 2002), 122, 131.
11. *NCA*, vol. 6, 745–52 (3815-PS).
12. D. Schenk, *Hans Frank: Hitlers Kronjurist und Generalgouverneur* (Frankfurt, 2006), 364–5.
13. *NCA*, vol. 6, 740–45 (3814-PS): various documents on the Frank affair in January 1945.
14. M. Steinert, 'The Allied Decision to Arrest the Dönitz Government', *Historical Journal*, 31:3 (1988), 651–63.
15. Speer, *Inside the Third Reich*, 486–7.
16. P. Padfield, *Himmler: Reichsführer-SS* (London, 1990), 600–607; Steinert, *Capitulation 1945*, 116–17.
17. Ibid., 1114–15; Speer, *Inside the Third Reich*, 496; L. Stokes, 'Otto Ohlendorf, the *Sicherheitsdienst* and Public Opinion in the Third Reich', in G. L. Mosse, ed., *Police Forces in History* (London, 1975), 258–9.
18. Steinert, *Capitulation 1945*, 238.
19. Matlock, ed., *Dänemark in Hitlers Hand*, 157–8.
20. Padfield, *Himmler: Reichsführer-SS*, 604–5.
21. Ibid., 604–5.
22. 'The Admiral's HQ', *Time*, 28 May 1945; Steinert, *Capitulation 1945*, 210–11.
23. Steinert, 'The Allied Decision', 659.
24. Ibid., 660.
25. Dolibois, *Pattern of Circles*, 85.
26. Weinberg, *A World at Arms*, 826.
27. Dolibois, *Pattern of Circles*, 100–135; also 'The Place of Judgement', *Time*, 6 August 1945.
28. Speer, *Spandau*, 20.
29. T. Schieder, ed., *The Expulsion of the German Population from the Territories East of the Oder-Neisse Line* (Bonn, n.d.), vol. 1, 129–30.
30. E. Scherstjanoi, ' "Vot ona prokliataia Germaniia!" Germany in Early 1945 through the Eyes of Red Army Soldiers', *Slavic Review*, 64:4 (Winter 2005), 165–89.
31. C. Merridale, *Ivan's War: Life and Death in the Red Army, 1939–1945* (New York, 2006), 301.
32. Ibid., 309; on the Wehrmacht see D. R. Snyder, *Sex Crimes under the Wehrmacht* (Lincoln, NE, 2007).
33. Merridale, *Ivan's War*, 284; Broekmeyer, *Stalin, the Russians and their War*, 120–22 (the case of Lev Kopelev), 126; on Kopelev, see L. Kopelev, *The Education of a True Believer* (New York, 1980).
34. Schieder, *Expulsion*, vol. 1, 136–7.
35. C. Kraft, 'Who Is a Pole and Who Is a German? The Province of Olsztyn in 1945', in P. Ther and A. Siljak, eds., *Redrawing Nations: Ethnic Cleansing in East-Central Europe, 1944–48* (Lathan, MD, 2001), 107–21, here 126; J. Kap, ed., *The Tragedy of Silesia, 1945–46* (Munich, 1952/3), 193.

36. Ibid., 198–9, 238–9; on ghettoes, see also Kraft, 'Who Is a Pole and Who Is a German?', 112.
37. Ther, 'A Century of Forced Migration', in Ther and Siljak, eds., *Redrawing Nations*, 55; Bryant, *Prague in Black*, 229–30.
38. S. Jankowiak, ' "Cleansing" Poland of Germans', in Ther and Siljak, eds., *Redrawing Nations*, 88–9.
39. J. Chuminski and E. Kaszuba, 'The Breslau Germans under Polish Rule, 1945–46: Conditions of Life, Political Attitudes, Expulsion', *Studia Historiae Oeconomicae*, 22 (1997), 87–101.
40. B. Frommer, *National Cleansing: Retribution against Nazi Collaborators in Postwar Czechoslovakia* (Cambridge, 2005).
41. E. Glassheim, 'National Mythologies and Ethnic Cleansing: The Expulsion of Czecho-slovak Germans in 1945', *Central European History*, 33:4 (2005), 463–86.
42. Ibid., 482; N. Naimark, *Fires of Hatred: Ethnic Cleansing in Twentieth Century Europe* (Cambridge, MA, 2001), 116; Bryant, *Prague in Black*, 238–9.
43. Naimark, *Fires of Hatred*, 130–33.
44. K. Kersten, 'Transformation of Polish Society', in Ther and Siljak, eds., *Redrawing Nations*, 78; Churchill cited in ibid., 6.
45. Wiskemann, *Germany's Eastern Neighbours*, 209–28.
46. A. Prazmowska, 'The Kielce Pogrom 1946 and the Emergence of Communist Power in Poland', *Cold War History*, 2:2 (January 2002), 101–24; D. Engel, 'Patterns of Anti-Jewish Violence in Poland, 1944–46', *Yad Vashem Studies*, 26 (1998), 43–87.
47. P. Ahonen, *After the Expulsion: West Germany and Eastern Europe, 1945–1990* (Oxford, 2003).

Chapter 17: We Europeans

1. J. Goebbels, 'Das Jahr 2000', *Das Reich*, 25 February 1945, 1–2, translated by Randall Bytwerk and available on his online German Propaganda Archive at http://www.calvin.edu/academic/cas/gpa/goeb49.htm. My thanks to Professor Bytwerk for permission to quote from this.
2. Ibid.
3. P. Herre, *Deutschland und die Europäische Ordnung* (Berlin, 1941), 196; E. Bramsted, *Goebbels and National Socialist Propaganda, 1925–1945* (East Lansing, MI, 1965), 303.
4. Ibid., 303–4.
5. Hitler, *Hitler's Second Book*, 109–16.
6. Goebbels, 'The Europe of the Future', 11 September 1940, in Neulen, *Europa und das 3. Reich*, 73–5.
7. P. Kluke, 'Nationalsozialistische Europaideologie', *Vierteljahrshefte für Zeitgeschichte*, 3:3 (1955), 240–75, here 259.
8. *DGFP*, 13, no. 327 (Statements by the Führer to Ambassador Abetz on 16 September 1941), 520.
9. *DGFP*, 13, no. 424 (Record of the Conversation between the Führer and Count Ciano at Headquarters on 25 October 1941), 692–4.
10. Speer, *Spandau*, 156.
11. Neitzel, ed., *Tapping Hitler's Generals*, 159, 175.
12. Boelcke, ed., *The Secret Conferences*, 113.
13. E. Beneš, 'The Organization of Postwar Europe', *Foreign Affairs*, 20:1 (January 1942), 226–42.
14. L. Curtis, 'World Order', *International Affairs*, 18:3 (May–June 1939), 301–20; see also D. Lavin, *From Empire to International Commonwealth: A Biography of Lionel Curtis* (Oxford, 1995). W. Lipgens, *A History of European Integration*, vol. 1 (1945–7) (Oxford, 1982).
15. Ibid., 62–5; Department of State, *Postwar Foreign Policy Preparation, 1939–1945*

(Washington, DC, 1949), 458–61 (Memo of 1 May 1940); Kennan, cited in J. L. Harper, *American Visions of Europe: Franklin D. Roosevelt, George F. Kennan, and Dean G. Acheson* (Cambridge, 1996), 182; R. Schlesinger, *Federalism in Central and Eastern Europe* (New York, 1945), ix.

16. Lipgens, *A History of European Integration*, vol. 1, 63–4; Schlesinger, *Federalism*, 478.
17. E. Ranshofen-Wertheimer, *Victory Is Not Enough: The Strategy for a Lasting Peace* (New York, 1942), 167–202.
18. Belgian opposition in T. Grosbois, 'Les Projets des petites nations de Benelux pour l'après-guerre, 1941–1945', in M. Demoulin, *Plans des Temps de Guerre pour l'Europe d'Après-Guerre, 1940–47* (Brussels, 1995), 120; S. Neumann, 'Fashions in Space', *Foreign Affairs*, 21:2 (January 1943), 276–88, here 288.
19. Schlesinger, *Federalism*, 447–9.
20. Strang cited in L. Kettenacker, 'The Anglo-Soviet Alliance and the Problem of Germany, 1941–1945', *Journal of Contemporary History*, 17:3 (July 1982), 435–58, here 449.
21. Lipgens, *A History of European Integration*, vol. 1.
22. G. Murashko and A. Noskova, 'Stalin and the National-territorial Controversies in Eastern Europe, 1945–1947', *Cold War History*, 1:3 (April 2001), 161–72.
23. D. Reynolds, 'Churchill, Stalin and the "Iron Curtain"', in *From World War to Cold War: Churchill, Roosevelt and the International History of the 1940s* (Oxford, 2006), 250–51.
24. Harper, *American Visions*, 188.
25. Steinert, *Capitulation 1945* (London, 1969), 6; Lipgens, *A History of European Integration*, vol. 1, 66 fn. 108, 104 fn. 21; W. Rostow, 'The European Commission for Europe', *International Organization*, 3:2 (May 1949), 254–68.
26. Lipgens, *History of European Integration*, vol. 1.
27. W. Mauter, 'Churchill and the Unification of Europe', *The Historian*, 61:1 (Fall 1998), 67–84; A. W. B. Simpson, *Human Rights and the End of Empire: Britain and the Genesis of the European Convention* (Oxford, 2001); A. Milward, *The European Rescue of the Nation-State* (London, 2000).
28. Schumann, 'Probleme der deutschen Aussenwirtschaft', 141–60.
29. L. Herbst, 'Die wirtschaftlichen Nachkriegspläne des SS, der Reichswirtschaftsministeriums und der Reichsgruppe Industrie im Angesicht der Niederlage (1943–45)', in Demoulin, *Plans des Temps de Guerre*, 15–24.
30. K. Tauber, *Beyond Eagle and Swastika: German Nationalism since 1945* (Middletown, CT, 1967), 208–9.
31. Ibid., 210–30.
32. Ibid., 925.
33. Speer, *Inside the Third Reich*, 307; Carlo Scorza, cited in C. Pavone, 'La continuità dello stato', in Pavone, *Alle origine della Repubblica*, 75.

Chapter 18: The New Order in World History

1. L. Namier, 'The German Finale to an Epoch in History', in *Vanished Supremacies*, 219.
2. F. Giddings (in *Democracy and Empire*) cited in D. P. Crook, *Benjamin Kidd: Portrait of a Social Darwinist* (Cambridge, 1984), 133–4.
3. C. K. Leith, 'The Struggle for Mineral Resources', *Annals of the American Academy of Political and Social Science*, 204 (July 1939), 42–8.
4. C. Schmitt, 'Grossraum gegen Universalismus', *Zeitschrift der Akademie für Deutsches Recht*, 9 (1939), 333–7 and the discussion in Herbert, *Best*, 271–5. See too C. Schmitt, *The Nomos of the Earth in the International Law of the Ius Publicum Europaeum* (New York, 2003), ch. 3.
5. J. Bendersky, *Carl Schmitt: Theorist for the Reich* (Princeton, 1983), 256–8.
6. R. Dumett, 'Africa's Strategic Minerals during the Second World War', *Journal of African History*, 26:4 (1985), 381–408.

7. A. Frye, *Nazi Germany and the American Hemisphere, 1933–1945* (New Haven, 1967); F. D. McCann, *The Brazilian–American Alliance, 1937–1945* (Princeton, 1973), 146; Weinberg, *A World at Arms*, 154.

8. G. Smith, *The Last Years of the Monroe Doctrine, 1945–1993* (New York, 1994), 35; Darwin, *After Tamerlane*, 419.

9. Weinberg, *A World at Arms*, 497; M. Lynch, *Mining in World History* (London, 2002), 286.

10. C. W. Spang and R.-H. Wippich, eds., *Japanese–German Relations, 1895–1945* (London, 2006), Introduction; M. Hauner, *India in Axis Strategy: Germany, Japan and Indian Nationalists in the Second World War* (Stuttgart, 1981), 278–9.

11. G. Weinberg, ed., *Hitlers Zweites Buch* (Stuttgart, 1961), 165; see, too, Reynolds, *From World War to Cold War*, 42–3.

12. As argued recently, for example, by K. Pomeranz, *The Great Divergence: China, Europe and the Making of the Modern World Economy* (Princeton, 2000); also C. Bayly, *The Birth of the Modern World, 1780–1914* (Oxford, 2004). For an older view, less convinced of the importance of the colonies, see P. O'Brien, 'European Economic Development', *Economic History Review*, 35:1 (February 1982), 1–18.

13. On extermination, for instance, see H. Johnston, 'The Empire and Anthropology', *Nineteenth Century and After*, 327 (July 1908) 133–46; C. Hart Merriam, 'The Indian Population of California', *American Anthropologist* (October–December 1905), 594–606; other quotations from S. Lindqvist, *Terra Nullius: A Journey through No One's Land* (New York, 2007), 35–6. Settler colonialism is examined in Elkins and Pedersen, eds., *Settler Colonialism in the Twentieth Century*.

14. Migration figures in K. J. Bade, 'From Emigration to Immigration: The German Experience in the 19th and 20th Centuries', *Central European History*, 28:4 (1995), 507–35; A. Perras, *Carl Peters and German Imperialism, 1856–1918: A Political Biography* (Oxford, 2004), 38.

15. C. Sauer, 'The Formative Years of Ratzel in the United States', *Annals of the Association of American Geographers*, 61:2 (June 1971), 245–54; Perras, *Carl Peters*, 31–3.

16. Perras, *Carl Peters*, 38, 44.

17. On German claims in South America, see R. Armstrong, 'Should the Monroe Doctrine Be Modified or Abandoned?', *American Journal of International Law*, 10:1 (January 1916), 77–103.

18. Harvey, 'Management and Manipulation', 106; T. Remeikis, ed., *Lithuania under German Occupation, 1941–1945: Despatches from the US Legation in Stockholm* (Vilnius, 2005), 46; Heiber, ed., *Hitler and his Generals*, 533–4.

19. Cited in D. Furber, 'Near as Far as in the Colonies: The Nazi Occupation of Poland', *International History Review*, 26:3 (September 2004), 541–79; H. Fischer, *Völkerkunde im Nationalsozialismus: Aspekte der Anpassung, Affinität und Behauptung einer wissenschaftlichen Disziplin* (Berlin, 1990), 133.

20. T. Bender, *A Nation among Nations: America's Place in World History* (New York, 2006), 222–3; Crook, *Benjamin Kidd*, 135.

21. Cited by S. Wolton, *Lord Hailey, the Colonial Office and the Politics of Race and Empire in the Second World War: The Loss of White Prestige* (London, 2000), 43.

22. E. Fischer, *Is This a War for Freedom?* (New York, 1940), 34; C. Wills, *That Neutral Island: A Cultural History of Ireland during the Second World War* (London, 2007), 71.

23. A. Césaire, *Discourse on Colonialism* (New York, 2000), 36.

24. Harrison quoted in R. W. Kostal, *A Jurisprudence of Power: Victorian Empire and the Rule of Law* (Oxford, 2005), 253; G. Gong, *The Standard of 'Civilisation' in International Society* (Oxford, 1984).

25. Neulen, *Europa und das 3. Reich*, 183.

26. On the League's reluctance to talk about annexation, see C. Schmitt, *The Concept of the Political*, trans. G. Schwab (New Brunswick, 1976), 73. More generally, M. Mazower,

'An International Civilization? Empire, Internationalism and the Crisis of the Mid-Twentieth Century', *International Affairs*, 82:3 (2006), 561–3.

27. Weinberg, ed., *Hitlers Zweites Buch*, 165–6.

28. Kostal, *A Jurisprudence of Power*, 470; Fitzjames Stephen in U. Singh Mehta, *Liberalism and Empire: A Study in Nineteenth-Century British Liberal Thought* (Chicago, 1999), 196; Neitzel, ed., *Tapping Hitler's Generals*, 174.

29. J. Reich Abel, 'Warring Internationalisms: Multilateral Thinking in Japan, 1933–1964', D.Phil. thesis, Columbia University, 2004, pp. 160–62; *I Documenti diplomatici*, ix, 546, Alfieri-Mussolini, 11 June 1943.

30. Hauner, *India in Axis Strategy*, 33, 342–5, 479, 497, 532–3. My thanks to Marilyn Young for this reference.

31. Goebbels, *The Goebbels Diaries 1942–43*, 212 (entry for 12 May 1942).

32. Cited in C. Boyd, *Hitler's Japanese Confidant: General Oshima Hiroshi and MAGIC Intelligence, 1941–1945* (Lawrence, KS, 1993), 81–2; H. Dobson, 'The Failure of the Tripartite Pact: Familiarity Breeding Contempt between Japan and Germany: 1940–1945', *Japan Forum*, 11:2 (1999), 179–90.

33. Boyd, *Hitler's Japanese Confidant*.

34. G. Orwell, 'Not Counting Niggers', *Adelphi* (July 1939).

35. Perham in H. Nicolson, 'The Colonial Problem', *International Affairs*, 17:1 (January–February 1938), 32–50; I. McLaine, *The Ministry of Morale* (London, 1979), 223–4; Wolton, *Lord Hailey*, 39–59.

36. Jennings, *Vichy in the Tropics*, 127.

37. C. Bayly and T. Harper, *Forgotten Wars: The End of Britain's Asian Empire* (London, 2007); P. Lagrou, 'The Nationalization of Victimhood: Selective Violence and National Grief in Western Europe, 1940–1960', in R. Bessel and D. Schumann, eds., *Life after Death: Approaches to a Cultural and Social History of Europe during the 1940s and 1950s* (Cambridge, 2003), 248 for an estimate of French civilians killed by the Germans during the occupation. For the colonial repressions, see R. Gildea, *France since 1945* (Oxford, 2002), 21–2.

38. R. Hyam, *Britain's Declining Empire: The Road to Decolonisation, 1918–1968* (Cambridge, 2006), 96; Darwin, *After Tamerlane*, ch. 8; Wolton, *Lord Hailey*, 123.

39. C. Elkins, 'Race, Citizenship and Governance: Settler Tyranny and the End of Empire', in Elkins and Pedersen, eds., *Settler Colonialism in the Twentieth Century*, 203–23.

40. H. Grimal, *Decolonization: The British, French, Dutch and Belgian Empires, 1919–1963* (Boulder, CO, 1978), 145.

41. Wolton, *Lord Hailey*, 47, 74.

42. R. E. Birchard, 'Europe's Critical Food Situation', *Economic Geography*, 24:4 (October 1948), 274–82.

43. Schacht in R. Overy, *Interrogations: The Nazi Elite in Allied Hands, 1945* (London, 2001), 535.

44. My thanks to Kiran Patel for discussing German and west European food policy with me. His forthcoming work will illuminate this badly neglected subject. On food intake and self-sufficiency, see H. Marmulla and P. Brault, *Europäische Intergration und Agrarwirtschaft* (Bonn, 1958), 326–31.

45. J. Herz, 'The Rise and Demise of the Territorial State', *World Politics*, 9:4 (July 1957), 473–93.

46. From an enormous literature on the USA as an empire, see C. Maier, *Among Empires: American Ascendancy and Its Predecessors* (Cambridge, MA, 2006); V. de Grazia, *Irresistible Empire: America's Advance through Twentieth Century Europe* (Cambridge, MA, 2005); and for the most recent period C. Johnson, *The Sorrows of Empire: Militarism, Secrecy and the End of the Republic* (New York, 2004).

47. J. Herz, 'The Territorial State Revisited: Reflections on the Future of the Nation-State', *Polity*, 1:1 (August 1968), 11–34.

48. A. Morris-Reich, 'Arthur Ruppin's Concept of Race', *Israel Studies*, 11:3 (Fall 2006), 1–30.
49. S. Reichman and S. Hasson, 'A Cross-Cultural Diffusion of Colonization: From Posen to Palestine', *Annals of the Association of American Geographers*, 74:1 (March 1984), 57–70; D. Penslar, *Zionism and Technocracy: The Engineering of Jewish Settlement in Palestine, 1870–1918* (Bloomington, IN, 1991); G. Shafir, 'Settler Citizenship in the Jewish Colonization of Palestine', in Elkins and Pedersen, eds., *Settler Colonialism*, 41–59.
50. G. Shafir, 'Tech for Tech's Sake', *Journal of Palestine Studies*, 21:4 (Summer 1992), 103–5; Y. Weiss, 'Central European Ethnonationalism and Zionist Binationalism', *Jewish Social Studies*, 11:1 (Fall 2004), 93–117.
51. Ibid., 102–3, 106–8; D. J. Penslar, *Israel in History: The Jewish State in Comparative Perspective* (Abingdon, 2007), 164–5; on Ruppin's caution see also S. Ilan Troen, *Imagining Zion: Dreams, Designs and Realities in a Century of Jewish Settlement* (New Haven, 2003), 179.
52. S. Della Pergola, 'Between Science and Fiction: Notes on the Demography of the Holocaust', *Holocaust and Genocide Studies*, 10:1 (Spring 1996), 34–51.
53. Data from J. Vernant, *The Refugee in the Post-War World* (London, 1953), 449; American Jewish Community, *American Jewish Yearbook* (various).
54. I. Zertal, *From Catastrophe to Power: Holocaust Survivors and the Emergence of Israel* (Berkeley, 1998), 215–62; S. Ilan Troen and N. Lucas, eds., *Israel: the First Decade of Independence* (Albany, 1995).
55. Ibid., 442; on the Iraqi case, see Y. Shenhav, 'The Jews of Iraq, Zionist Ideology and the Property of Palestinian Refugees of 1948: An Anomaly of National Accounting', *International Journal of Middle Eastern Studies*, 31:4 (November 1999), 605–30.
56. For preliminary thoughts on this process, see M. Mazower, 'The Strange Triumph of Human Rights, 1933–1950', *Historical Journal*, 47:2 (2004), 379–99; and idem., ' "An International Civilisation?" Empire, Internationalism and the Crisis of the mid-20th Century', *International Affairs*, 82:3 (2006), 553–66.
57. Cf. G. Agamben, 'Beyond Human Rights' in his *Means without Ends: Notes in Politics* (Minneapolis, 2000); Arendt, *The Origins of Totalitarianism*, ch. 9.
58. Cf. E. Borgwardt, *A New Deal for the World: America's Vision for Human Rights* (Cambridge, MA, 2005). I owe much on this point to discussions with Samuel Moyn, John Witt and Mira Siegelberg.
59. Paul Hoffman cited in O. A. Westad, *The Global Cold War: Third World Interventionism and the Making of Our Times* (Cambridge, 2007), 25; A. Weber, *Abschied von der bisherigen Geschichte* (Hamburg, 1946).

Bibliography

'A Citizen of Kharkiv', 'Lest We Forget: Hunger in Kharkiv in the Winter of 1941–42', *Ukrainian Quarterly*, 4 (Winter 1948), 72–9

Agamben, G. 'Beyond Human Rights', in his *Means without Ends: Notes in Politics* (Minneapolis, 2000)

Ahonen, P. *After the Expulsion: West Germany and Eastern Europe, 1945–1990* (Oxford, 2003)

Allen, M. T. *Hitler's Slave Lords: The Business of Forced Labour in Occupied Europe* (London, 2004)

Aly, G. *'The Final Solution': Nazi Population Policy and the Murder of the European Jews* (London, 1999)

—— *Hitler's Beneficiaries: Plunder, Racial War and the Nazi Welfare State* (New York, 2007)

Aly, G. and Heims, S. *Architects of Annihilation: Auschwitz and the Logic of Destruction* (Princeton, 2003)

Aly, G. and Roth, K. H. *The Nazi Census: Identification and Control in the Third Reich* (Philadelphia, 2004)

Aly, G. et al., eds. *Biedermann und Schreibtischtäter: Materialien zur deutschen Täter-Biographie* (Berlin, 1987)

American Jewish Community *American Jewish Yearbook*

American Jewish Conference *Nazi Germany's War against the Jews* (New York, 1947)

Ancel, J. *Documents Concerning the Fate of Romanian Jewry during the Holocaust* (New York, 1987)

—— *Transnistria 1941–1942: The Romanian Mass Murder Campaigns*, vol. 1 (Tel Aviv, 2003)

—— 'The German–Rumanian Relationship and the Final Solution', *Holocaust and Genocide Studies*, 19:2 (Fall 2005), 252–75

Anderl, G. 'Die "Zentralstellen für judische Auswanderung" in Wien, Berlin und Prag: Ein Vergleich', *Tel Aviver Jahrbuch für Deutsche Geschichte*, 23 (1994), 275–99

Anderson, T. 'Incident at Baranivka: German Reprisals and the Soviet Partisan Movement in Ukraine, October–December 1941', *Journal of Modern History*, 71:3 (September 1999), 585–623

—— 'A Hungarian *Vernichtungskrieg*? Hungarian Troops and the Soviet Partisan War in Ukraine, 1942', *Militärgeschichtliche Mitteilungen*, 58:2 (1999), 345–66

—— 'Germans, Ukrainians and Jews: Ethnic Politics in Heeresgebiet Süd June–December 1941', *War in History*, 7:3 (2000), 325–51

Andreyev, C. *Vlasov and the Russian Liberation Movement: Soviet Reality and Emigré Theories* (Cambridge, 1987)

Anfuso, F. *Da Palazzo Venezia al Lago di Garda (1936–1945)* (n. p., 1957), 196–210

Angrick, A. 'The Escalation of German–Rumanian Anti-Jewish Policy after the Attack on the Soviet Union', *Yad Vashem Studies*, 26 (1998), 203–39

Antonellis, G. de *Le Quattro Giornate di Napoli* (Milan, 1973)

Arad, Y. 'Alfred Rosenberg and the "Final Solution" in the Occupied Soviet Territories', *Yad Vashem Studies*, 13 (1979), 263–86

Arendt, H. *The Origins of Totalitarianism* (New York, 1951)

Armstrong, J., ed. *Soviet Partisans in World War II* (Madison, WI, 1964)

Armstrong, J. A. *Ukrainian Nationalism*, rev. edn (Littleton, CO, 1980)

Armstrong, R. 'Should the Monroe Doctrine be Modified or Abandoned?', *American Journal of International Law*, 10:1 (January 1916), 77–103

Arnaud, C. *Jean Cocteau* (Paris, 2003)

Arnold, K. J. 'Die Eroberung und Behandlung der Stadt Kiev durch die Wehrmacht im September 1941: Zur Radikalisierung der Besatzungspolitik', *Militärgeschichtliche Mitteilungen*, 58:1 (1999), 23–63

——*Die Wehrmacht und die Besatzungspolitik in den besetzten Gebieten der Sowjetunion: Kriegsführung und Radikalisierung im 'Unternehmen Barbarossa'* (Berlin, 2005)

Aronson, S. 'Heydrich und die Anfänge des SD und der Gestapo (1931–1935)', dissertation [Freie Universität Berlin, 1967]

——*Beginnings of the Gestapo System: The Bavaria Model in 1933* (Jerusalem, 1969)

Auswärtiges Amt, *Amtliches Material zum Massenmord von Katyn* (Berlin, 1943)

Backe, H. *Das Ende des Liberalismus in der Wirtschaft* (Berlin, 1938)

——*Um die Nahrungsfreiheit Europas: Weltwirtschaft oder Grossraum* (Leipzig, 1942)

Bacon, F. *Selected Writings of Francis Bacon* (New York, 1955)

Bade, K. J. 'From Emigration to Immigration: The German Experience in the 19th and 20th Centuries', *Central European History*, 28:4 (1995), 507–35

Balfour, M. *Helmuth von Moltke: A Leader against Hitler* (London, 1972)

Banning, C. 'Food Shortage and Public Health, First Half of 1945', *Annals of the American Academy of Political and Social Science*, 245 (May 1946), 93–110

Barasz, J. 'Un vichyste en Résistance, le général de la Laurencie', *Vingtième Siècle*, 94 (April–June 2007), 167–81

Bartov, O. *The Eastern Front, 1941–1945: German Troops and the Barbarization of Warfare* (New York, 1986)

——*Hitler's Army: Soldiers, Nazis and War in the Third Reich* (New York, 1991)

Baruch, M.-O. *Servir l'État Français: L'Administration en France de 1940 à 1944* (Paris, 1997)

Bar-Zohar, M. *Bitter Scent: The Case of L'Oréal, Nazis and the Arab Boycott* (New York, 1996)

Bassler, G. *Alfred Valdmanis and the Politics of Survival* (Toronto, 2000)

Battini, M. and Pezzino, P. *Guerra ai civili: occupazione tedesca e politica del massacro, Toscana 1944* (Venice, 1997)

Baudot, M. *L'Opinion publique sous l'Occupation: L'Example d'un département français (1939–1945)* (Paris, 1960)

Bauer, Y. 'The Death Marches, January–May 1945', *Modern Judaism*, 3:1 (1983), 1–21

Bayly, C. *The Birth of the Modern World, 1780–1914: Global Connections and Comparisons* (Oxford, 2004)

Bayly, C. and Harper, T. *Forgotten Wars: The End of Britain's Asian Empire* (London, 2007)

Bell, H. 'Monetary Problems of Military Occupation', *Military Affairs*, 6:2 (Summer 1942), 77–88

Bender, T. *A Nation among Nations: America's Place in World History* (New York, 2006)

Bendersky, J. *Carl Schmitt: Theorist for the Reich* (Princeton, 1983)

Beneš, E. 'The Organization of Postwar Europe', *Foreign Affairs*, 20:1 (January 1942), 226–42

Benjamin, L., ed., *Problema evreiasca in stenogramele Consiliului de Ministri* (Bucharest, 1996)

Benz, W. et al., eds. *Nationalsozialistische Besatzungspolitik in Europa, 1939–1945*, 9 vols. (Berlin 1996–9)

——*Die Bürokratie der Okkupation: Strukturen der Herrschaft und Verwaltung im besetzten Europa* (Berlin, 1998)

——*Einsatz im Reichskommissariat Ostland: Dokumente zum Völkermord im Baltikum und in Weissrussland, 1941–1944* (Berlin, 1998)

——*Kultur-Propaganda-Öffentlichkeit: Intentionen deutscher Besatzungspolitik und Reaktionen auf die Okkupation* (Berlin, 1998)

Benz, W. and Distel, B., eds. *Der Ort des Terrors: Geschichte der nationalsozialistischen Konzentrationslager*, vol. 5 (Munich, 2005)

Berkhoff, K. *Harvest of Despair: Life and Death in Ukraine under Nazi Rule* (Cambridge, MA, 2004)

Berlière, J.-M. 'L'Impossible Pérennité de la police républicaine sous l'Occupation', *Vingtième Siècle*, 94 (April–June 2007), 183–96

Bessel, R. and Schumann, D., eds. *Life after Death: Approaches to a Cultural and Social History of Europe during the 1940s and 1950s* (Cambridge, 2003)

Betz, A. and Martens, S., eds. *Les Intellectuels et l'Occupation: Collaborer, partir, resister, 1940–1944* (Paris, 2004)

Biddiscombe, P. '*Unternehmen* Zeppelin: The Deployment of SS Saboteurs and Spies in the Soviet Union, 1942–1945', *Europe–Asia Studies*, 52:6 (2000), 1115–42

Bilfinger, C. 'Streit um das Völkerrecht', *Zeitschrift für ausländisches öffentliches Recht- und Völkerrecht* 12 (1944), 1–34

Billig, J. *Alfred Rosenberg dans l'action idéologique, politique et administrative du Reich hitlérien* (Paris, 1963)

Birchard, R. E. 'Europe's Critical Food Situation', *Economic Geography*, 24:4 (October 1948), 274–82

Birn, R. B. *Die höheren SS- und Polizeiführer: Himmlers Vertreter im Reich und in den besetzten Gebieten* (Düsseldorf, c. 1986)

Black, P. 'Rehearsal for "Reinhard": Odilo Globocnik and the Lublin *Selbstschutz*', *Central European History*, 25:2 (1992), 204–26

Blackbourn, D. *The Conquest of Nature: Water, Landscape and the Making of Modern Germany* (London, 2006)

Blanke, R. 'An Era of "Reconciliation" in German–Polish Relations (1890–1894)', *Slavic Review*, 36:1 (March 1977), 39–53

——'The German Minority in Interwar Poland and German Foreign Policy: Some Reconsiderations', *Journal of Contemporary History*, 25 (1990), 87–102

——*Orphans of Versailles: The Germans in Western Poland, 1918–1939* (Lexington, KY, 1993)

Bloch, M. *Ribbentrop* (London, 1992)

Boelcke, W., ed. '*Wollt Ihr den totalen Krieg?*': Die geheimen Goebbels-Konferenzen 1939–1943* (Stuttgart, 1967)

——*The Secret Conferences of Dr Goebbels, the Nazi Propaganda War, 1939–1943* (New York, 1970)

Bohn, R., ed. *Die deutsche Herrschaft in den 'germanischen' Ländern 1940–1945* (Stuttgart, 1997)

Bonusiak, W. 'Die Landwirtschaftspolitik der sowjetischen Besatzungsmacht auf dem Gebiet des sog. westlichen Weissrusslands in den Jahren 1939–1949', *Studia Historicae Oeconomicae*, 24 (2001), 149–63

Borgwardt, E. *A New Deal for the World: America's Vision for Human Rights* (Cambridge, MA, 2005)

Borodziej, W. *Terror und Politik: Die deutsche Polizei und die polnische Widerstandsbewegung im Generalgouvernement, 1939–1944* (Mainz, 1999)

——*The Warsaw Uprising of 1944* (Madison, WI, 2006)

Bottai, G. *Diario, 1935–1944* (Milan, 1982)

Bottomore, T. and Goode, P., eds. *Austro-Marxism* (Oxford, 1978)

Botz, G. *Die Eingliederung Österreichs in das Deutsches Reich* (Linz, 1976)

Bowen, W. *Spaniards and Nazi Germany: Collaboration in the New Order* (Columbia, MO, 2000)

Bowles, B. 'Newsreels, Ideology and Public Opinion under Vichy: The Case of *La France en Marche*', *French Historical Studies*, 27:2 (Spring 2004), 419–63

Boyd, C. *Hitler's Japanese Confidant: General Oshima Hiroshi and MAGIC Intelligence, 1941–1945* (Lawrence, KS, 1993)

Bramsted, E. *Goebbels and National Socialist Propaganda, 1925–1945* (East Lansing, MI, 1965)

Brandes, D., Ivanickova, E. and Pesek, J., eds. *Erzwungene Trennung: Vertreibungen und Aussiedlungen in und aus der Tschechoslowakei 1938–1947 im Vergleich mit Polen, Ungarn und Jugoslawien* (Tübingen, 1999)

Brandt, K. *Management of Agriculture and Food in the German-Occupied and Other Areas of Fortress Europe: A Study in Military Government* (Stanford, 1953)

Bräutigam, O. *So hat es sich zugetragen . . . Ein Leben als Soldat und Diplomat* (Würzburg, 1968)

Brechtken, M. ' "La géographie demeure": Frankreich, Polen und die Kolonial- und Juden-frage am Vorabend des Zweiten Weltkrieges', *Francia*, 25:3 (1998), 25–60

Bree, G. and Bernauer, G., eds. *Defeat and Beyond: An Anthology of French Wartime Writing, 1940–1945* (New York, 1970)

Breitman, R. and Aronson, S. 'The End of the "Final Solution": Nazi Plans to Ransom Jews in 1944', *Central European History*, 25 (1992), 177–203

Breunis J. 'The Food Supply', *Annals of the American Academy of Political and Social Science*, 245 (May 1946), 87–92

Broekmeyer, M. *Stalin, the Russians and Their War, 1941–1945* (Madison, WI, 2004)

Broszat, M. *Nationalsozialistische Polenpolitik, 1939–1945* (Stuttgart, 1961)

Browder, G. *Hitler's Enforcers: The Gestapo and the SS Security Service in the Nazi Revolution* (Oxford, 1996)

Brown, K. *A Biography of No Place: From Ethnic Borderland to Soviet Heartland* (Cambridge, MA, 2004)

Browning, C. 'Unterstaatssekretär Martin Luther and the Ribbentrop Foreign Office', *Journal of Contemporary History*, 12:2 (April 1977), 313–44

—— *The Final Solution and the German Foreign Office* (New York, 1978)

—— *The Path to Genocide: Essays on Launching the Final Solution* (Cambridge, 1992)

—— 'A Final Hitler Decision for the "Final Solution": The Riegner Telegram Reconsidered', *Holocaust and Genocide Studies*, 10:1 (Spring 1996), 3–10

—— *Nazi Policy, Jewish Workers, German Killers* (Cambridge, 2000)

—— *The Origins of the Final Solution: The Evolution of Nazi Jewish Policy, September 1939–March 1945; With Contributions by Jürgen Matthäus* (Lincoln, NE, 2004)

Bryant, C. 'Either German or Czech: Fixing Nationality in Bohemia and Moravia, 1939–1946', *Slavic Review*, 61:4 (Winter 2002), 683–706

—— *Prague in Black: Nazi Rule and Czech Nationalism* (Cambridge, MA, 2007)

Brzeska, M. *Through a Woman's Eyes* (London, [1945])

Buchheim, C. 'Die besetzten Länder im Dienste der Deutschen Kriegswirtschaft während des Zweiten Weltkriegs', *Vierteljahrshefte für Zeitgeschichte*, 34:1 (1986), 117–45

Buchheim, H. 'Die höheren SS- und Polizeiführer', *Vierteljahrshefte für Zeitgeschichte*, 11 (1963), 362–91

Buchheim, H. et al., eds. *Anatomie des SS-Staates*, vol. 1 (Munich, 1967)

Buechler, Y. 'The Deportation of Slovakian Jews to the Lublin District of Poland in 1942', *Holocaust and Genocide Studies*, 6:2 (1991), 151–66

—— ' "Unworthy Behavior": The Case of SS Officer Max Täubner', *Holocaust and Genocide Studies*, 17:3 (Winter 2003), 409–29

Bullivant, K. et al., eds. *Germany and Eastern Europe: Cultural Identities and Cultural Differences* (Amsterdam, 1999)

Burdick, C. *Germany's Military Strategy and Spain in World War II* (Syracuse, 1968)

Burgwyn, H. J. *Empire on the Adriatic: Mussolini's Conquest of Yugoslavia, 1941–1943* (New York, 2005)

Burleigh, M. *Germany Turns Eastwards: A Study of Ostforschung in the Third Reich* (Cambridge, 1988)

Burleigh, M., ed. *Confronting the Nazi Past: New Debates on Modern German History* (London, 1996)

Burrin, P. *France under the Germans: Collaboration and Compromise* (New York, 1996)

—— *Living with Defeat: France under the German Occupation, 1940–1944* (London, 1996)

Calderwood, H. B. 'International Affairs: Should the Council of the League of Nations Establish a Permanent Minorities Commission?', *American Political Science Review*, 27:2 (April 1933), 250–59

—— 'International Affairs: The Proposed Generalization of the Minorities Regime', *American Political Science Review*, 28:6 (December 1934), 1088–98

Campbell, F. Gregory 'The Struggle for Upper Silesia, 1919–1922', *Journal of Modern History*, 42:3 (September 1970), 361–85

—— *Confrontation in Central Europe: Weimar Germany and Czechoslovakia* (Chicago, 1975)

Caplan, J. *Government without Administration: State and Civil Service in Weimar and Nazi Germany* (Oxford, 1988)

Carlyle, M., ed. *Documents on International Affairs, 1939–1946* (London, 1954)

Carsten, F. *The First Austrian Republic, 1918–1938: A Study Based on British and Austrian Documents* (Aldershot, 1986)

Cecil, R. *The Myth of the Master Race: Alfred Rosenberg and Nazi Ideology* (London, 1972)

Césaire, A. *Discourse on Colonialism* (New York, 2000)

Charles, J.-L. and Dasnoy, P., eds. *Les Dossiers secrets de la Police Allemande en Belgique: La Geheime Feldpolizei en Belgique et dans le Nord de la France*, 2 vols. (Brussels, 1972–3)

Chiari, B. *Alltag hinter der Front: Besatzung, Kollaboration und Widerstand in Weissrussland, 1941–1944* (Düsseldorf, 1998)

—— 'Reichsführer-SS: Kein Pakt mit Slawen: Deutsch-polnische Kontakte im Wilna-Gebiet 1944', *Osteuropa-Archiv* (April 2000), A134–A153

Chodakiewicz, M. *Between Nazis and Soviets: Occupation Politics in Poland, 1939–1947* (Lanham, MD, 2004)

Chuminski, J. and Kaszuba, E. 'The Breslau Germans under Polish Rule, 1945–46: Conditions of Life, Political Attitudes, Expulsion', *Studia Historiae Oeconomicae*, 22 (1997), 87–101

Ciano, G., *Ciano's Diary, 1939–1943*, ed. M. Muggeridge (London, 1947)

Cocteau, J. *Journal, 1942–45* (Paris, 1989)

Cohen, A. 'La Politique antijuive en Europe (Allemagne exclue) de 1938 à 1941', *Guerres mondiales*, 150 (1988), 45–59

Collotti, E. *L'amministrazione tedesca dell' Italia occupata* (Milan, 1963)

—— *L'Europa nazista: il progetto di un nuovo ordine europeo, 1939–1945* (Florence, 2002)

Collotti E. et al., eds. *Dizionario della Resistenza* (Turin, 2000–)

Colton, J. *Léon Blum: Humanist in Politics* (Durham, NC, 1987)

Cone, M. *Artists under Vichy: A Case of Prejudice and Persecution* (Princeton, 1992)

Connelly, J. 'Nazis and Slavs: From Racial Theory to Racist Practice', *Central European History*, 32:1 (1999), 1–33

Conway, M. *Collaboration in Belgium: Léon Degrelle and the Rexist Movement, 1940–1944* (New Haven, 1993)

Cook, W. 'Inside the Holiday Camp Hitler Built', *Observer*, 12 August 2001

Corni, G. *Hitler and the Peasants: Agrarian Policy of the Third Reich, 1930–1939* (New York, 1990)

—— *Il sogno del 'grande spazio': le politiche d'occupazione nell'Europa nazista* (Rome, 2005)

Cornwall, M. 'The Struggle on the Czech–German Language Border, 1880–1940', *English Historical Review*, 109:433 (September 1994), 914–51

Crook, D. P. *Benjamin Kidd: Portrait of a Social Darwinist* (Cambridge, 1984)

Curtis, L. 'World Order', *International Affairs*, 18:3 (May–June 1939), 301–20

Dallin, A. *Odessa 1941–1944: A Case Study of Soviet Territory under Foreign Rule* (Santa Monica, CA, 1957)

—— *German Rule in Russia, 1941–1945: A Study of Occupation Policies*, rev. edn (Boulder, CO, 1981)

Daric, J. 'Quelques aspects de l'évolution démographique aux Pays-Bas', *Population*, 1:3 (July–September 1946)

Darwin, J. *After Tamerlane: The Global History of Empire* (London, 2007)

David, J. *A Square of Sky: Memories of a Wartime Childhood* (London, 1992)

Deák, I., Gross, J. and Judt, T., eds. *The Politics of Retribution in Europe* (Princeton, 2000)

Deakin, W. *The Last Days of Mussolini* (London, 1962)

Dean, M. *Collaboration in the Holocaust: Crimes of the Local Police in Belorussia and Ukraine, 1941–44* (Basingstoke, 2000)

de Grazia, V. *Irresistible Empire: America's Advance through Twentieth Century Europe* (Cambridge, MA, 2005)

Delarue, J. *Trafics et crimes sous l'occupation* (Paris, 1968)

Deletant, D. *Hitler's Forgotten Ally: Ion Antonescu and His Regime, Romania 1940–1944* (London, 2006)

Della Pergola, S. 'Between Science and Fiction: Notes on the Demography of the Holocaust', *Holocaust and Genocide Studies*, 10:1 (Spring 1996), 34–51

Demoulin, M. *Plans des Temps de Guerre pour l'Europe d'Après-Guerre, 1940–47* (Brussels, 1995)

Department of State, *Postwar Foreign Policy Preparation, 1939–1945* (Washington, DC, 1949)

Deschner, G. *Reinhard Heydrich: Statthalter der totalen Macht* (Erslagen, 1977)

DeWeerd, H. A. 'Hitler's Plans for Invading Britain', *Military Affairs*, 12:3 (1948), 147–8

de Zayas, A. *Wehrmacht War Crimes Bureau, 1939–1945* (Lincoln, NE, 1989)

DiNardo, R. *Germany and the Axis Powers: From Coalition to Collapse* (Lawrence, KS, 2005)

Djilas, M. *Wartime* (New York, 1977)

Długoborski, W. et al., eds. *The Tragedy of the Jews of Slovakia: 1938–1945: Slovakia and the 'Final Solution of the Jewish Question'* (Oswiecim, 2002)

Dobroszycki, L., ed. *The Chronicle of the Lodz Ghetto, 1941–1944* (New Haven, 1984)

Dobroszycki, L. and Getter, M. 'The Gestapo and the Polish Resistance Movement', *Acta Poloniae Historica*, 4 (1961), 85–118

Dobson, H. 'The Failure of the Tripartite Pact: Familiarity Breeding Contempt between Japan and Germany: 1940–1945', *Japan Forum*, 11:2 (1999), 179–90

Dockrill, M. and Goold, J. D. *Peace without Promise: Britain and the Peace Conferences, 1919–1923* (London, 1981)

'Dokumentation: Rechtssicherheit und richterliche Unabhängigkeit aus der Sicht des SD', *Vierteljahrshefte für Zeitgeschichte*, 4 (1956), 398–422

Dolibois, J. *Pattern of Circles: An Ambassador's Story* (Kent, OH, 1989)

Dollmann, E. *The Interpreter: Memoirs of Doktor Eugen Dollmann* (London, 1967)

Dönhoff, M. *Before the Storm: Memories of My Youth in Old Prussia* (New York, 1990)

Dönhoff, T. and Roettger, J. *Weit ist der Weg nach Westen: Auf der Fluchtroute von Marion Gräfin Dönhoff* (Berlin, 2004)

Dreisziger, N., ed. *Hungary in the Age of Total War* (New York, 1998)

Dulic, T. *Utopias of Nation: Local Mass Killing in Bosnia and Hercegovina, 1941–1942* (Stockholm, 2005)

Dumett, R. 'Africa's Strategic Minerals during the Second World War', *Journal of African History*, 26:4 (1985), 381–408

Dwork, D. and Jan van Pelt, R. *Auschwitz: 1270 to the Present* (New York, 1996)

Eghigian, G. and Berg, M. P., eds. *Sacrifice and National Belonging in Twentieth Century Germany* (College Station, TX, 2002)

Ehrenreich, E. 'Ottmar von Verschuer and the "Scientific" Legitimization of Nazi Anti-Jewish Policy', *Holocaust and Genocide Studies*, 21:1 (Spring 2007), 58–60

Eichholtz, D. 'Die Ausbeutung der Landwirtschaft der faschistisch besetzten Gebiete durch die Okkupanten und die Taktik der materiellen Korrumpierung in Deutschland während des Zweiten Weltkrieges', *Studia Historiae Oeconomicae*, 14 (1982), 153–71

—— *Krieg und Wirtschaft: Studien zur deutschen Wirtschaftsgeschichte 1939–1945* (Berlin, 1999)

—— 'Öl, Krieg, Politik: Deutscher Ölimperialismus (1933–1942/43)', *Zeitschrift für Geschichtsgewissenschaft*, 51:6 (2003), 493–511

Eikel, M. ' "Weil die Menschen fehlen": Die deutschen Zwangsarbeitsrekruitierungen und -deportationen in den besetzten Gebieten der Ukraine, 1941–1944', *Zeitschrift für Geschichtswissenschaft*, 53:5 (2005), 405–34

Elkins, C. and Pedersen, S., eds. *Settler Colonialism in the Twentieth Century* (New York, 2005)

Ellman, M. and Maksudov, S. 'Soviet Deaths in the Great Patriotic War: A Note', *Europe–Asia Studies*, 46:4 (1994), 671–80

Engel, D. 'An Early Account of Polish Jewry under Nazi and Soviet Occupation Presented to the Polish Government-in-Exile, February 1940', *Jewish Social Studies*, 45:1 (1983), 1–16

—— 'Patterns of Anti-Jewish Violence in Poland, 1944–46', *Yad Vashem Studies*, 26 (1998), 43–87

Engel, G. *At the Heart of the Reich: The Secret Diary of Hitler's Army Adjutant* (London, 2005)

Epstein, F., ed. *Germany and the East: Selected Essays* (Bloomington, IN, 1973)

Erdely, E. *Germany's First European Protectorate: The Fate of the Czechs and the Slovaks* (London, 1942)

Falkenhausen, A. von *Mémoires d'outre-guerre* (Brussels, 1974)

Farbstein, E. 'Diaries and Memoirs as a Historical Source – The Diary and Memoir of a Rabbi at the "Konin House of Bondage" ', *Yad Vashem Studies*, 26 (1998), 87–129

Fedyshyn, O. *Germany's Drive to the East and the Ukrainian Revolution, 1917–1918* (New Brunswick, 1971)

Feldman, G. and Seibel, W., eds. *Networks of Nazi Persecution: Bureaucracy, Business and the Organization of the Holocaust* (New York, 2005)

Ferenc, T. *Quellen zur nationalsozialistischen Entnationalisierungspolitik in Slowenien, 1941–1945* (Maribor, 1980)

Fest, J. *The Face of the Third Reich: Portraits of the Nazi Leadership* (London, 1979)

Festgabe für Heinrich Himmler (Darmstadt, 1941)

Fiedor, K. 'Attitude of German Rightwing Organizations to Poland in the years 1918–1933', *Polish Western Affairs*, 14:2 (1973), 247–67

Fink, C. 'Stresemann's Minority Policies, 1924–1929', *Journal of Contemporary History* (1979), 403–22

—— *Defending the Rights of Others: The Great Powers, the Jews and International Minority Protection, 1878–1938* (Cambridge, 2004)

Fischer, B. *Albania at War, 1939–1945* (West Lafayette, IN, 1999)

Fischer, E. *Is This a War for Freedom?* (New York, 1940)

Fischer, F. *Germany's Aims in the First World War* (New York, 1967)

Fischer, H. *Völkerkunde im Nationalsozialismus: Aspekte der Anpassung, Affinität und Behauptung einer wissenschaftlichen Disziplin* (Berlin, 1990)

Fishman, S. et al., eds. *France at War: Vichy and the Historians* (New York, 2000)

Foerster, J. and Mawdsley, E. 'Hitler and Stalin in Perspective: Secret Speeches on the Eve of Barbarossa', *War in History*, 11:1 (2004), 61–103

Fong, G. 'The Movement of German Divisions to the Western Front, Winter 1917–1918', *War in History*, 7:2 (2000)

Fonzi, P. 'Nazionalsocialismo e nuovo ordine europeo: La discussione sulla "Grossraumwirtschaft" ', *Studi Storici*, 45:2 (2004), 313–65

Foot, M. R. D. 'Was SOE Any Good?', *Journal of Contemporary History*, 16:1 (January 1981), 167–81

Frank, H. *Die Technik des Staates* (Berlin, 1942)

Frei, N. *National Socialist Rule in Germany: The Führer State, 1933–1945* (Oxford, 1993)

Frevert, U. 'Europeanizing Germany's Twentieth Century', *History and Memory*, 17:1–2 (2005), 87–116

Friedlander, H. and Milton, S., eds. *Archives of the Holocaust: An International Collection of Selected Documents* (New York, 1989–)

Friedländer, S. *The Years of Extermination: Nazi Germany and the Jews, 1939–1945* (New York, 2007)

Friedrich, K.-P. 'Collaboration in a "Land without a Quisling": Patterns of Collaboration with the Nazi German Occupation Regime in Poland during World War II', *Slavic Review*, 64:4 (Winter 2005), 712–46

Frommer, B. *National Cleansing: Retribution against Nazi Collaborators in Postwar Czechoslovakia* (Cambridge, 2005)

Frumkin, G. *Population Changes in Europe since 1939* (New York, 1951)

Frye, A. *Nazi Germany and the American Hemisphere, 1933–1945* (New Haven, 1967)

Furber, D. 'Going East. Colonialism and German Life in Nazi-Occupied Poland', D.Phil. thesis, Pennsylvania State University, 2003

—— 'Near as Far as in the Colonies: The Nazi Occupation of Poland', *International History Review*, 26:3 (September 2004), 541–79

Garliński, J. *The Survival of Love: Memoirs of a Resistance Officer* (Cambridge, 1991)

Gatrell, P. *A Whole Empire Walking: Refugees in Russia during World War I* (Bloomington, IN, 2005)

Gebel, R. *'Heim ins Reich!' Konrad Henlein und der Reichsgau Sudetenland (1938–1945)* (Munich, 1999)

'Gegnerische Kriegsziele', in *Zeitschrift für ausländisches öffentliches Recht und Völkerrecht*, 11 (1942–3), 1–11

Geiss, I. *Der polnische Grenzstreifen, 1914–1918: Ein Beitrag zur deutschen Kriegszielpolitik im Ersten Weltkrieg* (Lübeck, 1960)

Gellately, R. *Backing Hitler: Consent and Coercion in Nazi Germany* (Oxford, 2001)

Geller, J. H. 'The Role of Military Administration in German-occupied Belgium, 1940–1944', *Journal of Military History*, 63:1 (1999), 99–125

Gerlach, C. *Kalkulierte Morde. Die deutsche Wirtschafts- und Vernichtungspolitik in Weissrussland, 1941 bis 1944* (Hamburg, 1999)

Gerlach, C. and Aly, G. *Das letzte Kapitel: Realpolitik, Ideologie und der Mord an den ungarischen Juden, 1944/45* (Stuttgart, 2002)

Germany. Auswärtiges Amt. *Amtliches Material zum Massenmord von Katyn* (Berlin, 1943)

—— *Documents on German Foreign Policy, 1918–1945*, Series D (1937–1945), 13 vols. (Washington, DC, 1949–83)

Geyl, P. *Encounters in History* (New York, 1961)

Gijsen, M., ed. *Belgium under Occupation* (New York, 1947)

Gildea, R. *Marianne in Chains: In Search of the German Occupation* (London, 2002)

—— 'Resistance, Reprisals and Community in Occupied France', *Transactions of the Royal Historical Society*, 13 (2003), 163–85

Gildea, R., Wieviorka, O. and Warring, A., eds. *Surviving Hitler and Mussolini: Daily Life in Occupied Europe* (Oxford, 2006)

Gillingham, J. 'The Baron de Launoit: A Case Study in the "Politics of Production" of Belgian Industry during Nazi Occupation' (Parts I and II), *Revue Belge d'Histoire Contemporaine*, 5 (1974), 1–59

—— 'The Politics of Business in the German *Grossraum*: The Example of Belgium', *Studia Historiae Oeconomicae*, 14 (1979), 23–4

——*Industry and Politics in the Third Reich: Ruhr Coal, Hitler and Europe* (London, 1985)

——*Coal, Steel and the Rebirth of Europe, 1945–1955* (Cambridge, 1991)

Giltner, P. '*In the Friendliest Manner*': German–Danish Economic Cooperation during the Nazi Occupation, 1940–1945 (New York, 1998)

Gisevius, H. N. *To the Bitter End* (London, 1948)

Glassheim, E. 'National Mythologies and Ethnic Cleansing: The Expulsion of Czechoslovak Germans in 1945', *Central European History*, 33:4 (2000), 463–86

Goda, N. W. *Tomorrow the World: Hitler, Northwest Africa and the Path toward America* (College Station, TX, 1998)

——'Black Marks: Hitler's Bribery of his Senior Officers during World War II', *Journal of Modern History*, 72:2 (June, 2000), 413–52

Goebbels, J., *The Goebbels Diaries, 1942–43*, ed. L. Lochner (New York, 1948)

——*The Goebbels Diaries, 1939–1941*, ed. F. Taylor (London, 1982)

——*Tagebücher*, ed, R. Reuth, 5 vols. (Munich, 1999)

——*Die Tagebücher von Joseph Goebbels*, ed. E. Fröhlich (Munich, 1996)

Goeschel, 'Suicide at the End of the Third Reich', *Journal of Contemporary History*, 41:1 (2006), 153–73

Goldyn, B. 'Disenchanted Voices: Public Opinion in Cracow, 1945–46', *East European Quarterly*, 32:2 (June 1998), 139–65

Gong, G. *The Standard of 'Civilisation' in International Society* (Oxford, 1984)

Goodman, N. 'Health in Europe', *International Affairs*, 20:4 (London, 1944), 473–80

Gordon, B. 'The Condottieri of the Collaboration: *Mouvement Social Révolutionnaire*', *Journal of Contemporary History*, 10:2 (April 1975), 261–82

Gott, V. 'The National Socialist Theory of International Law', *American Journal of International Law*, 32:4 (October 1938), 704–18

Gould, S. W. 'Austrian Attitudes toward Anschluss: October 1918–September 1919', *Journal of Modern History*, 22:3 (September 1950), 220–31

Graziosi, A. 'Il mondo in Europa: Namier e il "Medio oriente europeo", 1815–1948', *Contemporanea*, 10:2 (April 2007), 193–229

Gregor, N., ed. *Nazism, War and Genocide: Essays in Honour of Jeremy Noakes* (Exeter, 2005)

Gribaudi, G. *Guerra totale: tra bombe alleate e violenze naziste. Napoli e il fronte meridionale 1940–1944* (Turin, 2005)

Grimal, H. *Decolonization: The British, French, Dutch and Belgian Empires, 1919–1963* (Boulder, CO, 1978)

Grohmann, C. 'From Lothringen to Lorraine: Expulsion and Voluntary Repatriation', *Diplomacy and Statecraft*, 16 (2005), 571–87

Grondin, J. *Hans-Georg Gadamer: A Biography* (New Haven, 2003)

Groscurth, H. *Tagebücher eines Abwehroffiziers, 1938–1940* (Stuttgart, 1970)

Gross, J. *Polish Society under German Occupation: The Generalgouvernement, 1939–1944* (Princeton, 1979)

——*Neighbors: The Destruction of the Jewish Community in Jedwabne* (Princeton, 2002)

Gumz, J. 'German Counter-insurgency Policy in Independent Croatia, 1941–1944', *The Historian*, 61 (1998), 33–50

——'Stepping back from Destruction: Invasion, Occupation and Empire in Habsburg Serbia, 1914–1918', Ph.D. thesis, University of Chicago, 2006

Gumz, J. E. '*Wehrmacht* Perceptions of Mass Violence in Croatia, 1941–1942', *Historical Journal*, 44:4 (2001), 1015–38

Gutman, I. and Berenbaum, M., eds. *Anatomy of the Auschwitz Death Camp* (Bloomington, IN, 1994)

Haar, I. and Fahlbusch, M., eds. *German Scholars and Ethnic Cleansing, 1920–1945* (Oxford, 2005)

Haberer, E. 'The German Police and Genocide in Belorussia, 1941–1944. Part 1: Police

Deployment and Nazi Genocidal Directives', *Journal of Genocide Research*, 3:1 (2001), 13–29

Haestrup, J. *European Resistance Movements, 1939–1945: A Complete History* (London, 1981)

Hagen, W. *Germans, Poles and Jews: The Nationality Conflict in the Prussian East, 1772–1914* (Chicago, 1980)

Hahn, G. *Grundfragen europäischer Ordnung: Ein Beitrag zur Neugestaltung der Völkerrechtslehre* (Berlin, 1939)

Hahn, H. J. *The 1848 Revolutions in German-speaking Europe* (London, 2001)

Hammen, O. 'German Historians and the Advent of the National Socialist State', *Journal of Modern History*, 13:2 (June 1941), 161–88

Handelsman, M. *La Pologne: sa vie économique et sociale pendant la guerre* (Paris, 1933)

Hanson, J. *The Civilian Population and the Warsaw Uprising of 1944* (Cambridge, 1978)

Harper, J. L. *American Visions of Europe: Franklin D. Roosevelt, George F. Kennan, and Dean G. Acheson* (Cambridge, 1996)

Harriman, H. *Slovenia under Nazi Occupation, 1941–1945* (New York, 1977)

Harrison, E. D. R. 'The British Special Operations Executive and Poland', *Historical Journal*, 43:4 (2000), 1071–91

Harrison M. 'Resource Mobilisation for World War II', *Economic History Review*, 2 (1988)

Hart Merriam, C. 'The Indian Population of California', *American Anthropologist* (October–December 1905), 594–606

Harten, H. *De-Kulturation und Germanisierung: Die nationalsozialistische Rassen- und Erziehungspolitik in Polen 1939–1945* (Frankfurt, 1996)

Hartmann, C. ' "Massensterben oder Massenvernichtung": Sowjetische Kriegsgefangene im "Unternehmen Barbarossa" ', *Vierteljahrshefte für Zeitgeschichte*, 21 (2001), 102–58

——'Verbrecherische Krieg – verbrecherische Wehrmacht?' *Vierteljahrshefte für Zeitgeschichte*, 21 (2004)

Harvey, D. 'Lost Children or Enemy Aliens? Classifying the Population of Alsace after the First World War', *Journal of Contemporary History*, 34:4 (October 1999), 537–54

Hassell, U. von *The von Hassell Diaries, 1938–1944* (London, 1948)

Hauner, M. 'Did Hitler Want World Dominion?', *Journal of Contemporary History*, 13:1 (January 1978), 15–32

——*India in Axis Strategy: Germany, Japan and Indian Nationalists in the Second World War* (Stuttgart, 1981)

Hawes, S. and White, R., eds. *Resistance in Europe, 1939–1945* (Salford, 1973)

Hayes, O. *Industry and Ideology: I. G. Farben in the Nazi Era* (Cambridge, 1989)

Headlam, J. W. *A Memoir of the Paris Peace Conference, 1919* (London, 1972)

Heer, H. and Naumann, K., eds. *War of Extermination: The German Military in World War II, 1941–1944* (New York, 2000)

Heiber, H. 'Der Generalplan Ost: Dokumentation', *Vierteljahrshefte für Zeitgeschichte*, 6 (1958), 280–326

——, ed. *Hitler and His Generals: Military Conferences, 1942–45* (New York, 2003)

Heike, W.-D. *The Ukrainian Division 'Galicia', 1943–45: A Memoir* (Toronto, 1988)

Heinemann, I. *'Rasse, Siedlung, deutsches Blut': Das Rasse- und Siedlungshauptamt der SS und die rassepolitische Neuordnung Europas* (Göttingen, 2003)

Herbert, U. 'Labour and Extermination: Economic Interest and the Primacy of *Weltanschauung* in National Socialism', *Past and Present*, 138:2 (1993), 144–95

——*Hitler's Foreign Workers: Enforced Foreign Labor in Germany under the Third Reich* (Cambridge, 1997)

——*Best: Biographische Studien über Radikalismus, Weltanschauung und Vernunft, 1903–1989* (Bonn, 2001)

——, ed., *National Socialist Extermination Policies: Contemporary German Perspectives and Controversies* (New York, 2000) [*Nationalsozialistische Vernichtungspolitik, 1939–1945* (Frankfurt, 1998)]

Herf, J. 'The "Jewish War"': Goebbels and the Anti-Semitic Campaigns of the Nazi Propaganda Ministry', *Holocaust and Genocide Studies*, 19:1 (Spring 2005), 51–80

Herre, P. *Deutschland und die Europäische Ordnung* (Berlin, 1941)

Herwig, H. 'Tunes of Glory at the Twilight Stage: The Bad Homburg Crown Council and the Evolution of German Statecraft, 1917/1918', *German Studies Review*, 6:3 (October 1983), 475–94

Herz, J. 'The Rise and Demise of the Territorial State,' *World Politics*, 9:4 (July 1957), 473–93

—— 'The Territorial State Revisited: Reflections on the Future of the Nation-State', *Polity*, 1:1 (August 1968), 11–34

Herzstein, R. *When Nazi Dreams Come True: The Third Reich's Internal Struggle over the Future of Europe after a German Victory: A Look at the Nazi Mentality, 1939–45* (London, 1982)

Heydecker, J. *Un soldat allemand dans le ghetto de Varsovie 1941* (Paris, 1986)

Hiden, J. *The Baltic States and Weimar Ostpolitik* (Cambridge, 1987)

Hilberg, R. *The Destruction of the European Jews* (New York, 1985)

—— *The Destruction of the European Jews*, 3rd edn (New Haven, 2003)

Hildebrand. K. *Vom Reich zum Weltreich: Hitler, NSDAP und koloniale Frage, 1919–1945* (Munich, 1969)

—— *Deutsche Außenpolitik 1933–1945: Kalkül oder Dogma?* (Stuttgart, 1971)

Hill, A. *War behind the Eastern Front: The Soviet Partisan Movement in North-west Russia, 1941–1944* (London, 2005)

Hill, G. *Trends in the Oil Industry in 1944* (Washington, DC, 1944)

Hillgruber, A., ed. *Staatsmänner und Diplomaten bei Hitler* (Frankfurt, 1970)

—— 'England's Place in Hitler's Plans for World Dominion', *Journal of Contemporary History*, 9:1 (January 1974), 5–22

Himmler, H. *Reichsführer! Briefe an und von Himmler*, ed. H. Heiber (Stuttgart, 1968)

—— *Heinrich Himmler: Geheimreden 1933 bis 1945*, ed. B. Smith and A. F. Peterson (Berlin, 1974)

Hindley, M. 'Negotiating the Boundary of Unconditional Surrender: The War Refugee Board in Sweden and Nazi Proposals to Ransom Jews, 1944–45', *Holocaust and Genocide Studies*, 10:1 (Spring 1996), 52–77

Hionidou, V. *Famine and Death in Occupied Greece, 1941–1944* (Cambridge, 2006)

Hirschfeld, G., ed. *Policies of Genocide: Jews and Soviet Prisoners of War in Nazi Germany* (Boston, 1986)

—— *Nazi Rule and Dutch Collaboration: The Netherlands under German Occupation, 1940–1945* (Oxford, 1988)

Hitler, A., *Hitler: Speeches and Proclamations, 1932–1945*, ed. M. Domarus, 4 vols. (Wauconda IL, *c.* 1990–2004)

—— *Hitler's Second Book: The Unpublished Sequel to Mein Kampf*, ed. G. Weinberg (New York, 2006)

Hoare, M. A. *Genocide and Resistance in Hitler's Bosnia: The Partisans and the Chetniks, 1941–1943* (Oxford, 2006)

Hoettl, W. *The Secret Front: The Story of Nazi Espionage* (New York, 1954)

Hoffmann, S. 'Collaboration in France during World War II', *Journal of Modern History*, 40:3 (September 1968), 375–95

Hohenstein, A. *Warthelaňdisches Tagebuch aus den Jahren 1941/42* (Stuttgart, 1961)

Höhn, R. *Verfassungskampf und Heereseid; Der Kampf des Bürgertums um das Heer (1815–1850)* (Leipzig, 1938)

Höhne, H. *The Order of the Death's Head: The Story of Hitler's SS* (New York, 1970)

Hondros, J. *Occupation and Resistance: The Greek Agony, 1941–1944* (New York, 1983)

Hoover Institution, *France during the German Occupation, 1940–1944: A Collection of 292 Statements on the Government of Maréchal Pétain and Pierre Laval*, 3 vols. (Stanford, 1958–9)

Horne, C. F., ed. *Source Records of the Great War*, vol. 5 (New York, 1923)

Horthy, M. *The Confidential Papers of Admiral Horthy*, ed. M. Szinai and L. Szúcs (Budapest, 1965)

Höss, R. *Death Dealer: The Memoirs of the SS Kommandant at Auschwitz* (New York, 1996)

Housden, M. 'Ewalde Ammende and the Organization of National Minorities in Interwar Europe', *German History*, 18:4 (2000), 439–60

—— *Hans Frank: Lebensraum and the Holocaust* (New York, 2003)

Hull, C. *The Memoirs of Cordell Hull* (New York, 1948)

Hull, I. *Absolute Destruction: Military Culture and the Practices of War in Imperial Germany* (Ithaca, 2006)

Hüttenberger, P. *Die Gauleiter: Studie zum Wandel des Machtgefüges in der NSDAP* (Stuttgart, 1969)

Hutton, M. *Race and the Third Reich: Linguistics, Racial Anthropology and Genetics in the Dialectic of Volk* (Cambridge, 2005)

Hyam, R. *Britain's Declining Empire: The Road to Decolonisation, 1918–1968* (Cambridge, 2006)

Ilan Troen, S. *Imagining Zion: Dreams, Designs and Realities in a Century of Jewish Settlement* (New Haven, 2003)

Ilan Troen, S. and Lucas, N., eds. *Israel: The First Decade of Independence* (Albany, 1995)

Ingrao, C. and Szabo, F., eds. *The Germans and the East* (West Lafayette, IN, 2007)

International Military Tribunal *Trial of the Major War Criminals before the International Military Tribunal, 14 November 1945–1 October 1946*, 42 vols. (Nuremberg, 1947–9)

—— *Trial of the Major War Criminals before the Nuernberg Military Tribunals under Control Council Law No. 10*, 15 vols. (Washington, DC, 1949–53)

Irjud, A. 'La Germanisation des noms en Alsace entre 1940 et 1944', *Revue d'Alsace*, 113 (1984), 239–61

Italy, Ministero d'Affari Esteri *I Documenti Diplomatici* (Rome, 1953–)

Jäckel, E. *Frankreich in Hitlers Europa* (Stuttgart, 1966)

Jackson, J. *France. The Dark Years, 1940–1944* (Oxford, 2001)

—— *The Fall of France: The Nazi Invasion of 1940* (Oxford, 2003)

Jacobmeyer, W. 'Die polnische Widerstandsbewegung im General Gouvernement und ihre Beurteilung durch deutsche Dienststellen', *Vierteljahrshefte für Zeitgeschichte*, 25:4 (1977), 655–81

Jelinek, Y. 'Slovakia's Internal Policy and the Third Reich, August 1940–Feb. 1941', *Central European History*, 4:3 (1971), 242–70

Jennings, E. T. *Vichy in the Tropics: Pétain's National Revolution in Madagascar, Guadeloupe, and Indochina, 1940–1944* (Stanford, 2001)

Jensen, W. G. 'The Importance of Energy in the First and Second World Wars', *Historical Journal*, 11:3 (1968), 538–54

Jochmann, W., ed. *Adolf Hitler: Monologe im Führer-Hauptquartier, 1941–1944* (Hamburg, 1980)

Joerges, C. 'Europe a *Grossraum*? Rupture, Continuity and Re-configuration in the Legal Conceptualization of the Integration Project', *EUI Working Paper, Law no. 2002/2*, 13

—— 'Continuities and Discontinuities in German Legal Thought', *Law and Critique*, 14 (2003), 297–308

Joerges, C. and Ghaleigh, N. S., eds. *Darker Legacies of Law: The Shadow of National Socialism and Fascism over Europe and its Legal Traditions* (Oxford, 2003)

Johnson, C. *The Sorrows of Empire: Militarism, Secrecy and the End of the Republic* (New York, 2004)

Johnston, H. 'The Empire and Anthropology,' *Nineteenth Century and After*, 327 (July 1908), 133–46

Judt, T., ed. *Resistance and Revolution in Mediterranean Europe, 1939–1948* (London, 1989)

Kagan, J. and Cohen, D. *Surviving the Holocaust with the Russian Jewish Partisans* (London, 1997)

Kahrs, H. *Modelle für ein deutsches Europa: Ökonomie und Herrschaft im Grosswirtschaftsraum* (Berlin, 1992)

Kallay, N. *Hungarian Premier: A Personal Account of a Nation's Struggle in the Second World War* (London, 1954)

Kaminski, T. 'Bismarck and the Polish Question: The "Huldigungsfahrten" to Varzin in 1894', *Canadian Journal of History*, 22 (August 1988), 235–50

Kap, J., ed. *The Tragedy of Silesia, 1945–46: A Documentary Account with a Special Survey of the Archdiocese of Breslau* (Munich, 1952/3)

Kappeler, A. 'Ukrainian History from a German Perspective', *Slavic Review*, 54:3 (Autumn 1995), 691–701

Karny, M., Milotova, J., and Karna, M., eds. *Deutsche Politik im 'Protektorat Böhmen und Mähren' unter Reinhard Heydrich, 1941–1942: Eine Dokumentation* (Berlin, 1997)

Karski, J. *Story of a Secret State* (Boston, 1944)

Kaser, M., ed. *The Economic History of Eastern Europe, 1919–1975*, 3 vols. (Oxford, 1986)

Katz, J. A. 'The Concept of Overcoming the Political: An Intellectual Biography of SS Standartenführer and Professor Dr Reinhard Höhn, 1904–1944', MA thesis, Virginia Commonwealth University, 1995

Kay, A. *Exploitation, Resettlement, Mass Murder: Political and Economic Planning for German Occupation Policy in the Soviet Union, 1940–1941* (New York, 2006)

Kedward, H. R. *Resistance in France: A Study of Ideas and Motivation in the Southern Zone, 1940–1942* (Oxford, 1978)

——*In Search of the Maquis: Rural Resistance in Southern France, 1942–1944* (Oxford, 1993)

Kehrl, H. *Krisenmanager im Dritten Reich: 6 Jahre Frieden, 6 Jahre Krieg: Erinnerungen* (Düsseldorf, 1973)

Kennan, G. *From Prague after Munich: Diplomatic Papers, 1938–1940* (Princeton, 1968)

Kent, C. et al., eds. *The Lion and the Eagle: Interdisciplinary Essays on German–Spanish Relations over the Centuries* (London, 2000)

Kent, G. O. 'Britain in the Winter of 1940 as Seen from the Wilhelmstrasse', *Historical Journal*, 6:1 (1963), 120–30

Kershaw, I. 'Improvised Genocide? The Emergence of the "Final Solution" in the "Warthegau" ', *Transactions of the Royal Historical Society* (1994), 51–78

——*Hitler, 1889–1936: Hubris* (New York, 1999)

Kersten, F. *The Kersten Memoirs, 1940–1945* (London, 1956)

Kestling, R. W. 'Blacks under the Swastika: A Research Note', *Journal of Negro History*, 83:1 (Winter 1998), 84–99

Kettenacker, L. 'The Anglo-Soviet Alliance and the Problem of Germany, 1941–1945', *Journal of Contemporary History*, 17:3 (July 1982), 435–58

Kiss, G. 'Political Geography into Geopolitics: Recent Trends in Germany', *Geographical Review*, 32:4 (October 1942), 632–45

Kitson, S. 'From Enthusiasm to Disenchantment: The French Police and the Vichy Regime, 1940–1944', *Contemporary European History*, 11:3 (2002), 371–90

——*Vichy et la chasse aux espions nazis, 1940–1942: Complexités de la politique de collaboration* (Paris, 2005)

——'Spying for Germany in Vichy France', *History Today*, 56:1 (January 2006), 38–45

Klarsfeld, S., ed. *The Holocaust and the Neo-Nazi Mythomania* (New York, 1978)

Kling, H., ed. *Der nationalsozialistische Krieg* (Frankfurt, 1990)

Klingemann, C. 'Ursachenanalyse und ethnopolitische Gegenstrategien zum Landarbeitermangel in den Ostgebieten: Max Weber, das Institut für Staatsforschung und der Reichsführer SS', *Jahrbuch für Soziologiegeschichte* (1994), 191–203 .

Klinkhammer, L. *Zwischen Bündnis und Besatzung: Das nationalsozialistische Deutschland und die Republik von Salò, 1943–45* (Tübingen, 1993)

Kluke, P. 'Nazionalsozialistische Europaideologie', *Vierteljahrshefte für Zeitgeschichte* 3:3 (1955), 240–75

Klukowski, Z. *Diary from the Years of Occupation, 1939–1944* (Urbana, IL, 1993)

Knox, M. *Hitler's Italian Allies: Royal Armed Forces, Fascist Regime and the War of 1940–1943* (Cambridge, 2000)

Koch, H. W. *In the Name of the Volk: Political Justice in Hitler's Germany* (London, 1997)

Köchenhoff, G. 'Grossraumgedanke und Völkische Idee im Recht', *Zeitschrift für ausländisches öffentliches Recht und Völkerrecht*, 12 (1944), 34–82

Koehl, R. L. 'Colonialism inside Germany, 1886–1918', *Journal of Modern History*, 25:3 (September 1953), 255–72

—— 'A Prelude to Hitler's Greater Germany', *American Historical Review*, 59:1 (October 1953), 43–65

—— *RKFDV: German Resettlement and Population Policy 1939–1945: A History of the Reich Commission for the Strengthening of Germandom* (Cambridge, MA, 1957)

Kogan, A. 'Social Democracy and the Conflict of Nationalities in the Habsburg Monarchy', *Journal of Modern History*, 21:3 (September 1949), 204–11

Komjathy, A. and Stockwell, R. *German Minorities and the Third Reich: Ethnic Germans of East Central Europe between the Wars* (New York, 1980)

Kopelev, L. *The Education of a True Believer* (New York, 1980)

Koralka, J. 'Germany's Attitude to the National Disintegration of Cisleithania', *Journal of Contemporary History*, 4:2 (April 1969), 85–95

Kostal, R. W. *A Jurisprudence of Power: Victorian Empire and the Rule of Law* (Oxford, 2005)

Kotkin, S. 'World War Two and Labor: A Lost Cause?', *International Labor and Working-Class History*, 58 (Fall 2000), 181–91

Kramer, A. *Dynamics of Destruction: Culture and Mass Killing in the First World War* (Oxford, 2007)

Krausnick, H. and Broszat, M., eds. *Anatomy of the SS State* (London, 1973)

von Krockow, C. *Hour of the Women: Based on an Oral Narrative by Libussa Fritz-Krockow* (New York, 1992)

Kulischer, E. M. *Europe on the Move: War and Population Changes, 1917–1947* (New York, 1948)

Kunicki, M. 'Unwanted Collaborators: Leon Kozlowski, Wladyslaw Studnicki and the Problem of Collaboration among Polish Conservative Politicians in World War II', *European Review of History*, 8:2 (2001), 203–20

Kwiet, K. 'Vorbereitung und Auflösung der deutschen Militärverwaltung in den Niederlanden', *Militärgeschichtliche Mitteilungen*, 1 (1969), 121–53

Lamb, R. *War in Italy, 1943–45: A Brutal Story* (London, 1993)

Lanckoronska, K. *Michelangelo in Ravensbrück: One Woman's War against the Nazis* (New York, 2007)

Lang, J. von, ed. *Eichmann Interrogated: Transcripts from the Archives of the Israeli Police* (New York, 1999)

Lange, K. 'Der terminus "Lebensraum" in Hitlers "Mein Kampf" ', *Vierteljahrshefte für Zeitgeschichte*, 13:4 (1965), 426–37

Lannoy, F. de *La Ruée de l'Armée Rouge: Opération Bagration* (Bayeux, 2002)

Lavin, D. *From Empire to International Commonwealth: A Biography of Lionel Curtis* (Oxford, 1995)

Lebedeva, N. S. 'The Deportation of the Polish Population to the USSR, 1939–1941', *Journal of Communist Studies and Transition Politics*, 16:12 (2000), 28–45

Le Begnec, G. and Peschanski, D. eds. *Les Elites locales dans la tourmente* (Paris, 2000)

Lecoeur, S. F. 'The Italian Occupation of Syros and its Socio-Economic Impact, 1941–43', Ph.D. thesis, University of London, 2006

Legnani, M. 'Il "ginger" del generale Roatta: le direttive della 2a armata sulla repressione antipartigiana in Slovenia e Croazia', *Italia contemporanea*, 209–10 (December 1997–March 1998), 155–74

Leith, C. K. 'The Struggle for Mineral Resources', *Annals of the American Academy of Political and Social Science*, 204 (July 1939), 42–8

Lemkin, R. *Axis Rule in Occupied Europe: Laws of Occupation, Analysis of Government, Proposals for Redress* (Washington, DC, 1944)

Levai, E. *Black Book on the Martyrdom of Hungarian Jewry* (Zurich and Vienna, 1948)

Levine, H. S. 'Local Authority and the SS State: The Conflict over Population Policy in Danzig-West Prussia, 1939–1945', *Central European History*, 3 (1969), 331–55

——*Hitler's Free City: A History of the Nazi Party in Danzig, 1925–1939* (Chicago, 1973)

Levisse-Touzé, C., ed. *Paris 1944: Les Enjeux de la Libération* (Paris, 1994)

Lewis, N. *Naples '44* (London, 1978)

Liberman, P. 'The Spoils of Conquest', *International Security*, 18:2 (Autumn 1993)

——*Does Conquest Pay? The Exploitation of Occupied Industrial Societies* (Princeton, 1996)

Lindholm, R. W. 'German Finances in Wartime', *American Economic Review*, 37:1 (March 1947), 121–34

Lindqvist, S. *Terra Nullius: A Journey through No One's Land* (New York, 2007)

Linne, K. ' "New Labour Policy" in Nazi Colonial Planning for Africa', *International Review of Social History*, 49:2 (2004), 197–224

Lipgens, W. *A History of European Integration*, vol. 1 (1945–7) (Oxford, 1982)

——, ed. *Documents on the History of European Integration*, 4 vols. (Berlin, 1984–91)

Liulevicius, V. G. *War Land on the Eastern Front: Culture, National Identity and German Occupation in World War I* (Cambridge, 2000)

Loftus, J. *The Belarus Secret* (New York, 1982)

Lohr, E. *Nationalizing the Russian Empire: The Campaign against Enemy Aliens during World War I* (Cambridge, MA, 2003)

Loock, H.-D. 'Zur "Grossgermanischen Politik" des Dritten Reiches', *Vierteljahrshefte für Zeitgeschichte*, 8 (1960), 37–64

Lösener, B. 'Das Reichsministerium des Innern und die Judengesetzgebung', *Vierteljahrshefte für Zeitgeschichte*, 9:3 (1961)

Lossowski, P. 'The Resettlement of the Germans from the Baltic States in 1939/41', *Acta Poloniae Historica*, 92 (2005), 79–98

Lotnik, W. *Nine Lives: Ethnic Conflict in the Polish–Ukrainian Borderlands* (London, 1999)

Low, D. *The Anschluss Movement, 1918–1919 and the Paris Peace Conference* (Philadelphia, 1974)

Luciolli, M. *Palazzo Chigi: anni roventi, ricordi di vita diplomatica italiana dal 1933 al 1948* (Milan, 1976)

Luczak, C. 'Die Ansiedlung der deutschen Bevölkerung im besetzten Polen (1939–1945)', *Studia Historicae Oeconomicae*, 13 (1978), 193–205

——'Nazi Spatial Plans in Occupied Poland (1939–1945)', *Studia Historicae Oeconomicae*, 12 (1978)

——'Die Agrarpolitik des Dritten Reiches', *Studia Historicae Oeconomicae*, 17 (1982), 195–203

Lukas, R. *Forgotten Holocaust: The Poles under German Occupation, 1939–1944* (New York, 1990)

Lumans, V. *Himmler's Auxiliaries: The Volksdeutsche Mittelstelle and the German National Minorities of Europe, 1933–1945* (Chapel Hill, NC, 1993)

——*Latvia in World War Two* (New York, 2006)

Luyten, D. and Hemmerijckx, R. 'Belgian Labour in World War II: Strategies of Survival, Organisations and Labour Relations', *European Review of History*, 7:2 (Autumn 2000), 207–27

Lynch, M. *Mining in World History* (London, 2002)

MacDonald, C. *The Killing of SS Obergruppenführer Reinhard Heydrich, 27 May 1942* (London, 1989)

Machtan, L. ' "Bismarcks Varzin – Warcino heute": Betrachtungen zu einem Symbol politischer Kultur aus Preußen-Deutschland', *Zeitschrift für Geschichtswissenschaft*, 38:9 (1990), 771–86

Mackenzie, S. P. 'The Treatment of Prisoners of War in World War II', *Journal of Modern History*, 66:3 (September 1994), 487–520

Mackinder, H. 'The Geographical Pivot of History', *Geographical Journal*, 23:4 (April 1904), 421–7

Madajczyk, C. 'Deportations in the Zamosc Region in 1942 and 1943 in the Light of German Documents', *Acta Poloniae Historica*, 1 (1958), 75–106

——'Introduction to General Plan East', *Polish Western Affairs*, 3:2 (1962)

—— *Die Okkupationspolitik Nazideutschlands in Polen, 1939–1945* (Berlin, 1987)

——'Legal Conceptions in the Third Reich and its Conquests', *Michael*, 13 (1993), 131–59

——, ed. *Inter arma non silent musae: The War and Culture, 1939–1945* (Warsaw, 1977)

—— *Vom Generalplan Ost zum Generalsiedlungsplan* (Munich, 1994)

Magocsi, R. P. *Historical Atlas of East Central Europe* (Seattle, 1993)

Mai, U. *'Rasse und Raum': Agrarpolitik, Sozial- und Raumplanung im NS-Staat* (Paderborn, 2002)

Maier, C. *Among Empires: American Ascendancy and Its Predecessors* (Cambridge, MA, 2006)

Maisky, I. *Memoirs of a Soviet Ambassador: The War, 1939–1943* (London, 1967)

Makinen, G. A. 'The Greek Hyper-Inflation and Stabilization of 1943–46', *Journal of Economic History*, 46:3 (1986), 795–805

Malaparte, K. *Kaputt* (London, 1989)

Mamatey, V. and Luza, R., eds. *A History of the Czechoslovak Republic, 1918–1948* (Princeton, 1973)

Mankowski, Z. 'Die Agrarpolitik des Okkupanten im Generalgouvernement, 1939–1945', *Studia Historicae Oeconomicae*, 23 (1998), 255–68

Manoschek, W. *'Serbien ist judenfrei': Militärische Besatzungspolitik und Judenvernichtung in Serbien, 1941/42* (Munich, 1993)

Marmulla, H. and Brault, P. *Europäische Integration und Agrarwirtschaft* (Bonn, 1958)

Marples, D. 'Western Ukraine and Western Belorussia under Soviet Occupation: The Development of Socialist Farming, 1939–1941', *Revue Canadienne des Slavistes*, 27:2 (June 1985), 158–77

Marrus, M. and Paxton, R. *Vichy France and the Jews* (New York, 1981)

Martens, S. and Vaïsse, M., eds. *Frankreich und Deutschland im Krieg (Nov. 1942–Herbst 1944): Okkupation, Kollaboration, Resistance* (Bonn, 2000)

Martin, B. 'German-Italian Cultural Initiatives and the Idea of a New Order in Europe, 1936–1945', D.Phil. thesis, Columbia University, 2006

Mastny, V. *The Czechs under Nazi Rule: The Failure of National Resistance, 1939–1942* (New York, 1972)

Masur, N. *En jude talar med Himmler* (Stockholm, 1945)

Matlok, S., ed. *Dänemark in Hitlers Hand: Der Bericht des Reichsbevollmächtigten Werner Best über seine Besatzungspolitik in Dänemark mit Studien über Hitler, Göring, Himmler, Heydrich, Ribbentrop, Canaris u.a.* (Husum, 1988)

Maugue, P. *Le Particularisme Alsacien, 1918–1967* (Paris, 1970)

Mauter, W. 'Churchill and the Unification of Europe', *The Historian*, 61:1 (Fall 1998), 67–84

May, E. 'Nazi Germany and the United States: A Review Essay', *Journal of Modern History*, 41:2 (June 1969), 207–14

Mazower, M. 'The Strange Triumph of Human Rights, 1933–1950', *Historical Journal*, 47:2 (2004), 379–99

——'An International Civilization? Empire, Internationalism and the Crisis of the Mid-Twentieth Century', *International Affairs*, 82:3 (2006), 553–66

McCann, F. D. *The Brazilian–American Alliance, 1937–1945* (Princeton, 1973)

McElligott, A. and Kirk, T., eds. *Working towards the Führer: Essays in Honour of Sir Ian Kershaw* (Munich, 2003)

McLaine, I. *The Ministry of Morale* (London, 1979), 223–4

Mejer, D. *'Non-Germans' under the Third Reich: The Nazi Judicial and Administrative System in Germany and Occupied Eastern Europe with Special Regard to Occupied Poland, 1939–1945* (Baltimore, 2003)

Mendelsohn, J., ed. *The Holocaust: Selected Documents in Eighteen Volumes* (New York, 1982)

Merridale, C. *Ivan's War: Life and Death in the Red Army, 1939–1945* (New York, 2006)

Michalka, W., ed. *Nationalsozialistische Aussenpolitik* (Darmstadt, 1978)

—— *Der Zweite Weltkrieg: Analysen, Grundzüge, Forschungsbilanz* (Munich, 1989)

Mierzejewski, A. C. *The Collapse of the German War Economy, 1944–1945* (Chapel Hill, 1988)

—— 'A Public Enterprise in the Service of Mass Murder: The Deutsche Reichsbahn and the Holocaust', *Holocaust and Genocide Studies*, 15:1 (Spring 2001), 33–46

Militärgeschichtliches Forschungsamt, ed. *Das Deutsche Reich und der Zweite Weltkrieg* (Stuttgart, 1979–2004)

—— *Germany and the Second World War*, 7 vols. (Oxford, 1990–2006)

Miller, D. 'Colonising the Hungarian and German Border Areas during the Czech Land Reform, 1918–1938', *Austrian History Yearbook*, 34 (2003), 303–17

Milward, A. *The New Order and the French Economy* (Oxford, 1970)

—— *The Fascist Economy in Norway* (Oxford, 1972)

—— *The European Rescue of the Nation-State* (London, 2000)

Mommsen, H. 'The Dissolution of the Third Reich: Crisis Management and Collapse, 1943–45', *German Historical Institute (Washington): Bulletin*, 27 (Fall 2000), 9–23

—— *Third Reich between Vision and Reality: New Perspectives on German History, 1918–1945* (Oxford, 2001)

Mommsen, W. *Max Weber and German Politics, 1890–1920* (Chicago, 1984)

Moore, B., ed. *Resistance in Western Europe* (Oxford, 2000)

Morris-Reich, A. 'Arthur Ruppin's Concept of Race', *Israel Studies*, 11:3 (Fall 2006), 1–30

Moskowitz, M. 'Three Years of the Protectorate of Bohemia and Moravia', *Political Science Quarterly*, 57:3 (September 1942), 353–75

Mosse, G. L., ed. *Police Forces in History* (London, 1975)

Müller, N., ed. *Deutsche Besatzungspolitik in der UdSSR 1941–1944: Dokumente* (Cologne, 1980)

Müller, R.-D. *Der letzte deutsche Krieg, 1939–1945* (Stuttgart, 2005)

Müller, R.-D. and Volkmann, H.-E., eds. *Die Wehrmacht. Mythos und Realität* (Munich, 1999)

Mulligan, T. *The Politics of Illusion and Empire: German Occupation Policy in the Soviet Union, 1942–43* (New York, 1988)

Murashko, G. and Noskova, A. 'Stalin and the National-Territorial Controversies in Eastern Europe, 1945–1947', *Cold War History*, 1:3 (April 2001), 161–72

Murphy, R. et al., eds. *National Socialism: Basic Principles, Their Application by the Nazi Party's Foreign Organization and the Use of Germans Abroad for Nazi Aims* (Washington, DC, 1943)

Murray, W. *The Change in the European Balance of Power, 1938–1939: The Path to Ruin* (Princeton, 1984)

Musial, B. 'The Origins of "Operation Reinhard": The Decision-Making Process for the Mass Murder of the Jews in the *Generalgouvernement*,' *Yad Vashem Studies*, 28 (2000), 113–53

Myers, D. P. 'Berlin "Versus" Vienna: Disagreements about "Anschluss" in the Winter of 1918–1919', *Central European History*, 5:2 (June 1972), 150–75

Naasner, W., ed. *SS-Wirtschaft und SS-Verwaltung: 'Das SS-Wirtschafts-Verwaltungshauptamt und die unter seiner Dienstaufsicht stehenden wirtschaftlichen Unternehmungen' Und weitere Dokumente* (Düsseldorf, 1998)

Naimark, N. *Fires of Hatred: Ethnic Cleansing in Twentieth Century Europe* (Cambridge, MA, 2001)

Namier, L. *Vanished Supremacies: Essays on European History, 1812–1918* (London, 1962)

—— *1848: The Revolt of the Intellectuals* (Oxford, 1992)

Nazi Conspiracy and Aggression, 8 vols. (Washington, DC, 1946–8)

Neitze, S., ed. *Tapping Hitler's Generals: Transcripts of Secret Conversations, 1942–45* (Barnsley, 2007)

Neulen, H. W., ed. *Europa und das 3. Reich: Einigungsbestrebungen im deutschen Machtbereich, 1939–1945* (Munich, 1987)

Neumann, K. *Not the Way It Really Was: Constructing the Tolai Past* (Honolulu, 1992)

Neumann, S. 'Fashions in Space', *Foreign Affairs*, 21:2 (January 1943), 276–88

Nicolson, H. 'The Colonial Problem', *International Affairs*, 17:1 (January–February 1938), 32–50

Noakes, J. and Pridham, G., eds. *Nazism, 1919–1945: A Documentary Reader* vol. 3: *Foreign Policy, War and Racial Extermination* (Exeter, 1991)

Noble, A. 'The First *Frontgau*: East Prussia, July 1944', *War and History*, 13 (April 2006), 200–216

Nove, A. 'How Many Victims in the 1930s? II', *Soviet Studies*, 42:4 (October 1990), 811–14

O'Brien, P. 'European Economic Development', *Economic History Review*, 35:1 (February 1982), 1–18

Orwell, G. 'Not Counting Niggers', *Adelphi* (July 1939)

Otto, G. and Cate, J. H. ten, eds. *Das organisierte Chaos: 'Ämterdarwinismus' und 'Gesinnungsethik': Determinanten nationalsozialistischer Besatzungsherrschaft* (Berlin, 1999)

Overmans, R. *Deutsche militärische Verluste im Zweiten Weltkrieg* (Munich, 1999)

Overy, R. J. *Goering: The 'Iron Man'* (London, 1984)

—— *Why the Allies Won* (London, 1995)

—— *Interrogations: The Nazi Elite in Allied Hands, 1945* (London, 2001)

—— *The Dictators: Hitler's Germany, Stalin's Russia* (London, 2004)

——, ed. *War and Economy in the Third Reich* (Oxford, 1994)

Overy, R. J., Otto, G. and Cate, J. H. van, eds. *Die 'Neuordnung' Europas: NS-Wirtschaftspolitik in den besetzten Gebieten* (Berlin, 1997)

Padfield, P. *Himmler: Reichsführer-SS* (London, 1990)

Panayi, P. 'Exploitation, Criminality, Resistance: The Everyday Life of Foreign Workers and Prisoners of War in the German Town of Osnabrück, 1939–1949', *Journal of Contemporary History*, 40:3 (2005), 483–502

Paolino, E. N. *The Foundations of the American Empire: William Henry Seward and US Foreign Policy* (Ithaca, 1973)

Pare, J.-R. 'Les "Ecrits de jeunesse" du Max Weber: l'histoire agraire, le nationalisme et les paysans', *Canadian Journal of Political Science*, 28:3 (1995), 437–54

Parkinson, F., ed. *Conquering the Past: Austrian Nazism Yesterday and Today* (Detroit, 1989)

Parkinson, R. *Thirty Years in the South Seas: Land and People, Customs and Traditions in the Bismarck Archipelago and on the German Solomon Islands*, trans. J. Dennison (Honolulu, 1999)

Pavone, C., ed. *Alle origine della Repubblica: Scritti su fascismo, antifascismo e continuità dello Stato* (Turin, 1995)

Paxton, R. *Vichy France: Old Guard, New Order, 1940–1944* (New York, 1972)

—— 'Le Régime de Vichy était-il neutre?', *Guerres mondiales et conflits contemporaines*, 194 (1999), 149–62

Péan, P. *Une jeunesse française: François Mitterrand, 1934–1947* (Paris, 1994)

Penslar, D. J. *Zionism and Technocracy: The Engineering of Jewish Settlement in Palestine, 1870–1918* (Bloomington, IN, 1991)

—— *Israel in History: The Jewish State in Comparative Perspective* (Abingdon, 2007)

Perras, A. *Carl Peters and German Imperialism, 1856–1918: A Political Biography* (Oxford, 2004)

Pétain, P. *Discours aux Français: 17 juin 1940–20 août 1944*, ed. J.-C. Barbas (Paris, 1989)

Peterson, E. *The Limits to Hitler's Power* (Princeton, 1969)

Petrick, F., ed. *Die Okkupationspolitik des deutschen Faschismus in Dänemark und Norwegen (1940–1945)* (Berlin, 1992)

Petropoulos, J. and Roth, J. K., eds. *Grey Zones: Ambiguity and Compromise in the Holocaust and Its Aftermath* (New York, 2005)

Petrov, V. *Escape from the Future: The Incredible Adventures of a Young Russian* (Bloomington, IN, 1973)

—— 'The Politics of Occupation', *Air University Review* (March–April 1983)

Pilichowski, C. 'Verbrauch von Nahrungsmitteln durch jüdische Bevölkerung und Häftlinge der Okkupationslager in besetzten Polen', *Studia Historicae Oeconomicae*, 17 (1982), 205–15

Pinchuk, B. *Shtetl Jews under Soviet Rule: Eastern Poland on the Eve of the Holocaust* (Oxford, 1990)

Pinkus, O. *The House of Ashes* (London, 1991)

'The Place of Judgment', *Time*, 6 August 1945

Poiger, U. 'Imperialism and Empire in Twentieth Century Germany', *History and Memory*, 17:1 (2005), 117–43

Poliakov, L. and Wulf, J. eds. *Das Dritte Reich und seine Denker* (Wiesbaden, 1989)

Polish Fortnightly Review

Polish Ministry of Information, *The German New Order in Poland* (London, 1942)

Pollack, M. *The Dead Man in the Bunker* (London, 2006)

Pollock, J. K. *The Government of Greater Germany* (New York, 1938)

Pomeranz, K. *The Great Divergence: China, Europe and the Making of the Modern World Economy* (California, 2000)

Portelli, A. *The Order Has Been Carried Out: History, Memory and the Meaning of a Nazi Massacre in Rome* (London, 2003)

Präg, W. and Jacobmeyer, W., eds. *Das Diensttagebuch des deutschen Generalgouverneurs in Polen 1939–1945* (Stuttgart, 1975)

Prazmowska, A. 'The Kielce Pogrom 1946 and the Emergence of Communist Power in Poland', *Cold War History*, 2:2 (January 2002), 101–24

Prete, R. A. and Ion, A. H., eds. *Armies of Occupation* (Ontario, 1981)

Preuss, L. 'National Socialist Conceptions of International Law', *American Political Science Review*, 29:4 (August 1935), 594–609

Pringle, H. *The Master Plan: Himmler's Scholars and the Holocaust* (New York, 2006)

Prusin, A. 'A Community of Violence: The SiPo/SD and its Role in the Nazi Terror System in Generalbezirk Kiew', *Holocaust and Genocide Studies*, 21:1 (Spring 2007), 1–30

Raitz von Frentz, C. *A Lesson Forgotten: Minority Protection under the League of Nations: The Case of the German Minority in Poland, 1920–1934* (New York, 1999)

Ranshofen-Wertheimer, E. *Victory Is Not Enough: The Strategy for a Lasting Peace* (New York, 1942)

Rebentisch, D. *Führerstaat und Verwaltung im Zweiten Weltkrieg: Verfassungsentwicklung und Verwaltungspolitik, 1939–1945* (Stuttgart, 1989)

Rebentisch, D. and Teppe, K., eds. *Verwaltung contra Menschenführung im Staat Hitlers: Studien zum politisch-administrativen System* (Göttingen, 1986)

Reddaway, W. F., Penson, J. H., Halecki, O. and Dyboski, R., eds. *The Cambridge History of Poland: From Augustus II to Pilsudski (1697–1935)* (Cambridge, 1951)

Reich Abel, J. 'Warring Internationalisms: Multilateral Thinking in Japan, 1933–1964', D.Phil. thesis, Columbia University, 2004

Reichman, S. and Hasson, S. 'A Cross-Cultural Diffusion of Colonization: From Posen to Palestine', *Annals of the Association of American Geographers*, 74:1 (March 1984), 57–70

Rein, L. 'Local Collaboration in the Execution of the "Final Solution" in Nazi-Occupied Belorussia', *Holocaust and Genocide Studies*, 20:3 (Winter 2006), 381–409

Reitlinger, G. *The Final Solution* (London, 1953)

—— *The SS, Alibi of a Nation* (London, 1956)

—— *The House Built on Sand: The Conflicts of German Policy in Russia, 1939–1945* (London, 1960)

Remak, J. 'The Healthy Invalid: How Doomed was the Habsburg Empire?', *Journal of Modern History*, 41:2 (June 1969), 127–43

Remeikis, T., ed. *Lithuania under German Occupation, 1941–1945: Dispatches from the US Legation in Stockholm* (Vilnius, 2005)

Rempel, D. G. 'The Expropriation of the German Colonists in Southern Russia during the Great War', *Journal of Modern History*, 4:1 (March 1932), 49–67

Reynolds, D. *From World War to Cold War: Churchill, Roosevelt and the International History of the 1940s* (Cambridge, 2006)

Ribbentrop, J. von *The Ribbentrop Memoirs* (London, 1954)

Rich, N. *Hitler's War Aims*, vol. 1: *Ideology, The Nazi State, and the Course of Expansion*, vol. 2: *The Establishment of the New Order* (London, 1974)

Richter, J. H. 'Continental Europe's Prewar Food Balance', *Foreign Agriculture*, 6 (1942), 300–301

Rieber, A. 'Civil Wars in the Soviet Union', *Kritika*, 4:1 (Winter 2003), 129–62

Rieckhoff, H. van *German–Polish Relations, 1918–1933* (Baltimore, 1971)

Rieger, B. *Creator of the Nazi Death Camps: The Life of Odilo Globocnik* (London, 2007)

Riismandel, V. 'Soviet Law in Occupied Estonia', *Baltic Review*, 5 (June 1955), 23–42

Robbins, K. 'Konrad Henlein, the Sudeten Question and British Foreign Policy', *Historical Journal*, 12:4 (December 1969), 674–97

Robertson, E. M. *Hitler's Prewar Policy and Military Plans, 1933–1939* (London, 1963)

Rodogno, D. *Fascism's European Empire: Italian Occupation during the Second World War* (Cambridge, 2006)

Röhr, W. and Heckert, E., eds. *Die faschistische Okkupationspolitik in Polen (1939–1945)* (Berlin, 1989)

Roon, Ger van 'Graf Moltke als Völkerrechtler im OKW', *Vierteljahrshefte für Zeitgeschichte*, 18:1 (1970), 12–61

Rosenberg, A. *Schriften und Reden* (Munich, 1943)

—— *Letzte Aufzeichnungen: Ideale und Idole der nationalsozialistischen Revolution* (Göttingen, 1955)

Ross, R. 'Heinrich Ritter von Srbik and "Gesamtdeutsch" History', *Review of Politics*, 31:1 (January 1969), 88–107

Rossino, A. *Hitler Strikes Poland: Blitzkrieg, Ideology and Atrocity* (Lawrence, KS, 2003)

—— 'Polish "Neighbours" and German Invaders: Anti-Jewish Violence in the Bialystok District during the Opening Weeks of Operation Barbarossa', *Polin*, 16 (2003), 431–52

Rössler, M. 'Applied Geography and Area Research in Nazi Society: Central Place Theory and Planning, 1933 to 1945', *Environment and Planning*, 7 (1989), 419–31

Rössler, M. and Schleiermacher, S., eds. *Der 'Generalplan Ost': Hauptlinien der nationalsozialistischen Planungs- und Vernichtungspolitik* (Berlin, 1993)

Rostow., W. 'The European Commission for Europe', *International Organization*, 3:2 (May 1949), 254–68

Rothkirchen, L. 'The Final Solution in its Last Stages', *Yad Vashem Studies*, 8 (1970), 7–28

Ruehl, M. 'In This Time without Emperors: The Politics of Ernst Kantorowicz's *Kaiser Friedrich der Zweite* Reconsidered', *Journal of the Warburg and Courtauld Institutes*, 63 (2000), 187–242

Rutherford, P. T. ' "Absolute Organizational Deficiency": The *1. Nahplan* of December 1939 (Logistics, Limitations, and Lessons)', *Central European History*, 36:2 (2003), 235–72

—— *Prelude to the Final Solution: The Nazi Program for Deporting Ethnic Poles, 1939–1941* (Lawrence, KS, 2007)

Safrian, H. *Eichmann und seine Gehilfen* (Frankfurt, 1995)

Sakowicz, K. *Ponary Diary, 1941–1943: A Bystander's Account of a Mass Murder* (New Haven, 2005)

Sauer, C. 'The Formative Years of Ratzel in the United States', *Annals of the Association of American Geographers*, 61:2 (June 1971), 245–54

Sauvy, A. and Ledermann, S. 'La Guerre biologique (1933–1945): Population de l'Allemagne et des pays voisins', *Population*, 1:3 (July–September 1946)

Schechtman, J. P. *European Population Transfers, 1939–1945* (New York, 1946)

Schellenberg, W. *Hitler's Secret Service* (New York, 1956)

—— *Invasion 1940: The Nazi Invasion Plan for Britain*, introduced by J. Erickson (London, 2000)

Schenk, D. *Hans Frank: Hitlers Kronjurist und Generalgouverneur* (Frankfurt am Main, 2006)

Scherstjanoi, E. ' "Vot ona prokliataia Germaniia!" Germany in Early 1945 through the Eyes of Red Army Soldiers', *Slavic Review*, 64:4 (Winter 2005), 165–89

Schieder, T., ed. *The Expulsion of the German Population from the Territories East of the Oder-Neisse Line* (Bonn, n.d.)

Schlesinger, R. *Federalism in Central and Eastern Europe* (New York, 1945)

Schmidt, P. *Hitler's Interpreter* (London, 1951)

Schmitt, C. 'Grossraum gegen Universalismus' *Zeitschrift der Akademie für Deutsches Recht*, 9 (1939), 333–7

—— *Völkerrechtliche Grossraum-Ordnung mit Interventionsverbot für raumfremde Mächte* (Berlin, 1939)

—— *The Concept of the Political*, trans. G. Schwab (New Brunswick, 1976)

—— *The Nomos of the Earth in the International Law of the Ius Publicum Europaeun* (New York, 2003)

Schmokel, W. *Dreams of Empire: German Colonialism, 1919–1945* (New Haven, 1964)

Schöttler, P. 'Eine Art "Generalplan West": Die Stuckart-Denkschrift vom 14. Juni 1940 und die Planungen für eine neue deutsch-französische Grenze im Zweiten Weltkrieg', *Sozial Geschichte*, 18:3 (2003), 83–131

Schreiber, G. *Deutsche Kriegsverbrechen in Italien* (Munich, 1996)

Schulte, J. E. *Zwangsarbeit und Vernichtung: Das Wirtschaftsimperium der SS: Oswald Pohl und das SS-Wirtschafts-Verwaltungshauptamt, 1933–1945* (Paderborn, 2001)

—— 'Vom Arbeits- zum Vernichtungslager: Die Entstehungsgeschichte von Auschwitz-Birkenau 1941/42', *Vierteljahrshefte für Zeitgeschichte*, 50 (2002)

Schulte, T. *German Army and Nazi Policies in Occupied Russia* (New York, 1989)

Schulz, G. 'Zur englischen Planung des Partisanenkriegs am Vorabend des Zweiten Welt-krieges', *Vierteljahrshefte für Zeitgeschichte*, 30:2 (1982), 322–39

Schumann, W. 'Probleme der Deutschen Aussenwirtschaft und einer "Europäischen Wirt-schaftsplanung" ', *Studia Historicae Oeconomicae*, 14 (1979), 142–60

—— Schumann, W. et al., eds. *Europa unterm Hakenkreuz (1938–1945)*, 10 vols. (Berlin, 1988–94)

Schwendemann, H. ' "Drastic Measures to Defend the Reich at the Oder and the Rhine": A Forgotten Memorandum of Albert Speer of 18 March 1945', in *Journal of Contemporary History*, 38:4 (2003), 597–614

Semelin, J. *Unarmed against Hitler: Civilian Resistance in Europe* (London, 1993)

Shafir, G., 'Tech for Tech's Sake', *Journal of Palestine Studies*, 21:4 (Summer 1992), 103–5

Shenhav, Y. 'The Jews of Iraq, Zionist Ideology and the Property of Palestinian Refugees of 1948: An Anomaly of National Accounting', *International Journal of Middle Eastern Studies*, 31:4 (November 1999), 605–30

Shepherd, B. *War in the Wild East: The German Army and Soviet Partisans* (Cambridge, MA, 2004)

Simoni, L. *Berlino, Ambasciata d'Italia 1939–1943* (Rome, 1947)

Simpson, A. W. B. *Human Rights and the End of Empire: Britain and the Genesis of the European Convention* (Oxford, 2001)

Singh Mehta, U. *Liberalism and Empire: A Study in Nineteenth-Century British Liberal Thought* (Chicago, 1999)

Slepyan, K. *Stalin's Guerrillas: Soviet Partisans in World War Two* (Lawrence, KS, 2006)

Smelser, R. and Zitelman, R., eds. *Die braune Elite* (Darmstadt, 1993)
—— *The Nazi Elite* (London, 1993)
Smilovitsky, L. 'Righteous Gentiles, the Partisans and Jewish Survival in Belorussia, 1941–1944', *Holocaust and Genocide Studies*, 11:3 (Winter 1997), 301–29
—— 'A Demographic Profile of the Jews in Belorussia from the Prewar Time to the Postwar Time', *Journal of Genocide Research*, 5:1 (2003), 117–29
Smith, B. and Peterson, A., eds. *Heinrich Himmler: Geheimreden 1933 bis 1945* (Frankfurt, 1974)
Smith, G. *The Last Years of the Monroe Doctrine, 1945–1993* (New York, 1994)
Smith, L., *The Embattled Self: French Soldiers' Testimony of the Great War* (Cornell, 2007)
Smith, W. D. 'Friedrich Ratzel and the Origins of Lebensraum', *German Studies Review*, 3:1 (February 1980), 51–68
—— *The Ideological Origins of Nazi Imperialism* (Oxford, 1986)
Snyder, D. R. *Sex Crimes under the Wehrmacht* (Lincoln, NE, 2007)
Snyder, L. *The Blood and Iron Chancellor: A Documentary-Biography of Otto von Bismarck* (Princeton, 1967)
Snyder, T. 'The Causes of Ukrainian-Polish Ethnic Cleansing 1943', *Past and Present*, 179 (May 2003), 197–235
Sobieski, Z. 'Reminiscences from Lwow, 1939–1946', *Journal of Central European Affairs*, 6:4 (January 1947), 351–74
Sontag, R. J. and Beddie, J. S. eds. *Nazi–Soviet Relations, 1939–1941: Documents from the Archives of the German Foreign Office* (Washington, DC, 1948)
Spang, C. W. and Wippich, R.-H., eds. *Japanese–German Relations, 1895–1945* (London, 2006)
Spector, S. 'Aktion 1005 – Effacing the Murder of Millions', *Holocaust and Genocide Studies*, 5:2 (1990), 157–73
Speer, A. *Inside the Third Reich* (London, 1970)
—— *Spandau: The Secret Diaries* (London, 1976)
Stafford, D. 'The Detonator Concept: British Strategy, SOE and European Resistance after the Fall of France', *Journal of Contemporary History*, 10:2 (April 1975), 185–217
Stein, G. *The Waffen-SS: Hitler's Elite Guard at War, 1939–1945* (Ithaca, 1966)
Steinberg, J. 'The Third Reich Reflected: German Civil Administration in the Occupied Soviet Union, 1941–1944', *English Historical Review*, 110:437 (June 1995), 620–50
Steinert, M. *Capitulation 1945: The Story of the Dönitz Regime* (London, 1969)
—— 'The Allied Decision to Arrest the Dönitz Government', *Historical Journal*, 31:3 (1988), 651–63
Steininger, R., Bischof, G. and Gehler, M. eds. *Austria in the 20th Century* (New Brunswick, 2002)
Steinweis, A. and Rogers, D. E., eds. *The Impact of Nazism* (Lincoln, NE, 2003)
Stern, H. 'The Organisation Consul', *Journal of Modern History*, 35:1 (March 1963), 20–32
Stoakes, G. *Hitler and the Quest for World Dominion: Nazi Ideology and Foreign Policy in the 1920s* (New York, 1986)
Stokker, K. 'Hurry Home, Haakon: The Impact of Anti-Nazi Humor on the Image of the Norwegian Monarch', *Journal of American Folklore*, 109:433 (Summer 1996), 289–307
Streit, C. *Keine Kameraden: Die Wehrmacht und die sowjetischen Kriegsgefangenen, 1941–1945* (Bonn, 1997)
Stroble, G. *The Germanic Isle: Nazi Perceptions of Britain* (Cambridge, 2000)
Struye, P. *L'Evolution du sentiment publique en Belgique sous l'occupation allemande* (Brussels, 1945)
—— *Journal de guerre, 1940–1945* (Brussels, 2004)
Suval, S. 'Overcoming *Kleindeutschland*: The Politics of Historical Mythmaking in the Weimar Republic', *Central European History*, 3 (1969), 312–30
Swain, G. *Between Stalin and Hitler: Class War and Race War on the Dvina, 1940–1946* (London, 2004)

Sweet, P. R. 'Seipel's Views on Anschluss in 1928: An Unpublished Exchange of Letters', *Journal of Modern History*, 19:4 (December 1947), 320–23
—— 'The Historical Writing of Heinrich von Srbik', *History and Theory*, 9:1 (1970), 37–58
Sweets, J. *Choices in Vichy France: The French under Nazi Occupation* (Oxford, 1986)
—— 'Hold that Pendulum! Redefining Fascism, Collaborationism and Resistance in France', *French Historical Studies*, 15:4 (Autumn 1988), 731–58
Sword, K., ed. *The Soviet Takeover of the Polish Eastern Provinces* (London, 1991)
Symposium of the Commission of the Historians of Latvia. *The Hidden and Forbidden History of Latvia under Soviet and Nazi Occupation, 1940–1991* (Riga, 2005)
Szarota, T. *Warschau unter dem Hakenkreuz* (Paderborn, 1978)
—— *The Warsaw Ghetto: the 45th Anniversary of the Uprising* (Warsaw, 1987)
Tauber, K. *Beyond Eagle and Swastika: German Nationalism since 1945* (Middletown, CT, 1967)
Taylor, A. J. P. *The Origins of the Second World War* (London, 1961)
Taylor, L. *Between Resistance and Collaboration: Popular Protest in Northern France, 1940–1945* (Basingstoke, 2000)
Thamer, H.-U. *Verführung und Gewalt: Deutschland, 1933–45* (Berlin, 1986)
Ther, P. and Siljak, A., eds. *Redrawing Nations: Ethnic Cleansing in East-Central Europe, 1944–48* (Lathan, MD, 2001)
Thies, J. 'Hitler's European Building Programme', *Journal of Contemporary History*, 13 (1978), 413–31
Thomas, W. 'The Prussian-Polish Situation: An Experiment in Assimilation', *American Journal of Sociology*, 19:5 (March 1914), 624–39
Tims, R. W. *Germanizing Prussian Poland: The H-K-T Society and the Struggle for the Eastern Marches in the German Empire, 1894–1919* (New York, 1941)
Todorov, T. *A French Tragedy: Scenes of Civil War, Summer 1944* (Hanover, NH, 1996)
Tomosevich, J. *War and Revolution in Yugoslavia, 1941–1945: Occupation and Collaboration* (Stanford, 2001)
Tonnini, C. *Operazione Madagascar: La questione ebraica in Polonia, 1918–1968* (Bologna, 1999)
Tooze, A. *Wages of Destruction: The Making and Breaking of the Nazi Economy* (London, 2006)
Toynbee, A. and Toynbee, V., eds. *Survey of International Affairs: Hitler's Europe, 1939–1946* (London, 1954)
Trentmann, F. and Just, F., eds. *Food and Conflict in Europe in the Age of the Two World Wars* (Basingstoke, 2006)
Trevor-Roper, H. 'Hitlers Kriegsziele', *Vierteljahrshefte für Zeitgeschichte*, 8 (1960)
—— H., ed. *Hitler's War Directives, 1939–1945* (London, 1966)
—— *Hitler's Table Talk* (Oxford, 1988)
Trew, S. *Britain, Mihailovic and the Chetniks, 1941–42* (London, 1998)
Tucker, W. R. *The Fascist Ego: A Political Biography of Robert Brasillach* (Los Angeles, 1975)
Überschär, G. R., ed. *Orte des Grauens* (Darmstadt, 2003)
Überschär, G. R. and Wette, W., eds. *'Unternehmen Barbarossa': Der deutsche Überfall auf die Sowjetunion 1941: Berichte, Analysen, Dokumente* (Paderborn, 1984)
Umbreit, H. *Der Militärbefehlshaber in Frankreich 1940–1944* (Boppard am Rhein, 1968)
—— *Deutsche Militärverwaltungen 1938/39: Die militärische Besetzung der Tschechoslowakei und Polens* (Stuttgart, 1977)
Ungvary, K. *Battle for Budapest: One Hundred Days in World War II* (London, 2003)
USA, Office of the United States Chief of Counsel for Prosecution of Axis Criminality. *Nazi Conspiracy and Aggression*, 8 vols. and supplements (Washington, DC, 1946–7)
Valin, J., Mesle, F., Adamets, S. and Pyrozhov, S. 'A New Estimate of Ukrainian Population

Losses during the Crises of the 1930s and 1940s', *Population Studies*, 56:3 (November 2002), 249–64

Veillon, D. *Fashion under the Occupation* (Oxford, 2002)

Verna, F. P. 'Notes on Italian Rule in Dalmatia under Bastianini, 1941–1943', *International History Review*, 12:3 (1990), 441–60

Vernant, J. *The Refugee in the Post-War World*, (London, 1953)

Verschuer, O. 'Rassenbiologie der Juden', *Forschungen zur Judenfrage*, vol. 3 (1938)

Vick, B. *Defining Germany: The 1848 Frankfurt Parliamentarians and National Identity* (Cambridge, MA, 2002)

Vincent, P. 'Conséquences de six années de guerre sur la population française', *Population*, 1:3 (July–September 1946)

Vinen, R. *The Unfree French: Life under the Occupation* (New Haven, 2006)

Virgili, F. *Shorn Women: Gender and Punishment in Liberation France* (New York, 2002)

Volin, L. 'The Russian Food Situation', *Annals of American Academy of Political and Social Scientists*, 225 (January 1943), 89–91

Volkmann, H.-E. 'Landwirtschaft und Ernährung in Hitlers Europa, 1939–45', *Militärgeschichtliche Mitteilungen*, 35 (1984)

Wachsmann, N. *Hitler's Prisons: Legal Terror in Nazi Germany* (London, 2004)

Waite, R. *Vanguard of Nazism: The Free Corps Movement in Postwar Germany, 1918–1923* (New York, 1952)

Ward, J. ' "People Who Deserve It": Jozef Tiso and the Presidential Exemption', Nationalities Papers, 30:4 (2002), 571–601

Warlimont, W. *Inside Hitler's Headquarters, 1939–1945* (London, 1964)

Warmbrunn, W. *The Dutch under German Occupation, 1940–1945* (Stanford, 1963)

—— *The German Occupation of Belgium, 1940–1944* (New York, 1993)

Weber, A. *Abschied von der bisherigen Geschichte* (Hamburg, 1946)

Weber, W. *Die innere Sicherheit im besetzten Belgien und Nordfrankreich, 1940–1944* (Düsseldorf, 1978)

Wegner, B., ed. *From Peace to War: Germany, Soviet Russia and the World, 1939–1941* (Oxford, 1997)

Weinberg, G. *Germany and the Soviet Union, 1939–1941* (Leiden, 1954)

—— *World in the Balance: Behind the Scenes of World War II* (Hanover, NH, 1981)

—— *A World at Arms: A Global History of World War II* (Cambridge, 2005)

——, ed. *Hitlers Zweites Buch* (Stuttgart, 1961)

Weiss, Y. 'Central European Ethnonationalism and Zionist Binationalism', *Jewish Social Studies*, 11:1 (Fall 2004), 93–117

Weiss-Wendt, A. 'Extermination of the Gypsies in Estonia during World War II: Popular Images and Official Policies', *Holocaust and Genocide Studies*, 17:1 (Spring 2003), 31–61

Weizsäcker, E. *Die Weizsäcker-Papiere, 1933–1950*, ed. L. E. Hill (Frankfurt, 1974)

Westad, O. A. *The Global Cold War: Third World Interventionism and the Making of Our Times* (Cambridge, 2007)

Westermann, E. B. ' "Friend and Helper": German Uniformed Police Operations in Poland and the General Government, 1939–1941', *Journal of Military History*, 58:4 (October 1994), 643–62

Wildt, M. 'The Spirit of the Reich Security Main Office [RSHA]', *Totalitarian Movements and Political Religions*, 6:3 (December 2005), 333–49

——, ed. *Nachrichtendienst, politische Elite und Mordeinheit: Der Sicherheitsdienst des Reichsführers-SS* (Hamburg, 2003)

Williams, M. 'German Imperialism and Austria, 1938', *Journal of Contemporary History*, 14:1 (January 1979), 139–53

—— 'Friedrich Rainer e Odilo Globocnik: L'amicizia insolita e i ruoli sinistri di due nazisti tipici', *Qualestoria*, 1 (June 1997), 141–75

Wills, C. *That Neutral Island: A Cultural History of Ireland during the Second World War* (London, 2007)

Winiewicz, J. M. *Aims and Failures of the German New Order* (London, 1943)

Winter, C. 'The Long Arm of the Third Reich: Internment of New Guinea Germans in Tatura', *Journal of Pacific History*, 38:1 (2003), 85–124

Wiskemann, E. *Czechs and Germans* (Oxford, 1938)

——*Germany's Eastern Neighbours* (Oxford, 1956)

Witte, P. 'Two Decisions Concerning the "Final Solution to the Jewish Question"': Deportations to Lodz and Mass Murder in Chelmno', *Holocaust and Genocide Studies*, 9:2 (1995), 318–45

Witte, P. and Tyas, S. 'A New Document on the Deportation and Murder of Jews during "Einsatz Reinhardt" 1942', *Holocaust and Genocide Studies*, 15:3 (Winter 2001), 468–86

Witte, P. et al., eds. *Der Dienstkalendar Heinrich Himmlers 1941/42* (Hamburg, 1999)

Wollstein, G. *Das 'Grossdeutschland' der Paulskirche: Nationale Ziele der bürgerlichen Revolution 1848/49* (Düsseldorf, 1977)

Wolton, S. *Lord Hailey, the Colonial Office and the Politics of Race and Empire in the Second World War: The Loss of White Prestige* (London, 2000)

Wood, E. T. *Karski: How One Man Tried to Stop the Holocaust* (New York, 1994)

Wylie, N., ed. *European Neutrals and Non-Belligerents during the Second World War* (Cambridge, 2002)

Young, R. J. 'The Aftermath of Munich', *French Historical Studies*, 8:2 (Autumn 1973), 305–22

Zahra, T. 'Reclaiming Children for the Nation: Germanization, National Ascription and Democracy in the Bohemian Lands, 1900–1945', *Central European History*, 37:4 (2004), 501–43

——*Kidnapped Souls: National Indifference and the Battle for Children in the Bohemian Lands, 1900–1948* (Ithaca, 2008)

Zaloga, S. *Bagration 1944: The Destruction of Army Group Centre* (London, 1996)

Zertal, I. *From Catastrophe to Power: Holocaust Survivors and the Emergence of Israel* (Berkeley, 1998)

Zitelmann, R. *Hitler: The Policies of Seduction* (London, 1999)

Zylberberg, M. *A Warsaw Diary, 1939–1945* (London, 1969)

Index

Brest-Litovsk Treaty (1918), 26, 27, 145–6
Bretons, self-determination, 109
Briand, Aristide, 39
Britain
appeasement policy, 63
birth rate, 289
control of seas, 120, 480
Czech reserves, return, 263–4
and Danubian confederation, 564–5
decolonization, 593
as 'dominant race', 589
and eastern borders, 561
as European leader, 320, 561
and European union, 569–70
German cities, bombing, 124, 135
German invasion plans, 109, 111–12
and Greece, 518–19
Greece, guarantee to, 63, 67, 122
imperialism, 591
Mers-el-Kebir strike (1940), 421, 422
oil supplies, 290, 291
Operation Unthinkable, 566
Poland, guarantee to, 67, 122
and postwar Jewish resettlement, 601
raw materials, access to, 576–7, 581
resistance, aid, 480–81
retreat (1940), 102
Romania, guarantee to, 63
Somaliland, regained (1941), 340
Soviet alliance, 137, 406, 482
'Special Operations Executive' (SOE), 408, 480–81, 509, 511, 515
'Special Wanted List GB', 112–13
and Stalin, 131
and Sudetenland, 55
British Empire
exclusionary regime, 8
Hitler and, 112
and international law, 587
inter-war, 576
as model, 2, 3, 229, 581–2
racial policy, 3, 582, 585, 587–8, 591
Brjansk-Vjasma pocket, 159, 163
Brno, 545, 546
Brody, 459
Bromberg, ethnic Germans, 40
Brooke, Sir Alan, 566
Brown, Panama Al, 426
Brüning, Heinrich, 43, 46

Brussels, graffiti, 476–7
Buber, Martin, 599
Buchenwald camp
discovery, 408
Gustloff armaments works, 314–15
labour force, 316
population, 307, 308
Budapest
death toll (1944), 526
ghetto, 366
Jewish deportations halted (1944), 404–5
Red Army atrocities, 469, 541
Bukovina
Jewish deportations, 335–6
Jewish population, 337
Romanian retrieval, 331, 337
Soviet annexation, 88, 129, 130, 330, 334
Bulgaria
as ally, 329–30
Anti-Comintern Pact (1941), 323
anti-Jewish laws, 392
brutality, 330, 353
capitulation, 367
and common Jewish policy, 393
gains, 6, 130, 133, 329, 355
Greek Jews, 401, 403
Jewish labour battalions, 403
and Jewish nationals, 403
nineteenth-century expansion, 182
as occupier, 329–30
reasons for fighting, 327
switches sides, 403
voluntary workers, 295
wartime economic boom, 567
Yugoslavian federation plan, 565
Bundesgenossen, 248
Bürckel, Josef, 48–9, 52, 201, 227, 228
Bydgoszcz, violence, 68–9

Cahors, réfractaires, 491
California, German settlements, 583
Cameroon, backs De Gaulle, 578
Campania, Wehrmacht control, 499
camps
Allies liberate, 411
arms production, 314, 315–16
conditions in, 310–11
corruption in, 315

Hitler, Adolf – *cont.*
and Mediterranean, 113–14
and Middle East, 589
Molotov meeting (1940), 131–2
motorized tactics, preference, 141
and Mussolini, 340, 341–2, 362, 367
and nationalists, 247–8, 589–90
Nazi Party and, 226
and necessity of war, 54, 102
'Nero Decree', 526
and Netherlands, 105–6
'no retreat' policy, 522, 523, 525, 527
north African policy, 113–14, 116
and Norway, 104
'offer of peace' speech (1939), 80
officials, appointment, 223–4
Paris visit (1940), 428, 432
and Pavelič, 347, 348
personal power, 60, 75, 223, 226,
    227–8, 231
and Pétain, 114, 421
Poland, plans for, 66, 70–72, 73–4, 77,
    189, 191, 446
policy origins, 19
Polish invasion, 64–5, 71
political testament, 530–31
preparations for war, 63–4
radicalism, greater, demands, 486
raw materials, importance, 3, 578
on Red Army, 159
Reichstag speeches, 58, 247, 255, 586,
    597
reprisal quotas, 239, 242
and Romania, 331
and Rosenberg, 145, 146, 148, 150, 467
and Russian Liberation Army, 468–9
scorched earth policy, 526
and self-sufficiency, 259, 274–5, 292
and Slavs, 163, 198
and Slovenia, 203
Soviet invasion, 5–6, 133–6, 137, 138,
    139, 141–2, 144–5, 148–50, 164,
    320
Soviet Pact, 64, 137
and Soviet partisans, 168
and Soviet peace plan, 360
and Soviet POWs, 12, 161
and Soviet workers, 297
and Spain, 114–15
and SS recruitment, 457

strategic mistakes, 317
and Sudeten Germans, 54, 55
suicide, 530, 531
totalitarianism, 9–10
'transition to defence', 375
and Ukrainians, 152, 458
underground life, 321
and United States, 2, 556
utopianism, 211
and Versailles settlement, 43
war aims, 121
Wehrmacht purge (1944), 524
and western Europe, 268, 560
'Hitler salute', 93
Hitler Youth, 305, 455
Hoepner, General Erich, 143, 158
Hoeppner, Rolf-Heinz, 207–8
Höfle, Major Hermann, 384
Hohenzollern empire, 30, 41, 42
Höhn, Reinhard, 250
    career, 234–5
    and 1848ers, 16
    and ethnic homogeneity, 245
Holland *see* Netherlands
Homecoming (film), 179–80
Hong Kong, Japanese invasion, 580
Hoover, President Herbert, 548
Horthy, Admiral Miklos
    anti-Semitism, 393
    arrest, 536
    and ethnic Germans, 354
    and Jews, 398, 404–5
    nationalist mysticism, 328
    negotiations with Allies, 364–5, 365–6
    replacement (1944), 405, 524
    resignation, 366
    White Terror, 328
Höss, Rudolf, 28, 315, 532
hostages
    France, 249, 436, 437, 444
    Greece, 497, 518–19
    Italian policy, 349, 350
    Jewish, 172
    military guidelines on, 66, 69
    Odessa, 436
    policy, 172
    Polish, 90, 449, 471
    quotas, 239, 242
    release, 478
Huber, Franz Joseph, 233